MANAGEMENT ACCOUNTING

For Master of Business Administration (M.B.A.) Students.

&

A Reference book for M.Com, DBM, MCM, DHM & B.Pharm Students.

Prof. (Dr.) Mahesh A. Kulkarni

(M.Com, M.Phil (Com), LL.B.(Gen), LL.B (Third),
D.T.L., Ph.D. (Mgt).

G.E. Society's
RNC Arts, JDB Commerce & NSC Science College
Nashik Road.

MANAGEMENT ACCOUNTING

First Edition : July 2001
Second Edition : July 2006
Second Edition Reprint : September 2009

ISBN : 978-81-88739-37-0

Published By :
Nishad Deshmukh
Career Publications

Reg. Office :
432/B, Deshmukh Bunglow,
Vakil Wadi, Nashik - 422 001
Maharashtra, India

Communication Address :
First Floor, Kaveri Smruti,
Ashok Stambh, Nashik - 422 001
Maharashtra, India
Ph.: (0253) 2311210, 2310421, 2576175
E-mail : publications@careerandyou.com
Visit us : www.careerandyou.com

Pune Office :
First Floor, Gokhale Building,
Tilak Road, Pune - 411 030
Maharashtra, India
Ph. : (020) 24497602

Typesetting :
Career Publications

Printer :
Replica Printers
Nashik

Price : Rs. 350/-

This Book

is dedicated to

My Guru,
Brahmarshi Dnyanyogi
Shri. Datta Maharaj Kawishwar
Pune.

PREFACE TO FIRST EDITION

The subject of Management Accounting, which is neither in its infancy nor in its maturity, has become very popular among managers and academics alike in the last four decades in India. There are a number of books on the subject of "Management Accounting" available in the market, but they do not meet the requirements of MBA students. This book is written according to the syllabus prescribed for MBA Part I, by the University of Pune. Hence it will serve as good as a text book for these students. This book is also useful for M.Com, DBM, MCM, Diploma in Hospital Management, Diploma in Hotel Managements, D.T.L., Courses of the Institute of C.A. of India, the Cost Accountancy courses of ICWA of India and many other professional courses.

The book attempts to maintain a balance between conceptual and practical approaches to accounting. It presents the most contemporary issues in a very pragmatic and readable manner. Following each units are numerous questions and problems which are designed to reinforce concepts and procedures presented in the body of the unit. The coverage of text material is designed to satisfy the need of commerce and management students as well as practitioners in accounting.

I am thankful to Career publications, Nashik and their team, who took lot of pains to publish this book.

Any useful suggestions or modifications would be welcome. I have tried my level best to avoid errors. Nevertheless, some might have escaped my attention. I will be very thankful if these are pointed out to me.

Date : 9/7/2001
(Ganesh Chaturthi)

Dr. Mahesh A. Kulkarni

PREFACE

A number of changes have taken place in the subject of 'Management Accounting' studied by the students of University of Pune since the first edition of this book was published five years ago. This edition of 'Management Accounting' has taken into account all the changes made in the revised syllabus of University of Pune for MBA and PGDBM from June 2005. This edition has been significantly enlarged in order to accommodate the changes. Most of the chapters have been rewritten without disturbing its conceptual and practical thrust.

As earlier, a large number of experts have contributed to make this edition a reality. This daunting task could not have been completed without their strong support. I must express my gratitude to them. I am also thankful to Nishad Deshmukh and his team of Career Publication, my mother, wife and children who helped me all the way.

Previous editions of this book were well received by the students and scholars alike. I am sure that this edition will be accorded similar welcome.

In our constant endeavour to make this edition free of errors, we have incorporated the suggestions made by students and teachers. Despite indefatigable efforts to make this edition flawless, some errors may have crept in inadvertently. Therefore, with all humbleness, I seek suggestions from the teachers and students.

Dr. Mahesh A. Kulkarni

Syllabus

for

Master of Business Administration (M.B.A.) Part I, University of Pune.

1. Financial Accounting - Conventions and Concepts - Primary and Secondary books of accounts - Preparation of Trial Balance - Final Accounts, Bank Reconciliation Statement

2. Cost Accounting - Relationship with Financial Accounting - Cost management concepts.

3. Elements of Cost -
   a. Materials Cost - Materials purchasing, receiving, storing, issuing including pricing of issues
   b. Labour Cost - Time Keeping and Time Booking - Idle Time - Labour Turnover
   c. Overheads - Identifying the overheads with the cost center - Allocation, Apportionment and Absorption- Under Absorption and Over Absorption of Overheads
   d. Preparation of Cost Sheet.

4. Managerial Decision Making Techniques like -
   a. Marginal Costing - Cost Volume Profit Analysis-BEP
   b. Budgetary Control - Operating and Financial Budgets - Fiexible Budgets
   c. Standard Costing - Materials Cost and Labour Cost Variances only

Note - Problems should be covered on the following topics -
   a. Preparation of ledger accounts, trial balance and final accounts,
   b. Bank Reconciliation Statement
   c. Cost Sheet preparation
   d. Inventory Valuation
   e. Overheads - Allocation, Apportionment and Absorption - machine hour rate.
   f. Simple problems on concepts of Marginal Costing and Applications of Marginal Costing
   g. Budgets - Cash, Sales, Production
   h. Materials Cost and Labour Cost Variances

CONTENTS

* * * *

Unit No. 1

MANAGEMENT ACCOUNTING

Management Accounting : (Meaning & Concept)

Management Accounting is a segment of accounting that deals specifically with the accounting and reporting of information to management regarding the detailed operations of the company in order to helptake speedy for decisions in various areas of business. It is primarily oriented towards managerial control and other decision making groups inside the organisation. Management frequently requires timely financial information that deals with different aspects of the firm, ranging from special purpose reports for a specific department's operating performance to the preparation of annual budgets and forecasts which encompass the entire business.

Managers in all types of organisations need frequent information about business activities to plan accurately for the future, to control business results, to direct an enterprise toward achieving its goals and to make decisions that affect the operations of the business. Information is vital for the management process i. e. for functions carried out by the managers namely, planning, controlling and decision making. With the goal of providing information, managerial accounting identifies, collects, measures, classifies and reports information which is useful to managers in fulfilling the management process.

Management accounting is that field of accounting which deals with providing information including financial accounting information to managers for their use in planning, decision making, performance evaluation, control, management of cost and cost determination for financial reporting. Managerial Accounting contains reports prepared to fulfil the needs of management.

Management accounting was not known to the business world until 1950. The term was first formally described in a report entitled 'Management Accounting' in 1950. The report was published by the Anglo - American Council of Productivity Management Accounting Team after its visit to United States during April, May and June 1950. The team in its report defines Management Accounting as :

"the presentation of accounting information in such a way as to assist management in the creation of policy and in the day-to-day operation of an undertaking"

(Ref - Sizer J. An Insignt into Management Accounting, Pitman Publishing Ltd, London 1979)

Thereafter number of attempts were and are being made by various professional associations and authorities on the subject to define management accounting in its right perspective.

Important definitions of Management Accounting

Some important definitions on the subject are given below :

1) The National Association of Accountants (USA), in Statement. No. 1 A (Statements on Management Accounting 1982) has defined management accounting as :

"..... the process of identification, measurement, accumulation, analysis, preparation and communication of financial information used by management to plan, evaluate, and control within the organisation and to assure appropriate use and accountability for its resources."

2) The CIMA (UK) defines the term management accounting in the following manner :

"Management accounting is an integral part of management concerned with identifying, presenting and interpreting information used for :

1) formulating strategy 2) planning and controlling activities 3) decision making
4) optimising the use of resources 5) disclosure to shareholders and others external to the entity.
6) disclosure to employees 7) safeguarding assets

3) "Management accounting is the application of appropriate techniques and concepts in processing historical and projected economic data of an entity to assist management in establishing plans for reasonable economic objectives in the making of rational decisions with a view towards these objectives".

- American Accounting Association

4) "Management accounting is the application of accounting and statistical techniques to the specified purpose of producing and interpreting information designed to assist management in its functions of promoting maximum efficiency and in envisaging, formulating and co-ordinating their execution".

- ACCA, USA.

5) "The application of accounting knowledge to the purpose of producing and of interpreting accounting and statistical informations designed to assist management in its functions of promoting maximum efficiency and in formulating and coordinating future plans and subsequently in measuring their execution."

- H. M. Treasury

6) "Management Accounting is the term used to describe the accounting methods, system and techniques which, coupled with special knowledge and ability, assist management in its task of maximising profits or minimising losses."

- J. Batty

7) "Management Accounting is the application of professional knowledge and skill in the preparation of accounting information in such a way as to assist management in the formation of policies and in the planning and control of the operations of the undertaking."

- ICMA, London

8) "Management Accounting is more intimate merger of the two older professions of management and accounting wherein the informational needs of the manager determine the accounting means for their satisfactions."

- R. L. Smith

9) "Management accounting is concerned with the efficient management of a business through the presentation to management of such information as will facilitate efficient and opportune planning and control."

- Brown and Howard

10) "Management accounting is concerned with accounting information which is useful to management."

- Robert N. Athany

11) "The term 'Management Accounting' covers all those services by which the accounting department can assist top management and other departments in the formation of policy, the control of its execution and appreciation of its effectiveness."

- Broad and Carmichael

12) "Accounting which serves management by providing information as to the cost of profit associated with some portion of firm's total operations, is called Management Accounting."

- Shilling Law

13) "Management accounting is the adaptation and analysis of accounting information and its diagnosis and explanation in such a way as to assist management."

- T. G. Rose

14) "Management accounting is concerned with providing information to managers; that is to those who are inside the organisation and who are charged with directing and controlling its operations."

- R. H. Garrison.

15) "Any form of accounting which enables a business to be conducted more efficiently can be regarded as Management accounting."

- ICA England and Wales

All these definitions of Management Accounting reveal the following salient features :

1) It is a merger of 'management' and 'accounting'.
2) It is concerned with accounting information which is useful to management in maximising profits or minimizing losses.
3) It is concerned with the improvement in the efficiency of the various phases of management.

Briefly management accounting with all its paraphernalia, dose not supplant financial accounting as is erroneously misunderstood, but supplement the basic structure of traditional package of accounts to cater to the diversified requirements of modern management.

Thus Management Accounting emphasizes on the information that management requires to make specific intra-firm resource allocations. Such emphasis assumes that accounting must perform the two separate, distinct functions of financial and management reporting and that the data needs for each are often different. 'Few intelligent financial and economic decisions can be made in the absence of the information reservoir. Involvement with both time dimensions, past and future, places the executive near the centre of the control and decision-making processes in any organisation :

Scope of Management Accounting

Management accounting covers not only use of financial data and a part of costing theory but may extend beyond the boundaries of accounting and costing. It requires the aid of techniques of other disciplines such as economics, finance, mathematics, statistics and operations research. The following are some of the areas of specification included within the ambit of management accounting.

1) Financial Accounting

Financial accounting is an essential prerequisite of any discussion of management accounting. Financial statements contain enough information that is used by management of decision-making. Management accounting contains only tool and techniques and it gets the data for interpretation and analysis mainly from financial accounting. Thus, without efficient financial accounting system, management accounting cannot become operative.

2) Cost Accounting

Business executives depend heavily on accounting information in general and on cost information in particular because any activity of an organisation can be described by its cost. They make use of various cost data in managing organisations effectively. Cost accounting is considered as backbone of management accounting as it provides the analytical tools such as budgetary control, standard costing, marginal costing, inventory control, operating costing, etc. which are used by management to discharge its responsibilities efficiently.

3) Financial Statement Analysis

Frequently, the various users of financial statements may need access to information that can be obtained only be selecting individual numbers from the statements and by developing certain trends and ratios. Any attempt in this direction is referred to as financial statement analysis. A person can gain meaningful insights and conclusions about the firm with the help of analysis and interpretation of the information contained in financial statements. Numerous techniques have been developed which can be used for the proper interpretation and analysis of financial statements.

4) Forecasting and Budgeting

This refers to the formulation of budgets and forecasts, using standard norms in co-operation with operating and other departments of a business concern. The ultimate success of any budgeting depends on the proper setting of target figures in the budgets and the actual realization of the same in practice, even without a slight deviation due to external reasons beyond the control of the management.

5) Cost Control Techniques

These serve as effective tools for comparing the actual results with the predetermined figures as laid down in budgets. They greatly help in translating the budgets into operating plans.

6) Inflation Accounting

Inflation accounting attempts to identify certain characteristics of accounting that tend to distort the reporting of financial results during periods of rapidly changing prices. It devises and implements appropriate methods to analyse and interpret the impact of inflation on the financial information.

7) Management Reporting

Clear, informative, timely reports are essential management tools in making decisions that make the best use of a company's resources. Thus, one of the basic responsibility of management accounting is to keep the management well informed about the operations of the business. To discharge this responsibility efficiently, he has to prepare quarterly, half-yearly and other interim reports and submit the same to the management.

8) Quantitative Techniques

Modern managers believe that the financial and economic data available for managerial decisions can be more useful when analysed with more sophisticated analysis and evaluation techniques. Quantitative analysis methods allow managers to develop information from their financial database that is not otherwise available. The techniques such as time series, regression analysis and sampling techniques are commonly used for this purpose. Further, managers also use techniques such as linear programming, game theory, queuing theory etc. in their decision-making process.

9) Taxation

Taxation plays an important role in the profitability of a commercial concern. Therefore it is essential for a management accountant to have a complete knowledge of business taxation. The business profit and the tax thereon is to be ascertained as per the provision of taxation. The filling of tax returns and the payment of tax in due time is exclusively the responsibility of management accountant.

10) Internal Audit

The internal audit as a discipline of management accounting makes arrangements for performance appraisal of the company's various departments. Thus a management accountant must possess knowledge about the fixation of responsibilities and measurement of results.

11) Office Services

To discharge the responsibilities efficiently, a management accountant has to deal with data processing, filling, copying, duplicating. His area of responsibilities also includes the evaluation and reporting about the utility of different office procedures and machines.

Functions of Management Accounting

Broadly speaking the functions of management accounting embrace all activities concerning to satisfy the needs of different levels of management.

The primary objective of a management accounting system is to supply meaningful information to the management. To achieve this goal, it has to carry out many activities which are normally referred to as functions of management accounting. The major functions are summarised below :

1) Planning and Forecasting

Planning is an activity of the management that requires an efficient system of decision making. In any type of enterprise, plans should be made to guide future operations of the business. Thus, one of the major functions of the management accountant is to help management in the selection of company goals and in the formulation of policies and strategies to allocate resources to achieve these goals. Different accounting techniques are used by the management to discharge the function of planning efficiently. The important among them are financial statement analysis, budgeting, direct costing, capital budgeting and standard costing.

2) Furnishes information as per requirements

Management accounting furnishes statistical information according to the varying requirements of the different levels of management at periodic intervals. The three-tier management which is in vogue in the recent times requires information of various types at different intervals, e. g. the top level management requires information in a capsule form covering all aspects of the business at relatively long intervals whilst detailed analysis relating to a particular aspect of the business at short intervals will suffice the persons in the lower rings of the management ladder.

3) Not confine merely to financial data

Management accounting does not confine itself merely to financial data to assist the management in the decision making process but frequently draws upon various sources other than accounting for qualitative information which cannot be converted into monetary terms. For this purpose, engineering records, case studies, minutes of meetings, productivity reports, special surveys and other business documents are greatly relied upon.

4) Analysis and Interpretation

The economic and financial data as collected from various statements do not have much management utility unless it is properly analysed in light of the nature of the decisions. In fact process of analysis and interpretation puts life in available data to speak about future trends. The management accountant has to present the data with his comments and recommendations to the management. Thus the analysis & interpretations of data are considered as the backbone of Management Accounting.

5) Coordinating

The techniques such as budgeting, financial reporting and analysis and interpretation are commonly used by management accountants to coordinate efficiently the various activities of the business. The efficient control contributes to the efficiency of organisation which in turn increases the profitability of a concern.

6) Communication

The management accountant spends his maximum time in communicating to the management. He has to prepare various reports required by the management from time to time to meet the challenges of the business. The publication of company's annual report is also an important task of a management accountant.

7) Establishes standards of performance

Management accounting establishes standards of performance in the different realms of activities such that any deviation therefrom can be easily measured leading to further investigation of the causes and institution of prompt remedial measures for rectifying the same. This is made possible through budgetary control and standard costing which are essential adjuncts of management accounting.

8) Undertakes various special studies

Modern business is operating under such dynamic conditions where even a minor change in business can have a significant impact on the business results. Therefore, managements is always interested to know the areas of business which can contribute to the stability and profitability of the concern. To meet this objective, management accountant undertakes various special studies such as sales analysis, economic forecasts, price spread analysis, etc.

9) Tax Administration

In modern business organisations, the responsibilities of a management accountant also includes, the tax administration. This task involves submission of necessary documents and return to the tax authorities and supervision of all matters relating to tax administration.

10) Controlling

Management Accounting helps in the controlling by providing performance reportes and control reports which highlight variances between expected and actual performances. Such reports serves as a basis for taking necessary corretive action to control operations.

In short management accounting furnishes accounting data and statistical information required for the decision-making process in management which vitaly affects the survival & the success of the business.

Phases in the Evolution of Accounting

The history of accounting indicates the evolutionary pattern which focuses changing socio-economic conditions and enlarged purposes to which accounting is applied.

In the present situation seven phases in the evolution of accounting can be distinguished.

1) Stewardship Accounting
2) Financial Accounting
3) Cost- Accounting
4) Management Accounting
5) Social Responsibility Accounting
6) Inflation Accounting
7) Human Resource Accounting

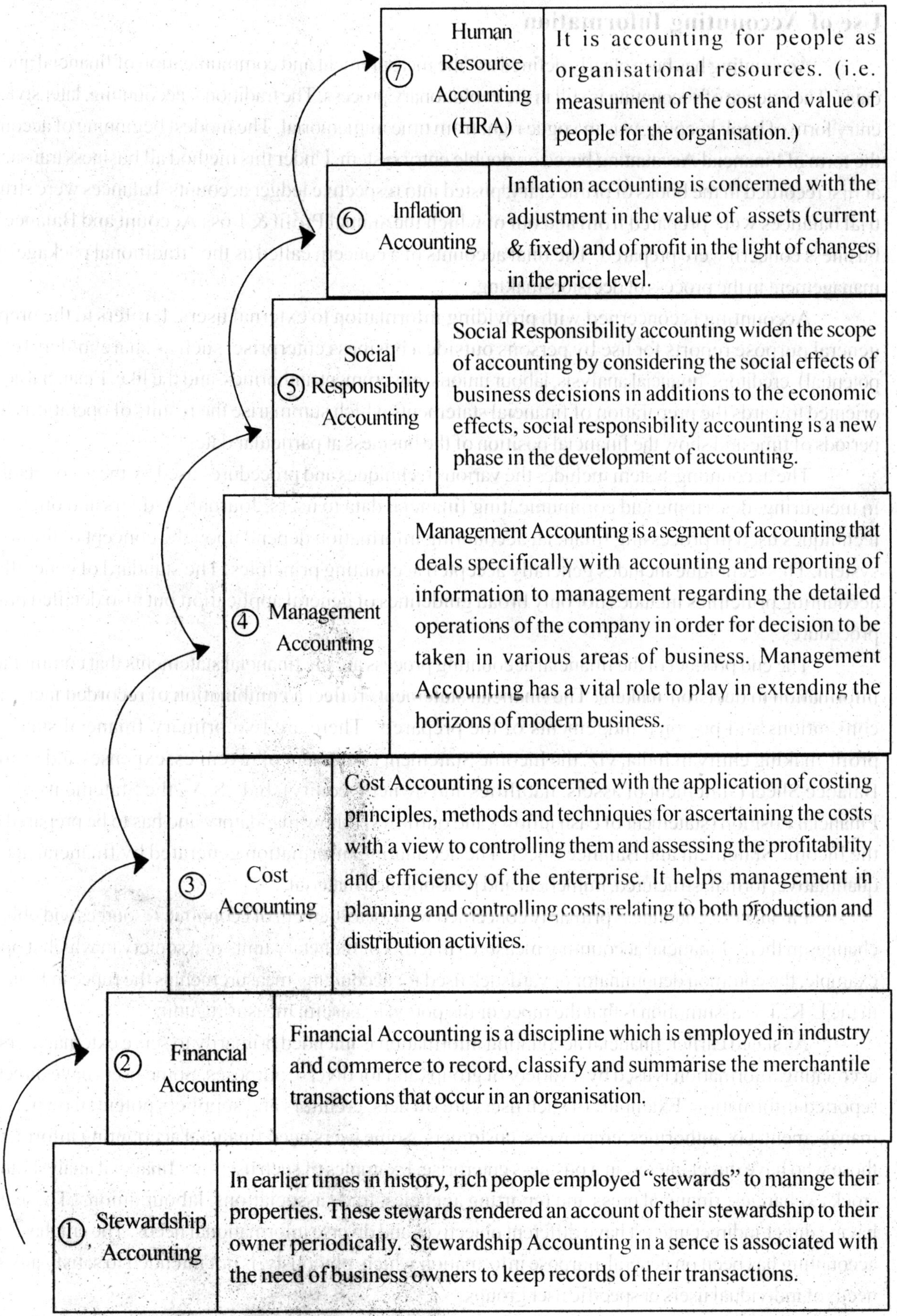

Phases in the Evolution of Accounting

Use of Accounting Information

Accounting has been clearly defined as "the measurement and communication of financial and economic data". The science of accounting is still in the evolutionary process. The traditional accounting, later styled as single entry form of book keeping, was in vogue right from time immemorial. The modest beginning of accounting took the form of Financial Accounting based on double entry system. Under this method all business transactions were at first recorded in the books of prime entry, posted into respective ledger accounts, balances were struck and the trial balances were prepared from and out of which the annual Profit & Loss Account and Balance Sheet of a business concern were prepared. The final accounts of a concern called as the "traditional package" helped the management in the process of decision-making.

Accounting is concerned with providing information to external users. It refers to the preparation of general purpose reports for use by persons outside a business enterprise, such as shareholders (existing and potential), creditors, financial analysis, labour unions, government authorities, and the like. Financial accounting is oriented towards the preparation of financial statements which summarise the results of operations for selected periods of time and show the financial position of the business at particular dates.

The accounting system includes the various techniques and procedures used by the accountant (preparer) in measuring, describing and communicating financial data to users. Journals, ledgers and other accounting techniques used in processing financial accounting information depend upon the concept of the double-entry system. This technique includes generally accepted accounting principles. The standard of generally accepted accounting principles includes not only broad guidelines of general application but also detailed practices and procedures.

The end product of the financial accounting process are the financial statements that communicate useful information to decision-makers. The financial statements reflect a combination of recorded facts, accounting conventions and personal judgements of the preparers. There are two primary financial statements for a profit-making entity in India, viz. the Income Statement (statement of revenues, expenses and profit), and the Balance Sheet (statement of assets, liabilities and owners' equity). In U.S.A., the Statements of Changes in Financial Position (statement of cash inflows and outflows) is now mandatory and has to be prepared along with the Income Statement and Balance Sheet. The accounting information generated by financial accounting in quantitative, formal, structured, numerical and post-oriented material.

Financial accounting is primarily concerned with measurement of economic resources and obligations and changes in them. Financial accounting measures in terms of monetary units of a society in which it operates. For example, the common denominator or yardstick used for accounting measurement is the rupee in India and pound in the U.K. The assumption is that the rupee or the pound is a useful measuring unit.

As stated earlier, financial accounting information is intended primarily to serve external users. Financial accounting information is used by a variety of groups and for diverse purposes. Some users have direct interest in reported information. Examples of such users are owners, creditors and suppliers potential owners, suppliers, management, tax authorities, employees, customers. Some users need financial accounting information to help those who have direct interest in a business enterprise. Examples of such users are financial analysts and advisers, stock exchanges, financial press and reporting agencies, trade associations, labour unions. These user groups having direct/indirect interest have different objectives and diverse informational needs. The emphasis in financial accounting has been on general-purpose information which, obviously, is not intended to satisfy any specialised needs of individual users or specific user groups.

Application of Accounting Information :

Accounting information is useful for : i) score-keeping ii) attention directing iii) problem solving.

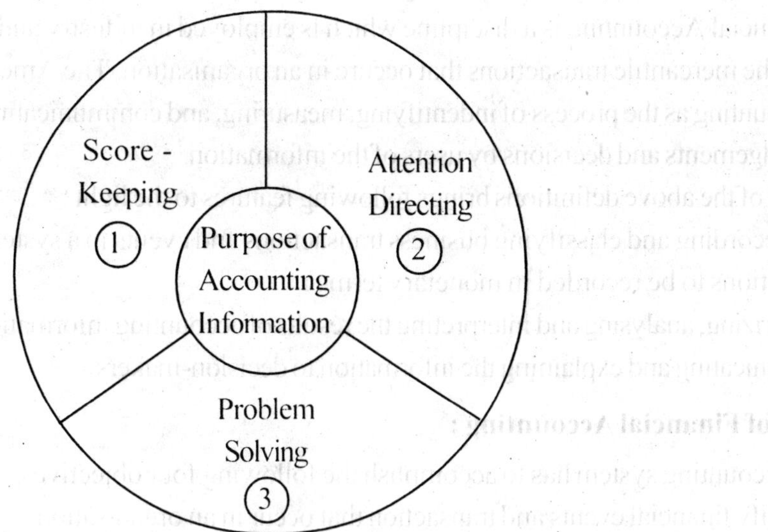

Fig.: Purpose of Accounting Information

1) Score keeping : The scorekeeping function in one of the purposes of accounting information. Score-keeping deals with the financial health of the business. Accounting in its score card role, accumulates information (data) and enables interested persons to understand and take stock of the organisation's performance.

2) Attention-directing : Attention-directing is nothing the process of giving a signal to the user of accounting informations about the necessity to take a decision. In this role accounting complements day-to-day operational planning control activities.

3) Problem-Solving : Accounting, in its problem solving role, data, enables quantification of the different alternative solutions, their relative pros and cons.

Structure of Accounting

Accounting plays a critical role in the efficient use of a firm's resources. Decision-makers operate in a complex economic environment that is constantly changing. Their information needs change with the environment, and accounting must adapt to satisfy these changing needs. The importance of sound financial information has always been recognized, but, in the light of today's conditions, such information has become crucial to the survival of business and industry.

Accounting can be broadly classified into three types a) Financial Accounting, b) Cost Accounting and c) Management Accounting. These three cannot be put in water-tight compartment classification. each one supplements the other. In fact, financial accounting provides the basis for cost accounting as well as management accounting and in the ultimate analysis management accounting includes part of cost accounting.

Financial Accounting

The American Institute of Certified Public Accountants has defined Financial Accounting as "the art of recording, classifying and summarising in a significant manner and in terms of money transactions and events which are in part at least of a financial character and interpreting the results thereof."

Accounting is the language effectively employed to communicate the financial information of a business unit to various parties interested in its progress such as proprietors, creditors, investors, employees, consumers, the Government etc. Financial accounting concerns that part of accounting which is meant to serve all parties externally to the operating responsibility of the firm, e.g. creditors, investors, employees, regulatory bodies and the general public. But management accounting is designed for use in the operational needs of the firm.

Financial Accounting is a discipline which is employed in industry and commerce to record, classify and summarize the mercantile transactions that occure in an organisation. The American Accounting Association has defined accounting as the process of indentifying, measuring, and communicating economic information to permit informed judgements and decisions by users of the information.

The analysis of the above definitions brings following features to the light :

i) Art of recording and classifying business transactions and events in a systematic manner ;

ii) Transactions to be recorded in monetary terms ;

iii) Summarizing, analysing and interpreting the results of accounting information ; and

iv) Communicating and explaining the information to decision-makers

Objectives of Financial Accounting :

A modern accounting system has to accomplish the following four objectives :

i) To identify financial events and transaction that occur in an organisation.

ii) To measure the value of these occurrences in terms of money.

iii) To organize the accumulated financial data into meaningful information, and

iv) To analyse, interpret and communicate that information to a broad range of persons and groups, both within and outside the organisation.

Functions of Financial Accounting

The major functions of financial accounting are summarised below :

1) Recording : Since all business transactions cannot be kept in memory, they have got to be systematically recorded and pass through journals, ledgers and work sheets before they could take the form of final accounts. This aspect of financial accounting has assumed considerable importance with the limitation of human memory.

2) Validating : With the universal acceptance and enforcement of accounting principles, every recorded entry in the books of accounts maintained by a business unit gives validity or authenticity to all such transactions so recorded.

3) Communicating : This is an important function of financial accounting. Accounting serves as a language for communicating the financial facts about the enterprise or activity most effectively to all concerned interested in using and interpreting them.

4) Interpreting : This aspect helps in unfolding the total financial picture of an undertaking and investing the same with more meaning.

Limitation of Financial Accounting

Financial Accounting like any other branch of knowledge, is not without limitations. The fast changing conditions and environmental factors have brought the limitations of financial accounting to the fore.

1) Financial accounting does not provide detailed cost information for different departments, processes, products, jobs in the production divisions. Similarly separate cost data are not available for different services and functions in the administration division. Management may need information about different products, sales territories and sales activities which are also not available in financial accounting.

2) Financial accounting does not set up a proper system of controlling materials and supplies. Undoubtedly, if material and supplies are not controlled in a manufacturing concern, they will lead to losses on account of misappropriation, misutilisation, scrap, defectives etc. They may, in turn, influence the reported net income of a business enterprise.

3) The recording and accounting for wages and labour is not done for different jobs, processes, products, departments. This creates problems in analysing the cost associated with different activities. This also does not provide a basis for rewarding workers and employees for the above-average performance.

4) Financial accounting contains historical cost information which is accumulated at the end of the accounting period. This accounting does not provide day-to-day information about costs and expense. This is the reason why much dissatisfaction has been shown with external financial reporting. The historical cost is not a reliable basis for predicting future earnings, solvency, or overall managerial effectiveness. Historical cost information is relevant but not adequate for all purpose. It is now rightly contended that current cost information should be reported along with historical cost information.

5) It is difficult to know the behaviour of costs in financial accounting as expenses are not assigned to the product at each stage of production. Expenses are not classified into direct and indirect and therefore cannot be classified as controllable and uncontrollable. Control of cost which is the most important objective of all business enterprises, cannot be achieved with the aid of financial accounting alone.

6) Financial accounting does not possess an adequate system of standards to evaluate the performance departments and employees working in departments. Standardisation is now applied to all elements of business. Standards need to be developed for materials, labour and overheads so that a firm can compare the work of labourers, workers, supervisors and executives with what should have been done in an allotted period of time.

7) Financial accounting does not provide information to analyse the losses due to various factors, such as idle plant and equipment, seasonal fluctuations in volume of business etc. It does not help management in taking important decisions about expansion of business, dropping of a product line, starting a new product, alternative methods of production, improvement in product, etc. The managerial decisions about these business matters have now become vital to the survival and growth of business enterprises.

8) Financial accounting does not provide cost data to determine the price of the product being manufactured or the service being rendered to the consumers. It is also not possible to prepare detailed cost reports for the purpose of comparison and analysis between two periods of time within an enterprise and also for making inter-firm comparison.

9) Change in the economic conditions of the country have direct impact on the business position of an organisation. The conditions of inflation or deflation change significantly the value of the business. Such a change is not depicted in the financial accounts as the accounts of the business have to be maintained on the basis of cost concept. With the result the balance sheet of an organisation fails to give true and fair view of the business.

10) The serious limitation to financial accounting is that it can be only understood by such persons who have accounting knowledge.

Cost Accounting

Cost accounting is an extension of general accounting system which have as a goal the gathering, classifying, and analysing to cost data that management needs in search for the most efficient methods of operating, achieving control of costs, and reducing expenses. 'Cost accounting is the provisions of such analysis and classification of expenditure as will enable the total cost of any particular unit of production to be ascertained with reasonable degree of accuracy and at the same time to disclose exactly how such total cost is constituted'.

According to the Institute of Cost and Works Accountnts (ICWA), London, cost accounting is "the process of accounting for cost from the point at which expenditure is incurred or committed to the establishment of its ultimate relationship with cost centres and cost units. In its widest usage it embraces the preparation of statistical data, the application of cost control methods and the ascertainment of the profitability of activities carried out or planned". W.J. Morse defines cost accounting as "the processing and evaluation of monetary and non-monetary data to provide information for external reporting, internal planning and control of bushiness operations and special analysis and decisions".

Thus cost accounting is the branch of accounting designed to determine the costs of manufactured products and to report cost information to management. It provides the means to gather the data needed to determine unit costs and to prepare reports, schedules, statements and analysis that are relevant to management. Cost accounting procedures and routines are used as a means of accumulating and allocating all elements of manufacturing cost in a manner that will produce meaningful data for the use of management.

Objectives of Cost Accounting

The main objectives of cost accounting are mentioned below :

i) To aid in the development of long-range plans by providing cost data that acts as a basis for projecting data for planning.

ii) To ensure efficient cost control by communicating essential data costs at regular intervals.

iii) To determine cost of products or activities.

iv) To identify profitable areas of business;

v) To provide management with information in connection with various operational problems.

Emergence of Management Accounting

With the advancement of science and technology more sophisticated equipments and gadgets have been put into operation in the realm of accounting as well. This has changed the accounting from a mere device of recording to a powerful tool of forecasting, budgeting and budgetary control. Thus, financial accounting has been supplemented with financial and cost control, budgeting and budgetary control and also production planning and control besides reporting on business performance. Precisely, it has led to the emergence of management accounting.

The term "Management Accounting" is of recent origin even in the U.S.A. This term was first coined and used by the British Team of Accountants that visited the United States in 1950 under the auspices of Anglo-American Productivity Council. Since then management accounting has grown into a full fledged subject and is looked upon as a subject distinct from accounting in recent years. It is also otherwise known as "Management-oriented Accounting" or "Accounting for Management".

Distinction Between Management Accounting and Financial Accounting

Though management accounting and financial accounting cannot be put in watertight compartment classification, it should be remembered that the former is only an off-shoot of the latter. Precisely, management accounting suppliments the functions of financial accounting in as much as it provides the necessary accounting data and statistical information needed by the management for improving the efficiency as a whole. Despite the close inter-relationship that exists, there are certain points of difference between the two and they are discussed below;

Sr.No.	Points	Financial Accounting	Management Accounting
1)	Primary users of information	The users of financial accounting statements are mainly external to the business enterprise. The financial statements prepared under financial accounting show how the resources have been used by a business enterprise during a specific period of time and thus are useful to external users in making sound economic decisions. These financial statements are relevant to managements but are not adequate for the purpose of planning, control and decision - making. External users include shareholders, creditors, financial analysts, government authorities, stock exchange, labour unions, etc.	Management accounting aims at preparing reports and supplying information to management for planning, controlling and decision-making. The information generated under the accounting system is used by members of management at different levels. The nature of internal reports and data varies for different levels of management in conformity with their information requirements for analysing business operations and for planning and control purpose. Thus, different sets of information could be developed under managerial accounting and supplied to different persons responsible for activities in the organisation.
2)	Nature	The historical nature of financial accounting serves a limited purpose of throwing light on the events and results of the past. The forward looking management accounting greatly helps the management in improving the results in future through various tools and techniques of budgeting and budgetary control, standard costing, profit planning etc.	Management accounting is mainly concerned with the future plans and policies, whereas financial accounting is concerned with historical records relating to the past. Management rely on the past records for formulation of future plans and hence, the interdependence of management accounting and financial accounting cannot be over-emphasised.
3)	Accounting method	Financial accounting follows the double-entry system for recording, classifying and summarising business transactions. This accounting process results in aggregate balances of all accounts maintained in a firm's books.	Management accountings is not based on the double-entry system. The data under management accounting may be gathered for small or large segments or activities of an organisation and monetary as well as other measures can be used for different activities in the firm. The only constraint regarding managerial accounting principles and methods is that they should be useful for management purposes.

Sr.No.	Points	Financial Accounting	Management Accounting
4)	Accounting principles	Financial accounting data is primarily meant for external users. The "generally accepted accounting principles" are important in financial accounting and are used extensively while recording, classifying, summarising and reporting business transactions. The use of GAAP adds creditability and reliability of financial statements and creates confidence among the financial statement users.	Management accounting is not bound to use the "generally" accepted accounting principles. It can use any accounting technique or practice which generates useful information. Besides, data developed in management accounting may be facts, estimates, projections, analysis. etc.
5)	Obligatory	It is more or less obligatory on the part of every business concern to adopt financial accounting for disclosing the results of the business to the rightful owners.	In modern times a business concern is free to install any system of management accounting.
6)	Time Span	Financial accounting data and statements are developed for a definite period, usually a year or a half-year. It requires that financial statements be developed and presented at regular time intervals. Company annual reports may be prepared semi-annually or quarterly but the important point is that they are prepared on a regular basis.	Management accounting reports and statements are prepared whenever needed. Reports may be prepared on a monthly, weekly or even daily basis. Frequency of reports is determined by particular planning, controlling and decision-making needs.
7)	Legal Formalities	Financial accounting statements are standardised and meant for external use. The preparation and presentation of annual final accounts of companies are governed by the provisions of the Companies & Income Tax Act in force.	Since a business concern is free to install the system of management accounting there is no statutory regulation fixing the norms and standards for preparation and presentation of accounting statements. Needless to state that these statements can be adapted to the changing needs of the management since they are meant for internal use.

Sr.No.	Points	Financial Accounting	Management Accounting
8)	Unit of measurement	All information under financial accounting is in terms of money. That is, transactions measured in terms of money have already occurred. In comparison managerial accounting applies any measurement unit that is useful in a particular situation.	Besides the monetary units, the management accountant may find it necessary to use such measures, as number of labour hours, machine hours and product units for the purpose of analysis and decision-making. The common objective in all measurement, reporting and data analysis in managerial accounting is usefulness for a particular purpose. Historical cost and past transactions are essential to financial accounting but may be secondary to managerial accounting as they are not of much use to management.
9)	Purpose of Report	Financial accounting produces information and reports which are general purpose reports in order to serve the informational needs of many external users such as shareholders, creditors, potential investors, customers, suppliers, regulatory authorities, employees and the general public. Financial accounting is concerned with overall firm performance rather than individual segments or departments.	The reports and data developed in management accounting are known as specific purpose reports designed for a particular user (manager) or particular decision. Managerial accounting uses internal reports to evaluate the performance of entities, product lines, departments and managers.
10)	Focus	Financial accounting focuses on the company as a whole. Sometimes, in financial accounting, some information is given about different products or lines of activity due to financial reporting requirements as provided in the Companies Act/ Other rules and regulations.	Management accounting provides detailed and disaggregated information about products, individual activities, divisions, plants, operations, tasks or any other responsibility centres.

Sr.No.	Points	Financial Accounting	Management Accounting
11)	Precision (Exactness)	In financial accounting precision is stressed greatly since the past result of the business are reflected through them.	Management accounting lays no emphasis on precision as the data and particulars compiled are merely estimates and relate to the future.
12)	Subject matter & Scope	Financial accounting, also known as external accounting, produces information and reports for external users. The subject matter and scope of managerial accounting and financial accounting are displayed in Figure 1.	Managerial accounting, also known as internal accounting, identifies, collects, measures, classifies and reports information that is useful to managers in planning, control and decision-making.

Tools and Techniques of Management Accounting

Management accounting is an information system designed to communicate meaningful economic and financial information to the management so that management may discharge its functions efficiently. The management accounting system consists of number of tools and techniques which are frequently used by the management accountant to meet the increasing needs of the business. The important among them are :

i) Financial Planning

Planning is necessary not only for efficient utilisation of available resources but also for better and progressive business results. It is more significant for finance function because finance plays a deciding role in managerial decision. Financial planning is the process of deciding in advance the financial objectives, policies, and procedures. An organisation can achieve long-term as well as short term financial objectives by employing financial planning. In the short term, it can help a concern in meeting its obligations by balancing flow of funds. At the same time, its proper application can ensure efficient utilisation of available financial resources in the long period.

ii) Statistical Analysis

Accountants frequently confront masses of data from which they would like to draw systematic and logical conclusions. Statistical analysis and, in particular, statistical sampling theory provides scientific method for drawing reliable and valid conclusions about the properties of an entire population when only a properly chosen sample of the population has been studied in detail.

iii) Cost Accounting

Cost accounting is a vital part of the total management accounting system. It includes the recording, classifying, analysing and reporting of all cost aspects of company performance. The cost accounting and procedures have to be designed with great care keeping in view the nature and requirements of the firm and the data required at the different levels of management for effective cost control and cost reduction.

iv) Standard Costing

Another major technique for operating control through management accounting is standard costing. Under this arrangement standard costs are used to control the major activities of the business. Standard costs are predetermined targets against which actual results are evaluated. This is the basis for a system of management

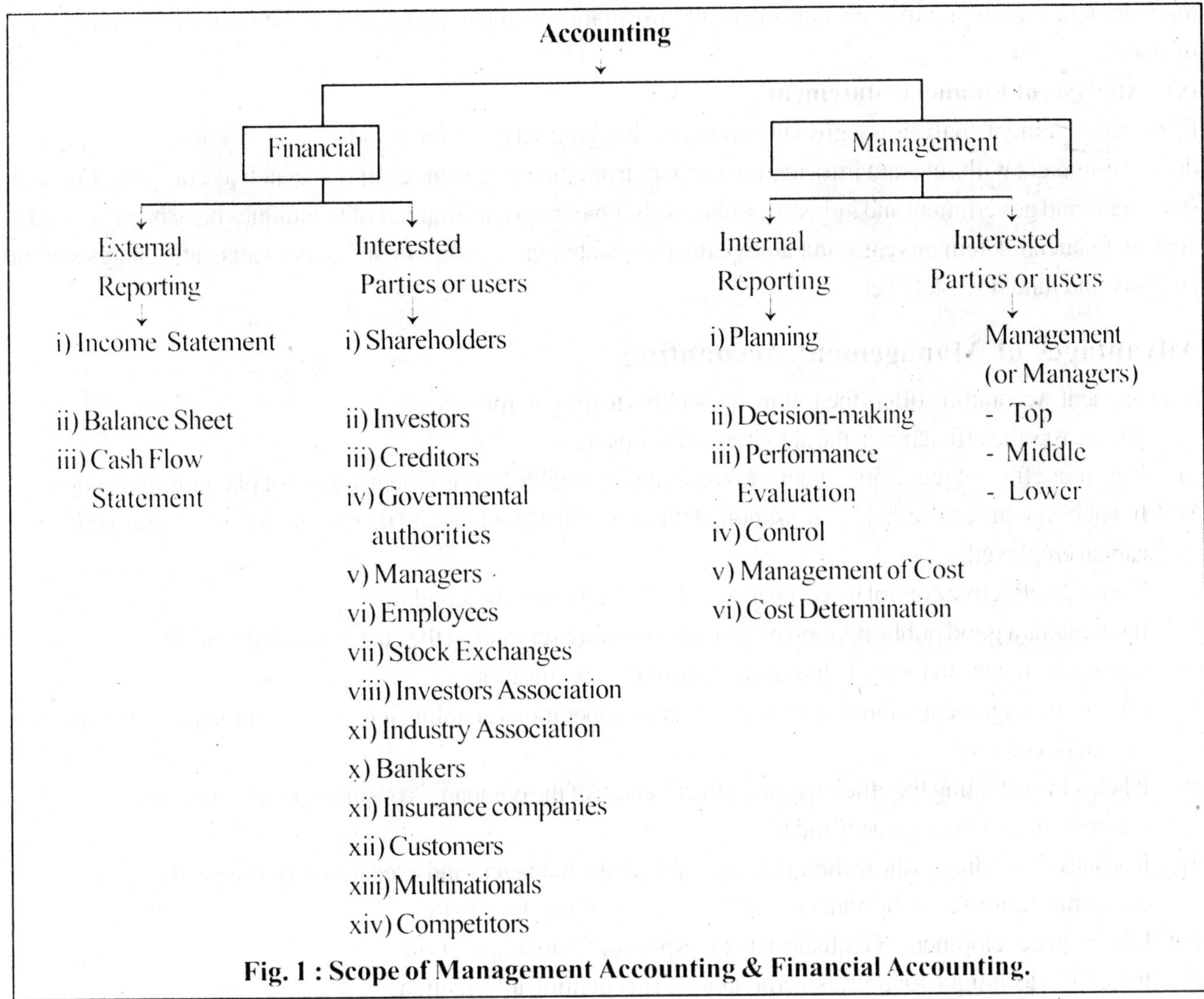

Fig. 1 : Scope of Management Accounting & Financial Accounting.

control, for which a proper monitoring of performance is a key factor. The variances between standard and actual costs are computed and reported to managements.

v) Marginal Costing

Marginal costing is a managerial technique that considers only variable costs in the additional output decisions. It is reporting system that values inventory and cost of sales at its manufacturing variable cost. It is frequently used as an internal management reporting system.

vi) Budgetary Control

Budgetary control refers to a system of business control that uses budgets to control the major activities of business. The budgets for all major activities of the business are prepared in advance. Generally the budget is prepared by updating the previous year's figures in the light of some forward projections.

vii) Funds Flow Analysis

Funds flow analysis attempts to highlight the causes of change in the financial condition of a business enterprise between two dates. Any statement prepared for this purpose refers to as funds flow statement. A funds flow statement helps management in the efficient planning and control of cash.

viii) Management Reporting

Management reporting is considered essential component of a well designed planning and control system. Decision-makers frequently require information on various aspects of business. Thus, it is the responsibility of the management accountant to communicate right information to the management at the right time and in a right manner.

ix) Analysis of Financial Statement

Financial statement analysis is a growing and ever changing set of systems and procedures designed to provide decision-makers with relevant information derived from the basic sources of data, such as company financial statements and government and industry publications. Over the years number of techniques have been devised to analyse financial statements e.g. comparative financial statements, common-size statements, ratio analysis, trend analysis, and fund flow statement.

Advantages of Management Accounting

Management Accounting offers the following benefits to the enterprise :

1) It increases the efficiency in the activities of the business.
2) It ensures efficient regulation of business activities by establishing efficient system of planning and budgeting.
3) It makes possible the efficient utilisation of the available resources and thereby increase the return on capital employed.
4) It ensures effective control by comparing actual results with the standards.
5) It maintains a good public relation by providing quality services to the customers of the business.
6) It provides means to motivate the employees of the organisation.
7) It keeps management informed about the on going operations enabling it to suggest remedical measures in case of deviations.
8) It helps in evaluating the efficiency and effectiveness of the company's business policies with the incorporation of management audit.
9) It is one of the "diagnostic techniques" available to the managers and executives for improving economic performance by realisation of the accounting system in use.
10) It helps in development of realistic data in respect of future transactions.
11) It provides technique for useful interpretation of accounting information.

A Overview of Planning, Organising, Control & Decision Making based on Accounting Information :

The Management process implies the four basic functions of (a) Planning (b) Organising (c) Controlling, and (d) Decision-making. Management accounting plays a vital role in these managerial functions performed by managers.

a) Planning : Planning is formulation of short term and long-term plans and actions to achieve a particular end. The long-term plan indicates management's expectation of the future during the next three to five years or perhaps even longer. Planning requires setting objectives and identifying methods to achieve those objectives. Planning involves activities such as setting selling prices, arranging for the financing of a plant expansion, and the development of new products. A budget is the financial planning showing how resources are to be acquired and used over a specified time interval.

Management accounting is closely interwoven in planning both because it provides information for decision-making and because the entire budgeting process is developed around accounting-related reports. Managerial accounting helps managers in planning by providing reports which estimate the effects of alternative actions on an enterprise's ability to achieve desired goals. For example, if a business enterprise determines a target profit for a year, it should also determine how to reach that target. For example, what products are to be sold at what prices ? The management accountant develops data that help managers identify the more profitable products.

Similarly, the effects of alternative prices and selling efforts (say, what will profit be if we cut prices by 10% and increase volume by 30% etc.) can easily be determined by the management accountant.

As part of the budgeting process, management accountants prepare budgeted (forecasted) financial statements, often called proforma statements. Among the most important is the budget of cash receipts and disbursements. Forecasts of cash requirements are used by the finance department to determine whether borrowing will be necessary. The management of cash is extremely critical; more companies fail because they run out of cash as a result of inadequate planning than because they are unable to make a profit. Making profits and maintaining cash are two very different things and managers must understand that success in one does not necessarily mean success in other."

b) Organising : Organising is a process of establishing an organisational frame work and assigning responsibility to people working in an organisation for achieving business goals and objectives. The type of organisational structure differs from one business enterprise to another. In some organisations there may be centralised structure and in others, organisational structure may be decentralised. In the organising process, departmentalisation can be done by setting up divisions, departments, sections, branches. Organising requires clarity about each manager's responsibility and lines of authority. The various departments and units are interrelated in a hierarchy, with a formal communication structure in which information and instructions are passed downwards to lower level management and upwards to top management level.

Management accounting helps managers in organising by providing reports and necessary information to regulate and adjust operations and activities in the light of changing conditions. For example, the reports under managerial accounting can be prepared on product lines on which basis managers can decide whether to add or eliminate a product line in the current product mix. Similarly management accountant can provide sales report, production report to the respective managers for taking suitable action about the sales and production position.

c) Controlling : Control is the process of monitoring, measuring, evaluating and correcting actual results to ensure that a business enterprise's goals and plans are achieved. Control is accomplished with the use of feedback. Feedback is information that can be used to evaluate or correct the steps being taken to implement a plan.

The functions of the controller in an organisation have not been structured and earmarked in crystal clear terms. In practice, the functions of the controlling depend more on the terms of the agreement that he has entered into with an undertaking. However, the Controllers Institute of America has drafted a seven point concept of modern controllership. The salient features of the concept are as follows :

1) To establish, co-ordinate and administer, as an integral part of management, a master plan for the control of operations providing for profit planning capital budgeting, sales forecasts, expenditure budgets, and standard costing along with procedures to the extent required in the business operations.
2) To compare performance with operating plans and standards and the report and interpret the results of operations to different levels of management and to the owners of business, including formulation and administration of accounting policy and the compilations of statistical records and special reports as required.
3) To consult with all segments of management responsible for policy or action concerning any phase of the operations of business so far as it relates to the attainment of objectives and the effectiveness of the policy, organisation structure and procedures.
4) To administer taxation policy and procedures.
5) To supervise and co-ordinate preparation to reports of Governmental agencies.
6) To assure fiscal protection to the assets of the business through adequate internal control and proper insurance coverage.

7) To continuously appraise economic and social forces and the Governmental influence and interpreting their effects on business.

The functions of the controller have been exhaustively spelt out by the Controllers Institute as well as the National Industrial Conference Board of the United States, in a greater detail. But all the same, they devolve mainly on the seven-point concept of modern controllership. But with the passage of time, the functions of the controller have been vastly expanded ensuring all accounting control over complex and cumbersome business operations.

Management accounting helps in the control function by producing performance reports and control reports which highlight variances between expected and actual performances. Such reports serve as a basis for taking necessary corrective action to control operations. The use of performance and control reports follows the principle of management by exception. In case of significant differences between budgeted and actual results, a manager will usually investigate to determine what is going wrong and possibly, which subordinates or units might need help.

d) Decision-making

Decision-making is a process of choosing among competing alternatives. Decision-making is inherent in each of three management functions described above, namely, planning, organising and controlling. A manager cannot plan without making decisions and has to choose among competing objectives and methods to carry out the chosen objectives. Only one of different competing plans can be selected by a manager.

Similarly in organising, managers need to decide on an organisation structure and on specific actions to be taken on day-to-day operations. In control function managers have to decide whether variance are worth investigating.

Before knowing the role of management accountant in the decision-making area, it is, first, necessary to understand the decision-making process. The decision-making process includes the following steps :

1) Identifying a problem requiring managerial action.
2) Specifying the objective or goal to be achieved (e.g. maximising return on investment).
3) Listing the possible alternative courses of action.
4) Gathering the information about the consequences of each alternative.
5) Making a decision, by selecting one of the alternatives.

Decision-making process, a vital function of the management, is highly facilitated by the information flowing from different sources, both from within and outside the organisation Information from outside the organisation is obtained primarily from customers, trade agencies, market research consultants and Government agencies whereas information from within represents movement of information upwards from lower levels. With the advancement in science and technology, large organizations install computers and other sophisticated equipments for getting quick information after due processing and analysis of information already fed into it. An important ingredient of the modern management information system (MIS) is the establishment of a 'data bank' in which all types of factual information, are stored which can be easily obtained subsequently by the management as and when required for decision-making process. It is well known that the electronic computers store data in "memories", add new data from time to time, perform bewildering variety of complex functions and then print answers required at a lightening speed undreamt of before.

Role of Management Accounting

Management accounting represents a happy blending of the two older professions of 'Management' and 'Accounting'. The two important elements in the success of a business concern are accounting control and management efficiency. These two determinants are completely merged in management accounting through the harnessing of accounting for improving the efficiency of management.

Management accounting greatly assists the management in achieving better results by making a clear shift in emphasis from mere recording of transactions to their analysis and interpretation to give a new vista to the management. It concerns with the tools and techniques of formulation of budgets and pre-setting of standards as well as evaluation of deviations in actual performance and also implementation of prompt remedial measures. In short, management accounting eliminates intuition from the field of business management and broadens the services of accounting to management.

The management accountant, often referred to as controller, is the manager of accounting information used in planning, control and decision-making areas. He is responsible for collecting, processing and reporting information that will help managers / decision makers in their planning, controlling and decision-making activities. He participates in all accounting activities within the organisation. He performs many vital responsibilities and functions within an organisation such as :

1) Providing help in the design of an accounting information system.
2) Collecting data.
3) Helping in the maintenance of accounting records, preparation of financial statements.
4) Helping in the budget preparation.
5) Preparation of performance reports, control reports, special managerial reports/analyses for planning, control and decision-making.
5) Coordinating budget-making and report preparation activities.
7) Interpreting accounting data based on the particular requirements of a manager in a given situation.
8) Ensuring that the accounting information system is adequate and useful in accordance with the budgets, plans, policies and decision requirements.

The role and responsibility of a management accountant is one of support. They provide help to these managers who have primary responsibility to fulfil basic managerial functions. Positions that have direct responsibility for the basic objectives of an organisation are known as line positions. Positions that are supportive in nature and have only indirect responsibility for an organisation's basic objectives are called staff positions. For instance, a manager of a production department holds a line position and has responsibility and authority to make decisions concerning his department. The production manager and similar other managers holding line positions formulate policies and goals and make decisions that have impact on production. The management accountant, however, has no authority over the production manager and other line positions managers. But since the management accountants have the responsibility of providing and interpreting accounting information, they can have significant influence on the policies and decisions made by production and similar line managers.

The management accountant should clearly understand that different decisions made in the organisation require different types of data. Short -run decisions need different data than long -run decisions. Similarly, decisions affecting the total company such as product lines to be added in the existing product mix need more aggregate data than some other decisions, say, the optimum use of a particular machine. Therefore, the management account should ensure that the information system of the organisation meets the needs of all decision makers within the organisation who require information for the performance of their jobs. For example, mangers responsible for the sales of particular product might need a weekly sales report for for each territory. Their supervisor, who also supervises other managers, might need a weekly report for a group of products. The chief sales executive may require monthly reports of sales by product group and sales territories. The management accountant must ensure that the information system meets these varying needs.

Because of the vital functions performed and role played by a management accountant in an organisation, the management accountant is often recognised as a member of the top-management team and encouraged to participate in planning, control and decision-making activities. Thus, it can be said that a management accountant is not only a service arm to management but also he is a part of the management.

From the above discussion it is clear that management accounting is no substitute for management. In the ultimate analysis the businessman like the general in a battle field confronted with a particular situation, must take a careful decision affecting the survival and success of the business. It is also highly imperative that a good management accounting department must be able to furnish all the necessary facts of the situation along with various alternatives open to the businessman in such a situation, and also the estimates of the various costs and benefits arising out of different courses of action suggested. Better the presentation of this information, easier is the decision-making for the management. It should also be remembered that on no account the management can delegate its vital function of decision-making to any department that provides counselling service to the management. It may however be noted that a management accountant may be authorised to deliberate on any issue concerning business management.

Limitations of Management Accounting

Following are the limitations of management accounting

1) **Psychological resistance**

The management accounting system spells a radical change in the management approach towards solving day-to-day problems confronted by it. This calls for a reorganisation of personnel as well as reorientation of their activities. This is bound to attract opposition especially from the labour force misconstruing it as a tool meant for their exploitation. Constant education about the benefits of such a new technique alone will allay the fears of the labour force by and large. Management accounting, as a new discipline, is no exception to this rule and it encountered psychological resistance at least in the initial stages.

2) **Expensive installation**

For installation of a system of management accounting in a business concern, an elaborate organisation and a large number of manuals are very essential. This in turn escalates the establishment charges such that only large scale organisations can afford to install it.

3) **Continuance of Intuitive Decision-making**

Management accounting eliminates the intuitive decision - making process of management and replaces it with scientific decision-making. Unfortunately, many managements are prone to take the easy and simple path of intuitive decision-making rather than the difficult but reliable scientific decision-making process in the day-to-day management.

4) **Broad-based scope :**

The scope of management accounting is wide and broad-based and this creates many difficulties in the implementation process. It is easy to record, analyse, and interpret an historical event converted into monetary terms in a most objective manner. But it will be difficult to perform the same functions in respect of future and unquantifiable situations in the light of the past records.

5) **Comprehensive coverage**

The fusion of a number of subjects like financial accounting, statistics, engineering, economics, taxation, etc. has culminated in the emergence of management accounting. Under the circumstances, should be emergence of management accounting. Under the circumstances, it more of these subjects will have its impact on the fixation of standards as well as solutions to the problems connected with the management performance.

6) **Evolutionary Stage**

Management accounting is a new discipline and a growing subject too. It is still in the infancy stage and undergoing evolutionary process. Naturally, it faces certain obstacles and impediments before achieving perfection and finality. This necessitates sharpening of the analytical tools and improving of techniques for removing the air of doubt as regards uncertainty in their applications.

7) **Persistent Efforts**

The conclusion drawn by the management accountant may not be readily and willingly implemented. For this purpose the management accountant has to strive to convince the staff members.

8) **Basic Records**

The management accounting collects the data from various sources like Financial Accounting, Cost Accounting, statistics and other operational records. If such data or information is incorrect or partial the decisions arrived at on the basis of such data may be incorrect and misleading.

9) **Principle of objectivity not followed**

The principle of objectivity is not followed in its real spirit in management accounting. The collection and analysis is considerably influenced by the personal bias of the management accountant.

10) **No substitute for Management**

Infact, Management Accounting is a mean to an end, the end being the successful business operations for achievements of business objectives. It cannot replace management as it is simply a tool or a technique in the hands of management and ultimate success in business depends upon the will and dedication of management.

However, number of the limitations from which management accounting is suffering can be overcome if the management is convinced about the importance of, and the necessity for management accounting. As well as these limitations do not undermine the significance of management accounting.

Questions for Self Study

1. What is Management Accounting ? Discuss the role of management accounting in the area of planning, control and decision making.
2. "Management Accounting is nothing more than the use of cost and financial information for management purpose". Explain the statement with illustrations.
3. Discuss the importance of management accounting for managerial decision making. State briefly the difference between managements accounting and financial accounting.
4. Define Management Accounting and explain its significance.
5. Describe how Management Accounting satisfies the various needs of management for arriving at appropriate business decisions.
6. What are the main limitations of financial statements ?
7. Explain the scope of Management Accounting.
8. How does management accounting differ from financial accounting ?

9. Explain the meaning of the term "Management Accounting" and state how it can be used as an instrument of higher control.

10. "A management accountant is both an information provider and a part of management". Explain.

11. Why is financial accounting subject to more strict rules and regulation than management / accounting ?

12. Explain the role of management accounting in a fast changing business environment. In what manner can management accounting is considered as an extension of financial accounting. Give salient points of distinction between the two.

13. Define 'Management Accounting' Describe the limitations of Management Accounting.

14. "Management Accounting is oftenly called as a tool for management" Discuss. Explain briefly the functions of Management Accounting.

15. What do you understand by the term "Management Accounting" ? Explain its usefulness in modern business.

16. Explain the important phases in the evolution of accounting.

17. What is the use of accounting information ? Explain the purposes of accounting information.

18. What is meant by Financial Accounting ? What are its objectives ?

19. Define the term "Financial Accounting". Explain its functions & limitations.

20. 'Management accounting plays a vital role in planning, organising, decision making & controlling functions performed by managers" Discuss.

21. Write short notes on :

    a) Functions of Management accounting

    b) Scope of management accounting

    c) Use of accounting information

    d) Objectives of financial accounting

    e) Cost accounting

    f) Limitations of management accounting.

22) Fill in the blanks with appropriate word given in the brackets.

    a) Management Accounting concentrates on.......... (opening of Books of Accounts/ preparation of financial statements/control of business activities).

    b) Financial accounting provides......purpose report (specific/general/specific & general both).

    c) The user of financial statements are mainly......to the business concern. (internal/external/internal & external both).

    d) Double Entry System is used in ....accounting (cost/financial/management).

    e) All business transactions are recorded in terms of money in....... accounting. (financial / cost / management/all type of).

    f) Planning and controlling are done by......(top management / middle management / lower level management / all levels of management).

    h) Decision making concerns the....(future/past/past & future both).

    i) Budgets are.....(past/present/future) financial plan to achieve the business objectives.

    j) Management Accounting emphasises on providing....... (historical/futuristic) data to managers.

    k) The function of management process that involves selecting one course of action from alternatives is referred to as......(organising /controlling /planning /decision making).

*****

UNIT NO. 2

FINANCIAL ACCOUNTING

Financial Accounting : Introduction

Accounting may be described as "the language of business" that can provide a partial history of activities of a particular business house - a history in which the recorded facts are generally expressed in terms of monetary units. Financial Accounting is the art and science of recording and summarising business transactions and of interpreting their effects on the affairs and activities of an economic unit. Financial Accounting is an important service activity in business and is concerned with the collecting, recording, evaluating and communicating the results of past events. Like any other functional management in a business concern (such as marketing, production etc.) "finance" is a vital functional organ of the business. If finance function does not operate well then whole organisational activity will be ruined. Hence it is essential that the finance function should be well organised in a firm.

Financial accounting concerns that part of accounting which is meant to serve all parties externally to the operating responsibility of the firm e.g. creditors, investors, employees, regulatory bodies, and general public.

Principles of Double Entry & Theoretical concepts of Accounting

Generally speaking there are two systems of book-keeping : Indian System and English System. Indian merchants have a tradition of keeping their accounts in their regional language. e.g. in Gujarati, Marathi, Urdu, Hindi etc. in special kinds of books called "bahis", hence the system is also called the "BAHIKHATA SYSTEM." Indian Merchants have a conventional system for recording and maintaining the books of accounts. Before the introduction of Double Entry System, accounts used to be kept either on Single Entry System or Cash System.

1) Single Entry System : There are many entrepreneurs having small scale business. Such small traders often deal exclusively in cash buying from wholesale markets and selling through local market stalls or hawking their products from house to house in vehicles adopted for the purpose. To such a trader there is really no need for written records, he conducts his entire affairs from his trouser's pocket. The records maintained are mainly regarding the cash transactions and personal accounts of debtors & creditors. Naturally, every entry has no double effect. The Nominal accounts and the Real accounts are not maintained. Since both the aspect of transactions are not kept in view, the system is called " Single Entry System" or "Incomplete accounts." Under this system greater importance is given to personal accounts. At best it may be known as a partial method of keeping accounts.

2) Cash System : The cash system of book-keeping is generally adopted by such organisations where all transactions that take place are for cash only. In this system debtors and creditors accounts are maintained, therefore there is no need for keeping personal ledger accounts. This system is used by institutions whose aim is not to create or earn profits. They generally prepare income & expenditure account with the help of cash book. This system is adopted by the institutions where the number of transactions are limited in number.

Double Entry Book-Keeping System

Book-keeping is based on the principles of double entry. Double entry book-keeping is the most scientific method of recording business transactions. In India, most of the business concerns have adopted this system. However there is some misunderstanding amongst the Indian business community of its being rigid and difficult. Therefore they adopt the Single Entry System with some modifications. The Mahajani system is being practiced in India for a considerably long time. Now a days also the same Mahajani System is rearly used in India.

History of Double Entry Book-Keeping System

Book keeping is as old as the trade or business itself. In its crude form, it has existed since time immemorial. But it was in 1494 that the modern system of book keeping took its birth in venice (Italy), for it was in that year that the first known work on book-keeping was published by an Italian Merchant named Lucas Pacioli. Thereafter this work was translated and published in English by Hugh Old Castle in 1543. A decade later, a work on "how to keep a perfect account of debtors and creditors" was published by James Pale. Thereafter a series of work was published. In 1795, Edward Jones, introduced the concept of Journal having two columns. Various other innovations were introduced later from time to time.

Nature of Double Entry System

Double entry system of book-keeping denotes that every business transaction has two fold effect. There cannot be business transaction unless it has effect atleast on two accounts or two parties. Whenever a piece of business is arranged, there are always two parties involved one is the 'giver' and another is the 'receiver'. "Every piece of business activity is called a transaction and millions of them occur every day. Every transaction must be recorded in two accounts one of which will be debited because it receives value. The other will be credited because it has given value.

Principles of Double Entry Book-Keeping :

The main and fundamental principles of Double Entry book-keeping are as under :

a) Each transaction has two fold aspects and affects two accounts.
b) In the two accounts affected, one account is the receiver of benefit under the transaction, and the other account is the giver of benefit under the same transaction of equal amount.

The rule for double entries is therefore as follows :

Debit the account that has received goods, or services or money.
Credit the account that has given goods, or services or money.

There are certain steps in recording any financial transactions :

a) Confirm that the thing to be recorded is a transaction and not only an event
b) Decide which two accounts are affected under a given transaction.
c) Decide which account receives benefit and which account parts with benefit under the same transaction.
d) Apply principles of debit and credit and record the transaction in the books of prime entry debiting one account and crediting the other account so affected.
e) Decide on the amount to be debited or credited.

For example

1) Rs.1000 are paid to Mr. Naresh :
This is a transaction. Here, the accounts affected are Cash account and Mr. Naresh account.
Mr. Naresh is the receiver of the benefit & Cash account is the giver of the benefit.

Thus, this transaction has two fold effect, and a complete record of both these effects can be kept only by recording the transaction in two accounts.

2) Sold goods on credit to Mr. Subhash of Rs. 200

This is a transaction. In this transaction, the customer (Mr. Subhash) receives the benefit and the goods have gone out. This transaction affects the two accounts viz. Customers Account and the Goods Account.

3) Paid Rs.20 for stationery.

In this transaction cash goes out of business and therefore, cash position changes. On the other hand, this amount is spent on stationery.

This method of writing every financial transaction in two accounts is called as Double Entry System of Book-keeping. This means for every debit accorded to any account, there is a corresponding credit to any other account.

It should, however be noted that some financial transactions may affect more than two accounts. But even then the total amount with which one or more accounts are debited and the total amount with which one or more accounts are credited would remain the same.

Naturally, the total of all the debits must agree with the total of all the credits. Therefore, this double entry book-keeping system enables us to check the arithmetical accuracy of the accounts.

Advantages of Double Entry System

Following are the advantages of Double Entry System :

a) Under this system both personal and impersonal accounts are maintained, therefore a complete record of transaction is possible.

b) It ensures arithmetical accuracy of books of accounts. For every debit, there is a corresponding credit. As such total debits and total credit have to be equal. This is ascertained by means of a Trial Balance.

c) Full information is readily available on the following points :
   i) Value of properties possessed by the proprietor.
   ii) The amount a trader owes to others or others owe to him.
   iii) Incomes, gains, expenses and losses from various items.

d) It affords an effective comparison of various items, such as purchases, sales, stocks, incomes, expenses, etc. of the current year with those of the past years to know whether there is any progress or not. This comparison tends to make substantial improvement in the nature of expenses to the benefit of business.

e) As Nominal Accounts are maintained, it is possible to prepare the Profit and Loss Account at the end of each year.

f) A statement of assets and liabilities (i.e. Balance Sheet) can be prepared showing the financial position of the business.

g) Under this system any errors made in recording the transaction can be easily checked and corrected.

h) A possibility of fraud is reduced. and if at all it is committed , the same can be easily detected.

In short, the Double Entry Book-Keeping is a procedure, perfect in all respects and offers all possible advantages in keeping books of accounts.

Disadvantages of Double Entry System

The double entry system though very scientific and accurate is not free from shortcoming or limitations. This system does not provide any method of detecting errors of the following types.

a) Omission of an entry in the books of original Entry : If any transaction is not recorded at all in the books of original entry, it may remain undiscovered.

b) ***Recording wrong amount in the books of original entry :*** If the amount of a transaction is wrongly recorded in the books of original entry, the mistake may not be found out.

c) ***Compensating errors :*** A compensating error may also remain undetected. These errors are of neutralising nature. One error is compensated by the other error or errors of opposite nature.

d) ***Entry in wrong account :*** If a wrong account is debited or credited, this error will not be disclosed by the Trial Balance.

Classification of Accounts

The true purpose of accounting is to maintain proper control of finances of the business. Accounting must be based on careful and efficient double entry book keeping.

An account, as we understand it is a ledger account opened in the ledger on separate pages. An account may be defined as a systematic and summarised record of transactions pertaining to any person or institution, any property or thing, any expense or income or any loss or gain. An account is always divided in two sides. The left hand side is known as the Debit side and the right hand side is known as Credit side.

The Proforma of 'Account' is as follows

Mr. Ramrao's Account (This is the title or name of the account)

Dr. (Debit side)-------------------------------------><------------------------------------(Credit side) Cr.

Date	Particulars	L.F.	Amount Rs.	P.	Date	Particulars	L.F.	Amount Rs.	P.

You should note the following points :

a) There is line at the top of every account page for the name or title of the Account.

b) The page is clearly divided down the middle and the two halves of the page are identical, each having columns for the date, particulars of transaction, folio number and the amount of money involved.

c) The two side of the page are respectively called the debit side and the credit side.

The debit side is always used when the person named at the top receives goods, services or money and thus becomes a debtors of the firm. The credit side is always used when the person gives goods, services or money to the firm and thus becomes a creditor.

Hence, in order to keep a complete record of the business transactions the businessman has to keep the accounts of persons or firms or institutions with whom he deals. He has to keep a record of his assets, liabilities and expenses, incomes, losses and gains.

Meaning of Classification :

The term classification means an act or a system of arranging in classes. The classification of accounts refers to the act of dividing various accounts into certain well defined classes.

The classification of accounts can be shown by way of chart as under.

1) ***Personal Accounts :*** These are the accounts of individuals, firms, limited companies, local authorities, associations with whom the businessman deals. These personal accounts may be of the customers who purchase the goods on credit, suppliers, who supply the goods on credit & other personal accounts like owners/ proprietors capital, lenders accounts. etc. A separate account is maintained for every person or firm or company.

2) ***Impersonal Accounts :*** These are the accounts which relate to other than persons. These are further divided into two types or groups :

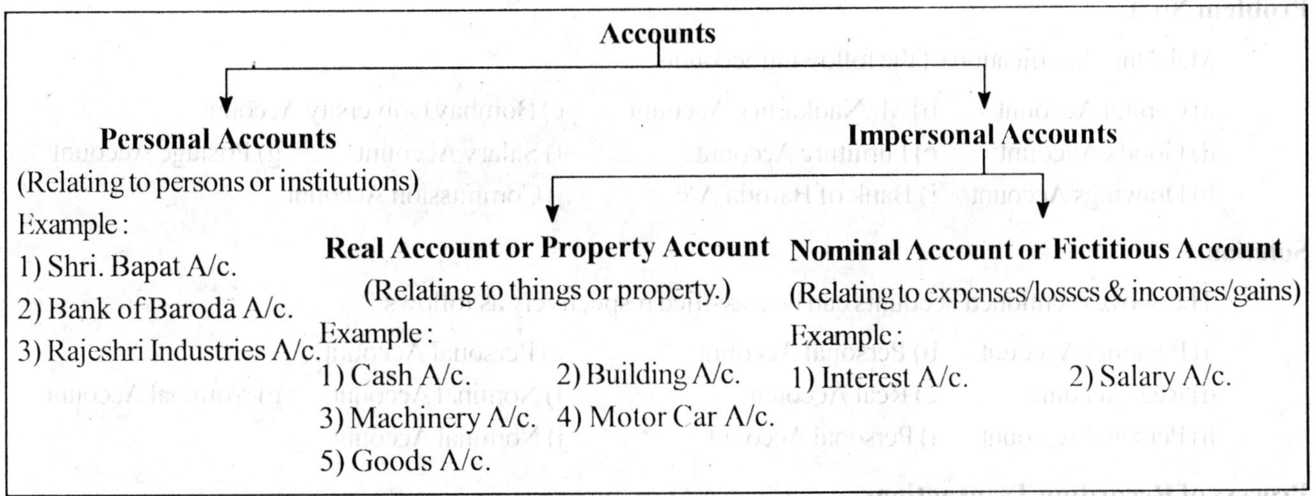

a) Real Account :- These are the accounts of properties, assets or professions of the businessman. These accounts are called Real Accounts because they represent something that really exists. A separate account is maintained for each class of property or assets. For example - Cash A/c, Furniture A/c, Goods A/c, Plant and Machinery A/c, Building A/c, Motor car A/c, Stock A/c etc.

b) Nominal Account :- Accounts representing expenses/losses and incomes/gains such as salary, rent, interest, commission etc. are called Nominal Accounts. The nominal accounts are so called as opposed to Real Accounts, because they exist in name only and they do not represent any tangible thing. They represent only services or uses or something intangible. A separate account is maintained for each head of expenses or losses or gain or income. For example - Rent, Salary, Interest, Electricity expenses etc.

Rules for Debit and Credit :

Under the double entry system of accounting every business transaction has minimum two aspects and these aspects are known as debit aspect and credit aspect. That means in every business transaction minimum one account is debited and one account is credited with the same amount. Following are the fundamental rules for recording business transactions in journal :

1) Personal Accounts :	a) Debit - the Receiver	b) Credit - the Giver
2) Real Accounts :	a) Debit - what comes in	b) Credit - what goes out
3) Nominal Accounts :	a) Debit - the expenses and losses	b) Credit - the gains and profits.

Chart showing Rules of Debit and Credit

Accounts

Personal Account	Real Account	Nominal Account
Debit ← Receiver	Debit ← What comes in	Debit ← Expenses & Losses
Credit ← Giver	Credit ← What goes out	Credit ← Incomes & Gains

Problem No. 1.-

Make the classification of the following accounts

a) Capital Account b) Mr.Nadkarni's Account c) Bombay University Account
d) Goods Account e) Furniture Account f) Salary Account g) Postage Account
h) Drawings Account i) Bank of Baroda A/c j) Commission Account

Solution

The above mentioned accounts can be classified respectively as follows

a) Personal Account b) Personal Account c) Personal Account
d) Real Account e) Real Account f) Nominal Account g) Nominal Account
h) Personal Account i) Personal Account j) Nominal Account

Process of Recording Transactions

Following are the steps or process for recording the business transactions.

1) Confirm that the thing to be recorded is a transaction.
2) Identify the nature of transaction.
3) Identify which two accounts are involved.
4) Identify the class or type of each account.
5) How each aspect of account is affected.
6) Find out the rule which is applicable for each aspect of transaction.
7) Find out which account is to be debited and which is to be credited.
8) Confirm the amount to be debited and credited.

For example : Purchased goods of Rs. 500 from Mr. Ramrao on Credit

1) This is a business transaction.
2) Credit Purchases.
3) Here, Real Account and Personal Account are involved.
4) Goods is a real account and Ramrao is a personal Account.
5) Goods comes in and Mr. Ramrao is a giver.
6) Here rule for real Account and Personal Account is applicable.
7) Goods Account will be debited because the goods comes in and Ramrao's Account will be credited because he is the giver.
8) Goods Account will be debited for Rs. 500 and Ramrao's Account will be credited for Rs. 500.

For easy understanding students should carefully study the following procedure for debit and credit under

Double Entry Book-Keeping

1) Ascertain which accounts are affected ?
2) Determine the nature of these two accounts that are affected or which type of accounts are they !
3) Apply the rules for different types of accounts !

Problem No. 2

A) Cash received from Mr. X (Proprietor) Rs. 10,000 as his capital to start business.

1) Ascertain, which accounts are affected ?

The two accounts affected are : i) Cash Account ii) X Capital account

2) Which types of accounts are they ? i) Real Account - because cash is an asset

ii) Personal Account 'X' is the giver of the capital amount

3) Rules which are to be applicable ?

   i) Real Account-Debit what comes in and credit what goes out-Here cash comes in hence debited to Cash A/c

   ii) Personal Account - Debit the receiver and credit the giver. - Here X is the giver of the cash to the business hence X capital Account is Credited.

B) Purchase of goods from Mr. Avinash on credit for Rs. 3,000.

1) The two accounts affected are : i) Goods Account ii) Mr. Avinash's Account

2) i) Real Account - Goods in stock on a particular date is an asset.

   ii) Personal Account - Avinash's Account is personal Account.

3) i) Rule of real account is debit what comes in and credit what goes out.

   ii) Rule of personal account is debit the receiver and credit the giver.

4) Hence - Goods Account is debited and Mr. Avinash's account is credited.

C) Received Commission in cash Rs. 100.

1) The two accounts affected are : i) Cash Account ii) Commission Account.

2) i) Real Account - Cash is an asset.

   ii) Nominal Account - Commission received is an income.

3) i) Rule of real account is debit what comes in and credit what goes out

   ii) Rule of Nominal account is debit the expenses and losses and credit incomes and gains.

4) Hence - Cash account is to be debited and commission account is to be credited.

D) Paid Salary to clerk in cash Rs.1000.

1) The two accounts affected are i) Salary Account ii) Cash Account

2) i) Real Account- When cash is paid as Salary, Cash goes out.

   ii) Nominal Account- Salary is an expenses

3) i) Rule of real account is debit what comes in and credit what goes out

   ii) Rule of Nominal account is debit the expenses & losses & credit incomes & gains.

4) Hence- Salary account is to be debited & cash account is to be credited.

E) Purchased a motor car for cash from Gujarat Motors Ltd.for Rs. 95000/-

1) The two accounts affected are : i) Motor Car Account ii) Cash Account.

2) i) Real Account -When motor car is purchased, it comes in

   ii) Real Account- Cash goes out on purchase of a motor car.

3) Rule of real account is debit what comes in & credit what goes out.

4) Hence- Motor Car Account is to be debited & cash Account is to be credited.

F) Borrowed Rs. 1000 from Shri Limaye

1) The two accounts affected are i) Cash Account ii) Limaye's Loan Account

2) i) Real Account - When loan is taken cash comes in ii) Personal Account- Mr. Limaye is the giver.

3) i) Rule of Real account is debit what comes in & credit what goes out.

   ii) Rule of personal account is debit the receiver and credit the giver.

4) Hence-Cash Account is debited & Limaye's Loan A/c is credited.

Accounting Concepts & Conventions

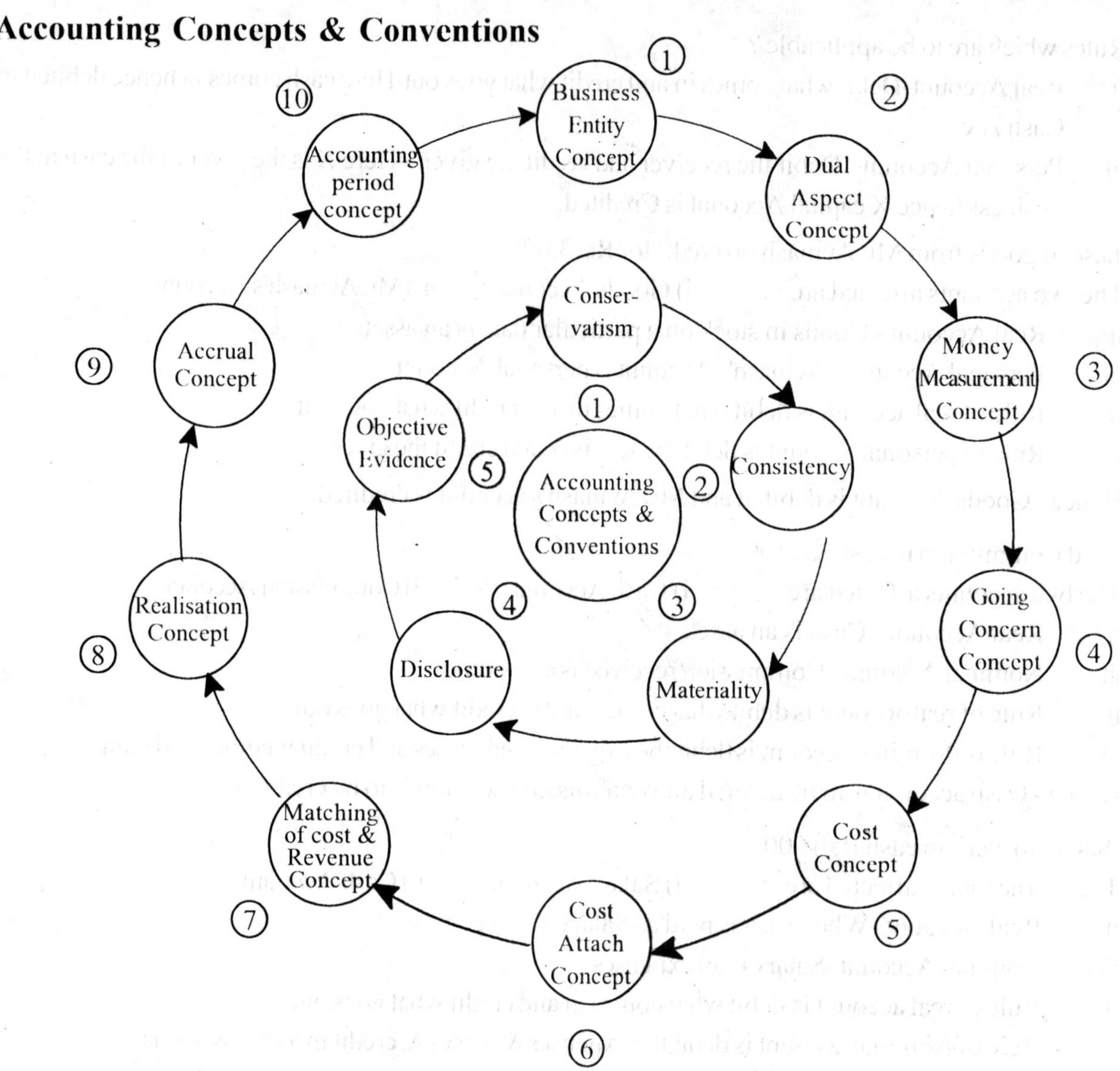

Accounting Concepts & Conventions

Introduction

The accounting process and financial statements are based on certain principles. In accounting terminology, principles means "a general law or rule, adopted or professed as a guide to action". The term "Accounting Principles" is a wide term and includes all practices, procedures, methods, techniques, concepts and conventions in accounting.

Accounting principles are widely accepted, if they satisfy the following criteria.

a) Utility : i.e. accounting statement should be meaningful.

b) Objectivity : i.e. accounting statements should be reliable for decision making on the basis of facts and figures shown in those statements.

c) Flexible : i.e. accounting principle should not be rigid.

d) Feasibility : i.e. accounting principle should have practicability.

Accounting principles are usually the concepts and conventions which have been adopted as a general guide by the accounting professional. There are 10 concepts in accounting and they are modified by 5 conventions.

A) Concept : A concept is a notion. The term 'concept' denotes the basic assumptions or propositions or predictions or conditions upon which accounting is based. Any abstract idea serving a systematised function may be termed as concept. It is an idea.

Accounting concepts are such ideas that are commonly associated with the theory and practice of accountancy. Concepts can be classified into 4 categories as follows.

a) Natural , i.e. Matching cost with revenue is a natural concept.
b) Real, i.e. practical
c) Ideal, i.e. theoretical
d) Borrowed concepts - i.e. concepts borrowed from other disciplines.

B) Convention : The term "Convention" denotes customs or traditions. Convention refers to "a statement or rule of practice which, by common consent express or implied, is employed in the solution of a given class of problems or guides behaviour in a certain kind of situation. Conventions are established usages or rules or statement of practice. "Debit on left hand side and credit on right hand side of an account, liability on left hand side and assets on right hand side of balance-sheet, expenditure on left hand side and Incomes on right hand side of profit and loss A/c are the examples of convention.

A) Accounting Concepts

1) Business Entity Concept

This concept is also called as "Separate Entity Concept." A firm or a business is regarded as separate and distinct from the owner. The business has its own entity and therefore its affairs are to be distinguished from the affairs of any body else even the owners. All the transactions of a business are recorded separately without mixing the private transactions of the owner. Even the proprietor is considered as a creditor to the business and hence his capital is shown as liability in the balance-sheet.

The business accounts are of business only and are not mixed up with the owners. For example; If the proprietor draws some goods from the business for personal use, it is not treated as a sale but the value of those goods consumed by the proprietor is debited to his 'drawing account' and reduced from his capital account.

2) Dual Aspect concept

All business transactions are regarded as having a dual aspect. The balance-sheet shows the financial position of the business at one point of time. It's Right hand side represents the assets being used by the business and left hand side represents the sources of these assets. The sources are of two types (a) owned sources i.e. capital and (b) borrowed sources i.e. liabilities or the claims of outsiders on the assets.

For example- (I) Mr. `X' the proprietor brings cash of Rs. 15,000 as his capital in the business. Here, the resource is X's capital and the form of resource is cash. Then the accounting equation will be as follows :

Owners Capital = Assets - Liabilities

Rs. 15,000 = Cash of Rs. 15,000

(II) He borrowed Rs. 10000 from A, and purchased a machinary of Rs. 20,000, then the accounting equation will be as follows.

Owners Capital + Liabilities = Assets in use.

Rs. 15,000 + 10,000 (Loan from A) = Machinery Rs. 20,000 + Cash Rs. 5,000

The assets are always equal to capital & liabilities. In this manner balance sheet should reconcile the amounts on both the sides. In other words one account is debited while the other account is credited with an equal amount. Every debit has a credit. That is, for every debit there is a corresponding credit.

3) Money Measurement Concept

All transactions are recorded in terms of money. Money had to act as a means of indicating the value of the commodity or prices. Money simplified the business of calculating the rate at which one commodity can be exchanged for another. Hence money is used as the measuring unit for financial reporting. This concept makes accounting information more meaningful and useful for analysis of financial statements. Thus money makes possible smooth exchanges.

For example - A business house has 40 acres of land, 20000 sq.ft. building, 10 horses, 1000 goats, 1000 tonnes of raw material etc. This does not give us a clear idea about its property. The real meaning will follow only when each commodity is accounted or valued in terms of money.

However some other things cannot be measured in terms of money such as, efficiency of management, sales and pricing policy of management, working conditions. etc. The limitation is that the qualitative aspect of the business cannot be recorded.

4) Going Concern Concept

This concept is also called as "The concept of permanancy "or" continuity concept". It implies that accounting is made on the assumption that a business will continue in future and will use its property in operations rather than sell them. Therefore, the market values or realisable values are recorded in the books of accounts.

Eric L. Kohler defines going concern as "a business enterprise in operation with the prospect of continuing operation in future, its assets, liabilities, revenues, operating costs, personnel policies and prospects, a concept basic to accounting of importance in the valuation of intangible assets and the depreciation of tangible and intangible assets" A dictionary for Accountants. Here, the assumption is that the business will continue trading over a long period of time. Accounting is to be done on the basis of this assumption or proposition and all transactions are entered at cost only.

Following are the main implications of this concept

a) The assets acquired need not be sold and are not meant for resale.
b) The revenue income is compared with revenue expenditure to ascertain the result from business.
c) The expenditure is classified into Capital & Revenue.
d) The assets are recorded at cost and shown in the balance sheet at cost less depreciation.
e) The principle of valuation of closing stock at cost or market price whichever is lower presumes that the concern is going to last for some more years.
f) Deferred revenue expenditure and unexpired costs are carried forward to the next year.
g) Estimated liabilities arising on future eventualities are also taken in to account.
h) The fluctuations in the market rates are ignored.

For example - When a machinery is purchased, proprietor has to presume or assume that machinery is going to last for a number of years and the business itself will continue. Therefore, on the basis of estimated life of the machinery, depreciation is to be calculated and debited to profit and loss account every year. If the continuity concept is not prevalent, the whole amount of asset would have been written off in the year in which the asset was purchased.

However, the following are the exceptions to this concept

a) In case of liquidation, a different approach to valuation is necessarily required and in such case market value which is realised may be taken in to consideration.
b) In case of constructual commitments, i.e. in case of contracts of construction obtained for a specific period, the cost of equipment purchased is charged to that contract, even though the same equipment may be useful for a longer period.

5) Cost Concept

This concept has been adopted for the purpose of convenience and feasibility. It implies that the resources of a business are to be recorded at their cost. Here, cost is the cash or the cash equivalent for an asset in a transaction.

The cost concept makes the accounting record objective because it does not allow transactions to be recorded at arbitrary value. It should not be recorded at market value. Similarly all transactions should be entered at cost only. Due to this concept the accounts will become more reliable, useful and comparable because the transactions are recorded at cost. The cost concept does not recognise the realisation value or the replacement value or the market value of an asset. According to this concept all assets and liabilities are recorded at their cost of acqusition.

Cost should be the basis for subsequent accounting also. It is shown at cost less depreciation. Even the intangible asset like goodwill is recorded at cost. If no amount is paid for an asset, it will not appear in the accounting records.

For example- A purchased a piece of land for Rs. 50,000 the market price of which is Rs. 59,000. While recording the same in the books of account, the entry must be made with Rs.50,000 only. Suppose subsequently the price of land falls to Rs. 32,000 still in the books of account the land will show of Rs. 50,000 only. Thus the transactions are recorded in the books at cost only.

However, there are certain limitations to this concept.

a) Price level changes are not reflected in the accounts and hence the current values of assets are ignored.
b) Depreciation is only an estimate. It cannot be calculated or ascertained accurately.
c) It ignores the true value of the asset to the business e.g. In many cases value of goodwill may be higher than the cost.
d) If the accounts are not converted at current values the inter firm comparison will be meaningless.

While considering the above limitations as such it is recommended to adhere to the cost concept only.

6) Cost Attach Concept

According to Ryall- "In practically, all cases, a cost is the sum of three groups or components : a) the purchase or transfer of material, b) the cost of hire of labour & c) the value of other disbursement made or expenditure incurred in achieving the desired product or result."

Thus, the total cost is the sum of material, labour cost & overheads.

Total Cost= Material Cost + Labour Cost + Overhead Cost.

When appropriate portion of material costs, labour costs and other overhead costs are added or merged together, product costs are obtained. Hence this concept is also known as 'Cost merge concept". However the total cost of production does not necessarily reveal the actual cost of the product. In fact, actual value will be determined by sales price which may be higher or lower than the cost. Subsequently, while cost remain unchanged, value changes depending upon the sale price.

7) Matching Costs and Revenue Concept

Firstly, the term" matching" indicates the close relationship that exists between the cost and revenue. The matching concept requires that the revenue and the cost incurred to obtain that revenue should be properly matched. This concept states that accounts should be presented at fixed intervals regularly. This will be helpful in measuring the business performance periodically. This concept is based on the accounting period. Therefore, it is also known as "the periodic matching with revenue concept".

For example : If the total cost is more than the sales value, it will result into a loss.

If the total cost is less than the sales value, it will result in to a profit.

Profit = Sales value - Total Cost & Loss = Total cost -Sales Value

Thus, the matching of costs and revenue is required to measure the positive or negative result of business operations in a particular accounting period. (The matching concept is related to accrual concept and realisation concepts also.)

8) Realisation Concept

According to the realisation concept, the profit on sale is generally regarded as earned at the time when the goods or services are passed on to the purchaser and the purchaser incurs the liability for that. No profit is considered to have been earned till it is either realised in cash or the other party involved is legally liable to pay the amount for sale of goods.

The concept of realisation does not only mean the receipt of income in cash, but the income is also said to be realised as a right to receive the income is created. The profit is to be credited only when it is actually realised.
For example : i) Cash sales of Rs.10,000, here the income is received in cash.

ii) Credit sales of Rs.50,000 to Ramrao, here the seller creates a legal right to receive the income.
Thus in credit sales though the income is not received in cash, still it is said to be realised.

However the following are the exceptions to this concept

a) Anticipated or unrealised profit should not be taken into account where as expected losses are taken into consideration.

b) Income like interest, rent etc. are credited to profit and loss account on accrual basis, though they are not realised.

c) In case of hire purchase sales, sales is said to have been made to the extent of cash received by way of instalment.

d) In case of assets, cost concept is adopted.

9) Accrual Concept

The concept of accruing income and expenses is fundamental in modern accounting method. It is also known as "Mercantile system of Accounting." The essential of the accrual concept is that, profit is measured by operating transactions that affect owners equity. When revenue is recognised at the time of sale rather than at the time of collection of cash, this is referred to as accrual basis of accounting. Accrual accounting means the system of recording revenues whether they are received in cash or not and expenses whether they are paid in cash or not. In other words, the outstanding, prepaid, prereceived expenses and income are considered under this concept. Because of this concept the net profit or loss of any period cannot be equal to corresponding cash increase or decrease. For this purpose, the necessary entries will be passed at the end of accounting year in respect of following items :

a) Income earned but not received.

b) Income received in advance.

c) Income received but pertaining to previous year.

d) Expenses due but not paid.

e) Expenses paid but not related to accounting period.

The American Accounting Association committee rightly pointed out that "Expenses is the expired cost, directly or indirectly related to a given fiscal period of the flow of goods or services into the market and of related operations. Recognition of cost expiration is based either on a complete or partial decline in the usefulness of assets or on the appearance of liability without corresponding increase in assets."

10) Accounting period concept

The term "periodicity" referes to segmentation of the existence of an organisation into time periods. This time period is called as "Accounting period." For the purpose of internal control, monthly, quarterly or half yearly accounts can be prepared. At the end of each such period the final accounts are drawn to find out the profit or loss during the period and the assets and liabilities at the end of the said period. Generally one year period of interval is accepted by the business concerns. This concept states that accounts should be presented regularly at fixed intervals.

Acceptance of this concept necessitates the closing of the books of accounts, particularly of revenue nature (i.e. incomes and expenses) for the accounting period ending and hence it requires the certain estimates, assumptions, or propositions which are mentioned as under :

a) Accounts should be maintained on accrual basis.
b) Unpaid incomes and expenses should be accounted for
c) Expenses paid in advance and income received in advance should be carried forward to the next year account.
d) Estimate of useful life of asset for the purpose of depreciation.
e) Rate of depreciation should be appropriate. (proper method should be adopted)
f) The expenditure should be properly segregated into capital & Revenue.
g) To accommodate the concept of realisation, assumptions should be made.

B) Accounting Conventions

1) Conservatism

The first convention is that "Anticipate no profit and provide for all possible losses". This indicate that think and provide for all probable losses and expenses but do not credit any probable future profit. On this basis, closing stock is valued at cost or market price whichever is lower, creating a provision for doubtful debts, a provision against fluctuations in the prices of investments and the profit is not credited unless it is realised, are all based on the conservatizm. This affects the current assets only. This concept thus presents the accounting information correctly and avoids unwarranted optimism in preparing Final Accounts. The following are the conservative accounting practices adopted in Accountancy :

a) Fixed assets are shown at cost minus depreciation.
b) Adopting accelerated method of depreciation.
c) Current assets are shown at cost or market price whichever is lower.
d) Charging stock of medicines, stock of stationery to profit & loss Account.
e) Showing joint life policies at surrender values instead of paid up values.
f) Amortising intangible assets.
g) Providing for doubtful debts and for discount of debtors.
h) Not providing for discount on creditors.

2) Consistency

Accounting policies, methods, rules and practices should remain unchanged from one year to another year. Then only the results of a business concern can be compared from one year to another. Consistency has to be followed in particular in respect of the following procedures :

a) Calculation of depreciation b) Valuation of material c) Treatment of revenue and capital expenditure.

Different business houses follow the different policies and methods.

1) Valuation of Raw material, work in progress, stores and spares and finished goods whether at cost or market

price whichever is lower or any other method.

2) Calculation of depreciation under straight line or reducing balance method etc.

3) Valuation of material issued under FIFO, LIFO, simple average, weighted average methods etc.

A change in these methods and policies will mean a change in the amount of expenditure or income and the value of asset. Hence the principle of consistency plays an important role, which says that; Once a method or policy is adopted by the business it should be consistently followed. Consistency helps comparison of results. Eric L Kohler in his dictionary for a accountants mentioned three type of consistencies.

Types of Consistencies

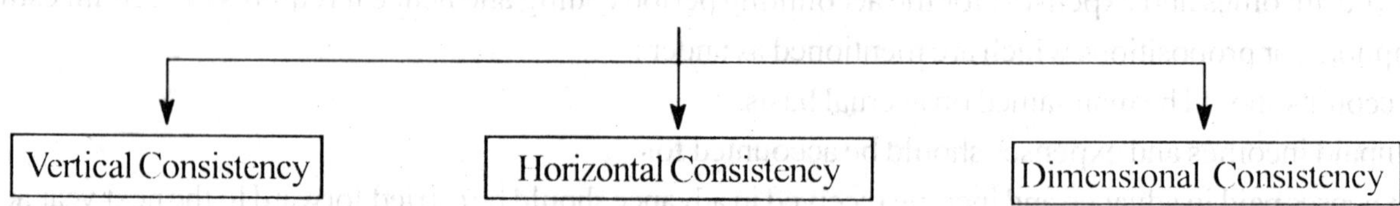

Consistency in interrelated statements. If 15% depreciation is charged in profit and loss account, the same percentage should be shown in the balance sheet also.

This helps comparison of results from one year to another in the same organisation . In the same orgainsation there should be consistency in final accounts from one year to another.

This helps comparison of results of one organisation with another organisation in the same industry. This refers to uniform accounting in the various organisation in the same type of industry.

3) Materiality

Eric L. Kohler in his dictionary for accountants defines materiality as "the characteristic attaching to a statement, fact or item where by its disclosure or the method of giving its expression is likely to influence the judgement of a reasonable person."

Materiality means the relative importance and is related to the convention of disclosure. Disclosure is necessary in financial accounts only for material facts. Materiality is of two kinds- materiality of information and materiality of accounts. This principle refers to the significance of transactions. The cost of accounting of a transaction is not more than the amount of transaction.

For example - While maintaining stock records there should be one head of account namely "Consumable stores" covering all items of small hardware etc. There is no need to make the entry for every screw, pin, or nails purchased etc. under different heads. Such separate individual entries are not material in business. Ultimately what is material and what is not, has to be decided on the basis of individual judgement. In other words, what is material in one account period may not be material in the next accounting period and what is considered to be material for one business may not be material to another business.

Materiality depends not only on the size of the amount spent but also on its nature.

4) Disclosure

All the material facts should be disclosed in the final accounts. In fact, the Companies Act has made several provisions for disclosure of essential information in Final Accounts. The object of disclosure is to make the financial statements more useful and to give less scope for misinterpretation. Even significant events occurring after the end of accounting year but before the preparation of balance sheet are to be disclosed. This will help the readers of financial statements to understand the performance of the business correctly.

The important items requiring disclosure are as under

a) Abnormal items. b) Contingent liabilities

c) Accounting methods and policies adopted by the company.

d) Changes in method or policies of accounting and their consequential effect on the profit.

e) Items of non-recording nature.

f) Significant difference between the cost and market value of stock .

g) Items pertaining to previous year i.e. prior period adjustments made in the current year.

5) Objective Evidence

The convention of objective evidence means that each and every transaction recorded in the accounts should be objective and variable. Unless some documentary evidence is obtained for business transaction no entry in the books is to be passed. The documents may be like voucher, bills, receipts, statements, bank pay in slip, contracts, cheques, correspondence and cash book etc. There is imperative need to make financial statements reliable and unbiased. In short, for every data furnished there should be a proper evidence and supported by objective documents, which can be verified by auditor at a later date. It is related to the evidence of each transaction necessary for accuracy and truth.

However, objective evidence may not be possible in the following cases :

a) Depreciation : It is calculated on the basis of estimated useful life of the asset.

b) Reserve for Doubtful Debts : It is also estimated by the proprietor.

c) Realisable value of inventory : It is also estimated.

d) Apportioning of overheads : On the basis of estimates only.

e) Amortisation of fictitious assets : In this case objective evidence may not be possible.

Statement showing meaning, examples & purpose of accouting concepts.

Following Accounting concepts make the maintenance of accounts and preparations of financial statements on uniform basis. Information gathered therefrom convey the same meaning.

	Concept	Meaning	Examples & Purpose
1)	Business Entity Concept	Business is regarded as distinct unit or entity from its owner. As business & businessman are two separate entities. (Distinction must be maintained between the proprietors and the firm)	i) Capital brought in by the owner is recorded as cash/asset coming in the business from the point of view of the business, where as, it is cash/asset going out from the point of view of businessman. ii) The owner may be having 3 different activities like a Grocery shop, a laundry and tea stall. The accountant must remember these 3 different entities and he should maintain three different sets of books of account. **Purpose :** This concept has led to good results. If the distinction is not kept the personal and business tranactions will get mixed and the accounting statements will become coufusing.
2)	Money Measurement Concept	In accounting only those things which can be expressed in terms of money are recorded to give a meaningful information. As money is accepted not only as a medium of exchange but also a store of value.	i) Merely saying that a business unit has 4 acres of land, 25000 sq. metre building, 2000 kgs of material etc. will not give us clear idea about its assets. The real meaning will follow only when all these are measured in common unit which is money. ii) A team of dedicated managers, no doubt is an asset of the business but it cannot be measured in terms of money and hence is not to be recorded in the books of account. iii) The state of health of the Managing Director of a company who has been the key contributor to the success of business is not recorded in the books. **Purpose :** Accounting record is concerned with amounts in terms of money.
3)	Continuity Concept (going concern concept)	This principle indicates that accounting is made on the assumption that a business will continue in future and will use its assets in operations rather than selling them. [This assumption is not applicable to terminable venture. (time or object)] The main implications of this concepts are: i) The expenditure is divided into Capital and Revenue. ii) The revenue income is compared with revenue expenditure to find the profit / gain.	i) Certain expenditure will give rise to benefits accruing over a long period, like expenditure on machinery and that it must be distinguished from the expenditure whose benefit will be exhausted within the year. ii) If the life of the venture is known in advance, the record will be from the point of view of the period of the life. (if some one engaged in one short-term contract only lasting less than a year there will be no distinction between expenditure whose benefits accrue over a long period and that those whose benefits are for a short period only.

	Concept	Meaning	Examples & Purpose
		iii) The capital expenditure (Assets) is shown at cost and not at market / realisable value vi) The fluctuations in the market rates are ignored.	iii) Depreciation (or amortisation) procedures rest up on this concept. **Purpose :** The concept holds that continuity of business activity is the reasonable expectation for the business unit for which accounting function is being performed.
4)	Cost concept / Objectivity concept.	It implies that the resources of a business are to be recorded at their cost. The market price, realisable value etc. should not be considered while recording the transations in the books. This means that the amount recorded should not depend on the wishes or whims of any particular individual, it should be based on objective evidence.	i) Purchased a plot for Rs. 80,000 the market price of which is Rs. 84,000 while recording it in the accounts, the entry must be made with Rs. 80,000 only. Suppose after few years the price of the plot falls to Rs. 70,000, still in the books the plot will show the amount of Rs. 80,000 only. **Purpose :** The most important purpose of this principle is to provide reliable, verifiable and definite accounting information. The cost concept meets all these basic criteria Relevance/Objectivity and feasibility.
5)	Accrual Concept	In accrual concept the revenue is reckoned (count) to the period in which it was realised (rather than received) and the cost applied to the period benefitting from the services (rather than when paid/incurred) In other words - the outstanding / prepaid prereceived expenses and incomes are considered under this concept.	i) Salary outstanding ii) Rent outstanding iii) Insurance premium paid in advance iv) Wages accured due v) Interest on loan unpaid vi) Taxes paid in advance. **Purpose :** Because of this concept the net profit / loss of any period can not be equal to corresponding cash increase or decrease. Outstanding Expenses Liability Income received in Advance Liability Outstanding Income Asset Prepaid Expenses Asset (Expenses paid in advance)
6)	Concept of Conservatism	This concept is based on the assumption that the recording is to be done for the expected losses, but not of anticipated gains. (Too rosy a picture of the financial affairs should not be conveyed by the financial statement)	i) Provision in accounts is made for all losses though not yet suffered e.g. provision for bad and doubtful Debts (RDD) ii) Profit is not credited unless it is realised e.g. the closing stock is valued at the market price or cost price whichever is less. iii) A customer has filed a suit for damages against the company in the court of law whether the judgement will be farourable or unfavourable to the company can not be determained for sure. Hence it will be prudent to provide for likely loss in the final Accounts.

	Concept	Meaning	Examples & Purpose
			Purpose : This concept presents the accounting data correctly and avoid unwarranted optimism in preparing financial statement.
7)	Materiality Concept	Materiality concept holds that item of small significance need not give strict theoratically correct treatment. In other words the cost of accounting of a transaction is not more than the amount of transaction. (what is material and what is not, has to be decided on the basis of individual judgement and common sense.)	i) While maintaining stock records, one can have one head as "consumable spare" covering all items of small hardware etc. There is no need to make the entry of every screw purchased, nails purchased etc. under different heads. ii) Purchase of stationery is recorded as an expenses unused stock of stationary is not recorded separately. **Purpose :** The concept referes to the significance of the transaction. It is not worthwhile to record every minute details in accounting as it will be cumbursome and uneconomical.
8)	Consistency Concept	There are different accounting policies and methods. Different business firms follow different policies and methods or certain rules and assumptions. In order to make the result of one year comparable with those of other years, the basis should not be changed.	i) The method for charging depreciation should remain unchanged from year to year, otherwise the profit of one year cannot be compared with the profit of other years. ii) Valuation of material issues under FIFO LIFO or simple average or weighted average methods etc. should not be changed. **Purpose :** The principle of consistency plays an important role, which says that once a method or policy adopted by the business, it should be consistently followed.
9)	Periodicity concept	According to this assumption, the life of an enterprise is divided into arbitrary period for preparing final accounts. (No businessman can wait for knowing the results of his business till its termination)	i) Now a days management, creditors, investors and government need results of the business more frequently, these can be prepared monthly, quarterly, half yearly or annually. ii) Generally financial statements are prepared annually for 12 months period starting on the 1st April and ending on 31st March. **Purpose :** This concept stated that accounts should be presented at fixed interval regularly.

Questions for Self Study

1) Explain the principle of double entry system of book-keeping.
2) Explain the statement "every debit has a corresponding credit."
3) State the advantages and disadvantages of double entry system.
4) Mention the classes into which ledger accounts are divided.
5) Give three examples of Personal account, Real account & Nominal accounts.
6) State whether the following accounts are Personal, Real or Nominal
   a) Capital b) Bad Debts c) Stock d) Cash e) Goods f) Interest
   g) Discount h) Loss by fire i) Printing & Stationery j) Bank of India k) Building
7) State with the help of a table, which account will be debited and which account will be credited. Give reasons
   a) Commenced business with Rs. 15,000.
   b) Purchased goods worth Rs. 1,000.
   c) Bought goods for cash Rs. 500.
   d) Paid rent to landlord Rs. 200.
   e) Opened an account with Bank of Maha. Rs. 500.
   f) Paid for office stationery Rs. 100.
   g) Paid for insurance premium of Rs. 200.
   h) Paid Rs. 400 to Amit on A/c.
   i) Cash Sales Rs. 800.
   j) Discount received Rs. 100 from supplier.
8) Fill in the blanks with suitable words.
   a) An account is always divided into .... sides
   b) The left hand side of the account is called............side.
   c) The accounts of properties and assets are called the .... account.
   d) Every transaction has a.............effect.
   e) Every...........has a corresponding ....
   f) Each transaction has at least ....accounts.
   g) An account which receives the benefit is ....and the account which gives the benefit is........
9) Say yes or no, stating your reasons.
   a) Machinery is a Real Account
   b) State Bank of India is a Real Account.
   c) Life Insurance Corporation is a Personal Account
   d) Loan Account is a Real Account
   e) Interest on Investment is a Personal Account
   f) Proprietor's capital Account is a Personal Account
   g) Postage account is a Nominal Account
   h) Commission paid is a Real Account
   i) Purchase account is a Nominal Account
   j) Drawing account is a Personal Account
10) Match the following :

a) Personal account is debited	1) When something is going out
b) Personal account is credited	2) For what is received
c) Real account is debited	3) When there is a gain
d) Real account is credited	4) When person is the giver
e) Nominal account is debited	5) When a person is the receiver
f) Nominal account is credited	6) For expenses

11) State whether the following classification is correct or not. Give the correct classification if necessary.

a) Anita Stores A/c	-	Nominal A/c	b) Loan A/c	-	Real A/c
c) Drawing A/c	-	Real A/c	d) Capital A/c	-	Personal A/c
e) Building A/c	-	Real A./c	f) Goods A/c	-	Real A/c
g) Conveyance A/c	-	Real A/c	h) Machinery A/c	-	Nominal A/c

i) Bank A/c - Real A/c

12) Briefly discuss basic accounting concepts and fundamental accounting assumptions.

13) Discuss conventions regarding financial statements.

14) Explain the difference between Concepts and Conventions

15) Write short notes on : a) Cost Concept b) The Accrual concept c) Realisation concept d) Business entity concept e) Money measurement concept

16) Match the following :

a) Concepts	1) Mercantile system
b) Convention	2) Basic assumption
c) Going concern concept	3) Cost merge concept
d) Cost attach concept	4) Permanency concept
e) Accrual Concept	5) Customs

17) Complete the following statements :

a) Profit = ...Value (-) Total Cost

b) Total Cost = Material Cost + ... Cost + Overhead Cost.

c) The first convention is that 'Anticipate no ....and provide for all possible ....'

d) Owners capital = ... (-) Liabilities.

e) Business entity concept is also called as.........

18) Multiple Choice Questions

a) Cash book is an example of-

a) General journal ( )

b) Special journal ( )

c) It is not a journal ( )

b) Commission received in advance is of the nature of -

a) Real account ( )

b) Nominal account ( )

c) Personal account ( )

c) Rebate on bills discounted account is of the nature of-

a) Personal account ( )

b) Real account ( )

c) Nominal account ( )

d) Patent rights account is of the nature of -

a) Nominal account ( )

b) Personal account ( )

c) Real account ( )

e) The sale of a business asset on credit is recorded in-

a) Sales journal ( )

b) General journal ( )

c) Cash Receipt journal ( )

f) The three columns on each side of the three columnar cash book represent-

a) Real and Nominl accounts ( )

b) Real and Personal accounts ( )

c) Real, Personal and Nominal accounts ( )

h) Ledger is a book in which-

a) Only real accounts are opened ( )

b) Only real and personal accounts are opened ( )

c) All the real, personal and nominal accounts are opend ( )

i) The trial balance shows-

a) Both debit and credit balances ( )

b) Only debit balances ( )

c) Only credit balances ( )

j) Rent prepaid account is of the nature of -

a) Real account ( )

b) Personal account ( )

c) Nominal account ( )

k) Subscription account (in case of clubs) is of the nature of-

a) Real account ( )

b) Personal account ( )

c) Nominal account ( )

Introduction, objectives, Importance & Utility of Book-Keeping

Introduction

This book deals with the subject "Book Keeping and Accountancy". The art of Book-Keeping deals with the question of how to keep a record of financial transactions. Before we start with what is meant by book-keeping it is necessary to clearly understand the meaning of the term "Transaction."

Transactions

An act of exchanging things, items or services between two parties is termed as a transaction.

Classification of transactions

Generally transactions are classified as : (a) Non-monetary transactions & (b) Monetary transactions.

a) Non-Monetary transactions : The transactions which do not involve an exchange of money or money's worth (i.e. things, items or services) directly or indirectly are known as Non-monetary transactions.

b) Monetary Transactions : A person's dealing in money or money's worth is termed as monetary transaction. It thus involves a transfer of money or its equivalent from one individual to another. Such dealings may be in exchange of cash, goods, services or debts.

In book-keeping, we are concerned with only monetary transactions of the business and therefore, whenever we come across the term 'business transactions', it means money transactions of the business. Certain examples of transactions are illustrated in the following chart.

Chart showing general classification of transactions :

Thus, the term "transaction" is applied in business for all dealings (whether with any individual or persons, in goods or things or money) involving exchange of money or money's worth.

Thus, the term "transaction" is applied in business for all dealings (whether with any individual or persons,

Events or Illustrations	Whether it is Monetary or Non- Monetary transaction.	Why it is a Monetary or Non-monetary transaction.
Ramesh gives his cycle to his friend Suresh for a single day use.	Non-Monetary Transaction	Here, Ramesh does not expect money or money's worth in return from Suresh as the use of cycle is allowed without any charge. Hence this transaction is called Non monetary transaction.
Ramesh gives his cycle to his friends Suresh on hire basis for a day.	Monetary Transaction	It becomes a monetary transaction because Ramesh receives hire charges from Suresh in return for the use of his cycle.
A mother gives her ornament to her daughter for the time being	Non-Monetary Transaction	It becomes a non-monetary transaction because the daughter is not expected to pay or give anything in return to the mother for the use of her ornament.
Shankar gives his bullock to Gopal in exchange of horse.	Monetary Transaction	It becomes a monetary transaction. Though exchange of money is not involved, money's worth is involved. One animal of value is exchangd for another animal of value.
Purchase of goods of Rs. 1000 by Manohar from Manikchand on Credit	Monetary Transaction	It becomes a monetary transaction because Manikchand has to receive money from Manohar for supply of goods.
Payment of wages of Rs. 500 to a worker.	Monetary Transaction	It becomes a monetary transaction because money is exchanged for the working hours spent by the worker.

in goods or things or money) involving exchange of money or money's worth.

Book-Keeping

Meaning

In simple words the term Book - Keeping means "it is an art and science of recording business transactions". But when the term is used as a method or system or a way of writing the books of accounts it is defined as under:

"Book Keeping is a scientific method of recording day to day business transactions in words and figures in the books of accounts so as to show correctly and clearly the financial position of a business".

"Book-Keeping is also defined as an art of recording transactions related to business or even non business so as to be able to show the significance of all transactions in a nut shell in terms of profit or loss and financial position by the end of a certain period".

L.C. Cropper has defined book-keeping as follows :- "Book-Keeping may be described as the science of recording transactions in money or money's worth in such a manner that, at any subsequent date, their nature and effect may be clearly understood, and that, when required, a combined statement of their result may be prepared."

R.N. Carter has defined book-keeping as follows :- "Book- Keeping is the science and art of correctly recording in books of accounts all those business transactions that result in the transfer of money or money's worth."

The above definitions indicate that book-keeping concerns itself with recording of financial transactions in the books of an economic entity. But to keep records is not an end in itself. Unless these records are classified and summarised, they are of little or no value. The science of accountancy concerns itself with the classification and summariasation of these records. Accountancy is the next stage of book-keeping. Accountancy begins where book-keeping ends. To find correct financial result of an economic unit, it is essential that all transactions be recorded, classified and summarised. It is as clear as sun shine that both book-keeping and accountancy help in achieving this target.

Accountancy has been defined as "The art of recording, classifying and summarising in a significant manner and in terms of money, transactions and events which are in part at least of financial character, and interpreting the results thereof." AICPA committee on terminology. (AICPA : American Institute of Certified Public Accountants)

This definition gives more emphasis on decision-making.

The records of transactions should be complete and properly set so that they can give the maximum information with minimum difficulties and trouble. One must understand the nature of transaction correctly and clearly by reading the record of that transaction.

Book Keeping : Objectives

It is to be appreciated that where a large number of transactions take place, it is impossible for a person to remember all these transactions. The basic idea behind maintaining books of account is to find the correct position regarding the financial condition of an economic entity. Further memory cannot be accepted as an evidence in case of the legal matters. Book-keeping serves as a permanent record of the business dealings and it can be produced as an evidence whenever & wherever required.

The primary object of book-keeping is to enable a businessman or a business house to know the following information accurately and with a minimum of time and efforts.

a) The amount of profits earned or losses sustained by his business during the accounting period.
b) What he owes to others and what others owe to him.
c) The amount of his capital in the business.
d) The financial position of his business which includes the amount of his assets and liabilities in the business at any particular date.

Apart from the above primary objectives, the following objectives are also served by book-keeping :

a) To meet the requirements of certain laws.
b) To know the progress of business by comparing present business results with those of past.
c) To determine the amount of liability to the government for various taxes such as Income Tax, Sales Tax, Professional Tax, etc.
d) To keep a check on the properties.
e) To review the progress of the business enterprise from year to year.
f) To maintain a permanent record of all transactions of business for future reference.
g) To know the amount due to his creditors at any time.
h) To know the amount due to him from each of his customers at any time.
i) To know at a glance the amount he has invested in the business i.e. his capital.
j) To prevent and minimise the errors and frauds by detecting them quickly.
k) To provide valuable information for legal purposes.
l) To help the management in making correct forecasts. Management wishes to know in advance what is likely to happen in the future. It helps them in preparing for the future events.
m) Book keeping and accountancy has developed tools through which efficiency of the economic unit can be measured. It enables the management to understand where they stand.

The accounting results are helpful for control purposes. Such information enables the businessman to exercise effective control over his business assets. He can take a precaution to see that the funds available are properly utilized and not unnecessarily lost.

Book Keeping : Importance

Book-keeping is of great importance to businessmen, book-keepers & accountants, business executives and government authorities. It is extremely important to a businessman. Book keeping is very essential for every business organisation and it is also compulsory by law.

Without a systematic record of transactions in set of books, it is impossible to find out :

a) The amount of profit or loss made by the organisation during a particular period.
b) The amount due to creditors and receivables from debtors.
c) The amount of expenses incurred by the business house for a particular objective.
d) The value of assets of the firm.

The importance of book-keeping in the present days is quite clear from the following points :

a) In the absence of book-keeping nobody can carry out the business successfully. He will not be in a position to know where he stands.
b) Book-keeping enables businessman to make proper record of all financial transactions. It also furnishes him with useful information enabling him to take proper decisions in his business.
c) Book-keeping helps a businessman to run his business smoothly and efficiently.
d) Its importance can also be seen from the point of view of its usefulness in deciding business policies.
e) Book-keeping can also educate the public in general and business community in particular, to be accurate, disciplined in finance and systematic in dealing with all financial matters.
f) Accounting procedures also provide some protection against theft and dishonesty.
g) By adopting the scientific approach in accounting, a businessman can rely upon the persons maintaining books of accounts.
h) With an accurate and scientific method of keeping the books of account, a businessman can exercise a great check on his finance.
i) Book-keeping guides the firm as to where to reduce expenses and as to what are its pitfalls.
j) By comparing the books of accounts with those of other similar concerns businessman comes to know his mistakes and errors.

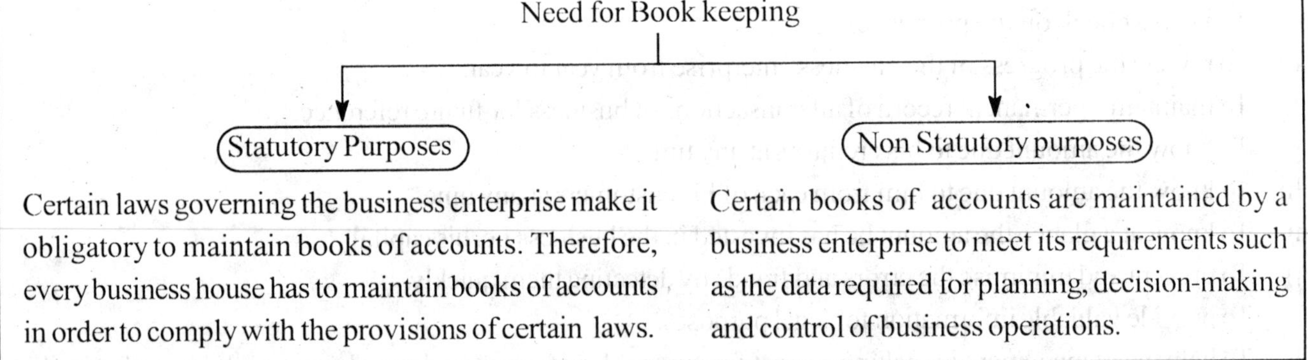

Utility of Book-Keeping

Utility of Book-Keeping (i.e. keeping the books of accounts in systematic manner) can be judged from the benefits book-keeping offers. The utility of book-keeping can be observed from various points of view. It is useful to different sections of the society, as described below

a) The main beneficiary of book-keeping is the businessman or the owner of the business. It would be almost difficult for a businessman to carry on a business without book-keeping.
b) Book-keeping enables the executive of business to control the activities of the business. The executive of the business arrives at certain conclusions by reading the accounts of the business.
c) If a legal action is required to be taken against any customer for recovery of debts due from him, the books of accounts are required to be produced in the court as an evidence.
d) In the case of insolvency the court may refuse or suspend the discharge of an insolvent who cannot produce the books of accounts.
e) In support of insurance claim lodged with the insurance company the relevant accounts are required to be submitted to the insurance company.
f) In absence of book-keeping a person invites risk of over payment to his creditors or wrong payment to a non-creditor.
g) Labour union gets necessary materials for the demand of their wage, bonus etc. from accounting reports.
h) Book-keeping helps price determination in case of sale of business.
i) Banks and depositors can have a good idea about the solvency or credit worthiness of the borrowers.
j) The government has to depend on the financial statements for administering any kind of control over the business organisations.
k) Prospective investors would try to know the financial strength, the profitability and the future prospects before taking the final decision.

Maintenance of books of accounts is not a question of one's will, it has become an indispensable requirement of any type of business. It may be an individual, a firm, a company or a body corporate or government whoever is having dealings in money or money's worth is required to keep the books of accounts in proper way to achieve successfully the predetermined objectives.

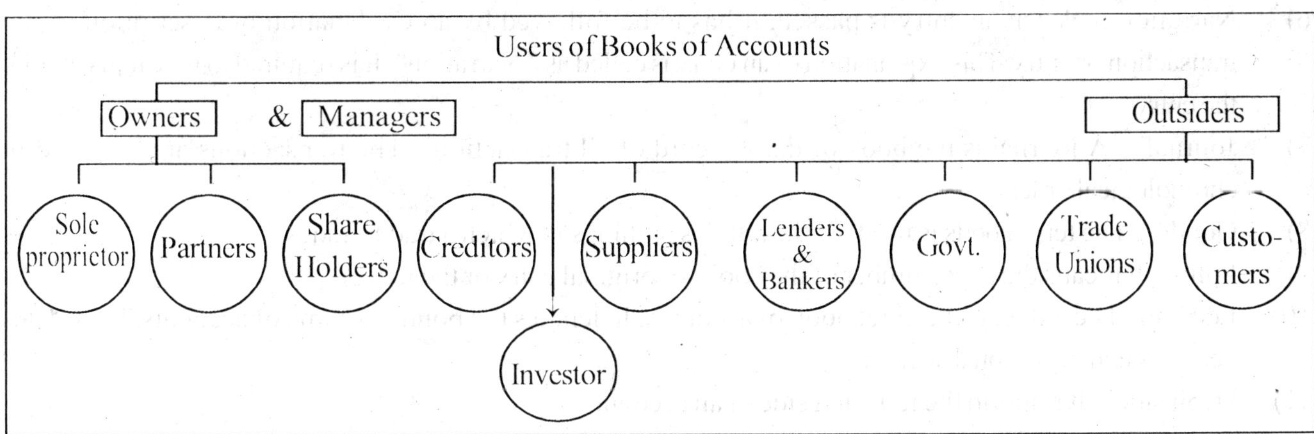

Book-Keeping is an Art and Science

The science of book-keeping deals with the art of keeping records of transactions of financial nature in a regular and systematic manner. However, there are controversial opinions and views regarding whether book-keeping is an art or a science. While art teaches us "to do", science teaches us "to know."

(A) Book keeping is a science because in book-keeping the book-keeper has to follow certain rules, regulations, restrictions, principles, norms, conventions and theories that have been established. Hence we can treat book keeping as a science. The science of book-keeping helps in understanding how the economic units have fared during a particular time period and whether their management has been proper or not. Without the science of book-keeping and accountancy, it would not have been possible to judge the efficiency of the organisation.

(B) Book-keeping is an art because in book-keeping the book-keeper has to use his discretion and judgement in recording transactions. Nicely presenting the books of accounts in good hand writing is also an art. There are certain entries such as depreciations, revaluation of assets and liabilities, valuation of good will & valuation of stock , apportionment of expenditure, where a book-keeper necessarily uses his own discretion although it may be directed by certain well-recognised norms and conventions. In manipulation of accounts a book-keeper may have a scope for using his own judgement and discretion. Hence book-keeping can also be treated as an art.

We therefore conclude by remarking that book-keeping is a mixture of an art and science or by saying that book-keeping is a science which deals with the art of keeping records of business transactions.

Basic Accounting Terms

We will explain below the meaning of some important technical terms used in book-keeping and accountancy.

1) Transaction :- An exchange of goods or services either for cash or on a credit basis is called as a transaction. A transaction requires a minimum of two parties.
2) Entry :- Entry is a record of a transaction in account books. It forms the very basis, for writing the books of accounts.
3) Account :- An account may be defined as a summarised record of all the transactions relating to any particular person or thing or any class of income or loss, which has been entered in, during a given period of time.
4) Head of account :- Head of Account is the name or title of the account.
5) Books of Original Entry- Books of original entry are those books in which the entries are first recorded. These books are also known as "the books of prime entry".
6) Narration :- When an entry is passed, it has to be followed by an explanation or description of the transaction or entry. This explanation of an entry is called as " Narration". It is required to give it just below the entry.
7) Journal :- A journal is the book of daily record of all transactions. The transactions are recorded in chronological order.
8) Goods :- The term goods is used for the articles or things in which a trader trades.
9) Folio :- It means the page number of the books of original entry or the ledger.
10) Ledger :- The ledger is the chief book of accounts. It denotes the bound volume of accounts. It includes personal and impersonal accounts.
11) Debit side :- It refers to the left hand side of an account.
12) Credit side :- It refers to the right hand side of an account.
13) To Debit :- It means passing entry on the debit side of an account.
14) To Credit :- It means passing entry on the credit side of an account.
15) Posting :- Transactions entered in the original books of entry are also to be recorded in the ledger. An act of recording the transaction in the ledger on the basis of the entry made in the original book is called "posting."
16) Casting :- Casting means the totalling of the books of accounts.
17) Capital :- Capital is the total amount invested in the business by the proprietor. The capital of a business is the claim of the owner to the business professions. In the accounting sense, capital is the excess of assets over liabilities.

18) Drawing :- Drawing is the withdrawal of money or goods by the proprietor from his business out of capital or out of profit for private purpose.

19) Assets :- All the properties, possessions and debits owing to a business house are known collectively as assets.

20) Liabilities :- Capital of the proprietor and the debts which are due by the firm, to other parties are known collectively as liabilities.

21) Expenses :- It means the expenditure whose benefit has been received and which belongs to the period under accounts. It is the amount spent on manufacturing and selling of goods and services.

22) Income :- Income or gain is the amount received in return of the service rendered.

23) Stock :- Goods unsold lying with a business on any given date are called stock.

24) Discount :- An allowance given on the sales price of goods. There are two kinds of discounts viz, Trade discount & Cash discount.

25) Bad Debts :- Debts which are irrecoverable are termed as Bad Debts.

26) Debtors :- A person who owes something. He is a person who has to pay to other person.

27) Creditors :- A creditor is a person to whom we owe something, he is the person to whom we have to pay.

28) Person :- The term person includes not only individuals but also institutions or associations like firms, companies, banks, co-operative societies etc.

Daily Books-Ledger-Trial Balance-Profit & Loss Account & Balance Sheet.

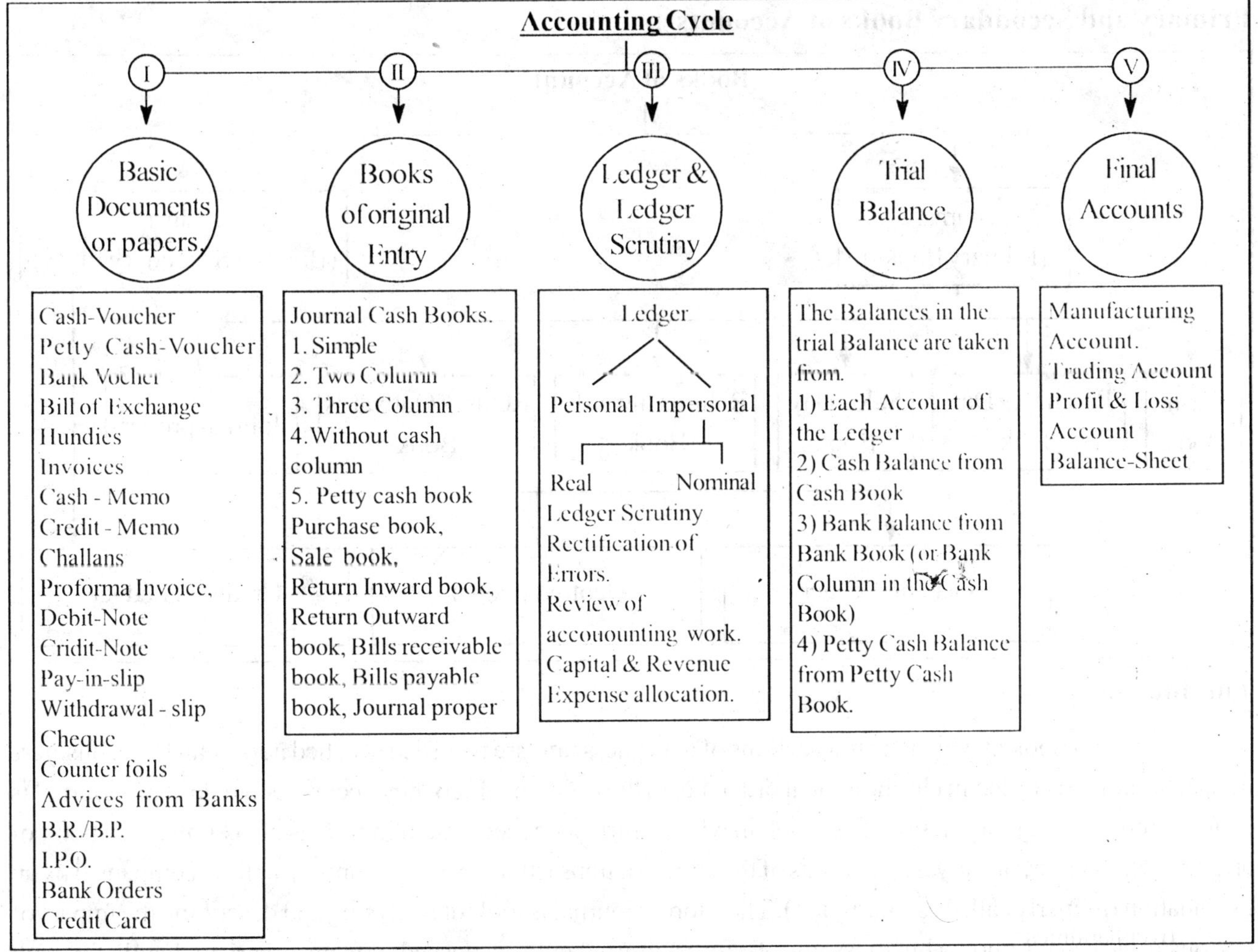

Accounting Cycle

We have studied so far what is to be recorded & what effect is to be given to the accounts affected. These accounting effects are given in the books of accounts. To know the results from the books of accounts a trial balance is prepared at the end of the period. (i.e. 6 months end or year ended or any period as the case may be) Preparation of Final Accounts is the last step as far as accounting treatment is concerned. Accounting cycle indicate the scope of accounting treatment.

Books of Original Entry

The recording of transactions in the books of original entry may be illustrated as follows :

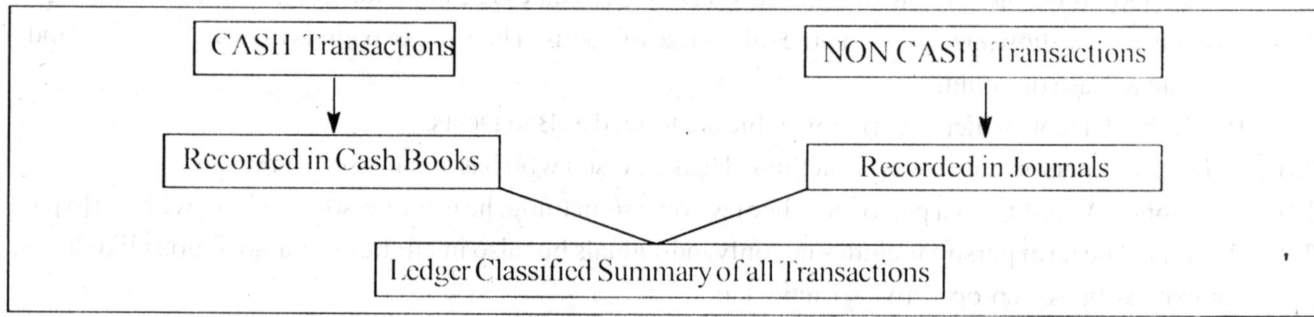

Normally in a business it is impossible to record every transaction as a journal entry. Hence special journal such as purchase book, sales book etc. which are mentioned above are used.

Primary and Secondary Books of Accounts

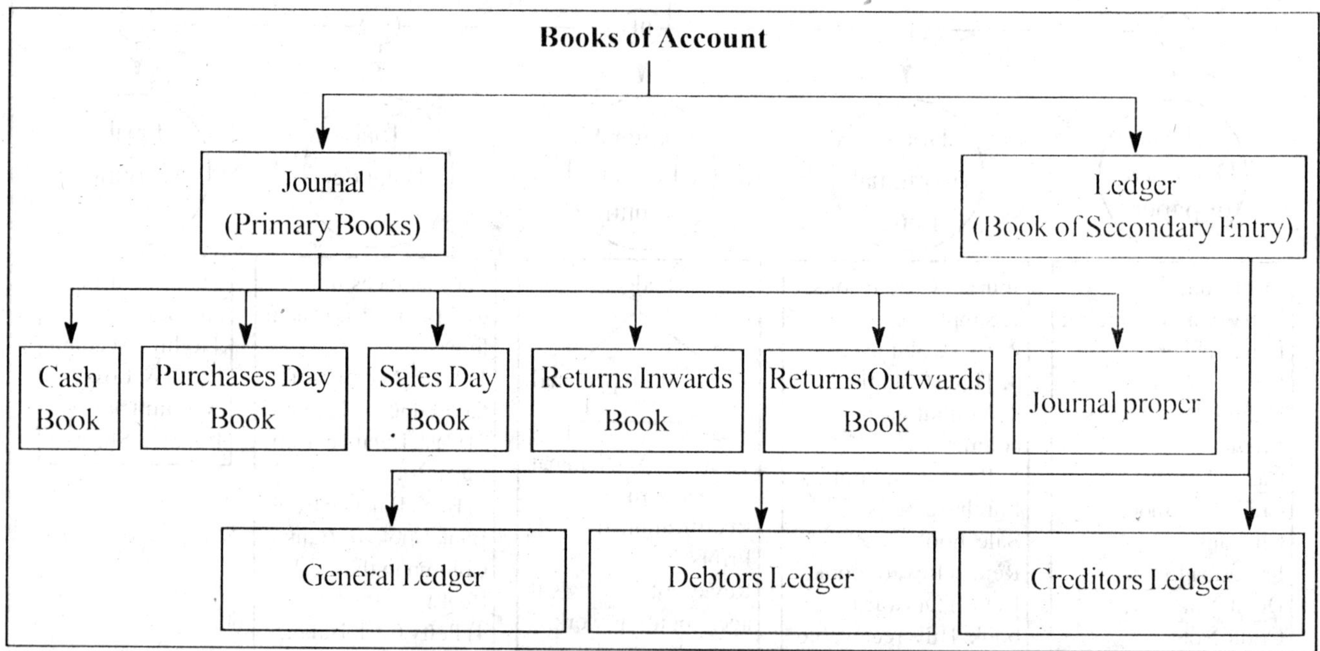

The Journal

The first book in which the transactions of a business unit are recorded is called a Journal. Here, business transactions are recorded in chronological order, i.e. in the order in which they occur. Each record in a journal is called an entry. As a journal is the first book in which entries are recorded, a journal is also known as a book of original entry. A journal entry is an analysis of the effects of transaction on the accounts, usually accompanied by an explanation (properly called as a narration). Therefore, a journal is tool for analysing and describing the impact of various transactions upon a business unit. Before a journal entry is passed, it is necessary to decide for each transaction, what are the accounts involved. It is also necessary that the accounts to be debited or credited are identified.

Ruling of a Journal

In its usual form, a Journal is divided by vertical lines into five columns in which to enter, in respect of each transactions : a) Date; b) Particulars; c) Ledger folio; d) Amount (debit); e) Amount (credit).

	Journal		Dr.	Cr.
Date	Particulars	L.F.	Amount	Amount
(a)	(b)	(c)	(d)	(e)

a) The date : The year is written at the top of the date column of each page of the journal. Thereafter, on the next line of the date column, the month and day of the first entry are written. Unless the month or year changes or until a new page is begun, neither the month nor the year is repeated on the page.

b) Particulars : The particulars column is the column for account titles and description. The name of the account to be debited is entered at the extreme left of the particulars column next to the date column. The symbol 'Dr.' is written at the right end of the particulars column on the same line of the account debited. The amount of the account debited is entered in the left hand money column. The name of the account to be credited is entered on the next line with a prefix 'To' and is indented to the right of the date column. The amount of the account credited is entered in the right hand money column. A short explanation of the transaction known as narration begins on the line immediately below the account credited. The narration should be adequate to explain the transaction and may include any data needed to identify the transaction.

c) Ledger folio (L.F.) : The ledger folio column to the right of the particulars columns is not filled in when transactions are recorded in the journal. When the debits and credits are posted in the ledger accounts, the page number of the ledger in which these accounts are appearing are listed in this column.

d) Amount (Debit) : The debit amount is recorded in the amount (Dr.) column opposite the title of the account debited. The unit of measurement, i.e. Rs is recorded at the top of this column on each page and this is not repeated.

e) Amount (Credit) : The credit amount is recorded in the amount (Cr.) column opposite the title of the account credited. Like the amount (Dr.) column, Rs is recorded at the top of this column on each page.

Example of a Journal Entry

This can be illustrated by means of an example. We suppose, on 1.5.2005, a trader sells goods for cash Rs. 8,000. Here, the accounts involved are cash account and sales account. Cash assount is to be debited and the sales account is to be credited.

Again, we suppose that on 2.5.2005 goods worth Rs.7000 were purchased for cash. Here, purchases account is to be debited and cash account is to be credited. The entries in the Journal will be as under:

		Journal			Dr.	Cr.
	Date	Particulars		L.F.	Amount	Amount
	2005					
Debit Account →	May 1	→ Cash Account	Dr.		8,000	
Credit Account →		→ To Sales Account				8,000
Narration →		→ (Being goods sold for cash)				
Month and Year →	2	Purchases Account	Dr.		7,000	
Not repeated		To Cash Account				7,000
		(Being goods purchased for cash)				

Limitations of Journals

When the number of transaction is large, it is practically impossible to record all the transactions through one journal because of the following limitations of journal :

1. The system of recording all the transactions in a journal requires (i) the writing down of the name of the account involved as many times as the transactions occur; and (ii) an individual posting of each account debited and credited and hence involves the repetitive journalising and posting labour.
2. Such a system does not provide the information on prompt basis.
3. Such a system does not facilitate the installation of an internal check system since the journal can be handled by only one person.
4. The journal becomes bulky and voluminous.

To overcome the shortcomings of the use of the journal only as a book of original entry, the journal is subdivided into special journals.

Subdivision of Journal

The journal is inadequate as the sole book of the original entry when the transactions are numerous. The nature of operations and the volume of transactions in the particular business determine the number and type of journals needed. A medium size business generally maintains the following types of journals :

1. Cash Book - to record cash transactions :
2. Sales Day Book - to record credit sales;
3. Purchases Day Book - to record credit purchases;
4. Sales Return Day Book - to record sales returns;
5. Purchases Return Day Book - to record purchases returns;
6. Bills Receivable Book - to record bill receivable;
7. Bills Payable Book - to record bills payable;
8. Petty Cash Book - to record petty cash payments; and,
9. Journal Proper - to record residuary transactions. It is also used for rectifying errors.

The Ledger

The ledger is the principal book of accounts where similar transactions relating to a particular person or thing are recorded. The journal is used to record the transactions in the chronological order. The owner of a business is not interested to know the effect of individual transaction on the financial statements, what he wants is the accumulated effect of each' Chart of Accounts'. Chart of accounts is an index to all accounts contained in double entry system. It allocates to each account a number and arranges accounts in logical subdivisions.

Subdivision of Ledger

When the size of the organisation is very large and number of accounts are numerous, it is found necessary to maintain a separate ledger for customers' accounts, suppliers' accounts and for other accounts. Generally, the following three kinds of ledgers are maintained by such organisations : a) Debtors' Ledger; b) Creditors Ledger; and c) General Ledger.

Debtors' Ledger : It may contain the accounts of all the customers to whom goods have been sold on credit. Entries in this ledger are made mostly from sales day books, sales returns book and cash book. This ledger is also called : Customers' Ledger or Sales Ledger.

Creditors' Ledger : It may contain the accounts of all the suppliers from whom goods have been purchased on credit. Entries in this ledger are made mostly from purchase day books, purchase returns book and cash book. This ledger is also known as : Suppliers' Ledger or Purchases Ledger.

General Ledger : It may contain all residual accounts, mainly real and nominal accounts. This ledger is also called Nominal Ledger.

Standard form of Ledger Account

'T' accounts are simplified representation of ledger accounts and is widely used. A 'T' account is divided into two sides, the left hand side represents the debit side and the right hand side represents the credit side. Each side of the ledger has columns of varying sizes for the following : a) Date; b) Particulars; c) Folio; and Amount.

Dr. Title of Account (Account No.) Cr.

Date	Particulars	Folio	Rs	Date	Particulars	Folio	Rs

Posting

The process of transferring of the debits and credits from the journal to the ledger accounts is called posting. Each amount entered in the debit column of the journal is posted by entering it on the debit side/column of an account in the ledger, and each amount entered in the credit column of the journal is posted by entering it on the credit side/column of an account in the ledger. Posting from journal to the ledger accounts are necessary in order to know how transactions have changed the account balances.

Balancing Ledger Accounts

Balance is the sum necessary to equalise the debit and credit totals of an account. Periodically, all the accounts in a ledger are balanced to ascertain the cumulative effect of entries on the accounts. The balance is an accounting term which means the difference between the two sides of an account, or the total of an account containing only debits and credits A computerised system will usually print the balance of the account after each transaction, but in a manual system we must calculate the balance.

Where the total of the debit side exceeds the total of the credit side the account is said to have a debit balance.

Where the total of the credit side exceeds the total of the debit side, the account is said to have a credit balance. Therefore, balancing is the process of bringing two sets of related figures into agreement.

At the end of a particular period (normally at the end of each month or year) the accounts are balanced. The steps taken for balancing are as follows :

1) Take totals of both the sides of the account on rough paper.
2) Work out the difference between the totals of both the sides.
3) Enter this difference in amount column of lighter (lesser) side and make the totals of two sides equal. This difference will be a balance of the account.
4) Write, in particulars column against this balance amount, words 'To Balance c/d' or 'By Balance c/d' as the case may be (c/d means carried down for next period).
5) Now total of two sides will tally. See that these totals appear on the same line.
6) Draw a line before writing such totals and draw double lines after writing such totals in amount columns only.
7) Bring down the balance for the next period or month on the opposite side of that account with the words "To alance b/d" (brought down) or "By Balance b/d" as the case may be.

Illustration of balancing of Cash Account is shown below -

Cash Account

Dr. Date	Particulars	JF	Amount Rs.	Date	Particulars	JF	Amount Rs. Cr.
2005				2005			
May 1	To Capital A/c		18,000	May 5	By Mohan A/c		2,000
18	To Sales A/c		8,000	10	By Purchase A/c		7,000
				28	By Rent A/c		1,500
				29	By Salary A/C		1,300
				31	By Balance c/d		14,200
			26,000				26,000
2005							
June 1	To Balance b/d		14,200				

TYPES OF BALANCES

There are three types of balances :

a) **Debit Balance (Dr.) :** When the debit side of an a/c is larger in amount than the credit side, it has a Dr. Balance.

b) **Credit balance (Cr.) :** When the credit side of an a/c is larger in amount than the debit side, it has a Cr. Balance.

c) **Nil Balance :** When the totals of Debits and Credits are equal, it has a Nil Balance. It occurs rarely.

1) **Personal A/c. :** If personal a/c. has a debit balance, it shows the total dues from him i.e. Debtor's A/c. If it has a credit balance it shows amount payable to him i.e. Creditor's A/c.

2) **Real A/c. :** All real accounts always have debit balances. They are treated as properties and assets.

3) **Nominal A/c. :** All expenses or losses have debit balances and all gains and incomes have credit balances.

With the help of above balances, the Trial Balances is prepared at the end of every month or every year (for detail study see unit-preparation of Trial Balance).

Problem-1

Yr. 2005

Jan. 1. Kishor started business by Rs. 8,000.

Jan. 8. Bought goods Rs. 2,100 from Atul on credit.

Jan. 12. Withdrew cash Rs. 200 for personal use.

Jan. 15. Paid Rs. 1500 to Atul on our account.

Jan. 24. Bought goods Rs. 800 by cash.

Jan. 28. Brought additional Capital Rs. 1,200/-.

Jan 30. Brought goods Rs. 1,000 from Atul on credit.

Solution :

In the books of Kishor Journal (Page No. 1)

Date	Particulars		LF	Debit Rs.	Credit Rs.
2005					
Jan 1	Cash A/c	Dr.	3	8,000	
	To Capital A/c		1		8,000
	(Being business started with cash)				
Jan 8	Purchases A/c	Dr.	4	2,100	
	To Atul's A/c		5		2,100
	(Being goods bought on credit)				
Jan 12	Drawings A/c	Dr.	2	200	
	To Cash A/c		3		200
	(Being cash withdrawn for personal use)				
Jan 15	Atul's A/c	Dr.	5	1,500	
	To Cash A/c		3		1,500
	(Being cash paid on account)				
Jan 24	Purchases A/c	Dr.	4	800	
	To Cash A/c		3		800
	(Being cash purchases made)				
Jan 28	Cash A/c	Dr.	3	1,200	
	To Atul's A/c		1		1,200
	(Being additional capital brought)				
Jan 30	Purchases A/c	Dr.	4	1,000	
	To Atul's A/c		5		1,000
	(Being goods bought on credit)				
		Total		14,800	14,800

Ledger Book

Dr. Capital Account (on page No. 1) Cr.

Date	Particulars	JF	Amount Rs.	Date	Particulars	JF	Amount Rs.
2005				2005			
Jan 31	To Bal c /d		9,200	Jan 1	By Cash A/c	1	8,000
				Jan 28	By Cash A/c	1	1,200
			9,200				9,200
				Feb 1	By Bal. b/d		9,200

Dr. Drawing Account (on page No. 2) Cr.

Date	Particulars	JF	Amount Rs.	Date	Particulars	JF	Amount Rs.
2005				2005			
Jan 12	To Cash A/c	1	200	Jan 31	By Bal. c/d		200
			200				200
Feb 1	To bal. b/d		200				

Dr.			Cash Account (on page No. 3)				Dr.
Date	Particulars	JF	Amount Rs.	Date	Particulars	JF	Amount Rs.
2005				2005			
Jan 1	To Capital A/c		8,000	Jan 12	By Drawing A/c	1	200
Jan 28	To Capital A/c		1,200	Jan 15	By Atul's A/c	1	1,500
				Jan 24	By Purchases A/c	1	800
				Jan 31	By Balance c/d		6,700
			9,200				9,200
Feb 1	To Bal b/d		6,700				

Dr.			Purchases Account (on page No. 4)				Dr.
Date	Particulars	JF	Amount Rs.	Date	Particulars	JF	Amount Rs.
2005				2005			
Jan 8	To Atul's A/c	1	2,100	Jan 31	By Bal. c/d		3,900
Jan 24	To Cash A/c	1	800				
Jan 30	To Atul's A/c	1	1,000				
			3,900				3,900
Feb 1	To Bal b/d		3,900				

Dr.			Atul's Account (on page No. 5)				Dr.
Date	Particulars	JF	Amount Rs.	Date	Particulars	JF	Amount Rs.
2005				2005			
Jan 15	To Cash A/c	1	1,500	Jan 5	By Purchases A/c		2,100
Jan 31	To Bal. c/d		1,600	Jan 30	By Purchases A/c		1,000
			3,100				3,100
				Feb 1	By Bal. b/d		1,600

Trial Balance as on 31st Jan 2005				
Sr. No.	Head of Accounts	JF	Dr. Bal. Rs.	Cr. Bal Rs.
1	Capital A/c	1		9,200
2	Drawing A/c	2	200	
3	Cash A/c	3	6,700	
4	Purchases A/c	4	3,900	
5	Atul's A/c (a creditor)	5		1,600
	Total		10,800	10,800

Problem 2

Journalise the following transactions in the Books of Shriram, and post them in to ledger.

May 1,2005, Started business with Cash Rs. 16,000/-.

5 Deposited in bank Rs. 1300/-.

9 Purchased goods for cash Rs. 800/- from S. Soham and Company.

11 Spent Rs. 15/- for postage.

17 Paid for travelling Rs. 32/-

19 Purchased machinery from M/s. Solkar Bros. Rs. 11,200/-

24 Paid salary by cheque Rs. 225/-.

28 Paid rent Rs. 230/-.

Solution

Journal of Shriram

Date	Particulars		LF	Debit Amount Rs.	Credit Amount Rs.
2005 May 1	Cash A/c	Dr.		16,000	
	To Capital A/c				16,000
	(Being capital brought in by the proprietor)				
5	Bank A/c	Dr.		1,300	
	To Cash A/c				1,300
	(Being amount depostied in Bank)				
9	Purchases A/c	Dr.		800	
	To Cash A/c				800
	(Being goods purchased for cash)				
11	Postage A/c	Dr.		15	
	To Cash A/c				15
	(Being amount spent for postage)				
17	Travelling Expenses A/c	Dr.		32	
	To Cash A/c				32
	(Being aount spent for travelling)				
19	Machinery A/c	Dr.		11,200	
	To Solkar Bros. A/c				11,200
	(Being machinery purchased from M/s. Solkar Bros)				
24	Salary A/c	Dr.		225	
	To Bank A/c				225
	(Being Salary paid by cheque)				
28	Rent A/c	Dr.		230	
	To Cash A/c				230
	(Being amount paid as rent)				
		Total		29,802	29,802

Ledger of Shriram

Cash Account

Dr.							Cr.
Date	Particulars	JF	Amount Rs.	Date	Particulars	JF	Amount Rs.
2005				2005			
May 1	To Capital A/c		16,000	May 5	By Bank A/c		1,300
				9	By Purchases A/c		800
				11	By Postage A/c		15
				17	By Travelling-Expenses A/c		32
				28	By Rent A/c		230
				31	By Bal/c/d		13,623
			16,000				16,00
June 1	To Bal b/d		13,623				

Capital Account

Dr.							Cr.
Date	Particulars	JF	Amount Rs.	Date	Particulars	JF	Amount Rs.
2005				2005			
May 31	To Bal c/d		16,000	May 1	By Cash A/c		16,000
			16,000				16,000
				June 1	By Bal b/d		16,000

Bank Account

Dr.							Cr.
Date	Particulars	JF	Amount Rs.	Date	Particulars	JF	Amount Rs.
2005				2005			
May 5	To Cash A/c		1,300	May 24	By Salary A/c		225
				31	By Bal. b/d		1,075
			1,300				1,300
June 1	To Bal. b/d		1,075				

Purchases Account

Dr.							Cr.
Date	Particulars	JF	Amount Rs.	Date	Particulars	JF	Amount Rs.
2005				2005			
May 9	To Cash A/c		800	May 31	By Bal. b/d		800
			800				800
June 1	To Bal. b/d		800				

Dr. **Postage Account** Cr.

Date	Particulars	JF	Amount Rs.	Date	Particulars	JF	Amount Rs.
2005				2005			
May 11	To Cash A/c		15	May 31	By Balance b/d		15
			15				15
June 1	To Bal. b/d		15				

Dr. **Travelling Expenses Account** Cr.

Date	Particulars	JF	Amount Rs.	Date	Particulars	JF	Amount Rs.
2005				2005			
May 17	To Cash A/c		32	May 31	By Balance b/d		32
			32				32
June 1	To Bal. b/d		32				

Dr. **Machinery Account** Cr.

Date	Particulars	JF	Amount Rs.	Date	Particulars	JF	Amount Rs.
2005				2005			
May 19	To Solkar Bros. A/c		11,200	May	By Balance b/d		11,200
			11,200				11,200
June 1	To Bal. b/d		11,200				

Dr. **Solkar Bros. Account** Cr.

Date	Particulars	JF	Amount Rs.	Date	Particulars	JF	Amount Rs.
2005				2005			
May 31	To bal. A/c		11,200	May 19	By Machinery A/c		11,200
			11,200				11,200
				June 1	By Bal. b/d		11,200

Dr. **Salary Account** Cr.

Date	Particulars	JF	Amount Rs.	Date	Particulars	JF	Amount Rs.
2005				2005			
May 24	To bank A/c		225	May 31	By Balance c/d		225
			225				225
June 1	To Bal. b/d		225				

Dr.			Rent Account				Cr.
Date	Particulars	JF	Amount Rs.	Date	Particulars	JF	Amount Rs.
2005 May 28	To Cash A/c		230	2005 May 31	By Balance c/d		230
			230				230
June 1	To Bal. b/d		230				

Trial Balance As on 31st May 2005				
Sr. No.	Particulars	LF	Dr. bal.	Cr. bal.
1	Cash A/c		13,623	-
2	Capital A/c		-	16,000
3	Bank A/c		1,075	-
4	Purchases A/c		800	-
5	Postage A/c		15	-
6	Travelling Exp. A/c		32	-
7	Machinery A/c		11,200	-
8	Solkar Bros. A/c (a creditor)		-	11,200
9	Salary A/c		225	-
10	Rent A/c		230	-
	Total		27,200	27,200

Problem 3

Prepare Ledger from the following transactions in the Books of Anil Bros.

Jan.1 2005. Started business with Cash Rs. 18,500/-

2	Opened an account with Bank of Baroda depositing Rs. 16,000/-
4	Purchased stationary Rs. 25/-
8	Purchased goods on credit from Reliance Sales Corporation Rs. 1,500/-
12	Purchased machinery from Meera Engineering Co. Ltd. for cash Rs. 750/-
15	Sold goods for cash Rs. 550/-
20	Paid salary to Mr. Laxmikant Rs. 250/-
22	Deposited in Bank of Baroda Rs. 500/-
26	Received commission from Mogal Rs. 100/-
28	Withdrew cash Rs. 100/- for personal use.
29	Paid to Reliance Sales Corporation Rs. 1,000/- by cheque.

Solution :

Ledger of Anil Bros.

Dr. **Cash Account** Cr.

Date	Particulars	JF	Amount Rs.	Date	Particulars	JF	Amount Rs.
2005				2005			
Jan 1	To Capital A/c.		18,500	Jan 2	By Bank of Baroda		16000
15	To Sales A/c.		550	4	By Stationary A/c.		25
26	To commission A/c.		100	12	By Machinery A/c.		750
				20	By Salary A/c.		250
				22	By Bank of Baroda		500
				28	By Drawings A/c.		100
				31	By Balance A/c.		1525
			19,150				19150
Feb 1	To Balance b/d.		1,525				

Dr. **Capital Account** Cr.

Date	Particulars	JF	Amount Rs.	Date	Particulars	JF	Amount Rs.
2005				2005			
Jan 31	To Balance c/d.		18,500	Jan. 1	By Cash A/c.		18,500
			18,500				18,500
				Feb 1	By Balance b/d.		18,500

Dr. **Bank of Baroda Account** Cr.

Date	Particulars	JF	Amount Rs.	Date	Particulars	JF	Amount Rs.
2005				2005			
Jan. 2	To Cash A/c.		16,000	Jan. 29	By Reliance Sales Corpn. A/c.		1000
22	To Cash A/c.		500				
			16,500	31	By Balance c/d/		15,500
Feb. 1	To Balance b/d.		15,500				16,500

Dr. **Sales Account** Cr.

Date	Particulars	JF	Amount Rs.	Date	Particulars	JF	Amount Rs.
2005				2005			
Jan. 31	To Cash A/c.		550	Jan. 15	By Cash A/c.		550
			550				550
				Feb 1	By Bal. b/d.		550

Stationary Account

Dr. Date	Particulars	JF	Amount Rs.	Date	Particulars	JF	Cr. Amount Rs.
2005				2005			
Jan. 4	To Cash A/c.		25	Jan. 31	By Balance c/d.		25
			25				25
Feb 1	To Balance b/d.		25				

Drawings Account

Dr. Date	Particulars	JF	Amount Rs.	Date	Particulars	JF	Cr. Amount Rs.
2005				2005			
Jan. 28	To Cash A/c.		100	Jan. 31	By Balance c/d.		100
			100				100
Feb 1	To Balance b/d.		100				

Purchases Account

Dr. Date	Particulars	JF	Amount Rs.	Date	Particulars	JF	Cr. Amount Rs.
2005				2005			
Jan. 8	To Reliance Sales Corp. A/c.		1,500	Jan. 31	By Balance c/d.		1,500
			1,500				1,500
Feb. 1	To Balance b/d.		1,500				

Reliance Sales Corporation Account

Dr. Date	Particulars	JF	Amount Rs.	Date	Particulars	JF	Cr. Amount Rs.
2005				2005			
Jan. 29	To Bank of Baroda A/c.		1,000	Jan. 8	By Purchases A/c.		1,500
31	To Balance c/d.		500				
			1,500				1,500
				Feb. 1	By bal. b/d.		500

Machinery Account

Dr. Date	Particulars	JF	Amount Rs.	Date	Particulars	JF	Cr. Amount Rs.
2005				2005			
Jan. 12	To Cash A/c.		750	Jan. 31	By bal. c/d.		750
			750				750
Feb 1	To Bal. b/d.		750				

Dr.			Salary Account				Cr.
Date	Particulars	JF	Amount Rs.	Date	Particulars	JF	Amount Rs.
2005 Jan. 20	To Cash A/c.		250	2005 Jan. 31	By bal. c/d.		250
-			250				250
Feb 1	To Bal. b/d.		250				

Dr.			Commission Account				Cr.
Date	Particulars	JF	Amount Rs.	Date	Particulars	JF	Amount Rs.
2005 Jan. 31	To Balance c/d.		100	2005 Jan. 26	By Cash A/c.		100
			100				100
				Feb 1	By balance b/d.		100

Questions for self Study

1) What do you understand by the term "Book-keeping" ?
2) What are the objects of Book-Keeping ?
3) Explain in detail the utility of Book-Keeping.
4) Explain in detail the term "Transaction".
5) Define book-keeping and explain it's importance.
6) Write short notes on - a) Book-keeping is an art and science b) Objectives of Book-Keeping.
7) Define a) Debtor b) Creditor c) Capital d) Assets e) Person.
8) Answer in one sentence.
   a) What is a transaction ? b) Who is called a debtor ? c) What is entry ?
   d) What is narration ? e) What is journal ?
9) State whether the following statements are true or false :
   a) A person to whom we owe something is our debtor.
   b) Big business can be run without the aid of book-keeping.
   c) Books of accounts cannot be produced as evidence in a court of law in case of any dispute.
   d) It would be difficult for a businessman to carry on a business without book-keeping.
   e) A person to whom we owe something is our creditor.
   f) A journal is the book of original entry.
   g) Entry means posting the transaction.
   h) Capital is the excess of liabilities over assets.
10) Match the pairs - (group A & B)

Group A	Group B
1) Debit Side	a) Right hand side of an account.
2) Credit Side	b) Left hand side of an account.
3) Journal	c) A person to whom we owe something.
4) Debtor	d) Book of original entry.
5) Creditor	e) A person who owe something.

I) Fill in the Blanks with appropriate words :

a) The journal is called a book of .... entry.

b) .... column of the journal is used for writing page number of Ledger.

c) At the end of each journal entry .... is written.

d) As per the principle of double entry the total of debit column must be .... to total of ....

e) .... discount does not appear in the books of accounts.

f) If the goods are distributed as free samples .... Account is credited.

g) A ledger is .... book.

h) The journal entries are posted in ....

i) Salary paid Rs. 100. Salary account is debited by Rs. 100 white Account will be credited with ....

j) Cash Account always shows .... balance.

k) If the total of debit side of an account is greater than the credit side, the account will show .... balance.

l) Discount allowed is debited to .... account while discount earned is credited to .... account.

II) State whether the following statements are true or false :

a) Journal is derived from a Latin word 'Jour'.

b) Journal is a book used for journalising the business transactions.

c) Journal is divided into debit and credit columns.

d) If two or more transactions take place on the same date having one or more common accounts we can pass a combined entry.

e) A person is said to be a solvent when his liabilities exceed his assets.

f) All expenses incurred on purchase of assets are debited to assets account.

g) Cash Account doesn't show a credit balance.

h) Rent account can show a credit balance.

i) A Journal entry can be posted to Debit and Credit of ledger account.

j) A ledger book is prepared only from a journal.

k) Balancing means strucking the total of Debit and Credit.

l) Drawing Account must show a Debit Balance.

III) Answer the following questions -

1) What is Journal ? Enumerate its importance in Double Entry Book-Keeping ?

2) Why is the Journal called a book of prime entry ?

3) Discuss the importance of ledger in Book-Keeping ?

4) How is posting made from Journal to Ledger ?

5) Explain the significance of 'Narration' in a Journal entry ?

IV) Journalise the following in the books of M/s. Kirankumar.

Jan. 2005
1 Started business with cash of Rs. 15,000
5 Purchased goods worth Rs. 5,000
8 Sold goods worth Rs. 6,000
10 Purchased goods from X & Co. on credit for Rs. 4,000
12 Paid to X ^& co Rs. 4000
15 Sold goods worth Rs. 3,000 to Y & Co.
18 Received Cash From Y & Co. Rs. 2,000
25 Paid carriage Rs. 50.

28 Paid rent Rs. 200 to landlord.

31 Interest Rs. 600/- received.

V) Journalise the following transactions, post them into Ledger and prepare a Trial Balance.

Feb. 1 Ashok started business with goods Rs. 10,000 and cash Rs. 5,000 borrowed from Sushil.

5 Bought goods worth Rs. 5,000 from Mr. Prasad.

6 Paid cash Rs. 150 to Deccan Queen Transport Co. for the carriage of goods.

7 sold gods worth Rs. 2,000 to Mira by cash

9 Bought goods from Avinash for Rs. 2,000.

11 Rs. 4,000 deposited into Bank of India.

15 Paid Rs. 1,000 to Avinash on account.

18 Sold goods for cash Rs. 3,000.

19 Paid commission Rs. 50 by cheque to Hira.

21 Paid telephone charges Rs. 150.

25 Cash Purchases Rs. 2,000.

28 Purchased a Cash counter from Deco Home for Rs. 1,500.

VI) Journalise the following transactions and post them into Ledger.

Mar. 2005 1 Commenced business with Rs. 15,000 Furniture Rs. 10,000 and goods worth Rs. 5,000 and Rs. 5,000 of cash borrowed.

3 A bank current account opened with United Western Bank with Rs. 10,000.

7 Bought goods from Vinayak worth Rs. 5,000.

9 Returned goods to Vinayak Rs. 2,000.

11 Sold goods to Swami Rs. 5,000 on credit.

13 Swami returned goods worth Rs. 500 to us.

17 Cash withdrawn from Bank Rs. 5000

19 Paid Rs. 2,000 to Vinayak as part payment by cheque.

20 Received a cheque of Rs. 3,000 from Swami and the same was deposited into Bank.

23 Paid building rent Rs. 500 to landlord.

25 Paid wages Rs. 50 for domestic servants.

27 Paid cartage Rs. 50 on goods.

29 Invoiced goods from Atmaram worth Rs. 1,500.

30 Invoiced goods to Kishor for Rs. 5,000.

VII) Journalise the following transactions in the Books of Pandit. Post them into the Ledger and prepare a Trial Balance.

May 1 Pandit started his business with cash Rs. 15,000 and machinery Rs. 20,000.

3 He paid Rs. 10,000 in the Central Bank of India's Current Account.

4 Bought goods on credit from Dinkar worth Rs. 5,000 off 10% T.D.

7 Invoiced goods to Diwakar Worth Rs. 6,000 less 10% T.D.

9 Diwakar returned goods worth Rs. 600 (Net).

11 Paid Rs. 3,000 to Dinkar on account.

13 Purchased 100 shares in Sunil Electrical Ltd. for Rs. 100 each.

15 Sold machinery for Rs. 500.

17 Sold goods worth Rs. 2,000 to Dinu and he paid us Rs. 1,500 of which Rs. 1,000 by cheque.

19 Drew from bank for personal use Rs. 2,000.

21 Paid salaries Rs. 500.

23 Paid electricity charges Rs. 75.

27 Paid rent Rs. 150.

29 Paid Rs. 50 for Life Insurance Premium.

VIII) Show how following transactions would be entered in the journal of Kulkarni.

2005

Dec. 1 Kulkarni commenced business with Cash Rs. 7,000, Furniture Rs. 5,000 and goods Rs. 8,000. The cash has been borrowed by him from the Bank.

5 Bought goods worth Rs. 2,000 less 20% T.D. from Sohani.

7 Sold half the above goods to Joshi at list price.

9 Paid carriage on goods on behalf of Joshi Rs. 30.

12 Bought goods worth Rs. 985 from Deshpande and he paid Rs. 15 carriage on account.

20 Drew cash for personal use Rs. 300.

22 Deposited into Bank Rs. 3,000 in cash and cheque of Rs. 1,000 received for Cash sales.

25 Paid the following expenses : Salaries Rs. 200, Rent Rs. 300 and Wages Rs. 500.

28 Sent goods worth Rs. 50 to Damle as free samples.

30 Paid rent of residential flat of Rs. 700.

31 Bought machinery worth Rs. 4,000 from H.M.T. co. and received their bill Rs. 4,800 including railway freight.

31 Goods worth Rs. 500 were damaged by fire which were not insured.

IX) Journalise following transactions in the books of Sapre :

2005

March 1 Bought goods worth Rs. 2,000 in auction sale and invoiced them to Kamat at 20% profit.

3 Bhave invoiced to Sapre goods worth Rs.1,000 less 10% T.D. and he despatched them for cash to Damle at list price less 2% C.D.

5 Received an order from Atre for goods worth Rs. 5,000.

7 Bought goods worth Rs. 5,000 from Khare, Received invoice from him of Rs. 4,500 at 10% T.d.

10 Executed the order received on 5th March by despatching the goods bought on 7th March.

20 Received Rs. 780 from Bhide on account of full settlement of Rs. 800/-

25 Bought goods worth Rs.1,000 less 10% T.D. and 2% Cash discount.

28 Purchased a TV. from National Agency for household use for Rs.3,000 and paid the half amount from office and the balance from private Bank Account.

X) Show how following transactions will appear in the respective journal of Taware and Kaware.

2005

Jan. 1 Taware bought goods worth Rs.10,000 from Kaware less 20% T.D.

3 Kaware bought furniture worth Rs. 4,000 from Taware.

8 Taware returned goods worth Rs. 400 to Kaware out of those bought on January 1.

12 Kaware paid Rs. 6,000 to Taware on account.

15 Taware advanced a loan to Kaware Rs. 2,000.

20 Taware sold goods for cash Rs. 1,400.

25 Kaware made cash purchases from Taware Rs. 16,000.

28 Kaware supplied goods to Taware for his household.

30 Taware repaired the roof of Kaware's residential flat for Rs. 1,000 and received cash from Kaware which he invested in his own business.

Different types of Cash Accounting Registers / Cash Books

According to the needs of business concerns, different types of cash books are used. There are generally following types of cash books maintained by the business concerns.

Modern Cash Books	1) Single column cash book- or simple cash book 2) Two column cash book or cash book with cash & bank column 3) Three column cash book or cash book with cash, discount & bank columns 4) Petty cash book 5) Cash book without cash column/cash book with only bank column. 6) Conventional cash book

Single Column Cash Book or Simple Cash Book or Cash Register

Importance : The cash register is the book of original entry for recording all cash transactions. The cash register is a very important controlling and recording device, especially for retail business. Most simple cash register at least accumulate individual sales & total sales for the day.

Where bills are paid in cash, the cash register becomes more important. In those instances, both sales & purchases should be recorded in the cash register. At the end of the day, the balance in the register's record will give you the position of cash in hand on that day.

The cash register is a control device, in that it functions as a check against missing sales receipts if used every time a sale is made. To carry out that control function properly, only the owner or manager should have the key to register & be able to clear its totals.

The cash Book is divided in two main parts, left hand side for cash receipts & right hand side for cash payments.

Contents of a Cash Book

Following are the contents of a Cash Book :

I) Debit side - (Receipt side) i.e. left hand side

a) Date
b) Receipt Number
c) Particulars
d) Folio
e) Amount

II) Credit side (Payment Side) i.e. right hand side

a) Date
b) Voucher Number
c) Particulars
d) Folio
e) Amount

Specimen of Cash Book/Cash Register

Debit Side Credit Side

Date	Receipt No.	Particulars	L.F.	Amount Rs.	P.	Date	Voucher No.	Particulars	L.F.	Amount Rs.	P.
		Total						Total			

Problem

The following are some of the transctions to be entered in the Cash Book with only cash column; for the month of March 200X.

Opening Balance on 1st of March 200X was Rs.2000.

March 200X 1. Drawing by the proprietor Mr. Ramesh Rs.2000

2. Received from Mr. Yashwant, a debtor Rs.3920 against bill No. 195

3. Rent paid Rs. 1000/- to the landlord Mr. Anand for Feb. 200X

4. Salary paid to workers for Feb. 200X Rs.4500

4. Cash withdrawn from Bank of Maharashtra Rs.4000
6. Received interest on Securities Rs.700
7. Cash sales during the day Rs.3540.
9. Paid to Mr. Pandurang a creditor Rs.1120
10. Telephone bill paid Rs.400

Dr. **Cash Book of Mr. Ramesh** Cr.

Date	Re. No.	Particulars	L.F.	Amount Rs.	Date	Vou. No.	Particulars	L.F.	Amount Rs.
March					March				
200X	--	To Balance b/d.		12,000	200X		By Drawing A/c.		2,000
1	01	To Mr.YashawatA/c.		3,920	1	01	(By proprietor Mr.		
2		(against bill No. 195)					Ramesh)		
	00	To Bank of		4,000	03	.02	By Rent A/c.		1,000
4		Maharashtra					(Paid for Feb.200X)		
		(withdrawn from bank)			04	03	By Salaries A/c.		4,500
	02	To Interest on security		700			(Paid to workers for		
6		(Received interst on					Feb.200X)		
		security.)			09	04	By Panduranga A/c.		1,120
	--	To Cash Sales A/c.		3,540			(paid against bill No..)		
7		(Cash sales as per cash			10	05	By Telephone A/c.		400
		memo No......to ....)					(Paid bill No...For.....)		
					* 10	--	By Balance c/d.		15,140
		Total		24,160			**Total**		24,160

* Generally the balancing of the Cash Book is made either daily or monthly. In the obove illustration as the details were given up to 10th of March. 200X, balancing is made on that date only.

Important points : While studying a simple Cash Book one can find the following :

a) In the simple cash book only the cash receipts & cash payments are recorded.

b) Total of the debit side will always be more than the total of the credit side of the cash book since the payments cannot exceed the available cash.

c) It is like an ordinary account.

d) It shows how much money the business has received & how much money it has paid away.

e) It shows how much money should be in balance in cash box at any given time.

f) For every entry in the cash book on the receipt side as well as on the payment side, reference number of the supporting documents must be given for which a separate small column is provided on both the side.

g) It provides a check on the cashier in that the businessman can compare the cash book with the cash box balance.

Two Column Cash Book or Cash Register

Importance : In the modern business, banking services have become essential for the business. A firm normally keeps the excess of its funds at a bank; money can be deposited and withdrawn at will, if it is a current account. Probably payments in to and out of the bank will be more numerous than strict cash transactions. There is only a little difference between cash in hand & money at bank. Therefore, it is very convenient if in the Cash Book on each side another column is added- to record money deposited at bank & payment made by the bank.

This book is the "book of original entry "for all receipts and payments, whether in cash or through bank (cheques).

Contents of the Cash book with Cash & Bank columns

Following are the contents of a cash book with two columns :

I) Debit side - (Receipts side)

a) Date

b) Receipt No.

c) Particulars

d) Ledger folio

e) Cash column

f) Bank column

II) Credit Side (Payment side)

a) Date

b) Voucher No.

c) Particulars

d) Ledger folio

e) Cash column

f) Bank column

If there are more than one bank accounts in the cash book there may be more than one bank columns for recording bank transactions.

Specimen or ruling of cash book with cash & bank columns :

Cash book of ....

Dr. Cr.

Date	Re. No	Particulars	L.F.	Amount		Date	Vou. No	Particulars	L.F.	Amount	
				Cash	Bank					Cash	Bank
				Rs.	Rs.					Rs.	Rs.
		Total						Total			

Problem

Enter the following transactions in the cash book of Mr. Ramesh (having cash book with cash & bank columns). March 200X,

1 Cash in hand Rs. 400 & at Bank Rs. 1000.

2 Sold goods to Suresh & Co. for Rs. 600 & received cash of Rs. 400 in part payment.

3 Purchased goods from Mr. Patel for Rs. 784 & paid the amount by issue of a cheque.

5 Transferred Rs. 500 from Private Banking A/c to Business Bank A/c.

10 Issued a cheque of Rs. 200 to Bharat Furniture work for the furniture purchased in the month of Feb. 200X.

12 Withdrew for personal use from Bank Rs. 100.

14 Issued a cheque to a petty cashier for Rs. 175.

15 Withdrew for office use Rs. 500.

18 Suresh & Co. informed that they paid directly into our bank account the remaining balance i.e. Rs. 200.

19 Bank collected interest on investments & credited to our account Rs. 200. Bank charged 1% commission.

20 Insured goods against fire for Rs. 40000 & paid Insurance premium 2% by cheque.

20 For Cash Sales received a cheque from M/s Manik & Sons for Rs. 500 & deposited into the bank A/c. immediately.

23 Cheque received from M/s. Manik & Sons was dishonoured.

25 Paid salary by cheque Rs. 300.

30 Purchased Govt. Securities of Rs. 800/- at 98%.

Cash Book of Mr. Ramesh

Date	Re. No	Particulars	L. F.	Bank Rs.	Cash Rs.	Date	Vou. No	Particulars	L. F.	Bank Rs.	Cash Rs.
March 200X						March 200X					
01		To Balance b/d.		1000	400	03	01	By Purchase A/c. (Issued cheque for purchases)		784	-- --
02		To Sales A/c. (Cash Sales)		--	400						
05		To Capital A/c. (Cash brought into business)		500	--	10	02	By Bharat Furniture Works (Issued cheque on A/c.)		200	--
15		To Bank Account (Withdrew for office use.)	C	--	500	12	03	By Drawing A/c. (Withdrew for personal use)		100	-- --
18.		To suresh & Co. A/c. (Direct deposit into bank)		200	--	14	04	By Petty Cash A/c. (Issued a cheque to cashier)		175	--
19.		To Interest on Investment A/c. (Collection by the bank)		200	--	15	05	By Cash A/c. (Withdrew for office use)	C	500	-- --
						19	--	By Bank charges Ac. (Commission charged by the Bank.)		02	--
20.		To Sales A/c. (Cash Sales)		500	--						
31.		To Balance c/d.		961	--	20	06	By Fire Insurance A/c. (Premium on Insurance of goods)		800	
						23	07	By Manik & SonsA/c. (Cheque of the party is dishonoured)		500	
						25	08	By Salaries A/c. (Paid by cheque)		300	
						30	09	By Investments A/c. (Purchase of Govt. Securities)			784
						31	--	By Balance c/d.			516
				3,361	1,300					3,361	1,300
April 200X,01		To Balance b/d.			516	April 200X,01		By Balance b/d.		961	

Important Points : While studying of Cash book with bank column one can see the following :

a) If a cheque is received by the proprietor, it is treated as cash & cash account is debited.

b) If a cheque received by the proprietor is paid in to the bank on the day of receipt, Bank account is debited as Bank is receiver.

c) If a cheque is dishonored the other accounts to be debited or credited is generally the account of the party who issued a cheque.However, if a cheque received or issued for a certain Nominal account, such as interest, commission etc. is dishonoured instead of party's account,that Nominal account should be debited/credited.

d) If a cheque received by the proprietor and endorsed to other party is dishonoured, no entry is to be passed in cash book. A journal entry will be passed in the journal or a reverse entry may be passed for cancelling the effect of the original entry.

e) If cash is paid in to bank, cash account is credited & bank account is debited. When cash is withdrawn from bank for office use, cash account is debited & the bank account is credited. As the cash account & the bank account are on the same page of the cash book the double entry of these transactions is effected on the same page on opposite sides. Therefore such entries are called **Contra Entries.** To show that it is a contra entry letter "C" is written in the L.F. column against such entry.

f) Cash is a real account & Bank is a personal account. Therefore cash account is debited when cash is received & it is credited when cash is paid . Bank account is debited when bank is receiver & it is credited when bank is giver.

Cash Book with cash, discount & Bank column

Importance : In some business concerns, discount is offered at the time of sale and at the time of receiving money while setlling the accounts of debtors. The discount allowed by manufactaurer or wholesellor to the other trader in the catelogue price is known as **Trade Discount**. The cash memo/credit memo is prepared only after deducting this discount. Hence the entries in the books are made with the amount after deducting the discount. Therefore no treatment other than this is needed in books for trade discount.

While on the other hand, cash discount is allowed for payment of dues within the time limit prescribed. It means that cash discount is allowed at the time of receipt of cash from the customers & cash discount is received at the time of payment of cash to the creditors. Hence it is found convenient to record the discount allowed & discount received in the cash book by providing two discount columns- one on each side of the cash book. Discount allowed by the proprietor being his losses are entered in the Disount Column on the debit side & discount received by the proprietor being his gains are entered under the Discount Column on the credit side.

Cash & Bank columns in the cash book represent cash account & bank account respectively and therefore their balances are extracted at the time of closing the cash book & also included in trial balance.

Contents of the cash book with cash, bank & discount columns :

I) Debit Side (Receipt Side)

a) Date
b) Receipt Number
c) Particulars
d) Ledger folio
e) Discount column
f) Cash column.
g) Bank Column

II) Credit Side (Payment Side)

a) Date
b) Voucher Number
c) Particulars
d) Ledger Folio
e) Discount Column
f) Cash Folio
g) Bank Column

Specimen or Ruling of Cash Book with, Cash, Bank & Discount Columns :

Cash Book of M/s............

Dr. Cr.

Date	Rc. No.	Particulars	L. F.	Discount Rs.	Cash Rs.	Bank Rs.	Date	V. No.	Particulars	L. F.	Discount Rs.	Cash Rs.	Bank Rs.
		Total							Total				

Problem

From the following particulars prepare a cash book with cash, bank & discount columns.

	Rs.
200X April, 1. Cash in Hand	200
2. Bank overdraft	3000
3. Issued a cheque in favour of Mr. Ramakant for Rs. 2500 in full settlement of	Rs.2600
5. Received a cheque from Suresh for Rs. 3250 in full settlement of Rs.3300 and deposited the cheque in to Bank	
7. Received an advice from the Bank stating that the Bank has paid Rs. 250 on Account of Insurance premium	
9. Paid to Petty Cashier	100
11. Made Cash Sales &	3500
Cash Purchases	900
15. Purchased Machinery for Rs. 7000 the amount being paid by cheque.	
19. Directly deposited by Mr. Jadhav	4800
26. Received crossed cheque from Mr. Parikh for Rs. 2000 in full settlement of	Rs. 2200
28. Paid office Expenses.	300
30. Paid office Rent by cheque	350

Important points

a) Balancing :- While balancing the cash book the cash column & bank columns are balanced. The discount column appearing on both the sides of the cash book is not to be balanced. Instead discount columns of both sides of the cash book are totalled separately, & then the totals are posted to the discount a/c in the ledger.

b) Cash books is a subsidiary journal with the distinctive feature that it is a journal as well as a ledger account.

c) Unlike other ledger accounts, cash account has a column for ledger folio & a narration is written after recording each entry.

d) Usually, when a payment is made, a document giving details of the payment is prepared. Such document is known as voucher.

e) If bank columns are not maintained in the cash book, it will be necessary to pass two entries on receipt of or on issue of a cheque, which means additional clerical & posting work. Such work is reduced with the introduction of bank column in the cash book.

f) When a businessman is running an 'overdraft' the balance in his cash book in the bank column will appear on the payment side as "By balance b/d" & not on the receipts side as in the case of a favourable balance.

Cash Book of............

(with Cash, Bank & Discount Columns)

Dr. | Cr.

Date	Re. No.	Particulars	L. F.	Discount Rs.	Cash Rs.	Bank Rs.	Date	Re. No.	Particulars	L. F.	Discount Rs.	Cash Rs.	Bank Rs.
200X April							200X April						
01		To Balance b/d.			200	--	2	--	By Balance b/d		-	-	3000
05		To Suresh A/c. (cheque received & deposited into the bank & discount allowed.)			--	3250	3		ByMr.Ramakant A/c (being paid to him by cheque & discount received)		100	--	2500
					--	--							
11		To Sales A/c. (being Received for sales)			3500	--	7		By Insurance Premium A/c. (Premium paid by Bank)		--	--	250
19		To Mr. Jadhav A/c. (Direct deposited by him.)			--	4800	9		By Petty Cash A/c. (being paid for petty cash)		--	100	--
26		To Mr. Parikh A/c. (being a crossed cheque received & allowed him a discount)			--	2000	11		By Purchases A/c. (being paid for purchases)		--	900	--
30		To Balance c/d.			--	3050	15		By Machinery A/c. (being purchases of machinery & paid by cheque)		--	--	7000
							28		By Office Exp. A/c. (paid for office Exp.)		--	300	--
							29		By Office Rent A/c. (being Rent paid by cheque)		--	--	350
							30		By Balance c/d.		--	2400	--
		Total			3700	13100			Total		100	3700	13100
May 1		To Balance b/d.			2400	--	May 1		By Balance b/d.		--	--	3050

Cash Book with bank column only or cash book without cash column

Importance : When a businessman deposits all cash receipts in the bank & makes all payments by cheques only, then he only keeps a Cash Book having Bank column. In such a case payments of petty expenses are made in cash. Such petty payments are entered in a separate book known as "Petty Cash Book."

In cash book without cash column type of cash book, a Bank column is provided on both sides. All sums received either in cash or by cheques are immediately banked & entered on the receipt side of the cash book . All payments are entered on the payment side of the cash book.

Contents of the cash book with bank column only :

I) Debit side (Receipt side)

a) Date

b) Receipt No.

c) Particulars

d) Ledger folio

e) Bank column

II) Credit Side (Payment side)

a) Date

b) Voucher No.

c) Particulars

d) Ledger folio

e) Bank column

Speciman of cash book with bank column or cash book without cash column :

Cash Book of M/s.......................

(Cash Book with bank column)

Dr. Cr.

Date	Re. No.	Particulars	L. F.	Bank Rs.	Date	V No.	Particulars	L. F.	Bank Rs.
		Total					**Total**		

Problem

From the following particulars given below, prepare a cash book with bank column.

			Rs
200X May	1	Balance at Bank	10,500
	3	Received from Mr. Suresh on A/c	825
	5	Purchased goods for cash & Paid by cheque	1,000
	8	Sold goods to Avinash & Co. for Cash	2,000
	10	Cash Sales	560
	13	Paid advance to Mr. Kulkarni	300
	18	Paid to Ramesh by cheque of Rs.	390
	21	Bank charges	5
	27	Paid to petty cashier	200
	29	Paid Salary	450
	30	Paid for stationery by cheque	50

Solution :

Dr. **Cash Book of M/s..............** Cr.

Date	Re. No.	Particulars	L. F.	Bank Rs.	Date	V No.	Particulars	L. F.	Bank Rs.
200X					200X				
May 1		To Balance b/d.		10500	May 5		By Purchases A/c. (being cash purchase, paid by cheque)		1,000
3		To Mr. Suresh A/c. (received cash from him)		825	13		By Advance A/c. (being advance paid to Mr. Kulkarni)		300
8		To Sales A/c. (being cash sales)		2,000	18		By Mr. Ramesh A/c. (Paid him on A/c.)		390
10		To Sales A/c. (Made cash sales)		560	21		By Bank Charges A/c (being amount charged by the bank)		5
					27		By Petty Cash A/c. (paid to petty cashier)		200
					29		By Salaries A/c. (paid for Salary)		450
					30		By Stationery A/c. (paid for stationery)		50
					31		By Balance c/d.		11,490
		Total		13,885			Total		13,885
June 1		To Balance b/d.		11,490					

Important points : a) Receipt Side : The amount entered in the bank column against each account head are to be individually credited to their respective ledger accounts

b) Payment side : The amounts entered in the bank column against each account head are to be individually debited to their respective ledger account.

c) The bank columns are to be balanced exactly like the cash columns at the end of a fixed period.

Petty Cash book

Importance : A businessman who deposits all receipts into the bank & makes all payments by means of issuing cheque generally maintains a Petty Cash Book." These minor cash payment are termed as "Petty cash payments or petty expenses".

The word "Petty" means small and these payments are certainly small in amount. Petty cash payments are small but numerous. If all these payments are to be recorded by the main cashier in the cash book, it will result in two main disadvantages. i.e. (1) The cashier will be overburdened & (2) the cash book size will become inconvenientely bulky with the record of all these petty cash payments. Petty cash book is a simple solution to solve this problem.

Types of petty cash books :

Following are the two types of petty cash book.

a) Simple petty cash book **b) Analytical or columnar petty cash book**

a) Simple petty cash book : A simple petty cash book is identical to cash book. Hence its format is also like that of a cash book. Whenever cash is received from the cashier, it is recorded on the receipt side & payments are recorded on the payment side; in order of their occurrence. All expense accounts are individualy debited in the ledger.

Format of simple petty cash book :

Simple petty cash book of ....

Amount Receivd Rs.	Cash Book Folio	Date	Particulars	Voucher No.	Ledger Folio	Amount Paid Rs.
					Total	

Problem of Simple petty cash book

Enter the following transactions in a simple petty cash book.

200X. April 1. Received cheque for Rs. 200 from the Head Cashier
4. Paid postage Rs. 10
8. Paid taxi fare Rs. 15
10. Paid wages Rs. 25
22. Paid for purchase of Stationery Rs. 35
26. Paid for coolie charges Rs. 70
30. Purchased revenue stamps Rs. 30

Solution :

Simple petty cash book of M/s ....

Amount Received Rs.	Cash Book Folio	Date	Particulars	Voucher No.	Ledger Folio	Amount Paid Rs.
200	01	April 200X, 01	To Bank	--	--	--
		04	By Postage	1	--	10
		08	By Taxi fare	2	--	15
		10	By Wages	3	--	25
		22	By Stationery	4	--	35
		26	By Coolie Charges	5	--	70
		30	By Revenue Stamps	6	--	30
		30	By Balance c/d	-	--	15
200					Total	200
15		May 200X, 01	To Balance b/d			

b) Analytical or columnar petty cash book : In this type of cash book each transaction is recorded separately in the respective columns. The columnar total is posted to the ledger A/c at the end of the accounting period. When a business is large petty cash payment of similar nature will be more in number. If these payments are recorded in the simple petty cash book it will become bulky, the burden of posting in to ledger will be also increased and the whole purpose of having petty cash book will be frustrated.

This problem is solved by an analytical petty cash book. Such petty cash book contains individual columns for recording different expenses.

Imprest System of Petty Cash

It is convenient to entrust a definite sum of money to the petty cashier in the beginning of a period & to reimburse him for payments made at the end of the period. Thus he will again have a fixed amount in the beginning of the new period. Such a system is known as the Imprest System of Petty Cash. This system is very useful specially if an analytical petty cash book is used. The book will have one column to record receipts of cash and other columns to record payments of various types. The total of the various columns will show why payments have been made & then the relevant accounts can be debited.

Format of Analytical Petty cash book

Receipts Rs.	Cash Book Folio	Date	Particulars	V. No.	Analysis of Expenditure				
					Total Rs.	Cartage Rs.	Stationery Rs.	Postage Rs.	Salary Rs.

Problem : Prepare a petty cash book on the imprest system from the following :

		Rs.	P.
Jan. 200X, 1.	Received Rs. 100 for petty cash		
2.	Paid bus fare	0	50
2.	Paid cartage	2	50
3.	Paid for Postage & Telephone	5	00
3.	Paid wages for casual labours	6	00
4.	Paid for stationery	4	00
4.	Paid tongs charges	2	00
5.	Paid for repairs to chairs	15	00
5.	Bus fare	1	00
5.	Cartage	4	00
6.	Postage and Telegrams	7	00
6.	Conveyance	3	00
6.	Cartage	3	00
6.	Stationery	2	00
6.	Refreshment to customers	5	00

Petty Cash Book of M/s.......

Receipts Rs.	Receipts Ps.	Date	Voucher No.	Particulars	Total Rs.	Total Ps.	Convey-ance Rs.	Convey-ance Ps.	Cart-age Rs.	Cart-age Ps.	Stati-onery. Rs.	Stati-onery. Ps.	Postage & Telegrams Rs.	Postage & Telegrams Ps.	Wages Rs.	Wages Ps.	Sund-ries Rs.	Sund-ries Ps.
		200X																
100	00	Jan 1	*	To Cash														
		2	1	By Conveyance	00	50	00	50	--		--		--		--		--	
		2	2	By Cartage	2	50	--		2	50	--		--		--		--	
		3	3	By Postage & Telegram	5	00	--		--		--		5	00	--		--	
		3	4	By Wages	6	00	--		--		--		--		6	00	--	
		4	5	By Stationery	4	00	--		--		4	00	--		--		--	
		4	6	By Conveyance	2	00	2	00	--		--		--		--		--	
		5	7	By Repairs to Furniture	15	00	--		--		--		--		--		15	00
		5	8	By Conveyance	1	00	1	00	--		--		--		--		--	
		5	9	By Cartage	4	00	--		4	00	--		--		--		--	
		6	10	By Postage & Telegram	7	00	--		--		--		7	00	--		--	
		6	11	By Conveyance	3	00	3	00	--		--		--		--		--	
		6	12	By Cartage	3	00	--		3	00	--		--		--		--	
		6	13	By Stationery	2	00	--		--		2	00	--		--		--	
		6	14	By General Exp.	5	00	--		--		--		--		--		5	00
					60	00	6	50	9	50	6	00	12	00	6	00	20	00
				By Balance c/d.	40	00												
100	00				100	00												
40	00			To Balance b/d.														
60	00			To Cash / Bank														

In the problem given above the journal entry & the relevant accounts will be as follows :

Date	Particulars		L. F.	Debit Rs.	Debit Ps.	Credit Rs.	Credit Ps.
Jan.200X,6	Conveyance A/c	Dr		6	50		
	Carriage A/c	Dr		9	.50		
	Stationery A/c	Dr		6	00		
	Postage & Telegram A/c	Dr		12	00		
	Wages a/c	Dr		6	00		
	Repairs A/c	Dr		15	00		
	General Expenses Account	Dr		5	00		
	To Petty Cash Account					60	00
	(Being the analysis of the petty Cash Book for the week ending Jan. 6th 200X)						
	Total			60	00	60	00

Important Points

a) The amount fixed for petty cash should be sufficient for the likely small payments of a relatively short accounting period, say, for a week, or a fortnight or a month.

b) The reimbursement should be made only when the petty cashier prepares a statement showing total payments supported by vouchers i.e. documentary evidence and should be limited to the amount of actual disbursement

c) No payment should be made without proper authorisation. Also payments above a certain specific limit should be made only by the head cashier.

d) The petty cashier should not be allowed to receive any cash except for reimbursement.

e) The vouchers should be filed in a serial order by the petty cashier.

f) A journal entry may first be prepared on the basis of the petty cash book, debiting the accounts, shown by the various analysis column & crediting the total of the payments to the petty cash accounts.

Conventional Cash Book

Importance : Even today the Cash book of conventional nature is maintained by the businessmen on a very large scale; particularly by the traders, retailers, wholesellers, professionals etc. The conventional cash book is the only primary book maintained in this method of accounting. Hence this cash book includes not only transactions of cash but also other transactions like- credit sales, credit purchases, cheques issued, cheques received, bank transactions, return inward, return outward, opening entries & adjustment entries. It means that any transaction will find a place in conventional cash book & every document will be entered in the conventional cash book. This method of maintaining the accounts is adopted generally by Gujrati's, Marathi's, Marwadis etc.

Contents of Conventional Cash Book

In this method the cash book is divided into two main parts- left hand side is called debit side & the right hand side is called credit side. Cash receipts are recorded on the left hand side & payments are recorded on the right hand side.

The opening balance is taken as the first item to the receipt side & the closing balance is taken to the credit side of the cash book. The book is generally printed with the details at the top of each page regarding the day, date and the year as per English & Indian calendars.

Each side of the cash book is further divided in to four small equal parts (or fold). The first part from the left is used for writing the amounts of receipts & the second one is used for showing the totals if any & remaining two are for writing the particulars of the transaction. In the similar way the right hand side of the cash book i.e. the payment side is written .There are no separate columns for date & ledger folio as are in modern cash book. The date is printed at the top & the ledger folio is written below the entry in circle. In this method of cash book as one page is separately provided for one day, the cash balance is made every day.

Specimen of Conventional Cash Book

<table>
<tr><td colspan="6" align="center">Saturday 21st January 2006
भारतीय शालीवाहन शके१९२७ संवत २०६२ मा पौष वद्य ७ ने शनिवार
मारवाडी मिती संवत २०३२ ना पौष वद्य ७ ने शनिवार ता. २१ जानेवारी २००६</td></tr>
<tr><td>५४०
१००</td><td>००
००</td><td>श्री. आरंभ शिल्लक
श्री. शंकर भांडवल खाते</td><td>३००</td><td>००</td><td>श्री. मालखरेदी खाते
(श्री. रमेश ह्यांचे कडून रोखपावती
क्र.......प्रमाणे रोख खरेदी)</td></tr>
</table>

Problem

Enter the following transactions in conventional cash book of Mr. Shankar on 31st March 2005 (Thrusday) in Marathi

1.	Opening Balance	Rs. 540	00
2.	Cash contributed by Mr. Shankar	Rs. 100	00
3.	Cash sales	Rs. 200	00
4.	Cash purchases from Mr. Ramesh	Rs. 300	00
5.	Credit sales to Mr. Abhay	Rs. 250	00
6.	Credit purchases from Mr. Narayanrao	Rs. 370	00
7.	Cash deposited in to the Bank	Rs. 500	00
8.	Cash withdrawn from the Bank	Rs. 20	00
9.	Cheque received from Mr. Bajaranga & deposited in to the Bank	Rs. 50	00
10.	Cheque issued to Mr. Chandrakant (Creditor)	Rs. 300	00
11.	Salary paid to Mr. Deshpande for March 2005	Rs. 50	00
12.	Commission received from Mr. Kashinath	Rs. 10	00
13.	Bank Interest credited by Bank	Rs. 25	00
14.	Bank Charges debited by the Bank	Rs. 1	50
15.	Goods returned by Mr. Abhay	Rs. 50	00
16.	Cheque received from Mr. Bajarang dishonoured	Rs. 50	00
17.	Depreciation on furniture to be charged	Rs. 50	00

Solution :

Conventional Cash Book of Mr. Shankar

गुरूवार दिनांक ३१ मार्च २००५ फाल्गुन वद्य षष्ठी शके १९२७

५४०	००	श्री. आरंभ शिल्लक	३००	००	श्री. मालखरेदी खाते (श्री. रमेश ह्यांचे कडून रोखपावती क्र.......प्रमाणे रोख खरेदी)
१००	००	श्री. शंकर भांडवल खाते			
२००	००	श्री. मालविक्री खाते (रोखपावती क्र.... प्रमाणे रोख जता)	२५०	००	श्री. अभय खाते (बिल नं.... प्रमाणे उधार विक्री.)
२५०	००	श्री. मालविक्री खाते (बिल क्र... प्रमाणे श्री अभय ह्यांस उधार विक्री)	३७०	००	श्री. मालखरेदी खाते (श्री. नारायणराव यांचेकडून बिल नं... प्रमाणे उधार खरेदी)
३७०	००	श्री. नारायणराव खाते (बिल क्र... प्रमाणे उधार खरेदी)			
२०	००	श्री. बँक खाते (धनादेश क्र... प्रमाणे रोख काढणे)	५००	००	श्री. बँक खाते (रू. ५०० चा रोख भरणा केला)
५०	००	श्री. बजरंग खाते (बिल क्र.... प्रमाणे धनादेश क्र... ने जमा)	५०	००	श्री. बँक खाते (श्री. बजरंग ह्यांचेकडून जमा झालेला धनादेश क्र... बँकेत भरला)
३००		श्री. बँक खाते (धनादेश क्र..... ने श्री. चंद्रकांत ह्यांस बिल नं... पोटी दिले)	३००	००	श्री. चंद्रकांत खाते (धनादेश क्र... ते बिल नं.... पोटी दिले)
१०		श्री. कमिशन खाते (श्री. काशिनाथ ह्यांचे कडून... कमिशन पोटी जमा)	५०	००	श्री. नोकरपगार खर्चखाते (श्री. देशपांडे ह्यांना मार्च २००५ चा पगार दिला)
२५		श्री. बँक व्याज खाते (मुदती खात्यावरील व्याज बँकेत जमा केल्याने)	२५	००	श्री. बँक खाते (मुदतीखात्यावरील व्याज बँकेत जमा)

रु.	पै.	तपशील	रु.	पै.	तपशील
१	५०	श्री. बँक खाते (बँकेचे कमिशन नांवे टाकल्याने)	१	५०	श्री. बँक कमिशन खाते (बँकेने कमिशन नांवे टाकल्याने)
५०	००	श्री. अभय खाते (त्यांचे कडून मालपरत आल्याने)	५०	००	श्री. विक्री माल परत खाते (श्री. अभय ह्यांचे कडून मालपरत आल्याने)
५०	००	श्री. बँक खाते (श्री. बजरंग ह्यांचे कडून जमा झालेला चेक न वटल्याने)	५०	००	श्री. बजरंग खाते (श्री. बजरंग ह्यांचा जमा झालेला चेक न वटल्याने)
५०	००	श्री. फर्निचरखाते (सन....साठी फर्निचर वर.... दराने घसारा आकारणी.)	५०	००	घसाराखाते (रु......फर्निचरवर....दराने सन....) साठीघसारा आकारणी.
			२०	००	श्री. अखेरची शिल्लक.
२०१६	५०		२०१६	५०	

Important points

a) This method of cash book is simple to understand & easy to operate. As we have seen in illustration, this cash book includes all transactions, it is the only record in which the businessman has to refer for any entry & he need not see a number of books for reference.

b) A small trader has a simple style of working like purchasing goods for cash & selling them again for cash. In such a case complications of business transactions are less & hence maintaining other primary books may not be essential.

c) In this method the businessman maintains only two books i.e. cash book & ledger.

d) As all transaction are entered in one book only, the cash book becomes bulky & finding the entries in the same may become difficult. There is no provision for writing voucher numbers in the cash book & as such finding the documents for a particular transaction may be difficult.

e) The method increases the clerical work for it involves two entries in this cash book for many transactions & their postings also. (i.e. Duplication of work)

Books of Accounts : (Other than Cash Books)

The Books of accounts maintained by the business house other than the cash book may be classified into Journal and Ledgers. The Journal is used as the book of original entry for all transactions which cannot be recorded in the cash book. In other words, all non cash transactions should be recorded in the journal. For practical purposes the journal is maintained by using a number of books called the 'Subsidiary Books'. They are also known as "Primary Books". In modern accounting method a businessman maintain a number of primary books which are as under :

1) Purchase Book
2) Purchase Return Book (Return Outward Book)
3) Sales Book
4) Sales Return Book (Return Inward Book)
5) Bills Receivable Book
6) Bills Payable Book.
7) Journal Proper.

Specimen formats of these books and brief explanation regarding their use are given as follows :

1) ***Purchase Book :*** Also known as Purchase Register. This book is used to record all credit purchases of goods only. The term "goods" covers only those items procured by the business for resale.

Specimen of Purchase Book .

Purchase Book of Mahaveer Enterprises.

Date	Name of Supplier	L.F.	Inward Invoice No.	Amount (Rs.)
200X April, 02	BYK Ltd.		426	20,740
April, 14	Sangita Enterprises		1407	2,100
April, 17	Gadgil & Sons.		1607	4,800
April, 18	Raghunath & Co.		2701	17,500
			Total	45,140

2) ***Purchase Return Book :*** This subsidiary book is used to record the goods purchased on credit and sent back to creditors or supplier because they do not conform to specifications or for some other reasons.

Specimen of Purchase Return Book

Purchase Return Book of Mahaveer Enterprises.

Date	Name of Supplier	L.F.	Debit Note No.*	Amount (Rs.)
200X April, 20	Sangita Enterprises.		21	700
April, 27	Gadgil & Sons.		22	900
			Total	1,600

* **Debit Note :** A note sent by the purchaser to the supplier informing the latter of the reduction in the amount due to him. e.g. When the purchaser rejects the goods, and returns goods he issue a debit note at the time of despatch of such goods.

3) ***Sales Book :*** Also known as Sales Register. This book is used to record all the sales of goods on credit. The sales of a business organisation may be of different items.

Specimen of Sales Book

Sales Book of Mahaveer Enterprises.

Date	Name of Customer	L.F.	Outward Invoice No.	Amount (Rs.)
200X April, 3	Bhalchandra Corporation		2001	14,700
April, 8	Vinayak Enterprises		2002	13,835
April, 16	Heramba Traders		2003	15,700
April, 20	Moreshwar & Co.		2004	13,100
			Total	57,335

4) ***Sales Return Book :*** This book is used to record the transactions relating to goods sold on credit and received from the customers as not confirming to the specification or for any other reason.

Specimen of Sales Return Book

Sales Return Book of Mahaveer Enterprises.

Date	Name of Customer	L.F.	Credit Note No.*	Amount (Rs.)
200X April, 11	Bhalachandra Corporation		09	670
April, 23	Vinayak Enterprises		10	200
April, 27	Heramba Traders		11	340
			Total	1,210

Credit Note : A note sent by the seller to the customer informing the latter of the reduction in the amount due from him. e.g. when goods are returned by the customer as not confirming to specifications, the seller will issue a credit note on receipt of the goods.

*5) **Bills Receivable Book :*** The bills receivable of a firm consist of all Bills of Exchange accepted by customers in respect of amount due from them. The Bills Receivable Book is used to record all Bills of Exchange accepted by customers.

Specimen of bills receivable book :

Bills Receivable Book of Mahaveer Enterprises.

S.No.	Date	From whom Received	Name of Acceptor	Date of Bill 200X	Term	Date of Maturity	Where Payable	Amount Rs.	How Disposed
	200X					200X			
1	April 24	Mahesh & Co.	Mahesh & Co.	April, 20	90 days	July 22	Bank of Baroda Nashik	13,100	Discounted with Banker on 27-4-200X
2	April 27	Shankar & Co.	Shankar & Co.	April, 23	60 days	June 25	Bank of India	11,700	–
							Total	24,800	–

Bill of Exchange : A bill of exchange is an order in writing by the creditor to the debtor to pay the amount specified there in, on the specified date called due date. Hence it is drawn by the creditor and accepted by the debtor.

*6) **Bills Payable Book :*** The bills payable consist of all Bills of Exchanges accepted by the business in respect of amounts owing to its suppliers. The Bills payable Book is used to record all such Bills of Exchange accepted by the business.

Specimen of Bills Payable Book

S.No.	Date	Name of the Drawer	Payee	Date of Bill	Term	Date of Maturity	Where Payable	Amount Rs.	Remarks
				200X		200X			
1	April 20	Sangita Enterprises	Sangita Enterprises	April 20	90 days	July 22	Punjab National Bank	1,400	
2	April 20	Raghunath & Co.	Raghunath & Co.	April 18	90 days	July 20	(Sangli)	17,500	
							Total	18,900	

7) ***Journal Proper :*** This book is used to record all transactions which cannot be included in the cash book or any of the other subsidiary books. The transactions that will be recorded in journal proper are, purchase or sale of fixed assets and investments on credit. Journal proper is also used to record :- Opening Entries, Transfer Entries, Closing Entries, Adjustment Entries, Entries related to dishonour of cheques and Bills of Exchange & Rectification of errors etc.

Journal proper is a book which is maintained in the usual journal form but it records only those transactions which cannot be recorded in the above subsidiary books. Generally trasactions connected with assets such as purchase and sale of asset or major repair to asset are recorded in the journal proper.

The transactions recorded in the journal are as follows :

1) Opening entries 2) Closing entries 3) Transfer entries 4) Rectification entries
5) Adjusting entries 6) Entries related to dishonour of cheques 7) Entries related to dishonour of bills

1) Opening Entries

These are passed when a businessman starts his new business and at the starting of each financial year to bring into account the opening balance of various assets and liabilities.

For example, Shri. Kamalakar commenced business with cash Rs. 30,000, Goods Rs. 10,000, Machinery Rs. 15,000 and Furniture Rs. 5,000 on 1-1-200X. The journal entry will be passed as under.

Date	Particulars	L.F.	Debit	Credit
1-1-200X	Goods A/c..........Dr.		30,000	
	Cash A/c.............Dr.		10,000	
	Machinery A/c.....Dr.		15,000	
	Furniture A/c.......Dr.		5,000	
	To Capital A/c.			60,000
	(Being assets introduced into business)			

When a businessman purchases an established business, the opening entry is passed as under :

Mr. X purchases the business by paying Rs. 80,000 to Mr. Y.

The assets and liabilities taken over as follows :

Machinery Rs. 40,000 Furniture Rs. 10,000 Stock : Rs. 30,000

Debtors : Rs. 12,000, Cash Balance : Rs. 3,000 and Creditors Rs. 20,000.

Date	Name of Supplier	L.F.	Debit	Credit
	Machinery A/c...................... Dr.		40,000	
	Furniture A/c....................... Dr.		10,000	
	Stock A/c............................ Dr.		30,000	
	Debtors A/c......................... Dr.		12,000	
	Cash A/c............................. Dr.		3,000	
	Goodwill A/c....................... Dr.		5,000	
	To Creditors A/c.			20,000
	To X's Capital A/c.			80,000
	(Being assets and liabilites taken over and difference transfered to Goodwill)			

Opening entry is also passed at the begining of every year to brought forward the balance of personal and real accounts appearing in the last year's Balance Sheet of Shri. Gosavi as at 31-03-200X was as under :

Balance Sheet of Shri. Gosavi As at 31st Match, 200X

Liabilities	Rs.	Assets	Rs.
Creditors	15,000	Cash	1000
Bank Overdarft	25,000	Stock	11,000
Gupte's Capital A/c.	40,000	Debtors	4,000
		Plant and Machinery	60,000
		Furniture	4,000
	80,000		80,000

2) Closing Entries :

At the end of financial year final accounts are prepared like Trading Account, Profit and Loss Account and Balance Sheet.

Accounts relating to goods such as opening stock, purchases, sales, return inward, return outward and direct expenses. such as carriage inward, wages, power etc. are transferred to Trading Account by passing the closing entry.

All nominal accounts expenses and incomes are transferred to Profit and Loss Account and for this purpose journal entry is necessary.

The following balances appeared in the ledger of Shir. Ashok as on 31.3.200X.

	Debit Balance (Rs.)	Credit Balance (Rs.)
Opening Stock	1,00,000	
Purchases	4,00,000	
Wages	1,50,000	
Direct Expenses	50,000	
Sales		10,00,000
Office Expenses	1,00,000	
Selling Expenses	50,000	

Journal

Date	Particulars	L.F.	Debit (Rs.)	Credit (Rs.)
31.3.200X	Trading A/c........Dr.		7,00,000	
	To Opening Stock			1,00,000
	To Purchases			4,00,000
	To Wages			1,50,000
	To Direct Expenses			50,000
	(Being the transfer of balance to Trading A/c.)			
31.3.200X	Sales A/c...........Dr.		10,00,000	
	To Trading A/c.			10,00,000
	(Being the transfer of sales to Trading A/c.)			
31.3.200X	Profit and Loss A/c.....Dr.		1,50,000	
	To Office Expenses A/c.			1,00,000
	To Selling Expenses A/c.			50,000
	(Being the transfer of balances to Profit & Loss A/c.)			

3) Transfer Entries

Transfer entries are passed in the journal when balance of one account is to be transfeared to some other account e.g. If Mr. B has given the loan of Rs. 1,00,000 to the business & now it is to be transferred to his capital account, the following entry will be passed.

Date	Particulars	L.F.	Debit (Rs)	Credit (Rs)
	B's Loan A/c..........Dr.		1,00,000	
	To B's Capital A/c			1,00,000
	(Being the transfer of B's Loan A/c to B's Capital A/c)			

4) Rectification entry

When an error is made while passing the entry and such error is to be eliminated, then a rectification entry is passed in the journal. (In detail we will discuss later in the unit)

5) Adjustment Entries

In order to arrive at the correct profit or loss at the end of year some adjustments are required to be made. Such adjustment are made by passing suitable journal entries. (All such adjusting entries we will discuss later in the unit)

6) Entries related to dishonour of cheques

If cheque is returned dishonoured, all entries passed in connection with it must be cancelled by means of a reverse entries. Discount allowed or received must also be cancelled. i.e. cheque received from a customer entered in cash column is dishonoured a reverse entry is to be passed on payment side of cash book in the cash column debiting customer's account.

7) Entries related to dishonour of bills

When the bill is dishonoured by non-payment on maturity, all entries passed in connection with it must be cancelled by means of reverse entries. In the books of drawer. Drawee account should be debited and Bills (Receivable) Account should be credited.

Capital & Revenue Expenditure

· Of the total expenditure incurred, a portion is charged against revenue while preparing the Profit & Loss Account and the remaining amount is shown in the balance sheet as asset. The expenses shown in the profit & loss account are called revenue expenses & the amounts shown as assets are known as capital expenditures.

Meaning of Capital Expenditure

Capital expenditure is the cost incurred in acquiring an assets or improving on existing asset in order to enhance its profit earning capacity. Building, Machinery, & Office equipment such as computers & typewriters, are examples which easily spring to mind.

Capital expenditure normally yields benefit over a long period. The following types of expenditure are capital expenditure.

a) Expenditure incurred to acquire a tangible asset.
b) The expenditure which results in the acquisition of a permanent asset.
c) Expenditure in connection with the purchase, receipt or erection of a fixed asset.
d) Expenditure for the extension of or improvement, modification in fixed asset.
e) Expenditure incurred to acquire the right to carry on business.

Examples of Nature of Capital Expenditure

a) ***Expenditure incurred to acquire a tangible asset*** : Even if the asset does not prove to be profitable, the expenses incurred on it is treated as Capital Expenditure.

b) ***The expenditure which results in the acquisition of a permanent asset*** : All money spent for acquiring an asset are capital expenditure. An assets means anything which can be either used for a long time or which can be converted in to cash later.

c) ***Expenditure in connection with the purchase, receipt or erection of a fixed asset*** : All expenses in addition to purchase price, incurred for making the assets ready for use, are added to the cost of asset and thus are known as Capital Expenditure. For example - wages paid to workers for erecting machinery, the cost of the platform on which the machine will be fixed, interest on the loan raised to purchase a fixed assets etc.

d) ***Expenditure for the extension of or improvement in fixed assets*** : If because of any expenditure the profit earning capacity is increased the expenditure incurred for extension, modification, in fixed asset are known as Capital Expenditure.

e) ***Expenditure incurred to acquire the right to carry on business*** : The expenses necessary for establishing the business, such as preliminary expenses or expenses for obtaining licence will be Capital Expenditure. Similarly the cost of a patents, that is the right to produce certain goods in a certain manner will be capital expenditure. Only initial expenditure is capital. Renewal fees are revenue.

Meaning of Revenue Expenditure

Expenditure which, on the other hand, aims at maintaining revenue earning capacity, is revenue expenditure, properly chargeable to profit & loss account.

The expenses of occupying premises, such as rent, rates, taxes insurance & repairs or the cost of buying raw material, paying wages, salaries, selling & distributing such as advertising & delivery, or of administration, such as postage, telegraphs, and stationery are all items of revenue expenditure.

The following types of expenses are included in the category of revenue expenditure :

a) Expenditure incurred on purchase of stocks of materials and goods to the extent these are used up during the year, the remaining amount will be an asset.

b) Expenditure incurred for day to day running of the business. For example, Salaries, Rent, Wages etc.

c) Expenses incurred for the upkeep of fixed assets for example repairs and maintenance.

d) Depreciation on fixed assets or expired cost of fixed assets.

Difference between Capital & Revenue Expenditure

The points of difference between Capital Expenditure & Revenue Expenditure are summarised as follows.

Capital Expenditure	Revenue Expenditure
Earning capacity	
Capital expenditure increases the earning capacity of the business or reduces working expenses.	Revenue expenditure does not increase earning capacity of the business.
Accounting period	
Capital expenditure affects the business more permanently in the sense its effect lingers on the next accounting period.	Effect of revenue expenditure is over with specified accounting period. Say-one year.
Recurring & Non Recurring	
These expenses are of non-recurring nature i.e. they are incurred once in very long time	These expenses are of recurring nature & repeated in accounting year.
Carry forward	
These expenses are carried forward to the next period (year)	These expenses are not carried forward to next period (year)
Purpose of spending	
These expenses are incurred for increasing production, reducing cost or increasing profit of the business	These expenses are incurred for day to day operations of the business.
Deduction from the profit	
These expenses are not deducted from the profit of thebusiness but they show the financial position of the business	These expenses are deducted from the profit of the business during the year.
Period of Benefit	
Capital expenditure creates a benefit for a long period of time i.e. more than a year	Revenue expenditure creates a benefit for a small period which is less than one year
Accounting treatment	
These expenses are shown in the balance sheet	These expenses are shown in the Profit & Loss account.
Possibility of realisation	
Such expenses cannot be recovered in cash again & realisation of such spending is not possible.	These expenses are realisable & encashed afterwords

Deferred Revenue Expenditure

Where revenue expenditure is incurred, the benefit of which is not restricted to the year in which the expenditure is made, but extend over a determined future period, it is termed as **Deferred Revenue Expenditure.** It falls to be written off over a period of benefit, thus relieving one year of an amount of charge disproportionate to the amount of, and possibly in excess of, the benefit felt in that year.

Advertising is an example of this type of expenditure. The portion of such expenditure relating to the current year is declared as expenditure while finding the profit of the year & the balance of the expenditure for the next years is treated as an assets.

The loss of a building because of an earthquake" may be treated in this manner. This type of loss is also treated as deferred revenue expenditure.

Expenses which appear to be revenue expenses but they are really capital expenditure.

a) Expenses incurred on the repairs & white washing for the first time on the purchase of an old building. Since these expenses are necessary to make the building usable.

b) Wages paid to workers to produce a tool to be used by the factory itself or to fix a machine.

c) Expenses incurred in connection with purchase of a land or building, such as fees paid to the lawyer or registration charges.

d) Interest on loan raised to acquire an asset up to the point of time, it is ready for use.

Problem : Find out Capital/Revenue expenditure in following assets.

1) Second hand furniture worth Rs. 7000 was purchased, repainting of the furniture cost Rs. 500. The furniture was installed by own workers, wages for this being Rs. 100.

Answer : The total cost of the furniture should be treated as Rs. 7600. i.e. all the amounts mentioned should be capitalised since without such expenditure the furniture would not be available for use.

2) Expenses in connection with obtaining a licence for running the cinema were Rs. 10000. During the course of the year cinema company was fined Rs. 100 for contravening rules. Renewal fee Rs. 200 for next year also paid.

Answer : The licence for running the cinema house is necessary. Hence its cost should be capitalised. But the fine of Rs. 100 is revenue expenditure. The renewal for the next year is also revenue nature expenditure but it pertains to the next year. Hence it is prepaid expenses.

3) Temporary huts were constructed costing Rs. 1000. They were necessary for the construction of the cinema. They were demolished when the cinema was ready.

Answer : Since the temporary huts were necessary for the construction of the cinema, their cost should be added to the cost of cinema hall & thus capitalised.

4) During the first week of the cinema running, free tickets were distributed. These numbered 5000, the average value being Rs. 2 per ticket.

Answer : The cost of the tickets distributed free for advertisement purpose is revenue expenses. But since no payment has been made the amount should either be ignored or debited to the Advertisement Account & credited to revenue account. The entry will be -

Advertisement A/c	Dr. 10,000	
To revenue A/c		10,000

Since the advantage of the advertisement may accrue for a few years, the cost may be spread over three or four years. It means that the initial advertisement may be treated as "deferred revenue expenditure."

5) Rs. 4000 expended on discounting, removing & reinstalling plant & Machinery to a more convenient place & Rs. 700 paid for removal of stock to the new site.

Answer : The expenses for removal of a factory from one place to another should be treated as deferred revenue expenditure.

6) Before removal to the new site a machine which stood in the books of account at Rs. 2000 was found obsolete & sold as scrap for Rs. 800. A new machinery was installed in its place at the new site at a cost of Rs. 4200 & Rs. 200 paid on the erection of the new machinery.

Answer : The loss on old machine Rs. 1200 which has been scrapped should be treated as revenue loss. The cost of the new machine Rs. 4200 should be capitalised & the cost of erection Rs. 200 should be capitalised by adding to the cost of the machine.

7) ABC company erect a factory building some years ago at a cost of 450000. A few years later owing partly to defects in construction & partly to the need of a larger building, extensive remodelling was undertaken and completed at a cost of 250000 It was estimated that out of Rs. 250000 now spent Rs. 40000 were for repairs to old building. How would you apportion the expenditure between Capital & Revenue?

Answer : Rs. 40000 will be debited to the Profit & Loss Account since it has been spent on the repairs of the old building The remaining amount of Rs. 210000 being cost of remodelling should be treated as Capital Expenditure.

8) State which of the following expenses/incomes are of revenue nature :

a) Salary paid	b) Wages paid	c) Telephone bill paid	d) Telephone Deposit
e) Rent deposit	f) Electricity bill	g) Electrical installation	h) Building repairs
i) Construction of premises	j) Wages for erection of machinery		k) Interest received
l) Commission received	m) Sale of goods	n) Discount received	o) Bank loan received
p) Share capital raised.			

Answer : Following are revenue incomes : (k), (l), (n)
Following are revenue expenses : (a), (b), (c), (f), (h), (i)

9) State which of the following items would be charged to capital & which to revenue.

a) Salary	b) Purchase of land	c) Wages	d) Construction of building
e) Electrical bill	f) Purchase of machinery	g) Printing	h) Purchase of tools
i) Stationery	j) Purchase of vehicle		

Answer : Item No. : (a), (c), (e), (g), (i) are revenue expenditure &
Item No. : (b), (d), (f), (h), (j) are capital expenditure.

Important Note : We have studied from the above illustrations that how capital expenditure are different from revenue expenditure. However, students should not think that the distinction is very easy. Suppose a cinema house converts its ordinary screen in to a cinema scope screen. Is the expenditure capital or revenue?

Since the seating capacity of the cinema house has not increased the expenditure should be treated as only revenue expenditure. But now there is a greater chance for the house being full or more often, profit will thus increase and therefore, the expenditure may be treated as capital expenditure. There is truth in both the views.

Throughout his audit the auditor must be alert to detect any incorrect allocation of expenditure. If capital expenditure is charged to revenue the profit will appear diminished or the loss increased. Ultimately the balance sheet will fail to show the correct figure's for fixed assets. If revenue expenditure is treated as capital expenditure the profit will be overstated, or the loss diminished and assets over stated. Incorrect allocation between capital & revenue can result in false figure for profit or loss, incorrect taxation & the possibility of dividend being unlawfully paid.

Assets Account

Assets are basically of two types- those that are meant to be used by the business over a long period & not sold and those that are meant to be converted in to cash as quick as possible. The former type of assets are called **"Fixed Assets"** & the latter type of assets are called **"Current Assets."** Assets are anything owned by a business that is used in its operation.

Meaning of Fixed Assets

These are assets which are not "turned over" and sold at a profit but are "fixed" in the business and retained over a very long period. They are often called "Capital Assets", since they form part of the permanent capital equipment in use. For example - Land & Buildings, Plant & Machinery, Furniture & Fittings, Motor vehicles etc

Fixed Assets are further classified as under :

Fixed Assets

Intangible Assets	**Tangible Assets**	**Investment**
a) Development Costs	a) Land & Building	a) Shares in Group Companies
b) Patents	b) Plant & Machinery	b) Long term loans to group or related company.
c) Trade Marks	c) Fixtures & Fittings	c) Other Permanent Investments.
d) Licences	d) Tools	
e) Goodwill	e) Equipments	
f) Similar rights & Assets	f) Furniture	
	g) Vehicles	
	h) Payments on account & Assets in course of construction.	

Tangible & Intangible Assets

Tangible Assets are those which can be seen & felt like building machinery, furniture etc. Intangible Assets cannot be seen or felt, like goodwill of the business. Both the assets are valuable.

Current Assets

These are sometimes called " Circulating Assets" as they are assets which are continually being turned over. The word "Current" comes from the French Word "Courrant" meaning running.

The following figure illustrates the better position of Current Assets :

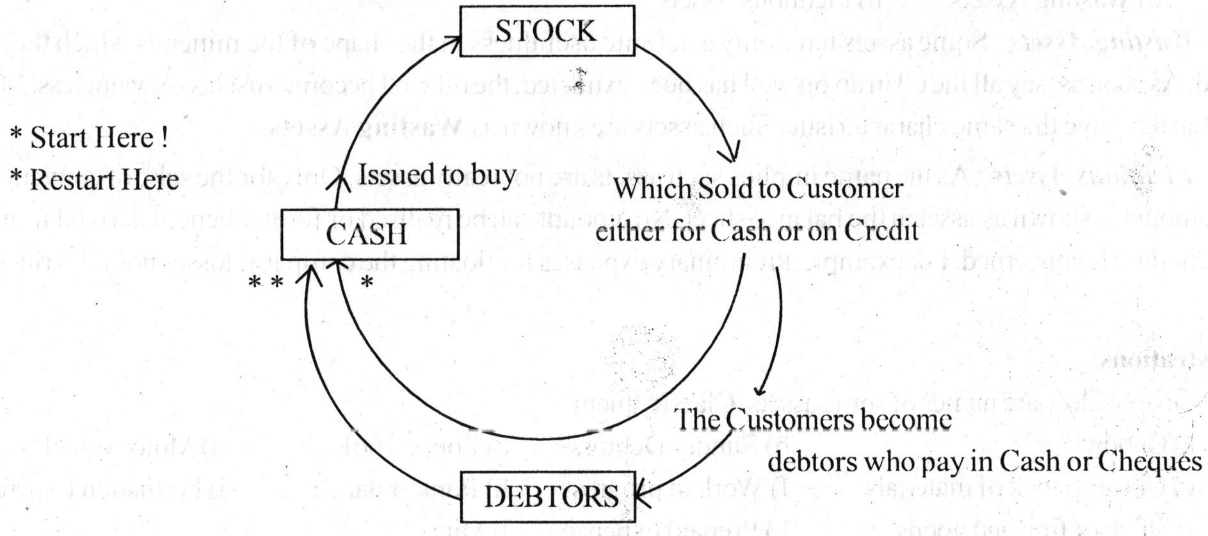

Fig.: Position of Current Assets

Current Assets are further classified as under :

Current Assets

Stock	Debtors	Investments	Cash at Bank & Cash in hand
a) Raw Material & consumables	a) Trade Debrors	a) Investments in Govt.Securities	a) Cash in hand
b) Work in Progress	b) Amount owed by group Co.	b) Investments in shares.	b) Petty cash Balance
c) Finished Goods	c) Amount owed by Related Co.	c) Other Investment.	c) Cash at Bank Current Accounts Saving Accounts
d) Goods for resale	d) Other Debtors	d) Investments in fixed deposit with bankers	
e) Payments on Account	e) Called up share * Capital not paid		
	f) Prepayment & * accrued Incomes		

* These items may be shown separately in the balance sheet

Other types of Assets

a) Wasting Assets b) Fictitious Assets

a) Wasting Assets : Some assets have only a definite usefulness in the shape of the minerals which they can yield. As soon as, say all the oil in an oil well has been extracted, the oil well becomes useless & valueless. Mines & quarries have the same characteristic. Such assets are known as **Wasting Assets**.

b) Fictitious Assets **:** As the name implies such assets are not really assets. Only for the sake of convenience the amount is shown as asset in the balance sheet. No amount can be realised or further benefit derived from the expenditure is concerned. For example-Preliminary expenses for floating the company, losses not yet written off etc.

Illustrations

1) Given below are names of some assets. Classify them.

a) Goodwill b) Sundry Debtors c) Loose Tools d) Motor vehicles
e) Closing stock of materials f) Work in progress h) Bank Balance. i) Formation Expenses
j) Stock of finished goods k) Prepaid expenses l) Mines

<u>**Answer**</u> **:** i) Fixed Assets : (a), (c), (d), ii) Fictitious Assets : (i)
iii) Current Assets : (b), (e), (f), (h), (j), (k) iv) Wasting Assets : (l)

2) Find out Current Assets & Fixed Assets from the following items

a) Cash in hand b) Furniture & Fixtures c) Cash at Bank d) Land & Building
e) Bills Receivables f) Plant & Machinery g) Sundry Debtors h) Patents rights
i) Closing Stock j) Free hold premises

Answer : Current Assets : (a), (c), (e), (g) (i)   Fixed Assets : (b), (d), (f), (h), (j)

Rectification of Errors

Types of Errors

While maintaining the books of account some mistakes may be committed by the accountant. These mistakes are of different types and are grouped under the following heads.

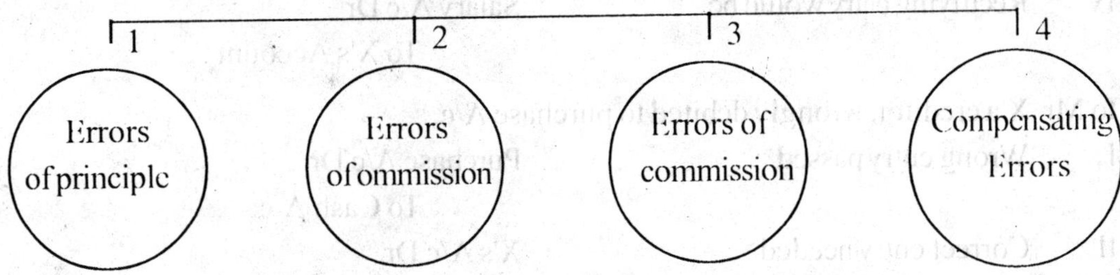

A) Errors of Principle

This error is for violation of the accounting principles. For Example :- A capital expenditure is treated as revenue or vice-versa or expenditure of personal nature debited to business expenditure account etc. In short, while entering the transactions in the books, the accountant does not observe the accounting principles. These errors can be rectified by passing an entry. These errors do not affect the total of trial balance.

B) Errors of Omission

These errors occur when some transactions are omitted from the books of accounts either fully or partly. When the transaction is totally omitted from the books, it will have no effect on the totals of the trial balance. But if a part of the transaction is omitted and a part of the transaction is recorded in the books, it may have the effect on the totals of trial balance. For example a purchase is not recorded at all. This error is the example of total omission. If effect to the creditors account only is given, it becomes the example of part omission. The rectification of total omission is made by passing the entry omitted and the rectification for part omission can be made by giving the second effect omitted.

C) Errors of Commission

These errors are more or less clerical errors. Entries are made with proper principles but the procedural mistakes are committed. For Example- Error in the side of posting to an account or Error in amount of posting, Error in totalling or balancing of subsidiary books or ledger etc. These errors can be rectified by correcting the wrong side, amount, balance or total. Generally no entry is passed for such corrections.

D) Compensating Errors

As the name indicates these errors are such that the effect of one wrong is compensated or nullified by the effect of another wrong. The trial balance therefore agrees even though such error exists. For example- Wrong totalling of the debit side of one account may be compensated by similar wrong totalling of credit side of another account. For rectifying such error also no entry is generally passed.

Now let us see the process of rectification by taking some examples

1) Salary paid to X wrongly debited to X's Account

The Error is of the account head. Credit effect is correctly given (to cash or bank Account) Instead of debiting "Salary A/c" Mr. X's account is wrongly debited. Hence rectification is needed to the debit part only. While rectifying the entry one should follow the following process.

I	Wrong entry made	X's A/c Dr To Cash A/c Cr
II	Correct Entry	Salary A/c Dr To Cash A./c
III	Wrong is with the debit side and hence wrong debit given to X's account is to be nullified by crediting that account with similar amount and debiting the correct account head, "Salary".	
IV	Rectifying entry would be	Salary A/c Dr To X's Account .

2) Paid to Mr. X a creditor, wrongly debited to purchase A/c.

I	Wrong entry passed	Purchase A/c Dr To Cash A/c
II	Correct entry needed	X's A/c Dr To Cash A/c
III	Wrong is with the debit side, hence purchase A/c needs rectification	
IV	Rectifying entry would be	X's A/c Dr To Purchase A/c

3) Wages for installation of Machinery wrongly debited to Wages A/c

I	Wrong entry passed	Wages A/c Dr To Cash A/c
II	Correct entry needed	Machinery A/c Dr To Cash A/c
III	Wrong is with the debit side hence correction is needed to wages account.	
IV	Rectifying entry would be-	Machinery A/c Dr To Wages A/c

4) Cash purchase from Ramrao wrongly debited to Ramrao A/c

I	Wrong entry passed	Ramrao A/c Dr To Cash A/c
II	Correct entry needed	Purchase A/c Dr To Cash A/c
III	Wrong is with the debit side hence Ramrao A/c needs rerectification	
IV	Rectifying entry would be	Purchase A/c Dr. To Ramrao's A/c

5) Received from D a debtor, Credited to sales Account

I	Wrong Entry	Cash A/c Dr To Sales A/c
II	Correct Entry needed	Cash A/c Dr D's A/c
III	Wrong is with the credit side hence rectification is needed to sales A/c	
IV	Rectifying Entry would be	Sales A/c Dr To D's A/c

6) Received from X, Credited to Y's A/c.

I	Wrong entry	Cash a/c Dr To Y's A/c
II	Correct entry needed	Cash A/c Dr To X's a/c
III	Wrong is with credit side, hence rectification is needed to B's A/c	
IV	Rectifying entry would be	Y's A/c Dr To X's A/c

7) a) Cheque received and deposited into Bank A/c But the name of the party is not known and hence not entered in the books.

I	Wrong Entry	No entry passed
II	Correct entry needed	Bank A/c Dr To Suspense A/c
III	This is the error of ommission which can be rectified by passing above correct entry.	

b) Afterwords the name of the party giving the cheque was ascertained as Mr. Shyamrao.

I	Wrong entry passed	Bank A/c Dr To Suspense A/c
II	Correct entry needed	Bank A/c Dr To Shyamrao A/c
III	Wrong is with the credit side hence suspense account needs rectification	
IV	Rectifying Entry	Suspense A/c Dr To Shyamrao A/c

Some entries are such that for their rectification no entry is required to be passed. Their rectification is made by correcting the side of the account, the amount, the totals or the balance. For example :

1) Cash Received from X entered in the cash book correctly but posted to the debit side of X A/c

In such a case entry made to the debit side X's A/c will have to be cancelled and correct posting will have to be made to the credit side of X A/c.

2) Purchase Register is undercast by Rs.100

Here the mistake is of totalling. Hence debit given to purchase A/c is short by Rs.100 which can be rectified by correcting the total of purchase register and the amounts posted to purchase A/c

3) Mr.X's balance calculated is Rs.2300 instead of Rs. 3300.

The error is of balancing. It can be rectified by cancelling the incorrect balance and writing the correct balance in the account.

4) While posting the amount to A's A/c Rs. 178 is entered instead of Rs. 187.

This is also a clerical error regarding amount. It can be rectified by cancelling the incorrect figure and writing the correct figure in the account.

A Transaction sometimes may be wrongly recorded in wrong subsidiary book. For Example Purchase bill entered in Sales book, cheque received entered in cash book (cash column) etc.

Let us see how these wrongs can be rectified :

1) Purchase bill of Mr. XYZ of Rs. 1000/- entered in sales book.

I Wrong entry Passed — XYZ A/c Dr. 1000
To Sales A/c 1000

II Correct entry needed — Purchase Dr. 1000
To XYZ A/c 1000

III Wrong is on both sides i.e. debit as well as credit side hence wrong debit given to XYZ can be cancelled by crediting it once and the correct credit required to XYZ can be given by crediting it again or credit to XYZ may be with double the amount (Rs. 2000)
Similarly wrong credit given to sales to be cancelled by debiting it and debit to purchase A/c not given should now be given in rectifying entry.

IV Rectifying entry would be — Sales A/c Dr 1000
Purchase A/c Dr. 1000
To XYZ A/c 2000

2) Cheque received from Mr. A of Rs. 500 entered in cash column and credited to B's A/c

I Wrong entry — Cash A/c Dr
To B's A/c

II Correct entry needed — Bank A/c Dr
To A's A/c

III In the entry passed, both the effect are wrong which can be rectified by giving reverse effects to the accounts and the correct effects should be given in rectifying entry.

IV Rectifying entry should be — Bank A/c Dr 500
B's A/c Dr 500
To Cash A/c 500
To A's A/c 500

Questions on Section

1) What is Cash Book ? What are the different types of Cash Books ?
2) Give the specimen of different types of Cash Books.
3) Explain the contra entries in the Cash Book.
4) What is Petty Cash Book ? Why is it written in addition to the Cash Book ?
5) Differentiate between modern cash book & conventional cash book.
6) What is conventional cash book ? When it is used ? What are its limitations?
7) Write short notes on :
   a) Cash book with cash & discount column.
   b) Simple cash book.
   c) Cash book with cash & bank column.
   d) Cash book without cash column.
   e) Petty cash book.
8) What do you understand by the imprest system of petty cash ? Explain giving the illustrations.

9) Enter the following transactions in cash book with discount columns.

200X June	1	Cash in hand	Rs. 1500
	5	Paid to Ramrao	Rs. 300
		Discount allowed by him	Rs. 10
	8	Purchased goods	Rs. 400
	9	Received from Gopal	Rs. 980
		Discount allowed	Rs. 20
	16	Sold goods	Rs. 400
	21	Paid to Shankar	Rs. 275
		Discount Received	Rs. 5
	25	Paid wages	Rs. 50
	30	Paid to Narayan in full settlement of his account which shows a credit Balance Rs. 400	Rs. 390

10) Prepare a two column cash book from the following transaction of Mr. Ramachandra.

June 200X	1	Mr. Ramchandra commenced business with cash.	Rs. 8000
	2	He bought goods for cash.	Rs. 5000
	3	Sold goods for cash.	Rs. 100
	6	Received cash from Mr. Mohan Kumar.	Rs. 360
	8	Allowed him discount.	Rs. 20
	10	Paid into Bank.	Rs. 3000
	15	Paid cash to Mr. Harikishan.	Rs. 215
	15	Discount allowed.	Rs. 10
	17	Sold goods for cash.	Rs. 1500
	19	Paid for stationery.	Rs. 35
	22	Paid for office furniture.	Rs. 185
	24	Received from Mr. Kailashchand.	Rs. 680
	24	Allowed him Discount.	Rs. 20
	25	Paid for Advertisement.	Rs. 90
	26	Purchased Postage stamps.	Rs. 8
	29	Paid Electricity charges.	Rs. 115

11) Insert the following transactions in Tabular Petty cash book the imprest is Rs. 40

			Rs.	Ps.
Feb. 200X	1	Chaukidar's wages	15	00
	2	Pencils	5	25
	4	Railway Freight on account books	2	30
	12	Postal Stamps	1	25
	14	Telegrams	6	00
	15	Sundry Expenses	0	80

12) Enter the following transaction in a Three Column Cash Book.

			Rs.
Jan.200X	1	Started business with cash	20000
	2	Opened current Account with Bank of Maharashtra	8000
	3	Bought goods by cheque	150
	4	Received cheque from Mr. Ram	200
	4	Allowed him discount	10
	5	Sold goods for Cash	40
	7	Paid in to Bank. Cash	300
	10	Paid to Mr. Shamrao by cheque	345
		Discount received	5
	12	Paid carriage by cheque	180
	15	Drew from Bank for office use	200
	30	Paid wages by cheque	600

13) Make the following entries in Three Column Cash Book

			Rs.	Ps.
Jan 200X	1	Cash in Hand	3151	20
	1	Cash at Bank	91401	10
	2	Discounted a bill for Rs. 1000 at 1% through Bank		
	5	Bought goods for Rs. 2000 paid cheque for them Discount allowed 1%		
	7	Paid trade expenses	120	00
	17	Paid taxes (Sales Tax)	400	00
	19	Paid Insurance Charges	100	00
	25	Sold goods for Rs. 12,500 Received cheque for them discount allowed 1%		
	27	Received cheque from Joshi & Co.	6000	00
	30	Purchased 100 articles for Rs. 100 each at Rs. 75 each & paid for them by cheque		

14) From the undermentioned particulars, write out petty cash book on the imprest systems.

On 1st Jan. 200X a cheque was drawn of Rs.75 for petty cash. On 2nd Jan. Postal stamps valued at Rs. 10=50 were purched. On 3rd Jan. a telegram was sent at a cost of Rs. 5=10 and stationery bought for Rs. 8=25 Auto charges paid Rs. 10=50 & ink purchased Rs. 4=00. On 4th Jan. Rs. 2=50 paid for Auto & Rs. 1=50 for carriage. On 5th Jan. carriage on goods sold paid Rs. 5=00 & On 6th Jan. charges of printing amounting to Rs. 7=25 were paid.

15) Given below is the list of some items of expenses of a family budget. Find out the Capital & Revenue expenses from the list.

a) Milk	b) Purchase of Radio.	c) Grocery	d) Purchase of Scooter.
e) Vegetables	f) News Paper	g) Electrical Fittings	h) Purchase of fan
i). Rent	j) Laundry Expenses	k) Purchase of T.V.	l) Electricity bill
m) Fruits.	n) Municipal Taxes	o) Purchase of Furniture	

16) Enter the following transactions in Conventional Cash book.

Date		Particulars		Amount
Jan. 200X	1	Opening Balance	Rs.	2500
	2	Cash Sales	Rs.	2000
	3	Cash purchases from Mr. Diwan	Rs.	2000
	5	Credit sales to Mr. Amar	Rs.	2500
	7	Credit purchases from Mr. Abhijeet	Rs.	3700
	9	Cash withdrawn from Bank	Rs.	700
	10	Goods return by Mr. Amar	Rs.	500
	11	Cheque received from Mr. Amar	Rs.	2000
	16	Salary paid to Mr. Deshpande	Rs.	500
	17	Commission received from Mr.Kumbhojker	Rs.	1500
	18	Bank charges debited by Bank	Rs.	15

17) Explain the factors on the basis of which the capital expenditure is distinguished from the revenue expenditure.

18) What do you understand by capital & revenue expenditure ? Some times it is difficult to make a distinction between Capital & Revenue Expenditure. Explain this statement.

19) What are deferred revenue expenses ?

20) Out of the following pick the Revenue Expenses, the others are Capital Expenditure.

i) Replacing the wooden floor by tiles in the office.

ii) Special tax paid on land which is to be used for construction purposes.

iii) The overhauling expenses of machines.

iv) Expenses incurred to set right defects in a new machine before it is used.

v) The cost of erecting new machine.

vi) The cost of changing the foundation of a machine.

vii) Getting a car converted in to a delivery van.

viii) Cost of repainting machines.

ix) Cost of repainting the ceiling of the building

x) Purchase of land for new plant.

21) State which of the following expenses/income are of revenue nature.

a) Share capital raised b) Bank loan received c) Discount received

d) Sale of Goods e) Commission earned f) Interest received

g) Wages for installation of machinery h) Construction of Building

i) Building Repairs j) Electricity bill k) Rent deposit

l) Telephone bill m) Rent n) Wages

o) Salaries p) Telephone deposit q) Discount paid

22) State which of the following items would be charged to capital & which are to revenue :

a) Rs. 5000 Paid on the painting of the new factory.

b) Rs. 200 paid on the erection of the new machine.

c) Rs. 1800 Paid for removal of stock to the new site.

d) Rs. 7800 paid for removal & reinstallation of plant & machinery to a more convenient place.

e) Rs. 1000 paid for a new machine installation at new site.

f) Rs. 2000 paid for repairs to the old building.

g) Rs. 1500 paid for painting to a old building.

h) Rs. 1000 paid for fire insurance premium

i) Rs. 1200 paid for construction of temporary huts. They were necessary for construction of the factory building.

k) Rs. 9000 paid for purchase of second hand furniture.

23) ABC company Ltd., erected a factory building 5 years ago at a cost of Rs. 5,00,000 At the completion of 3 years later owing partly to defects in construction and partly to the need of a factory for larger building. Extensive remodelling & renovation was undertaken and completed at a cost of Rs. 2,50,000. It was estimated that out of Rs. 2,50,000 now spent on the same Rs. 90,000 were for repairs to the old building. How would you apportion the expenditure between Capital & Revenue?

24) Explain the following expenditure, capital or revenue expenditure with reasons.

a) Goods purchased of Rs. 10000

b) Octroi charges paid for machinery bought during the year Rs. 1000

c) Labour charges paid of Rs. 4000 for installing the machine purchased.

d) Advance insurance of Rs. 250 paid e) Travelling expenditure Rs.500/-

f) Paid for repairs to old building of Rs. 6000

h) Paid Rs. 10,000 for purchase of a second hand motor car

i) Wages paid Rs. 600

j) Paid deposit of Rs. 10,000 to the landlord.

k) Paid Insurance premium of Rs. 1,000.

25) Classify various assets, giving examples.

26) What do you understand by wasting assets & fictitious assets?

27) What is meant by "Tangible & Intangible Assets".

28) Give the meaning of Fixed Assets & classify them, giving examples.

29) Explain the term " Current Assets" & classify them, giving examples.

30) Complete the following sentences :

A) All assets which are valueless are called.........

a) Intangible Assets b) Fictitious Assets c) Wasting Assets

B) 'Leasehold premises' can be classified as

a) Fixed Assets b) Floating Assets c) Liquid Assets

C) Govt. securities can be classified as

a) Fixed Assets b) Fictitious Assets c) Liquid Assets

D) "Copy right of the Book" having no demand can be classified as.

a) Intangible Assets b) Fictitous Assets c) Wasting Assets

E) Those assets whose value decreases because of use are

a) Intangible Assets b) Fictitious Assets c) Wasting Assets

F) "Goodwill" can be classified as

a) Intangible Assets b) Fictitious Assets c) Wasting Assets

G) Stone Quarries can be classified as

a) Intangible Assets b) Fictitious Assets c) Wasting Assets

31) Explain the types of Assets, giving examples.

32) Following are the names of some assets, classify them properly.

1) Sundry Debtors 2) Goodwill 3) Loose tools 4) Motor vehicle 5) Closing stock of material
6) Work in progress 7) Mine 8) Bank Balance 9) Prepaid Expenses 10) Stock of finished goods

BANK RECONCILIATION STATEMENTS

Introduction

The word 'reconcile' means 'to make compatible. It frequently happens in business that two sets of figures which should agree, for some reason do not. For example we might estimate that certain profit should be made in a given period but in fact we fail to achieve this expected profit. A good accountant would seek to reconcile the two sets of figure, examining the reasons for the discrepancy.

Perhaps the commonest of all such situations is the reconciliation of the Bank Account, as shown in our ledger, with the Bank Account in the bank's ledger, when the bank sends us a bank statement.

By reconciliation, the Cash Book balance can be proved by comparing it with the bank statement. Bank Reconciliation is an important part of the internal control system over cash balance lying in the bank. At present, the major Indian banks are in the process of switching to a computerized system which is changing the way in which bank statements are rendered to customers. However, this is unlikely to affect the need for bank reconciliation statements.

Meaning, need and importance of Bank reconciliation statements

When a bank agrees to permit a customer to open a current account by paying in an initial sum of money, and gives him a cheque book so that he may make any payments through the cheque system, it does not undertake to correspond with the customer every time a transaction takes place. Some banks hardly ever write to their customers at all, except when the customer fails to keep enough funds in his account to ensure that the bank will always be able to honour any cheques presented. Similarly the customer never writes to the bank to tell them he is making out a cheque. Every now and then the customer may ask for a bank statement, or the bank, feeling the a sufficiently large collection of paid cheques has accumulated on its files, will render a statement to the customer. Since the banker is the trustee of the customer, the bank provides to its customer a Bank Statement at regular intervals (generally during the 1st week of each month). Which summarizes payments as well as deposits and other charge for the period In fact, Bank statement is a copy of the customer's account in the Bank's Ledger.

There are several reasons why the bank statement may differ from the Bank Account in our three-column cash book, and in practice it will rarely be always due to a lack of knowledge of what the other person has been doing. To ascertain the bank balance a concern has two sources of information.

a) Bank column of the cash book and b) Bank Statements (Pass Book).

On principle, the two balances should be equal and opposite on a stated date, But usually these two balances do not agree. The main reason for the difference in balances is owing to the fact that no party intimates the other every time a transaction takes place. It is interesting to know that many of the transactions of the customer are intimated to the banker by a third party (for instance, when a cheque is presented).Disagreement in balances may also arise owing to mistake or mistakes in the Cash Book or Bank Statement.

Since the two balances are different, if all the facts are brought together, it should be possible for them to be reconciled by means of a Bank Reconciliation Statement.

a) Meaning

Bank Reconciliation Statements is a statement which contains a complete and satisfactory explanation of the differences in balances as per the Cash Book and Bank Statement.

The preparation of Bank Reconciliation Statement is not a part of the double entry bookkeeping system. It is just a procedure to prove the Cash Book balance.

It should be noted that : a) a Bank Reconciliation Statement is to be prepared whenever a Bank Statement is received; and b) it is prepared on a stated day

b) Need for Bank Reconciliation Statement :

1) It reflects the actual bank balance position. (Plus or minus)
2) It helps to detect any mistake in the Cash Book and in the Pass Book.
3) It prevents frauds in recording the banking transactions.
4) It explains any delay in the collection of cheques.
5) It identifies valid transactions recorded by one party but not by the other.

c) Importance of Bank Reconciliation

As a prudent policy, Bank Reconciliation should be done by a person who is not in charge of the Cash book. The -- functions of bank reconciliation and recording cash transactions are separated from each other. With this separation of functions, the system of check automatically operates and chances of pilferage or embezzlement are reduced. The employees cannot prepare unauthorised cheques, and get them encashed, without entering the transaction in the account If they want to, they should enter into collusion with each other, which is more circuitous and, therefore, difficult then when both the jobs are entrusted to the same person. Therefore, cash recording and cash dealing with the books should be in separate hands, help the management and for cash controlling.

Bank reconciliation is an important mechanism of internal control or internal check of cash inflow and outflow. Both of them must tally as per cash book with the Bank Pass Book (or bank statements). This brings in to focus errors and irregularities in the business. Therefore, preparation of Bank reconciliation statement is an usual practice of almost all business houses. The process of reconciliation is helping in finding out the reasons for the difference in the balance (i.e. bank balance shown in the Cash Book and balance shown in Bank Book).

Reasons for difference in bank balance as per cash Book & balance as per pass Book

The reasons may be divided into three groups :

a) Differences arising from the bank's actions, about which we have not been notified.
b) Differences arising from the time-lag which is inevitable whenever cheques are sent in payment of debts, or are received and paid into the bank for clearing through the banker's clearing house.
c) Errors, either by the bank, or by our own cashier.

Such errors are unlikely to occur frequently, because the banks usually institute careful checks on their figure, and a cashier is usually a responsible member of the staff. Inevitably though, mistakes do occur from time to time.

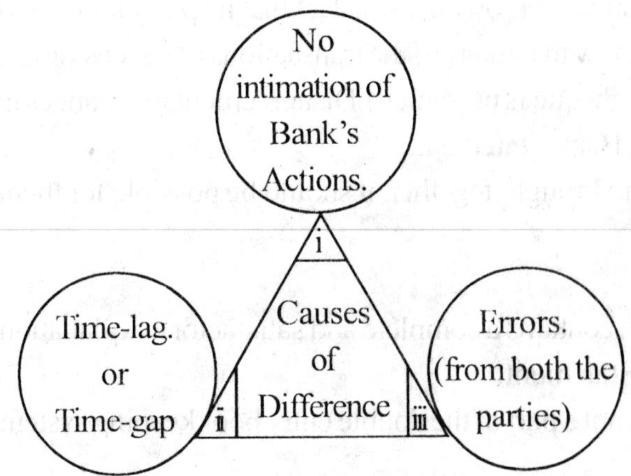

Fig. : Causes of differences in the two balances

The same reasons are presented in different manner by some authors as follows :

The differences in the two balances arise from the following three causes.

i) No intimation of Bank's Actions. ii) Time-lag.
iii) Errors. (from both the parties).

i) No intimation of Bank's actions

For some transactions, the bank has earlier knowledge and it adjusts its records before the business. Some differences may arise from the bank's actions that have not been intimated to the customer. For example, interest credited by the bank or bank charges debited by the bank.

The customer comes to know of these transactions only when he receives the Bank Statement or Bank Pass-Book.

ii) Time-lag

There may be a time gap between recording transactions in the customer's book and bank's book. For example, when a cheque is issued to a party, it is recorded immediately in the customer's book, but the bank will record it only when it makes payment against that cheque.

Similarly, when a cheque is deposited, it is recorded in the Cash Book immediately, but the bank will record it only when it collects money in respect of that cheque.

iii) Errors (from both the parties)

Some differences in balance may arise owing to errors committed by the bank or by the person responsible for preparing the Cash Book. For this reason, the books are to be properly rectified.

Common items frequently cause a difference

There are some common items which frequently cause a difference in the two balances.

1) **Cheques deposited but not credited by the bank :** Whenever a person receives a cheque from a third person and deposits it, he debits Bank Account in his own books, and credits the account of the person from whom the cheque has been received. His bank balance, therefore, is increased. The bank, however takes some time in collecting the cheque; and it would credit the customer's account only when the amount has been realised. Until the cheque has been collected, the balance appearing in the Pass Book would be less than the balance appearing in the Bank Account or Cash Book.

2) **Cheques issued but not presented for payment :** When a cheque is issued to a supplier or a third party, it is immediately entered in the Cash Book by crediting the bank and this has the effect of reducing the bank balance in the depositor's book. But the receiving party may not present the cheque to the bank for payment immediately. The bank debits the customer's account only when the cheque has been presented and paid for. So long as it is not presented, the balance shown in the Pass Book or Bank Statements is more than the balance shown by the depositor's Cash Book.

3) **Standing Order :** A standing order is an instruction to a bank by a customer to make a fixed payment regularly on stated days to some third party (ies). When a business unit requires to make regular payments for an item like salaries, the business unit may save itself the trouble of remembering to write several cheques and hand these over to the employees each month by making a standing order at the bank to pay salaries to its employees. The bank will then automatically pay the employees the same amount of money each month until further notice is received from the business unit. Since the business unit does not prepare cheques for its employees each month, these will be unrecorded in the cash book. When the business unit receives the bank statement, it will check that salaries have been paid in accordance with standing orders and then make the necessary double entries in the ledger.

Most people remember to deduct these sums from the Bank Account if they are monthly payments, for example mortgage payments or payments for rates. The less regular ones may be overlooked, such as annual contributions to bodies like the Automobile Associations, or to professional bodies.

4) **Interest credited by Bank not entered in the Cash Book :** When the bank allows interest to a customer, it credits the customer's account and his bank balance would increase. But the customer comes to know about it only at the end of the month, and then the would pass an appropriate entry. Until then the bank balance as per the Pass Book would be more than the balance as per the Cash Book.

5) **Bank Charges debited by the bank but not recorded in the Cash Book :** The bank charges some amount from each customer by way of incidental charges, collection charges, and the like and debits his account for this reason from time to time. As soon as these charges are made, the bank debits the customer's account in its own books and this reduces the bank balance. But the customer learns about these charges only, when he receives the Bank Statement or Pass Book and then he credits Bank Account in his own books. Until then, the bank balance as per the Pass Book would be less than the bank balance as per the Cash Book.

6) **Amount directly deposited in to Bank by Debtors :** When any amount is directly deposited by a debtor into the Bank Account of the depositor, the bank would credit the depositor's account immediately but the customer would know about it only after receiving advice from his bank. Until then, the bank balance, as per the Pass Book would show more than the balance as per the Cash Book.

7) **Credit transfer :** The receipt of sums by credit transfer, either from debtors or, more usually, from investments. For example, the ICICI Bank which manages the dividend yield security market on behalf of the investor, prefers, to pay interest on securities directly into the investor's bank account, rather than send him a cheque for the amount due. This credit transfer will appear on the Bank Statement as a deposit, increasing the balance on the account.

When the bank collects dividends, it would credit the customer's account and his bank balance will increase. But the customer would know about it only after receiving advice form the Bank. Until then, the bank balance as per the Pass Book would be more than the balance as per the Cash Book.

8) **Direct Debit :** Direct debit is an instruction given to a bank by its customer to allow charges to be made periodically to the account at the instance of some third party. Therefore, a direct debit is also a standing order with the exception that the receiver can alter the date or the amount of payment.

Payment through standing order / direct debit will lead to difference between the balance as per Cash Book and Pass Book. For example, when the bank pays insurance premium on behalf of its customer, it would debit the cutomer's account and his bank balance would decrease. But the customer will know about it only after receiving advice from the bank. Until then, the bank balance as per the Pass Book will be less than the balance as per the Cash Book.

9) **Errors and Omissions :** Errors and omissions either in the Cash book or in the Pass Book may lead to differences between the bank balance as per the Pass Book and Cash Book. Mostly, totalling and balancing mistakes in the cash book and in the Pass Book lead to differences between bank balance as per Cash Book and Pass Book.

Specimen of Bank Reconciliation statement

The specimen of Bank Reconciliation statement is as under.

Bank Reconciliation Statement of ______________________ Bank an on / /200

	Rs.	Rs.
Bank balance as per Cash Book		xxx
Add 1) Cheques issued but not debited by the Bank in Pass Book.	xxx	
2) Interest credited by the bank not entered in the cash book.	xxx	
3) Cheque/cash directly deposited by the party in the bank account not entered in the Cash Book (e.g. dividend, bills collected by the Bank).	xxx	
4) Cheque issued by us but cancelled or dishonoured subsequently.	xxx	
5) Excess balance shown by the bank due to mistake in totalling or balancing.	xxx	(+) xxx
		xxxx
Less 1) Cheques deposited but not credited by the bank in the pass book.	xxx	
2) Cheque deposited into the bank and dishonoured by the party.	xxx	
3) Interest charged by the bank not entered in the cash book.	xxx	
4) Bank charges/commission/postage debited by the bank not entered in the cash book.	xxx	
5) Direct payments made by the bank (i.e. insurance premium etc.) not entered in the cash book.	xxx	
6) Less balance shown by the bank due to mistake in totalling or balancing Bank Balance as per Bank Pass Book.	xxx	(-) xxxx
		xxxx

Preparation of Bank Reconciliation statement

Before preparing the bank reconciliation statement, The following steps may be taken in to consideration:

Steps in Reconciliation :

The following steps may be taken for such a reconciliation :

Step I — Confirm that the opening bank balance tallies with opening balance shown in the pass book. If it does not tally with the pass book the items of reconciliation of the previous period should be carried forward.

Step II — Check the totals and balancing of bank column of cash book.

Step III — Check the totals and balancing of bank pass book.

Step IV — Compare each item of the payments side of bank column in the cash book with the payment side (withdrawal) of pass book.

Step V — Compare every item to the debit side of bank column in the cast book with the deposit side of bank pass book.

Step VI — The comparison of the items as shown in step no. VI & V will reveal some entries which are entered only in either of the two or there may be difference in the amounts entered.

Step VII — Such differences or omissions should be enlisted on a piece of paper.

Step VIII — Then prepare bank reconciliation statement.

Reconciliation statement is nothing but systematic presentation of the reasons (with amounts) for difference in the two balances. This statement starts with the bank balance either as per cash book or as per pass book. The reasons for difference as pointed out in step VII & VIII above are either added or deducted as per their nature to the balance taken; so that the resultant figure tallies with the balance as per Cash Book or Bank Book. The decision whether to add or deduct a particular amount depends on simple logic. For example, cash book shows bank balance of Rs. 1000 and in the pass book a cheque deposited of Rs. 200 is not credited. If we start the reconciliation by taking balance as per cash book of Rs. 1000, the omission of Rs. 200 in the pass book means less balance shown by the bank, it must be deducted from the balance of Rs. 1000 to find balance as per pass book. If a cheque of Rs. 500 issued by us is not debited by the bank, it will mean that the bank has not deducted Rs. 500 from the balance in our account. In other words bank balance must be more in the pass book. Hence it is required to be added to our balance of Rs. 1000 to find the balance as per pass book. Similarly interest credited by bank in the pass book of Rs. 30 is not entered by us in our books. This means that the balance as per cash book is less than the balance as per pass book by Rs. 30. Hence Rs. 30 should be added to the balance of Rs. 1000 to reach the balance as per pass book.

Such a logic can be applied for different reasons found in steps V & VI above. The specimen of such reconciliation statement is as given above.

One can start with the bank balance as per bank pass book also and reach to the balance as per cash book. In this process the items mentioned above naturally would have reverse effects i.e. the items shown under the heading "Add" will come under the heading "Less" & vice versa. If bank account is overdrawn and the balance at the end is overdraft balance, again the reverse effects to above items may be necessary.

It could be seen from the above items that some of them are nullified in due course automatically. For example : 1) Cheque issued not debited by bank or 2) Cheque deposited not credited by bank.

These debits and credits may be given in the net period because some time is required for cheque clearance. Hence for such items not entries are required to be made in the books of accounts.

Some other items are such that for them entry must be made in the cash book to nullify the difference in the two balances. Such items may be :

a) Direct credits in the bank accounts.
b) Direct payment made by the bank from the account.
c) Bank interest debited or credited by bank.
d) Bank charges debited be bank.
e) Cheque issued, dishonoured or cancelled.
f) Cheque deposited & dishonoured.

Unless the entries for the above items are passed in the cash book there is no much use of preparing the reconciliation statement, because otherwise the balances of different accounts to that extent will not show the correct position. For example - A cheque dishonoured by the party if not cancelled by passing an entry in cash book, the party's balance shall be incorrect. After passing these entries the following items shall only remain in the reconciliation statement :

a) Cheque issued debited by the bank in the next period.
b) Cheque deposited credited by the bank in the next period.
c) Totalling or balancing mistake in bank pass book.

In the trial balance such rectified bank balance as per cash book after passing the entries for the above items, should be taken, so that the profit and loss account and the balance sheet will show a true and fair picture of the business.

Chart for helping the students in solving the problems

Following chart should be refered by the students while solving the practical problems. In example there

Reasons	When Balance is given as per Cash Book (a)	When Balance is given as per Pass Book (b)	When Overdraft Balance is given as per Cash Book (c)	When Overdraft Balance is given as per Pass Book (d)
Nature of Balance	Dr.	Cr.	Cr.	Dr.
1) Cheque deposited into bank but not credited.	(-)	(+)	(+)	(-)
2) Cheque issued but not presented for payment.	(+)	(-)	(-)	(+)
3) Bank Charges debited in Pass Book only.	(-)	(+)	(+)	(-)
4) Interest credited in Pass Book only.	(+)	(-)	(-)	(+)
5) Interest debited in Pass Book Only.	(-)	(+)	(+)	(-)
6) Payments made by bank recorded in Pass Book only.	(-)	(+)	(+)	(-)
7) Direct payment by customers in bank recorded in pass book only.	(+)	(-)	(-)	(+)
8) B. R. Discounted with bank being dishonoured, recorded in pass book only.	(-)	(+)	(+)	(-)
9) Cheque deposited into bank being dishonoured, not recorded in Cash Book.	(-)	(+)	(+)	(-)

are 4 possibilities.

1) Bank balance as per cash book is given & students have to calculate bank balance as per pass book.
2) Bank balance as per pass book is given & students have to calculate bank balance as per cash book.
3) Overdraft balance as per cash book is given & students have to calculate overdraft balances as per pass book.
4) Overdraft balance has per pass book is given & students have to calculate overdraft balance as per cash book.

Problem

a) When Bank Balance is given as per Cash Book

Problem : 1

The cash book of Mrs. Gujarathi Showed a debit balance of Rs. 5400 on 31st March 2001. But her Bank Pass Book showed all together a difference balance and on comparing her Cash Book and Pass Book you find the following reasons :

i) Cheques amounting to Rs. 3,200 issued but not presented for payment before 31st March 2001.

ii) Cheques paid into bank but not collected and credited before 31st March 2001, amounted to Rs. 1700.

iii) Bank charges Rs. 20 debited in the Pass Book, did not appear in Cash Book.

iv) Interest credited by bank Rs. 350 did not appear in Cash Book. You are requested to prepare a bank reconciliation statement so as to show bank balance as per bank pass book.

Solution

In the books of Mrs. Gujarathi

Bank Reconciliation Statement as on 31st March, 2001

b) When bank balance is given as per Bank Pass Book

	Rs.	Rs.
Bank Balance as per Cash Book as on 31.03.2001.		5,400
Add :		
Cheques issued but not presented for payment before 31.03.2001.	3,200	
Interest credited by bank but not entered in cash book.	350	(+) 3,550
Less :		8,950
Cheques paid into bank but not collected and credited by bank before 31.03.2001.	1,700	
Bank charges debited in the pass book but not entered in the cash book.	20	(-) 1,720
Bank Balance as per Bank Pass Book as on 31.032001.		7,230

Problem : 2

M/s. Thanewala Co's Pass Book showed a credit balance of Rs. 9750 or 31st May, 2001. From the following particulars prepare a Bank Reconciliation Statement showing the balance as per Cash Book as on 31st May, 2001.

1) Out of the cheques of Rs. 4,200 deposited into bank till 31st May 2001, cheques worth Rs. 1,500 were realised upto 31st May, 2001.
2) Cheques issued prior to 31st May, 2001 but presented after that date amounted to Rs. 3,700.
3) Pass Book shows that a bill receivable of Rs. 3,000 has been collected by bank for which no entry appears in the cash book.
4) Bank paid Rs. 250 for Chamber of Commerce subscription for the year, for this no entry in the cash book.
5) Bank charges Rs. 30 were wrongly recorded as Rs. 300 in cash book.
6) Interest credited by bank Rs. 450 does not appear in cash book.

Solution

In the books of M/s. Thanewala Co. Ltd.

Book Reconciliation Statement as on 31st May, 2001

Particulars	Rs.	Rs.
Bank Balance as per Pass Book as on 31.05.2001.		9,750
Add :		
Cheques deposited into bank but not collected and credited before 31.5.2001.	2,700	
Chamber of commerce subscription paid by bank debited in Pass Book not entered in cash book.	250	(+) 2,950
Less :		12,700
Cheques issued but not presented for payment before 31.5.2001	3,700	
Bill receivable collected and credited by bank was not entered in cash book.	3,000	
Bank charges wrongly credited in cash book	270	
Interest credited by bank but not entered in cash book	450	-7,420
Bank Balance as per Cash Book as on 31st May, 2001		+ 5,280

c) When overdraft balance is given as per Cash Book

Problem : 3

From the following particulars, prepare a bank Reconciliation Statement showing the balance that would appear in the Pass Book of Mrs. Puja as on 31st March, 2001.

1) The overdraft as per Cash Book on 31st March, 2001 was Rs. 8,450.
2) Interest on overdraft for six months ending 31st March, 2001 Rs. 370, did not appear in the Cash Book.
3) Bank charges Rs. 70 for the above period debited in the Pass Book were not yet recorded in the Cash Book.
4) Cheques issued but not presented for payment before 31st March, 2001 amounted to Rs. 3,500.
5) A bill for Rs. 1,000 discounted at the bank appears in cash book in full amount, whereas the bank had deducted discounting charges Rs. 40.
6) Cheques amounting to Rs. 5,500 deposited into the bank but a only cheque of Rs. 1,200 was collected and credited before 31st March, 2001.
7) Bank has paid final call on 100 shares of Sunita Ltd. at Rs. 20 per share according to standing instructions to them. It is not entered in the cash book.

Solution :

In the books of Mrs. Puja

Bank Reconciliation Statement

As on 31st March, 2001

Particulars	Rs.	Rs.
Bank overdraft as per Cash Book as on 31.03.2001		
Add :		8,450
Interest on overdraft debited in pass book not entered in cash book.	370	
Bank charges debited in pass bok not entered in cash book.	70	
Discount on B. R. was debited in the pass book but was not considered in the cash book	40	
Cheques deposited into bank but collected and credited before 31.03.2001	4,300	
Final call on shares paid by bank debited in pass book not entered in cash book	2,000	+ 6,780
Less :		15,230
Cheques issued but not presented for payment before 31.03.2001		3,500
Bank overdraft as per bank pass book as on 31.03.2001		11,730

d) When overdraft balance is given as per Pass Book

Problem : 4

Prepare the Bank Reconciliation Statement of Mrs. Patankar, Pune from the following data. Its on 31st May 2001.

1) Balance as per pass book on 31st May 2001 (debit) Rs. 12,100.
2) Cheques drawn on 31st May 2001 but not cleared till June 2001 Rs. 7,450, Rs. 9,500 and Rs. 14,200.
3) Cheques received on 29th May 2001, entered in the cash book but not deposited in the bank till October, Rs. 34,000.
4) A periodic payment of Rs. 150 by bank under standing instructions not entered in cash book.
5) There was a debit in the pass book Rs. 100 for bank charges and Rs. 1500 for interest on overdraft which was not entered in cash book.
6) Cheques of Rs. 15,000 deposited in the bank was finally dishonoured was not entered in cash book.

7) Bankers have made a mistake in balancing by showing overdrawn balance in excess by Rs. 1000 on 31st May 2001.

Solution :

In the Book of Mrs. Patankar,

Bank Reconciliation Statement as on 31st May 2001

Particulars	Rs.	Rs.
Bank overdraft balance as per Bank Pass Book as on 31.05.2001		12,100
Add :		
Cheques issued but not presented for payment before 31.5.2001		(+) 31,150
Less :		43,250
Cheques received and entered in Cash Book are not deposited into bank before 31.05.2001	34,000	
Periodic payment by bank debited in pass book not entered in cash book	1,500	
Bank charges debited in pass book not entered in cash book	100	
Interest on O.D. in pass book not entered in cash book	1,500	
Cheques deposited into bank and dishonoured not recorded in cash book	15,000	
Bank's mistake in balancing by showing overdraft balance in excess.	1,000	(-) 53,100
Bank Balance as per Cash Book as on 31.5.2001		(-) 9,850

c) When abstracts from the Cash Book and the Pass Book are given

In such a case there can be two situations :

i) When the abstracts relate to the same period : In such a case such transactions should be found which are not common in both the abstracts. These constitute the causes of difference.

ii) When the pass book relates to the suceeding period : In such a case compare those transactions which are common in both the abstracts. These constitute causes of difference.

Problem : 5

The following are the Cash Book and Bank Pass Book of Mirali for the month of April, 2001

Cash Book (Bank Column)

Date	Particulars	Rs.	Date	Particulars	Rs.
1.4.2001	To Balance b/d	12,500	1.4.2001	By Salaries A/c (Ch. No. 183)	4,000
4.4.2001	To Sales A/c	8,000	6.4.2001	By Purchases A/c (Ch. No. 184)	3,200
8.4.2001	To Parimal A/c	1,500	11.4.2001	By Machinery A/c (Ch No. 185)	6,000
13.4.2001	To Mahim A/c	3,400	15.4.2001	By Om Prakash A/c (Ch. No. 186)	1,000
18.4.2001	To Kamal A/c	4,600	19.4.2001	By Drawing A/c (Ch. No. 187)	800
21.4.2001	To Furniture A/c	1,200	23.4.2001	By Kishore A/c (Ch. No. 188)	2,000
25.4.2001	To Sales A/c	3,800	27.4.2001	By Suresh A/c (Ch. No. 189)	1,000
30.4.2001	To Firoz A/c	3,000	30.4.2001	By Printing A/c (Ch. No. 190)	500
			30.4.2001	By Balance c/d	19,500
		38,000			38,000

Bank Pass Book

Date	Particulars	Deposit	Withdrawal	Balance
1.4.2001	Balance			12,500
2.4.2001	Cheque No. 183		4,000	8,500
6.4.2001	Cash	8,000		16,500
6.4.2001	Cheque No. 184		3,200	13,300
10.4.2001	Cheque	1,500	1,500	14,800
16.4.2001	Cheque	3,400		18,200
17.4.2001	Cheque No. 187		800	17,400
20.4.2001	Cheque	4,600		22,000
24.4.2001	Cheque	3,800		25,800
28.4.2001	Cheque No. 185		6,000	19,800
28.4.2001	Cheque No. 189		1,000	18,800
30.4.2001	Interest	100		18,900
30.4.2001	Deposit (Firoz)	3,000		21,900
30.4.2001	Charges		10	21,890

You are required to prepare a Bank Reconciliation Statement as on 30th April, 2001

Solution

Bank Reconciliation Statement of Mirali as on 30th April, 2001

Particulars		(Rs.)	(Rs.)
Balance as per Cash Book		19,500	
Less : Amount deposited but not credited			1200
Add : Cheques drawn but not presented			
Cheque No. 186	1,000		
Cheque No. 188	2,000		
Cheque No. 190	500	3,500	
Add : Interest allowed by bank but not posted in Cash Book		100	
Less : Charges debited by bank but not posted in Cash Book			10
		23,100	1,210
Balance as per Pass Book		21,890	

I) Fill in the Blanks :

1) Trader records his banking transactions in the __________ column of his Cash Book while the banker records the same transactions in his __________.
2) Banking transactions recorded to the receipt side of cash book would be recorded by bank to the __________ side of pass book.
3) __________ represents a copy of the customer's account as it appears in the bank's ledger.
4) If banking transactions are recorded in Cash Book as well as in Pass Book, both the books must show __________ balance.
5) Bank Reconciliation Statement is prepared at the end of __________.

II) Write True or False :

1) Bank Reconciliation Statement is a Ledger account.
2) Bank Reconciliation Statement is prepared without comparison of cash book with Pass Book.
3) Bank Reconciliation Statement must be prepared every month.
4) Bank Reconciliation Statement is neither a Journal nor a Ledger.
5) Bank Reconciliation Statement is also prepared by Bank.

III) Answer the following :

1) Why does the balance of Bank column of Cash Book differ from the Pass Book ?
2) What is Bank Reconciliation Statement ?
3) How is a Bank Reconciliation Statement prepared ?

IV) Prepare a Bank Reconciliation Statement as on 31st December 2004 from the Bank Pass Book and Cash Book (Bank column only).

Bank Pass Book

Date	Particulars	Withdrawals Rs.	Deposits Rs.	Dr. / Cr.	Balance Rs.
2004					
Dec. 1	By Balance b/d			Cr.	11,500
Dec. 4	By Mahesh A/c		750	"	12,250
Dec. 7	By Santosh A/c		1,000	"	13,250
Dec. 10	To Prakash A/c	850		"	12,400
Dec. 15	To Cash A/c	2,400		"	10,000
Dec. 20	By Vikas A/c		500	"	10,500
Dec. 23	To Vishal's A/c	700		"	9,800
Dec. 26	To Insurance Premium A/c	500		"	9,300
Dec. 31	To Bank Charges A/c	50		"	9,250
Dec. 31	To Interest A/c		110	"	9,360
Dec. 31	By Interest on Investment A/c		640	"	10,000

Cash Book (Bank column only)

2004		2004			
Dec. 1	To Balance c/d	11,500	Dec. 10	By Raviraj A/c	1,000
Dec. 1	To Mahesh's A/c	750	Dec. 12	By Prakash A/c	850
Dec. 5	To Santosh's A/c	1,000	Dec. 15	By Cash A/c	2,400
Dec. 16	To Kumar's A/c	600	Dec. 18	By Vishal's A/c	700
Dec. 26	To Dinanath's A/c	600	Dec. 25	By Gune's A/c	400
			Dec. 28	By Shinde's A/c	600
			Dec. 31	By Bal. c/d	8,500
		14,450			14,450

V) Prepare a Bank Reconciliation Statement : A merchant opened current account in bank with Rs. 15,000 on 1st March 2005. During March he deposited cheques of Rs. 8,750/- in the account out of which cheques of Rs. 6,875/- were cleared by the end of the month. He also issued cheques of Rs.4,750/- in March of which cheques of Rs. 500/- was returned as dishonored on 1st April. The bank charges Rs. 10/- and commission Rs. 5/- not recorded in his cash book.

VI) From the following particulars, prepare a Bank reconciliation Statement as at 28th February 2005. The Bank Pass Book showed a credit balance of Rs. 9,400/- on that date.

a) A cheque of Rs. 579/- was deposited in the bank on 14th February, collected in due course, but the same was not recorded in the Cash Book.

b) The Bank had in accordance with the standing instruction paid life insurance premium of Rs. 500/- for which no entry was made in Cash Book.

c) Out of the total cheques for Rs. 1,600/- issued during the month, cheques for Rs. 340/- were presented for payment in March, one cheque Rs. 160/- issued to one party was lost in transit.

d) One customer directly deposited in the Bank Rs. 1,000/- for which no entry is recorded in Cash Book.

e) The Cash Book (Bank column) did not show the bank charges Rs. 12/- and interest on deposit Rs. 60/-.

VII) Prepare a Bank Reconciliation Statement from the following particulars on 30th June, 2005. Bank balance as per Cash Book Rs. 34,000/-.

a) Cheques issued but not presented for payments Rs. 2,400/-.

b) Cheques deposited but not cleared Rs. 3,000/-.

c) Cheques debited in Cash Book but not banked Rs. 1,540/-.

d) Cheques issued in June but presented for payment in July Rs. 800/-.

e) Interest credited in Pass Book only Rs. 360/-.

f) Bank charges debited in Pass Book only Rs. 30/-.

VIII) You are given the following extracts of the cash book (bank column only) and the pass book of the M/s Laxmi Stores who opened a bank account on 1st July with Rs. 30,000 prepare a Bank Reconciliation Statement on 31st July 2005.

Cash Book (Bank column only)

2005			2005		
July 1	To Cash A/c	30,000	July 4	By Salaries A/c	1,000
July 6	To Anurag's A/c	4,450	July 6	By Rent A/c	300
July 9	To Sales A/c	3,280	July 9	By Drawing's A/c	700
July 12	To Baban's A/c	2,520	July 12	By Purchases A/c	2,850
July 18	To Interest	300	July 15	By Engle's A/c	1,825
July 21	To Chandrakant's A/c	1,400	July 18	By Fizee's A/c	400
July 25	To Digu's A/c	1,200	July 24	By Gujar's A/c	2,425
			July 29	By Harun's A/c	1,700
			July 31	By Bal. c/d	31,950
		43,150			43,150

Pass Book

Date	Particulars	Rs.	Date	Particulars	Rs.
2005			2005		
July 4	To Salaries A/c	1,000	July 1	By Cash A/c	30,000
July 6	To Rent A/c	300	July 9	By Sales A/c	3,280
July 9	To Drawing's A/c	700	July 15	By Baban's A/c	2,520
July 12	To Purchases A/c	2,850	July 18k	By Interest A/c	300
July 20	To Engle's A/c	1,825	July 29	By Digu's A/c	1,200
July 29	To Gujar's A/c	2,425	July 30	By Moti's A/c	500
July 31	To Digu's A/c	1,200	July 31	By interest on investment A/c	300
July 31	To Bank Charges	25			
July 31	To balance c/d	27,775			
		38,100			38,100

IX) The Pass Book of M/s. Mico Trading Co. showed that the balance as on June 30, 2005, in account of State Bank, Poona is Overdraft of Rs. 4,390/-. This did not agree with the firms books of accounts and you found the following.

a) A cheque for Rs. 150/- issued was reported lost by postal authorities.

b) Two cheques of Rs. 1,000/- and Rs. 5,500/- deposited in June were cleared on July 5th.

c) The bank had collected interest on investments Rs. 500/- on June 24, and had debited its charges Rs. 15/- but the entry in respect there of was not passed in books of accounts. Interest on overdraft Rs. 250/- debited in Pass Book on July 1, had been adjusted in Cash Book on 30th June.

X) From the following particulars ascertain the balance that would appear in the Cash Book of Anand on 31st December, 2004.

a) The Bank Overdraft as per Pass Book on 31st December 2004 Rs. 9,400/-.

b) Interest on overdraft for 6 months ending 31st December, 2004 Rs. 190/- is debited only in Pass Book.

c) Cheques issued but not cashed prior to this date amounted to Rs. 1,100/-.

d) Cheques paid into bank not cleared before this date were for Rs. 6,170/-.

e) Interest on investments collected by the Bank and credited in the Pass Book Rs. 900/-.

f) Bank charges for the above period debited by Bank in the Pass Book Rs. 40/-.

TRIAL BALANCE

Introduction

Under Double Entry Book-Keeping system every debit has a corresponding credit. If various accounting entries are recorded correctly in various accounting books, a total of all debit balances of different accounts on a particular date must be equal to the total of all the credit balances of different accounts. Before preparing a Trial Balance all ledger Accounts must be totalled and balanced properly.

Meaning & Purpose of Trial Balance

For every transaction in the double entry system, equal rupee amounts of debits and credits are recorded in the books of account. If all the transactions have been recorded perfectly, we can say that the total of the debits should be equal to the total of the credits. Similarly, if all the account have been correctly balanced the total of the account with debit balances, must be equal to the total of the accounts with credit balances.

Balance of account is the difference between the total of the balance and similarly, if the credit side total is greater it is called a credit balance. Let us study the following account :

Dr.		Cash Account	Cr.
	Rs.	Particulars	Rs.
To Capital A/c	1,50,000	By Purchases A/c	80,000
To Sales A/c	90,000	By Salary A/c	15,000
		By Electricity A/c	11,000
		By Rent A/c	12,000

If we add up both the sides we get :

Debit side total	Rs. 2,40,000
Credit side total	Rs. 118,000
Difference	Rs. 122,000

This difference of the bank account will be called a 'debit' balance because the debit side total is more. At the time of balancing an account the 'balance' is first entered on the side whose total is less, then it is brought down on the proper side to show the actual nature of the 'Balance'. After balancing, the above cash Account will read as follows :

Dr.		Cash Account	Cr.
	Rs.	Particulars	Rs.
To Capital A/c	1,50,000	By Purchases A/c	80,000
To Sales A/c	90,000	By Salary A/c	15,000
		By Electricity A/c	11,000
		By Rent A/c	12,000
		By Balance c/d	1,22,000
	2,40,000		2,40,000
To Balance b/d	1,22,000		

The account balances are used to prepare the final accounts. An attempt is first made to check the accuracy of the recording and posting of each transaction as well as the correct balancing of an account by means of preparing a schedule of balances of all accounts known as the Trial Balance. A Trial Balance is simply a list of the names and balances of all the accounts in the ledger and cash book and listed in the order in which they appear in the ledger.

Features of a Trial Balance :

1. It is a list of balances of all ledger accounts and cash book.
2. It is not a part of the double-entry system of bookkeeping, it is just a working paper.
3. It can be prepared any time during the accounting period.
4. It serves as an instrument for carrying out the job of checking and testing.
5. Arithmetical accuracy of posting of entries from journal to ledger can be ensured.
6. Some errors are not revealed by the Trial Balance, for example, errors of principle. Compensating error.
7. An aggregation of Trial Balance is not a conclusive proof that there is no fraud or mistake.

Purposes in Drawing up a Trial Balance

1. It facilitates the preparation of the Trading, Profit and Loss Accounts and the Balance Sheet by making available the balances of all the accounts at one place.
2. It also ensures that the balance of each account, whether debit or credit, has been transferred properly to the respective columns of the trial balance and that the Trial Balance has been correctly added.
3. Some of the errors in the books of account can be detected by the Trial Balance and they can be rectified before the preparation of the final accounts.
4. It ensures that all transactions have been recorded with identical debit and credit amounts and the balance of each account has been computed correctly.
5. If serves as an instrument for verifying books of accounts and ledger posting.
6. It helps in ascertaining the nature and value of assets of a business.
7. It helps to find out the financial solvency of an enterprise.
8. It helps in ascertaining the nature and value of liabilities of a business.

Preparation of Trial Balance

'A trial balance is a statement or list of debit and credit balances of all the ledger accounts as on a given date'.

A Trial Balance is usually prepared on loose sheets of ruled papers. It is just like a page of the Journal or Ledger. Generally there are four columns, for particulars, ledger folio, Debit balance & Credit balance. Date column is not necessary as the date on which the trial balance is prepared can be stated at the top of the sheet as 'Trial Balance as on ___. The name of each account is entered in the particular column and the balance shown by it is entered against it in the appropriate column i.e. debit balance in the Debit Column and Credit Balance in the Credit Column.

For the purpose of preparing the Trial balance from a given list of ledger balances, the following rules should be followed :

1. The balances of all accounts relating to : a) Assets; b) Expenses; c) Losses; d) Drawings; and e) Debtors, should be placed in the debit column of the Trial Balance.
2. The balances of all accounts relating to : a) Liabilities; b) Income and Revenue; c) Gain; and d) Creditors, should be placed in the Credit column of the Trial Balance.

Treatment of Closing Stock in Trial Balance

Generally, closing stock does not appear in the Trial Balance because a separate account for this is not opened in the general ledger. Closing stock represents the balance of goods unsold, out of opening stock and purchases. When goods are purchased, the double-entry is completed with Purchases Account and Cash / Creditor account.

The closing stock appears in the Trial Balance only when it is adjusted against purchases by the entry.

Closing Stock Account Dr.
To Purchases Account

Specimen of Trial Balance

If all the transactions are correctly recorded in the ledger accounts and if the balances of the accounts have also been struck correctly, the debit and credit columns of the Trial Balance should agree. Therefore, a Trial

Balance essentially proves the arithmetical accuracy of the books of accounts. A Trial Balance is prepared at regular intervals, such as monthly, half-yearly or yearly, as desired. A specimen of a Trial Balance is given below :

Trial Balance of XYZ Co. as at 31.3.2xxx

Sl. No.	Heads of Account	L. F.	Debit Balance Rs.	Credit Balance Rs.
1	Cash in hand		10,000	
2	Cash at bank of Maharashtra		30,000	
3	Purchases		200,000	
4	Wages		25000	
5	Rent		15,000	
6	Sales			2,20,000
7	Capital			50,000
8	Loan from Bank			10,000
	Total		2,80,000	2,80,000

Preparation of Trial Balance from given balances of accounts

There are three methods of constructing a Trial Balance : a) Trial Balance with balances; b) Trial Balance with totals and c) Trial Balance with balances and totals.

a) Trial Balance with Balances

Under this method, the Trial Balance can be prepared on a loose sheet that may have five columns : a) Serial Nos. : b) Heads of Account; c) ledger folio (L.F.); d) Debit Balance; and e) Credit Balnce. For the preparation of a Trial Balance, the following steps are followed :

Step 1 : Calculate the balances of the cash book and all ledger accounts.

Step 2 : Write down the heading - 'Trial Balance of   as at   ' at the top of the loose sheet.

Step 3 : Write down : a) Serial numbers of the accounts in the 1st column. b) Names of the accounts in the 2nd column; c) L.I. number in the 3rd column; and d) The balances in the respective columns.

Step 4 : Add both the debit and credit columns to see whether they agree.

Problem : 1

Enter the following transactions in the ledger of Mr. Amit.

2005		Rs.	2005		Rs.
Jan. 1	Started business with cash	8,000	Jan. 19	Sold goods for cash	350
Jan 4	Bought goods for resale	500	Jan. 20	Bought stationery	80
Jan. 7	Bought stationery	50	Jan. 21	Paid wages	100
Jan. 10	Bought goods for resale	750	Jan. 23	Bought goods for resale	200
Jan. 12	Paid wages	100	Jan 24	Sold goods for cash	600
Jan. 15	Sold goods for cash	350	Jan. 25	Paid postage	80
Jan. 16	Sold goods for cash	300	Jan. 26	Paid for advertisement	30
Jan. 17	Paid electricity Bill	70	Jan. 31	Sold goods for cash	700
			Jan. 31	Paid wages	150

You are required to extract a Trial Balance as on 31st January 2005.

Solution :

Cash Account Ledger of Mr. Amit

Dr. **Cr.**

Date	Particulars	Rs.	Date	Particulars	Rs.
2005			2005		
Jan. 1	To Capital A/c	8,000	Jan. 4	By Purchases A/c	500
Jan. 15	To Sales A/c	350	Jan. 7	By Stationery A/c	50
Jan. 16	To Sales A/c	300	Jan. 10	By Purchases A/c	750
Jan. 19	To Sales A/c	350	Jan. 12	By Wages A/c	100
Jan. 24	To Sales A/c	600	Jan.17	By Electricity Charges A/c	70
Jan. 31	To Sales A/c	700	Jan. 20	By Stationery A/c	80
			Jan. 21	By Wages A/cs	100
			Jan. 23	By Purchases A/c	200
			Jan. 25	By Postage A/c	80
			Jan. 26	By Advertisement A/c	30
			Jan. 31	By Wages A/c	150
			Jan 31	By Balance C/d	8,190
		10,300			10,300

Purchases Account

Dr. **Cr.**

Date	Particulars	Rs.	Date	Particulars	Rs.
2005			2005		
Jan. 4	To Cash A/c	500	Jan. 31	By Balance c/d	1,450
Jan. 10	To Cash A/c	750			
Jan 23	To Cash A/c	200			
		1,450			1,450

Sales Account

Dr. **Cr.**

Date	Particulars	Rs.	Date	Particulars	Rs.
2005			2005		
Jan. 31	To Balance c/d	2,300	Jan. 15	By Cash A/c	350
			Jan. 16	By Cash A/c	300
			Jan. 19	By Cash A/c	350
			Jan. 24	By Cash A/c	600
			Jan. 31	By Cash A/c	700
		2,300			2,300

Capital Account

Dr. **Cr.**

Date	Particulars	Rs.	Date	Particulars	Rs.
2005			2005		
Jan. 31	To Balance c/d	8,000	Jan. 1	By Cash A/c	8,000

Stationery Account

Dr. Cr.

Date	Particulars	Rs.	Date	Particulars	Rs.
2005			2005		
Jan. 7	To Cash A/c	50	Jan. 31	By Balance c/d	130
Jan. 20	To Cash A/c	80			
		130			130

Wages Account

Dr. Cr.

Date	Particulars	Rs.	Date	Particulars	Rs.
2005			2005		
Jan. 12	To Cash A/c	100	Jan. 31	By Balance c/d	350
Jan. 21	To Cash A/c	100			
Jan. 31	To Cash A/c	150			
		350			350

Electricity Charges Account

Dr. Cr.

Date	Particulars	Rs.	Date	Particulars	Rs.
2005			2005		
Jan. 17	To Cash A/c	70	Jan. 31	By Balance c/d	70

Postage Account

Dr. Cr.

Date	Particulars	Rs.	Date	Particulars	Rs.
2005			2005		
Jan. 25	To Cash A/c	80	Jan. 31	By Balance c/d	80

Advertisement Account

Dr. Cr.

Date	Particulars	Rs.	Date	Particulars	Rs.
2005			2005		
Jan. 26	To Cash A/c	30	Jan. 31	By Balance c/d	30

Trial Balnce of Mr. Amit as at 31.01.2005

Sl. No.	Heads of Account	L. F.	Debit Balance Rs.	Credit Balance Rs.
1	Cash Account		8,190	
2	Purchases Account		1,450	
3	Sales Account			2,300
4	Capital Account			8,000
5	Stationery Account		130	
6	Wages Accounts		350	
7	Electricity Charges Account		70	
8	Postage Account		80	
9	Advertisement		30	
	Total		10,300	10,300

b) Trial Balance with totals

Under this method, the trial balance is prepared by taking the total of each side of the accounts without balancing the accounts. This method of preparing a trial balance is not commonly used because it cannot help in the preparing of trading, profit and loss account and the balance sheet.

This method of preparing a trial Balance is similar to trial balance with balances method, except that the debit balance and credit-balance columns are replaced by debit total and credit total columns respectively.

c) Trial balance with balances and totals

Under this method, the trial balance is prepared by combining the first and second methods. In this method, there are columns for debit balance and credit balance along with columns for debit total and credit total. The following specimen will clarify this method.

Trial Balance of XYZ.... as on ....

Sr. No.	Heads of Account	L. F.	Debit Balance Rs.	Credit Balance Rs.	Debit total Rs.	Credit total Rs.

Limitations of a Trial Balance

An agreed Trial Balance does not prove that :

1. All transactions have been correctly analyzed and recorded in the proper accounts. If for example : the wages paid for the installation of plant had been erroneously recorded by debiting the wages account in place of the plant account, the Trial Balance would still agree
2. All transactions have been recorded in the books of original entry. If, for example, a purchase bill were to be completely omitted from being recorded in the purchase book, the error would not be disclosed in the Trial Balance.

In short, we can say that a Trial Balance should not, therefore, be regarded as a conclusive proof for the correctness of the books of account.

Problem :

State whether the balances of the following accounts should be placed in debit column or credit column of the Trial Balance.

1. Plant and machinery
2. Furniture
3. Salary
4. Discount allowed
5. Bank overdraft
6. Cash in hand
7. Creditors
8. Sundry debtors
9. Carriage inwards
10. Carriage outwards
11. Sales
12. Purchases
13. Discount received
14. Interest paid

Solution :

Trial balance as at ...

Sl. No.	Heads of Account	Logic	Debit Balance Rs.	Credit Balance Rs.
1	Plant and Machinery Account	Asset	✓	
2	Furniture Account	Asset	✓	
3	Salary Account	Expense	✓	
4	Discount Allowed Account	Expense	✓	
5	Bank Overdraft Account	Liability		✓
6	Cash in Hand Account	Asset	✓	
7	Creditors Account	Liability		✓
8	Sundry Debtors Account	Asset	✓	
9	Carriage Inward Account	Expense	✓	
10	Carriage Outward Account	Expense	✓	
11	Sales Account	Income		✓
12	Purchases Account	Expense	✓	
13	Discount Received Account	Income		✓
14	Interest Paid Account	Expense	✓	

Panchasutri of Trial Balance

The trial balance contains all of the account balances from the ledger. It includes assets, liabilities, expenses, income, capital and drawings. Students should remember following five points (panchasutri).

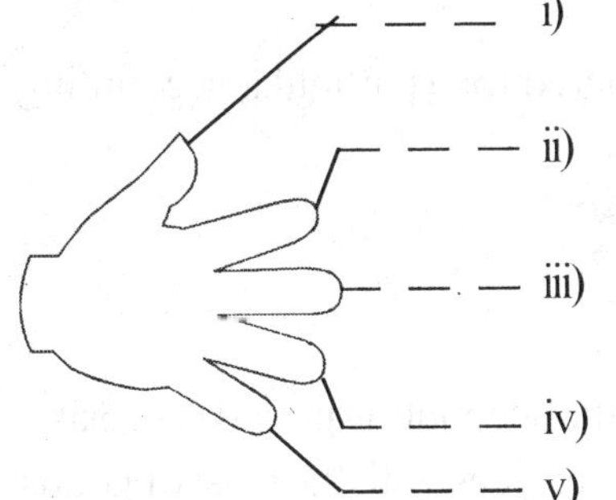

i) Debit balances usually represent either assets, expenses or drawings and these are always shown in the left hand column of the Trial Balnce.

ii) Credit balances are usually either income, liabilities or capital and these are always shown in the right hand column of the Trial Balnce.

iii) The expenses and income are shown in the Trading Account and Profit and Loss Account.

iv) Assets, liabilities, capital and drawing are shown in the Balance Sheet.

v) Additional information given by way of a note have not been recorded in the Ledger Accounts and consequently will require both a debit and a credit entry (which is usually effected by entering them in both the Trading and Profit and Loss Account and the Balance Sheet). Accounts appearing in the Trial Balance will be shown in the Trading Account or Profit and Loss Account or Balnce Sheet. No double entry is required for these Accounts.

FINAL ACCOUNTS OF A PROPRIETORY CONCERN

Introduction

In earlier unit we saw that the first level of maturity in accounting is to reach the Trial-Balance level of work, where the student can enter transactions in the ledger, balance off the accounts at the end of a period and prepare a Trial Balance of the ledger, getting the two sides to agree.

The second level of work in accounting is called 'Final-Accounts' level, because the student moves on past the Trial Balance to prepare two Final Accounts: the *Trading Account* and the *Profit* and *Loss Account*. The first of these is used to discover what is known as the gross profit or overall profit. The second is used to prepare the net profit or clean profit of the business. This net profit of course belongs to the owner, or owners, of the business, and will be handed over to the sole proprietor, or shared among the partners or shareholders, as a reward for the enterprise they have shown.

Final-Accounts work is therefore concerned with discovering the profits of an enterprise, and paying them over to the person or persons entitled to enjoy them.

Preparation of Final Accounts involves the following :

a) Preparation of a Trading Account;

b) Preparation of a Profit and Loss Account: and

c) Preparation of a Balance Sheet.

Trading Account is prepared to know the gross profit or overall profit. Profit and Loss Account discloses net profit or clear profit of the business. The Balance Sheet shows the financial position of the business in a given date-generally on the last date of the accounting period.

Preparation of Trading Account

After preparing a tallied trial balance at the end of an accounting period, the next step is to prepare Trading Account.

Meaning of Trading Account

Trading account is one of the financial statements which shows the result of buying and selling of goods and/or services during an accounting period.

Heading of Trading Account

Trading Account is a flow statement and not a static statement. It is prepared for a particular accounting period and not at a particular point of time/. Hence, it is headed as follows :

"Trading Account for the period ended......."

Purpose of Trading Account

Trading account is prepared to know the gross profit or gross loss during the accounting period. The basis for the preparation of this account is the matching of selling prices of goods and services with the Cost of goods sold and services rendered. In accounting parlance, gross profit means overall profit. Gross Profit is the difference between sale proceeds of a particular period and the cost of the goods actually sold. Since gross profit means overall profit, no deduction of any sort is made, i.e. general, administrative or selling and distribution expenses. Gross Profit is said to be made when the sale proceeds exceed the cost of goods sold conversely. When sale proceeds are less than the cost of the goods sold, gross loss is incurred.

Passing of Closing Entries

While preparing a Trading account, one important point must be kept in mind that a closing journal entry is to be made in the journal proper. At the end of each accounting period, revenues and expenses account (direct) are closed by transferring their balances to Trading Account. The balances of these accounts disappear once they are absorbed by Trading Account. The entries required for such transfer are called 'Closing Entries', since such entries will close the accounts of all the concerned items. The following closing entries are passed to give affect to such transfer of balance :

Account (s) to be closed	Accounting Entry to be passed	
a) Purchases Returns Account	Purchase Returns A/c	Dr.
	To Purchases A/c	
b) Opening Stock Account, Purchases Account and Accounts of Direct Expenses (e.g., wages, carriage Inwards, freight inwards)	Trading A/c	Dr.
	To Opening Stock A/c	
	To Purchases A/c	
	To Direct Expenses A/c	
c) Sales Returns or Return Inwards Account	Sales A/c	Dr.
	To Sales Returns A/c	
d) Sales	Sales A/c	Dr.
	To Trading A/c	

Closure of Trading Account

The Trading Account is closed by transferring its balance to the Profit and Loss Account by passing the following entry :

Nature of the Balance in Trading Account	Accounting Entry to be passed	
a) In case of Gross Profit (i.e., when the credit side exceeds the debit side)	Trading A/c	Dr.
	To Profit and Loss A/c	
b) In case of Gross Loss (i.e., when the debit side exceeds the credit side)	Profit and Loss A/c	Dr.
	To Trading A/c	

Format of a Trading Account

Trading Account can be prepared either in horizontal format ('T' form) or vertical format. The horizontal format of a Trading Account and the usually appearing entries therein are shown below. A general format of a Trading Account is shown below :

Trading Account of ... for the Period Ending on

Dr.	Cash Account				Cr.
Particulars		Rs.	Particulars		Rs.
To Opening Stock		xxx	By Sales	xxx	
To Purchases	xxx		Less : Return Inwards	xxx	xxx
Less : Returns outwards	xxx	xxx	By Closing Stock		xxx
To Direct Expenses		xxx	By Abnormal Loss of Stock		xxx
To Wages and Salaries		xxx	By Gross Loss transferred to P & L A/c		xxx
To Freight Inward		xxx			
To Carriage Inward		xxx			
To Cartage Inward		xxx			
To Gross Profit transferred to P & L A/c		xxx			
		xxx			xxx

* Either Gross Profit or Gross Loss shall appear.

The vertical format of a Trading Account is given below. Now-a-days, this format is more commonly used for Profit statements and reporting

Trading Account of X for the accounting year ended 31st March 2XXX

Particulars	Rs.	Rs.	Rs.
Sales			XXXX
Less : Returns inwards			XXX
			XXXX
Opening Stock		XXX	
Purchases	XXXX		
Less : Returns outwards	XXX	XXX	
Direct expenses :			
Freight & carriage	XXX		
Customs & insurance	XXX		
Wages	XXX		
Gas, water & fuel	XXX		
Factory expenses	XXX		
Royalty on production	XXX	XXX	
		XXX	
Less : Closing Stock		XXX	
Cost of Goods Sold			XXXX
Gross Profit			XXXX

Trading Account Items

Debit Side

1. Opening Stock : In case of a merchandising business; the opening stock consists of different types of finished goods. In case of a manufacturing concern, opening stock consists of raw materials, work-in-progress and finished goods. Where a separate manufacturing account is prepared, opening stock consists of only finished goods. In case of a newly set up business, there will be no opening stock ___ at the beginning of the first year. The amount of the opening stock is available in the Trial Balance.

Opening stock refers to the closing stock of unsold goods at the end of previous accounting period which has been brought forward in the current accounting period.

2. Purchases : The balance of the Purchase Account, as appeared in the Trial Balance, shows the total purchases made during the a accounting period which includes both cash and credit purchases. In respect of purchases the following points must be noted :

i) Purchase of capital asset should not be added with the purchases. If it is already included in purchases, it should be deducted therefrom.

ii) If some of the goods purchased are still in transit at the year end, it is better to debit Stock-in-transit' Account and credit Cash or Supplier's Account.

iii) If the amount of purchases include goods received on consignment, or on approval or on hire purchase, these should be excluded from purchases.

iv) Cost of goods sent on consignment must be deducted from the purchases in case of a trading concern.

The following items are shown by way of deduction from the amount of total purchases:

a) Purchases Returns or Return Outwards (i.e., goods returned to suppliers)

b) Goods withdrawn by the proprietor for his personal use.
c) Goods distributed by way of free samples.
d) Goods given as charity.

3. Direct Expenses : Direct expenses are shown separately in the Trading Account. Direct expenses are those expenses which are directly attributable to the purchase of goods or to bring the goods in saleable condition. Some examples of direct expenses are as under :

a) Freight and insurance : Freight and insurance paid in connection with acquiring goods or making them saleable is debited to Trading Account. Freight and insurance paid in connection with the sale of goods is charged to Profit and Loss Account. Freight and insurance paid for acquisition of fixed assets must be capitalised.
b) Carriage inwards : Carriage paid for bringing the goods to the godown is treated as carriage inwards and it is debited to Trading Account.
c) Octroi : When goods are purchased within municipality limits, generally octroi duty has to be paid on it. It is debited to Trading Account.
d) Fuel. power and lighting expenses : Fuel and power expenses are incurred for running the machines These are considered as direct expenses since directly related with the production and debited to Trading Account. Lighting Expense of factory is also charged to Trading Account but lighting expenses of administrative office or sales office are charged to Profit and Loss Account.
e) Packing charges : There are certain types of goods which cannot be sold without a container or proper packing. These form a part of the finished product. One examples is ink, which cannot be sold without a bottle. These type of packing charges are debited to Trading Account. But if the goods are packed for their safe despatch to customers, i.e. packing meant for transportation or fancy packing meant for advertisement will appear in the Profit and Loss Account.
f) Duty on Purchases : Any duty paid in connection with the purchase of goods is debited to Trading Account.
g) Wages : Wages incurred in a business is direct, when it is incurred on manufacturing or merchandise or on making it saleable Other wages are indirect wages. Only direct wages are debited to the trading Account. Other wages are debited to the Profit and Loss Account. If it is not mentioned whether wages are direct or indirect, it should be assumed as direct and should appear in the Trading Account.

Credit Side

1) Sales : The balance of the sales account, as appearing in the Trial Balance, shows the total sales made during the accounting period which includes both cash and credit sales. In respect of sales, following points must be noted :

a) If the goods are sold but yet to be despatched, it should not be included in sales, but the closing stock will be increased by the cost of such goods (if the property in goods has not yet been transferred).
b) If sale of fixed asset is included in sales, it should be deducted from sales.
c) Goods sold on approval or on consignment or on hire purchase, should be recorded separately. If these are included in sales, these should be deducted. Sales Returns or Returns Inwards (i.e., goods returned by customers) are shown by way of deduction from the amount of total sales.

2) Closing Stock : Refers to the stock of unsold goods at the end of the current accounting period. According to convention of conservatism, stock is valued at cost or net realisable value (NRV) whichever is lower. The rationale behind this practice is to provide for anticipated losses. Closing Stock is accounted for as under :

I	If the Closing Stock appears outside the Trial Balance.	The following entry is passed to incorporate the Closing Stock in the books. Stock A/c To Trading A/c As a result, the Closing Stock appears both on the credit side of the Trading Account and on the Assets side of the Balance Sheet.
II.	If the Closing Stock appears inside the Trial Balance.	a) Closing Stock will not be shown in the Trading Account since the Closing Stock has already been taken into Account while computing the adjusted purchases/cost of goods sold. b) Closing Stock will be shown in the Balance Sheet.

In case of a merchandising business, the closing stock consistys of different types of finished Goods. In case of manufacturing concern closing stock consists of raw materials, work-in-progress and finished goods. Where a separate manufacturing account is prepared. closing stock consists of only finished goods.

MANUFACTURING ACCOUNT

Manufacturing Account is prepared by an enterprise engaged in manufacturing activities. It is prepared to ascertain the cost of goods manufactured during an accounting period. This account is closed by transferring its balance to the debit of the Trading Account. A general format of a Manufacturing Account is shown below :

Dr. Manufacturing Account of... for the Period Ending on... Cr.

Particulars		Rs.	Particulars	Rs.
To Opening Work-in-progress		xxxx	By Sale of Scrap	xxxx
To Raw material Consumed :			By Closing Work-in-progress	xxxx
Opening Stock	xxx		By Trading Account	xxxx
Add : Purchases	xxx		(Cost of goods produced transferred)	
Add : Cartage Inward	xxx			
Add : Freight Inward	xxx			
Less: Closing Stock	xxx	xxxx		
To Wages		xxxx		
To Salary of Works Manager		xxxx		
To Power, Electricity and Water		xxxx		
To Fuel		xxxx		
To Postage and Telephone		xxxx		
To Depreciation on :				
Plant and Machinery		xxxx		
Factory Land and Building		xxxx		
To Repairs to :				
Plant and Machinery		xxxx		
Factory Land and Building		xxxx		
To Rent and Taxes		xxxx		
To General Expenses		xxxx		
To Royalty based on production		xxxx		
		xxxx		xxxx

Note : The amount of depreciation and expenses which has been debited to Manufacturing Account, shall not again be debited to Trading or Profit and Loss Account.

Balancing of Trading Account

After recording the above items, in the respective sides of the Trading Account, the balance is calculated to ascertain Gross Profit or Gross Loss. If the total of credit side is more than that of the debit side, the excess represents Gross Profit. Conversely, if the total of debit side is more than that of the credit side, the excess represents Gross Loss. Gross Profit is transferred to the credit side of the Profit and Loss Account and Gross Loss is transferred to the debit side of the Profit and Loss Account.

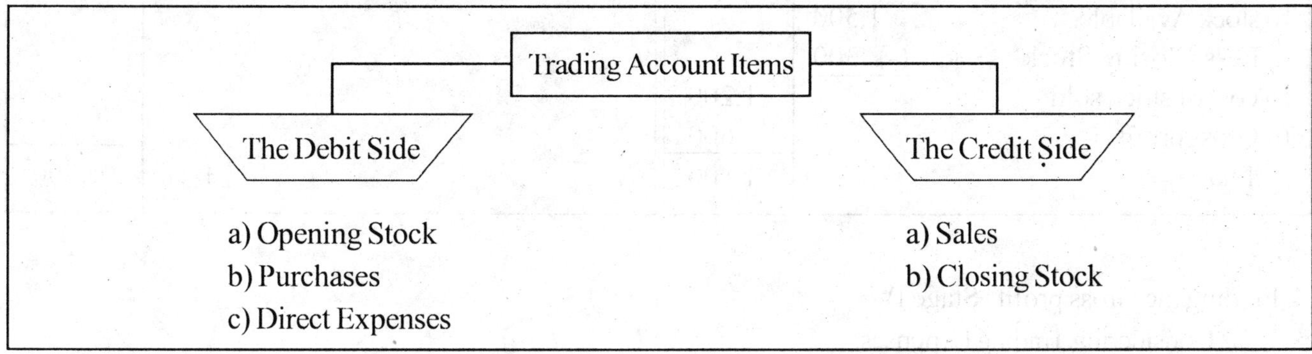

Accounting treatment for finding of a gross profit from Trading Account

For finding of a gross profit following four stages are followed.

1. Finding of Gross profit : Stage I.

Gross profit = Sales - Purchases (Cost of sales)

Trading A/c. (For the period ending....)

Dr.	Manufacturing Account of... for the Period Ending on...		Cr.
Particulars	**Rs.**	**Particulars**	**Rs.**
To purchases (Cost of sales)	2,550	By Sales	3,200
To Gross Profit.	650		
Rs.	3,200	Rs.	3,200
		By Gross profit	650

2. Finding of Gross Profit : Stage II.

Net Sales - N Purchases = Gross profit.

Dr.		Trading A/c. (For the period ending....)			Cr.
Particulars		**Rs.**	**Particulars**		**Rs.**
To purchases A/c	1,400		By Sales	1,895.00	
Less purch. Return	(-) 100		Less return	95.00	
To Net purchases (Costs Sales)		1,300	Net Sales (Turnover)		1,800
To Gross Profit		500			1,800
		1,800	By Gross profit		500

3. Finding of Gross profit : Stage III

Considering stock at the beginning & stock at the closing for the calculation of Gross Profit.

Dr.	Trading A/c. (For the period ending....)			Cr.
Particulars		Rs.	Particulars	Rs.
To opening stock	200		By Sales 1895.00	
To purchases 1400			Less return 95.00	
Less Returns (-) 100	(+)1,300		by By Net sales (Turnover)	1,800
(Net purchases).				
To stock Available.	1,500			
Less Closing Stock	(-) 300			
To cost of stock sold		1,200		
To Gross profit		600		
Total		1,800	Total	1,800

4. Finding the Gross profit : Stage IV.

Considering Trading Expenses.

Dr.	Trading A/c. (For the period ended .....)				Cr.
Particulars		Rs.	Particulars		Rs.
To opening stock		200	By Sales	1895.00	
To purchases	1,400		Less returns	(-) 95.00	
+ Carriage Inward	(+) 30				1,800
	1,430				
Less return	(-) 100	1,330			
To total stock available		1,530			
Less closing stock	(-)	300			
To cost of stock sold		1,230			
To warehouse wages	(+)	100			
To warehouse Exp.	(+)	56			
		1,386			
To Gross profit		414			
	Total	1,800		Total	1,800
			By Gross profit		414.00

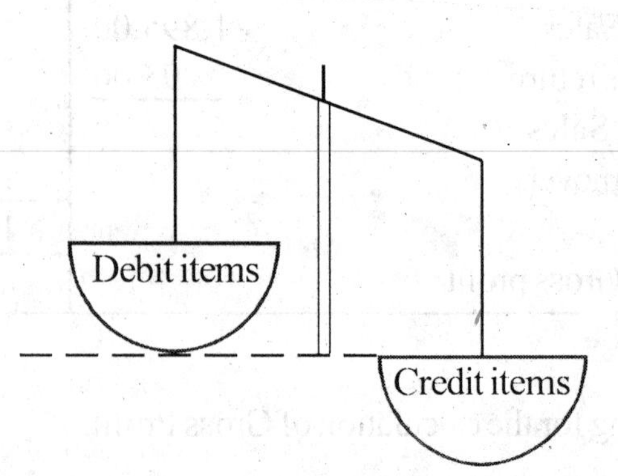

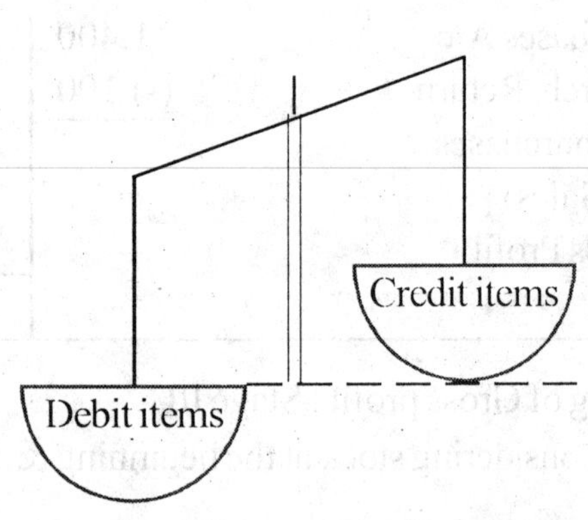

Excess Credit items over Debit items = Gross Profit   Excess Debit items over Credit items = Gross Loss

Preparation of Profit and Loss Account

After preparing a Trading Account, the next step is to prepare Profit and Loss Account with a view to ascertain net profit or net loss of the business during an accounting period.

Meaning of Profit and Loss Account

The Profit and Loss account is one of the financial statement. It shows the financial performance of business during an accounting period. The Profit and Loss Account can be defined as a report that summarises the revenues and expenses of an accounting period to reflect the changes in various critical areas of firm's operations. As pointed out earlier, the balance of the Trading Account (gross profit or gross loss) is transferred to the Profit and Loss Account, which is the starting point of the preparation of this account. This is why, Trading Account, is treated as a subsection of the Profit and Loss Account. Profit and Loss Account shows the profit or loss on ordinary activities, profit or loss on the sale of a capital asset, other abnormal losses and gains but excludes the payment of taxation, transfer to or withdrawal from reserves or from the business and the distribution of profit.

Treatment for sources of other incomes and expenditure in Profit and loss A/c:- After transferring the Gross Profit or Gross Loss from the Trading Account to the Profit and Loss Account, the sources of other incomes like commission or discount received are shown on the credit side of the Profit or Loss Account. The credit side also includes the nontrading income like interest on the bank deposits or securities, dividend on shares, rent of property let-out, profit arising out of sale of fixed assets, etc. On the debit side, all other expenses appearing in the Trial Balance which cannot find a place in the Trading Account, will appear. The debit side will also include the losses arising out of sale of assets and any abnormal losses.

Treatment for Prepaid and outstanding incomes & expenditure in Profit and loss A/c:- The Profit and Loss Account measures net income by matching revenues and expenses according to the accounting principles. Net income is the difference between total revenues and total expenses. In this connection, we must remember that all the expenses, for the period are to be debited to this account --- whether paid or not. If it is paid in advance or outstanding, proper adjustment are to be made. Likewise all revenues, whether received or not are to be credited. Revenue if received in advance or accrued but not received, proper adjustment is required.

After transferring all the nominal accounts from the Trial Balance to the Profit and Loss Account, it is necessary to balance the Profit and Loss Account. If the credit side is more than the debit side, it indicates net loss for the period

Heading of Profit and Loss Account

Profit and Loss is a flow statement and not a static statement. It is prepared for a particular accounting period and not for a particular point of time. Hence it is headed as follows:

"Profit and Loss Account for the period ended ...."

Purpose of Profit and Loss Account

The Profit and Loss Account is prepared to ascertain the Net Profit earned or net Loss incurred by the business entity during an accounting period.

Net Profit means the excess of all revenue (whether operating or nonoperating) over expenses and losses (whether operating or non-operating) or it is an excess incomes over expenditure. Therefore it is also known as revenue profit.

Operating Profit means the excess of operating revenues over operating expenses and losses. It arises as a result of carrying out operating activities. Operating activities are the principal revenue producing activities of the enterprise and other activities that are known as investment or financial activities. For example, Sales and

Purchases of buildings by Builders and property dealers are operating activities. Granting loans to third parties by them are investment activities. Taking loans from third parties by them are financial activities.

Passing of Closing Entries

The preparation of the Profit and Loss Account requires (a) to bring down the gross profit / gross loss and (b) to pass the necessary entries to transfer the balance of accounts of all the concerned items to the Profit and Loss Account. The entries required for such transfer are called closing entries since such entries will close the accounts of all the concerned items. The following closing entries are passed to give effect to such transfer of balances :

Accounts to be closed	Accounting Entry to be passed
a) To close the accounts of indirect revenue expenses and losses (i.e., other than those shown on the debit side of the Trading Account).	Profit and Loss A/c Dr. To Respective Items of expenses and losses (Individually).
b) To close the accounts of indirect revenue incomes and gains (i.e., other than those shown on the credit side of the Trading Account).	Respective Items of Income and gains Dr. (Individually) To Profit and Loss A/c ------------------

Closure of a Profit and Loss Account

The Profit and Loss Account is closed by transferring its balance to the Capital Account of the proprietor (in case of a proprietory concern) or of the partners (in case of a partnership firm) by passing the following entry :

Nature of Balance in P & L A/c	Accounting Entry to be passed
a) In case of Net Profit (i.e., when the credit side exceeds the debit side).	Profit and Loss A/c Dr. To Capital A/c -------------------------
b) In case of Net Loss (i.e., when the debit side exceeds the credit side).	Captial A/c Dr. To Profit and Loss A/c ------------------

Format of a Profit and Loss Account

Like Trading Account, Profit and Loss Account can also be prepared either in horizontal format or vertical format. The horizontal format of a Profit and Loss Account is given below :

Dr.	Profit and Loss Account of.... for the Peirod Ending on...		Cr.
Particulars	**Rs.**	**Particulars**	**Rs.**
To Gross Loss b/d	xxx	By Gross Profit b/d	xxx
To Salaries and Wages	xxx	By Interest earned	xxx
To Rent. Rates and Taxes	xxx	By Commission earned	xxx
To Fire Insurance Premium	xxx	By Rent earned	xxx
To Repairs and Maintenance	xxx	By profit on sale of fixed assets	xxx
To Depreciation	xxx	By Income from investments	xxx
To Audit Fees	xxx	By Sale of Scrap	xxx
To BankCharges	xxx	By Miscellaneous Incomes	xxx
To Legal Charges	xxx	By * Net Loss transferred to	
To Miscellaneous Expenses	xxx	Capital Account *	xxx
To Discount Allowed	xxx		
To Carriage Outward	xxx		

To Freight Outward	xxx		
To Commission to Salemen	xxx		
To Travelling Expenses	xxx		
To Entertainment Expenses	xxx		
To Sales Promotion Expenses	xxx		
To Advertising and Publicity	xxx		
To Bad Debts	xxx		
To Packing Expenses	xxx		
To Interest on Loan	xxx		
To Loss by Theft	xxx		
To Loss by Fire	xxx		
To Loss by Embezzlement			
To *Net Profit transferred to Capital Account	xxx		xxx
	xxx		xxx

* Either Net Profit or Net Loss shall appear.

The vertical format of a Profit and Loss Account is given below. This, too is more commonly used for profit statement and reporting.

Profit and Loss Account of X for the accounting year ended 31st March 2005.

Particulars	Rs.	Rs.	Rs.
Gross Profit			xxx
Add : Other Income :			
Discount received	xxx		
Commission received	xxx	xxx	
Add : Non-Trading Income			
Bank Interest	xxx		
Rent of property let out	xxx		
Dividend from shares	xxx	xxx	
Add : Abnormal Gains :	xxx		
Profit on sale of machinery	xxx		
Proft on sale of investments	xxx	xxx	xxx
			xxx
Less : Management expenses	xxx		
Salaries (administrative)	xxx		
Office rent, rates and taxes	xxx		
Printing and stationery	xxx		
Telephone charges	xxx		
Postage and telegrams	xxx		
Insurance	xxx		
Audit fees	xxx		
Legal charges	xxx		
Electricity charges	xxx	xxx	

Less : Maintenance expenses	xxx		
Repairs & renewals	xxx		
Depreciation on :			
Office equipment	xx		
Office furniture	xx		
Office buildings	xx	xxx	
Less : Selling and Distribution expenses			
Salaries (selling staff)	xxx		
Advertisement	xx		
Godown rent	xx		
Carriage outward	xx		
Bad debts	xx		
Provision for bad debts	xx		
Selling commision	xx	xxx	
Less : Financial expenses			
Bank charges	xx		
Interest on loans	xx		
Discount on bills	xx		
Discount allowed to customers	xx	xxx	
Less : Abnormal losses			
Loss on sale of machinery	xxx		
Loss on sale of investment	xxx		
Loss by fire	xxx	xxx	xxx
Net Profit (transferred to Capital A/c)			xxxx

Profit and Loss Account Items

The Debit Side

The items that will appear in the debit side of a Profit and Loss Account can broadly be classified as under:

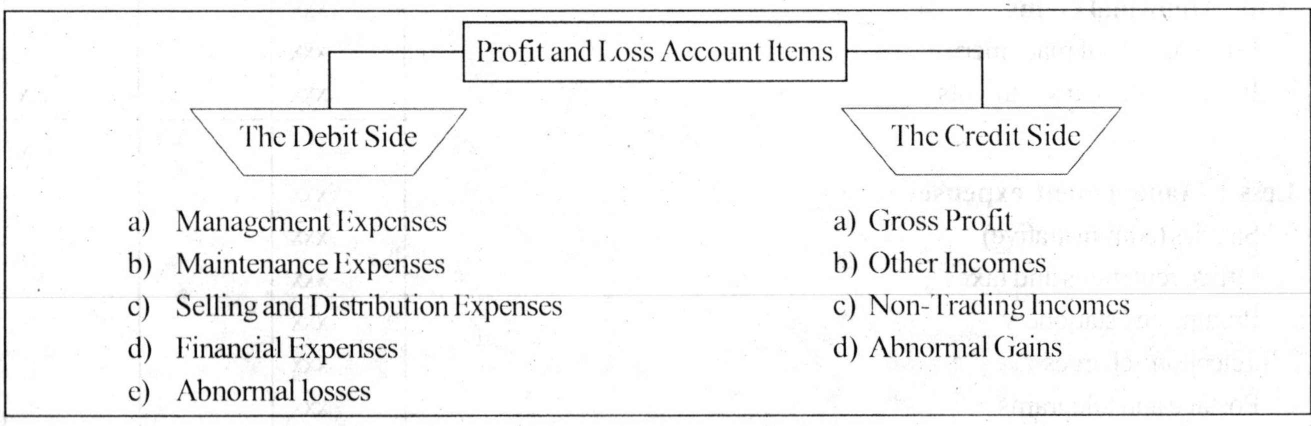

a) **Management Expenses :** These are the expenses incurred for carrying out the day-to-day administration of a business. Expenses under this head include office salaries, office rent and lighting, printing and stationery and telegrams, telephone charges, courier service charges, internet charges, etc.

b) **Maintenance Expenses :** These expenses are incurred for maintaining the fixed assets of the administrative office in a good condition. They include repairs and renewals, etc.

c) **Selling and Distribution Expenses :** These expenses are incurred for promoting sales and distribution of sold goods. Example of such expenses are godown rent, carriage outwards, advertisement, cost of after sales service, selling agents' commission, baddebts, R D D etc.

d) **Financial Expenses :** These expenses are incurred for arranging finance necessary for running the business. These include interest on loans, discount on bills, brokerage and legal expenses for raising loan, etc.

e) **Abnormal Losses :** There are some abnormal losses that may occur during the accounting period. All types of abnormal losses are treated as extraordinary expenses and debited to Profit and Loss Account. Examples are goods lost by fire and not covered by insurance, loss on sale of machinery, cash defalcation etc.

Expenses not appearing in the Profit and loss Account

Following are the expenses which do not appear in the Profit and Loss Account.

i) Domestic and household expenses of proprietor or partners (i.e. expenses for daughter's marriage).

ii) Drawings in the form of cash, goods by the proprietor or partners.

iii) Personal income tax and life insurance premium paid by the firm on behalf of proprietor or partners.

Events to be considered to ascertain the amount of expenses

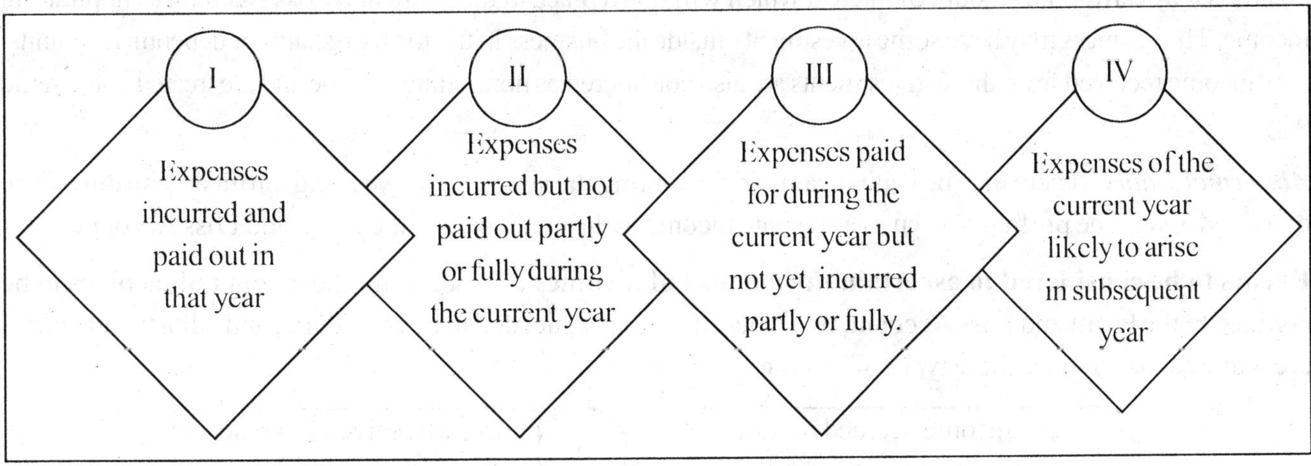

To ascertain the amount of expenses to be debited to the Profit and Loss Account, four types of events are needed to be considered and the cash payment made in connection with these events. They are as under:

i) Expenses incurred and paid out in that year : If an expenditure is incurred in one year and also paid for in the same year, the transaction becomes simplest and least troublesome. Most of the expenses for a period are generally paid before the accounting period is over. Here, when the expenses are incurred and payment is made, we debit expenses account and credit cash or bank account. At the year end, the Expense Account cannot have any balance, since closed by transferring it to the Profit and Loss Account by debiting Profit and Loss Account and crediting the Expense Account. (As we discussed the closing entries earlier).

ii) Expenses incurred but not paid out, partly or fully, during the current year: There are some expenses, which are incurred in the current accounting period, but not paid for partly or fully, by the end of the period, are called 'Outstanding expenses'.

Outstanding expenses include outstanding salaries, interest, rent, wages and other expenses.

iii) Expenses paid for during the current year, but not yet incurred, partly or fully : Sometimes, it happens that some expenses are paid for during the current year, but not yet incurred, partly or fully, are known as 'Prepaid Expenses'. Prepaid Expenses include prepaid insurance premium, rent, taxes, interest, etc. A prepaid expense is an asset and will be shown in the Balance Sheet.

iv) Expenses of the current year likely to arise in subsequent period: Sometimes, an expense or a loss may arise in the future in connection with current years' business. In such a case, we make a provision of the anticipated loss and a charge is created against the profit for the current period. This provision is shown either as a liability or as a contingent asset, i.e. it appears in the Balance Sheet as a deduction from some other asset.

Example of this anticipated expense is provision for bad debts.

The Credit Side

The items that appear on the credit side of a Profit and Loss Account can broadly be classified as under :

(a) Gross Profit; (b) Other incomes; (c) Nontrading income; and (d) Abnormal gains.

Gross Profit : This is the balance of the Trading Account transferred to the Profit and Loss Account. If the Trading Account shows a gross loss, it will appear on the debit side.

Other Incomes : During the course of the business, other than income from the sale of goods, the business may have some other income of financial nature. The examples are discount or commission received.

Nontrading Income : The business may have various transactions with the bank. At the end of the year, the business may earn some amount of interest which will find a place in the Profit and Loss Account as nontrading income. The business may have some investment outside the business in the form of shares or debentures or units. Any income received from these investments are also considered as nontrading income and are treated in the same way.

Abnormal Gains : There may be capital gains arising during the course of the year, e.g. profit arising out of sale of a fixed asset. The profit is shown as a separate income in the credit side of the Profit and Loss Account.

Events to be considered to ascertain the amount of incomes : To ascertain the amount of incomes to be credited to the Profit and Loss Account, two types of events are needed to be considered and adjustment entries are required to recognise these types of incomes.

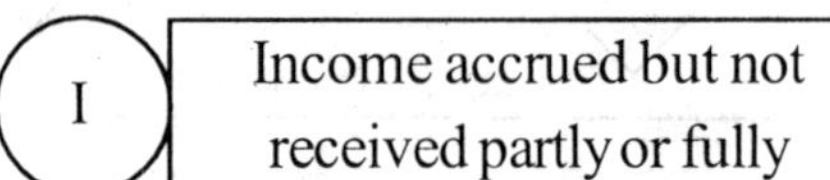

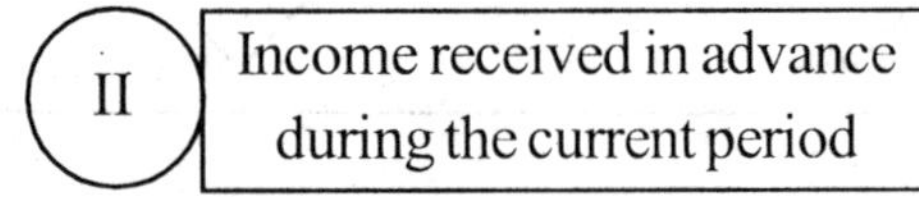

All the other incomes or abnormal gains are to be credited to the Profit and Loss Account if they arise or accrue during the period. Similarly, income received in advance is to be deducted from the income. The following adjustments are to be considered :

i) Income accrued but not received, partly or fully: Accrue means increase. Certain income such as interest on debentures, dividend or shares accrued during the accounting period but are not received. Adjusting entry is required to recognise these unrecorded increases (accruals) in income. For recording, the following entry will be passed :

Accrued Income Account	Dr. (Will be shown in the Assets side of the Balance Sheet)
To Income Account	(To be credited to Profit and Loss Account)

ii) Income received in advance during the current period : Income received in advance is not the revenue of the current accounting period. It will be recognised as income in the coming year. Income received in advance is treated as a liability and shown in the Balance Sheet. The adjusting entry will be :

Income Account Dr. (balance to be credited to Profit and Loss Account)

To Income Received in Advance Account (to be shown in the liability side of the Balance Sheet)

Balancing the Profit and Loss Account

The balance in the Profit and Loss Account represents the net profit or net loss. If the credit side is more than the debit side, it shows the net profit, and if the debit side shows more than the credit side, it shows net loss.

When the Profit and Loss Account shows a net profit, we pass the following entry :

Profit and Loss Account Dr.

To Net Profit Account

If the Profit and Loss Account shows a net loss the entry will be reverse.

Preparation of Balance Sheet

After preparing the Profit and Loss Account, the next step is to prepare a Balance Sheet.

Meaning of Balance Sheet

A Balance Sheet is one of the financial statement. A Balance Sheet is a statement of assets and liabilities of an enterprise at a given date. It is called a Balance Sheet because it is a sheet of balances of those ledger accounts which have not been closed till the preparation of the Trading and Profit and Loss Account.

A Balance Sheet is a list of assets and claims of a business at some specific point of time and is prepared from an adjusted Trial Balance. It shows the financial position of a business by detailing the sources of funds and the utilisation of these funds. A Balance Sheet shows the assets and liabilities grouped properly classified and arranged in a specific manner. After a Trial Balance is prepared and adjusting entries are passed and incorporated in the Trial Balance, some accounts are closed by transferring to the Trading Account and some accounts are transferring to the Profit and Loss Account. These accounts are in the nature of expenses and revenues. With the remaining accounts lying in the Trial Balance, which mainly represent assets and liabilities and adjusting accounts, a Balance Sheet is prepared in the unadjusted Trial Balance, has to be shown either in the Trading Account or in the Profit and Loss Account or in the Balance Sheet.

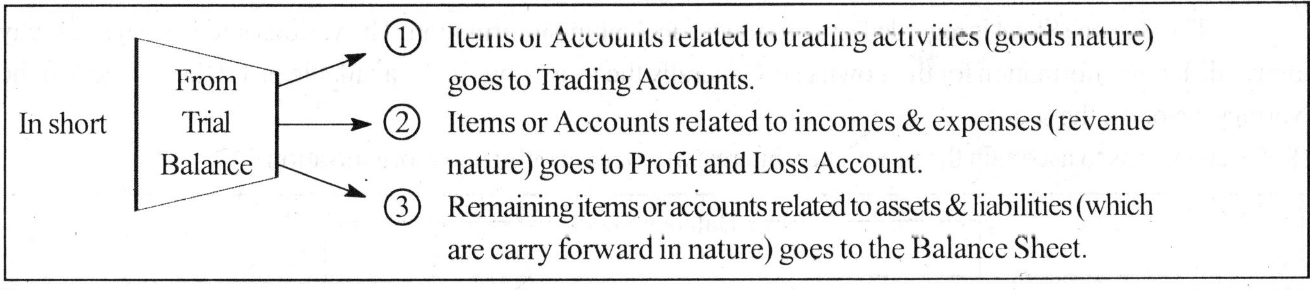

However, an adjusting accounts figures are to be shown both in the trading / profit and loss account and in the balance sheet.

The Balance Sheet summarises the incomplete transactions of the business. The Balance Sheet accumulates the various financial data in accordance with the basic accounting equation, Assets - Liabilities = Capital. The left hand side of the Balance Sheet shows the sources from which cash can be obtained and the right hand side shows the forms in which cash has been invested.

Features of a Balance Sheet

The Features of a Balance Sheet are summarized as under :

1. A Balance Sheet is **only a statement and not an account.** It has no debit side or credit side. The heading of the two sides are 'Assets' and 'Liabilities'.
2. A Balance Sheet is prepared **at a particular point of time and not for a particular period**. The information contained in a Balance Sheet is true only at the particular point of time at which it is prepared.
3. It is a summary of various assets provided to the business and the claims to these assets. It provides information regarding the assets owned by the business and the debts owed to the outsiders, and indicates the capital of the owners in the business.
4. A Balance Sheet is a **summary of balances** of those ledger **accounts** which have **not** been **closed** by transfer to the Trading and Profit and Loss Account.
5. A Balance Sheet **shows the nature and value of assets and the nature and the amount of liabilities** at a given date.

Heading of Balance Sheet

Balance Sheet is a static statement and not a flow statement. Balance Sheet is prepared at a particular point of time and not for a particular period. Hence it is headed as follows:

"Balance Sheet as at ....." or "Balance Sheet as on ......"

Purposes of preparing Balance Sheet

The purpose of preparing a Balance Sheet are as follows :

1. To ascertain the nature and value of assets of a business
2. To ascertain the nature and amount of liabilities of a business.
3. To find out the financial solvency of an enterprise. An enterprise is considered to be a solvent if its assets exceed its external liabilities. The solvency of a firm is measured by ascertaining the relationship of total assets to total liabilities and indicates the firm's ability to meet eventually all its short and long term debts.
4. To ascertain the working capital of a business to serve as a measure of liquidity.

Uses of the Balance Sheet

The Balance Sheet is regarded as a prominent accounting information. The various interested parties may derive different information for their own use. Generally the following can be available in a Balance Sheet to the various factors of the society.

1. It enables us to ascertain the proprietary interest of a person or business organisation.

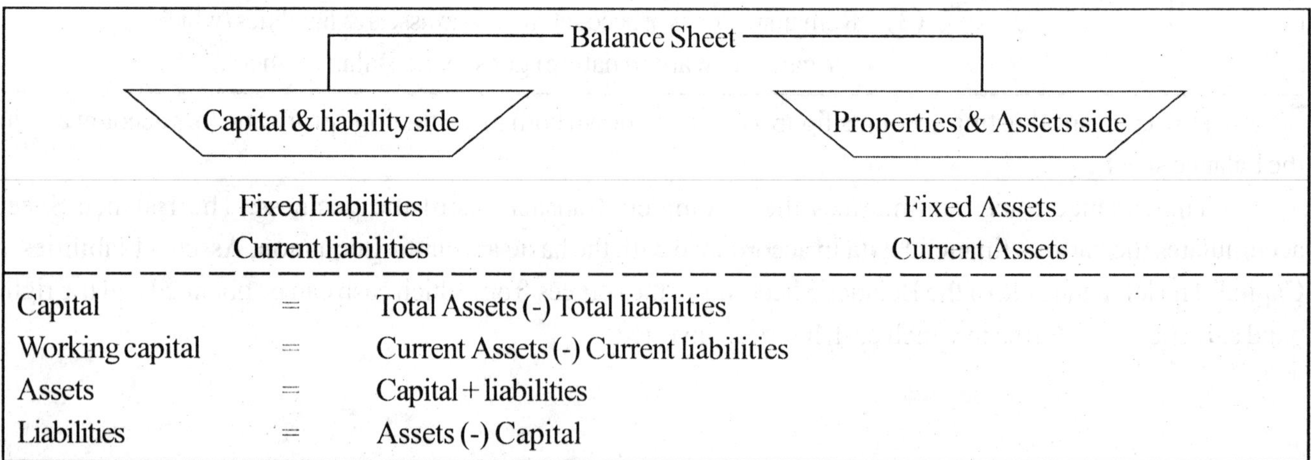

2. It enables us to calculate the actual capital employed in the business.
3. The lender or supplier can ascertain the financial position of the business for extending lending facilities.
4. It may serve as the basis for determining purchase consideration of the business.
5. The trends of working capital of the business can be determined by comparing the Balance Sheet of successive years and corrective measures can be taken, where necessary.
6. Different ratios can be calculated from the Balance Sheet and these ratios can be utilised for better management of the business and they can be helped for proper financial decision making.

Contents of Balance Sheet

In India the right hand side of a Balance Sheet is called the 'Assets' side and the left hand side is called the 'Liabilities' side. In some of the other countries (for example **America**) the right hand side of a Balance Sheet is called the 'Liabilities' side and the left hand side is called the 'Assets' side. The various items which are shown on the assets side and liabilities side are as given below :

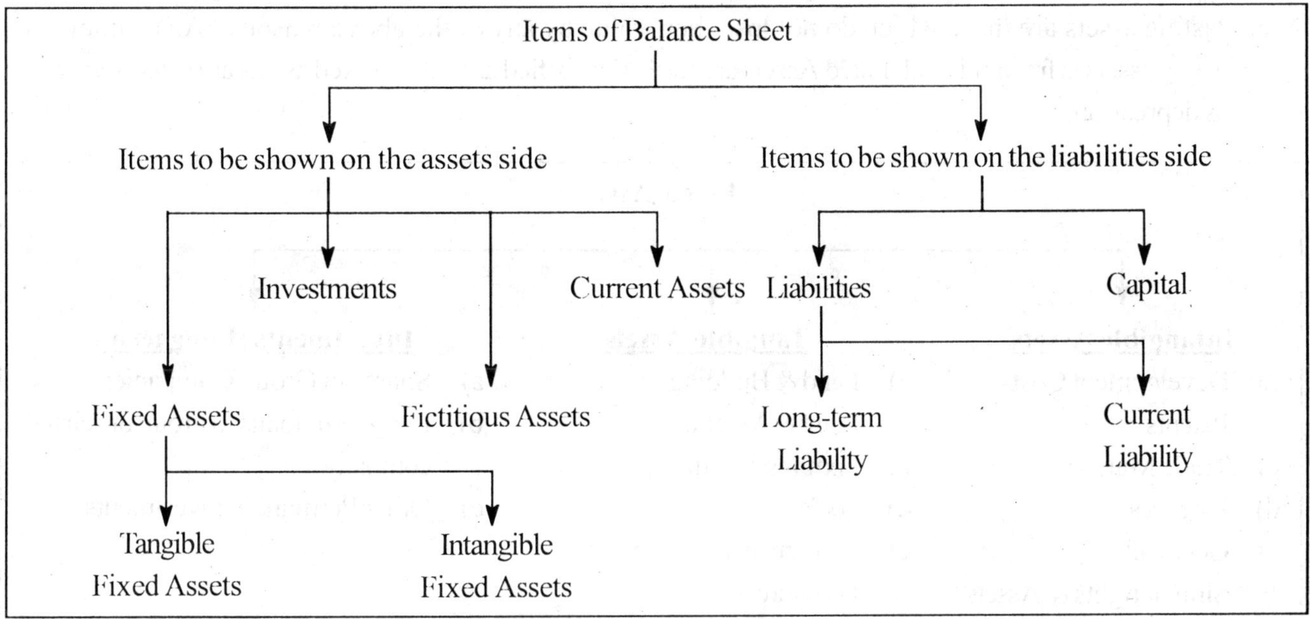

Items to be shown on the Assets side of Balance Sheet : The debit balances of those ledger accounts which have not been closed till the preparation of the Trading and Profit and Loss Account, are shown on the 'Assets' side of the Balance Sheet.

Assets refer to tangible objects or intangible rights owned by an enterprise and carrying probable future benefits. Usually the following items are included in the Assets :

Assets Account

Assets are basically of two types - those that are meant to be used by the business over a long period & not sold and those that are meant to be converted in to cash as quick as possible. The former type of assets are called "**Fixed Assets**" & the latter type of assets are called **"Current Assets."** Assets are anything owned by a business that is used in its operation.

Meaning of Fixed Assets

These are assets which are not "turned over" and sold at a profit but are "fixed" in the business and retained over a very long period. They are often called "Capital Assets", since they form part of the permanent capital equipment in use. For example - Land & Buildings, Plant & machinery, Furniture & Fittings, Motor vehicles etc.

Fixed assets are defined by the CIMA Terminology (Chartered Institute of Management Accountants) as:

'Any asset .... acquired for retention by an entity for the purpose of providing a service to the business, and not held for resale in the normal course of trading.'

These assets are tangible in nature ----- relatively long lived resources of a business. A business generally require these types of assets in order to use them in the production of goods and services. If the assets are held for re-sake they are classified as inventories, even though they are long lived. Therefore, fixed assets are long lived assets whose usefulness is likely to extend beyond one accounting period in the operations of the business. Fixed assets appear in the Balance Sheet at their historical costs minus accumulated depreciation. The expression "accumulated depreciation" means the portion of the original cost of the asset which has already been charged as an expense in the previous years as a cost of doing business.

The example of fixed assets are land and building, plant and machinery, furniture and fixtures, etc. Fixed assets are generally divided into wasting assets and non-wasting assets. Wasting assets lose their value by wear and tear (plant and machinery) or by the passage of time (leasehold land) or through being worked (mines). Non-wasting assets are those which do not lose their value by any of the above reasons,. An example of a non-wasting assets is freehold land. Fixed Assets are further classified as under : Fixed assets are usually valued at cost less depreation.

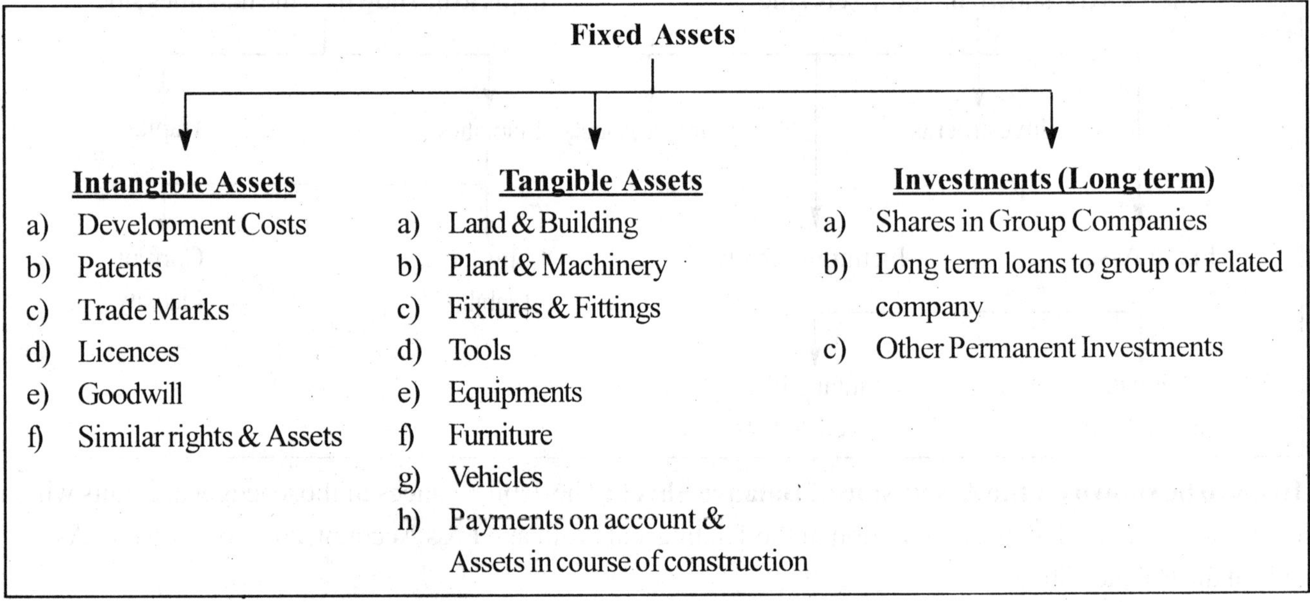

Tangible & Intangible Assets

Tangible Assets are those which can be seen & felt like building, machinery, furniture etc. Intangible Assets cannot be seen or felt like goodwill of the business. Both the assets are valuable. Tangible assets have physical identification, intangible assets do not have physical identification. Bankers or lenders accept tangible assets as security for a loan given, on the other hand, lenders do not accept intangible assets as security for a loan given. Tangible assets can be lost due to fire, flood, but intangible assets cannot be lost due to fire, flood etc.

Current Assets : Current assets are defined by the CIMA Terminology as :

'Cash or other asset, e.g. stock, debtors and short term investments, held for conversion into cash in the normal course of trading'.

These assets are reasonably expected to be realised in cash or consumed during normal operating cycle of the business. The distinction between fixed assets and current assets is important. The essence of the distinction is time. Current Assets are those that is owned by the business generally not for more than a year from the Balance

Sheet date whereas fixed assets are those that are expected to be owned for more than one year. Following are the examples of the current assets :

i) Stock is the inventory of raw materials, work in progress and finished goods. Stock is needed by a business either for sale in the ordinary course of business, or for use in the process of production for such sale or are to be currently consumed in the production of goods and services to be available for sale,. Stock is recorded in the Balance Sheet at its cost or current market value which ever is lower.

ii) Sundry Debtors are amounts owed to the business generally by its customers arising out of credit sales. Sundry debtors appear in the Balance Sheet at their net expected realisable value i.e. at their book values less an allowance for that portion of the amount owed which is not expected to be collected.

iii) Bills Receivable are acknowledgments of debts of the customers. When the amount owed by debtors are evidenced by a written acknowledgments of obligation, it would appear not under the head "Sundry Debtors" but under the head "Bills Receivable". Generally, Bills Receivable is a method of converting sundry Debtors into acceptor of bills.

iv) Investments are easily marketable securities and are generally converted into cash within the accounting period. A business invests money, which is temporarily idle, to get some return in cash. Investments are valued in the Balance Sheet at cost or current market value, whichever is lower. It is valued at cost only when the decline in the market value is believed to be only temporary.

v) Prepaid expenses and deferred charges represent certain kinds of assets, usually of an intangible nature, usefulness of which will expire with the near future. In fact, these are expenses which are already incurred, but the entire portion could not be recognised in the current accounting period because the benefit is spread over to more than one accounting period.

vi) Cash consists of funds which are readily available for disbursement without restriction. Most of these funds are usually on deposit with the banker (known as bank balance) and the balance in the temporary storage facilities (in cash box position) on the business campus.

Current Assets : These are sometimes called "Circulating Assets" as they are assets which are continually being turned over. The word "Current" comes from the French Word "Courrant" meaning running.

"The following figure illustrates the better position of Current Assets :

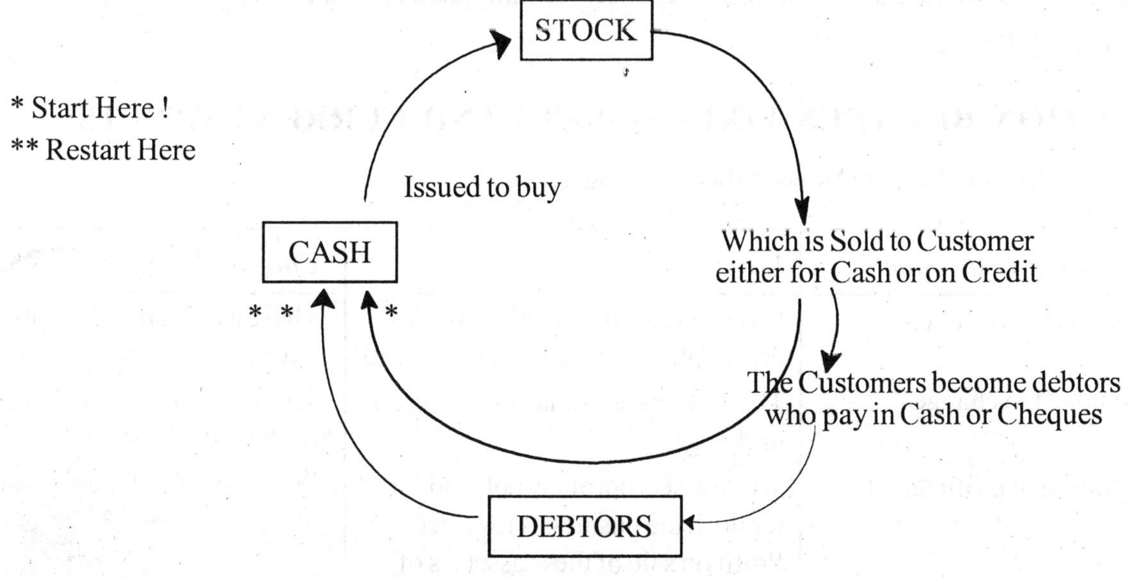

Fig : Position of Current Assets

Current Assets are further classified as under :

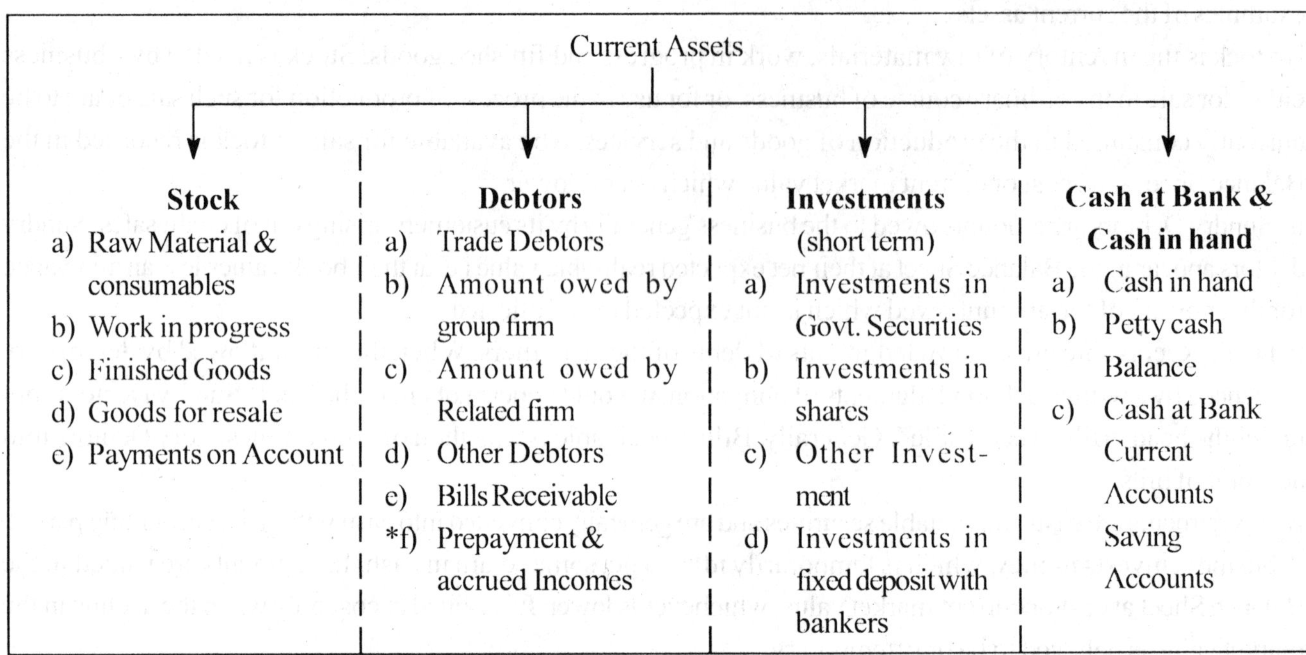

* These items may be shown separately in the balance sheet

Current assets are those assets which are held :

i) in the form of cash e.g. cash in hand and cash at bank,
ii) for their conversion into cash e.g., stock of finished goods, debtors, Bills Receivable, Accrued Income.
iii) for their consumption in the production of goods or rendering of services in the normal course of business e.g., Stock of raw material, Works in progress.

Current Assets are usually valued at cost or market price whichever is less on the basis of Prudence (or Conservatism) Principle.

Fictitious Assets : These are intangible properties which are not represented by anything concrete. The examples of fictitious assets are preliminary expenses, accumulated losses, etc. These also include deferred revenue expenditure.

DISTINCTION BETWEEN FIXED ASSETS AND CURRENT ASSETS

Fixed Assets differ from Current Assets in the following respects :

S.No.	*Basis of Distinction*	*Fixed Assests*	*Current Assets*
1.	Valuation of Asset	Fixed assets are valued at cost less depreciation. (at their historical cost)	These assets are valued at cost or market price whichever is lower.
2.	Subject to change	These assets are usually not subject to change.	These assets are usually subject to change.
3.	Nature of profit on sale	These assets normally not held for resale in the business. However Profit on sale of these assets is of Capital Nature.	Profit on sale of these assets are of Revenue nature.

S.No.	Basis of Distinction	Fixed Assests	Current Assets
4.	Purposes of holding	These are the assets which are held for the purpose of providing or producing goods or services	These are the assets which are held-in the form of cash, for their conversion into cash & for their consumption in the production of goods or rendering of services in the normal course of business.
5.	Charges	Fixed charges can be created on such type of Assets.	Floating charges can be created on these assets.
6.	Creation of Revaluation Reserves	If, fixed assets are appreciated revaluation reserve is created.	If current assets are appreciated, revaluation reserve cannot be created.
7.	Source of finance	These assets are financed out of long-term funds.	These assets are mainly financed out of short-term funds.
8.	Requirement in Business & Retained in Business	"Fixed Assets". are often called capital assets they form part of permanent capital equipment in use and retained over a very long period.	Current Assets are called "Circulating Assets" which are continually being turned over for a very short period (generally not more than a year)

Contingent Asset : Contingent asset has been defined by Kohler as "An asset, the existence, value and ownership of which depend upon the occurrence or non-occurrence of a specific event or upon the performance or nonp-erformance of a specified act; contrasts with contingent liability, often growing out of such a liability. Suppose the firm has filed a suit for some property now in the possession of someone else. If the suit is decided in the firm's favour, the firm will get the property; at the moment it is a contingent asset.

Items to be shown on the Liabilities side of a Balance Sheet : The credit balances of those ledgers accounts which have not been closed till the preparation of the Trading and Profit and Loss Account are shown on the 'Liabilities' side of the Balance Sheet.

Liabilities : Liabilities refer to the financial obligations of an enterprise other than owner's funds. Liabilities are obligations which arise from transactions or other events that have already been occurred. It involves an enterprise in a probable future transfer of cash, goods or services or the forgoing of a future cash receipt. The amount of the liability and the date of settlement of such liabilities are the claims of the outsiders against the business or the amounts that the business owes to some person or persons other than its owners.

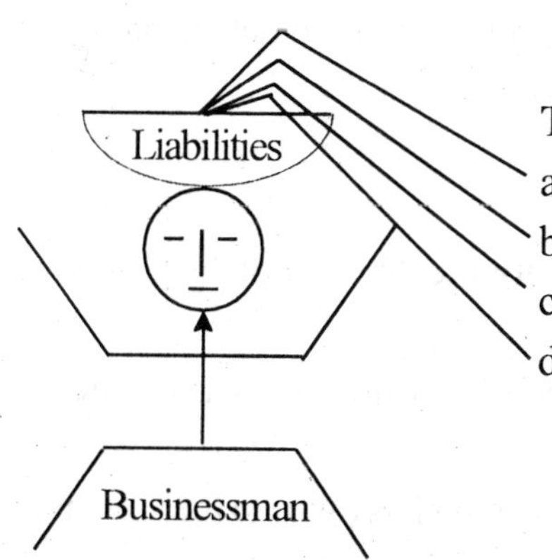

The liability of the business may take one of the following forms :

a) those with fixed amounts and date of payment

b) those with fixed amount but date of payment is estimated.

c) those for which the amount and the date of payment are estimated

d) those arise from the advances made by the customers.

Liabilities of a business can be classified into : (a) Fixed Liabilities; (b) Current Liabilities; and (c) Contingent Liabilities.

Figure

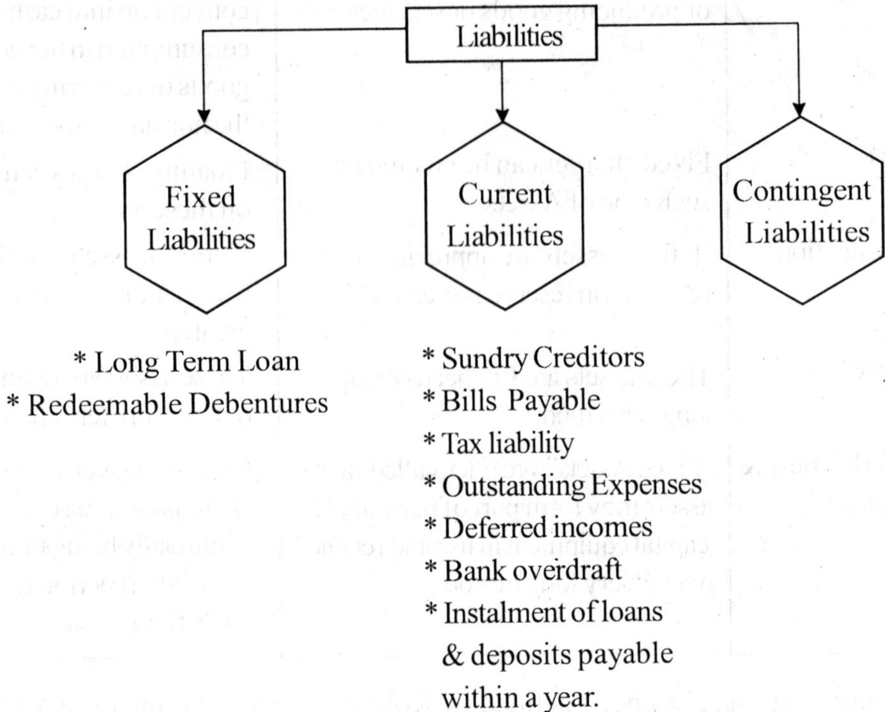

* Long Term Loan
* Redeemable Debentures

* Sundry Creditors
* Bills Payable
* Tax liability
* Outstanding Expenses
* Deferred incomes
* Bank overdraft
* Instalment of loans & deposits payable within a year.

(a) Fixed Liabilities : Fixed liabilities are not defined as such by CIMA Terminology but these are long-term liabilities which are generally redeemed after a long period of time. These include long-term loan, redeemable debentures of a company, etc.

(b) Current Liabilities : Current liabilities are defined by CIMA Terminology as :

'Liabilities which fall due for payment within one year. They include that part of the long term loans due for repayment within one year'.

These are obligations of the business which are payable in the near future, usually within the next accounting period. Therefore, a liability which is expected to have been paid within one year from the date of the Balance Sheet, is termed as "Current Liability".

Current liabilities are generally obligations for the items which are entered into the operating cycle of a business, such as sundry creditors and bills payable in the acquisition of inventory, supplies to be used in the production cycle, collection received in advance against the delivery of goods, debts which arise from operations directly relating to the operating cycle such as outstanding salaries, wages, commission, royalty, rent and so forth. It also includes income tax and other freight and taxes.

Following are the examples of current liabilities.

(i) Sundry creditors are the claims of the suppliers against the business for the delivery of the goods on credit which may not be evidenced by a written acknowledgment of debt.

(ii) Bills payable are the claims of the suppliers which is evidenced by a note or some other written acknowledge of debt.

(iii) Liability for taxes are the provisions made for the estimated tax liability which is owed to the government for taxes.

(iv) Outstanding expenses are expenses which are already incurred but not paid for. These are the converse of prepaid expenses. These liabilities may be intangible in nature in the sense that they are evidenced by a legal document. The examples of outstanding expenses are outstanding wages and salary, outstanding rent, etc.

(v) Deferred Income represents the short term liability of a business that arises because the business has received money in advance for a service to be rendered in future. An example is rent received in advance, which means rental payment is received by the business in advance for which the business agrees to permit the tenant to make use of property during near future.

Contingent Liabilities : These liabilities are conditions which exist at the Balance Sheet date, the outcomes of which can only be confirmed on the occurrence or non-occurrence of one or more uncertain future events. A contingent liability may also exist when a current situation may result in a future liability, but the amount of the liability in the monetary terms cannot be reasonably anticipated on the Balance Sheet date. They do not include uncertainties connected with accounting estimates, e.g. provision for doubtful debts or provision for discount on debtors.

Really, contingent liabilities have two characteristics: (i) uncertainty as to whether the amount will be payable at all; (ii) uncertainty about the amount involved. It is sufficient for the amount of contingent liability to be stated on the face of the balance sheet by way of a note, unless there is a probability that a loss will materialize and its reasonable estimate can be made. In that event, it is no more a contingent liability and a specific provision should be made therefor.

The examples of contingent liabilities not provided for include the following:

(i) Arrears of dividends on cumulative preference shares;

(ii) Bills of exchange discounted

(iii) Guarantees given by the company to companies under the same management; and

(iv) Suit for damages against the company which it is defending.

An example of contingent liability usually provided for is the one in respect of gratuities payable to staff on retirement or death.

An example, not involving loss, is the amount due on partly paid shares or the amount payable on a contract for construction works. On payment, a corresponding assets will come into existence.

Contingent liabilities are not recorded in the books of account; hence it does not appear on the liability side of the Balance Sheet. They are disclosed as a footnote at the bottom of the Balance Sheet.

Capital - Capital is the excess of assets over external liabilities. It refers to the amount invested in an enterprise by the proprietor (in case of a proprietorship concern) or partners (in case of a partnership concern), which is increased by the amount of profit earned and further contribution by a proprietor.

In the accounting sense, capital is the money contributed by the owner to an organisation to enable it to function. It is measured by the excess of assets over liabilities. Capital can be brought in by a person into the business in different forms - cash or kind. When capital is brought in the form of cash, it is spent away on various items of assets that make the business a running concern. Capital of the business is thus, represented by the amount of money invested in a business or net value of assets of a trader.(i.e. assets (-) liabilities).

In a sole proprietorship, capital is represented by the account which indicates the accountability of the business to the owner. When the owner brings in capital (or further capital) to his business, the amount is credited to the Capital Account. Likewise, the net profit for a period is credited to the Capital Account. When drawings are made by the owner, Capital Account is debited. Therefore, if the drawings are less than that of the income, the capital is increased by the difference.

Capital --- A Liability of Business

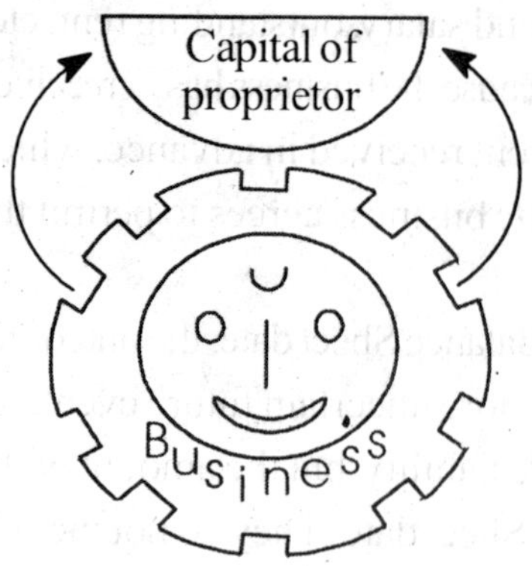

Capital is a liability of the business.

The owner of a business provides loan to the business when the initial capital of a business is invested by him and any additional capital injected into it at a later date. Any loan to the business is something which must be repaid in future, because it is a liability. This concept applies equally to the capital invested by the owner. Since we regard a business as quite a distinct entity from its owners, it can be seen clearly that capital is a loan to the business and that the business owes money to whomsoever loaned it. Hence, capital is a liability of the business. In accounting language, liabilities are of two fold, liability to outsiders and liability to the owner. The liability to outsiders is termed as 'liabilities' while liability to the owner is termed as 'Capital'.

Balance Sheet Formats

A Balance Sheet may be prepared in one of two forms : (i) Horizontal (Traditional) format and (ii) Vertical format.

Horizontal (Traditional) Format

Under this format, the left hand side lists liabilities of the business as on the last day of the accounting period well as details of its capital position; and on the right hand side are listed various assets of the enterprise. A Balance Sheet is so designed that it discloses the financial interest of the owner(s) in the business and its liabilities to outsiders --- and how those amounts are represented by its various assets. Therefore, the Balance Sheet includes the net profit or net loss as disclosed by the Profit and Loss Account.

Arrangement of Assets and Liabilities

The assets on the right-hand side and liabilities and capital on the left-hand side must be properly marshalled, i.e. they should be shown in a certain order. Subject to any particular law, which requires the assets and liabilities are to be shown in certain order, assets and liabilities can be arranged in any form that exists in the particular organisation. There are two common ways in which the assets and liabilities can be arranged. They are as under :

a) In the order of liquidity or dischargeability

According to this basis, assets are arranged in order of the case with which they can be converted into cash. Here, the cash in hand will come first, then cash at bank followed by other assets and land and building at the bottom of the list. In regard to the liabilities, they are so arranged in the order they are to be discharged, Bills payable appears first, then trade creditors and followed by loans, outstanding expenses. Thereafter, reserves and surplus will appear and capital at the bottom. Under this method, assets and liabilities are arranged as under :

Balance Sheet as at .....

Liabilities	Rs.	Assets	Rs.
Bills Payable		Cash in hand	
Trade Creditors		Cash at Bank	
Bank overdraft		Government Securities	
Loans		Other Investments	
Outstanding Expenses		Bills Receivable	
Reserves & Surplus		Sundry Debtors	
Capital		Stock	
		Furniture & Fixtures	
		Plant & Machinery	
		Land & Building	
		Good will	

b) In the order of permanence

According to the second basis, assets are listed in order of permanence, i.e. starting with those least 'realisable' and working down to the most 'liquid' assets. Liabilities are also recorded in order of their permanence, i.e. the liability which will have to be discharged last is shown first. On the assets side, the most fixed asset is land and building, will come first followed by plant and machinery, furniture and fixture, stock, debtors and cash in hand at the bottom. In regard to the liabilities, capital account heads the list, followed by reserve and surplus, and then by any creditors, for outstanding expenses. Thereafter, loans from outsiders, followed by creditors will appear and bills payable at the bottom. Under this method, assets and liabilities are arranged as under :

Balance Sheet as at .....

Liabilities	Rs.	Assets	Rs.
Capital		Good will	
Reserves & Surplus		Land & Building	
Outstanding Expenses		Plant & Machinery	
Loans		Furniture & Fixtures	
Trade Creditors		Stock	
Bills Payable		Sundry Debtors	
Bank overdraft		Bills Receivable	
		Other Investments	
		Government Securities	
		Cash at Bank	
		Cash in hand	

In this connection, following are the points to be noted :

1. Assets of the same class are grouped together ---- all fixed assets together and all current assets together.
2.

A Schedule of Proprietor's Funds

	Particulars	Rs.	Rs.
A.	Capital in the beginning		xxxx
B.	Add : Additional Capital Introduced	xxxx	
	Interest on Capital	xxxx	
	Salary to Partner	xxxx	
	Profit for the current accounting period	xxxx	xxxx
C.	Less: Drawings	xxxx	
	Interest on Drawings	xxxx	
	Loss for the current accounting period	xxxx	xxxx
D.	Capital at the end of the year (A+B-C)		xxxx

3. The term 'Grouping' means putting together items of a similar nature under a common heading. For example, under the heading 'Trade Creditors' the balances of the ledger accounts of all the suppliers from whom goods have been purchased on credit, will be shown.

4. The term 'Marshalling' refers to the order in which the various assets and liabilities are shown in the Balance Sheet. The assets and liabilities can be shown either in the order of liquidity or in the order of permanency.

c) Vertical Format

The Balance Sheet presentation used so far is known as the horizontal format. The disadvantages with the above presentation is that it does not show the value of the organisation. The networth of an organisation to the owner is the value of the owner's capital. The vertical format clearly displays the networth of the business to the owner ---- i.e. the capital. This format also displays the amount of investment in the fixed assets and in working capital (which is the difference between the current assets and current liabilities).

The vertical format merely involves a re-arrangement of the information shown by a Balance Sheet presented in Horizontal format. Many non-accountant managers are now required to make decisions based on accounting information. The vertical format is intended to help them gain a better understanding of the financial information presented by the accountants and therefore improve their decision-making.

Balance Sheet of ---------- as at -------

	Particulars	Rs.	Rs.	Rs.
A.	**Sources of Funds**			
	(a) Proprietor's Funds			XXXX
	(b) Long-term Debts			XXXX
				XXXX
B.	**Application of Funds**			
	(a) Net Working Capital			
	(i) Current Assets			
	Cash in hand	XXXX		
	Cash at bank	XXXX		
	Bills receivable	XXXX		
	Accrued income	XXXX		
	Debtors	XXXX		
	Stock	XXXX		
	Prepaid Expenses	XXXX	XXXX	
	(ii) Less: Current Liabilities			
	Bank Overdraft	XXXX		
	Accrued expenses	XXXX		
	Bills payable	XXXX		
	Trade creditors	XXXX		
	Income received in advance	XXXX	XXXX	XXXX
				XXXX
	(b) Investments			
	(c) Fixed Assets			
	Furniture & Fixtures		XXXX	
	Patents& Trade Marks		XXXX	
	Plant & Machinery		XXXX	
	Building		XXXX	
	Goodwill		XXXX	XXXX
				XXXX

Treatment of some items from trial balance for which no specific information is given. In such cases students should follow the following table for solving the problem.

Items	If item appears on debit side	If item appears on credit side	If it is not given whether debit or credit
(a) Returns	Shown on the credit side of Trading A/c by way of deduction from the amount of Sales	Shown on the debit side of Trading A/c by way of deduction from the amount of Purchases	It may be assumed as Returns Inward or Returns outward by giving an assumption to that effect.
(b) Discount	Shown on the debit side of P&L A/c as Discount Allowed.	Shown on the credit side of P& LA/c as Discount Received.	It may be assumed as Discount Allowed or Received by giving an assumption to that effect.
(c) Commission	Shown on the debit side of P&L A/c as Commission Allowed.	Shown on the credit side of P & L A/c as Commission Earned	It may be assumed as Commission Allowed or Commission earned by giving an assumption to that effect.
(d) Interest	Shown on the debit side of P&L A/c as Interest Allowed	Shown on the credit side of P & L A/c as interest Earned	It may be assumed as Interest Allowed or Earned by giving an assumption to that effect.
(e) Rent	Shown on the debit side of P&L A/c as Rent Paid	Shown on the credit side of P &L A/c as Rent Earned.	It may be assumed as Rent paid or rent earned by giving an assumption to that effect.
(f) Apprenticeship Premium	Shown on the debit side of P&L A/c as Apprenticeship Premium paid	Shown on the credit side of P & L A/c as Apprenticeship Premium received	It may be assumed as Apprenticeship Premium paid or received by giving an assumption to that effect.
(g) Carriage	Shown on the debit side of Trading A/c (if assumed as carriage on purchases) or P&L A/c(if assumed as carriage on sales).	---	It may be assumed as carriage on purchases or carriage on sales by giving an asumption to that effect.
(h) Freight	Shown on the debit side of Trading A/c (if assumed as Freight Inwards) or P&L A/c(if assumed as Freight outwards).	---	It may be assumed as Freight Inwards or Freight outwards by giving an assumption to that effect.
(i) Wages & Salaries	Shown on the debit side of Trading A/c	---	-----
(j) Salaries & Wages	Shown on the debit side of P&L A/c	---	-----

Effect of Adjustments

(a) Closing Stock

Closing stock refers to the stock of unsold goods at the end of current accounting period which is carried forward in the next accounting period as opening stock. The stock of finished goods is valued at cost or net realisable value whichever is lower. Its accounting treatment is summarized as under:

I.	Adjusting Entry to be passed	Closing Stock Dr. To Trading A/c
II.	Treatment in Trading A/c	Shown on the Credit side
III.	Treatment in Balance Sheet	Shown on the Assets side as a Current Asset.

Note: If closing stock already appears in the Trial Balance, then no adjusting entry is required to be passed since it has already been taken into account while computing the amount of 'Adjusted Purchases' or 'Cost of Goods Sold', such closing stock will still be shown only in the Balance Sheet and not in the Trading Account.

(b) Depreciation

Depreciation is the process of allocating the cost of a tangible fixed asset over its estimated life in a rational and systematic manner. Depreciation is generally charged to such assets as Plant and Machinery, Building, Furniture, Equipment, etc. Initially the cost of the assets including installation cost is debited to the particular asset. In each accounting period a portion of the cost expires and it needs adjustment for showing correct profit of the period and correct value of the asset.

Depreciation represents that portion of the cost of a fixed asset which has been used in the business for the purpose of earning profits. Its accounting treatment is summarised as follows:

I.	Adjusting Entry to be passed	Depreciation A/c Dr. To Respective Asset A/c
II.	Treatment in P&L A/c	Shown on the debit side as a separate item
III.	Treatment in Balance Sheet	Shown on the assets side by way of deduction from the value of respective fixed assets.

Note: If depreciation already appears in the Trial Balance, then no adjusting entry is required to be passed since it has already been taken into account while computing the closing book value of the relevant fixed asset. Such depreciation will be shown only in the Income Statement and not in the Balance Sheet. Following adjustment entries are passed

(a) When asset account is maintained at written down value:

(i) Depreciation Account Dr.
To Asset Account
(Being depreciation charged)

(ii) Profit and Loss Account Dr.
To Depreciation Account
(Being depreciation transferred to Profit and Loss Account)

(b) When asset account is maintained at cost price :

(i) Depreciation Account Dr.

To Provision for Depreciation Account

(Being depreciation charged)

(ii) Profit and Loss Account Dr.

To Depreciation Account

(Being depreciation transferred to Profit and Loss Account)

Total accumulated depreciation is shown in the Balance Sheet liabilities side. Alternatively, it can be shown by way of deduction from the original cost of asset in the assets side.

(c) Bad and Doubtful Debts

A provision for doubtful debts refers to a provision created to cover the loss of possible bad debts by means of a predetermined percentage of net debtors (i.e. debtors less bad debts) with a view to bring in a certain element of certainity in the amount of bad debts charged for each accounting period. Its accounting treatment is summarised as follows:

I.	Adjusting Entry to be passed	Profit & Loss A/c Dr. To Provision for Doubtful Debts A/c
II.	Treatment in P&L A/c	Shown on the debit side as a separate item
III.	Treatment in Balance Sheet	Shown on the assets side by way of deduction from the amount of Sundry Debtors (i.e Net of additional bad debts).

Bad Debts

For achieving the maximum sales, goods are often sold to known customers on credit. Some of these customers fail to pay their debts due to insolvency. These debts which cannot be recovered are called Bad Debts. It is a loss to the business and an adjustment is needed.

The required entry will be :

Bad Debts Account Dr. (To be shown in the Profit and Loss Account)

To Sundry Debtors Account (In the Balance Sheet, Sundry Debtors is shown after deducting this bad debt)

It should be noted here that no adjustment is required for any bad debt which is appearing already in the Trial Balance. The bad debts which is appearing in the Trial Balance only to be debited to Profit and Loss Account of the period.

Accounting entry will depend upon the situation whether provision for bad debts appearing in the Trial Balance or not appearing in the Trial Balance.

Situation 1 *When Provision for Bad Debts Not Appearing in the Trial Balance:*

The accounting entry will be :

Profit and Loss Account Dr.

To Provision for Bad Debts Account [To be shown in the Balance Sheet as a deduction from Debtors]

Situation 2 *When Provision for Bad Debts Appearing in the Trial Balance :*

At first, calculate the amount of provision to be created at the end of the period in the same way as above. Now compare the provision with the provision appearing in the Trial Balance.

(a) If the new provision is more than the provision appearing in the Trial Balance, pass the following entry:

Profit and Loss Account Dr.
To Provision for Bad Debts [New provision less old provision]

(b) If the new provision is less than the provision appearing in the Trial Balance pass the following entry:

Provision for Bad Debts Account Dr.
To Profit and Loss Account [Old provision less new provision]

(d) Provision for discount on debtors & creditors

Provision for Discount on Debtors refers to the provision created to provide for discount likely to be allowed on good debtors (i.e. Sundry Debtors less additional bad debts given outside the Trial Balance and the provision for doubtful debts). Its accounting treatment is summarised as under :

I.	Adjusting Entry to be passed	Profit & Loss A/c Dr. To Provision for Discount on Debtors A/c
II.	Treatment in P&L A/c	Shown on the debit side as a separate item
III.	Treatment in Balance Sheet	Shown on the assets side of the Balance Sheet by way of deduction from the Sundry Debtors

Reserve for discount on creditors refers to the reserve created for discount likely to be earned from creditors on their payments. Its accounting treatment is summarised as under:

I	Adjusting Entry to be passed	Reserve for Discount on Creditors A/c Dr. To Profit & Loss A/c
II	Treatment in P&L A/c	Shown on the Credit side as a separate item.
III	Treatment in Balance Sheet	Shown on the Liabilities side by way of deduction from the Sundry Creditors.

Note: *According to Prudence Principle, discount likely to be earned from creditors being on unrealized gain should not be accounted for.*

If goods are purchased on credit and cash paid to creditors in time, creditors allow cash discount. It is an income of the business. For this, following entries are passed:

(i) Creditors Account Dr.
To Bank Account
To Discount Received Account

(ii) Discount Received Account Dr.
To Profit and Loss Account

Out of the creditors, at the end of the accounting year, we may expect certain discount but such discount will be received in the next year though it actually related to current period. An adjustment is required for the expected discount from creditors and which should be reflected in the accounts at the year end as follows:

Step 1

Calculate probable amount of discount to be received from creditors. Generally, it is calculated by applying a percentage on outstanding creditors.

Step 2

Pass the following entry to record it:

Reserve for Discount on Creditors Account Dr.

To Profit and Loss Account

Step 3

Show this Reserve for Discount on Creditors in the Balance Sheet by way of deduction from creditors.

In the next year, when actual discount is received, the following entry is to be passed:

(i) Creditors Account Dr.

To Bank / Cash Account

To Discount Received Account

(ii) Discount Received Account Dr.

To Reserve for Discount on Creditors Account

(e) Outstanding Expenses

Outstanding Expenses refer to those expenses which have been incurred but not paid during the current accounting period. Its accounting treatment is summarized as follows:

I	Adjusting Entry to be passed	Concerned Expenses A/c Dr. To Outstanding Expenses A/c
II	Treatment in Trading A/c (if it is a direct expense)	Added to the concerned expenses (e.g., wages) on the debit side.
III	Treatment in P & L A/c (if it is an indirect expense)	Added to the concerned expenses (e.g.Salaries) on the debit side.
IV	Treatment in Balance Sheet	Shown on the liabilities side as Current Liability.

Note: *If outstanding expenses already appear in the Trial Balance, then no adjusting entry is required to be passed since these expenses have already been taken into account while computing the amount of relevant expenses. Such outstanding expenses will be shown only in the Balance Sheet and not in the Income Statement.*

In fact, on the date of the final accounts, outstanding expenses, both an expense and a liability exist without having been recorded in the books of account. For recording it, the following entry is to be passed:

Expenses Account Dr. (Will be shown in the Profit and Loss Account)

To Outstanding Expenses Account (Will appear in the liabilities side of the Balance Sheet)

Example

Salaries paid during the year Rs.25,000; Salaries outstanding at the end of the accounting period Rs.500/-

Ledger Accounts

(a) Before Adjusting Entry

Dr. Outstanding Salaries Account Cr.

	Rs.		Rs

Dr. Salaries Account Cr.

	Rs.		Rs.
To Cash A/c	25,000		

(b) After Adjusting Entry is posted

Dr. Outstanding Salaries Account Cr.

	Rs.		Rs
To Balance c/d	500	By Salaries	500

Dr. Salaries Account Cr.

	Rs.		Rs.
To Cash A/c	25,000	By P/L A/c	25500
To Out Salary A/c	500		
	25500		25500

Balance Sheet

Liabilities	Rs.	Assets	Rs.
Outstanding Salaries	500		

Dr Profit & Loss Account Cr.

	Rs.		Rs.
To Salaries A/c	25500		

Note: At the begining of the next accounting year, a reverse entry will be passed:

Outstanding Salaries Account Dr Rs.500

To Salaries Account Rs.500

(f) Prepaid Expenses:- (OR Unexpired Expenses)

Prepaid expenses refer to those expenses which have been paid during the current accounting period but the benefit of which will accrue in the subsequent accounting period or periods.

Its accounting treatment is summarised as follows:

I	Adjusting Entry to be passed	Prepaid Expenses A/c Dr. To Respective Expenses A/c
II	Treatment in Trading A/c (if it is a direct expense)	Deducted from the respective expenses (e.g., wages) on the debit side.
III	Treatment in P & L A/c (if it is an indirect expense) e.g., Insurance Premium	Deducted from the respective expenses (e.g.Insurance Premium) on the debit side.
IV	Treatment in Balance Sheet	Shown on the liabilities side as Current Asset.

For recording prepaid expenses, following entry is to be passed

Prepaid Expenses Account Dr. (To be shown as asset in the Balance Sheet)

To Expenses Account (Balance of this account is to be debited to Profit & Loss Account)

Example:

On 30th June, 2004 insurance premium paid for one year Rs. 1,800. The accounts are prepared on 31st December, 2004.

Out of Rs. 1,800 only Rs. 900 is related to the accounting year 2004 and the remaining Rs.900 should be carried forward to the next period.

Ledger Accounts

(a) Before Adjusting Entry

Dr.	Insurance Premium Account		Cr.
	Rs.		Rs
To Bank A/c	1,800		

Dr.	Prepaid Insurance Premium Account		Cr.
	Rs.		Rs.

(b) After Adjusting Entry is posted:

Dr.	Insurance Premium Account		Cr.
	Rs.		Rs
To Bank A/c	1,800	By Prepaid Insurance Premium A/c	900
		By Profit & Loss A/c	900

Dr.	Prepaid Insurance Premium Account		Cr.
	Rs.		Rs.
To Ins.Prem. A/c	900	By Balance	900

Balance Sheet			
Liabilities	Rs.	Assets	Rs.
		Prepaid Ins Prem	900

Dr	Profit & Loss Account		Cr.
	Rs.		Rs.
To Ins.Prem. A/c	900		

Note: At the begining of the next accounting year, a reverse entry will be passed:

Insurance Premium A/c	Dr.	Rs.900	
To Prepaid Insurance Premium Account			Rs.900

(g) Accrued Income

Accrued income refers to that income whcih has been earned but not received during the current accounting period. Its accounting treatment is summarised as follows:

I	Adjusting Entry to be passed	Accured Income A/c Dr. To Respective Income A/c
II	Treatment in P&L A/c	Added to the respective income on the credit side
III	Treatment in Balance Sheet	Shown on the assets side as a Current Asset.

Note: *If Accrued Income already appears in the Trial Balance then no adjusting entry is required to be passed since it has already been taken into account while computing the amount of relevant income. Such accrued income will be shown only in the Balance Sheet and not in the Income Statement.*

Example

Interest on debenture received during the year Rs.1,000. Interest accrued but not received during the year Rs.200

Ledger Accounts

(a) Before Adjusting Entry

Dr.	Interest Received Account		Cr.
	Rs.		Rs.
		By Cash A/c	1,000

Dr.	Accrued Interest Account		Cr.
	Rs.		Rs.

(b) After Adjusting Entry is posted

Dr.	Interest Received Account		Cr.
	Rs.		Rs.
To Profit & Loss A/c	1,200	By Cash A/c	1,000
		By Accrued Int.A/c	200
	1,200		1,200

Dr.	Accrued Interest Account		Cr.
	Rs.		Rs
To Int. Recd. A/c	200	By Balance c/d	200
	200		200

Dr.	Profit & Loss Account		Cr.
	Rs.		Rs.
		By Int.Recd.A/c	1,200

Balance Sheet			
Liabilities	Rs.	Assets	Rs
		Accrued Interest	200

(h) Income Received in Advance :-(Unaccrued income or Unearned income)

Unaccrued income refers to that income which has been received but not earned during the current accounting period. Its accounting treatment is summarised as follows:

I	Adjusting Entry to be passed	Concerned Income A/c Dr. To Unaccrued Income A/c
II	Treatment in P&L A/c	Deducted from the concerned income on the credit side
III	Treatment in Balance Sheet	Shown on the liabilities side as a Current Liability.

Note: *If unaccrued Income already appears in the Trial Balance, then no adjusting entry is required to be passed since it has already been excluded while computing the amount of relevant income. Such unaccrued income will be shown only in the Balance Sheet and not in the Income Statement.*

Example

On November 1, 2004 A & C0. leases one of its Buildings to the B & Co, for one year. B & Co. paid Rs. 9,000 rent for one year in advance. The Books are being closed on December 31, 2004.

Out of Rs. 9,000 received as rent, only Rs. 1,500 (November + December) should be treated as revenue for the year 2004 and the balance of Rs. 7,500 should be treated as rent received in advance for 2005, so Rs. 7,500 should be carried to next accounting period.

Ledger Accounts

(a) Before Adjusting Entry

Dr.	Rent Received in Advance Account		Cr.
	Rs.		Rs

Dr.	Rent Received Account		Cr.
	Rs.		Rs.
		By Cash A/c	9,000

(b) After Adjusting Entry is posted:

Dr. Rent Received in Advance Account Cr.

	Rs.		Rs
To Balance c/d	7,500	By Rent Recd.A/c	7,500
	7,500		7,500

Dr. Rent Account Cr.

	Rs.		Rs.
To Rent Recd.A/c	7,500	By Cash	9,000
To Profit & Loss A/c	1,500		
	9,000		9,000

Balance Sheet

Liabilities	Rs.	Assets	Rs.
Rent Recd.in Adv	7,500		

Dr Profit & Loss Account Cr.

	Rs.		Rs.
		By Rent Recd.A/c	1,500

Note: At the beginning of the next accounting year a reverse entry will be passed:

Rent Received in Advance Account Dr. Rs.7,500

To Rent Received Account Rs.7,500

Effects of other adjustments

(i) Interest on Capital

Interest on capital means the cost of using the capital invested in an enterprise by the proprietor (in case of a proprietorship concern) or partners (in case of a partnership concern). Its accounting treatment is summarised as follows:

I	Adjusting Entry to be passed	Interest on Capital A/c Dr. To Capital A/c
II	Treatment in P&L A/c	Shown on the debit side as a separate item.
III	Treatment in Balance Sheet	Shown on the liabilities side by way of addition to the capital.

(ii) Interest on Drawings

Interest on drawings means the cost of using the sum of money or other asset (e.g. goods) withdrawn by the proprietor (in case of proprietorship concern) or partners (in case of a partnership concern). Its accounting treatment is summarised as follows:

I	Adjusting Entry to be passed	Capital A/c Dr. To interest on Drawings A/c
II	Treatment in P&L A/c	Shown on the credit side as a separate items.
III	Treatment in Balance Sheet	Shown on the liabilities side by way of deduction from the Capital.

(iii) Abnormal loss of stock

The abnormal loss of stock is an avoidable loss and is usually caused by fire, theft, abnormal spoilage/ leakage/breakages/pilferage. etc. Its accounting treatment is summarised as follows:

I	Adjusting Entry to be passed	Loss of Stock A/c Dr. To Trading A/c
II	Treatment in Trading A/c	Total value of abnormal loss (whether, recovered or not) is shown on the credit side as a separate item.
III	Treatment in P&L A/c	Total value of irrecovered loss of stock (i.e. total loss less amount if any, recovered from Insurance Co.) is shown on the debit side as a separate item.
IV	Treatment in Balance Sheet	The amount if any, due from the Insurance Co. is shown on the Assets side as a 'Current Asset'.

(iv) Income Tax

Income tax is not an expense to earn revenue. Therefore, while ascertaining the profit of a concern, income tax is not treated as an expense to be deducted from the profit. For a sole proprietor, income tax is payable by the owner and not by the business. Therefore, if income tax appears in the 'Trial Balance, it should be treated as drawings and should be deducted from capital. Following are the entries to be passed

(a) Income Tax Account Dr. (When paid)
To Cash / Bank Account

(b) Drawings Account Dr.
To Income Tax Account

(v) Advance Tax

For a sole proprietor, advance tax is payable by the owner and not by the business. Therefore, if the advance tax appears in the Trial Balance, it should be treated as drawings and should be deducted from capital. The following are the entries to be passed:

(a) Advance Tax Account Dr. (When paid)
To Cash / Bank Account

(b) Drawings Account Dr.
To Advance Tax Account

(vi) Interest on Advance Tax

If any interest is received on advance tax, it is not the income of the business. It is the income of the proprietor. Therefore, if the interest on advance tax appears in the 'Trial Balance (it is shown in the credit column of the Trial Balance) it should be added with the capital.

The following are the entries to be passed:

(a) Bank Account Dr.
To Interest on Advance Tax Account

(b) Interest on Advance Tax Account Dr.
To Capital Account

Problem 1 : From the following particulars prepare Trading Account as on 31st December 200X.

Opening Stock	50,000
Purchases	2,20,000
Carriage inward	12,000
Freight	17,000
Return outward	20,000
Sales	5,17,000
Custom Duty	20,000
Return Inward	7000
Closing Stock	53,000

Solution :

Dr. **Trading Account as on 31.12.200X** **Cr.**

Particulars	Rs.	Particulars	Rs.
To Opening Stock	50,000	By Sales 5,17,000	
To Purchases : 2,20,000		Less Return Inward 7,000	5,10,000
Less Return Outward : 20,000	2,00,000		
To Carriage Inward	12,000	By Closing Stock	53,000
To Freight	17,000		
To Custom duty	20,000		
To Gross Profit c/d	2,64,000		
Total	5,63,000	Total .	5,63,000

Problem 2 :

Prepare Trading Account as on 31.12.200X

Particulars	Rs
Sales	7,00,000
Purchases	2,70,000
Stock on 1.1.200X	1,80,000
Stock on 31.12.200X	1,49,000
Carriage inward	79,000
Freight	81,000
Custom Duty	9,100
Return Inward	25,000
Return Outward	12,000

Solution :

Trading Account As On 31.12.200X

Dr. **Cr.**

Particulars		Rs.	Particulars		Rs.
To opening Stock		1,80,000	To Sales	7,00,000	
To Purchases :	2,70,000		Less Return Inward	25,000	6,75,000
Less Return Outward :	12,000	2,58,000	By Closing Stock {Stock on 31.12.200X (-)}		1,49,000
To Carriage Inward		79,000			
To Freight		81,000			
To Custom duty		9,100			
To Gross Profit C/D		2,16,900			
Total		8,24,000	**Total**		8,24,000

Problem 3

From the following particulars prepare Trading and Profit and Loss Account for the period ended 31.12.200X

Opening Stock	2,00,000	Sales	12,00,000
Wages	2,00,000	Sales Return	60,000
Salaries	2,50,000	Interest paid	20,000
Carriage Inward	30,000	Rent Paid	10,000
Carriage Outward	40,000	Discount Received	25,000
Purchases	6,00,000	Printing and Stationery	70,000
Purchase Return	30,000	Travelling expenses	10,000
		Closing Stock	5,00,000

Solution :

Dr. **Trading Account for the period ended 31.12.200X** **Cr.**

Particulars		Rs.	Particulars		Rs.
To Opening Stock		2,00,000	To Sales	12,00,000	
To Wages		2,00,000	Less : Return Inward	60,000	11,40,000
To Carriage Inward		30,000			
To Purchases	6,00,000		By Closing Stock		5,00,000
Less : Return Outward :	30,000	5,70,000			
To Gross Profit c/d		6,40,000			
Total Rs.		16,40,000	Total Rs.		16,40,000

Profit And Loss Account for the period ended 31.12.200X

Dr. **Cr.**

Particulars	Rs.	Particulars	Rs.
To Salaries	2,50,000	By Gross Profit b/d	6,40,000
To Carriage Outward	40,000		
To Interest Paid	20,000	By Discount Received	25,000
To Rent Paid	10,000		
To Printing and Stationary	70,000		
To Travelling Expenses	10,000		
To Net Profit	2,65,000		
Total Rs.	6,65,000	Total Rs.	6,65,000

Problem 4 :

From the following particulars prepare Profit and Loss Account for the period ended 31.12.200X

Dr. **Cr.**

Gross Profit	22,00,000	Carriage outward	50,000
Travelling Expenses	1,70,000	Advertisement	2,70,000
Bad debts	1,00,000	Commission Received	1,80,000
Salary	3,00,000	Insurance paid	2,10,000
Rent Paid	2,00,000	Printing and stationery	1,10,000

Solution

Profit And Loss Account for the period ended 31.12.200X

Dr. **Cr.**

Particulars	Rs.	Particulars	Rs.
To Salary	3,00,000	By Gross Profit b/d	22,00,000
To Rent Paid	2,00,000		
To Carriage Outward	50,000	By Commission Received	1,80,000
To Advertisement	2,70,000		
To Insurance Paid	2,10,000		
To Printing and Stationary	1,10,000		
To Travelling Expenses	1,70,000		
To Bad Debts	1,00,000		
To Net Profit	9,70,000		
Total	23,80,000	Total	23,80,000

Problem 5

From the following particulars, Prepare Balance Sheet as at 31.12.200X

Plant and Machinery	50,00,000	Closing Stock	5,50,000
Cash in hand	10,00,000	Sundry Creditors	10,00,000
Bills Receivable	12,50,000	Bank Overdraft	20,00,000
Debtors	25,00,000	Capital	81,00,000
Investments	7,00,000	Drawings	1,00,000

Solution : **Balance Sheet as at 31.12.200X**

Liabilities		Rs.	Assets	Rs.
Capital	81,00,000		Cash in hand	10,00,000
(+) Net Profit	---		Bills Receivable	12,50,000
			Sundry Debtors	25,00,000
	81,00,000		Investments	7,00,000
(-) Drawing	1,00,000	80,00,000	Plant & Machinery	50,00,000
Bank O/D		20,00,000	Closing Stock	5,50,000
Sundry creditors	---	10,00,000		
Total		110,00,000	**Total**	110,00,000

Important Adjustments of Final Account (At a glance)

- ***For every item given in the trial balance only single effect should be given (It should be written only for one time) i.e. either in Trading A/c., Profit & Loss A/c or in Balance Sheet.***
- ***For every item given in adjustments double effect should be given.***

1) Closing Stock

Closing Stock means item of stock given in adjustment . Effect of closing stock should be given as under.Its double effect should be as follows :

a) First Effect = Balance Sheet - Asset Side

b) Second Effect = Trading Account - Credit Side

2) Interest on Capital

Interest on capital should be calculated by applying given % (rate) to opening balance of capital.

a) First Effect Add in amount of capital in balance sheet

b) Second Effect Profit and Loss Account Debit side

3) Interest on Drawings

b) First Effect Add in amount of drawing (ultimately both drawings and interest on drawing should be deducted from capital)

b) Second Effect Credit side (It should be shown on credit side of Profit and Loss account)

4) Goods distributed as free sample

a) First Effect Trading amount Credit side

b) Second Effect Profit and Loss Account Debit side

5) Goods lost by fire

a) First Effect Trading Account : Credit side

b) Second Effect Profit and loss Account : Debit side

6) **Goods lost by Fire and Insurance Company Admitted a claim for it**

Example - Goods costing Rs.1000 lost by fire and Insurance company admitted claim of Rs.700

a) Trading Account : Credit : Rs.1000

b) Profit & Loss Account : Debit side : Rs.300 (1000-700) (Part effect on Profit & Loss A./c.)

c) Balance sheet : Assets side : Rs. 700 (Part effect on Balance Sheet)

7) **R.D.D. (Reserve for Doubtful debt)**

If R.D.D. is given only in trial balance then only single effect should be given i.e. profit and loss Account credit side

If R.D.D. is given in adjustments then apply percentage of R.D.D. on amount of Debtors (after deducting amount of bad debt from debtors if bad debts are given in adjustment) and following effect should be given

a) First Effect Profit and Loss Debit side

b) Second Effect Deduct from Debtors in Balance Sheet

R.D.D. is also called as Reserve for Bad Debts or provision for Bad and Doubtful Bebts.

8) **Bad Debts**

If bad debts are given in trial balance then- Profit and Loss Account Debit side only single effect should be given. If bad debts are given in adjustment then

a) First Effect Profit and Loss Debit Account (add in bad debts)

b) Second Effect Deduct from Sundry Debtors in Balance Sheet

If Bad debt and R.D.D. both are coming together in same problem then give first effect of Bad Debt and then of R.D.D. as shown above.

9) **Outstanding Expenses**

If Outstanding expenses are given in trial balance then - Balance Sheet, Liability side- only single effect

If outstanding expenses are given in adjustment then

a) First Effect Add in original expenses in Profit and Loss Account

b) Second Effect Balance Sheet - Liability side

10) **Prepaid Expenses**

If prepaid expenses are given in trial balance then only single effect i.e. Balance Sheet Assets side.

When prepaid expenses are given in adjustments then :

a) First Effect Deduct from original expenses in Profit and Loss Account

b) Second Effect Balance sheet Assets side

11) **Trade Expenses and General Expenses**

When only trade expenses are given then Profit and Loss Account Debit

When only general expenses are given then Profit and Loss Account Debit

When both are given in same problem then

Trade Expenses - Trading Account Debit

General Expenses - Profit and Loss Account Debit

12) **Depreciation**

Calculate amount of depreciation by applying given percentage to the amount of assets and then

a) First Effect Deduct the same amount from value of assets and

b) Second Effect Profit and Loss account debit side (Transfer the same amount)

Practical Problems

Problem 1 :

From the following Trial Balance of Shri Bharat Bhushan prepare the final account as on 31st March 200X

	Dr. (Rs.)	Cr. (Rs.)
Bharat's Capital		2,00,000
Land and Building	87,000	
Plant and Machinery	17,500	
Goodwill	20,000	
Bharat's Drawing	22,600	
Cash in hand	1,795	
Stock on 1st April 200x	27,000	
Wages	10,000	
Purchases Less Returns	69,000	
Carriage Inward	600	
Traveller's Commission and Expenses	6,000	
Insurance premium	2,000	
Motor Car	3,000	
Carriage outward	1,400	
Sales : Less Returns		94,000
Salaries	15,000	
Bank charges	105	
Reserve for Doubtful Debts		1,500
Debtors	20,000	
Creditors		7,500
Total	3,03,000	3,03,000

The following adjustments are to be considered :

a) On 31st March 200x the stock was valued at Rs.46,000.

b) Insurance Premium amounting to Rs.800 is prepaid. c) Outstanding Salaries amount to Rs.1000.

d) Depreciation Plant and Machinery @ 10% and Motor Car 20%

e) Create a Reserve for Doubtful Debts at 10% on Debtors.

Solution :

In the books of Shri Bharat Bhushan

Trading, and Profit and Loss Account for the period ended 31.3.200X

Particulars		Rs.	Particulars		Rs.
To Opening Stock		27,000	By Sales		
To Wages		10,000	Less : Return	———	94,000
To Purchases			By Closing Stock		46,000
Less : Return	———	69,000			
To Carriage Inward		600			
To Gross Profit c/d		33,400			
Total		1,40,000	Total		1,40,000

Particulars		Rs.	Particulars	Rs.
To Salary	15,000		By Gross Profit	33,400
(+) Outstanding	1,000	16,000		
To RDD		2,000	By Reserve for Doubtful Debts	1,500
To Traveller's Commission & Exp.		6,000		
To Insurance	2,000			
Less : Prepaid	800	1,200		
To Carriage Outward		1,400		
To Bank charges		105		
To Total Depreciation		2,350		
To Net Profit		5,845		
		34,900		34,900

Balance Sheet of Bharat Bhushan as on 31.3.200X

Liabilities		Rs.	Assets		Rs.
Capital	2,00,000		Cash in hand		1,795
(-)Drawing	22,600		Land & Building		87,000
	1,77,400		Plant & Machinery	17,500	
(+) Net Profit	5,845	1,83,245	(-)10% Depreciation	1,750	15,750
Outstanding Salaries		1,000	Goodwill		20,000
Creditors		7,500	Motor Car	3,000	
			(-)20% Depreciation	600	2,400
			Debtors	20,000	
			(-)10% R.D.D.	2,000	18,000
			Closing Stock		46,000
			Prepaid Insurance		800
		1,91,745			**1,91,745**

Problem 2

The following balances were extracted from the books of Smt.Deepali Deshpande as on 30th June 200X. Prepare Trading and Profit and Loss Account for the year ended 30th June 200X and the Balance Sheet as on that date after taking into account the following adjustments :

Particulars	Dr. (Rs.)	Cr. (Rs.)
Deepali's Capital	--	3,30,000
Deepali's Drawings	24,450	
Opening Stock	2,00,000	
Bills Receivable	25,000	
Purchases	2,75,000	
Sales		4,20,000
Bills Payable		60,000
Returns outwards		4,500
Returns Inward	5,000	
Plant & Machinery	1,00,000	
Loose Tools	25,000	

Patents	25,000	
Sundry Debtors	1,25,000	
Sundry Creditors		1,40,000
Cash at Bank	7 7,550	
Salaries and Wages	50,000	
Repairs & Renewals	7,500	
Insurance	3,000	
Power & Fuel	3,500	
Printing & Stationery	2,000	
Miscellaneous Expenses	6,500	
Total	9,54,500	9,54,500

Adjustments

a) Closing stock was worth Rs. 1,30,000.

b) Depreciate Plant & Machinery by 5% and Patents by 15%.

c) Revalue Tools at Rs.20,000.

d) Provide for Bad and Doubtful Debts at 5% on Debtors.

e) Provide for outstanding expenses as follows :

i) Salaries Rs.2,500.

i) Wages Rs. 1,000.

f) Insurance paid in advance to the extent of Rs.750.

In the Books of Smt. Deepali Deshpande

Dr. **Trading and Profit and Loss Account for the year ended 30.6.200X** Cr.

Particulars		Rs.	Particulars		Rs.
To Opening Stock		2,00,000	By Sales	4,20,000	
To Purchases	2,75,000		Less : Return Inward	5,000	4,15,000
Less : Return Outward	4,500	2,70,500			
To Power & Fuel		3,500			
To Gross profit c/d		71,000	By Closing Stock		1,30,000
		5,45,000			5,45,000
To Salaries & Wages	50,000		By Gross Profit b/d		71,000
(+) Outstanding	3,500	53,500	By Net Loss		20,750
To Repairs & Renewals		7,500	(Transferred to capital)		
To Insurance	3,000				
Less :Prepaid	750	2,250			
To Miscellaneous Expenses		6,500			
To Printing & Stationery		2,000			
To Provision for R.D.D.		6,250			
To Depreciation on :					
Plant & Machinery		5,000			
Patents		3,750			
Tools		5,000			
		91,750			91,750

Balance Sheet of Smt. Deepali Deshpande as on 30.6.200X

Particulars		Rs.	Particulars		Rs.
Capital	3,30,000		Cash in Bank		77,550
Less : Drawing	24,450		Plant & machinery	1,00,000	
	3,05,550		Less : 5% Depreciation	5,000	95,000
Less : Net Loss	20,750	2,84,800	Loose Tools	25,000	
			Less : Depreciation	5,000	20,000
			Patents	25,000	
			Less : 15% Depreciation	3,750	21,250
			Sundry Debtors	1,25,000	
			Less : 5% P.B.D.D.	6250	1,18,750
Bills Payable		60,000	Bills Receivable		25,000
Sundry Creditors		1,40,000	Closing Stock		1,30,000
Outstanding Salaries and Wages		3,500	Prepaid Insurance		750
		4,88,300			4,88,300

Promlem 3

The Trial Balance of Mr.Eknath Mahashabde as on 30th Sept. 200X was as follows :

	Dr. (Rs.)	Cr. (Rs.).
Capital Account		2,50,000
Drawings	7,500	
Investments	1,00,000	
Motor Vehicles	80,000	
Office Furniture	20,000	
Office Equipments	60,000	
Cash in hand	5,500	
Purchases	4,75,000	
Sales		7,55,000
Returns	15,000	10,000
Carriages	3,500	
Opening Stock	1,40,000	
Customs, duties & clearing charges	30,000	
Debtors	1,76,000	
Salaries	25,000	
Trade Expenses	3,000	
General Expenses	6,000	
Bad Debts	2,500	
Reserve for Bad Debts		7,500
Discount	1,000	500
Creditors		1,26,000
Prepaid Insurance	1,000	
Outstanding Salaries		2,000
Total	11,51,000	11,51,000

Adjustments

a) Closing Stock was valued at Rs.80,000.

b) Depreciation Motor Vehicle and Office Furniture at 5% and Office Equipments at 10%.

c) Create 5% Reserve for Doubtful Debts & Debtors.

d) Goods costing Rs.1000 was taken for personal use by Mr. Mahashabde and it was included in Debtors.

e) Goods worth Rs.10000 were destroyed by fire and the Insurance Company admitted claim for Rs. 8000.

Solution

In the Books of Mr. Eknath Mahashabde

Trading and Profit and Loss Account for the period ended 30.9.200X

Particulars		Rs.	Particulars		Rs.
To Opening Stock		1,40,000	By Sales	7,55,000	
To Purchases	4,75,000		Less : Returns	15,000	7,40,000
Less : Returns	10,000	4,65,000			
To Carriage		3,500	By Closing Stock		80,000
To Trade Expenses		3000	By Goods Destroyed by Fire		10,000
To Gross profit c/d		2,18,500			
		8,30,000			8,30,000
To Salaries		25,000	By Gross Profit b/d		2,18,500
To Custom Duties		30,000	By Reserve for Bad Debts		7,500
To General Expenses		6,000	By Discount received		500
To Bad Debts		2,500			
To Discount (Allowed)		1000			
To Reserve for Bad & Doubtful Debt		8,800			
To Depreciation on :					
Motor Vehicle		4,000			
Office Furniture		1,000			
Office Equipments		6,000			
To Loss by Fire		2,000			
To Net Profit (transferred to capital)		1,40,200			
		2,26,500			2,26,500

Balance Sheet of Mr. Eknath Mahashabde As On 30.9.200X

Liabilities		Rs.	Assets		Rs.
Capital	2,50,000		Cash in hand		5,500
Less : Drawing	7,500		Motor Vehicles	80,000	
	2,42,500		Less : 5% Depreciation	4,000	76,000
Less : Goods taken for			Investment		1,00,000
personal use	1,000		Office Furniture	20,000	
	2,41,500		Less : 5% Depreciation	1,000	19,000
(+)Net Profit	1,40,200	3,81,700	Prepaid Insurance		1,000
			Closing Stock		80,000

Outstanding Salaries	2,000	Office Equipments	60,000	
Creditors	1,26,000	Less : 10% Depreciation	6,000	54,000
		Insurance Claim		8000
		Debtors	1,76,000	
		Less : 5% R.B.D.D	(-) 8,800	
			1,67,200	
		Less : Goods Taken for personal use	(-)1,000	1,66,200
	5,09,700			5,09,700

Problem 4

Following is the Trial Balance of Anupam Traders for the year ended 31.3.2005 Prepare Trading & Profit and Loss Account for the year ended 31.3.2005 & the Balance Sheet as on that date.

Trial Balance

Name of the Account	Debit (Rs.)	Credit (Rs.)
Rent Received		10,000
Sales		5,12,000
Creditors		56,600
Bank Overdraft		1,40,000
Bills Payables		23,000
Capital		4,05,000
Opening Stock	72,000	
Purchases	2,20,000	
Carriage Inward	8,000	
Wages	80,000	
Goodwill	30,000	
Free hold Land	60,000	
Lease hold Land	1,00,000	
Building	2,20,000	
Plant & Machinery	1,80,000	
Vehicles	70,000	
Furniture	20,000	
Advertisement	10,000	
Salaries	38,000	
Stationery	8,300	
Office Expenses	4,100	
Bank Charges	100	
Carrige Outward	3,700	
Cash in Hand	400	
Debtors	12,000	
Interest on Bank Overdraft	10,000	
	11,46,600	11,46,600

Adjustments

1. Lease to run for 10 years from 1.4.2004.
2. Depreciate Plant & Machinery at 15% Vechicle at 20% & Furniture at 10%.
3. Stock of 31.3.2005 is valued at Rs. 58,000
4. Outstanding wages are Rs. 3800 & Outstanding salaries are Rs. 4,500
5. Interest on Bank Overdraft, for the last quarter of the year Rs. 4,600 is not recorded so far.
6. Provide 5% on debtors for Doubtful Debts.

Solution :

Anupam Traders

Trading Account & Profit & Loss Account

For the Year Ended 31st March, 2005

Dr. Cr.

Particulars		Rs.	Particulars	Rs.
To Opening Stock		72,000	By Sales	5,12,000
To Purchase		2,20,000	By Closing Stock	58,000
To Carriage Inward		8,000		
To Wages	+ 80,000			
Add Outstanding	3,800	83,800		
To Gross Profit c / d		1,86,200		
		5,70,000		5,70,000
To Advertisment		10,000	By Gross Profit	1,86,200
To Salaries	+ 38,000		By Rent received	10,000
Add Outstanding	4,500	42,500		
To Stationery		8,300		
To Office Expences		4,100		
To Bank Charges		100		
To Carriage Outward		3,700		
To Interest on Bank Overdraft	+ 10,000			
Add Outstanding	4,600	14,600		
Leasehold Land		10,000		
To Depreciation on :				
Plant & Machinery		27,000		
Vehicles		14,000		
Furniture		2,000		
To R.D.D.		600		
To Net Profit Transferred to Capital Account		59,300		
		1,96,200		1,96,200

Anupam - Traders. Balance Sheet As On 31st Match 2005

Liabilities		Rs.	Assets		Rs.
Outstanding Wages		3,800	Cash in hand		400
Outstanding Salaries		4,500	Closing Stock		58,000
Bills Payable		23,000	Debtors	12,000	
Creditors		56,600	Less : R.D.D.	600	11,400
Bank overdraft	1,40,000		Vehicles	70,000	
Add : outstanding interest	+ 4,600		Less : Depreciation	14,000	56,000
		1,44,600	Furniture	20,000	
Capital	4,05,000		Less : Depreciation	2,000	18,000
Add : Net Profit	+ 59,300		Plant & Machinery	1,80,000	
		4,64,300	Less : Depreciation -	27,000	1,53,000
			Leasehold land	1,00,000	
			Less : Depreciation	10,000	90,000
			Building		2,20,000
			Freehold Land		60,000
			Goodwill		30,000
		6,96,800			6,96,800

Problem 5 : Following is the Trial Balance of Mr. Ashok for the year ended 31.3.200X. Prepare Final Accounts.

Trial Balance

Name of the Account	Debit (Rs.)	Credit (Rs.)
Purchases	98,000	
Wages	21,000	
Stock on 1.4.200X	25,000	
Printing & Stationery	17,000	
Insurance (Paid one year from 1.10.200X to 30.9.200X)	2,200	
Salaries	32,000	
Sales		2,12,000
Carriage Inward	10,000	
Carriage Outward	12,000	
Advertising	14,000	
Capital		1,10,000
Land & Building	35,000	
Machinery	60,000	
Debtors & Creditors	30,000	35,000
Return Inward & Return Outward	2,000	2,300
Cash	2,300	
Loan from Mr.Bhagwan (taken on 1.12.200X @12% per annum)		18,000
Patents	20,000	
Rent received		3,200
	3,80,500	3,80,500

Adjustments

1) Closing Stock is valued at cost price Rs. 32,000 & at market price Rs. 26,000.
2) Depreciate machinery at 10% per annum & patents are revalued on 31.3.200X at Rs. 18,200.
3) A part of the building is let out at Rs. 1000 per month form 1.12.200X.
4) Printing bill of Rs. 1,200, Wages of Rs. 1,800 & Salaries of Rs. 3,800 are outstanding.

Solution

Dr. Mr.Ashok : Trading & Profit and Loss Account For the Year Ended 31st March 200X

Particulars		Rs.	Particulars		Rs.
To Opening Stock		25,000	By Sales	2,12,000	
To Purchase	98,000		Less : Return Inward	2,000	2,10,000
Less : Return outward	2,300	95,700	By Closing stock		26,000
To Wages	21,000				
Add : outstanding	1,800	22,800			
To Carriage Inward		10,000			
To Gross Profit c/d.		82,500			
		2,36,000			2,36,000
To Printing & Stationery	17,000		By Gross Profit		82,500
Add : Outstanding	1,200	18,200	By Rent received	3,200	
To Insurance	2,200		Add : Outstanding	800	4,000
Less : Prepaid	1,100	1,100	By Net Loss transferred to		3,120
Transferred to B/s			Capital A/c		
To Salaries	32,000				
Add : Outstanding	3,800	35,800			
To Carriage Outward		12,000			
To Advertising		14,000			
To Outstanding interest on loan					
from Mr. Bhagwan		720			
To Depreciation on					
Machinery		6,000			
Patents		1,800			
		89,620			89,620

Balance Sheet of Mr. Ashok as on 31st Match 200X

Liabilities		Rs.	Assets		Rs.
Outstanding Expenses :			Cash in Hand		2,300
Printing	1200		Outstanding rent on bulding		800
Wages	1800		Prepaid Insurance		1,100
Salaries	3800	6,800	Closing Stock		26,000
Creditors		35,000	Debtors		30,000
Loan From Bhagwan	18,000		Patents	20,000	
Add : Out standing Interest	720	18,720	Less : Depreciation	1,800	18,200
Capital	1,10,000		Dep. Machinery	60,000	
Less : Net Loss	3,120	1,06,880	Less : Depreciation	6,000	54,000
			Land & Building		35,000
		1,67,400			1,67,400

Working Notes

1) Closing stock is valued at cost or market price whichever is less. Therefore value of closing stock is taken as Rs. 26,000.

2) Insurance is paid for one year up to 30.9.200X out of which from 1.4.200X to 30.9.200X i.e. for 6 months, it is prepaid.

3) Loan is taken on 1.12.200X i.e. from 1.12.200X to 31.3.200X i.e. for 4 month interest is outstanding on it.

4) Rent receivable on building from 1.12.200X to 31.3.200X for 4 month at Rs. 1000 per month is Rs. 4000, out of which Rs. 3,200 is already received & therefore Rs. 800 is outstanding.

Questions for self-study

I) Fill in the blanks with proper words

a) The chief objects of book-keeping is to find out ________ .

b) Trading, Profit & Loss Account are final accounts as they are prepared ________ .

c) Trading Account is a sub-part of ________ Account.

d) For ascertaining net profit or loss ________ account is prepared.

e) Trading Account is ________ Account.

f) Unrecorded items to be entered in Trial Balance or in final accounts are known as ________ .

g) Closing stock and loss of goods are recorded to the ________ side of ________ accounts.

h) The balance of Trading Account is known as ________ or ________ .

i) The balance of Profit & Loss Account is known as ________ or ________ .

j) Balance sheet is a ________ and not account.

II) State whether following statements are True or False

a) Final Accounts are prepared when business is to be closed.

b) Balance sheet is prepared to ascertain the Profit of the Business.

c) Unexpired expenses are not recorded in profit & Loss Account.

d) Closing stock does not appear in Trial Balance.

e) Adjusted Trial Balance is an Original Trial Balance.

f) Direct expenses are recorded in Profit & Loss Account.

g) Final Accounts are balanced.

h) When Credit side of Trading Account is more than debit it indicates Gross Profit.

i) Financial position is revealed by Balance-sheet.

j) When any adjustment is shown by way of deduction in final accounts it is consolidating entry.

III) Write Short Notes

a) Final Accounts,

b) Adjusted Trial Balance,

c) Trading Account,

d) Balance Sheet,

e) Adjustments in Final Accounts.

Problem 1

From the following Trial Balance of Mr. Chavan you are required to prepare Trading, Profit & Loss A/c for the year ended 31st December, 2004 and the Balance Sheet as on that date after taking into account the necessary adjustments.

Trial Balance		
Particulars	Debit Rs.	Credit Rs.
Chavan's capital		3,30,000
Chavan's drawing	24,450	
Stock on 1.1.2004	2,00,000	
Bills receivable	25,000	
Purchases	2,75,000	
Sales		4,00,000
Bill payable		60,000
Sales returns	5,000	
Purchases returns		4,500
Plant & Machinery	1,00,000	
Loose tools	25,000	
Patents	25,000	
Sundry debtors	1,25,000	
Sundry creditors		1,40,000
Cash at bank	77,550	
Wages	19,000	
Salaries	17,500	
Rates & Taxes	7,500	
Insurance	3,000	
Printing & Stationery	2,000	
Power & Fuel	3,500	
	9,34,500	9,34,500

Adjustments

1) Depreciate plant and machinery by 5% and patents by 15%.
2) Provide for bad and doubtful debts at 5% on Sundry Debtors.
3) Prepaid insurance Rs. 750/-.
4) Outstanding expenses (a) Salaries Rs. 2,500/-, (b) Wages Rs. 1,000/-, (c) Printing & Stationery Rs. 500/-.
5) Stock as at 31st December, 2004, Rs. 1,30,000/-.

Problem 2

From the following Trial Balance of Mr. Promod, Prepare a Trading, Profit & Loss Account for the year ended 31st March, 2005 and Balance-sheet as on that date.

Trial Balance as on 31st March 2005			
Particulars	Rs.	Particulars	Rs.
Opening stock	20,000	Capital Account	30,000
Purchases	1,30,200	Sales	1,70,500
Sales Returns	500	Purchases Returns	3,200
Debtors	20,000	Commission	300
Wages	6,000	Provident Fund	2,000
Royalties	1,000	Interest on Provident fund Investment	200
Furniture	5,000	Reserve for doubtful debts	500
Machinery	30,000	Creditors	20,000
Advertisement for 4 years	4,000	Bills payable	4,000
Salaries	3,000		
Provident fund contribution	500		
Provident fund investment	2,000		
Insurance	500		
Cash	3,000		
Drawings	5,000		
	2,30,700		2,30,700

Adjustments

1) Closing stock : Cost price Rs. 25,000 Market price Rs. 30,000.
2) Prepaid insurance amounted Rs. 100.
3) Depreciate furniture by 15% and machinery by 20%.
4) Write of Rs. 4,000 Bad debts and maintain the reserve for doubtful debts at 3% on debtors.

Problem 3

The Trial Balance of Mr. Kapil on 30th June 2005 was as follows.

Trial Balance		
Particulars	Debit Rs.	Credit Rs.
Capital Account		25,000
Building	20,000	
Drawing	750	
Plant & Machinery	6,000	
Cash at Bank	550	
Purchase & Sales	47,000	75,500
Returns	1,500	1,000
Carriage	850	
Stock as on1.7.2004	11,000	
Wages	6,000	
Postage & Telegram	200	
Debtors & Creditors	17,600	12,600
Salaries	2,500	
Rent & Insurance	400	

Bad Debts	250	
Discounts	100	50
Reserve for bad debts		750
Outstanding salaries		100
Trade Expenses	300	
	1,15,000	1,15,000

Adjustments

1) Reserve for bad debts and doubtful debts is to be maintained at 5% on the debtors.
2) Depreciate building at 5% and Plant & Machinery at 10% p.a.
3) Stock on 30th June 2005 was valued at Rs. 8,000. Prepare a Trading & Profit & Loss Account for the year ended 30th June 2005 and Balance-sheet as on that date.

Problem 4

You are required to prepare the Trading and Profit and Loss account of Mrs. Patel for the year ended 30th September 2005 and a Balance sheet as at that date. The following is a list of Balances extracted from the books.

Particulars	Debit Rs.	Credit Rs.
Bills payable		25,000
Bills receivable	15,000	
Cash in office	10,000	
Loans		20,000
Land & Building	12,000	
Furniture & Fixtures	8,000	
Capital		72,000
Dead Stock	14,400	
Stock (1.10.04)	12,800	
Salaries	7,200	
Lease hold premises	48,000	
Purchases	1,52,000	
Carriage outwards	1,000	
Balance at bank	15,000	
Trade debtors	14,000	
Reserve for bad debts		560
Returns outward		4,800
Carriage inwards	4,000	
Discount allowed	2,800	
Sales		2,08,000
Returns inwards	8,400	
Trade creditors		16,000
Discount received		2,240
Drawings	20,800	
Insurance	2,000	
Rent	1,200	
	3,48,600	3,48,600

Adjustments

1) The stock on hand on 30th September 2005 was valued at Rs. 14,400.
2) Dead stock to be depreciated by 10%.
3) Salaries due but not paid amount to Rs. 600.
4) From trade debtors a sum of Rs. 2,000 is to be written off as bad debts.
5) Provision for bad and doubtful debts is to be raised to Rs. 1,200/-.
6) Insurance paid in advance amounts to Rs. 400/-.
7) Prepaid rent amount to Rs. 800/-.

Problem 5

From the following Trial Balance of Sunil prepare Trading and Profit & Loss Account for the year ended 31st December, 2004 and the Balance-sheet as at that date after making the adjustments given below :

Particulars	Debit Rs.	Credit Rs.
Capital		2,00,000
Land & Building	87,000	
Plant & Machinery	17,500	
Goodwill	20,000	
Drawings	22,600	
Deposits	1,000	
Stock in Trade (1.1.04)	27,000	
Wages	10,000	
Purchases less returns	69,000	
Carriage inwards	600	
General expenses	4,000	
Rent & Taxes	2,000	
Motor car	3,000	
Carriage outwards	1,400	
Sales less returns		84,000
Salaries	3,100	
Bank charges	105	
Bad debts written off	2,100	
Reserve for bad debts		1,500
Debtors & Creditors	19,800	7,500
Bank Account	795	
Printing & Stationery	2,000	
	2,93,000	2,93,000

1) Closing stock was Rs. 4,600.
2) Stock worth Rs. 3,000 uninsured has been destroyed by fire.
3) Plant & Machinery to be depreciated by 7.1/2% p.a. and motor car 15% p.a. and reserve for Bad Debts to be increased to Rs. 2,000.
4) Rent and taxes prepaid were Rs. 800.

Problem 6

The following is the Trial Balance of Ram on March 31st 2005 Prepare Trading and Profit & Loss A/c. and Balance sheet as on 31st March, 2005.

Debit Balances	Rs.	Credit Balances	Rs.
Bank	7,500	Bills Payable	50,000
Salaries	21,000	Loan	1,00,000
Carriage on sale	2,500	Sales	36,00,000
Carriage on purchase	2,000	Discount	2,000
Purchases	34,96,000	Commission	500
Lighting	1,500	Sundry Creditors	1,00,000
Buildings	1,35,000	Capital	2,00,000
Rates & Taxes	2,000		
Sundry Debtors	40,000		
Furniture	30,000		
Cash in hand	1,250		
Bill Receivable	7,500		
Opening Stock	3,06,250		
	40,52,500		40,52,500

Rates have been prepaid to the extent of Rs. 600. During the year bad debts amounted to Rs. 2,500 provision of 5% has to be made on debtors. Building have to be depreciated at 2% and Furniture at 10%. Closing stock was Rs. 2,00,000.

Problem 7

From the following balances extracted from the books of Mr. Ravi Shastri and the subjoined information you are required to prepare the Profit & Loss Account for the year ended on 30th June 2005 and the Balance-sheet on that date.

Particulars	Debit Rs.	Credit Rs.
Stock on July 1, 2004	60,500	
Purchases & Sales	90,300	1,37,200
Returns	2,200	1,300
Capital Account		30,000
Drawing Account	4,500	
Land & Buildings	30,000	
Furniture & Fittings	8,000	
Sundry Debtors & Creditors	25,000	45,000
Cash in hand	3,500	
Investment	10,000	
Interest		500
Commission		3,000
Total direct expenditure	7,500	
Postage, Stationery & Phones	2,500	
Fire Insurance Premium	2,000	
Salaries	11,000	
Bank overdraft		40,000
	2,57,000	2,57,000

Information

1) Closing stock on 30.6.2005 was valued Rs. 6.500.
2) Interest on Investment Rs. 500 is yet to be received.
3) Prepaid insurance Rs. 500 for quarter ending September 2005
4) Depreciation to be provided on land & Building @5% and on furniture and fittings @ 10%.
5) Provide provision for doubtful debts @5% on Sundry debtors.

Problem 8

From the following Trial Balance draft Trading, Profit & Loss Account for the Year ended 31st December 2004 and a Balance sheet as on that date taking into consideration the following adjustments.

1) Closing stock Rs. 9,500.
2) One quarter of a insurance premium falls in next year,
3) Provide 10% Depreciation on furniture,
4) Loan to X carries 8% interest p.a.
5) Loan from Y carries 6% interest p.a.
6) Goods worth Rs. 500 have been taken by proprietor for private use,
7). Provide 5% for bad and doubtful debts,
8) Salaries includes salaries to proprietor @ Rs. 200 per month.

Debit Balances	Rs.	Credit Balances	Rs.
Stock 1.1.04	6,000	Capital	40,000
Salaries	6,000	Returns outward	500
Drawings	6,000	Loan from Y	5,000
Carriage inward	1,000	Rent outstanding	100
Carriage outwards	500	Creditors	13,000
Return Inwards	800	Liabilities for the expenses	1,900
Loan to X	3,000	Provision for bad debts	1,000
Rent	1,200	Discount	300
Purchases	60,000	Sales	73,700
Debtors	30,000	Rent by sub-lettmg	500
Advertisements	3,000		
Bad Debts	500		
Discount	600		
Cash	200		
Furniture	3,000		
Goodwill	5,000		
Wages	100		
Insurance Premium	600		
Bank	8,500		
	1,36,000		1,36,000

Problem 9

The Trial Balance as on 31st December, 2004 is given below. Prepare Trading & Profit & Loss A/c and Balance Sheet after taking into A/c the given adjustments.

Particulars	Rs.	Particulars	Rs.
Purchases	98,000	Capital	70,000
Patent rights	4,000	Provident Fund	7,000
Buildings	1,00,000	Creditors	45,000
Stock (1/1/04)	15,000	Bank loan	12,000
Printings & Stationary	1,750	Sales	1,58,000
Sundry Debtors	35,000	Res. for doubtful debts	250
Wages & Salaries	11,000	Purchase returns	3,500
Audit fees	700		
Sundry expenses	3,500		
Furniture & fixtures	8,000		
10% Investments (Purchased 30/6/04)	10,000		
Cash	4,000		
Provident fund contribution	800		
Carriage Inwards	1,300		
Trade Expenses	2,700		
	2,95,750		2,95,750

Adjustments

1) Closing Stock is valued at cost Rs. 15,000 while its market price Rs. 19,000.
2) On 31st December, 2004 the stock of stationery was Rs. 500.
3) Reserve for bad and doubtful debts at 5% on debtors.
4) Depreciation building at 5% and patents at 10%.
5) Interest on capital is to be provided at 5%.
6) Goods worth Rs. 10,000 were destroyed by fire. The Insurance Co. admitted a claim for Rs. 8,000.

Problem 10

Prepare Trading & Profit & Loss A/c from following Trial Balance as on 31/12/2004

Trial Balance
As on 31/12/2004

Particulars	Rs.	Particulars	Rs.
Loose Tools	2,320	Commission	4,000
Carriage	2,000	Interest	4,200
Opening Stock	30,760	Sales	92,000
Salary	2,000	Bill Payable	5,000
Wages	1,000	Purchase Return	3,800
Audit fees	2,000	Sundry creditors	22,400
Discount	500	Outstanding salary	400
Interest	750	Capital	1,00,000
Motive Power	4,500		
Motor Van	28,000		
Bad debts	1,920		
Buildings	34,000		
Debtors	20,000		
Goodwill	4,800		
Cash at Bank	9,000		

Machinery	10,000		
Investments	12,000		
Purchases	60,250		
Drawings	6,000		
	2,31,800		2,31,800

Adjustments

1) Outstanding Wages Rs. 400.
2) Provide depreciation at 10% p.a. on Building and Motor Van.
3) Accrued interest on investment Rs. 360.
4) Provide 5% R.D.D. on Debtors.
5) Stock on 31st December, 2004 was valued : market Rs. 40,000. Cost price Rs. 50,000.

Problem 11

The following is a Trial Balance of Mr. Shaha as on 31st March 2005.

Particulars	Debit Rs.	Credit Rs.
Goodwill	24,000	
Investments	4,800	
Bad Debts	490	
Shaha's Capital		1,00,000
Shaha's Drawings	10,000	
Provision for Bad Debts		1,000
Typewriter as on 1st April 2004	4,300	
Sale of Typewriters on 1st April 2004		800
Machinery as on 1st April 2004	4,000	
Additions to Machinery on 1st Oct 2004	1,600	
Rent	1,800	
Sundry Debtors & Creditors	16,280	14,600
Purchases and Sales	1,62,400	1,97,000
Rate and Taxes	1,250	
Salaries	12,800	
Cash and Bank balance	14,830	
Returns	1,000	1,300
Office Expenses	2,860	
Opening Stock	52,290	
	3,14,700	3,14,700

Prepare Trading and Profit and Loss Account for the year ended 31st March 2005 and Balance Sheet as on that date after making following adjustments.

1) The closing Stock is valued for Rs. 40,000.
2) New R.D.D. to be provided for Rs. 2,160.
3) Provide for outstanding liabilities Rates & Taxes Rs. 1,000 and Salaries Rs. 170, Audit fees Rs. 400.

4) The book value of Typewriter sold Rs. 1,300.

5) Depreciate Typewriter at 20% p.a. Machinery at 15% p.a.

Problem 16

Prepare Final Account from the following Trial Balance

Trial Balance As on 31st December, 2004			
Particulars	**Rs.**	**Particulars**	**Rs.**
Land & Building	22,250	Capital Account	50,000
Plant (Addition Rs. 1,500 on 1st OCt. 2004)	4,875	Sales	28,500
Drawings	2,500		
Opening Stock	13,000	Sundry Creditors	4,700
Wages	2,500	R.D.D.	250
Purchases	17,250	Outstanding expenses	250
Carriages	350	Interest	50
Office-expenses	1,135		
Rent, Rates & Taxes	875		
Insurance	240		
Motor Van	10,000		
Salaries	875		
Bad debts	475		
Sundry Debtors	7,300		
Cash at Bank	125		
	83,750		83,750

Adjustments

1) Closing Stock - Cost Price Rs. 20,000. Market Price - Rs. 25,000.

2) Charge 10% p.a. interest on Capital.

3) Charge interest on Drawings Rs. 125.

4) Depreciate plant at 10% p.a.

5) Sanjay (owner) withdrew goods worth Rs. 500 for his personal use but it is not recorded in the Books.

Distinction Between Book-keeping and Accounting

Book-keeping	Accounting
Book-keeping involves - identifying the transactions, measuring the identified transaction, recording the measured transactions, and classifying the recorded transactions.	Accounting in addition to Book-keeping involves - summarizing the classified transactions, analysing the summarized results, interpreting the analysed results and communcating the interpreted information to the interested parties
Book-keeping is primary stage of Accountacy, It is the basis of Accounting.	Accounting is the secondary stage. It starts where book-keeping ends. It is a next stage of book-keeping.

The basic objective of book-keeping is to maintain systematic records of financial transcations.	The basic objective of accounting is to ascertain net results of operations and financial position and to communicate information to the interested parties.
Book-keeping work is performed by junior staff. (Now a days by computer)	Accounting work is performed by senior staff. (Required advance knowledge)
The book-keeper is not required to have higher level of knowledge than that of an accoutant.	The accountant is required to have higher level of knowledge than that of book-keeper.
The book-keeper may or may not possess analytical skill.	An accountant is required to possess analytical skill.
The job of a book-keeper is often routine and clerical in nature.	The job of an accountant is analytical in nature.
It does not cover designing of accounts system.	It covers designing of accounting system.
The book-keeper does not supervise and check the work of an accountant.	An accountant supervises and checks the work of a book-keeper.
Book-keeping has no branch.	Accounting has several branches e.g. Financial Accounting, Cost Accounting etc.
Book-keeping is the recording phase of an accounting system.	Accounting is the summarising phase of an accounting system.
Personal judgement of the book-keeper is not required.	Personal judgement of the accountant is essential

Capital Expenditures	**Revenue Expenditures**
Capital expenditures are incurred for more than one accounting period	Revenue expenditures are incurred for a particular accounting period.
Capital expenditures are of non-recurring nature.	Revenue expenditures are of recurring nature.
All capital expenditures eventually become revenue expenditures.	Revenue expenditures are not generally capital expenditures.
Capital expenditures are not matched with capital receipts.	All revenue expenditutes are matched with revenue receipts.
Capital expenditures are incurred before or after the commencement of the business.	Revenue expenditures are incurred always after the commencement of the business.

Capital Receipts	Revenue Receipts
Capital receipts are not available for distribution as profits .	Revenue receipts are available for distribution as profits only after deducting revenue expenses.
Capital receipts cannot be utilised for creating a reserve fund.	Revenue receipts can be utilised for creating a reserve fund after deducting revenue expenses.
A business can survive without any capital receipts during an accounting period.	The survival of a business mainly depends on the revenue receipts during an accounting period.
Capital receipts are the sources for creating capital reserves.	Revenue receipts are the sources for creating revenue reserves.

Journal	Ledger
It is book of original or prime entry.	It is book of final or secondary entry.
It is prepared on the basis of source documents of transactions.	It is prepared on the basis of journal.
Recording in the journal is the first stage.	Recording in the ledger is the second stage.
It is prepared to record all transactions in chronological order.	It is prepared to know the net effect of various transactions affecting a particular account.
In journal, there are five column: 1. Date 2. Particulars 3. Ledger Folio 4. Debit Amount 5. Credit Amount	In ledger there are identical four column on debit side and credit side 1. Date 2. Particulars 3. Folio 4. Amount
Journal is not balanced.	All ledger accounts (except nominal account) are balanced in the ledger.
Narration is written for each entry.	No narration is given.
The process of recording in journal is called **'journalizing'**.	The process of recording in the ledger is called **'posting'**.
Journal directly does not serve as basis for the preparation of final accounts.	Ledger serves the basis for the preparation of final accounts.

Trade discount	Cash discount
It is a reduction granted by a supplier from the list price of goods or services on business considerations (such as quantity bought, trade practices, etc.) other than for prompt payment.	A reduction granted by supplier from the invoice price in consideration of immediate payment or payment within a stipulated period.
It is allowed to promote the sales or as trade practice.	It is allowed to encourage the prompt payment.
It is allowed on purchase of goods.	It is allowed on immediate payment or payment or within a specified period.
It is shown by way of deduction in the invoice itself.	It is not shown in the invoice.
Trade discount account is not opened in the ledger.	Cash discount account is opened in the ledger.
It may vary with the quantity purchased.	It may vary with the period within which the payment is made.

Main Cash Book and Petty Cash Book

1. In the main cash book all cash receipts are recorded whereas in the petty cash book only Cash Receipts from Main Cashier are recorded.
2. In the main cash book all cash payments except payments of petty cash expenses, are recorded whereas in the petty cash book only payments of petty cash expenses are recorded.

Manufacturing Account	Trading Account
It is prepared to ascertain the cost of goods manufactured.	It is prepared to ascertain the gross profit or gross loss.
It is closed by transferring its balance to the debit side of the Trading Account.	It is closed by transferring its balance to the debit side (in case of gross loss) or credit side (in case of gross profit) of the Profit and Loss Account.
It does not show the opening and closing stock of Finished Goods.	It shows the opening and closing stock of finished goods.
It is prepared by a manufacturing concern only.	It is prepared by every business concern.

Tangible Assets	Intangible Assets.
These assets have physical identity	These assets do not have physical identity.
Fixed tangible assets are depreciated.	Intangible assetss are amortized.
Tangible assets can be fixed or current asset.	Intanginle assets usually fall in the category of fixed assets.
Lenders accept such assets as security for a loan given.	Lenders usually do not accept such assets as security for a loan given.
The assets may be lost due to fire.	These assets cannot be lost due to fire.

Fixed Assets	Current Assets.
These are the assets which are held for the purpose of providing or producing goods or services and those which are not held for resale in the normal course of business.	These are the assets which are held - (a) in the form of cash (b) for their conversion into cash (c) for their consumption in the production of goods or rendering of services in the normal course of business.
Fixed assets are valued at cost less depreciation.	These assets are valued at cost or market price whichever is lower.
These assets are usually not subject to change.	These assets are usually subject to change.
Fixed charge can be created on these assets.	Floating charge can be created on these assets.
Profit on sale of these assets is of capital nature.	Profit on sale of these assets is of revenue nature.
In case of appreciation in the value of such assets, revaluation reserve can be created.	In case of appreciation in the value of such assets, revaluation reserve cannot be created.
These assets are financed out of long term funds.	These assets are mainly financed out of short-term funds.

Trading and P&L A/c	Balance Sheet
The Trading and Profit & Loss A/c is prepared to ascertain the results of business operation during an accounting period.	The Balance Sheet is prepared to know the financial position of an enterprise at a particular time.
The balances of all the ledger accounts of revenue nature are shown in the Trading and Profit and Loss A/c.	The balances of only those ledger accounts which have not been closed till the preparation of Trading and Profit and Loss A/c, are shown in the Balance Sheet.
The Trading and Profit and Loss A/c is a ledger account. It has debit side and a credit side. It is closed by transferring its balance to the Capital Account.	The Balance Sheet is only a statement and not an account It has no debit side and credit side. The heading of the two sides are 'Liabilities' and 'Assets'.

Trial Balance	Balance Sheet
It is prepared to check the arithmetical accuracy of the posting of transactions to the ledger.	It is prepared to know the financial position of an enterprise at particular point of time.
All the ledger accounts are shown in the Trial Balance.	The balances of only those ledger accounts which have not been closed till the preparation of Trading and Profit and Loss Account are shown in the Balance Sheet.
The heading of the two columns are 'debit balance' and 'credit balance'(in case of a Trial Balance by Balance Method)	The headings of the two sides are 'Liabilities' and 'Assets'.

Trial Balance	Balance Sheet
Generally, the closing stock does not appear in the Trial Balance whereas the opening stock appears.	In a Balance Sheet, only the closing stock appears on the Assets side as a current assets.
It can be prepared without incorporating the items of adjustments. Information about net profit/net loss is not provided in a Trial Balance.	It cannot be prepared without incorporating the items of adjustments. Information about net profit/net loss is provided.
It can be prepared periodically (say) at the end of a month/quarter/half-year. Its preparation can be dispensed with.	It is generally prepared at the end of an accounting period. Its preparation cannot be dispensed with.

Outstanding Expenses	Prepaid Expenses
It refers to an expense incurred but not paid during the current accounting period.	It refers to an expense paid but not incurred during the current accounting period.
It is yet to be paid	It has already been paid.
It has already been incurred.	It is yet to be incurred.
It is an item of the current year	It is an item of the following year.
It is shown by way of addition to the relevant item.	It is shown by way of deduction from the relevant item.
It is shown on the liabilities side as a current liability.	It is shown on the asset side as a current asset.

Accrued Income	Unaccrued Income
It refers to an income earned but not received during the current accounting period	It refers to an income received but not earned during the current accounting period.
It is yet to be received.	It has already been received.
It has already been earned.	It is yet to be earned.
It is an item of the current year It is shown by way of addition to the	It is an item of the following year. It is shown by way of deduction from the
relevant item. It is shown on the assets side as a current asset.	relevant item. It is shown on the liabilities side as a current liability.

Debit Note

It is a commercial document notifying a person that a debit has been made to his accounts. For example, if the goods are sold on credit and a part of that is returned, a debit note might be issued for the value of the goods returned.

Credit Note

It is a document evidencing that a credit entry has been made to a debtors account. For example, if a customer returns a part of the goods previously sold on credit, a credit note may be issued.

*****

Unit No. 3

ESSENTIALS OF COST ACCOUNTING

Cost Accounting

Introduction

In today's world of competition, cost consciousness is the key factor for determining the growth of the industrial economy. Ours is a developing country where we have mixed economy and hence mixed problems. We are facing acute inflation problem, depression in the industries and stagnation in the economy. Hence cost reduction has become the need of the hour. Therefore, the industrialists must have a perfect knowledge of costs so that they can make various decisions regarding planning, pricing, budgeting, policy making of the company regarding fixation of wages etc.

Thus, the study of cost accounting is of utmost importance in our country because unless we reduce the costs, we cannot stand in the competitive world and have progress of our economy.

Definition and Scope of Cost Accounting

Various authors have defined Cost ; 'Cost Accounting' and 'Cost Accountancy' in different ways. According to Shellinglaw - 'Cost represents the resources that have been or must be sacrificed to attain a particular objective.' The terminology of Cost Accountancy published by the Institute of Cost and Works Accountants, London defines Costing as "The techniques and processes of ascertaining costs ".

H.J. Wheldon has defined it as , " The classifying, recording and appropriate allocation of expenditure for the determination of the costs of products or services; the relation of these costs to sales values; and the ascertainment of profitability."

The definition given by Van Sickle is "Cost accountancy is the science of recording and presenting business transactions pertaining to the production of goods and services, whereby these records become a method of measurement and a means of control."

Difference between Costing, Cost Accounting & Cost Accountancy

The three terms i.e. Costing, Cost accounting and Cost Accountancy are often used interchangeably. But there is distinct difference between all three terms :

Costing : It consists of the principles and rules which are used to find out :-

a) The cost of manufacturing a product. b) The cost of providing a service

Example of products : Pen, Watches, etc. Example of Services : Banking, Insurance etc.

Cost Accounting

In this case the costs of producing the articles or services rendered are ascertained and controlled. It is thus the application of accounting and costing principles, methods and techniques by which the ascertainment of cost is possible which can be compared with the set standards to find out whether there is any saving or excess spending of amount.

Thus in 'Costing', there is cost finding only whereas in 'Cost accounting', use is made of the accounting mechanism by which the costs can be ascertained.

Cost Accountancy

It includes all aspect of costs, i.e. costing, cost accounting, cost control and cost audit. Cost accountancy is used for planning and controlling the utilisation of the scarce resources. Cost Accountancy is therefore useful in taking managerial decision from the information collected, analysed and interpreted.

Scope of Cost Accouting

In today's world of competition, it is absolutely necessary to conduct business with maximum efficiency, otherwise, it becomes difficult to exist. We have scarce resources and their maximum use should be made to obtain the best results. Thus we see in every business that the main aim is to get maximum output from a given input. The comparison is made between the cost of input and the value of output produced, i.e. the price of a product in the market for which people are willing to pay for it. The businessman should know how to incur the least cost of input so that the sales price can be fixed which will give sufficient profits to the company as well as it will be most competent in the market to compete with the sales price of other companies. In the case of of service industry also, the cost of providing the services should be less than the value of it being paid by the customer.

Thus the owner of any business or organisation is always interested in knowing :

a) what is the cost per unit b) how to achieve maximum efficiency ? c) where to have improvements ?
d) how to control the costs ? e) how to reduce the costs ?

All these questions can be answered by Cost Accountancy and hence the need for Cost Accountancy is felt very much in the business world today.

Cost Accountancy helps to solve the management problems. In the recent past, there is so much of its development that it has become difficult to spell out its scope precisely.

Thus Cost Accountancy has a wide scope and it is said that Cost Accountancy is the science art and practice of a Cost Accountant.

It is regarded as a science because it is a body of systematic knowledge which has certain principles which a cost accountant should be familiar with in order to carry out his duties effectively. It is regarded as an art because it is the skill and ability of the cost accountant to apply the various principles of cost accountancy to solve the decision making problems of the management.

By practice we mean that the cost accountant should keep himself abreast about all the latest developments which take place in the techniques and methods of costing. Hence he should make continuous efforts so that his theoretical knowledge can be applied to solve the various new problems which arise in the business. For this he need practical training also.

Objectives of Cost Accounting

The main objectives of cost accounting are as follows :

a) ***For formulating or fixing operating policies*** : Cost accounting helps the management to formulate the operating policies such as :

i) whether to continue a business at loss or to close down the business totally.

ii) whether to buy certain components from outside or to make them in the own factory.

iii) whether to go in for improved and sophisticated technology or to continue with the existing methods of production.

iv) whether to have hi-tech systems by importing certain machinery so that production can be made at reduced costs.

v) finding out the relationship between cost of production, sales and profit for taking important decision such as continuing a certain product or not, etc.

b) ***Ascertainment of costs :*** The very purpose of cost accounting is the finding out of the costs which is known as cost ascertainment. For cost ascertainment, various techniques, tools and methods are used under various situations. This is the skill of getting the information at the time from all the departments so that the costs which are ascertained can be utilized for cost control and also for taking managerial decisions.

c) ***Control of Costs :*** By cost control we mean reducing costs and increasing the efficiency. Reduction in costs is important because unless there is competitive price offered for the products in the market, one cannot stand in world of competition. Hence cost control has gained much importance in the recent years.

d) ***Help the organisation for preparation of financial statements :*** For every business it is very much necessary to have constant review of production, sales as well as the operating results. For the preparation of the financial statements it is necessary to find out the stock values for a particular period for which the financial statements are to be prepared. If costing records are not maintained for the stocks, it takes a long time to verify the stock physically and for which the business has to be closed down till the physical verification is completed. But where there is a system of keeping cost accounting records, the ascertainment of the value of closing stock as regards the raw materials partly, finished goods as well as the finished goods can be made. This helps the organisation to prepare the financial statements either weekly, fortnightly, monthly or quarterly.

e) ***Management's guide for decision making :*** Cost Accounting helps the management to run the business with greatest efficiency. Cost data helps the management to take vital decisions as regards make or buy decisions, diversification of products, introduction of new products, closing down a line of product which does not have any contribution towards profits, to sell the products at lower price, utilization of excess capacity etc.

Thus it helps the business to find out whether the activities are carried out profitably or not so that the unprofitable areas can be looked into and improvements suggested.

Thus from the above we find that there are a number of decisions which can be taken by the management with the help of costing if the cost records are maintained by the organisation.

Uses of Cost Accounting

The necessity and importance of cost accounting is felt in every industry in the modern business practices because cost accounting has various uses and advantages which help the management to take important decisions at every level of activity. The following are the uses of cost accounting :

a) It helps the management to decide on the future plan of action and capital to be employed for further expansion.
b) When there is competition, the prices can be reduced upto point where only the costs would be recovered from selling the articles.
c) It helps the management to find out the exact cost of each product.
d) Cost accounting helps to analyse the cost of each product and hence the profitable and unprofitable activities can be located.
e) Cost comparisons can be made of various items and hence comparison with other industries is possible. This enables to improve the efficiency.
f) It can reveal the wastages and prevent them .
g) Idle capacity of plants can be located and utilized.
h) Efficiency of the machines which are old can be compared with the new machines in the market and replacement decisions can be taken.
i) It enables the management to fix the selling price correctly.

j) The causes of high/low profit or loss as shown by the financial accounts can be found out and analysed.

k) Standards can be set up for each item of activity and then compared with the actuals to find out the efficiency.

l) Stock and inventory control techniques are applied so that minimum stock is maintained. Hence less amount of capital is blocked up.

m) An efficient systems of communication of cost information at various levels of management in desired forms can be set up and maintained. It means that any person in the organisation can get the cost records as required by him anytime.

n) It helps to conduct cost audit of the costing records of a company whenever the Govt. instructs cost audit to be conducted.

o) Quotations and tenders can be submitted by quoting the exact prices.

p) It helps the management to make cost calculation for the new designs of existing products or a totally new product.

q) Various incentive schemes can be introduced on the productivity and cost saving made by the workers.

Thus cost accounting is useful not only to the management but is also advantageous to the workers, creditors and investors, customers, society and the Government.

Limitations

Cost accountancy suffers from many limitation also. This is because costing is based mostly on the estimates and other conventions and factors which are flexible. Hence we cannot have definite or accurate costs. Each cost varies under different circumstances. For example :

a) Classification of costs cannot be made accurately.

b) Procedure of material issue to production differs from industry to industry.

c) The allocation and apportionment of costs are sometimes made on adhoc basis.

d) Segregation of costs into fixed, variable and semi-variable differs from unit to unit.

e) The definition of normal and abnormal costs as well as controllable and uncontrollable costs differ.

f) No exact bifurcation of expenses which can be included or excluded from costs can be made.

Thus cost accounting cannot be termed as an exact science like Physics for Maths, but it is a subjective art which is practised based on the accounting theories, reasoning and most importantly the common sense. Hence all decisions of the management are based upon the best judgement of the cost accountants who take into account the various factors while preparing the cost statements, which may not be the same with other cost accountants. The management sometimes gets confused about the different cost statements submitted to it for different purposes. For example, the costs differ in case of slack season or recession of the industry, the standards vary from the actuals etc.,

But apart from the above limitations, costing helps the management to take vital decisions with valuable cost figures without which todays management could not have solved the complex business problems.

Cost Concepts

The concept of cost is not something definite and care must be taken to qualify it according to its context. For managerial decision making a cost accountant is mainly concerned with the following cost concepts :

(1) **Total Cost :** It is the sum of all the items of expenses - whether paid or not - which have been incurred in the production, sale or distribution or in the rendering of a service to a customer.

(2) **Direct Cost :** It is the aggregate of a marginal cost and a portion of fixed cost that can be traced or allocated to products - Direct costs are, therefore, all traceable costs.

(3) **Marginal Cost :** Marginal Cost is the total of variable cost. ICMA, London-defines it as, "the variable

cost of one unit of product or a service i.e. a cost which would be avaoided if the unit was not produced or provided. It consists of all direct costs and variable overheads. It is based on the distinction between fixed and variable costs. Fixed costs are ignored and only variable costs are taken into consideration for determining the cost of products and value of work in progress and finished goods. Thus, marginal cost is the additional cost of producting additional units.

(4) **Standard Cost :** This is a pre-determined estimated cost which an organisation tries to attain under standard normal conditions. Thus, estimates of costs are made before incurring them and then the actual results are compared with the standards to find out the efficiency of a business.

(5) **Conversion Cost :** This term is used to denote the sum of direct labour and overhead costs in the production of a product. It is the total cost of 'converting' a raw material into finished product. In other words it is works cost minus cost of direct materials.

(6) **Sunk Cost :** The National Association of Accountants defines a sunk cost as, an expenditure for equipment or productive resources which has no economic relevance to the present decision making process". As the name implies it is historical in nature. It is a cost which has been created by a decision that was made in the past which cannot be changed by any decision that will be made in the future. These costs are not relevant for decision-making about the futute. Thus, the book value of an asset currently being used is not relevant in making the decision to replace it.

(7) **Opportunity Cost :** ICMA, London-defines it as, "the value of benefit sacrificied in favour of an alternative course of action". Edward Hermanson and Salmonson defines it as "the benefit lost by rejecting the best competing alternatives to the one chosen". Thus, Opportunity cost is the sacrifice involved in accepting the alternative under consideration. This concept is used in the problems of alternative choices. Opportunity cost is a pure decision-making cost and is not entered in the books of account. Suppose a company owns a building which is proposed to be used for a special project, the likely rent of building is the Opportunity Cost which should be taken into consideration that evaluates the profitability of the project.

(8) **Out of Pocket Cost :** These are the costs which require cash payments to be made (such as wages, rent etc.) whereas many costs do not require cash outlay (such as depreciation). Out-of-pocket costs are those costs that involve cash outlays or require the utilisation of current resources. Out-of-pocket cost may be either fixed (such as manager's salary) or variable such as raw material, direct wages etc). This cost is frequently used as an aid in make or buy decisions, price fixation during recession and many other vital decisions.

(9) **Replacement Cost :** It is the current market price of replacing an existing asset. The present market price is always considered for taking any decision for buying a machine and not the original cost at which it was bought.

(10) **Imputed Cost :** ICMA, London defines it as, "a hypothetical cost taken into account to represent a benefit enjoyed by the undertaking in respect of which no actual expense is incurred". They are computed for decision-making purposes. These are the built-up costs which are imaginary. These are the non-cash items. Examples of imputed costs are : rent of owned land, salary of owner, interest on owned capital etc.

(11) **Differential (or incremental) Cost :** It is the increase or decrease in the total cost which results from taking alternative decisions by the management from among the various choices. Thus the difference between two alternative course of action is known as "Differential Cost".

(12) **Avoidable and Unavoidable Cost :** Avoidable costs are those which can be eliminated if a particular product or department with which they are directly related, is discountinued. For example, salary of the clerks employed can be eliminated if a particular depatment in which they are employed is decided to be

discontinued. Unavoidable cost are those costs which cannot be eliminated with the discontinuation of a particular product or department. Such costs are merely allocated if the product or department is discontinued. for example, salary of factory manager or factory rent cannot be eliminated even if a product is eliminated.

(13) **Joint Cost :** When two or more products are produced from the use of a single raw material, we get either two main products from it or one may be a main product and the other be a by-product. But the cost to produce is the combined costs. Then the management can take decisions whether to take up manufacture of joint products or to go in for processing of the by-products further so that the total costs can be reduced.

(14) **Relevant and Irrelevant Cost :** Relevant costs are those costs that would be changed by the decision. Irrelevant costs are those costs that would not be affected by the decision. It means a relevant cost is cost whose magnitude will be affected by a decision being made. Management is concerned only with those things which it can affect. For example, management cannot change the cost of equipment purchased in 1980. It can change future costs by its current decisions. Hence, relevant costs are future costs that will differ depending on the action of the management. For each decision the management must decide which costs are relevant. For example, when a manufacturer decided to close a certain unit, the wages associated with the maintenance of such unit is relevant cost as wage payment cease if the unit is closed. but rent which was already paid under lease agreement which cannot be recovered is irrelevant cost.

(15) **Discretionary costs :** These are also called managed costs or programmed costs and consist of fixed costs that arise from periodic appropriation decisions that directly reflect top management policies.

(16) **Engineered Costs :** These are costs which vary directly with the level of production. these are opposed to managed or discretionary costs.

(17) **Shut down Cost :** A cost which will still be incrurred although a plant is shut down temporarily, e.g., rent, rates, depreciation, maintenance of plant, etc.

(18) **Traceable Cost :** A cost which can be easily identified with cost unit or cost centres. The term is used to distinguish it from joint or common costs.

Relationship of cost and financial accounting

Financial accounting is that part of accounting which covers the classification and recording of actual transactions of an entity in monetary terms in accordance with established concepts, principles, accounting standards as well as legal requirements and presents as accurate a view possible of the effect of those transctions over a period and at the end of that period. It originated to fulfill the stewardship function of a business and serves the basis of external reporting

Financial accounting provides information to business managers and also to the outsiders including shareholders, suppliers, customers, employees, government departments, and general public.

The main function of financial accounting is classification, recording and analysis of business transactions in a subjective manner according to nature of expenditure so as to facilitate preparation of profit and loss account and balance sheet for depicting the result of business operation as a whole.

All accounting practices treats costs, but whilst the financial accounting does this very broadly, cost accounting does this in much greater detail. Cost accounts show, by analysis and localisation, the unit costs and profit or losses of different product lines, whereas financial accounts reveal the profit or loss of the business as a whole during a particular period.

Cost accounting rests on the same principles concerning debits and credits that are found in financial accounting. The same records are used; but over and above these financial books of accounts there is imposed another group of forms and records dealing more specifically with aspects of costs constituting the field study of cost accounting.

Cost accounting is thus a much more detailed application of the principles of accounting. The distinction between the objectives of cost accounting and financial accounting at first resulted in the use of two entirely separate accounting systems, each producing a figure of profit or loss which did not agree with the corresponding total disclosed by the other.

Thus, compared with finanacial accounting, cost accounting is relatively a recent development. In fact, cost accounting started as a branch of financial accounting, but now it may be well regarded as a profession in its own right. The vital importance that cost accounting has acquired in modern age is because of the growth of complexities in modern industry.

It may be observed that finanacial accounts safeguard the interest of the business, its proprietors, shareholders, present and prospective creditors and the Government particularly Income-tax, Excise and other authorities. Cost accounts, on the other hand, render information for the guidance of the management for proper planning, operation, control, profitability study and decision-making. Thus in case of materials, financial accounts show whether purchases have been correctly accounted and paid for and closing stocks have been valued 'at cost or market value whichever is lower' for the purpose of preparing balance sheets. Cost accounts, however, maintain detailed account for each material, report management regarding effectiveness of material utilization and inform the variations from budget as regards price and consumption with reasons for such variances. Similar considerations apply with regard to utilization of labour, machines and capital resources.

It may be pointed out that where financial accounts end cost accounts start Thus, when purchases of raw matercials are made, the financial accounts keep records of purchase and creditors meticulously but do not keep any record of raw materials. The cost accounts keep detailed records in respect of each material showing receipts, issues and balances in terms of quantity and value. The cost accounting is concerned with the computation of actual product costs for stock valuation and profit measurement.

Difference between Financial and Cost Accounting

In the financial accounting system recording of all money transactions are made on the principle of double entry system in a set of books for the preparation of the financial statement i.e. the profit and loss account and the Balance Sheet.

Cost accounting refers to the system of cost ascertainment, classification, analysis and cost presentation for managerial decisions and control, In both the systems i.e. financial as well as costing we find that the same expenses are made use of in different ways for their own purposes. Due to the complexities of large scale production in the modern business activities, the financial accounting falls short of meeting these challenges. Hence cost accounting has come into existence to solve all the managerial problems.

The following are the differences between financial accounting and cost accounting :-

Financial Accounting	Cost Accounting
1) It is concerned with the total business concern.	1) It is concerned with the transaction relating to certain specific activities only. e.g. production, sales, services etc.
2) It relates to pure financial and commercial matters.	2) It relates to the transactions for manufacture of goods and services.
3) Labour efficiency cannot be measured and ideal time cannot be located and hence incentives cannot be offered.	3) Accurate time sheets are prepared from which efficiency of labour can be found out and suitable incentives scheme can be formulated.
4) There is no system of material control i.e. analysis is not made about the high cost paid, inefficient handling of materials etc.	4) It reveals inefficiency in material handling, inventory control etc. It also fixes the standard for purchase, issue and storage of materials.
5) Costs are not broken up according to their nature and functions.	5) The costs are analysed according to their nature and functions for further analysis and control.
6) There is no system of bifurcation of costs fixed and variable or controllable and uncontrollable	6) Since there is bifurcation of costs into controllable and uncontrollable costs, the management can reduce the controllable costs. The distinction between fixed costs and variable costs also help the management to take vital decision.
7) It can find out the total profit or loss of the business.	7) Profit/loss for each job product or service can be found out.
8) It deals with the actual figures i.e. the actual expenses incurred.	8) It deals with the actuals as well as the estimates.
9) It is concerned with the external transactions i.e. the out siders e.g. creditors, shareholders etc.	9) It is concerned with the internal transactions and is not connected with cash.
10) Financial statements i.e. P & L A/c and Balance Sheets are prepared at the end of the financial year.	10) Cost data can be prepared anytime and reported to the management either weekly, fortnightly, monthly, quarterly, half yearly or even yearly.
11) The creditors, investors and the Govt. cannot get detailed records from the financial accounts for further analysis of figures.	11) Cost records provide detailed information.
12) Framing of pricing policy on a sound and accurate basis is not possible.	12) Prices can be fixed more accurately from the cost data.
13) Inter firm or Intra firm comparison cannot be made.	13) It is possible to make inter firm Intra-firm comparison
14) It deals with the transaction which have already been over (historical costs) and hence no action can be taken to correct the situations if there are any mistake.	14) It deals with both type of costs i.e. historical as well as the estimate.
15) Stocks are valued at cost or market price whichever is less.	15) Stocks are valued at costs.

Questions for Self-Study

Cost Accounting

1) Define 'Cost Accounting'. Explain the scope of cost accounting.
2) Define 'Cost Accounting' & Distinguish between Costing, Cost Accounting & Cost Accountancy.
3) Explain the term 'Cost Accounting'. State in brief objectives of Cost Accounting.
4) What are the uses of Cost Accounting ? How is it advantageous to the various sections of the economy ?
5) State the difference between Financial and Cost Accounting.
6) State whether following statements are true or false :-
   a) The study of cost accounting is of utmost importance in our country.
   b) Cost Accounting does not help to solve the management problems.
   c) Cost Accounting enables the management to fix the selling price correctly.
   d) The allocation and apportionment of costs are some times made on adhoc basis
   e) Cost Accounting can find out the total profit or loss of the business.
   f) In Cost accounting stock are valued at cost or market price whichever is less.
7) Match the pairs.

Group A		Group B	
1)	Costing	a)	Concern with the total business
2)	Cost Accounting	b)	Includes all aspect of costs.
3)	Cost Accountancy	c)	Cost can be ascertained
4)	Financial Accounting	d)	Cost Finding only.
		e)	Single Entry system.

8) Fill in the gaps.

a) Costing is based mostly on the..... (actuals/estimates/past performance)

b) Cost Accounting cannot be termed as an exact. .... (Science/Arts/Commerce)

c) Cost accountancy suffers from many..... (advantages/benefits/limitations)

d) Cost accounting has come into existence to solve all.... problems (Administrative/Managerial/Financial)

e) Cost accounting referes to the system of... (cost management/financial management/marketing management).

ELEMENTS OF COST

Introduction

The natural process of classifying costs means that all costs of a product should be grouped. In a manufacturing concern, the total cost of a product includes the following elements. 1) Direct materials 2) Direct labour 3) Direct expenses 4) Factory overheads, 5) Selling Distribution & Administrative overheads.

Material - Labour and Other Expenses

Only the knowledge of total cost control is not sufficient to meet the requirements of the management. For necessary control and decision by the management the cost data should be provided in such a way that they can be analysed and classified further. Hence the total cost is analysed according to the elements of cost. It means that the costs are analysed and classified according to their nature. There are basically three elements of cost i.e. materials, labour and other expenses. Again they are further analysed into different elements i.e. direct and indirect materials, direct and indirect labour and direct and indirect expenses. Indirect expenses are also termed as overheads. The overheads are production or works oveheads, administration overheads, selling overheads and distribution overheads.

The different elements of costs can be shown with the help of the following chart :-

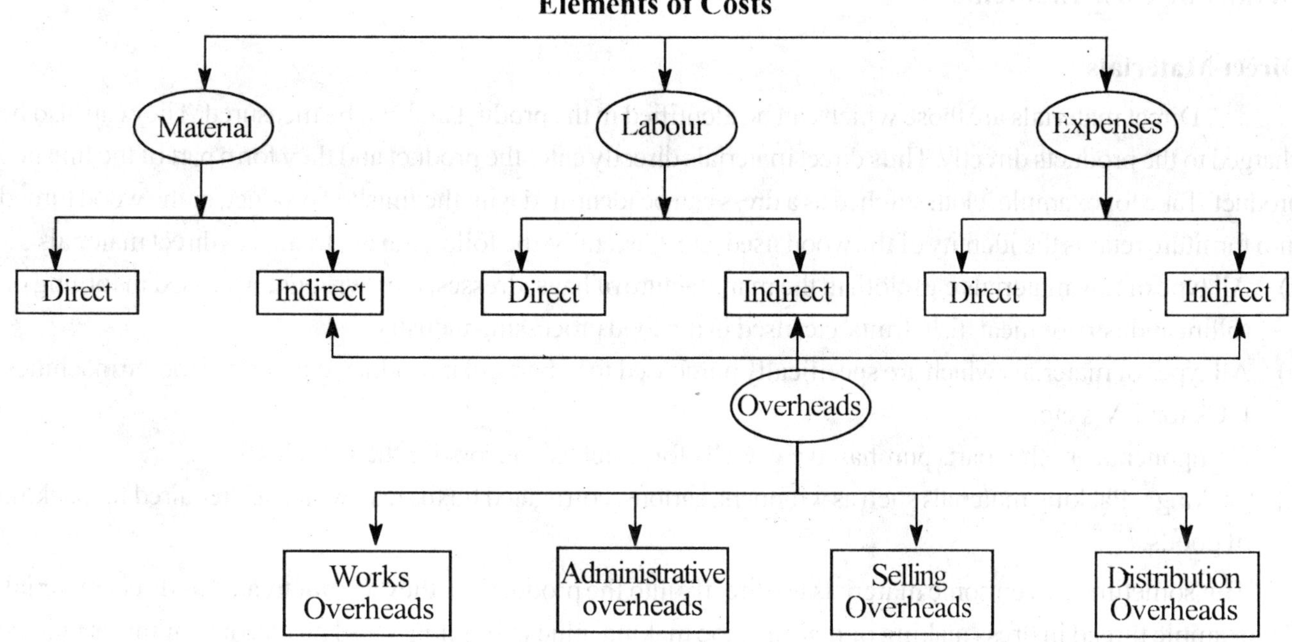

Divsions of Costs

Cost division constitute the different types of elements of costs in the following manner :

A) ***Prime cost*** : Direct Material plus Direct Labour and Direct expenditure gives us what is known as the 'Prime Cost'

B) ***Works/ Factory Cost*** : Prime cost plus production/ works overheads gives us the `Works/Factory Cost'

C) ***Cost of Production*** : Works cost plus administrative overheads gives us the 'Cost of Production'.

D) ***Total Cost*** : Cost of production plus selling overheads plus distribution overheads gives us the `Total Cost.' or which is also known as 'Cost of Sales.'

Statement (Chart)Showing components of Selling price :

Direct Material		x
plus. Direct labour		x
plus. Direct Expenses		x
	Prime Cost	xxx
Add : Production / Works overheads		x
	Factory Cost	xxxx
Add : Administrative overheads		x
	Cost of production	xxxxx
Add : Selling and Distribution overheads		x
	Cost of Sales	xxxxxx
Add / Deduct : (Profit/Loss)		x

Selling Price xxxxxxx

Details of Cost Elements

Direct Materials

Direct materials are those which can be identified in the product and can be measured. They can also be charged to the products directly. Thus direct materials directly enter the product and they form part of the finished product. Take for example, cloth stitched as a dress can be identified with the finished product, or the wood turned into furniture retains the identity of the wood used, etc. Generally, the following are treated as direct materials :

a) All type of raw materials e.g. cloth in the manufacture of bags, dresses, etc., wrought iron used in forging or rolling industry or meat, fish, fruits, etc. used in the food processing industry.

b) All types of materials which are specifically purchased for a particular product, e.g. screws for the machines, I. Cs for T.V's etc.

c) Components or other parts purchased e.g. Cells for watches, mirrors for the vehicles, etc.

d) Packing :- Packing materials such as wrappers, cartons, corrugated boxes, etc. which are required for packing of goods.

But sometimes, even some materials go directly into the production, they are not treated as direct material. For example thread in dress making or nails in shoe making, glue in binding, etc. The reasons for this is that the value of these materials is very less and the quantity used is also negligible. Hence attempt is not made to analyse their costs which will otherwise be time consuming and will add to extra cost because of spending more time on them, while their value being negligible. Thus such materials, should conveniently be treated as indirect materials.

Direct Labour

It has been defined as "all labour expended in altering the construction composition, confirmation of condition of the product. In other words direct labour is that labour which can be easily identified with and allocated directly to a particular job, product or process, e.g. wages paid to workers working on machine which manufactures toys. Thus direct labour is utilised for converting the raw materials into finished products. The wages paid to such workers are known as direct wages. Thus the direct wages are the payments made for the actual manufacture of a commodity. The labour engaged in helping the manufacture i.e. for supervision, maintenance etc.or the wages paid to inspector, foremen, chargemen, analysts, etc. who are directly connected with such production. Though the wages paid to the supervisors, inspectors, etc. are not direct labour, they can be treated as direct labour if they can be easily identified with the products. Sometimes the wages are paid to the trainees or apprentices, when engaged by the concerns. These wages may not be treated as direct labour cost if they are not very high.

Direct Expenses

Direct expenses include all types of expenses other than direct materials, direct labour, which are incurred specifically for a particular product or process. Direct expenses form a part of the prime cost. The following are the example of direct expenses :

a) Excise duty paid b) Research expenditure c) Architect's fees. d) Royalty paid
e) Cost of drawings and patterns. f) Repairs and maintenance of plants and equipment taken on hire.

Indirect Material

Indirect materials are those which do not form part of the finished products. It is defined as 'Materials which cannot be allocated , but which can be apportioned to or absorbed by cost centres or cost units." For example, lubricants, oils, cotton wastes, small tools etc. But sometimes the cost of small items which have less value like the nails in furniture, or thread in the dress manufactured are treated as indirect materials though they go directly into production. Hence all the indirect materials costs which relate to the factory form part of the factory overhead.

Indirect Labour

The wages which cannot be charged directly to production are known as indirect wages, Thus the wages which cannot be allocated but which can be apportioned to or absorbed by cost centres or cost units is known as direct labour. Examples of indirect labour are :

Salaries and wages paid to foremen, supervisors, chargemen, inspectors, maintenance workers, clerical staff in the production department, overtime and night shift allowance paid and any other benefits paid.

Indirect Expenses

The expenses which are neither indirect material nor indirect labour are known as indirect expenses. These expenses are not charge directly to production.

Indirect expenses cannot be allocated but they can be apportioned to cost absorbed by cost centres or cost units. Examples of indirect expenses are : rent, taxes, salary of the General Manager, staff welfare expenses, canteen expenses, telephone expenses, lighting, power, fuel etc.

Overheads

Overheads are defined as "the aggregate of indirect materials cost, indirect wages and indirect expenses. Terminology of cost Accountancy (I.C.W.A., London) :

Overhead costs are the operating costs of a business enterprise which cannot be identified with particular units of output. Some items of overheads may be found directly connected with a machine or department, but will be indirect as regards the output is concerned. Thus overheads costs are indirect costs and can be found in all departments, while direct costs are found only in the production departments. Thus overheads cannot be allocated but can be apportioned to the cost units. Overheads consists of all expenses incurred for or in connection with the general organisation of the entire concern or a part of it, i.e. cost of operating supplies and services used by the undertaking. It may also include maintenance of capital assets.

There are 4 main types of overheads as given below :

A) Production or Works Overheads

These overheads cover all types of indirect expenses incurred by a concern right from the receipt of order to the final dispatch of goods to the customer or for storing the finished goods in the godowns.

Thus all the expenses incurred from the receipt of an order to the final delivery of goods, other than the direct materials, direct labour and direct expenses are classified as manufacturing expenses. The other names for the indirect expenses are -works on cost, factory overhead, production overhead or works overhead.

The following is the list of such expenses :-

a) Electricity charges including gas, coal, steam, compressed air etc.
   Wages of indirect workers i.e. the supervisory staff e.g. salary of the supervisor or Works Manager.
b) Repairs and maintenance of fixed assets .
c) Rent, Rates and Insurance of factory premises, plant and machinery and other fixed assets .
d) Medical services such as hospital and dispensary expenses incurred for the factory workers.
e) Workers' welfare services e.g. canteen and recreation club expenses.
f) Factory telephone and other stationery items like postages, stamps telegram charges etc., of the works office.
g) Expenses incurred for the purchase of stores, store keeping expenses, cost of consumable stores and normal

loss of material.

B) *Administration overheads*

These are the indirect expenses incurred for formulating the policies, for planning and controlling the functions and directing and motivating the personnel in an organisation to attain its objectives. In other words, these expenses included all the expenses incurred by the administrative office i.e. for the secretarial work done, accounts, and costing department expenses and other managerial costs incurred for financial control.

The examples of administration overheads are :-

a) Salaries, allowances and other benefits paid to the office staff. b) Stationery, postage stamps, etc.
c) Taxes paid on office building. d) Office rent, light etc.
e) Repairs and maintenance of office building and equipment.
f) Insurance of office building and other equipments. g) Legal charges,
h) Audit Fees i) Director's fees .
j) Salary paid to General Manager, Finance Manager, Accountant, Secretary etc.
k) Depreciation of office building, furniture equipment etc.
l) Expenses of the share department and the secretarial department.
m) Membership fees of Trade Associations and other professional bodies.

C) *Selling Overheads*

Selling overheads are the indirect expenses which are incurred i.e. indirect material , indirect labour and indirect expenses for getting new customers and retaining (maintaining) the existing customers. It is the skill of any business to attract new customers by offering some extra facilities and services, by giving them free samples of the products, etc., so that they get attracted to the company. Similarly, the existing customers, should be retained by providing the best services for which certain expenses are necessary. Thus, if a concern wants to expand its business it must incur selling expenses which cannot be avoided. Examples of selling overheads are :-

a) Salary of the sales staff, sales manager and salesman, b) Fees paid to the Marketing Director.
c) Commission paid to Salesman and selling agents. d) Fancy packing on cartons.
e) Advertisement charges, hoarding, publicity etc. f) Mail order house expenses.
g) Free catalogues, pamphlets and price lists. h) Free gifts and samples.
i) Show room expenses. j) Free advice on technical matters.

D) *Distribution Overheads*

These consist of all the expenses incurred from the stage the goods are finished in the factory till they reach the final consumers. It means that distribution overhead includes all indirect material, indirect wages and indirect expenses incurred upto the point of packing the product for making it available for dispatch and ends with making the reconditioned returned empty packages and tins available for reuse. The actual definition of distribution expenses is "the cost of the sequence of operations. Which begins with making the packed product available for despatch and ends with making the reconditioned returned empty package, if any available for reuse."

The following are the examples of Distribution overheads :

a) Salary of warehouse keeper and others. b) Warehouse rent and insurance.
c) Cost of maintenance of vehicles. d) Insurance of goods in transit.
e) Cost of transportation of goods. f) Carriage outward
g) Loading expenses. h) Depreciation of delivery vehicles.
i) Special packing expenses.
j) Losses in warehouse stocks and finished goods damaged in transit.

k) Cost of repairing and reconditioning of empty boxes, cartons, cylinders etc.,

Types of Costs

The concept of cost is not very clear and hence it's classification should be made according to the function it performs. The following are the various types of costs :

A) *Total Cost*

It includes all the expenses related to production or services rendered whether actually incurred or not. Hence whatever items of expense enters into production of an article or whatever expenses are incurred for providing the services to a customer are included in the total cost.

B) *Marginal Cost*

It is the variable cost of a product. It consists of all direct cost and variable overheads. Marginal cost is the additional cost of producing additional units. But the marginal cost per unit remains the same irrespective of the volume of output.

For example if the cost of producting 10 washing machines is gives as -

Total Variable cost		Rs.	40,000 00
(i.e. Marginal cost)	Fixed cost	Rs.	10,000 00
	Total Cost	Rs.	50,000 00

If the output is increased by one unit of washing machine the cost will be as follows :

Total variable cost (i.e. Marginal cost = 11 x Rs. 4000)		Rs.	44,000 00
Fixed Cost		Rs.	10,000 00
	Total Cost	Rs.	54,000 00

Thus the additional cost of producing one additional Washing machine is Rs. 4000 which is known as the Marginal cost.

C) *Standard Cost*

This is predetermined estimated cost which an organisation tries to attain under standard normal conditions. Thus estimates of costs are made before incurring them and the actual results are compared with the standards to find out the efficiency of a business.

D) *Conversion Cost*

It means the cost incurred in converting the raw materials into finished products, i.e. it consists of only the Direct wages paid and the production expenses incurred, but excludes the cost of raw materials.

Other Type of Costs

Apart from the above costs, the management requires various other types of costs for taking vital decisions. They are as follows :-

A) *Out of Pocket Costs*

These are the actual expenses incurred in cash for the payment of wages, rent, etc. but do not include non-cash expenses such as depreciations etc. This concept of out of pocket costs helps the management in taking decisions as regards make or buy decisions or for fixing the prices during depreciation or trade recession.

B) *Opportunity costs*

It is cost for not using the other alternatives. For example the use of the scarce resources like men, materials, capital etc. can be used for a particular purpose. But if the same resources are utilized for some other purpose the original benefits lost for utilizing the second alternative is known as the opportunity cost. For example if Rs. 5.00 lacs are kept in a bank which can earn interest @ 7% p.a. are utilized for investment in an industry then the interest lost on this deposit is known as the opportunity cost.

C) Sunk costs

These are the costs which are already incurred and which cannot be recovered. Thus it has no importance in a particular decision making process. Sunk cost is calculated when an old asset is replaced by a new one, For example if a machine costs Rs.10,000 and its present book value is Rs.3000 is replaced by a new one then the loss is Rs.3,000 which is the undepreciated value of the old machine. Thus this undepreciated book value of the old machine is the sunk cost and is not considered in taking the decision to buy the new machine.

D) Replacement Cost

It is the current market price of replacing an existing asset. The present market price is always considered for taking any decisions for buying a machine and not the original cost at which it was bought.

E) Differential / Incremental Costs

It is the increase or decrease in the total cost which results from taking alternative decisions by the management from among the various choices. Thus the difference between two alternative course of action is known as the Differential cost.

F) Imputed Costs

These are the built up costs which are imaginary. They are computed for decision- making purposes. These are the non-cash items. Imputed costs are just like opportunity costs. Many a times, capital is invested for the new projects for which the return from various alternatives are studied. Hence considering the less investment with equal return is preferred in taking decision from the various alternatives. This is because the interest burden will be less in case of lower investment which is deducted from the additional income derived from the new investment.

G) Joint Costs

When two or more products are produced from the use of a single raw material, we get either two main products from it or one may be a main product and the other a by - product. But the cost to produce is the combined cost whether there are two products or one main product and one by product.

Thus the management can take decision whether to take up manufacture of joint products or to go in for processing of the by-products further so that the total costs can be reduced.

H) Traceable Costs

These are the costs which can be easily identified with a cost unit/cost centre. These are different from the terms "joint costs" or "Common costs."

Cost Sheet

Cost sheet is a statement which is prepared to show the details of all the costs incurred to produce the total output for a given period of time. Thus it means that the costs are segregated and put in a statement form with definite classifications. For example the first part of the cost sheet shows the 'Prime Cost', which we have already seen earlier, consists of the Direct materials cost, Direct labour cost and Direct expenses. To the prime costs is added the works overheads to arrive at the 'Works Cost'. To the Works Cost, we add the Administration overheads to get the 'Cost of Production.' By adding the Selling and Distribution overheads to the Cost of production, we arrive at the 'Total cost of production' or the 'Cost of Sales'.

Cost sheet is prepared in order to find out the total cost of production or the value of output which is offered for sale. Thus it does not include the financial items such as interest on loan taken or discount allowed etc. Hence it is not a part of the Double entry system of book keeping. To have cost comparisons between the present and the past performances and also with the standard costs fixed for the current production, the cost sheets are usually provided with 2/3 extra columns. In the cost sheet the cost per unit is also shown at the different stages of production.

Cost sheet is therefore useful to the management for keeping an eye on the expenses and for finding out the costs so that control on costs is possible at each and every stage of production.

Thus a cost sheet is a statement prepared by showing the item of cost of production and services which are analysed by their nature, elements, functions and behaviour i.e. whether they are fixed in nature or variable. It should also be noted that the non-cost items like the dividends and income tax paid should not be included in the cost sheets because these are the appropriations of profits. Generally speaking a cost sheet does not include the sales and the profit figures But if they are included, then the statement is called 'Statement of cost and profit.'

There are various benefits of cost sheets which are enumerated below :-

a) It shows both the total cost as well as the unit cost of production during a given period.

b) It helps the management to frame a suitable production policy.

c) It helps the management to have a detailed scrutiny of the costs so that control can be exercised at each and every stage of production.

d) With the comparison of costs with the past data as well as the standards, we can find out the variance in the costs and eliminate those costs which are unnecessary.

e) The selling price can be fixed more accurately as per the Govt. directives.

f) In case of severe competition, the management can reduce the price to a low level i.e. up to the cost of production so that the firm remains in the business just to recover the costs.

Important points for preparation of Cost Sheets

While preparing the cost sheets there are certain points which are of vital importance should be noted. They are as follows :

A) Consumption of Raw Materials

Opening Stock of raw materials	Rs.	xxx
Add : Purchases	Rs.	xxx
Carriage Inward	Rs.	xxx
	Rs.	xxx
Less: Closing stock of raw materials	Rs.	xxx
Value of consumption of raw materials	Rs.	xxx

B) Work in progress

Work in progress means the incomplete jobs lying in the production on which some work has been done, but which are not complete as finished goods. Work in progress is valued on the basis of the Works Cost (i.e. Prime Cost + Works Overheads). Sometimes it is also valued at the Prime cost basis. But it depends upon the management as to which method should be chosen. If it is valued at the works cost, then the following working is necessary :

Direct material	Rs.	xxx
Direct Labour	Rs.	xxx
Direct Expenses	Rs.	xxx
Prime Cost	Rs.	xxx
Add : Factory Overhead	Rs.	xxx
Add : Work in progress (Opening)	Rs.	xxx
Less : Work in progress (Closing)	Rs.	xxx
Work Cost	Rs.	xxx

C) Finished Goods

In most of the concerns all the stocks produced are not sold. Hence there are always the opening and closing balances of finished goods. Hence the opening and closing stock of finished goods should be adjusted before calculating the cost of goods sold. The treatment is as under:-

Value of Cost of Production	Rs.	xxx
Add :Opening stock of finished goods	Rs.	xxx
Less: Closing Stock of finished goods	Rs.	xxx
Cost of goods Sold	Rs.	xxx

D) Sale of Scrap

Before calculating the works cost, the amount received by way of sale of scrap is to be deducted from the works/ factory ovehead.

Proforma of Cost Sheet

Cost Sheet

Period Ending	Rs.	Units Produced Total Cost (Rs.)	Per Unit Cost (Rs.)
DIRECT MATERIAL :			
Opening Stock of raw material	xxxxxx		
Add : Purchases	xxxxxx		
	xxxxxx		
Less : Closing Stock of raw materials	xxxxxx		
Materials consumed	xxxxxx	xxxxxx	xxxxxx
Direct Wages		xxxxxx	xxxxxx
Direct Expenses		xxxxxx	xxxxxx
(a) Prime Cost		xxxxxx	xxxxxx
Works/Factory overheads :			
Fuel, Power and Water (Factory)	xxxxxx		
Heating and Lighting	xxxxxx		
Indirect Material	xxxxxx		
Wages of supervisors foremen and other indirect labourers	xxxxxx		
Works, Office Expsenses	xxxxxx		
Rent, Taxes and Insurance (factory)	xxxxxx		
Depreciation :			
Factory land and building	xxxxxx		
Plant and Machinery	xxxxxx		
	xxxxxx	xxxxxx	
Less: Sale of scrap	xxxxxx		
Add: Opening work in progress	xxxxxx	xxxxxx	
Less: Closing work-in progress		xxxxxx	

Table continued on next page

	Rs.	Total Cost (Rs.)	Per Unit Cost (Rs.)
(b) Works Cost		xxxxxx	xxxxxx
Administrative Overheads :			
Rent, Taxes, and Insurance (Office)	xxxxxx		
Lighting and Cleaning (Office)	xxxxxx		
Salary (Office)	xxxxxx		
Telephone (Office)	xxxxxx		
Printing & Stationery	xxxxxx		
Legal fees, Audit fees etc.	xxxxxx		
Director's fees/ Remuneration	xxxxxx		
General Manager's Salary	xxxxxx	xxxxxx	xxxxxx
(c) Total Cost of Production		xxxxxx	xxxxxx
Add: Opening Stock of finished goods		xxxxxx	xxxxxx
Less: Closing Stock of of finished goods		xxxxxx	xxxxxx
		xxxxxx	xxxxxx
Selling & Distribution Overheads :			
Expenses on show room	xxxxxx		
Salaries and commission of salesmen	xxxxxx		
Warehouse rent and other expenses	xxxxxx		
Advertising expenses	xxxxxx		
Delivery expenses	xxxxxx		
Carriage Outward	xxxxxx		
Discounts allowed	xxxxxx		
Bad debts		xxxxxx	xxxxxx
(d) Cost of Sales		xxxxxx	xxxxxx
Profit		xxxxxx	xxxxxx
(e) Selling Price		xxxxxx	xxxxxx

Practical Problems

Problem 1

From the following information supplied for A Ltd, prepare a statement showing the cost of production and goods sold for the period from 1.1.200X to 31.1.200X.

Stock of raw material as on 1.1.200X	Rs.	40,00,000
Raw materials purchased during the month	Rs.	5,00,00,000
Wages paid	Rs.	2,50,00,000
Factory overheads	Rs.	80,00,000
Work in progress (1.1.200X)	Rs.	10,00,000
Work in -progress (31.1.200X)	Rs.	20,00,000
Closing Stock of raw materials as on (31.1.200X)	Rs.	30,00,000
Opening Stock of finished Goods (1.1.200X)	Rs.	80,00,000
Closing Stock of finished Goods (31.1.200X)	Rs.	70,00,000
Selling & Distributions Overheads	Rs.	10,00,000
Administrative Overheads	Rs.	25,00,000
Sales	Rs.	10,00,00,000

Solution

In the books of A Ltd.

Statement of Cost for the month ended 31.1.200X

Direct Material	**Rs.**	**Rs.**
Stock as on 1.1.200X	40,00,000	
Purchases during the month	5,00,00,000	
	5,40,00,000	
Less : Closing Stock as on 31.1.200X	30,00,000	5,10,00,000
Direct wages		2,50,00,000
Prime Cost :		7,60,00,000
Factory overheads		80,00,000
		8,40,00,000
Add : Work in progress (1.1.200X)		10,00,000
		8,50,00,000
Less : Work in progress (31.1.200X)		20,00,000
Works Cost :		8,30,00,000
Administrative Overheads		25,00,000
Cost of Production :		8,55,00,000
Add : Opening Stock of finished goods (1.1.200X)		8,000,000
		9,35,00,000
Less : Closing stock of finished goods (31.1.200X)		70,00,000
		8,65,00,000
Selling and Distribution Overheads		1,00,00,000
Cost of Sales :		8,75,00,000
Sales		10,00,00,000
Profit		1,25,00,000

Problem 2

M/s Sunit & Vinayak Co. manufactures plastic jars and furnish you with the following particulars. You are required to prepare a Cost Sheet for the period ended 31.12.200X. Showing therein the Prime Cost, Works Cost, Cost of Production and Cost of Sales alongwith Cost per unit and percentage of each element of cost to total cost.

Units Produced **1,000**	**Rs.**
Material consumed	10,000
Wages paid to workers	4,000
Power and fuel (factory)	2,000
Repairs of Machines	800
Depreciation-Machinery	600
Depreciation-Office Furniture	200
Supervision expenses (factory)	200
Hire charges for machines of special purposes	400

Units Produced	1,000	Rs.
Wages paid to maintenance workers		2,000
Audit Fees		150
Director's fees		750
Bad debts		250
Office expenses		350
Salaries		200
Rent, Rates and Taxes (factory)		500
Sales		30,000
Salesmen Salary		800
Advertising expenses		200
Delivery van expenses		800
Warehouse Rent		600
Printing & Stationery		100
Direct expenses		800

Solution

Sunit & Vinayak Co.
Cost sheet for the period ended 31.12.200X

Elements of Cost	Cost/Unit (Rs.)	% to total cost Rs.	Total Rs.
Material Consumed	10.00	42.37	10,000
Wages paid to workers	4.00	16.95	4,000
Hire charges for machines	0.40	1.69	400
Direct expenses	0.80	3.39	800
Prime Cost	**15.20**	**64.40**	**15,200**
Manufacturing Overheads :			
Wages paid to maintenance workers	2.00	8.47	2,000
Repairs to machines	0.80	3.39	800
Supervision expenses (factory)	0.20	0.85	200
Depreciation -Machinery	0.60	2.54	600
Rent, rates and taxes (factory)	0.50	2.12	500
Works cost Administrative Overheads	**19.30**	**81.77**	**19,300**
Depreciation - Office furniture	0.10	0.42	100
Audit Fees	0.15	0.64	150
Directors fees	0.75	3.18	750
Office Expenses	0.35	1.48	350
Salaries	0.20	0.85	200
Printing & Stationery	0.10	0.43	100
Cost of Production	**20.95**	**88.77**	**20,950**

Selling and Distribution Overheads			
Salesman's Salary	0.80	3.39	800
Advertising expenses	0.20	0.85	200
Bad debts	0.25	1.06	250
Delivery van Expenses.	0.80	3.39	800
Warehouse Rent	0.60	2.54	600
Cost of Sales/Total Cost	**23.60**	**100.00**	**23,600**
Profit	**6.40**		**6,400**
Sales	**30.00**		**30,000**

Problem 3

From the following particulars of Finolex Co. prepare a Cost Sheet showing a) Prime cost b) Factory cost c) Total Cost of production and d) Cost of Sales for the period ended 30.6.200X

	Rs.
Raw material consumed	25,000
Wages paid to workers	10,000
Direct expenses incurred for production	1,250
Consumable stores	250
Supervisor's wages	1,000
Wages paid to shop floor helper	300
Electric Power (Factory)	400
Electric Power (Office)	250
Rent (factory)	2,500
Rent (office)	1,000
Repairs and Renewals on :	
Plant and Machinery	2,500
Renovation of office building	500
Depreciation on Plant and Machinery	250
Depreciation on Office building	100
Manager's Salary	1,500
Telephone charges	100
Printing & Stationery	200
Postage and Telegram	75
Director's fees	400
Advertisement	400
Travelling Exps.	150
Salesmen's Salary and commission	500
Warehouse rent	450
Delivery van Expenses.	500
	49,575

Solution

Finolex Co.

Cost Sheet for the period ended 30.6.200X

			Rs.
Direct Material	:	Raw material consumed	25,000
Direct labour	:	Wages paid to workers	10,000
Direct expenses	:	Expenses incurred for production	1,250
		(I) Prime Cost	36,250
Add : Factory overheads :			
Indirect Materials	:	Consumable stores	250
Indirect labour	:	Supervisors wages	1,000
		Wages paid to shop floor helper	300
Indirect Expenses :			
Electric power (Factory)			400
Rent (Factory)			2,500
Repairs and Renewals :			
Plant and Machinery			2,500
Depreciation :			
On Plant and Machinery			250
		(II) Factory Cost / Works Cost	43,450
Add : Administrative Expenses :			
Electric power (Office)			250
Rent (Office)			1,000
Renovation of office building			500
Depreciation			100
Manager's Salary			1,500
Telephone charges			100
Printing & Stationery			200
Postage and Telegrams			75
Directors fees			400
		(III) Total cost of Production	47,575
Add : Selling and Distribution Overheads :-			
Advertisement			400
Travelling Expenses			150
Salesman's Salary and Commission			500
Warehouse Rent			450
Delivery van Expenses.			500
		(IV) Cost of Sales	49,575

Problem 4

M/s Ganesh Foundry Works Ltd. Produce machine parts. From the following particulars prepare Cost Sheet for the period ended 31.12.200X

	Rs.
Opening stock of raw materials	20,00,000
Raw material purchased	70,00,000
Closing Stock of raw materials	15,00,000
Direct Labour Cost (20% of Factory on Cost). Factory on Cost	30,00,000
Administrative Overheads (10% of Works Cost). Selling and Distribution Expenses	10,00,000

Details of the finished goods are as follows :-

Opening stock of finished goods	2000 units	Rs. 25,00,000
Finished goods produced during the period	20,000 units	
Closing Stock of finished goods	4000 units	

You are required to find out the profit made during the year @ 10% on the Selling price

Note : a) There was no balance of opening or closing stock of work-in-progress

b) Show the working of profit how ascertained.

Solution

M/s Ganesh Foundry Work Ltd.

Cost Sheet for the period ended 31.12.200X

Unit produced - 20,000

Element of Cost		**Cost/Unit (Rs.)**	**Total Cost (Rs.)**
Raw Material consumed :-			
Opening stock of raw material	Rs. 20,00,000		
Add : Purchases	Rs. 70,00,000		
	Rs. 90,00,000		
Less : Closing Stock	Rs. 15,00,000	375	75,00,000
Direct Labour Cost (20% of Factory on Cost) i.e. $\frac{20}{100} \times \frac{30,000}{1}$		030	6,00,000
Prime Cost		405	81,00,000
Add : Factory on Cost		150	30,00,000
Works Cost		555	1,11,00,000
Add : Administrative Overheads (10% of Works Cost) $\frac{10}{100} \times \frac{1,11,00,000}{1}$		055	11,10,000
Cost of Production		610	1,22,10,000

WORKING OF PROFIT

	Units	Cost (Rs.)
Opening Stock of finished goods	2,000	25,00,000
Produced during the period	20,000	1,22,10,000
	22,000	1,47,10,000
Less : Closing Stock (Value 4,000 x Rs.6.10)	4,000	24,40,000
	18,000	1,22,70,000
Add : Selling and Distribution expenses		10,00,000
Cost of goods sold	18,000	1,32,70,000
Add : Profit (10% on selling price)		14,74,400
Sales	18,000	1,47,44,400

Working of Profit - Calculation :

Let the Selling price be Rs. 10,000

and the profit given is 10% (-) Rs. 1,000

Then the Cost Price is Rs. 9,000

Thus with simple arithmetic we can find out the Total Profits as :

When Rs. 9,000 is the cost .... Rs. 1,000 the profit

∴ When Rs. 1,32,70,000 is the cost ....?

$$\text{Profit} \quad \frac{1{,}000}{9{,}000} \frac{\times 1{,}32{,}70{,}000}{\times \quad 1} \quad \text{Rs. } 14{,}74{,}400$$

Problem 5

AVM Ltd. manufacturer produces two types of Washing Machines i.e. Local model and Semi auto model. He sells both the models at the same price of Rs.12,000 per piece. From the following details prepare a statement showing cost and profit per washing machine sold.

	Local Model	Semi Auto Model
Direct Material	Rs.15,00,000	Rs. 21,25,000
Direct Labour	Rs.10,00,000	Rs. 13,75,000
Works Overhead :	60% on Labour cost	
Administrative Overhead :	20% on Works cost	
No. of pieces sold :		
Local Model :	400 Nos.	
Semi-Auto Model :	500 Nos.	

Solution

Statement of Cost and Profit of AVM Ltd.,

	Local Model Sold : 400 Units		**Semi Auto Model Sold : 500 Units**	
	Per Unit Rs.	**Total Rs.**	**Per Unit**	**Total Rs.**
Direct Material	3,750	15,00,000	4,250	21,25,000
Direct Labour	2,500	10,00,000	2,750	13,75,000
Prime Cost	6,250	25,00,000	7,000	35,00,000
Works Overhead (60% on labour cost)	1,500	6,00,000	1650	8,25,000
Work Cost	7,750	31,00,000	8,650	43,25,000
Administrative Overheads (20% on Works Cost)	1,550	6,20,000	1,730	8,65,000
Cost of Production	9,300	37,20,000	10,380	51,90,000
Profit	2,700	10,80,000	4,620	8,10,000
Sales	12,000	48,00,000	12,000	60,00,000

Problem 6

The accounts of Himatlal Co. Ltd. for the year ended 31.3. 2004 show the following :

	Rs.
Design Office Salaries	65,000
Counting-House-Salaries	1,26,000
Cash-Discount Allowed	29,000
Carriage and Cartage Outwards	43,000
Carriage and Cartage Inwards	71,500
Bad Debts written off	65,000
Repairs of Plant, Machinery and Tools	44,500
Rent, Rates, Taxes and Insurance (Factory)	85,000
Rent Rates taxes Insurance (Office)	20,000
Sales	46,11,000
Stock of Materials 31.3.2003	6,28,000
31.3.2004	4,80,000
Materials Purchased	18,50,000
Travelling Expenses	21,000
Traveller's Salaries and Commission	77,000
Productive Wages	12,60,000
Depreciation - Plant, Machinery and Tools	65,000
- Furniture	3,000
Director's Fees	60,000
Gas and Water (Factory)	12,000
Gas & Water (Office)	4,000
Manager's Salary (3/4 Factory and 1/4 office)	1,00,000
General Expenses	34,000
Income-tax	10,000
Dividend	20,000

Prepare a statement giving the following information :

(i) Materials consumed (ii) Prime cost (iii) Factory on cost and the percentage on wages (iv) Factory cost (v) General On Cost and the Percentage on Factory Cost (vi) Total Cost (vii) Net Profit

Solution : Himatlal Co.. Ltd. Statement of Cost for the year ended 31.3.2004

	Rs.
Stock of Materials on 31.3.2003	6,28,000
Add : Materials purchased during the year	18,50,000
Add : Carriage and Cartage Inwards	71,500
	25,49,500
Less : Stock of Materials on 31.3.2004	4,80,000
(I) Materials Consumed	20,69,500
Productive Wages	12,60,000
(II) Prime cost	33,29,500
Factory Overheads :	
Design Office Salaries	65,000
Repairs of Plant, Machinery and Tools	44,500
Depreciation on Plant, Machinery and Tools	65,000
Rent, Rates, Taxes and Insurance- Factory	85,000
Gas and Water-Factory	12,000
Manager's Salary 3/4 Factory (i.e. 3/4 of Rs. 1,00,000)	75,000
(III) Factory on Cost	3,46,500
(IV) Factory Cost	36,76,000
General Overheads :	
A) Administrative Overheads :	
Counting House Salaries	1,26,000
Rent, Rates, Taxes and Insurance -Office	20,000
Depreciation on Furniture	3,000
Directors fees	60,000
Gas and Water Office	4,000
Manager's Salary (Office) 1/4 of Rs. 1,00,000	25,000
General Expenses	34,000
	2,72,000
B) Selling and Distribution Overheads :	
Carriage and Cartage Outward	43,000
Bad Debts Written Off	65,000
Travelling Expenses	21,000
Traveller's Salaries and Commission	77,000
(V) General on Costs	4,78,000
(VI) Total Cost	41,54,000
(VII) Net Profit	4,57,000
Sales	46,11,000

Note : General overheads includes administrative and Selling and Distribution overheads.

A) Percentage of Factory Overheads to Wages : $\frac{3,46,500 \times 100}{12,60,000}$ = 27.5%

B) Percentage of General overheads on Factory Cost : $\frac{4,78,000 \times 100}{36,76,000}$ 13%

Problem 7

A factory produces a standard product. The following information is given to you from which you are required to prepare Cost Sheet for the period ended 31. 7.200X

Consumable Materials :		Rs.
Opening Stock		10,00,000
Purchases		85,00,000
Closing stock		4,00,000
Direct Wages		20,00,000
Other Direct expenses.		10,00,000
Factory Overheads	100% of Direct labour	
Office overheads	10% of Works Cost	
Selling and Distribution Expenses	Rs. 2 per unit sold	
Units of Finished Products :		
In hand at the beginning of the period	1000	(Value Rs. 16,00,000)
Produced during the period		10,00,000
In hand at the end of the period		2,00,000

Also find out the selling price per unit on the basis that profit mark up is uniformly made to yield a profit of 20% of the selling price. There were no work-in-progress either at the beginning or at the end of the period.

Solution

COST SHEET (for the period ending 31.7.200X)

		Per Unit (Rs.)	Total (10,000 Units) (Rs.)
Opening stock	10,00,000		
Add : Purchases	85,00,000		
	95,00,000		
Less :- Closing Stock	4,00,000		
Material Consumed		910	91,00,000
Direct Wages		200	20,00,000
Direct Exps.		100	10,00,000
Prime Cost		1210	1,2100,000
(Factory Ovehead 100% of works-cost		141	20,00,000
Work cost		1410	1,41,00,000
Office overheads (10% of works costs)		200	14,10,000
Cost of production Statement of Profit (Sales 9000 Units)		1551	1,55,10,000
Cost of Prouduction			1,55,10,000
Add: Opening Stock of finished products			16,00,000
			1,71,10,000
Less: Closing Stock of finished product @ Rs. 15.51 per unit)			31,02,000
Cost of Goods sold			1,40,08,000
Profit (20% on sales)			39,52,000
Sales			1,79,60,000

Selling Price per unit 1,79,60,000 ÷ 9,000 Rs. 1,79,69,000

Problem 8

Prepare a Statement of Cost from the following information relating to Mumbai Traders, Mumbai for the year ended 31-03-200X.

	Rs.
Cost of Direct materials	2,00,000
Sales	4,00,000
Direct Wages	1,00,000
Office Indirect Materials	5,000
Cost of special patterns	40,000
Postage and Telegrams	2,000
Factory Rent and Insurance	5,000
Outstanding Chargeable Expenses	2,000
Carriage Outward	2,500
Interest on Loan	2,150
Printing and Stationery	500
Factory Indirect wages	3,000
Selling on cost	4,000
Travelling salesman's salary	4,000
Factory Indirect Material	1,000
Royalties	8,000
General Works Overhead	2,000
Bad debts written-off	1,000

Also calculate the percentage of profits earned to sales.

Solution

In the books of Mumbai Traders, Mumbai

Statement of Cost for the year ended 31-03-200X

Particulars		Amount Rs.	Amount Rs.
Cost of Direct Materials		2,00,000	
Add : Direct Wages		1,00,000	
Add : Direct Expenses			
(1) Cost of Special Patterns		40,000	
(2) Outstanding Chargeable Expenses		2,000	
(3) Royalties		8,000	
PRIME COST	(1)	3,50,000	3,50,000
Add : Factory Expenses :			
(1) Factory Rent and Insurance		5,000	
(2) Factory Indirect Wages		3,000	
(3) Factory Indirect Material		1,000	
(4) General Works Overheads		2,000	
FACTORY COST	(2)	3,61,000	3,61,000

Add : Office Expenses :			
(1) Office Indirect Materials		5,000	
(2) Postage and Telegrams		2,000	
(3) Printing and Stationery		500	
COST OF PRODUCTION	(3)	3,68,500	3,68,500
Add : Selling and Distribution Expenses :			
(1) Carriage Outward		2,500	
(2) Selling on Cost		4,000	
(3) Travelling Saleman's Salary		4,000	
(4) Bad debts written-off		1,000	
TOTAL COST	(4)	3,80,000	3,80,000
Add : PROFITS FOR THE YEAR	(5)	20,000	20,000
Sales		**4,00,000**	4,00,000

Calculation and Notes

(1) calculation of percentage of profits earned to sales

For Rs. 4,00,000 Sales Rs. 20,000 profits.

100 = ?

$$\frac{100 \times 20,000}{4,00,000}$$

5%

(N.B. : Interest on loan is an item to be excluded from cost)

Problem 9

From the following particulars relating to M/s Chandmal Bros., Chinchwad, prepare Cost-Sheet showing (a) Prime Cost, (b) Factory Cost, (c) Cost of Production, (d) Cost of Sales, (e) Profit & Loss for the period, for six months ended 31 - 03 - 200X.

	Rs.
Cost of materials consumed	40,000
Oil and waste	100
Operating labour	9,000
Wages of Foreman	1,000
Direct expenses	2,000
Store keepers wages	500
Sales	1,00,000
Commission paid to the partner, Mr. Chandmal	350
Electric Power	200
Salary paid to the partner, Mr.Rajmal	650
Consumable stores	1,000
Direct wages payable	1,000

Lighting:	
(i) Factory	500
(ii) Office	200
Carriage Outward	150
Rent:	
(i) Office	1,000
(ii) Factory	2,000
Warehouse charges	200
Repairs and Renewals :	
(i) Factory Plant	500
(ii) Machinery	1,000
(iii) Office Premises	200
(iv) Warehouse	100
Advertising	400
Depreciation:	
(i) Office Premises	500
(ii) Machinery	200
Travelling expenses	200
Office Manager's salary	2,250
Salesmen's commission and salaries	500
Director's fees	500
Printing and Stationery	200
Telephone charges	50
Postage	100
Bad Debts	450

Solution

In the books of Chandmal Bros. Chinchwad

Cost-Sheet

for the six months ended 31-03-200X

Particulars		Amount Rs.	Amount Rs.
Cost of materials consumed		40,000	
Add : Direct Labour :			
(1) Operating labour		9,000	
(2) Direct wages payable		1,000	
Add : Direct expenses		2,000	
PRIME COST	(a)	52,000	52,000
Add : Factory Expenses:			
(1) Oil and waste		100	
(2) Wages of Foreman		1,000	
(3) Store keepers wages		500	

(4) Electric power		200	
(5) Consumable stores		1,000	
(6) Factory lighting		500	
(7) Factory Rent		2,000	
(8) Repairs and Renewals - Factory Plant		500	
(9) Repairs and Renewals - Machinery		1,000	
(10) Depreciation - Machinery	+	200	
FACTORY COST	(b)	59,000	59,000
Add : Office Expenses:			
(1) Office Lighting		200	
(2) Office Rent		1,000	
(3) Repairs and Renewals - Office Premises		200	
(4) Depreciation - Office Premises		500	
(5) Office Manager's Salary		2,250	
(6) Director's Feers		500	
(7) Printing and Stationery		200	
(8) Telephone charges		50	
(9) Postage	+	100	
COST OF PRODUCTION	(c)	64,000	64,000
Add : Selling and Distribution Expenses :			
(1) Carriage Outward		150	
(2) Warehouse charges		200	
(3) Repairs and renewals - Warehouse		100	
(4) Advertising		400	
(5) Travelling Expenses		200	
(6) Salesmen's commission and salaries		500	
(7) Bad Debts	+	450	
COST OF SALES	(d)	66,000	66,000
Add : PROFIT FOR THE PERIOD	(e) +	34,000	34,000
SALES		1,00,000	1,00,000

(N.B.: Commission paid to the partner Mr. Chandmal and salary paid to the partner Mr.Rajmal are the items to be excluded from cost).

Problem 10

The expenditure incurred in the manufacturing and selling of product X' for the three months ended 31-03-200X is as given below :

	Rs.
Direct material cost	30,000
Engineers fees	1,000
Power and Fuel	7,000
Wages payable	2,000
Office salary	5,000
Trade Discount	500

Chargeable Expenses	4,000
Haulage	3,000
General on cost	1,000
Catalogue Expenses	1,500
Process and Operating Wages	13,000
Time-keeping expenses	2,000
Electricity charges	2,000
Donations for Kargil Fund	1,000
Tendering Expenses	1,000
Commission on Sales	2,500

Tons manufactured and sold - 1000

Prepare a Cost-Sheet of Modern Mnufacturers. Malad showing the cost for each element, the total cost per ton and the profits if the sales are made at Rs. 100 per ton.

Solution

In the books of Modern Manufacturers, Malad

Cost-Sheet for Product X'

for the three months ended 31-3-200X

Units Produced - 1000 Tons

Units Sold - 1000 Tons

Particulars			Amount Rs.	Amount Rs.
Direct Material Cost			30,000	30.00
Add : Direct Labour:				
(1) Process and Operating Wages		13,000		
(2) Wages payable	+	2,000	15,000	15.00
Add : Direct Expenses:				
(1) Engineers Fees		1,000		
(2) Chargeal Expenses	+	4,000	5,000	5.00
		+		
PRIME COST	(1)		50,000	50.00
Add : Factory Expenses :				
(1) Power and Fuel		7,000		
(2) Haulage		3,000		
(3) Time-keeping expenses	+	2,000	12,000	12.00
		+		
FACTOR COST	(2)		62,000	62.00
Add : Office Expenses :				
(1) Office salary		5,000		
(2) General cost		1,000		
(3) Electricity charges	+	2,000	8,000	8.00

Table continued on next page

COST OF PRODUCTION	(3) +		70,000	70.00
Add : Selling and Distribution Expenses:				
(1) Catalogue Expenses		1,500		
(2) Tendering Expenses		1,000		
(3) Commission on Sales	+	2,500	5,000	5.00
TOTAL COST	(4)		75,000	75.00
Add : PROFITS	(5)	+	25,000	25.00
Sales : (1,000 tons x Rs. 100			1,00,00	100.00

(N.B.: Trade discount and donations for Kargi Fund are the items to be excluded from cost).

Problem 11

The following is the Trading and Profit Loss A/c of Sarabhai chemicals Ltd. Sion for the year ended 31-03-200X.

	Rs.	Rs.		Rs.	Rs.
To Opening Stock of Raw Materials		18,000	By Sales	5,10,000	
To Purchases of Raw Materials	2,52,000		Less : Returns Inward	- 10,000	5,00,000
Less : Returns Outward	2,000	2,50,000	By Closing Stock of Raw Materials		10,000
To direct wages		1,02,000	By Sale of scrap of raw materials		1,000
To Carriage		25,000			
To Royalty		7,200			
To Gas and Water		19,000			
To Custom charges		8,000			
To Wages Payable		8,000			
To Chargeable expenses outstanding		2,800			
To Heating and Lighting		11,000			
To Gross Profit C/D*		60,000			
		5,11,000			**5,11,000**
To Carriage		5,000	By Gross Profit B/D		60,000
To Preliminary expenses		5,500	By Discount received		10,000
To Underwriting commission		4,500	By Interst on investment		12,000
To Commission on Sales		7,600	By Commission		8,000
To Sales Report Expenses		2,400			
To Discount on issue o f shares		6,000			
To salaries		16,000			
To Bad debts provision		1,000			
To Property tax on Office Buildings		2,000			
To Income Tax		5,000			
To Depreciation on Office Furniture		2,000			
To Donations		4,000			
To Net Profit C/D*		29,000			
		90,000			**90,000**

You are required to prepare a Cost-Statement for the year ended 31-03-200X showing

(1) Cost of materials consumed	(2) Prime Cost
(3) Works Cost	(4) Cost of Production
(5) Total Cost	(6) Profits for the year

Also calculate the precentage of profit on sales.

Solution

In the books of Sarabhai Chemicals Ltd,; Sion
Cost-Statement
for the year ended 31-03-200X

Particulars			Amount Rs.	Amount Rs.
Opening Stock of Raw Materials			18,000	
Add : Purchases of Raw Materils			2,52,000	
Add : Expenses for Purchases:			33,000	
(1) Carriage		25,000		
(2) Custom charges	+	8,000		
		+	3,03,000	
Less : Closing stock of Raw Materials		-	10,000	
Less : Sale of Scrap of Raw Materials		-	1,000	
Less : Returns Outward		-	2,000	
COST OF MATERIALS CONSUMED	(1)		2,90,000	2,90,000
Add : Direct Labour :				
(1) Direct wages		1,02,000		
(2) Wages payable	+	8,000	1,10,000	
Add : Direct expenses :				
(1) Royalty		7,200		
(2) Chargeable expenses outstanding	+	2,800	10,000	
PRIME COST	(2)		4,10,000	4,10,000
Add : Factory Expenses:				
(1) Gas and Water		19,000		
(2) Heating and Lighting	+	11,000	30,000	
WORKS COST	(3)		4,40,000	4,40,000
Add : Office Expenses :				
(1) Salaries		16,000		
(2) Property Tax on Office Buildings		2,000		
(3) Depreciation on Office Furniture	+	2,000	20,000	
COST OF PRODUCTION	(4)		4,60,000	4,60,000
Add : Selling and Distribution Expenses:				
(1) Carriage		5,000		
(2) Commission on Sales		7,600		
(3) Sales Depot expenses	+	2,400	15,000	
TOTAL COST	(5)		4,75,000	4,75,000
Add : PROFIT FOR THE YEAR	(6)	+	25,000	25,000
Sales			5,00,000	5,00,000

Calculation and Notes

(1) calculation of percentage of profit on sales

If Rs. 5,00,000 Sales   Rs. 25,000 profits.

100   = ?

$$\frac{100 \times 25,000}{5,00,000} = 5\%$$

(N.B. Preliminary Expenses, Underwriting Commission, discount on issue of Shares, Bad debts provision, Income Tax, Donations given, Discount received, Interest on Investment, Commission received etc. are the items to be excluded from cost)

Problem 12

The cost of turnover of a particular product is made up of the following cost as on 31-03-200X

	Rs.
Loading and unloading on Materials Purchased	950
Productive wages payable	900
Materials used in factory	2,100
Sales of scrap - Raw materials	750
Salary to watch and ward staff	1,100
Materials used in office	600
Godown Rent	3,500
Materials used in manufacturing-direct	55,750
Labour required for factory supervision	1,800
Cost of special drawings	3,300
Expenses of management	1,200
Materials used in selling and distribution	1,500
Freight Inward	4,050
Delivery van running expenses	1,000
Hire of plant	1,700
Labour required in production-direct	9,100
Office supplies and expenses	2,200
Materials used in primary packing	10,000

Assuming that all goods manufactured are sold, what should be the selling price to obtain a profit of 20% on value of turnover?

Prepare a Cost-Sheet of Super Ltd., Saswad showing :

(1) Direct material Cost

(2) Prime Cost

(3) Factory Cost

(4) Cost of Production

(5) Cost of Turnover

(6) Selling Price

Solution

In the books of super Ltd., Saswad
Cost-Sheet
for the year ended 31-03-200X

Particulars			Amount Rs.	Amount Rs.
Materials used in manufacturing-direct			55,750	
Add : Materials used in primary packing		+	10,000	
Add : Expenses on purchases of materials :				
(1) Loading and unloading			950	
(2) Freight Inward		+	4,050	
			70,750	
Less : Sale of scrap-raw materials		-	750	
DIRECT MATERIAL COST	(1)		70,000	70,000
Add : Direct Labour				
(1) Labour required in Production-Direct	+	9,100		
(2) Productive wages payable	+	900	10,000	
Add : Direct Expenses:				
(1) Cost of special drawings		3,300		
(2) Hire of plant	+	1,700	5,000	
PRIME COST	(2)		85,000	85,000
Add : Factory Overheads :				
(1) Materials used in factory			2,100	
(2) Salary to watch and ward staff			1,100	
(3) Labour required for factory supervision	+		1,800	
FACTORY COST	(3)		90,000	90,000
Add : Office Overheads :				
(1) Materials used in office			600	
(2) Expenses of Management			1,200	
(3) Office supplies and expenses		+	2,200	
COST OF PRODUCTION	(4)		94,000	94,000
Add : Selling and dsitribution Overheads :				
(1) Godown rent			3,500	
(2) Material used in selling and distribution			1,500	
(3) Delivery Van running expenses		+	1,000	
COST OF TURNOVER	(5)		1,00,000	1,00,000
Add : Profits (20% on value of turnover)		+	25,000	25,000
SELLING PRICE	(6)		**1,25,000**	**1,25,000**

Calculation and Notes

(1) calculation of profit i.e. 20% on value of turnover.

SP	=	CP + P
i.e. value of turnover 100	=	80 + 20
If 80 CP	=	20 P
Rs. 1,00,000 C.T.	=	?
	=	$\frac{1,00,000 \times 20}{80}$
	=	Rs. 25,000

Problem 13

The following data have been extracted from the books of M/s Sunshine Industries Ltd., Solapur for the calender year 200X.

	Rs.
Opening stock of Process Materials	25,000
Wages - Direct	70,000
Rent and Taxes	5,500
(Factory - 10/11, Office - 1/11)	
Freight on purchases of Raw Materials	5,000
Indirect Materials	500
Sales promotion charges	2,000
Purchases of Raw Materials	85,000
Interest on Debentures	5,200
Depreciation :	
(i) Plant and Machinery	1,500
(ii) Office Equipment	1,000
Closing Stock of Process Materials	35,000
Wages - Indirect	10,000
Cost of designs and drawings	12,000
Salaries :	
(i) Office Staff	2,500
(ii) Travelling Salesmen	2,000
Production Expenses	3,000
Defective materials returned - process material	5,000
Other works on cost	5,700
Office overheads	4,900
Manager's Remuneration	
(i) Works	2,300
(ii) Office	6,100
Productive Wages due but not paid	5,000
Irrecoverable debts	1,000
Sales	2,50,000
Debt collection charges	1,100
Advance payment of income tax	20,000
Selling on cost	3,900

Prepare a Statement of cost showing profits earned during the year 200X.

Solution

In the books of M/s Sunshine Industries Ltd. Solapur
Statement of Cost
for the calender year 200X

Particulars		Amount Rs.	Amount Rs.
Opening Stock of Process Materials		25,000	
Add : Purchases of Raw Materials		85,000	
Add : Freight on purchases of Raw Materials		5,000	
		1,15,000	
Less: Closing Stock of Process Materials		35,000	
Less: Defective Material returned - Process Materials		5,000	
COST OF MATERIALS CONSUMED	(1)	75,000	75,000
Add : Direct Labour :			
(1) Wages - Direct		70,000	
(2) Productive wages due but not paid		5,000	
Add : Direct Expenses :			
(1) Cost of designs and drawings		12,000	
(2) Productive expenses		3,000	
PRIME COST	(2)	1,65,000	1,65,000
Add : Factory Expenses:			
(1) Rent and Taxes - Factory (10/11 x Rs. 5,500)		5,000	
(2) Indirect Materials		500	
(3) Depreciation on Plant and Mchinery		1,500	
(4) Wages - Indirect		10,000	
(5) Other works on cost		5,700	
(6) Works Manager's Remuneration		2,300	
WORKS COST	(3)	1,90,000	1,90,000
Add : Office Expenses :			
(1) Rent and Taxes - Office (1/11 x Rs,5,500)		500	
(2) Depareciation on Office Equipments		1,000	
(3) Salaries - Office staff		2,500	
(4) Office overheads		4,900	
(5) Office Manager's Remuneration		6,100	
COST OF PRODUCTION	(4)	2,05,000	2,05,000
Add : Selling and Distribution Expenses :			
(1) Sales promotion charges		2,000	
(2) Salaries - Travelling salesmen		2,000	
(3) Irrecoverable debts		1,000	
(4) Debts collection charges		1,100	
(5) Selling on cost		3,900	
TOTAL COST	(5)	2,15,000	2,15,000
Add : PROFITS EARNED	(6)	35,000	35,000
Sales		2,50,000	2,50,000

(N.B. Interst on Debentures, Advance payment of Income-Tax etc. are the items to be excluded from cost)

Questions for Self-Study

1) Discuss the various elements of cost and draw a chart and a statement to illustrate your answer.

2) Define and distinguish between Direct and Indirect Expenditure.

3) What do you mean by Direct Material ? Explain with suitable examples.

4) What are the main types of overheads ? Explain Production Overheads & Administrative Overheads.

5) State any five examples of each of the following expenses :-

   a) Production Overheads   b)Administrative   c) Selling   d) Dsitribution Expenses

6) What are the different types of classification by nature or element?

7) What is cost sheet ? Give a proforma of a cost heet.

8) Write short notes on :

   a) Direct Material   b) Direct Labour   c) Direct Expenses   d) Selling Overheads

   e) Administrative Overheads   f) Distribution Overheads   g) Types of Cost   h) Cost Sheet

   i) Imputed Cost   j) Joint Cost   k) Benefits of Cost Sheet.

9) State following statement are true or false :-

   a) The wages which cannot be charged directly to production are known as indirect wages.

   b) Indirect materials are those which do form part of finished product.

   c) The expenses which are neither indirect material, nor indirect labour are known as indirect expenses.

   d) Salary of the sales manager is an example of administrative overhead .

   e) Warehouse rent and insurance is an example of direct expenditure.

   f) The first part of the cost sheet shows the cost of production.

10) Match the pairs :

Group A	**Group B**
1) Marginal Costs	a) Predetermined Cost
2) Standard Costs	b) Variable Cost
3) Sunk Costs	c) For decision making process
4) Imputed costs	d) Undepreciated value
5) Joint Costs	e) Use of single raw material
6) Traceable Costs	f) Common cost
	g) Related with cost unit

Group I	**Group II**
a) Works Overheads	1) Showroom Expenses
b) Administrative Overheads	2) Gas, Coal, Oil
c) Selling Overheads	3) Office rent
d) Distribution Expenses	4) Carriage outward
e) Direct Material	5) Super vision Exp.
f) Direct Labour	6) Screws for machines
g) Direct Expenses	7) Audit Fees
	8) Excise Duty Paid

11) Fill in the gaps .

a) Direct materials form part of the...........(Administrative Cost /Finished Product / Selling Cost.)

b) Indirect materials are those which ....form of the finished product (do/do not/always)

c) Salaries and Wgaes paid to foremen is ....expenditure. (Direct Labour /Indirect Labour/Not at all)

d) Expenses incurred for purchases of stores are ....Work Overheads / Administrative Overheads / Selling Overheads).

e) The Variable Cost of a product is nothing but ....(Marginal Cost /Standard Cost /Conversion Cost)

f) Cost Sheet is prepared in order to find out the ....Cost of production. (Raw material /labour / Total)

Problem 1

The accounts of Dorabjee manufacturers, Deolali for the year ended 31-3-200X shows the following

	Rs.
Stock of Raw materials as on 1-4-200X	67,200
bad debts written-off	9,100
Raw materials purchased	2,59,000
Motive Power	320
Traveller's Commission	10,780
Depreciation on Office equiments	420
Carriage Inwards	720
Interest on Bank Loan	380
Factory Taxes	11,900
Production wages	1,76,400
Director's Travelling Expenses	8,400
Coal and Coke	560
General Overheads	4,760
Gas and Water - Factory	1,680
Packing charges	940
Sales of finished goods	6,00,000
Manager's salary (Factory - $^{2}/_{3}$, Office - $^{1}/_{3}$)	15,000
Delivery van expenses	4,060
Depreciation on Factory Buildings	18,200
Publicity charges	2,000
Repairs to Plant	6,340
Carriage Outward	7,120
Hire charges of special machinery	9,010
Office Rent	2,800
Surveyor's Fees	590
Legal charges	620
Stock of Raw materials as on 31-03-200X	87,920

Prepare a Cost-statement giving the following details for the year ended 31-03-200X

(1)	Cost of material consumed	(2)	Prime Cost
(3)	Works Cost	(4)	Cost of Production
(5)	Total Cost	(6)	Net Profit for the year.

Problem 2

Following details have been obtained from the cost records of Colgate Ltd., Calcutta for the year ended 31-03-200X.

	Rs.
Stock of operating materials as on 1-4-200X	30,000
Wages paid to direct workers	55,000
Interim dividend paid	12,000
Purchase of raw materials	87,000
Heating and Lighting	6,000
Counting house salaries	20,000
Carriage and cartage on purchases of raw materials	3,000
Commission on Sales	5,000
Wages payable	5,000
Technical Director's Fees	10,000
Stock of operating material as on 31-03-200X	40,000
Show-room Expenses	7,000
Establishment on cost	12,000
Share Transfer Fees	2,000
Expenses of Testing Labs.	4,000
Branch Office Expenses	8,000
After-Sales service Expenses	8,000
Sales	2,50,000

Prepare a Cost-Sheet showing :

(1) Cost of raw materials consumed (2) Prime Cost

(3) Works Cost (4) Cost of Production

(5) Total Cost (6) Profit or Loss

Also calculate the percentage of

(1) factory overheads to direct wages

(2) office on-cost to works cost

(3) selling and distribution expenses to cost of production.

2. Calculation of percentage of Office on Cost to Works Cost.

If Rs. 1,60,000 W.C. Rs. 40,000 O.O.C.

∴ 100 ?

$$\frac{100 \times 40,000}{1,60,000}$$

= 25%

3. Calculation of percentage of Selling and distribution expenses to Cost of Production.

If Rs. 2,00,000 C.O.P Rs. 20,000 S. & D.E.

$$\therefore \quad 100 = \frac{100 \times 20,000}{2,00,000}$$

= 10%

(**N.B.** : Interim dividend paid, share transfer fees etc. are the items to be excluded from cost).

Problem 3

Following information of Finolex Ltd. relates to a commodity for the year ending 31-03-200X.

	Rs.
Opening stock as on 1-4-200X	
(i) Raw Materials	5,000
(ii) Work-in-Progress	1,200
(iii) Finished goods (1,000 Tons)	4,000
Closing Stock as on 31-03-200X	
(i) Raw Materials	3,000
(ii) Work-in-Proggress	3,200
(iii) Finished goods(2,000 Tons)	9,000
Purchases of Raw Materials	35,000
Prime Cost Labour	25,000
Excise duty on purchases of Raw Materials	2,000
Administration Overheads	8,000
Cost of factory supervision	12,000
Income Tax	5,000
Carriage and Cartage	1,000
Management Expenses	1,000
Accountancy charges	1,000
Preliminary expenses	3,200
sales of finished goods	1,17,500

Advertising, Bad debts and selling on cost amounted to 50 paise per ton sold. 16,000 tons of commodities were produced during the year 2002-200X.

Prepare a Cost-sheet showing

(1) Cost of materials consumed, (2),Prime Cost, (3) Works Cost,
(4) Cost of Production, (5) Cost of goods sold, (6) cost of sales,
(7) Profits for the period, (8) Profits per ton of commodity sold.

2. Calculation of profits per ton of commodity sold-

If 15,000 Tons Profits Rs. 30,000

1 Ton ?

$$\frac{1 \text{ ton x } 30,000 \text{ Rs.}}{15,000 \text{ tons}}$$

Rs. 2 per ton

(**N.B.** : Income tax, Preliminary Expenses etc. are the items to be excluded from Cost).

Problem 4

The cost accounts of Eagle Ltd. Allahabad for the year ended 31-03-200X showed the following information.

Types of Stock	As on 1-4-2000	As on 31-03-200X
Raw Materials	65,000	50,000
Work-in-Progress	10,000	7,500
Finished Stock	15,000	5,000

	Rs.
Underwritting commission	10,000
Purchase of Raw Materials	2,60,000
Selling overheads	8,000
Drawing office salaries	12,000
Productive Labour	1,65,000
Audit Fees	7,000
Establishment on Cost	2,000
Steam, Gas and Water	1,500
Sales	5,50,000
Rent	15,000
(Factory-66 $^2/_3$%, Office-33 $^1/_3$%)	
Architect's Fees	10,000
Wages Outstanding	5,000
Octroi and Duty	5,000
Distribution on Cost	2,000

Prepare Cost-sheet showing

(a) Cost of materials consumed, (b) Basic cost, (c) Works cost,

(d) Cost of production, (e) Cost of turnover, (f) Profit

Problem 5

Jindal manufacturers, Jalgaon furnished the following data relating to the manufacture of a standard product during the month of March 200X.

	Rs.
Carriage on purchase of basic materials	200
Raw Materials Stock as on 31-03-200X	2,850
Sale of Scrap-Raw Materials	150
Operating wages payable	600
Stock of Raw Materials as on 01-03-200X	1,200
Royalty	1500
Machine hour rate	2.50
Purchases of Raw Materials	14,600

Administration overheads : 10% of Work Cost

Selling and Distribution on cost : Rs. 3.60 per unit

Direct Labour charges	4,400
Cost of Layout	500

Operation of machine hours - 1,600

Monthly production - 1,000 units

Units sold - 900 units (@ Rs. 40 per unit)

You are required to prepare a Cost-Sheet showing total cost per unit for the month ended 31-03-200X. Also calculate profit for the month and profit per unit sold.

Problem 6

The following information has been obtained from the records of Quality Manufacturing Co. Ltd., Bharatpur for the year ended 31-03-200X.

Summary of Stock Position

Types of Stock	As on 1-4-2004 Rs.	As on 31-03-200X Rs.
Finished Goods-stock	50,000	75,000
Raw Materials	20,000	25,000
Stock of work-in-progresss	5,000	7,000

OTHER PARTICULARS	**Rs.**
Purchase of raw materials	1,30,000
Wages outstanding	3,000
Indirect material	12,000
Discount on issue of debentures	8,000
Freight Inward	15,000
Property Tax on Factory Buildings	8,000
Director's Travelling Expenses	8,000
Carriage on Sales	5,000
Defective raw materials returned	5,000
Direct chargeable expenses	2,000
Workshop Rent	7,000
Expenses for participating in Industrial Exhibition	3,000
Value of Sales	3,00,000
Office cleaning charges	2,000
Sales promotion charges	6,000
Miscellaneous overheads	7,000
Upkeep of Delivery Vans	1,000
Motive Power	5,000
Productive wages	60,000
Postage and Telegrams	3,000

Prepare a statement of cost showing

1. Value of raw materials consumed, 2. Direct Cost, 3. Manufacturing Cost, 4. Cost of Production , 5. Cost of goods sold, 6. Cost of Turnover, 7. Profit.

Also calculate the percentage of profit on cost price and on selling price separately.

MATERIAL COST

Introduction

Material is an important element of cost and constitutes major factors of production. The term material may be defined as "anything that can be stored, stocked or stockpiled". It refers to all commodities that are consumed in the process of manufacture. Materials cost constitutes a substantial portion of the capital invested in factories and hence, material management is very important, as far as cost of the product is concerned.

Material include raw materials, factory supplies such as oil, grease etc. purchased parts and finished parts. All these materials are collectively described as "stores". It may be classified in the following groups.

a) Direct materials : Material which actually form a part of the finished product are known as direct materials. These can be conveniently identified with particular cost units. Examples of direct materials are metal sheet used in manufacturing utensils, timber in furniture, clay in bricks, cotton in clothes etc.

b) Indirect Materials: When materials are consumed in production but cannot be specifically assigned to a particular job or unit of product, they are known as indirect materials. Examples of indirect materials are nuts and bolts, screw, thread, paints, cotton wastes, consumable stores. They constitute a major part in factory overheads, administrative overheads as well as in selling and distribution overheads.

c) Factory supplies: such as oil grease, soap, rags, cleaning materials etc.

d) Finished parts: In the case of automobiles, serving machines, refrigerators, television etc. some parts may be manufactured in advance and stored.

e) Purchased parts: Finished parts may be purchased instead of being produced by the enterprise. The success of business concern depends to a great extent upon efficient purchasing, storage accounting, control and consumption of materials. We have seen that almost in every manufacturing concern, the cost of materials constitutes a major portion of the cost of production. Hence, it becomes necessary and important to keep the cost of materials per unit of product, as low as possible. The objective is obtained by efficient materials management and material control.

Material control is a system that assures the continuous availability of all types of material in right quantities and of requisite quality but without blocking excessive investment in raw materials and inventories. Material control is defined as, "a systematic control over purchasing, storing and consumption of materials, and at the same time, avoiding overstocking or understocking".

Thus, it is seen from the above definition that material control is a wide function bringing within its scope control of all factors concerning materials, i.e. purchase, receipt, inspection, storage, consumption and price.

Objectives of Scientific Purchasing

Purchasing is an art. Wrong purchases increase the cost of materials. Hence, it is imperative that purchases should be effectively, efficiently and economically performed. Dr. Walter defines scientific purchasing as, "the procurement by purchase of the proper materials, machinery, equipments and supplies of stores used in the manufacture of product adapted to marketing in the proper quantity and quality at the proper time and the lowest price consistent with the quality desired".

Major objectives of scientific purchasing can be enumerated as follows :

1) Continuous flow of materials: Purchasing should be in such a way that production is not held up for want of raw-materials. In other words, there should be continuous flow of materials. Stoppage of production due to want of materials results into increasing cost.

2) No understocking : Understocking leads inevitably to materials running out of stock. Shortages of material may arise at the needed time causing delay in production or stoppage in production. It may result in loss or profit. So purchasing should be made in such a manner that there should be no understocking.

3) No overstocking : There should not be excessive investment in stocks. Investment in material must be kept as low as possible, considering the production requirements and financial resources of the business. Overstocking of materials unnecessarily locks up capital and causes high storage cost, thus, adversely affecting the profits. So purchasing should be made in such a way that there should be no overstocking.

4) Proper type and quality of material: Purchasing should be made of those materials which suits the object of their procurement. Again, while purchasing weightage should be given to the quality. For different kinds of products particular quality of material is needed. There should be no inferior quality or very superior quality. So while purchasing, taking into consideration the objects of productions, proper type and proper quality of materials should be purchased.

5) Economy in purchasing: Purchase of materials at the cheapest (economical) price reduces the cost of products, leading to increase demand for the product in the competitive market. So by purchasing of materials at reasonable prices, the purchaser is able to make a valuable contribution to the success of a business.

6) Proper advise to the management: By scientific purchasing, the purchase Department may give advise to the management regarding introduction of newly profitable lines of products, use of substitute materials, change in market trends etc.

7) Supply of information about materials: By giving scientific approach to the purchasing system, it becomes possible for the storekeeper to supply information about materials to the management. It helps the management in framing plans and policies relating to scheduling of production and marketing. Thus, the main object behind the scientific purchasing may be served as the procurement of materials of the right quality, in the right quantity, at the right time, from the right source and at a right price can be made.

Functions of Purchasing Department

Purchasing is of an extreme importance particularly to a manufacturing concern because it has its bearing on every vital factor concerning the manufacture, i.e. quality, quantity, cost, volume of production, prompt delivery, efficiency, economy etc. It is by the purchasing Department that much money can be saved or lost. The work of purchasing materials should be handled by a separate purchase department, under an official designated as Purchase Manager.

The Purchasing Department obtains the required materials, supplies, machines, tools etc. at the most favourable terms, consistent with maintaining the desired standard of quality and continuity in service.

In order to ensure procurement of materials of requisite quantity at economic prices following points should be noted :

i) Purchasing should be centralised i.e. no purchases should be made except by the purchasing Department.

ii) Full co-operation between Purchase Department and other departments is necessary.

iii) The Purchasing Officer should have good technical knowledge of the industry.

iv) No purchases should be made unless the purchasing department receives a duly signed purchase requisition.

1) **Purchase of quality materials :** While purchasing, Purchasing Department should keep in mind that raw materials should be of proper quality to meet the requirement of the market for which the final product is intended. For different kinds of products different types of material is needed. Unnecessary increase in quality of raw materials or components increase the cost of product. So Purchase Manager must know the exact specification of materials which are used in the production.

2) **Purchase of materials in right quantities :** We have seen that material cost may account for as much as 50% to 70% of the total cost producing a product. Hence, while purchasing materials, Purchasing Department Should purchase the materials strictly as per requisition of the various departments. It means that materials should be purchased in required quantities only.

3) **Buying at right price :** The price to be paid for the purchases of materials must be reasonably low but quality must not be sacrificed in doing so. This will be secured from market quotations and reports, catalogue prices issued by different suppliers.

4) **Timely supply of materials :** Time element is an important factor in purchase procedure. It should be remembered that material purchased for a particular job must be obtained in the right time, so that there should not be delay in production. So while doing an agreement with supplier, Purchasing Department must mention that timely supply of material will be one of the important condition of the agreement. While specifying the time limit lead time should also be considered

5) **Determination of purchase Budget :** Preparation of a Purchase Budget is one of the most important duty of purchasing Department. While preparing purchase budget requisitions and specification of material should be taken from various departments. For prompt and correct payment of purchase bills, there should be close liaison with the account department and stores department. This purchase budget guides the purchase manager in knowing what he has to buy, what should be the quantity and size and also when he has to buy.

6) **Selection of suppliers :** After receiving the purchase requisition, the Purchase Department starts exploring the sources of materials and suppliers. Various sources are examined for the purpose of securing the best materials at the lowest possible price. Due consideration is also given to factors like terms of payments, date of delivery and reliability of suppliers in the past.

7) **Issue purchase orders to suppliers :** After selecting the supplier the purchase manager prepares a Purchase Order and place them to the selected supplier. Once the Purchase Order is issued to a supplier it is obligatory on the part of the Purchase Manager to take delivery of materials and arrange for the payment of invoice. The purchase order must be carefully prepared including all essential elements of purchases to be made.

8) **Verification of quality and quantity of materials received :** On receipt of materials purchasing department should verify the materials obtained in respect of quality and quantity and be reassured that it is as per the purchase order only.

9) **Approving Invoices :** After verifying materials received, Purchasing Department, should verify and check the invoices and approve them for payment.

10) **Maintenance of proper record :** Keeping up-to-date information about the best markets, best seasons, new and improved materials, spare parts, components, equipments etc. is also one of the important function of the purchasing department. It is necessary for efficient operation of the purchase department.

11) **Co-ordination with other departments :** For smooth and efficient functioning of purchase department it must be co-ordinated with stores, accounts and industrial engineering departments. Purchase Manager should also take part in departmental conferences for planning, formulation of policies and other purposes.

Methods of Purchasing

The Purchase Department is the custodian of buying efficiently. The best buying system in a given situation is one that gives the best efficiency speed, accuracy and economy. Following are the different methods of purchasing.

1) Centralised Purchasing : Centralising of purchases refers to purchase of materials under one purchase department headed by a competent purchase manager.

Advantages of Centralised Purchasing

1) Centralised purchasing ensures better control over purchases.
2) It avoids excessive reckless buying by several persons.
3) Regular supply and favourable treatment from the supplier is obtained.
4) Bulk purchasing results in reduced price of materials on account of trade discount, cash discount facilities.
5) It eliminates possibility of overstocking and locking up of capital in stock of materials.
6) Standardisation of materials is facilitated.
7) Free home delivery under this system is available due to bulk purchasing.
8) Expert purchasing staff can be concentrated in one purchasing department.
9) It ensures uniformity in purchasing policies, practices and procedures.
10) It can take advantage of market changes.

Disadvantages of Centralised Purchasing

1) The buying procedure becomes rigid.
2) Working capital gets locked-up.
3) Benefits of local purchases cannot be enjoyed.
4) Distribution to consumption centres involves transportation cost.
5) Creation of a separate purchasing department is a costly affair.
6) It involves delay in receiving and settling discrepancies and it may create misunderstanding between the purchasing department and various departments.

2) Decentralised Purchasing : Under this system a separate purchase department is established to make purchases independently. This method is applicable to those manufacturing concerns which operate for acquiring different types of materials. Each purchase department will have a purchase authority who enjoys the freedom of making purchases of materials required for his department. The purchasing authority in each department reports to the Chief Purchase Officer who establishes the general purchase policies and co-ordinates the purchasing functions in all plants.

Advantages of Decentralised Purchasing

1) It is more prompt and flexible.
2) Personal contacts with suppliers are easily developed.
3) Local knowledge of the market helps in locating the right purchases.
4) It avoids delay in procurement of materials.
5) It is more convenient for uncommon items which are specific to units or departments.
6) It avoids incurrence of certain costs connected with store-keeping and running of the Purchase Department.

Disadvantages of Decentralised Purchasing

1) Many times the losses incurred may be more than savings effected due to this system.
2) Inefficiency in purchasing may creep in due to want of necessary information about sources of supplies, prices, demand and supply conditions in market etc.

3) Centralised - decentralised systems : This method is applicable to those concerns where there are more than one plant. Though such plants produce different products there are some materials which are common to all plants. Under such circumstances, it is desirable to partially centralise and partially decentralise the purchase function. Under this system it is necessary to make clear that which type of materials are to be purchased by the decentrialised system. For the successful operation of this system, the following points should be noted.

1) The Chief Purchase Manager has to establish common policies, procedures, record keeping methods and exercise control over all departments.

2) All decentralised purchases must be reported immediately to the central office.

3) The decentralished purchase department must buy materials for his plant only within the budget sanctioned for them.

4) Approval of the central office must be made compulsory for special and excess quantity purchases.

Purchase procedure

Purchasing is one of the important elements of material control. It starts with the initiation of purchase requisitions and ends with the receipt of materials into stores and the payment of bill for purchases.

The procedure of purchasing materials varies from one business to another depending upon size, conditions and orders. But, normally the following procedure for purchasing materials is adopted by the Purchase Department.

1) **Purchase Budget :** The Purchase Manager with the help of production planning department, prepares a Purchase Budget in the beginning of the year. This Purchase Budget guides him in knowing what he had to buy and when

2) **Purchase Requisition :** Purchasing starts when someone in the organisation decides that a particular material is needed. Request for purchase of materials in a particular form to Purchase Department is termed as "Purchase Requisition'. Purchase Requisition may be received from :

a) Storekeeper
b) Production Control Department
c) Plant and Maintenance Department
d) The Heads of the various Service Departments

The purchase requisition may be prepared in different shade of colours.

i) Original copy is sent to the Purchasing Department.
ii) Second copy is retained by the Department preparing it.
iii) Third copy is retained by the Department preparing it.

Purchase requisition serves the following purposes :

a) It is a notification of the need of the department for particular materials to the purchasing department.
b) It provides a written record of details of materials and date when required.
c) It provides data for reference when responsibility for shortage of materials is to be established.

The Purchase Requisition should give clearly and completely all the information that is required for initiation of the purchase procedure. These particulars ensure that the purchases can be made with speed and accuracy It must contain the following essential information.

a) Name and exact description of materials required.
b) Quantity of materials required.
c) Date on which materials are needed.
d) The place of delivery of goods after receiving inspection department's reports.
e) Signature of the authority initiating the purchase requisition.

A specimen form of Purchase Requisition is given in unit 'Purchase Documentation'.

3) **Decision regarding exact quantity, quality and time for purchasing :** Before proceeding towards Purchase of materials, the Purchase Manager has to decide the quality, Quantity, price and time at which materials are to be purchased.

a) **Buying the proper quality :** Buying proper quality of materials depends upon the accurate specification of materials required and placing the order with a reliable supplier. Definiteness in the specification of materials always tend to minimise cost of materials.

b) **Buying proper quantity :** As a rule the quantity of material to be purchased had to be specified in the purchase requisition. But the quantity may be changed to take advantage of market or speculative purchasing. Quantity of materials to be purchased are determined by taking into account the sales forecast, customer's order, production authorisation, time taken to supply etc.

c) **Buying at proper price :** In order to purchase materials at reasonable price, the purchase manager must obtain and record the price. Materials prices may be classified into :

i) Prices obtained from market reports and newspapers.

ii) Prices listed catalogues.

iii) Price quoted by the suppliers when tenders are issued.

4) **Locating source of materials :** Locating source of materials :

After determining the quality and quantity of materials to be brought, the sources of supply are to be tapped. The following are the important sources of supply of materials.

i) Trade directories   ii) Telephone directories   iii) Periodicals
iv) Newspapers and Commerce Magazines   v) Catalogues   vi) Suppliers Index Files
vii) Exhibitions and Trade Shows   viii) Market Survey   ix) Quotations

While considering suitable source of supply the following points should be considered.

i) Whether to purchase from a single supplier or a multiple of them.

ii) Whether to purchase from the local sources or from some distant places.

iii) Whether to purchase directly from the manufacturer or through wholesaler.

5) **Selection of suppliers :** When there are more than one supplier dealing with materials, the purchase manager had to select the best supplier with whom the purchase manager has confidence as to quality of materials, ability to deliver the materials promptly at the cheapest price and with better terms of sale. The purchase department usually maintains for each type of materials a list of the tenders to them. On receipt of the quotations from the supplier, a comparative statement of various quotations received should be prepared and the desirable supplier should be selected.

6) **Preparing and placing Purchase Order :** After selecting the proper supplier, the purchase manager prepares a Purchase Order. A purchase order is a contractual document which authorises the supplier to supply the materials. Once the purchase order is issued to supplier, it is obligatory on the part of the purchase manager to take delivery of materials and arrange for the payment of invoice. The purchase order must be carefully drafted by precisely including all essential elements of purchases to be made. It must be prepared in such a manner so as to avoid future misunderstanding and minimise the necessity of correspondence.

Generally, five copies are prepared for sending each to :

i) The Supplier   ii) The Receiving department,
iii) The Department which initiated purchase requisitions   iv) The Accounts department
v) The Filing department for reference.

A specimen of Purchase Order is given in unit 'Purchase Documentation'.

7) **Follow-up :** It is very important to follow-up purchase orders so as to ensure timely delivery. Lack of follow-up measures may cause delay in arrival of materials resulting in stoppages in production for want of materials. It is thus the important duty of the purchase department to :

a) Obtain an acknowledgment or acceptance of the orders.

b) Obtain a promise of delivery according to requirements,

c) Watch the progress of filling up of orders particularly for important items.

d) Check up finally that the delivery promise is maintained.

Follow-up action is taken either by sending copies of purchase order from time to time until delivery is effected or by sending reminders. Follow-up is as important as placing the order.

8) **Receipt of materials :** In a large enterprise, there is generally a separate Receiving Department. But in a small concern, the receipt and inspection of goods may be done by one person.

When ordered goods are received, the receiving clerk checks whether the packages and their contents are intact or not and compares the quantity and particulars with suppliers delivery note and a copy of purchase order.

The receiving clerk is not expert in checking the quality of goods, but he will just weigh, count or measure the quantity of materials received by him and if this quantity agrees with the Delivery Note and Purchase Order and the goods which are in perfect condition, then he will accept them and will sign the documents acknowledging the receipt of material. It is termed as "Materials Received Note".

Materials Received Note serves the following purposes :

i) It informs the storekeeper or other requisitionist about the receipt of materials.

ii) It notifies the accounting department that the materials have been received and that a voucher can be prepared..

iii) When it includes cost column, it can serve as a source of entry in the stores ledger.

The materials received Note contains the following :

i) The Serial Number and Date. ii) Suppliers Name and Address.

iii) Description, Code and quantity of goods received. iv) Order Number, Inspection Report, bin no. etc.

v) condition in which materials are received. vi) Type of Container.

vii) Mode of Transportation.

A separate 'materials received note' is prepared for materials requiring laboratory testing.

The number of copies required depends upon the size and organisation of the firm. Generally Materials Received Note is prepared in quadrauplicate and sent as follows :

1) The first copy to Purchasing Department.

2) The second copy accompanying the goods to the Department or stores to which they are sent.

3) The third copy is sent to the Accounts Department.

4) The fourth copy is retained by the receiving Department for future reference.

9) **Inspection of Materials :** The responsibility to see that goods have been received according to purchase order specification is that of the Inspection Department. In large manufacturing concerns there may be a separate Inspection and Testing Department to test the quality of materials purchased. In small factories inspection function is performed by the receiving clerk or by the storekeeper himself. The results of the tests are intimated to the authorities by means of the Testing Reports. Generally, necessary columns are provided in the Material Received Note about the goods passed or rejected on the basis of tests conducted. But when the inspecting function is of great importance a special Inspection Report is preferred. This report contains information order number, name of the supplier etc. it clearly mentions that the quantity of goods received, accepted/rejected and the reasons for the rejections. Generally, this report is prepared in inspection or Production Department, and the Third copy is retained by it for future reference.

A specimen form of Inspection Report is given in unit "Purchase Documentation".

10) **Return of Rejected Materials :** If the goods received are according to the purchase order in respect of quality, quantity etc. they are sent to the stores alongwith a copy of materials Received Note.

But when materials are not in accordance with the specifications which are given clearly in the purchase order or received in damaged conditions, these are usually returned to the suppliers along with a Debit Note, informing him that his account has been debited with the value of materials returned and reasons. When such a claim is accepted by the supplier, he signifies his acceptance by the issue of a Credit Note. The rejected material may be returned to the supplier immediately or they may be held pending for his instruction.

The Debit Note may be prepared by the purchase Department on the basis of the inspection report. Original copy is sent to the supplier. Second copy is sent to accounts department for adjustment entry and the third copy is retained for Purchase Department file.

11) **Passing the Invoice and Payment of Bills :** This is the last step in the purchase procedure. The invoice is checked with the purchase order and the materials received note. The rates and terms of invoice are compared with those of purchase order. Similarly, quantity received must tally with the quantity ordered. It is equally important to check totals. For adjustment of discrepancies, the inspection report and materials received note should be compared with the invoice. Finally, if everything is in proper order and O.K., the invoice is approved by the Purchase Manager and forwarded to the accounts department for payment. All related document like Purchase Order, materials Received Note etc. are marked with the Invoice Number to preclude the passing of a possible duplicate invoice.

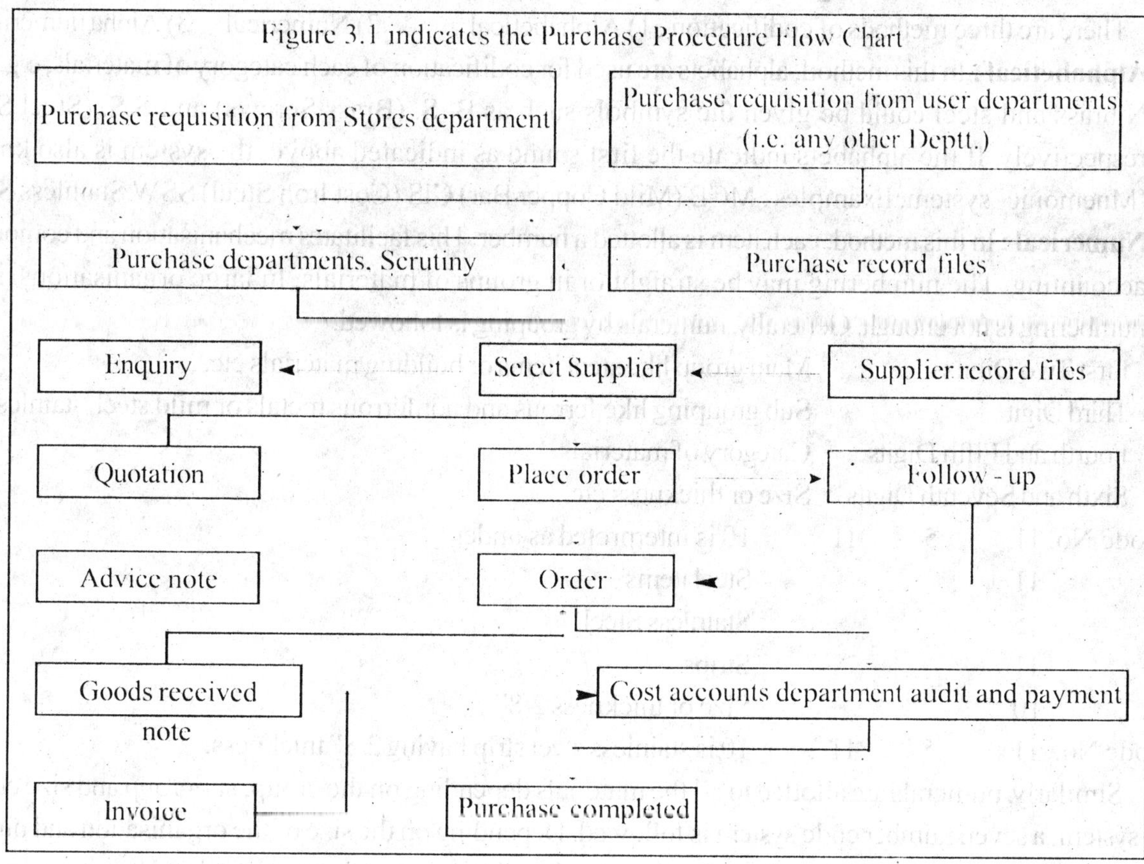

Classification and codification

Classification relates to grouping of materials and codification covers the process of assigning codes or symbols to various groups and kinds of materials. Codification facilitates the identification of materials and is convenient in the case of bill of materials and other materials documents. Codification is advantageous not only to the purchase department and production department, but also to the cost accounting department. It ensures the economy in space and facilitates machine accounting. Secrecy can also be maintained. A good system of classification and codification is chracterised by its simplicity, brevity, aid to memory, elasticity and certainity.

Basic Principles of Coding

While assigning codes, the following principles should be kept in mind :

1) Exclusive : Each code number should relate to only one type of materials and there should be no duplication.

2) Certain : The code must identify the materials without any ambiguity, simplicity is essential for coding.

3) Brief : Codes should be brief, as long codes take longer time to write and are more subject to error.

4) Elastic : The code should be such that new materials can be added easily and logically.

5) Menmonic : As far as possible, codes should be easier to remember such as HCB for Hard Copper Bar, MCB for Mild Copper Bar.

Procedure for Classification and Codification

Firstly, materials are grouped under various categories such as steel items, building materials, petrol, diesel, lubricants, metals, spares and other consumable materials. It may be further classified into subgroups like ferrous metals and nonferrous metals under the main head metals. Then, the codes or symbols are allotted. These may be further categorised as indigenous and imported.

There are three methods of codification : 1) Alphabetical 2) Numerical 3) Alpha numerical

1) **Alphabetical :** In this method, alphabets are used for codification of each category of materials, e.g. screws N brass and steel could be given the symbols such as B. S. (Brass Screws) and S.S. (Steel Screws) respectively. If the alphabets indicate the first sound as indicated above, the system is also known as 'Mnemonic' system. Examples : MCB (Mild Copper Bar) CIS (Cost Iron Steel) SSW Stainless Steel)

2) **Numerical :** In this method, each item is allotted a number. This facilitates mechanisation and computerised accounting. The numbering may be straight or in groups of materials. In large organisations, straight numbering is not enough. Generally, numerals by grouping is followed.

First Two Digits	Main group like steel items or building materials etc.
Third Digit	Sub grouping like ferrous and nonferrous metals or mild steel, stainless etc.
Fourth and Fifth Digits	Category of materials
Sixth and Seventh Digits	Size or thickness etc.

e.g. Code No. 11 5 11 10 is interpreted as under :

11	Steel items
5	Stainless Steel
11	Strips
10	Size or thickness 2/8"

i.g. Code No. 11 5 11 10 is stainless steel strip having 2/8" thickness.

Similarly, numerals are allotted to all the materials depending on the group, subgroup and size etc. In the above system, a seven number code system is followed. Depending on the size of the organisation and number of categories of materials, the numbers in code may be reduced to 5 or may be increased to 10.

For example, in a factory following code may be assigned.

Aluminium	:	11	Bronze :	12	Coal	:	13
Copper	:	14	Steel :	15	Wool	:	16

Further, physical features can be indicated in the code by decimals. This is shown below for Aluminium of which numerical code as shown above is 11.

Aluminium Sheets	:	11.1	Aluminium Bars	:	11.2
Aluminium Granules	:	11.3	Aluminium Wire	:	11.4
Aluminium Tubes	:	11.5			

Subdivision of, say, Aluminium bars into various grades may be coded as follows :

Aluminium bar grade A : 11.21 Aluminium bar grade B : 11.22

Aluminium bar grade C : 11.23

This is a combination of numerical and alphabetical methods. In the above example,-SS 10 may indicate steel screws 2/8". Following are some examples :

Mild copper Bar of 6' length MCB6 Brass strips of 1/4" thickness BS14

Cost Iron sheets 2' x 2' CIS 22

The code of materials should appear on all documents relating to the movement and use of materials and should be marked against the appropriate bins. In fact, codes must be handled with extreme care. If a slight mistake is made in quoting the correct code, the entire work order may have to be scrapped, entailing considerable loss to the organisation.

Advantages of Classification and Codification

A good system of classification and codification offers the following advantages :

1) It facilitates the identification of various store resulting in prompt issue of stores.
2) It helps in maintaining secrecy
3) It helps in material control.
4) It reduces clerical work and effects economy in space.
5) It helps in maintaining mechanised accounts (make easy for computerisation).

Forms and documents used in stores

Maintaining accurate and upto date records of material received, issued, rejected, disposed and quantity on hand of all the items, are the three main activities. i.e. receipts, stocking and issue of material, various documents are used in stores management.

Stores Records :

The stores records include

1) The Basic Perpetual Inventory Records 2) The Various documentations

1) **The perpetual Inventory Records :** On these is entered the pattern of movement of stores i.e. the receipts and issues and also the balances in stock. Bin card and Store ledger are the two basic perpetual inventory records.
2) **The Documents :** These are used to authorise movement of materials into the out stores. These are goods Received Note, Store Requisition Note, Bill of Materials, Materials Return Note etc.

Bin Card

A Store Keeper often maintains a record of quantity of each material, such record is known as Bin Card. The Bin Cards show the details of receipts and issues of materials and the balance in stock at any time. This record is of immense help to the storekeeper in controlling the stock position.

A bin card is attached to the bin, drawer or any other container in which material is stored. An entry made at the time of each receipt or issue and the new balance in stock is calculated. All these entries of receipts and issues are supported by documents such as Goods Received Note, Material Return Note, Stores Requisition Note etc.

As a storekeeper has usually to initiate purchase requisitions, the maximum and minium stock levels are shown on the bin card along with ordering level and quantity. This information helps the storekeeper in preparing the necessary purchase requisition when the stock reaches ordering level.

Bin Card

Description : ______	Bin No. : ______	Minimum Level :	Material Code No. :
Grade : ______	Ordering Level : ______	Unit : ______	Location :
Ordering Quantity : ______	Stores Ledger Folio : ______		

Date	Receipts		Issues		Balance of Stock	Stock Verification	
	Ref. No.	Quantity	Ref. No.	Quantity	Quantity	Date	Initial

Figure - Bin Card

Utilities of bin Card

a) It is used for entering the receipts, issues and the closing balance of each item of stores.

b) It is used for controlling the stock by watching the maximum and minium level stated on the card.

c) It helps in requisitioning the materials when the recorder level is reached.

d) Since the Economic Order Quantity is also stated on the card it enables the store keeper as to how much quantity he has to requisition.

e) Location code of the material in Bin Card helps in proper storage keeping with greater efficiency and identifying store easily.

f) It helps in the implementation of the perpetual inventory system as the Bin card contains the quantitative record of receipts, issues and closing balance of each item of stores.

g) Bin card provides an independent check on the stores ledger.

Bin card as a tool for controlling the stock : Bin means a rack, container, or space where goods are kept. For each kind of materials, inventory tag is attached to the bin and bin card is maintained. A bin Card is quantitative record of receipts, issue and closing balances of each item of stores. The Bin cards are used not only for entering the receipts and issues, but also for controlling the stock by watching maximum and minimum levels stated on the card. When the ordering level is reached storekeeper has to send the requisition for further supplies. For each entry, whether relating to receipt or issue, the balance quantity is calculated and recorded in the 'Balance' column should agree with the physical balance in Bin and Stores ledger balances.

Two Bin System : In large concerns , a two bin system is adopted. In this system two bins are maintained for each material. One bin contains the minimum quantity or reserve quantity or no issues are made from this bin except under in emergency when the other bins are empty. Another bin contains the balance quantity from which issues are made usually. This system facilitates the physical verification of stores as well as pacing the purchase requisitions.

Triple Bin System : While the double bin system is followed for material control and reduces the risk of shortage of material under normal circumstances, sometimes necessity may arise when the double bin system may be modified to triple bin system. It has been shown in the following diagram along with double bin system.

Double Bin System

A Minimum Level	B

Triple Bin System

Minimum Level		
A1 Danger Level	A2	B

The sum of A1 + A2 + B is the total stock level and indicates the need for fresh supplies. Material of A1 + A2 portion are equal to the minimum stock level and A1 portion is equal to danger stock level. If fresh supplies have not been received and materials of A2 portion are also consumed, it indicates the danger level and any delay in receiving the material will lead to interruption in production with its concomitant evils. Then, the firm should take emergency action to procure materials even paying slightly higher prices so as to keep production going.

Reordering level is useful to know when a fresh order is to be placed. While the double bin system is useful to know the minimum level and consequential necessity for fresh supplies, the triple bin system has the added advantage of identifying an emergency situation for procuring the materials on a top priority basis.

Problem : The following is the history of receipts and issues of material in a factory during March 200 X.

1 Opening stock 20 kg

3 Received from supplier S_1 40 kg (GRN No. 548)

8 Issued to production department 24 kg (S. R. No. 783)

10 Issued to production department 16 kg (S. R. No. 797)

12 Received from supplier S_2 50 kg (G. R. No. 555)

15 Issued to production department 40 kg (S. R. No.821)

16 Received from supplier S_3 25 kg (G. R. No.2)

(GRN denotes Goods Received Notes. SR Denotes Stores Requisition)

The minimum stock level of material X is 20 kg, Re-order level is 35 kg and re-order quantity is 50 kg. Prepare a Bin Card No. 83 for material X with all necessary details showing the transactions in January 200X.

Bin Card

Description : A   Bin No. : 83   Minimum Level : 20   Code No.

Re-order Level : 35   Unit : kg.   Re-order Quantity : 50   Stores Ledger Folio :

Date 200X March	Ref. No.	Quantity Kg.	Issues		Balance	Stock Verification
			Ref. No.	Quantity	Quantity Kg.	
1	----	----	----	----	20	
3	GRN No. 548	40	----	----	60	
8	----	----	SR No. 783	24	36	
10	----	----	SR No. 797	16	20	
12	GRN No. 555	50	----	----	70	
15	----	----	SR No. 812	40	30	
16	GRN No. 561	25	----	----	55	
19	GRN No. 562	50	----	----	105	
21	----	----	SR No. 840	25	80	
24	----	----	SR No. 850	26	54	
28	----	----	SR No. 874	35	19	

Stores Ledger

This record gives the same information regarding stores as that of bin card and in addition it gives the money values of materials. Separate ledger folios are maintained in it for each item of material. The ledger sheets may be in loose leaf form or separate bindings may be used for each type of material.

The stores ledger is maintained in the cost accounting department and is one of the basic records for materials accounting in a cost system. There are mainly three sections on this ledger i.e. receipts, issues and balance, each of these with appropriate subdivisions showing date, quantity, unit price and total cost. Two additional sections are usually included materials On Order and Materials Reserved. The On Order column prevents placing of Materials On Order and Materials Received. The On order column prevents placing of duplicate orders and Reserve column indicates the materials reserved for a specific job order.

The entries in the receipts and issues columns are made from the same documents which are used for posting in bin card i.e. Goods Received Note and Stores Requisition Note, etc.

It is often contended that maintenance of bin card along with Stores ledger is an unnecessary duplication of work but the necessity for it arises from the fact that stores ledger constitutes a check on the quantity shown in the bin card. Moreover, bin cards are not accounting records and are kept with the stores in the storeroom. For costing purpose, it becomes necessary to maintain stores ledger.

Generally, stores ledger is maintained in a loose sheets. The number cards are the same as in the case of Bin Cards which are dependent upon the number of kinds and classes of materials. If a new Bin Card is opened or any Bin Card is closed, the information should be sent by the storekeeper so that similar action is taken in Cost Accounting Department also in respect of opening or closing of stores ledger cards. The posting is done in the same way as in the case of Bin Cards. In large organisations, the line number of Bin Cards is also indicated in the Material document so that the document is valued and posted in the same line number in the stores ledgers also. It facilitates the reconciliation between Bin card and stores ledger in such a way that balance after every entry in the bin card tallies with that in the stores ledger. By following the system of serial number of documents as mentioned before and the line numbers, missing vouchers, if any, are called from the Stores Department by the Cost Accounting Department.

Materials Accounting and Pricing of Issues

Difference between Bin Card and Stores Ledger Card :

Bin Card	Stores Ledger Card
1) It is record of quantities only.	1) It is record of the both quantities and values.
2) It is kept inside the Stores.	2) It is kept in the Costing Department.
3) Posted before the transaction takes place.	3) Posted after the transaction takes place.
4) It is maintained by the Storekeeper.	4) It is maintained by the Cost Accountant.
5) Each transaction is individually posted.	5) Transactions are summarised and posted monthly.
6) Balance in Bin Card is compared with the physical quantity.	6) Balance in Stores Ledger Card is compared with Bin Card quantity.
7) No need of reconciliation with general ledger as it contains quantities only.	7) Total value of all these cards is to be reconciled with general ledger.

In stores, the stock consists of materials purchased in different lots at different times and at different prices. However, when materials are to be issued to production, what price should be charged for costing the unused stock in hand. Whether it should be original purchase price or the average price or the current market price on the date of issue or some other price that should be used for the accounting treatment. This problem of pricing the issue of material is important. Because the pricing directly affects the amount of profit or loss for the accounting period if the method chosen puts higher value to closing stock, it will ultimately result in higher profit, and vice versa, lower valuation of closing stock will result in lower profits.

The Figure shows a form of Stores Ledger Account

Stores Ledger Account

Description : ____________ Unit : __________ Maximum : __________ Ordering Level : ________ Code No. : ____________

Bin No. : ____________ Location : ____________ Minimum : ________ Ordering quantity: ____________

On Order			Reserved			Receipts						Issues					Balance			Stock Verification	
Date	Ref. No.	Qty.	Date	Ref. No.	Qty.	Date	Ref. No.	Qty.	Rate Rs.	Amt. Rs.	Ref. No.	Qty.	Rate Rs.	Amt. Rs.	Qty.	Rate Rs.	Amt. Rs.	Date	Initials

Methods of Pricing Material Issues

The various methods of pricing the issue of materials are as follows. The various methods used are based on different assumptions. Such methods are classified as those based on :

i) Actual cost price ii) Average price and iii) Notional price This is shown in following table.

Methods of Pricing Material Issue			
A) Actual cost on the Principle of	**B) Average price**	**C) Notional Prices**	**D) Other Methods**
1) First in First Out (FIFO)	1) Simple Average price	1) Standard price	1) Specific price
2) Last in First Out (LIFO)	2) Periodic Simple Average price	2) Inflated price	
3) Highest in First Out (HIFO)	3) Moving Simple Average price	3) Replacement price or market price	
4) Next in First Out (NIFO)	4) Weighted Average price	4) Re-use price	
5) Base stock price	5) Periodic Weighted Average price		
	6) Moving Weighted Average price		

A-1 First In First Out (FIFO)

This method is used under the assumption that the materials which are received first are issued first. Hence, the price of the first batch/lot purchased is charged for all the issues until the stock of that batch/lot is exhausted. In other words, the issues are priced in the chronological order of receipt. In this case, issues to production/maintenanace are valued at historical price and stock is valued at the latest purchase price.

Advantages

1) This method is easy to understand and operate if prices do not fluctuate too often.
2) The value of closing stock represents for current market price.
3) Issues are charged at actual cost and hence, no adjustment for profit or loss is necessary.
4) This method is useful in the case of slow-moving materials, bulk items and materials of high unit cost.
5) Issues are priced in the same order in which the materials are issued.

Disadvantages

1) Useful comparison of material cost of one job to another is not possible if the prices fluctuate too often.
2) If the prices fluctuate too often, this method will involve more calculations with resultant clerical errors.
3) Sometimes, more than one price has to be adopted for pricing a single issue of materials.
4) In case the materials are found defective after their issue to production, credit adjustment will be required when such defective materials are returned to suppliers and it will affect the pricing of next new issues.
5) When the excess material is returned from production to stores, the adjustment will create complications in the case of issues with more than one price as mentioned in (3) above.

A-2 Last in First Out (LIFO)

This method uses the price of the last batch purchased for all issues until stock of that batch is exhausted. Hence, issues are valued at current prices and stock is valued at historical prices. As the issues are valued at current prices, this method is also called replacement cost method. Here also, the physical flow of materials does not concern the Cost Accountant. This method was first introduced in U.S.A. during the Second World War, in order to get the advantage of rising prices.

Advantages

1) Issues are valued at current prices and hence charge to production is more appropriate.
2) This method is useful when the prices are on the rising trend.
3) Like the FIFO system, this method is also easy to understand and operate, if the prices do not fluctuate too often.
4) Like the FIFO system, issues are charged at actual cost and hence no adjustment for profit or loss is necessary.

Disadvantages

1) As the stock is valued at historical prices, it will not be reflected in the Balance Sheet at realistic value and thus, false working capital position is shown in the Balance Sheet. Secret Reserve will be created.
2) Issues are not valued in the same order in which the materials are issued.
3) During the periods of falling prices, the issues are priced at lower rates and the stock value will be at higher prices. In such cases, it requires some adjustment on the principle of valuation of stock at the cost or market price whichever is lower.
4) Like the FIFO system, useful comparison of material cost of one job to another is not possible if the prices fluctuate too often.
5) Like the FIFO system, this method also will involve more calculations with resultant clerical errors, if the prices fluctuate too often.
6) Like the FIFO system, sometimes more than one price has to be adopted for pricing a single issue of materials.
7) If the latest receipt rate is not finalised, the work of pricing of issues will be held up.

A-3 Highest In First Out (HIFO)

Under this method, issues are valued at the highest price paid for a lot/batch of materials until stock of that lot/batch is exhausted and so on. It has the effect of overvaluing production and undervaluing stock, i.e. stock should always remain at the lowest value. Thus, Secret Reserve will be created. This method is complicated to administer and hence it has not become popular. This method is mainly used in the case of monopoly products or cost plus contracts.

A-4 Next In First Out (NIF)

Under this method, issues are valued at the price estimated or expected for the next purchase. This is similar to replacement price. The problem will arise if the price ruling at the time of supply differs from the purchase order price.

A-5 Base Stock Method

This method is usually used with FIFO and LIFO method by assuming a fixed minimum stock of materials which is called the Base Stock. The minimum stock is not used except under an emergency. This method is suitable in smelting, tanning, and oil refining industries where it is necessary to keep minimum stock of basic raw materials because of long period of processing. Issues are valued at actual cost. As this method is used with FIFO or LIFO, all the advantages and disadvantages of FIFO or LIFO will apply depending on the method followed. It is not an independent method as it is used with FIFO or LIFO.

B-1 Simple Average Price

Under this method, issues are valued at simple average price which is the average of number of prices (available at the time of issue) without any regard to quantities. Issues are not, therefore, charged at actual cost and hence profit or loss may be incurred by adopting this system. It is useful when the materials are purchased in uniform quantities and prices do not fluctuate.

Advantages

1) It is easy to operate 2) Cost distortion is not much because of adoption of average price.

Disadvantages

1) When the price rise sharply, the closing stock may show a minus balance.
2) As in case of FIFO and LIFO, the value of closing stock cannot be reconciled.
3) As the quantities are not considered, the system may produce incorrect results.
4) As the issues are not valued at actual cost, profit or loss may arise.
5) Cumulative receipt column and cumulative issue column are to be adopted to ensure the average number of prices available at the time of issues.
6) Price has to be calculated at each issue of material made.

B-2 Periodic Simple Average Price

Under this method, simple average price will be calculated periodically (normally a month) and not at each issue of material. A simple average of all the receipts during a month will be arrived at and applied to all the issues during the month. The opening does not enter into the calculation because it was not purchased during the current period.

Advantages

1) As there is only issue rate for the whole period (normally a month) it is very easy to operate.
2) This system can be utilised in process industries.

Disadvantages

1) This system is not useful to jobbing industry.
2) Though it is only one issue rate, it requires a lot of time to calculate.
3) The disadvantages as 1 to 4 of simple average price will apply here also.

B-3 Moving Simple Average Price

Under this method, the issues are valued at price which is calculated by dividing the total of the simple periodic average prices are given number of periods. It takes into account the average price of the current period and also the average price for a given number of preceding periods. Generally, odd number of months, say 3, 5 to 7 is used. This method evens out price fluctuations over a number of periods and cost distortion from one job to another job is reduced. In the case of rising prices, the stock is overvalued. Profit or loss may aries due to approximations.

B-4 Weighted Average Price

Under this method, issues are valued at a price which is calculated by dividing the total cost of the material in the stock by the total quantity of material in that stock. This method averages prices after multiplying by their quantities. A new average price has to be worked out on each and every purchase of materials and this weighted average price is to be applied to all the issues till another purchase is made. To achieve accuracy, the issue price has to be calculated upto 4 decimal places.

Advantages

1) This method is suitable where there are wide fluctuations in purchase prices and it evens out prices over the whole period of accounting because of considering the quantities also.
2) Since the receipts are much frequent than issues, number of calculations are not many as the weighted average price is calculated on the receipt of materials and not on the issue of material.

3) Value of closing stock under this method can be accepted for the purpose of Balance Sheet.

4) It is easy to calculate.

Disadvantages

1) As the issue are not valued at actual cost, profits or loss may arise.
2) If the receipts are many, this method requires lot of calculation.
3) Issue may not be at current prices.
4) Issue prices may be calculated upto 4 decimal points.
5) Inventory on hand does not represent current economic values.

B-5 Periodic Weighted Average Price :

Under this method, the issues are valued at price which is calculated by dividing the total cost of the materials obtained during that period by the quantity purchased. It is the weighted average price of material purchased during that period. A new average price is calculated at the end of the period, normally a month, and is applied to all the issues in that month.

Advantages

1) It is useful in process industries where accounting entries can be made at the end of a period.
2) Only one calculation is required at the end of the period normally a month and hence it is easy to operate.
3) As the quantities and the cost are considered, this method is much more accurate than the periodic simple average price.
4) It is usually employed where the prices of material fluctuate considerably.
5) It evens out wide fluctuations in a particular period.

Disadvantages

1) This method is not useful to jobbing industry.
2) The value of closing stock does not represent either the actual cost or current market price.
3) This method involves considerable delay in pricing material issues and a heavy burden of clerical work at the end of the period. This can be avoided if the weighted average price of one period is used in the subsequent period.
4) Profit or loss may arise as the issues are not valued at actual cost or current market price.

B-6 Moving Weighted Average Price

To obtain the Moving Weighted Average Price, the total of the weighted average price of the current period and weighted average price of a given number of preceeding periods is to be divided by the number of periods (i.e. current + preceeding periods). This price is to be applied to all the issues in the current period. It is more or less similar to the moving simple average methods excepting that this is a Moving Weighted Average Price and hence all the advantages and disadvantages of Moving Simple Average Method are applicable here also.

C-1 Standard Cost Method

It is a pre-determined price fixed on the basis of a specification of all the factors affecting the price of materials in future period. Such factors include :

1) The quantity of materials on hand.
2) The quantity of materials to be purchased.
3) Quantity discounts.
4) Prices normally paid or payable.
5) Normal purchasing cost involved.
6) The likelihood of a rise or fall in prices due to market conditions.
7) Changes in production requirements.
8) Charging of containers, freight and warehousing expenses to the price of materials.

A standard price will be set for each material and is applied for all the issues in a period, normally a year.

It is compared with the actual price paid. Profit or loss may arise under this method also but it is not due to average prices.

It is on account of variances from a pre-determined price set for each material. If the actual price paid exceeds standard, it is adverse variance and if the actual price is less than standard, it is favourable variance. All receipts under this method are posted at actual prices and issues at standard prices for each material. The difference between standard and actuals is disposed of through price variance account.

This method can be utilised in most of industries in general and steel industry in particular where material transactions are numerous, even though a system of standard costing is not in operation. Standard price should not be set on a long-term basis. It should be determined for short term only and revised as and when necessary.

Advantages

1) It is easy to operate because all the issues are priced at the same standard rate.
2) Useful comparison of one job / process with another job / process can be made.
3) Efficiency of purchase department can be measured.
4) It reduces the clerical costs as the standard price will be applied to all the issues in a period, normally a year.

Disadvantages

1) It is very difficult to fix a standard price during the period of inflation or when prices fluctuate widely from time to time.
2) Issues may not be at current economic values and hence profit or loss may arise which has to be adjusted in the accounts.
3) The value of closing stock may show absurd figures.
4) The trend of actual prices may not be reflected.

C-2 Inflated Price

It is a price which includes a charge designed to cover the cost of contigencies or related costs. Normally, the invoice price includes the cost, freight, insurance and taxes less discounts. Other expenses like cost of receiving, inspection, storing and carrying, handling of materials and losses arising out of evaporation and breaking up bulk, etc., are treated as production overheads. Under this method, all these expenses are added to determine the cost of issues. Hence, inflated price will recover the full cost of materials. This is not a separate method of pricing. Any of the prices-actual, average or notional may be inflated for the purpose of valuation of issues.

C-3 Replacement Price or Market Price

Under this method, issues are valued at the replacement price prevailing in the market on the date of issue. The method presupposes the determination of replacement cost of material at the time of each issue which may involve considerable work.

Advantages

1) It is easy to operate as there are no calculations of issue prices. It ascertains the market price and charge the issues accordingly.
2) The issues are priced at the current market prices.

Disadvantages

1) It is not so easy to get market quotations.
2) Issues are not priced at actual cost.
3) It is difficult to get the market prices daily for all the issues made on that day. In such cases, current prices are to be estimated.

4) The valuation of stock will not be at current market prices. In times of rising prices, the value of closing stock may show a negligible amount or even a negative amount, because of charging issues at higher market prices. In times of falling prices, the stock value becomes alarmingly high.

5) This method causes an element of unrealised profit or loss which has to be adjusted in accounts.

C-4 Re-Use Price

It is the price which is used to value a material in its re-use. This price is adopted for the issue of materials to other departments for an alternative use. Profit or loss may arise because the issues are not valued at actual cost and it has to be adjusted in accounts.

D) Other Methods

D-1 Specific Price : or Identifiable Cost Method

Materials which are purchased exclusively for certain jobs are to be issued and charged at the specific price. This method is used in case of non-standard and special materials required for such jobs.

Of course, this method has only a limited application. But it enjoys the advantages of pricing the materials at actual cost and thus is desirable from costing point of view. This method has a special application in job order industries where non standard materials are purchased for specific job.

Accounting for Issue of Material

Following procedure of accounting for issue of materials is followed by the costing department in an organisation.

After the posting of the stores requisition in the issue column of Bin-Card one copy is sent to costing department for necessary posting in stores ledger, pricing of issues and accounting thereof. These stores requisitions may be for Direct Material or for indirect material. If it is for Direct Material, Job No. or work order No is to be mentioned. If it is for indirect material, standing order No. is to be mentioned in case of factory and Cost Account No is to be mentioned in case of administration, Selling and Distribution Departments.

Journal Entries

For Direct Materials	:	Debit Work in Progress A/c Credit Stores Ledger Control A/c
(Subsidiary Book	:	Debit or process or product as the case may be)
For indirect material	:	Debit Factory / Administration / Selling / Distribution overhead Control A/c Credit Stores Ledger Control A/c

Accounting for shortage found during physical verification, Excess found during physical verification material returns from production department to stores department, material return to suppliers, pricing of material transfers has been given as follows :

A) Shortage found during physical verification

The quantity of shortage found during physical verification is to be entered in the issue column and valued at the issue price depending on the method, i.e. FIFO, LIFO, Weighted Average etc. followed by the organisation.

Journal Entry

Debit	:	Factory Overhead A/c
Credit	:	Stores Ledger Control A/c (If the shortage is normal)
Debit	:	Cost Profit and Loss A/c
Credit	:	Stores Ledger Control A/c (If the shortage is abnormal)
Debit	:	Work-in-progress A/c
Credit	:	Stores Ledger Control A/c

(If it is ascertained that the shortage was on account of wrong counting or weighing at the time of original issue of materials of a particular job).

B) Excess found during physical verification

The excess quantity found during physical verification should be entered in the receipt column and valued at the latest purchase price or market price. If it is not ascertainable, it should be valued at the latest issue price.

Journal Entry

Debit : Stores Ledger Control A/c
Credit : Factory Overhead A/c (If the excess is due to normal causes)
Debit : Stores Ledger Control A/c
Credit : Costing Profit and Loss A/c (If the excess due to abnormal circumstances)
Debit : Stores Ledger Control A/c
Credit : Work-in-Progress A/c

(If it is ascertained that the excess at the time was on account of wrong counting or weighing at the time of original issue)

C) Pricing of material returned from Production Department to Stores Department

The excess material drawn from the Stores Department may be returned by the Foreman of the Production Department to the Stores Department. The quantity of material returned should be entered in the receipt column and valued at the price at which the materials were originally issued. If the original issue is not ascertainable, the latest issue price can be adopted for pricing the materials returned.

Journal Entry

Debit : Stores Ledger Control A/c   Credit : Work-in-Progress A/c (i.e. job / process / product)

D) Materials returned to suppliers

Generally, the accepted quantity only should be entered in the receipt column. Depending on the technical condition of the material, it is to be inspected over the machines for a certain number of hours and if it is found not acceptable after testing on the machines etc., the same has to be returned to the suppliers. Then the quantity should be entered in the issue column and valued at the price at which it was originally purchased from the supplier.

E) Pricing of Material transfers

Sometimes, foreman may not return the excess material drawn which is meant for one particular job. Instead, he may use this material for another similar job. In such case, he need not return the material to the Storekeeper but he has to inform the Costing Department by way of Material Transfer Note for valuation and accounting thereof. In Cost Ledger, no transfer entry is required but in the Subsidiary Register of Jobs, the job where this excess material is used has to be debited by crediting the job where from the material has been transferred.

Adjustment of Unusual Balances in Stores Ledger

Some unusual balances are often revealed in the Stores Ledger because of pricing of issues at average rates and their accounting adjustments are as follows :

Table showing nature of balance, treatment and account entries regarding unusual balances in stores ledger

No.	Nature of Balance	Treatment	Journal Entry
1)	Plus Quantity nil or minus value	Quantity on hand should be valued	Debit : Stores Ledger Control A/c Credit : Factory Overhead A/c
2)	Minus Quantity	There should not be minus quantity. This may be due to error. It should be located and rectified.	No Journal Entry
3)	Nil Quantity plus Value	Value should be wiped out.	Debit : Factory Overhead A/c Credit : Stores Ledger Control A/c Debit : Stores Ledger Control A/c Credit : Factory Overhead A/c

Problem : 1

The following particulars have been extracted in respect of Material-Bee of Royal Co., Kolkatta for the month of March, 200X. Prepare Stores Ledger Account pricing the material issues on the basis of Last In First Out Method.

1st	Opening stock - 100 units @ Rs. 1.75	5th	Purchases - 150 units @ Rs. 1.50
8th	Issues - 200 units	12th	Purchases - 300 units @ Rs. 1.60
18th	Issues - 250 units	22nd	Purchases - 400 units @ Rs. 1.70
29th	Issues - 400 units	30th	Spoilage - 10 units.

Ascertain the value of closing stock.

Solution : LIFO

In the books of Royal Co., Kolkatta
Stores Ledger Account of Material-Bee for the month ended 31-03-200X

Maximum Level : Minimum Level :
Reorder Level : Reorder Quantity :

Date 200X March	Particualrs	Receipts				Issues				Balance			Remarks
		GRN No.	Qty. units	Rate Rs.	Amt. Rs.	MRN No.	Qty. units	Rate Rs.	Amt. Rs.	Qty. Rs.	Rate Rs.	Amt. Rs.	
1st	Opening Stock									100	1.75	175	
5th	Purchases	---	150	1.50	225					100 150	1.75 1.50	175 225	
8th	Issues					---	150 50	1.50 1.75	225 87.50	50	1.75	87.50	
12th	Purchases	---	300	1.60	480					50 300	1.75 1.60	87.50 480	
18th	Issues					---	250	1.60	400	50 50	1.75 1.60	87.50 80.00	
22nd	Purchases	---	400	1.70	680					50 50 400	1.75 1.60 1.70	87.50 80.00 680	
29th	Issues					---	400	1.70	680	50 50	1.75 1.60	87.50 80.00	
30th	Spoilage						10	1.60	0.16	50 40	1.75 1.60	87.50 64.00	Spoilage

Valuation of closing stock

Closing stock is 90 units which consists of two lots viz.

i) 50 units - @ Rs. 1.75 - Rs. 87.50 ii) 40 units - @ Rs. 1.60 - Rs. 64

Hence, 90 units are valued at Rs. 157.50

Problem : 2

The following are the receipts and issues of Material in Amon Co. Ltd. Ahmednagar, during the month of March 200X.

1 Opening stock 2,000 units @ Rs. 46 per unit

4 Issued 1,400 units

6 Purchased 3,500 units @ Rs. 45 per unit

8 Condemned due to deterioration in quantity and hence transferred to scrap 300 units

9 Issued 800 units

14 Issued 2,100 units

17 Purchased 2,000 units @ Rs. 48 per unit

20 Issued 1,200 units

25 Purchased 1,800 units @ Rs. 47 per unit

28 Issued 2,800 units

31 Excess found in stock 430 units due to wrong weighing during the month.

The maximum level fixed is 4,000 units, the minimum 750 units and the reorder level is 1,000 units. Show the Stores Ledger Account under Last In First Out Method.

Solution : LIFO

In the books of Amon Co. Ltd., Ahmednagar

Stores Ledger Account of Material-Bee for the month ended 31-03-200X

Maximum Level : 4,000 units Minimum Level : 750 units

Reorder Level : 1,000 units Reorder Quantity :

Date 200X March	Particualrs	Receipts				Issues				Balance			Remarks
		GRN No.	Qty. units	Rate Rs.	Amt. Rs.	MRN No.	Qty. units	Rate Rs.	Amt. Rs.	Qty. Rs.	Rate Rs.	Amt. Rs.	
1st	Opening Stock									2,000	46	92,000	
4th	Issues					---	1,400	46	64,400	600	46	27,600	
6th	Purchases	---	3,500	45	1,57,500					600 3,500	46 45	27,600 1,57,500	
8th	Condemned due to deterioration					---	300	45	13,500	600 3,200	46 45	27,600 1,44,000	Scrap
9th	Issues					---	800	45	36,000	600 2,400	46 45	27,600 1,08,000	
14nd	Issues					---	2,100	45	94,500	600 300	46 45	27,600 13,500	
17th	Purchases	---	2,000	48	96,000					600 300 2,000	46 45 48	27,600 13,500 96,000	
20th	Issues					---	1,200	48	57,600	600 300 800	46 45 48	27,600 13,500 38,400	

Date 200X March	Particualrs	Receipts				Issues				Balance			Remarks
		GRN No.	Qty. units	Rate Rs.	Amt. Rs.	MRN No.	Qty. units	Rate Rs.	Amt. Rs.	Qty. Rs.	Rate Rs.	Amt. Rs.	
25th	Purchases	---	1,800	47	84,600					600 300	46 45	27,600 13,500	
										800 1,800	48 47	38,400 84,600	
28th	Issues						1,800 800 200	47 48 45	84,600 38,400 9,000	600 100	46 45	27,600 4,500	
31th	Excess in	---	430	47	20.210	---				600 100 430	46 45 47	27,600 4,500 20,210	Excess in Stock

N.B. : Excess found in stock on 31st March due to wrong weighing during the month, is valued at Rs. 47 per unit as the latest purchase price

Problem : 3

The stock on hand of material as on 01 - 01 - 200X was 500 units @ Re. 1 per unit. The following purchases and issues were subsequently made. Prepare Stores Ledger Account of material in Ballarpur Ltd., chandrapur for the three months ended 31 - 03 - 200X under Last In First Out Method.

Purchases

6-1-200X	:	100 units @ Rs. 1.10	20-1-200X	:	700 units @ Rs. 1.20
27-1-200X	:	400 units @ Rs. 1.30	13-2-200X	:	1,000 units @ Rs. 1.40
20-2-200X	:	500 units @ Rs. 1.50	17-3-200X	:	400 units @ Rs. 1.60

Issues

9-1-200X	:	500 units	22-1-200X	:	500 units
30-1-200X	:	500 units	15-2-200X	:	500 units
22-2-200X	:	500 units	11-3-200X	:	500 units

On 29-03-200X the stock verifier reported that there was a breakage of 15 units.

Solution : LIFO

In the books of Ballapur Ltd.; Chandrapur

Stores Ledger Account for the month ended 31-03-200X

Maximum Level : ______ Minimum Level : ______ Reorder Level :

Reorder Quantity : ______

Date 200X March	Particualrs	Receipts				Issues				Balance			Re-marks
		GRN No.	Qty. units	Rate Rs.	Amt. Rs.	MRN No.	Qty. units	Rate Rs.	Amt. Rs.	Qty. Rs.	Rate Rs.	Amt. Rs.	
1-1	Stock on hand	---								500	1	500	
6-1	Purchases	---	100	1.10	110					500 100	1 1.10	500 110	
9-1	Issues					---	100 400	1.10 1	110 400	100	1	100	
20-1	Purchases	---	700	1.20	840					100 700	1 1.20	100 840	

Date 200X March	Particualrs	Receipts				Issues				Balance			Re-marks
		GRN No.	Qty. units	Rate Rs.	Amt. Rs.	MRN No.	Qty. units	Rate Rs.	Amt. Rs.	Qty. Rs.	Rate Rs.	Amt. Rs.	
22-1	Issues					---	500	1.20	600	100 200	1 1.20	100 240	
27-1	Purchases	---	400	1.30	520					100 200 400	1 1.20 1.30	100 240 520	
30-1	Issues					---	400 100	1.30 1.20	520 120	100 100	1 1.20	100 120	
13-2	Purchases	---	1,000	1.40	1,400					100 100 1,000	1 1.20 1.40	100 120 1,400	
15-2	Issues					---	500	1.40	700	100 100 500	1 1.20 1.40	100 120 700	
20-2	Purchases	---	500	1.50	750					100 100 500 500	1 1.20 1.40 1.50	100 120 700 750	
22-2	Issues					---	500	1.50	750	100 100 500	1 1.20 1.40	100 120 700	
11-3	Issues					---	500	1.40	700	100 100	1 1.20	100 120	
17-3	Purchases	---	400	1.60	640					100 100 400	1 1.20 1.60	100 120 640	
29.3	Breakage					---	15	1.60	24	100 100 385	1 1.20 1.60	100 120 616	Break-age

Problem : 4

The following transactions relate to purchase and issue of material, CM-105 in Vicco Goa during March, 200X. Prepare a Stores Ledger Account under, LIFO method of charging materials.

1st Opening balance - 500 units @ Rs. 25
3rd Issued 70 units
4th Issued 100 units
8th Issued 80 units
13th Received from vendor 200 units @ Rs. 24
14th Refund of surplus from a work order 15 units @ Rs. 24
16th Issued 180 units
20th Received from vendor 240 units @ Rs. 23
24th Issued 304 units
25th Received from vendor 320 units @ Rs. 23.50
26th Issued 112 units

27th Refund of surplus from a work order 12 units @ Rs. 25

29th Received from vendor 100 units @ Rs. 24

A stock verifier noted that on 15th he had found a shortage of 5 units and on 28th a damage of 8 units.

Solution : LIFO

In the books of Vicco, Goa

Stores Ledger Account of Material CM-105 for the month ended 31-03-200X

Maximum Level : .... Minimum Level : ....

Reorder Level : .... Reorder Quantity : ....

Date 200X March	Particualrs	Receipts				Issues				Balance			Re-marks
		GRN No.	Qty. units	Rate Rs.	Amt. Rs.	MRN No.	Qty. units	Rate Rs.	Amt. Rs.	Qty. Rs.	Rate Rs.	Amt. Rs.	
1st	Opening Balance									500	25	12,500	
3rd	Issues					---	70	25	1,750	430	25	10,750	
4th	Issues					---	100	25	2,500	330	25	8,250	
8th	Issues					---	80	25	2,000	250	25	6,250	
13th	Purchases	---	200	24	4,800					250 200	25 24	6,250 4,800	
14th	Refund of surplus	---	15	24	360					250 215	25 24	6,250 5,160	Refund *
15th	Shortage					---	5	24	120	250 210	25 24	6,250 5,040	Shortage *
16th	Issues					---	180	24	4,320	250 30	25 24	6,250 720	
20th	Purchases	---	240	23	5,520					250 30 240	25 24 23	6,250 720 5,520	
24th	Issues					---	240 30 34	23 24 25	5,520 720 850	216	25	5,400	
25th	Purchases	---	320	23.50	7,520					216 320	25 23.50	5,400 7,520	
26th	Issues					---	112	23.50	2,632	216 208	25 2.50	5,400 4,888	
27th	Refund of surplus	----	12	25	300					216 208	25 23.50	5,400 4,888	Refund *
28th	Damage					---	8	25	200	12 216 208 4	25 25 23.50 25	300 5,400 4,888 100	Damage *
29th	Purchases	---	100	24	2,400					216 208 4 100	25 23.50 25 24	5,400 4,888 100 2,400	

Problem : 5

On 1st March, 200X the stock of a component in the stores was 500 units @ Rs. 300 per hundred. During the three months the receipts and issues were as folows :

Purchased

March	:	400 units @ Rs. 400 per hundred
April	:	500 units @ Rs. 500 per hundred
May	:	600 units @ Rs. 600 per hundred

Issued

March : 300 units April : 400 units May : 500 units

When stock was taken on 31st May 200X, a discrepancy of 50 units was revealed. Prepare a Stores Ledger Card under First In First Out Method in the books of National Ltd., Pune.

Solution : FIFO

In the books of National Ltd., Pune

Stores Ledger Card of a component for three months ended 31-05-200X

Maximum Level : ______________ Minimum Level : ______

Reorder Level : ______________ Reorder Quantity : ______

Date	Particualrs	Receipts				Issues				Balance			Re-
200X March		GRN No.	Qty. units	Rate Rs.	Amt. Rs.	MRN No.	Qty. units	Rate Rs.	Amt. Rs.	Qty. Rs.	Rate Rs.	Amt. Rs.	marks
1-3	Opening Stock									500	3	1,500	
1-3	Purchases	---	400	4.00	1,600					500	3	1,500	
										400	4	1,600	
31-3	Issues					---	300	3	900	200	3	600	
										400	4	1,600	
1-4	Purchases	---	500	5.00	2,500					200	3	600	
										400	4	1,600	
										500	5	2,500	
30-4	Issues					---	200	3	600	200	4	800	
							200	4	800	500	5	2,500	
1-5	Purchases	---	600	6.00	3,600					200	4	800	
										500	5	2,500	
										600	6	3,600	
31-5	Issues					---	200	4	800	200	5	1,000	
							300	5	1,500	600	6	3,600	
31-5 *	Discrepancy					---	50	5	250	150	5	750	Discrep
										600	6	3,600	ancy *

Problem : 6

Prepare a Stores Ledger Account on the basis of First In First Out method of pricing the issue of stores using the following infomation about material G-7 of Deep Co. Panvel for March, 200X.

Date : 200X March	Particulars	Quantity units	Rate per unit (Rs.)
1st	Materials on hand	300	9.70
3rd	Purchases	250	9.80
11th	Issues	390	---
14th	Shortage	10	---
15th	Purchases	300	10.05
18th	Purchases	150	9.60
20th	Issues	210	---
24th	Purchases	110	9.90
25th	Issues	300	---
28th	Purchases	150	10.30
29th	Issues	210	---

Solution : FIFO

In the books of Deep Co., Panvel

Stores Ledger Account Material G-7 for the month ended 31-03-200X

Maximum Level : ____________ Minimum Level : ____________

Reorder Level : ____________ Reorder Quantity : ____________

Date 200X March	Particualrs	Receipts				Issues				Balance			Re-marks
		GRN No.	Qty. units	Rate Rs.	Amt. Rs.	MRN No.	Qty. units	Rate Rs.	Amt. Rs.	Qty. Rs.	Rate Rs.	Amt. Rs.	
1st	Materials on hand									300	9.70	2,910	
3rd	Purchases	---	250	9.80	2,450					300	9.70	2,910	
										250	9.80	2,450	
11th	Issues					---	300	9.70	2,910	160	9.80	1,568	
							90	9.80	882				
14th	Shortage						10	9.80	98	150	9.80	1,470	Shortage *
15th	Purchases	---	300	10.05	3,015					150	9.80	1,470	
										300	10.05	3,015	
18th	Purchases		150	9.60	1,440					150	9.80	1,470	
										300	10.05	3,015	
										150	9.60	1,440	
20th	Issues					---	150	9.80	1,470	240	10.05	2,412	
							60	10.05	603	150	9.60	1,440	
24th	Purchases	---	110	9.90	1,089					240	10.05	2,412	
										150	9.60	1,440	
										110	9.90	1,089	
25th	Issues					---	240	10.05	2,412	90	9.60	864	
							60	9.60	576	110	9.90	1,089	
28th	Purchases	---	150	10.30	1,545					90	9.60	864	
29th	Issues									110	9.90	1,089	
										150	10.30	1,545	
						---	90	9.60	864	140	10.30	1,442	
							110	9.90	1,089				
							10	10.30	103				

Problem : 7

The stock in hand as on 1st January 200X was 500 units @ Rs. 10 per unit. From the following transactions of purchases and issues of Ideal Co. Ltd., Mumbai, prepare a Stores Ledger Account under First In First Out Method.

Purchases :

6th Jan. 100 units @ Rs. 11	20th Jan.700 units @ Rs. 12	27th Jan.400 units @ Rs. 13
13th Feb.1,000 units @ Rs. 14	20th Feb.500 units @ Rs. 15	17th Feb.400 units @ Rs. 16

Issues :

9th Jan. 500 units	22nd Jan.500 units	30th Jan. 500 units	15th Feb. 500 units
22nd Feb. 500 units	11th Mar.500 units	30th Mar. Missing units 20.	

Solution : FIFO

In the books of Ideal Co. Ltd. Mumbai

Stores Ledger Account of Material Fox for the three months ended 31-03-200X

Maximum Level : ________________ Minimum Level :

Reorder Level : ________________ Reorder Quantity :

Date 200X March	Particualrs	Receipts				Issues				Balance			Re-marks
		GRN No.	Qty. units	Rate Rs.	Amt. Rs.	MRN No.	Qty. units	Rate Rs.	Amt. Rs.	Qty. Rs.	Rate Rs.	Amt. Rs.	
1-1	Stock in hand									500	10	5,000	
6-1	Purchases	---	100	11	1,100					500	10	5,000	
										100	11	1,100	
9-1	Issues					---	500	10	5,000	100	11	1,100	
20-1	Purchases	---	700	12	8,400					100	11	1,100	
										700	12	8,400	
22-1	Issues					---	100	11	1,100	300	12	3,600	
							400	12	4,800				
27-1	Purchases	---	400	13	5,200					300	12	3,600	
										400	13	5,200	
30-1	Issues					---	300	12	3,600	200	13	2,600	
							200	13	2,600				
13-2	Purchases	---	1,000	14	14,000					200	13	2,600	
										1,000	14	14,000	
15-2	Issues					---	200	13	2,600	700	14	9,800	
							300	14	4,200				
20-2	Purchases	---	500	15	7,500					700	14	9,800	
										500	15	7,500	
22-2	Issues					---	500	14	7,000	200	14	2,800	
										500	14	7,000	
11-3	Issues					---	200	14	2,800	200	15	3,000	
							300	15	4,500				
17-3	Purchases	---	400	16	6,400					200	15	3,000	
										400	16	6,400	
30-3	Missing					---	20	15	300	180	15	2,700	
										400	16	6,400	Missing

Problem : 8

Prepare a Stores Ledger Account of material ICS from the following particulars adopting First-In-First-Out Method of pricing of material issues in the books of Komal Co. Ltd. Thane for March, 200X.

1st Opening stock - 200 pieces @ Rs. 2

Purchases :

5th 100 pieces @ Rs. 2.20 - Goods Received Note - 7

10th 150 pieces @ Rs. 2.40 - Goods Received Note - 12

20th 180 pieces @ Rs. 2.50 - Goods Received Note - 15

29th 120 pieces @ Rs. 2.30 - Goods Received Note - 24

Issues :

2nd 150 pieces - Material Requisition Note - 6

7th 100 pieces - Material Requisition Note - 10

12th 100 pieces - Material Requisition Note - 17

28th 200 pieces - Material Requisition Note - 23

31st Defectives - 15 pieces

Solution :

In the books of Komal Co. Ltd. Thane

Stores Ledger Account of Material Ic5 for the month ended 31-03-200X

Maximum Level : ____________ Minimum Level : ____________

Reorder Level : ____________ Reorder Quantity : ____________

Date 200X March	Particualrs	Receipts				Issues				Balance			Re-marks
		GRN No.	Qty. units	Rate Rs.	Amt. Rs.	MRN No.	Qty. units	Rate Rs.	Amt. Rs.	Qty. Rs.	Rate Rs.	Amt. Rs.	
1st	Opening stock									200	2	400	
2nd	Issues					6	150	2.00	300	50	2	100	
5th	Purchases	7	100	2.20	220					50 100	2 2.20	100 220	
7st	Issues					10	50 50	2 2.20	100 110	50	2.20	110	
10th	Purchases	12	150	2.40	360					50 150	2.20 2.40	110 360	
12th	Issues					17	50 50	2.20 2.40	110 120	100	2.40	240	
20th	Purchase	15	180	2.50	450					100 180	2.40 2.50	240 450	
28th	Issues					23	100 100	2.40 2.50	240 250	80	2.50	200	
29th	Purchases	24	120	2.30	276					80 120	2.50 2.30	200 276	
31st *	Defectives					---	15	2.50	37.50	65 120	2.50 2.30	162.50 276	Defective

Problem : 9

Show the following information relating to material - INFO, in Stores Ledger Account of Bharat Co. Ltd., Igatpuri on Simple Average Rate Method.

Receipts :

Date	Particulars	Quantity (Units)	P. O. No.	Rate per unit Rs.
1-1-200X	Opening Balance	200		2
5-1-200X	Purchases	100	67	2.20
10-1-200X	Purchases	150	71	2.40
20-1-200X	Purchases	180	75	2.60

Issues :

Date	Particulars	Quantity (Units)	M. R. N. No.
6-1-200X	Issues	150	51
11-1-200X	Issues	100	54
21-1-200X	Issues	200	62

On 13-01-200X the stock verification revealed a shortage of 10 units.

Solution :

Simple Average Rate Method

In the books of Bharat Co. Ltd., Igatpuri

Stores Ledger Account of Material - INFO for the month ended 31-01-200X

Maximum Level : ____________ Minimum Level : ____________

Reorder Level : ____________ Reorder Quantity : ____________

Date 200X March	Particualrs	Receipts				Issues				Balance		Re-marks
		P.O. No.	Qty. units	Rate Rs.	Amt. Rs.	MRN No.	Qty. units	Rate Rs.	Amt. Rs.	Qty. Rs.	Amt. Rs.	
1st	Opening Balance									200	400	
5th	Purchases	67	100	2.20	220					300	620	
6th	Issues					51	150	2.10	315	150	305	
10th	Purchases	71	150	2.40	360					300	665	
11th	Issues					54	100	2.20	220	200	445	
* 13th	Shortage						10	2.30	23	190	422	Shortage
20th	Purchases	75	180	2.60	468					370	890	
21st	Issues					62	200	2.40	480	170	410	

Calculation and Notes

1) Calculation of Simple Average Rate

6th $= \frac{\text{Rs. } 2 + \text{Rs. } 2.20}{2} = \frac{\text{Rs. } 4.20}{2} = \text{Rs. } 2.10$

11th $= \frac{\text{Rs. } 2 + \text{Rs. } 2.20 + \text{Rs. } 2.40}{3} = \frac{\text{Rs. } 6.60}{3} = \text{Rs. } 2.20$

13 $= \frac{\text{Rs. } 2.20 + \text{Rs. } 2.40}{2} = \frac{\text{Rs. } 4.60}{2} = \text{Rs. } 2.30$

21 $= \frac{\text{Rs. } 2.20 + \text{Rs. } 2.40 + \text{Rs. } 2.60}{3} = \frac{\text{Rs. } 7.20}{3} = \text{Rs. } 2.40$

Problem :10

Prepare a Stores Ledger Account from the following receipts and issues of Material Lee-45 of Liril Co. Ltd. for March, 200X pricing it on Weighted Average Rate Method.

Receipts

Date	Quantity (Units)	P. O. No.	Rate Per Unit (Rs.)
1st	1,000	8	10
15th	1,500	12	9
30th	500	20	8

Issues

Date	Quantity (Units)	M. R. N. No.
3rd	500	6
9th	250	8
20th	1,250	13
31st	500	19

Solution

Weighted Average Rate Method

In the books of Liril Co. Ltd.,

Stores Ledger Account of Material Lee - 45 for the month ended 31- 03- 200X

Maximum Level : ____________ Minimum Level : ____________

Reorder Level : ____________ Reorder Quantity : ____________

Date 200X March	Particualrs	Receipts				Issues				Balance			Re-marks
		GRN No.	Qty. units	Rate Rs.	Amt. Rs.	MRN No.	Qty. units	Rate Rs.	Amt. Rs.	Qty. Rs.	Rate Rs.	Amt. Rs.	
1st	Purchases	8	1,000	10	10,000					1,000	10	10,000	
3rd	Issues					6	500	10	5,000	500	10	5,000	
9th	Issues					8	250	10	2,500	250	10	2,500	
15st	Purchase	12	1,500	9	13,500					1,750	9,143	16,000	
20th	Issues					13	1,250	9,143	11,429	500	9,143	4,571	
30th	Purchases	20	500	8	4,000					1,000	8,571	8,571	
31st	Issues					19	500	8,571	4,28550	500	8,571	4,28550	

Calculation and Notes :

Calculation of weighted Average Rate :

1st $= \dfrac{(1{,}000 \text{ units} \times \text{Rs. } 10)}{1{,}000 \text{ units}} = \dfrac{\text{Rs. } 10{,}000}{1{,}000 \text{ units}} = \text{Rs. } 10$

15th $= \dfrac{(250 \text{ units} \times \text{Rs. } 10) + (1{,}500 \text{ units} \times \text{Rs. } 9)}{250 \text{ units} + 1{,}500 \text{ units}} = \dfrac{\text{Rs. } 2{,}500 + \text{Rs. } 13{,}500}{1{,}750 \text{ units}} = \dfrac{\text{Rs. } 16{,}000}{1{,}750 \text{ units}} = \text{Rs. } 9.143$

30th $= \dfrac{(500 \text{ units} \times \text{Rs. } 9{,}143) + (500 \text{ units} \times \text{Rs. } 8)}{500 \text{ units} + 500 \text{ units}} = \dfrac{\text{Rs. } 4{,}571 + \text{Rs. } 4{,}000}{1{,}000 \text{ units}} = \dfrac{\text{Rs. } 8{,}571}{1{,}000 \text{ units}} = \text{Rs. } 8.571$

Questions for Self-Study

1) What do you understand by classification and codification of materials? State the advantages of a good system of classification and codification.
2) What is Codification? What are the basic principles of coding?
3) Explain the methods of Codification.
4) What is classification of materials? How are the materials classified?
5) What are the objectives of good store keeping?
6) Explain in detail the forms and documents used in stores?
7) What is a Bin Card? Explain the utilities of Bin Card.
8) "Bin card is an effective tool for controlling the stock" Discuss.
9) What is Stores ledger? Discuss the utility of stores ledger.
10) Discuss the general nature and uses of stores ledger.
11) What is the difference between Bin Card and Stores ledger card.
12) Explain the various methods of pricing of material issued from stores.
13) Explain briefly the various factors which are considered before adopting a particular method of pricing of meterial issues from stores.
14) Explain the advantages and disadvantages of First In First Out Method of pricing of material issues.
15) Discuss the effects of rising prices and falling prices on Last In First out method of pricing of materials issues.
16) Explain the advantages and disadvantages of Simple Average Method of pricing of material issues.
17) Distinguish between simple Average Method and Weighted Average Method of pricing of material issues.
18) What is Inventory Control System? Explain the important objectives of an effective inventory control system?
19) From the following prepare Stores Ledger Account under : i) FIFO ii) LIFO methods

Purchases:

1st Jan.	Opening Stock	200 pieces @ Rs. 2 each
5th Jan.	Purchases	100 pieces @ Rs. 2.20 each
10th Jan.	Purchases	150 Pieces @ Rs. 2.40 each
20th Jan.	Purchases	180 pieces @ Rs. 2.50 each
Issues :		
2nd Jan.	Issues	150 Pieces
7th Jan.	Issues	100 Pieces
12th Jan.	Issues	100 Pieces

28th Jan. Issues 200 Pieces

20) The following is the record of receipts and issues of certain material in the factory during a week :

1st April	Opening Stock	50 tons @ Rs. 10 per ton
1st April	Issued	30 tons
2nd April	Received	60 tons @ Rs. 10.20 per ton
3rd April	Issued	25 tons (Stock verification reveals loss of one ton)
4th April	Received from orders	10 tons (previously issued at Rs.9.15 per ton
5th April	Issued	40 tons
6th April	Received	22 tons @ Rs. 10.30 per ton
7th April	Issues	38 tons

At what prices will you issue the materials ? Use FIFO and LIFO methods and show the comparative results.

21) A manufacturer used cost price as the basis for charging out the materials to jobs. The receipt side of the stores ledger accounts shows the following particulars :

500	articles	bought	at	Rs. 3 each
700	articles	bought	at	Rs. 3.10 each
400	articles	bought	at	Rs. 3.20 each
800	articles	bought	at	Rs. 3.10 each

Successive issues were made of 300, 1000 and 200 articles. At what price per article should each of these issues be charged under FIFO method?

22) Show the following in Stores Ledger Account on FIFO basis.

Date	Particulars	Unit	Rate Rs.
1-1-200X	Opening Balance	100	3.80
4-1-200X	Purchases	800	4.00
15-1-200X	Purchases	500	4.20
16-1-200X	Issues	600	-
21-1-200X	Purchases	800	4.60
22-1-200X	Issues	1,200	-
24-1-200X	Purchases	1,400	4.40
25-1-200X	Received back from completed job (Issued on 16-1-200X)	50	-
27-1-200X	Issues	900	-
30-1-200X	Issues	450	-

On 20th January stock verification revealed a shortage of 20 units.

23) The following are the receipts and issues of coal in a factory during March, 200X.

March	1	Opening stock 200 tons at Rs. 460 per ton
	4	Issues 140 tons
	6	Purchases 350 tons at Rs. 450 per ton
	8	Condemned due to deterioration in quantity and transferred to scrap 30 tons
	9	Issues 80 tons
	14	Issues 210 tons
	17	Purchases 200 tons at Rs. 480 per ton

20 Issues 120 tons

25 Purchased 180 tons at Rs. 470 per ton

28 Issues 280 tons

31 Excess found in stock - 43 tons due to wrong weighing during the month

The maximum level fixed is 400 tons, the minumum 75 tons and the re-order level is 100 tons. Show the stores Ledger Account under LIFO system.

24) From the following records of receipts and issues of materials, write up Stores Ledger Account for the month of January, 200X by LIFO method.

1 Opening Balance 500quintals @ Rs. 25.

3 Issued 70 quintals

4 Issued 100 quintals

8 Issued 800 quintals

13 Received from vendor 200 quintals @ Rs. 24

14. Refund of surplus from a work order 15 quintals @ Rs. 24.

16. Issued 180 quintals.

20 Received from vendor 240 quintals @ Rs. 23.

24. Issued 304 quintals.

25. Received from vendor 320 quintals @ Rs. 25.

26. Issued 112 quintals

27. Refund of surplus from a work order 12 quintals @ Rs. 25

29. Received from vendor 100 quintals @ Rs. 24.

A stock verifier of the factory noted that on 15th January he had found a shortage of 5 quintals and on 28th January another shortage of 8 quintals.

25) The following particulars have been extracted in respect of "Material A". Prepare Stores Ledger Account pricing,the material issue on the basis of First In first Out (FIFO) method and Last In First Out (LIFO) method :

Receipts

1-3-200X	Opening Stock	100 units at Rs. 1.80
5-3-200X	Purchased	150 units at Rs. 1.50
12-3-200X	Purchased	300 units at Rs. 1.60
22-3-200X	Purchased	400 units at Rs. 1.70

Issues

8-3-200X	Issued 200 units
18-3-200X	Issued 250 units
29-3-200X	Issued 400 units

26) The following transactions took place in respect of material item.

Date	Receipt Quantity	Rate Rs.	Issues Quantity
2-3-200X	400	2.00	-
10-3-200X	300	2.20	-
15-3-200X	-	-	250
18-3-200X	250	2.40	-
20-3-200X	-	-	200

Prepare Stores Ledger Account on the basis of :

a) Simple Average Method

b) Weighted Average Method

27) During January 200X, The Jagat Engineering Co. Ltd. effected the purchase of a certain item of stores as under:

Purchases

Date	Units	Total amount in Rs.
2-1-200X	100	190
15-1-200X	150	333

During the same period the details of the issues of the item were as under :

Issues

Date	Units
8-1-200X	50
20-1-200X	100

Besides on 1-1-200X there was an Opening Balance of 160 units valued for Rs. 200.

Enter the above transactions in the Stores Ledger under the Weighted Average price Method.

28) The following figures relate, to Material 'X'. Prepare Stores Ledger Account showing receipt and issue, pricing the issue on the basis of Weighted Average.

1-1-200X	Opening Stock 200 units @ Rs. 3.50 per unit.
3-10-200X	Purchases 300 units @ Rs. 4 per unit
5-10-200X	Issued 400 units
13-10-200X	Purchases 900 units @ Rs. 4.30 per unit
15-10-200X	Issued 600 units
23-10-200X	Purchases 600 units @ Rs. 3.80 per unit
25-10-200X	Issued 500 units

29) From the following information prepare Stores ledger account under :

i) Simple Average method, and ii) Weight Average method for the month of March 200X.

1st March : Opening Stock 300 pieces at Rs. 2 each

Purchases

5th March	:	400 pieces at Rs. 2.20 each
10th March	:	150 pieces at Rs. 2.40 each
20th March	:	180 pieces at Rs. 2.60 each

Issues

6th March	:	250 pieces
11th March	:	100 pieces
21st March	:	200 pieces

On 31st March 200X the stock verifier reported that there was shortage of 10 pieces.

30) The following are details supplied by Modern Company Ltd., in respect of its raw materials for the month of March 200X.

Date 200X March	Receipts		Issues Units kg.
	Units kg.	Price per kg. Rs.	
1.	2,000	5	
7.	1,000	6	
10			2,500
15	2,000	7	
31.			2,200

Show the Stores Ledger Account under FIFOand LIFO system.

LABOUR COST

Labour cost is the second major element of cost in most of the manufacturing undertakings. Proper accounting and control of labour cost, therefore constitutes one of the most important problems of management. In controlling labour cost, the problem is complicated by the human element. This is so because labour consist of a lot of different individuals, each with a different mental and physical capacity and each with a different personality.

Proper control over labour costs involves the following :

1. Satisfactory systems for recruitments and selections, training and placement of workers to job.
2. Satisfactory methods of labour remuneration.
3. Healthy working conditions, consistent with legal requirements and competitive undertaking.
4. Methods of assuring efficient labour performance.

Direct and Indirect Labour

Labour cost is divided into direct and indirect.

Direct labour cost is the cost of all labour expended in altering the construction, composition or condition of the product. Direct labour is directly engaged on production work and can be conveniently identified or attributed wholly to a particular job, product or process. For example, in furniture factory, wages of workers who cut and plan lumber and those who assemble the parts into finished furniture items are considered direct labour costs.

Indirect labour cost, on the other hand, is the wages paid to those workers who are not directly engaged in covering raw material into finished products. Such costs cannot be conveniently identified with a particular job, product or process. Supervisors, inspectors, work checkers, instructors, peons, watchmans are examples of indirect workers.

Organisation for accounting and control of labour cost

There are mainly five departments in an organisation which deals with labour, these are :

1) Personnel Department 2) Engineering Department 3) Time Keeping Department
4) Payroll Department 5) Cost Accounting Department

1) **Personnel Department** This is a service department and is mainly concerned with the proper selection and training of workers and placing them to jobs for which they are best suited.

2) **Engineering Department :** This department prepares, plans and specifications of job, makes job analysis, conducts time and motion studies, makes provisions for safe working conditions and supervises production activities.

3) **Time Keeping Department :** This department is concerned with recording of workers time. The recording of time put in by workers is required not only for attendance and wage calculations purpose but also for the purpose of cost analysis and apportionment of labour cost over various jobs.

4) **Payroll Department :** This department maintains a record of job classification and wage rate of each employee and performs the function of consumption of wage payable to them by preparing payroll or wage sheet. It is also responsible for disbursement of wage payments.

5) **Cost Accounting Department:** This department accumulates and classifies all cost data of which labour is one important element. It analysis the payroll and prepares routine and special labour cost reports for submission to managements so that proper control may be exercised on labour cost.

Time Records

The Time Keeping department is an important part of a firm's system of accounting and control of labour costs. The main function of this department is to accurately record each worker's time of arrival and departure in the factory and also the time spent on different jobs or processes. Thus, it embraces two functions :

a) Time-keeping i.e. recording time for attendance purpose and for calculation of wages, and

b) Time booking i.e. recording time spent for different jobs or processes for determining labour cost of job / processes.

The purpose of time recording is to provide basic data for :

i) Preparation of pay roll.

ii) Attendance records to meet statutory requirements.

iii) Computing labour cost of a job or process.

iv) Computing overhead cost of jobs, if based on wages or labour hours.

v) Statistical analysis of labour records, for determining productivity and control of labour cost.

Time- keeping : The essentials of a good time-keeping systems are as follows :

1) The system should be economical.
2) The system should be simple, smooth or quick.
3) Time-keeper should be there to avoid proxy attendance and ensure strict adherence to the prescribed procedure.
4) Late coming and early going should also be recorded.
5) Time-recording clocks should be correctly adjusted from time to time.
6) Monthly summary should be prepared correctly as this will be the basic data for the preparation of the payrolls.
7) False or fundamental entries should be avoided.
8) No proxy attendance.

Methods of Time-Keeping : Following are the different methods of recording attendance of workers :

a) Attendance Registers b) Metal Token or disc methods

c) Time recording clocks d) Other types of time recorders.

a) Attendance Registers

In this method, attendance of each worker is recorded in the register, maintained for this purpose. This register provides sufficient number of columns for attendance of each worker. Entries in the arrival and departure columns may be made by the foreman or the worker himself. If the workers are literate, they should be required to sign against their entries to avoid any dispute later on, separate attendance registers may be maintained in each department if the number of the workers is large, otherwise one register serve the purpose.

This method is quite simple and cheap. But is can be used only when the number of workers is very small. In such cases generally, there is no need for a separate time keeper as the work is done by the foreman himself.

b) Metal Token or disc method

Whenever a worker is employed a number will be allotted to him. Under this method, metal token bearing the worker's number is placed on the hook on 'OUT' board kept at the entrance of the factory. The worker on entering say at 8.00 a.m., removes this token and places it on 'IN' board. After completion of grace time, say at 8.10 a.m., the 'IN' board will be locked and workers will be allowed to enter the factory by keeping their token on 'Late' board, say upto 9.00 a.m. Beyond 9.00 a.m., workers will not be allowed. They have to apply for leave. At the time of departure, workers will keep their tokens on 'OUT' board in the order of numbers and leave the factory. On the basis of the above arrangement, daily attendance is compiled giving the details of normal attendance, late attendance and absentees. Details of overtime and early going from the factory are also collected daily. Then monthly summary is prepared for the preparation of pay rolls.

c) Time recording clocks

This is a mechanical method of recording attendance and proves quite useful when the number of workers is fairly large.

Each worker is allotted a clock card bearing his identification number, name, department, etc. These cards are kept in a rack in a serial order. There are usually two racks, an In Rack and an Out Rack. On arrival the worker will pick up his card from the 'Out' rack, put it in the slot of the clock, press a button and the exact time is printed on the card. After this the card is put in the 'In' rack. An inspection of the 'Out' racks will reveal absentees. A similar procedure is followed if workers leave the factory at the mid-day for lunch or in the evening at closure time. Clocks are adjusted so that late arrivals, early or late leavings, overtime etc. are automatically printed in red. The time-keeper must take care to see that no worker places friend's card in the clock in addition to his own, so as to avoid proxy. At the end of the week, the cards are sent to the pay office and a fresh set of cards for ensuing week is placed in the racks.

CLOCK CARD

Name .... Department ....

No. .... Week ending ....

Day	Beforenoon		Afternoon		Overtime		Total Hours	
	In	Out	In	Out	From	To	Normal	Overtime
Monday								
Tuesday								
Wednesday								
Thursday								
Friday								
Saturday								
						Total		

Wage Rate Rs. .... Time -keeper

Total Wage Rs. ....

Less : Deductions Rs. ....

(Signature)

Net Pay Rs. ....

MONTHLY CLOCK CARD

Ticket No. : Name :

Month : Department :

Only Clock stamping will be recognised

					Overtime			Total
Date	In	Out	In	Out	In	Out	Ordinary Time	Over Time
1								
2								
3								
4								
5								
6								
7								
8								
9								
10								
11								
12								
13								
14								
15								
16								
17								
18								
19								
20								
21								
22								
23								
24								
25								
26								
27								
28								
29								
30								
31								

TOTAL TIME

Days	Hours		Rate	Rs.	Ps.
		Regular Time Overtime Extra Time Lost time			
			Total		

Advantages : The main advantages of installing time recording clocks are :

1) The method is quite economical for large concerns as the initial heavy capital expenditure in installing clocks is recovered by savings in operating expenses i.e. economy in wages of time recording staff.
2) Chances of dispute are reduced as clocks provide more authentic records than hand written documents.
3) Work in connection with the preparation of wage sheets becomes more easier because clock cards may be utilised for calculation of wages.

Disadvantages : The main shortcoming of this method is that heavy initial capital investment is required which small concerns may find very difficult to afford.

Some organisations may follow 4 recordings of time i.e.

1) While entering the factory 2) While going for lunch 3) While coming after lunch

4) While leaving the factory and two recordings for overtime i.e.

a) While starting at overtime and b) At the time of completion of overtime.

Monthly cards are also used for the purpose of time recording and preparation of pay rolls.

d) Other types of Time Recorders

Besides time recording clocks, there are two types of time recorders which do not make use of clock cards.

1) **Dial Recorder :** This consist of a mechanism with a dial having a number of holes around the circumference. Each hole represents a number which corresponds to the clock number of workers. All that a worker has to do is to swing a radical arm mounted on the clock and place it into the hole alloted to him. This automatically records the time on a roll of paper placed within the machine against his clock number.

2) **Key Recorders :** This is mechanism with a number of keys, each key bearing the number of worker. The worker inserts the key in the key hole, and gives a turn, the clock number and the time are recorded on a sheet of paper placed inside the recorder.

An advantage of the above two records is that the rolls of the paper on which recordings are made form part of the payroll and so timing of the arrival and departure are not to be copied out.

These two methods of recording suffer from the following limitations :

a) The capacity of these is limited as the number of holes and keys is about 150 only.

b) Worker's time of arrival and departure are widely separated on the paper and calculation of each worker's total time becomes cumbersome.

Time Booking

In addition to recording worker's time of arrival and departure, it is necessary to record the particulars of work done by the workers and the time spent on each job or process. Recording of worker's time spent on different jobs is known as Time Booking. The objects of time booking are :

i) to ensure that the time for which a worker is paid is properly utilised;

ii) to ascertain the labour cost of work done; iii) to provide a basis for apportionment of overheads;

iv) to ascertain the idle time so as to control it.

Methods of Time Booking

The following are the common methods of Time Booking :

a) Daily Time-Sheets

In small works, each worker is provided with a daily time sheet. This system is useful in the case of small works and when a worker attends to several jobs in a day of 8 hours, he has to record the particulars of time spent on each separate job and hand it over to the foreman for his checking and signature.

DAILY TIME-SHEET

Worker's Name _______ Token No. _______ Machine No. _______ Date:

Works Order No.	Work done	Time		Hours	Rate	Rs.	Ps.
		Start	Finish				

Signed	Certified	Office
Worker :	Foreman :	Ref. :

Advantages

1) Simple and easy to understand.
2) These sheets are suitable even in the case of maintenance work or services.
3) Foreman will know the quantum of work performed by each worker in a day.
4) There is a close check on the correctness as the foreman signs daily.
5) In case of a number of jobs to be performed by a worker in a day, the paper work is less voluminous compared to the job card system.

Disadvantages

1) Accuracy cannot be relied upon as the entries are made by the individual workers.
2) There is a scope for mixing the idle time with the time booked for job or services.
3) Paper work be voluminous where workers are engaged on one job for several days.

The first two disadvantages can be avoided if the entries are made in the foreman's office and greater accuracy may be obtained.

b) Weekly Time Sheets

Weekly Time Sheets record almost the same particulars as the Daily Time Sheets. A worker has to enter the time spent on several jobs in a week. The foreman countersigns the sheet at the end of the week. This method has all the advantages and disadvantages of the Daily Time Sheets. In addition, there may be delay in posting the entries i.e. entries may be made once in two or three days or once in a week. Thus, there will be delay in sending the data to the cost office for ascertaining the labour cost of jobs and other particulars.

It is extensively used by the builders, decorators and civil engineering contractors. A different coloured stencil may be used for each trade i.e. fitter, machinists, welders etc.

WEEKLY TIME SHEETS

Workman : Clock No.

Dept : Week ending : Token No. Hourly rate.

Day	Beforenoon		Afternoon		Overtime		Hours	
	In	Out	In	Out	In	Out	Regular	Overtime
Sunday								
Monday								
Tuesday								
Wednesday								
Thursday								
Friday								
Saturday								

WEEKLY SUMMARY

At regular rate :	hrs @ Rs.	Rs.
At overtime rate :	hrs @ Rs.	Rs.
	Total	Rs.
Signed :	Certified :	Office
(Worker) :	(Foreman) :	Ref :

c) Job Card

Separate job card may be used whenever the workman starts on any new job or operation. When the job is finished, he has to surrender the card to the foreman after completing the entries regarding the completion time of job etc. Then he is issued another job card for entering the starting time and completion time of the job and so on. This method ensures automatic analysis of job time but it requires reconciliation of attendance time and job time plus idle time. Use of mechanical aid will ensure better accuracy and convenience of analysis. The job cards are sent to the cost office for ascertaining the labour cost of the various jobs.

JOB CARD

Work Order No :	Shop/Dept :	Time Allowed :	Date :
Drawing No :	Operation No :	Machine No :	

Job No.	Description	Time		Hours	For Cost Office	
		On	Off		Rate	Amount

Worker No. :

Signature :	Certified :	Ref :
(Worker) :	(Foreman) :	Date :

If the worker is not allotted another job as soon as he finished a job, an idle time card may be given to him for noting the idle time along with the reason there for.

Note : Standing orders are used for maintenance and other services.

Advantages

1) The information is recorded fully and correctly as per the proforma.
2) Worker has to fill up the required columns only. His portion of writing is negligible
3) It provides the useful link between production control and costing.
4) The information is suitable for cost analysis.

Disadvantages

1) Where a worker has to perform several jobs every day the paper work will become heavy and voluminous.
2) The foreman will not know, at a glance, The quantum of work performed by each worker in a day.
3) If idle time is not booked properly, the reconciliation with attendance of worker becomes very difficult.

d) Labour Cost Card

This card is meant to record the time taken on the various operations on the job by all the workers employed on it. Instead of allotting one card to each worker. The same card is circulated along with the job and the time taken by each worker on that job is recorded for different operations. Hence, it is also called as the 'Circulating Job Card'.

LABOUR COST CARD

Order No. Quantity :

Drawing No. Time allowed for the job :

Description of job : Special instruction :

Operation	Particulars of operation	Clock No.	Hours	Rate Rs.	Cost	Timing	Worker
1	Rough Planning	Off		2.50			B
		On					
2	Rough Turning	Off					B
		On					
3	Turning	Off					B
		On					
4	Planning	Off					B
		On					
5	Grinding	Off					B
		On					
6	Finishing	Off					
		On		2/-			A
7	Packing	Off					A
		On					
Material required		Checked by Foreman/Inspector			Cost office Reference		

Advantages

1) This card facilitates the computation of labour cost of the job.
2) The time taken can be compared with the time allowed which is recorded on it and any excessive time can be easily seen from the card. The comparision will assist in the labour cost control.

Disadvantages

1) If a job runs for a longer period reconciliation with attendance of the worker becomes difficult.
2) Where worker enters the details of the time taken, he may understate it to avoid the excessive time taken. In such cases, he may get inflated bonus on the basis of excessive time saved which is not correct saving of time. For this purpose, it is suggested that the entries should be made in foreman's office and the greater accuracy may be obtained.

c) Piece-work Card

Generally, the time taken for jobs on piece rate system is not recorded. But it is useful to record the time taken in case of differential piece work system of Taylor, Merrick etc. In this case, each worker will be given a piece work card. The details of quantity of work done, time taken and number of rejections etc. are recorded. Finally, wages payable after reducing the penalty for rejections will be calculated.

PIECE WORK CARD

Date :

Worker 's Name : Token No : Order No :

Department : Job Ledger

Nature of work : Entered on Abstract :

Description	Quantity	Rate	Amount Rs.	Amount Ps.	Time Taken
Less : Rejections Net :					
Signature of Foreman :		Posted to Job Ledger :	Entered on wages Sheets :		

f) Time-Cum-Job Card with Idle Time

It records all the three items i.e. the attendance time, job time and idle time on a single card record. This facilitates reconciliation and discrepancy, if any, is brought out. As usual, these may be filled either manually or with the help of clock recorders.

TIME-CUM-JOB CARD WITH IDLE TIME.

Name : Token No : Department :

Trade and Grade : Week ending : Hourly rate of pay :

Job No.	Day	Clock In	Time Out	Job Start	Time Finish	Ordinary Time	Over Time	Job Time	Idle Time
	Sunday Monday Tuesday Wednesday Thursday Friday Saturday								
					Total :				

Total Wages : Signed :

Difference between Time-keeping and Time-booking

Time-Keeping	Time-Booking
1. It is the recording of attendance time of workers.	1. It is the recording of the timespent by the worker on different jobs during his period of attendance.
2. It is the recording of the time for the purpose of attendance and wage calculations.	2. It is recording time for the purpose of cost analysis and apportionment of labour cost.
3. It helps to maintain discipline in attendance.	3. It helps to minimise the idle time.
4. Attendance time can be recorded through register disc or token system or time recording clocks.	4. Worktime can be recorded through daily time sheet, weekly time sheet, job card or labour cost card.
5. An efficient system of time-keeping should be smooth and quick.	5. An efficient system of time-booking should provide instructions for filling the work-time records correctly.

LABOUR TURNOVER

Labour turnover is the loss of employment in an organisation. It is a national problem of every nation and leads to high costs and low productivity. The extent of labour turnover varies according to industry , structure of employment in country , ratio of male and female in labour force, and infrastructure of a particular organisation. Although the cost of labour turnover is high in these days, very little effort has been made to collect, classify and compare the cost of labour turnover. A detailed study of the causes of labour turnover, analysis and comparision of cost of such turnover may help in controlling the situation.

In all business organisation, it is a common feature that some workers leave the employment and the new workers join in place of those leaving. This change in work force is known as Labour Turnover. Labour turnover is thus defined as the rate of change in the labour force in the organisation. Labour turnover varies greatly between different trades and industries. For example, where part time and seasonal labour is employed, the rate will be higher.

Measurement of Labour Turnover

To facilitate the comparisons between different periods and different undertakings, labour turnover may be expressed in a rate. There are three alternative methods by which this rate is computed. Once a particular method is used, it should be consistently followed for comparative analysis. The methods are :

1) Separation Method

This method takes into account only those workers who have left during a particular period. The formula is :

$$\text{Labour Turnover Rate} = \frac{\text{No. of workers left during a period}}{\text{Average no. of workers during the period}} \times 100$$

$$\text{Average Number} = \frac{\text{No. of workers in the beginning} + \text{No. of workers at the end of the period}}{2}$$

Multiplication by 100 in the above formula indicates rate in percentage.

2) Replacement Method

This method takes into account only those new workers who have joined in place of those who have left. Its formula is :

$$\text{Labour Turnover Rate} = \frac{\text{No. of workers replaced during the period}}{\text{Average no. of workers during the period}} \times 100$$

If new workers are engaged for expansion program or any other such purpose they are not considered for this computation.

3) Flux Method

This shows the total change in the composition of labour force due to separation and additions of workers. The formula is :

$$\text{Labour Turnover Rate} = \frac{\text{No. of workers left + No. of workers replaced}}{\text{Average no. of workers}} \times 100$$

Problem

Bharat Foods Product Ltd. supplies you the following information

No. of workers on 1 April 2002	80
No. of workers on 30 April 2002	100
No. of workers resigned	07
No. of workers discharged	02
No. of replacements	08

Calculate labour turnover rate.

Solution

Average No. of workers $= \frac{80 + 100}{2} = 90$ No. of workers left $= 7 + 2 = 9$

1) Separation Rate $= \frac{9}{90} \times 100 = 10\%$

2) Replacement Rate $= \frac{8}{90} \times 100 = 8.8\%$

3) Flux Rate $= \frac{9 + 8}{90} \times 100 = 18.8\%$

Causes of Labour Turnover

Labour turn over reports should be prepared regularly to be placed before manager giving a breakdown of the causes as why the workers left. The causes may be classified into three broad categories :

1) Avoidable causes 2) Unavoidable causes 3) Personal causes

1) Avoidable causes

These includes :

a) Redundancy due to seasonal fluctuations, shortage of raw materials, contraction in market demand, government and technological unemployment etc.

b) Dissatisfaction with

i)low remuneration ii) job iii) long hours of work iv) bad working condition v) locality or environment.

c) Discrimination between one worker and another.

d) Bad relation with subordinates, fellow workers, supervisors and management

e) Lack of :

i) transport ii) accommodation iii) proper recreational facilities iv) proper welfare measures

v) proper training facilities and vi) proper promotional avenue.

f) Inadequate protection from accidents

g) Dispute between rival trade unions

2) Unavoidable Causes

These are due to

a) Personal betterment b) Retirement c) Sickness d) Accidents e) Death
f) Domestic responsibility g) Pregnancy or marriage h) Move from locality
i) National service j) Dismissal or discharge due to insubordination, negligence, inefficiency ,unauthorised long absence,criminal prosecution etc.

3) Personal Causes

Workers may leave employment purely on personal grounds. Example

a) Dislike for the job, locality or environments b) Domestic troubles and family responsibilities
c) Personal betterment d) Retirement due to old age or illness
e) Marriage of girls.

Effect of Labour Turnover

A certain amount of labour turnover will always take place. To a limited extent this may be welcome particularly at the lower management level in that it creates vacancies for internal promotions and maintains the high moral for the young and ambitious. Moreover, new workers bring new ideas and methods of doing work from other concerns.

Labour turnover is expensive and generally it should be minimized because it results in increased cost of production for reasons stated below.

Labour turnover due to avoidable causes is not only a loss to the individual but also a loss to the organisation, industry and the nation as a whole.

High Labour Turnover

High Labour Turnover results in increased cost of production due to the following reasons :

a) Increased cost of selection, training the new workers.
b) Costs connected with new entrants such as accidents, breakage of tools, spoilage of finished products etc.
c) Delay in production.
d) Efficiency of new workers becomes very low and hence productivity will also be low.
e) Increase in cost of scrap, defective work and additional supervision etc.
f) Decrease in overall production due to lack of desired efficiency of new workers and due to time lost between the leaving of staff and recruitment of new workers. In addition there will be reduction in sales and loss of goodwill with customers.

Low Labour Turnover

In the senior grades of factory, employment may not be good thing because there will be few possibilities of promotion for young workers who will be forced to leave the organisation for future advancement. This also results in increased labour cost per unit of production because of high wages of the existing senior workmen.

Cost of Labour Turnover

The cost of labour turnover may be broadly classified into two broad categories :

i) Preventive costs, and ii) Replacement costs.

i) Preventive costs : These costs are those which are incurred to keep the work force satisfied and to prevent or discourage them from leaving the organisation. These include :

a) Cost of personnel management : Only that portion of the cost which can be attributed to the efforts of the personnel department in maintaining good relation between management and workers.

b) Cost of welfare activities and services, example canteen, meal, co-operative stores, educational and transport facilities, housing schemes etc.

c) Cost of medical services.

d) Pension schemes to provide security and retirement benefits.

e) Extra bonus and other perquisites (in excess of those given by other similar concerns) to discourage their defecting by the other undertakings.

ii) Replacement cost

These cost includes all such losses and wastage arising because of the inexperienced new labour force replacing the existing one as well as the cost of the recruitment and training of the new workers. These include :

a) Cost of recruitment and selection of new employees.

b) Cost of training of new workers.

c) Loss of output due to some time gap in obtaining new workers.

d) Loss due to inefficiency of new workers.

e) Cost of accidents due to lack of experience of new workers.

f) Cost of scrap and defective work of new workers.

g) Cost of tools and machines breakdown due to faulty handling by new worker.

Reduction and Control of Labour Turnover

Labour turnover may be reduced by taking action on the basis of avoidable causes given earlier. The following steps may be taken in this regard :

1. Divising a suitable and satisfactory wage policy.
2. Providing working conditions conducive to health and efficiency.
3. Impartial and sympathetic attitude of personnel management.
4. Introducing financial and nonfinancial incentive plans.
5. Providing promotional opportunities.
6. Encouraging labour participation in management.
7. Introducing an effective grievance addressing procedure.
8. Strengthning the welfare measures.

Treatment of Cost of Labour Turnover

The preventive cost of labour turnover should be apportioned to various departments on the basis of number of workers in each department.

Regarding the replacement costs, if the replacement is due to the fault of a particular department it should be directly charged to that department. If the labour turnover is due to the defective management policy, the replacement cost should be apportioned to various departments on the basis of number of workers in each department.

Working Cost of Labour Turnover

1) The cost of labour turnover may be worked out as a percentage of sales or per worker employed as follows

$$\frac{\text{Total cost of labour turnover}}{\text{Sales}} \times 100 \quad \text{or} \quad \frac{\text{Total cost of labour turnover}}{\text{Average number of workers employed}}$$

2) Preventive costs should be apportioned to the different departments in proportion to the number of employees in each department.

3) Replacement costs are to be allocated to the concerned departments on the basis of the number of persons engaged in that department.

Idle Time

Idle time represents time lost by time workers. When workers are paid on time basis, some difference between the time for which they are paid and that which they actual spend upon production is bound to arise. This difference is known as idle time. Idle time represents the time for which they are paid but no production is obtained. For example, time lost between factory gate and the department, time when production is interrupted by machine maintenance, tea breaks, etc.

Causes

Idle time may occur owing to.

a) Productive causes b) Administrative causes c) Economic causes

Productive causes: The productive causes are classified as follows :

a) Idle time due to machine breakdown b) Power failures c) Waiting for tools and/or raw materials
d) Waiting for work e) Waiting for instructions.

Idle time due to productive causes is usually controllable by proper planning, strict supervision and proper maintenance of plant and machinery.

Administrative causes: Idle time is sometimes caused by administrative decisions. Thus when there is a surplus capacity of plant and machinery which the management decides not to work, there may be some idle time due to administrative decision. This usually happens during depressions when some of the machines have got to work below normal capacity and the regular workers are paid full amount of wages. This is because the management does not want to get rid of trained workers temporarily. Such idle time arises out of abnormal situations and is generally not controllable.

Economic causes: Idle time may also be caused by fall in the demand of products, say due to severe competition, seasonal nature of certain industries like woolen goods, ice cream industry, etc, where production cannot be evenly distributed throughout the year. In such cases, it is not possible to get rid of workers during slack season. Such surplus labour force is usually utilised for doing some other jobs and if such complimentary jobs cannot be found, there will be some idle time which is beyond control.

Treatment of idle time

From the point of view of treatment, idle time is classified as normal and abnormal.

Normal idle time: This is that wastage of labour time which cannot be avoided and has to be borne by the employer. For example, the time which, out of necessity, elapses between the completion of one job and the commencement of the next, the time taken in going from the factory gate to the department in which the worker is engaged, personal needs, time spent in setting machines etc. The cost of normal idle time may be treated in one of the following two ways :

a) It is charged to factory overhead. For this purpose, idle time is classified according to causes and each type of idle time is allotted a separate standing order number. This helps in its effective control.

b) Wage rate may be inflated, so as to make allowance for normal loss of labour time. Thus, if a worker's production time is only 7 hours and 8 hours a day and his hourly rate of pay is Rs. 10, the inflated wage rate will be $\frac{8}{7} \times 10$ = Rs. 11.43 per hour.

The second method is not considered very desirable as the cost of idle time should be treated separately instead of being absorbed as a part of direct labour cost. In this way it can prove more helpful for the purpose of controlling and reducing it to the minimum.

Abnormal idle time: This is that idle time which arises due to reasons in no way connected with the usual routine of manufacture and for which employer must pay. For example, time lost due to breakdown of machinery, strikes and lockouts, time lost in waiting for tools and for raw materials, accidents etc. Abnormal idle time is attributed to defective planning, inefficiency or bad luck, payment for such idle time is not included in cost and is adjusted through the costing Profit and Loss Account.

IDLE TIME CARD

Worker's No------------------ Date -------------------

Worker's Name-------------- Department ------------

Reason for Idle time	Standing Order No.	Time		No. of Hours	Cost	
		From	To		Rate Rs.	Amount Rs.
Machine breakdown Power failure Waiting for tools Waiting for materials Waiting for instructions Strikes Other reasons :						

Control of Idle Time

From control point of view, idle time should be divided into controllable and uncontrollable. Idle time arising due to controllable causes should be properly analysed and responsibility should be fixed on appropriate individuals. It is advisable to prepare an Idle Time Card showing the analysis of idle time so that action may be taken where necessary. It may be prepared as shown above

The following steps may be taken to control idle time.

a) Production should be properly planned so that imbalances in production are avoided or reduced.
b) Repairs and maintenance of plant and machinery should be regularly undertaken so as to avoid breakdown.
c) Raw materials, tools and instructions should reach the worker well in time so that no time is wasted in their waiting.
d) Supervision should be tightened.

Questions for Self-Study

1) Distinguish between direct labour and Indirect labour.
2) Define the term 'Labour Cost'. How you will control the labour cost ?
3) What is Time Keeping ? Explain the essentials of a good time keeping system.
4) Define the term "Time keeping". Explain in brief the methods of time keeping.
5) What is Time Booking ? Explain in brief the methods of time booking
6) Explain the difference between "Time keeping" and "Time booking"
7) What are the important duties of Time keeping department ? Explain the methods of time recording in the factory.

8) Explain the term 'Labour Turnover'. What are the causes responsible for Labour turnover ?

9) Define 'Labour Turnover'. What is the effet of Labour Turnover on the cost of production?

10) "The Cost of Labour Turnover is always reflected in Product Cost". Discuss.

11) What are the reasons why labour turnover should be kept within limits?

OVERHEADS

Overhead is defined as the aggregate of indirect material cost, indirect wages and indirect expenses. The word 'Indirect' is that which cannot be allocated, but which can be apportioned to or absorbed by the cost centres or cost units. All expenses over and above the prime cost are known as 'Overhead' charges.

Broadly speaking, overhead may be divided into four main functions as follows :

Overheads = Indirect material + Indirect wages + Indirect expenses.

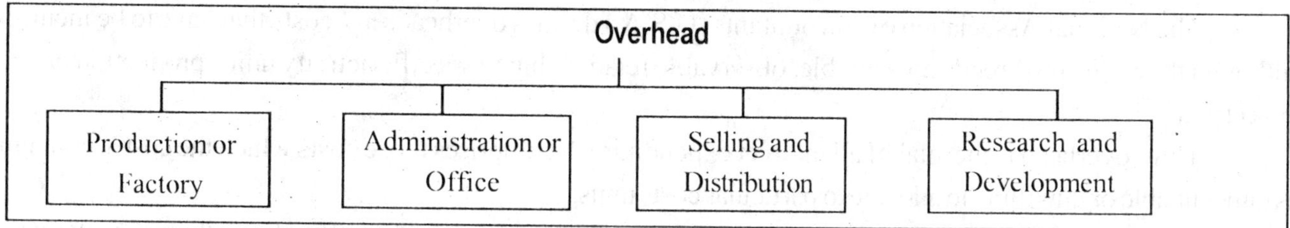

Production overhead is a part of cost of production and which is incurred inside the factory. Incurring of production overhead is must in order to complete the finished product. After completion of the finished product, it is transferred from the factory to the warehouse. Other three overheads are incurred outside factory depending on the management policy. It is, therefore, optional.

When the marginal costing principles are applied, the overheads are to be classified according to their behaviour with changes in volume of overheads of output such as fixed overheads, variable overheads and semivariable overheads which are sub divided into fix and variable.

Flow chart of overheads

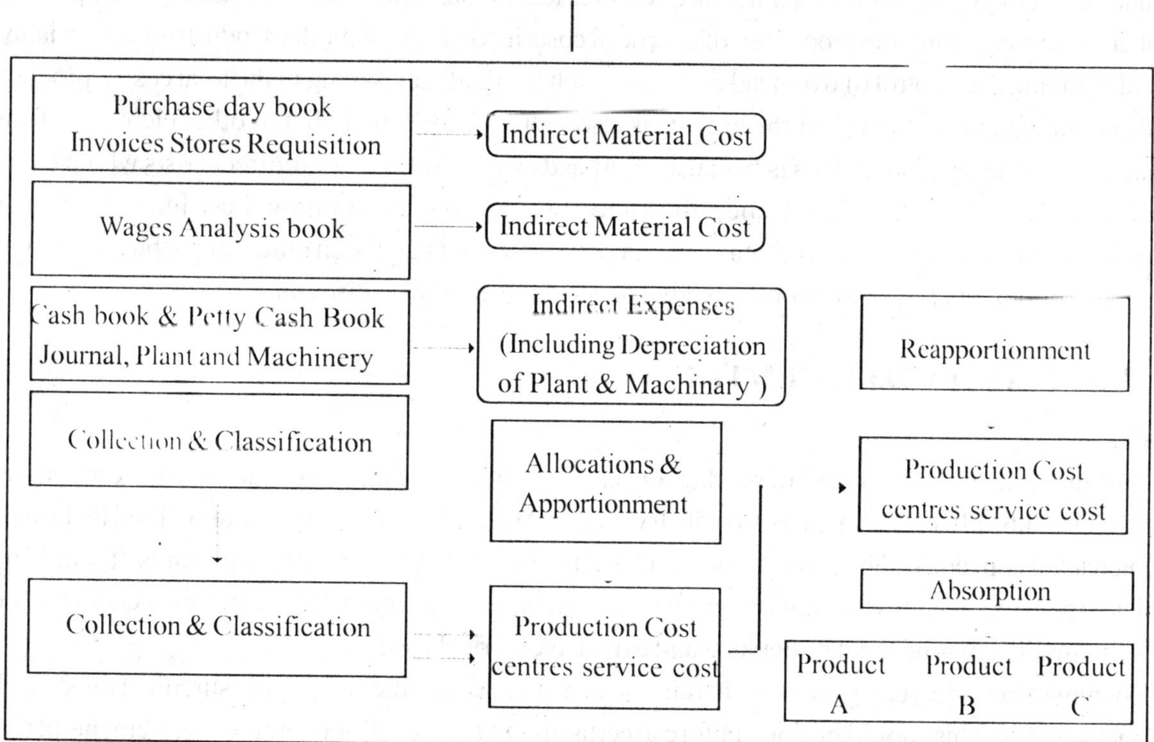

MEANING AND CLASSIFICATION OF OVERHEAD COSTS

Meaning of Overheads

Total cost is broadly divided into direct cost and indirect cost. The total of all direct costs (i.e. direct materials, direct wages and direct expenses) is termed as Prime Cost and the total of all indirect costs (i.e. indirect materials, indirect wages and indirect expenses) is known as Overheads.

A simple definition of overhead has been given by C.I.M.A. London, according to which overhead is "an aggregate of indirect materials, indirect wages and indirect expenses".

According to Blocker and Weltmer in their Cost Accounting, "Overhead costs are the operating costs of a business enterprise which cannot be traced directly to a particular unit of output".

In the words of Wheldon in his Cost Accounting and Costing Methods, "Overheads may be defined as the cost of indirect materials, indirect labour and such other expenses, including services which cannot conveniently be charged direct to specific costs units. Alternatively, overheads are all expenses other than direct expenses".

The National Association of Accountants (U.S.A.) defines overheads as "costs that have to be incurred although they have no directly measurable, observable relationship to specific activity units, production or cost objectives".

Thus, overhead is the total of all indirect expenditure. It comprises those costs which the cost accountant is either unable or unwilling to allocate to particular costs units.

In the United States, the word 'burden' is used in place of overhead. "So difficult and thorny are the some problems relating to overheads and its treatment in cost accounts that one may perhaps be pardoned for saying that the cost accountant's "burden" is overhead. Other terms in use for overhead are 'oncost', 'supplementary cost', 'non productive costs', etc. Of all the terms, overhead is the most common and C.I.M.A. London does not recommend the use of the terms 'oncost' and 'burden'.

Overhead is becoming an increasingly important element of cost in today's environment as a result of several factors such as increased mechanization, plant automation and other advances in technology. Use of costly plant and machinery results in higher overhead costs because of higher amount of plant depreciation, repairs and maintenance etc. Use of automatic machines also requires less human effort thereby resulting in employment of less number of workers. Thus, the proportion of overhead costs in total cost in modern industry is appreciably high and careful planning and control of overhead costs can result in significant saving in the total cost of production.

Accounting and control of overhead costs is also more complex than that of other elements of cost i.e. direct material and direct labour. This is because overheads by definition, are indirect costs which cannot be conveniently allocated to costs units. Hence, the knotty problem of apportioning these indirect costs to cost centers and costs units. Ascertainment of total cost of a cost unit would have been quite simple but for problems of allocation, apportionment and absorption of overhead costs has become bit difficult.

COST UNIT AND COST CENTRE

Cost Unit

Cost unit is a quantitative unit of product or service or time in relation to which costs are ascertained or expressed. Cost units differ from industry to industry. The unit selected should be the most natural to the business and accepted to all concerned. Therefore, utmost care should be taken while selecting cost units. It should neither too small nor too large. If unit is too large, significant cost trends may pass unnoticed, due to averaging of cost. If the unit is too small, it may necessitate detailed and expensive clerical work.

Costing means measuring the costs in relation to a unit. Hence, the unit of measurement must be clearly defined and selected. This should be done before ascertainment of costs. For example, in a cement factory, the cost per ton of cement is found out ; in a cloth mill, the cost per meter is ascertained ; in case of machine, the cost per machine hour is found out etc. Thus, here, tonne, metre and machine hour become the cost units. Hence, we can say that a cost unit is nothing but a unit of measurement of cost.

In case of a service unit, it is difficult to find out and decide a suitable cost unit. For example, in case of a transport undertaking the costs may be either related to the distance travelled in k.m. or the weight carried i.e. tonnes. While selecting proper cost unit for the transport including both factors i.e. distance and weight should be considered. Hence, tonne k.m. or passenger k.m. will be a proper unit.

Each industry has a different cost units, some of which are given below :

Industry/ Product	Cost Unit	Industry/Product	Cost Unit
1) Automobile	Number	12) Transport	Ton km/Passenger km
2) Bricks	Thousand	13) Utensils	KG/Ton
3) Cotton/Jute	Bale	14) Cement	Ton
4) Chemicals	Litre, Gallon, K.G. Tonne	15) Cable	Meter or km
5) Electricity	K W H	16) Fertilizer	Per ton
6) Furniture	Number	17) TV/Radio/VCR	Per Set
7) Gas	Cubic meter	18) Building	Per sq. ft. / Per sq.mtr.
8) Hotel/Hospital	Room per day/per bed	19) Nuts and Bolts	Gross
9) Mines	Ton	20) Sugar and Flour Mills	Quintal
10) Steel	Ton	21) Timber	Cubic foot
11) Shoes	Pair	22) Water Supply	Thousand litres/Gallon

Cost Centre

According to ICMA, London, Cost Centre is defined as, "a location, person or item of equipment (or group of these) for which costs may be ascertained and used for the purpose of control".

Thus, a Cost Centre is a part of the business to which costs can be attributed or charged. It may be a location (a department, sales area etc), an item of equipment (a delivery van, lathe machine etc) or a person (a machine operator, salesman etc)

The finding out of a proper cost centre and analysis of costs for each cost centre is necessary for cost comparison and cost control. To find out the cost of each product or service, expenses should be separated according to each cost centre. For each cost centre one person is held responsible who is supposed to control the cost of that particular cost centre. How many cost centres be, what should be their size, who will be responsible for the cost centre, will be decided according to the nature of the organisation i.e. the expenses incurred by the organisation as well as the requirement of the management. A large number of cost centres tend to be expensive but having too few cost centres defeat the basic purpose of cost control.

Types of Cost Centres

1) Production Cost Centre : It is a cost centre connected with production i.e. machine shop, welding shop, assembly shop etc. The manufacturing and non-manufacturing costs are charged to product cost centres.
2) Service Cost Centre : A Service Cost Centre is one which provides services to the other cost centres.Only non-manufacturing costs are charged to service cost centre. Examples of service cost centre are canteen, machinery maintenance department, office service etc.
3) Personal Cost Centre : Personal Cost Centre consists of a person or group of persons. Personal Cost Centre follows the organisational structure of a factory. Under this type of cost centre, costs are analysed and accumulated by Works manager, Sales Manager, Store-Keeper, Foreman etc.

4) Impersonal Cost Centre : It consists of a location or item of equipment. A cost centre relating to location may represent a region of sales, a warehouse, or store-room. Cost Centre relating to an item of equipment could be a machine or group of machine.

5) Operation Cost Centre : It is a cost centre which consists of machines/persons carrying out similar operations i.e. machines and operations engaged in welding, turning or matching.

6) Process Cost Centre : It is a cost centre which consists of a specific process or continuous sequence of operations.

Whatever may be the type of cost centre, it is determined by taking into consideration the following factors:

i) The volume of work to be performed. ii) The extent of cost control that can be exercised.

iii) Responsibilities to be identified. iv) The uses of cost centres to the cost accounting department.

Classification of Overheads Costs

Overhead costs may be classified according to :

a) Functions b) Elements c) Behaviour.

a) Classification according to Functions

The main group of overheads on the basis of this classification are :

1) Production overheads 2) Administration overheads

3) Selling overheads 4) Distribution overheads.

1) **Production Overhead :** Also termed as factory overhead, works overhead or manufacturing overhead. It means indirect expenditure incurred in connection with production operations. It is the aggregate of factory indirect material cost, indirect wages and indirect expenses. Unlike direct material and direct labour, production overhead is an invisible part of finished product. Examples of these cost are : Lubricants, consumables, indirect wages, factory power and light, depreciation of plant and machinery, depreciation of factory building, insurance of plant and factory building, storekeeper expenses, repairs and maintenance etc.

2) **Administration Overhead :** This constitutes all expenses incurred in the direction, control and administration (including secretarial accounting and financial control) of an undertaking which is not related directly to production, selling and distribution functions. Examples are : General management salaries, audit fees, legal charges, postage and telephone, stationery and printing, office rent and rates, office lighting and salaries of office staff etc.

3) **Selling Overhead:** These are the costs of seeking to create and stimulate demand or of securing orders. Examples : Advertising, salaries and commission of sales personnel, showroom expenses, travelling expenses, bad debts, catalogues and price lists etc.

4) **Distribution Overhead :** It comprises all expenditure incurred from the time product is completed in factory until it reaches its destination or customer. It includes : packing costs, carriage outward, delivery van costs, warehousing costs etc.

Both selling and distribution costs are incurred after the production work is over and thus taken together these are known as "After Production Costs".

b) Classification according to Elements

The classification is based on the definition of overheads given below. The main classes under this head are : indirect materials, indirect wages, and indirect expenses.

1) **Indirect Materials :** The aggregate of indirect material cost, indirect wages and indirect expenses incurred in the factory for purpose of production is called factory overhead. In the course of manufacture of a product, indirect materials do not form part of finished product. The indirect materials are the consumable items, electrodes, coolants, cotton waste etc. which are required for the completion of finished product. Indirect materials cost is the material costs which cannot be allocated, but which can be apportioned to or absorbed by the cost centers or cost units.

2) **Indirect wages :** Indirect wages of a factory are the wages and the overtime paid for all labourers (other than direct labourers) in the factory, viz. helpers in factory, foremen, supervisors, inspection staff and production manager etc. who do not directly contribute in converting raw material into finished product.

3) **Indirect Expenses :** Indirect expenses of factory are all expenses of the factory such as rent, rates, taxes and insurance of factory, repairs of factory, machinery power etc. including depreciation of plant, machinery, equipment, loose tools and factory building.

c) Classification according to Behaviour

Different overhead costs behave in different ways when the volume of production increases or decreases. On the basis of behaviour, overheads may be classified into

1) Fixed Overhead 2) Variable Overhead, and 3) Semi-fixed or Semi-variable Overheads.

1) **Fixed Overhead :** These overheads remain unaffected or fixed in the total amounts by fluctuations in volume of output. Examples are rent and rates, managerial salaries, building depreciation, postage, stationery, legal expenses etc.

2) **Variable Overhead :** This is the cost which, inaggregate, tends to vary in indirect proportion to changes in the volume of output. Variable overhead per unit remain fixed. Examples are indirect materials, indirect labour, salesman's commission, power, light, fuel etc.

3) **Semi-variable Overhead :** This overhead is partly fixed and partly variable. In other words, such costs vary in part with the volume of production and in part they are consistent, whatever be the volume of production. Examples : supervisory salaries, depreciation, repairs and maintenance, telephone bills, electricity bills etc.

Methods of Segregating Semi-variable Costs

The main purpose of classifying overhead costs into fixed and variable is to help the organization in decision making and control of expenditure. As such the semi-variable costs may present some problems and thus cost accountant must segregate them into fixed and variable components. The cost accountant has to determine an extent to which an item of semi-fixed or semi-variable cost is fixed or variable. The following methods are used for determining the fixed and variable elements in semi-variable costs.

Methods of segregating semi-variable costs are as follows :

1) Scatter Diagram Method 2) Simultaneous Equation Method 3) Average Method

4) High and Low Point Method 5) Least Square Method

1) Scatter Diagram Method

This is graphic method and gives approximate results. In this method, the amount of semi-variable or semi-fixed costs at various levels of activity are plotted on a graph in which X-axis represents the units of output (or direct labour, hours, or direct wages, or machine hours, or percentage of capacity) and Y-axis represents the various cost figures. The following data has been assumed to illustrate this method.

Problem : 1

Year	Units of Output	Semi-variable cost
1999	270	6,550
2000	380	8,200
2001	430	8,950
2002	400	8,500
2003	420	8,800
2004	450	9,250
Total	**2,350**	**50,250**
Average (Total ÷ 6)	**391.66**	**8,375**

Solution

Following figure shows the graphical presentation of a sector Diagram.

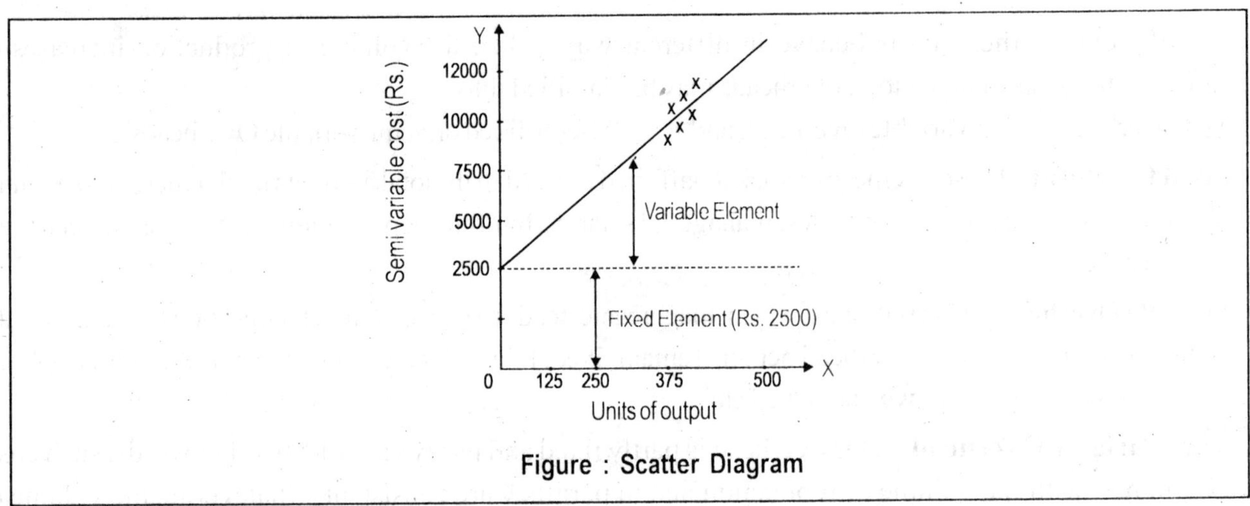

Figure : Scatter Diagram

The yearly figures are plotted on a scatter diagram as shown above. The preceding figures are plotted on this diagram and straight line is drawn which appears to be the "line of best fit". This line of best fit represents the trend shown by the majority of the data points and will leave roughly as many points on one side of the line as on the other.

The point where this line of best fit cuts the vertically- Y-axis marks the fixed cost. From the given diagram, it can be easily found that the fixed cost is approximately Rs. 2,500 (with average figures).

Semi Variable Cost - Fixed Cost = Variable Element : Rs. 8,375 - Rs. 2,550 = Rs. 5,875

$$\text{Variable Cost per unit} = \frac{\text{Average Variable Element}}{\text{Average No. of units of output}} = \frac{\text{Rs. } 5,875}{\text{Rs. } 391.66} = \text{Rs. } 15 \text{ (Approx)}$$

2) Simultaneous Equation Method

In this method, two simultaneous equations are used to segregate fixed and variable elements in semi-variable costs. Two equation are used in respect of two periods or level of production.

The equation is : $Y = MX + C$

where,

Y = Total semi-variable cost M = Variable cost per unit

X = Units of output C = Fixed cost

Problem : 2

Applying this equation to figures of previous illustration

2000 = 8,800 = 420 M + C ---------------------- (i)

2001 = 9,250 = 450 M + C ---------------------- (ii)

Subtracting (i) from (ii) 9250 = 450

ie (+) 8800 - 420

450 = 30

$M = \frac{450}{30}$ ∴ M = Rs. 15

Putting the value of M in equation (i),

8,880 = 420 x 15 + C C = 2,500

The results will be same when value of M is put in equation (ii)

Thus, in 2000 Fixed element = Rs. 2,500 Variable Element = Rs. 6,300

Semi- variable costs = Rs. 8,800

3) Method of Averages

This method is similar to Scatter diagram and high and low points method. Instead of fitting in the line of best fit by inspection or calculating mathematically, the cost is ascertained by taking the average of selected groups.

Problem : 3

Taking the figure of Illustration 1

	Units of Output	Semi- Variable Cost (Rs.)
Average I 2002-2003	325	7,375
Average II 2004-2005	435	9,025
Difference	**110**	**1,650**

Solution :

Variable cost per unit = $\frac{1,650}{110}$ = Rs. 15 Fixed cost = 7,375 - (325 x 15) = Rs. 2,500.

Following figure shows the graphical presentation of separating fixed and variable cost by methods of averages.

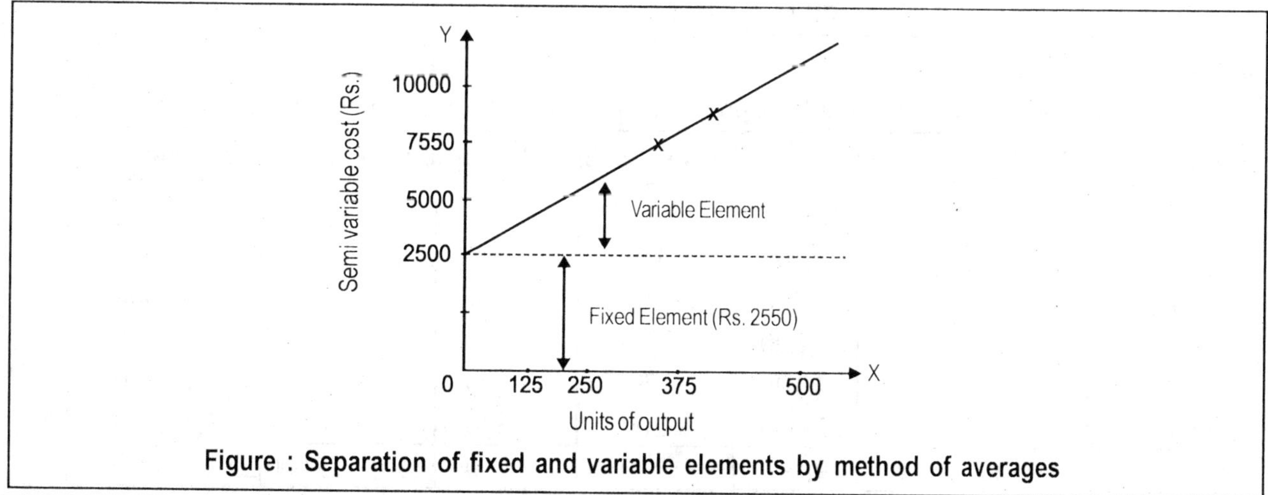

Figure : Separation of fixed and variable elements by method of averages

4) High and Low Points Method

In this method, the difference between the highest and the lowest volume of output and the difference of the corresponding costs are worked out and the variable and fixed elements are separated as illustrated below. (The figures of illustration 1 have been taken).

Problem : 4

	Output	Semi-Variable Cost (Rs.)
Highest 2000	450	9,250
Lowest 2001	270	6,550
Difference	**180**	**2,700**

Solution

Variable cost per unit 2,700 ÷ 180 Rs.15

	Highest (Rs.)	Lowest (Rs.)
Semi-Variable cost	9,250	6,550
Less : Variable element @ Rs. 15 (per unit)	6,550	4,050
Fixed element	2,700	2,500

The calculations in this method are simple but the method suffers from a disadvantage that it determines cost behaviour based only on two data points-the highest and the lowest. When the highest and the lowest points are the extremes, the results obtained are not likely to be accurate. In such cases, other methods based on a larger number of points are likely to prove better.

5) Method of Least Squares

This method gives the most accurate results of all methods. Here the line of best fit is determined by the use of statistical methods (In scatter diagram, this line is determined by inspection). As the method may lead to complicated calculations, simple figures have been taken to illustrate it as follows :

Problem : 5

Year	Units of Output	Semi-Variable cost (Rs.)
2000	150	2,900
2001	200	3,200
2002	300	3,800
2003	350	4,100
2004	500	5,000

Solution

The following type of table should be prepared in using least squares method.

Year	Units of Output		Semi-Variable Deviation of Cost Output from			
	(X)	(Y)		(Y)	(X²)	(XY)
2000	150	2,900	- 150	- 900	- 22,500	1,35,000
2001	200	3,200	- 100	- 600	10,000	60,000
2002	300	3,800	0	0	0	0
2003	350	4,100	+ 50	+ 300	2,500	15,000
2004	500	5,000	+ 200	+ 1,200	40,000	2,40,000
Total	1,500	19,000	0	0	ΣX² 75,000	ΣXY 4,50,000

Mean 1,500 ÷ 5 = 300 units 19,000 ÷ 5 = Rs. 3,800

Variable cost per unit $= \frac{\Sigma xy}{\Sigma x^2} = \frac{\text{Rs. } 4,50,000}{75,000} =$ Rs. 6

Fixed cost = Mean cost - (Variable rate x Mean output) = Rs. 3,800 - (6 x 300) = Rs. 2,000

Line of best fit (regression line) y = 6x + 2,000

2000 - 2,900 = 6 x 150 + 2,000

2001 - 3,200 = 6 x 200 + 2,000 and so on.

It is interesting to note that results obtained under the various methods are identical. This is because there is a linear relationship between output and variable overhead cost, i.e. for each unit of output, the same amount of variable overhead cost is incurred. In practice, it may not always be so and final separated figures for fixed and variable elements may differ widely under different methods.

Importance of Classifying Costs into Fixed and Variable

The fixed-variable cost classification is of great importance in planning, decision making and control as discussed below :

1) Decision Making

As most of the problem of decision-making relate to changes in volume, this classification acquires a special importance in managerial decision making. This is so because fixed and variable costs behave in different ways when volume of output change.

2) Control of costs

From control point of view, cost may be controllable or uncontrollable. The fixed costs are mostly uncontrollable and if, at all, any control can be exercised, it can be done by the top management. Variable costs, on the other hand, are the most controllable. For example, rent for building (fixed) is not easily controllable but cost of materials (variable) may be controlled by purchasing in economic lots, seasonal purchasing etc. Classifying costs into fixed and variable, therefore, helps in effective control of cost by pointing out where management should concentrate to control.

3) Preparation of Budget

This classification helps in the preparation of budget. For instance, when flexible budgets are prepared for different level of activity, the fixed costs remain constant at all levels of activity, whereas variable costs varies according to the actual level of output.

4) Absorption of Overhead

By classifying cost into fixed and variable, separate rates of absorption of overhead may be used for fixed and variable overheads. The under / over absorption arising out of two types of overheads are different in nature and need different managerial action. For example, under absorption of fixed overhead means the existence of surplus or idle capacity so that suitable steps may be taken to effectively utilise idle capacity.

5) Marginal Costing and Break Even Analysis

This technique is totally dependant on segregation of cost into fixed and variable.

6) Other uses

In addition to the above stated , fixed-variable cost classification is useful in many other areas. For example, while planning capital expenditure, effect of the project on total fixed and variable costs should be studied. Moreover, differential and comparative cost analysis are based on this classification.

Steps in dealing with Factory Overheads

There are five main steps in dealing with the factory overheads in a cost accounts :

a) Collection b) Classification c) Allocation d) Apportionment e) Absorption

a) Collection

There are seven main sources of cost data relating to factory overheads :

1) Purchase day book
2) Invoice
3) Stores requisitions, these three are meant for collection of indirect material cost book
4) Wages analysis book for indirect wages
5) Cash book and petty cash book
6) Journal entries
7) Other registers like plant and machinery.

These three are meant for collection of indirect expenses including depreciation of plant and machinery.

b) Classification

There may be three broad categories of factory overheads :

1) Plant overheads
2) Overheads relating to production cost centres and
3) Overheads relating to service cost centres.

All the factory overheads are to be classified to suit the purpose of cost accounting. Whether itemwise i.e. rent, insurance, depreciation etc. or functionwise. Standing order numbers are used for covering the factory overheads. Cost account numbers are used for covering the administration, selling and distribution overheads.

c) Allocation

Allocation is the allotment of whole items of cost to cost units, whether they may be production cost centres or service cost centres. For example, indirect wages of production department A is to be allocated to Deparment 'A' only. Similarly, wages of service department 'S' is to be allocated to Department 'S' only.

d) Apportionment

Apportionment is the allotment of proportion of items of cost to cost centers or cost units on suitable basis after they are collected under separate standing order numbers. It may be the basis of services rendered by a particular item of expense to different departments or by survey method. Sometimes, the basis will be the 'Ability to pay method' i.e. ability of department to bear such share of items of overheads.

e) Absorption

Changing overheads to individual product or job is known as absorption. Thus, purpose behind is that expenses allocated or apportioned to departments or cost centres should be absorbed in the cost of output of the given period.

Standing Order Numbers

After overheads are classified, it is found useful to allot each group of expenses a number of symbols so that each group is easily distinguished from others. Such number of symbols are codes for overheads and are sometimes called as standing order numbers. Each standing order number denotes a particular type of expenditure so that items of expenses of similar nature, as and when they are incurred are appropriately classified into one of these. A schedule or manual is maintained enlisting all standing order numbers. There cannot be a standard list of standing order number as the number and the type under which overheads may be sub-grouped vary with the

a) size of the factory, b) type of expenses, and c) the extent of control necessary.

An essential requisite for an effective system of standing order number is that such numbers should be clearly defined so that individuals responsible for booking expenditure may easily understand the classification. Secondly, the classification into standing order numbers should have the quality of flexibility, so that as and when the need arises, suitable changes can be incorporated without seriously dislocating the existing system.

Methods of Allotting the Standing Order Numbers

Each standing order number is identified by a code number or symbol. The allocation of number or symbol can be done by any of the following methods :

Methods of Coding

1) Serial number system
2) Decimal system
3) Alphabetical system
4) Combination of alphabetical and numerical system.

1) Serial Number System

In this method, each type of expenditure is allotted a number in serial order as shown in table below:

S.O. Number	Expenditure
01	Furnace oil
07	Work's Manager Salary
23	Power
34	Factory Lightning
52	Factory Rent

A group of numbers is set apart to classify the items under a broad head. For example, 1 to 20 for indirect materials, 21 to 40 for indirect labour, and so on.

2) Decimal System

This is also a numerical system with the difference that instead of full numbers, decimals are used. The whole numbers are used to indicate the main group and the decimal represent the sub-groups. For example,

Sr. No.	Item	S.O.No.	Item
1	Factory Overhead	1.2	Indirect Labour
1.1	Indirect material	1.2.1	Inspectors
1.1.1	Furnace oil	1.2.2	Foremen
1.1.2	Lubricating oil	1.2.3	Sweepers
1.1.3	Cotton waste	1.2.4	Repair worker's wages
1.1.4	Repairs and maintenance of stores	1.2.5	Idle time wages
1.1.5	Tools for general use		

Similarly			
2	Administration Overheads	2.2	Accounting Services
2.1	Office expenses	2.2.1	Salaries
2.1.1	Travelling expenses	2.2.2	Depreciation of plant & machinery
2.1.2	Salaries/Honorarium		
2.1.3	Maintenance of cars	2.2.3	Stationery, Xerox
2.1.4	Telephone expenses	2.2.4	Postage / Courier

3) Alphabetical System

This system has the advantage that it may be formed into a memonic code.

For Example : P = Purchases

PD = Purchase discount　　PM = Purchase manager　　PO Purchase outdoor

PR = Purchase of raw material　　PI = Purchase indoor　　PC - Purchase - Components

On account of limited number of alphabets, this method has a limited coverage and lacks flexibility.

4) Combination of Alphabets and Numbers System

The alphabet denotes the main group and the sub-group or type of expenditure is indicated by the numerical 1.

The following codes illustrate this method :

R1	Repairs to plant and machinery	D1	Depreciation of plant and machinery
R2	Repairs to building	D2	Depreciation of building
R3	Repairs to delivery vans	D3	Depreciation of delivery vans
R4	Repairs to office cars	D4	Depreciation of office cars

ALLOCATION OF OVERHEADS

Meaning of Allocation

After the collection and classification of overheads is done, the next step is to allocate / apportion the expenses to the cost centres. The other name for this is "Departmentalization of overheads" or "Primary distribution of overheads".

Direct costs are charged direct to the cost centre or cost unit without difficulty. But this is not possible in overhead costs. Distribution of overhead costs to cost units is one of the complex problems of cost accounting. This is because overhead costs cannot be identified with individual cost units and there are no accounting means of exact distribution. Therefore, such costs are analysed and distributed to various cost centres and cost units on arbitrary basis. For example, it is not possible to exactly calculate the amount off rent that should be charged to a particular cost unit and thus it has to be distributed on the same arbitrary basis. The cost accountant is constantly searching for equitable bases to distribute overhead costs to units in this regard. For instance, he may apportion rent to various departments of the factory on the basis of the area occupied by each such department. Similarly, labour welfare expenses may be apportioned on the basis of number of workers in each department.

The procedure of distribution of overhead costs is discussed below :

Steps in Overhead Accounting

Unlike direct materials and direct wages, overheads cannot be allocated to cost units directly. The various steps taken for distribution of overhead costs are as follows :

1) Classification and collection of overheads.
2) Allocation and apportionment of overheads to production departments and service departments.
3) Re-apportionment of service department costs to production department.
4) Absorption of overheads of each production department in cost units.

These steps are explained below :

Collection of Overheads

The procedure of classification of production overheads and of assigning standing order (code) numbers has already been discussed. Such classification and codification are prerequisite to the collection of overheads.

Production overheads should be collected for understanding order numbers. The main source from which overhead costs are collected are as follows :

a) **Invoice :** for collection of indirect expenses like rent, insurance etc.
b) **Stores requisitions :** for collection of indirect materials.
c) **Wages analysis sheet :** for collection of indirect wages.

d) **Journal entries :** for collection of those overheads items which do not result in current cash outlay and need some adjustment. Example, depreciation, charge in lieu of rent, outstanding rent etc.

Departmentalisation of Overheads

After overhead costs have been collected under various standing order number, the second step is to allocate and apportion the overhead to production and service departments. This is also known as departmentalization or primary distribution of overhead.

Departmentalization of overhead is the process of allocation and apportionment of overhead to different departments or costs centres. For smooth and efficient working, a factory is sub-divided into a number of departments each of which denotes a particular activity of the factory. Example purchase department, Stores department, time keeping department, personnel department, melting shop etc. These departments are mainly of two types :

a) Production department and b) Service departments.

The following factors are taken into account while organising a concern into a number of departments.

1) Similarity of operation, processes, machines and equipment in a department.
2) Location of operations and processes and the sequence of operations.
3) Division of responsibility for control of production and control of cost.
4) Optimum number of centres. Too many cost centres make the system of cost accounting detailed and quite expensive whereas too few cost centres will not be able to provide requisite cost information and thus will fail to serve the main objectives of cost accounting.

Need of Departmentalisation of Overheads

Departmentalisation of overheads is necessary for the reasons given below :

1) **Control of overhead cost :** Effective control of overhead costs is possible because departmentalisation makes the incurrence of cost in a department or costs centres the responsibility of some one who heads the department or the cost centre. Thus, with the help of departmentalisation, responsibility of accounting can be effectively introduced for control purposes.
2) **Forecasting and Estimating :** Because of greater accuracy in cost ascertainment and cost control, deparmentalisation ensures more accurate forecasting and estimating and decision making.
3) **Ensures greater accuracy in cost ascertainment :** For accurate costing of each functions or operation, overhead absorption rates should be determined separately for each cost centres. This is possible only with the help of departmentalisation.
4) **Use of different methods of absorption :** Basis of absorption of overhead may be different for different cost centres. Example machine hour rate may be suitable for one cost centre whereas direct labour hour rate may be more appropriate for another cost centre. Different basis may be used for different cost centres only when overheads are departmentalised.
5) **Valuation of work in progress :** Correct cost of work in progress cannot be ascertained unless overheads are departmentalised.
6) **Cost of service departments :** Departmentalisation helps in ascertaining the cost of various service departments which is useful for making estimates and submitting quotations for those items which make use of the services of various cost centres.

Allocation of Overheads

Certain items of overhead costs can be directly identified with a particular department or cost centre as having been incurred for that cost centre. Allotments of such costs to departments or cost centres is known as allocation. Thus, allocation may defined as "the allotment of whole item of cost to cost centres or cost units". In other words, allocation is charging to a cost centre those overheads that results solely from the existence of that cost centre. A point to be clearly understood is that the allocation can be made only when the exact amount of overhead incurred in the cost centre is definately known. For example, rent cannot normally be allocated since rate is payable for the factory as a whole and exact amount for each department cannot be known. Indirect materials, on the other hand, can be easily allocated to various department in which they are incurred. Other items which are allocated includes indirect wages, overtime and idle time cost, power (when sub-metres are installed in departments), depreciation of machinery, supervision etc.

In brief, in order that an overhead can be allocated, it should meet both of the following conditions :

a) The cost centre must have caused the overhead to be incurred; and

b) The exact amount incurred in a cost centre must be known.

APPORTIONMENT OF OVERHEADS

Meaning of Apportionment

Certain overhead costs cannot be directly charged to a department or cost centre. Such costs are common to a number of cost centers or departments and do not originate from any specific department. Distribution of such overhead cost to various department is known as apportionment. Thus, apportionment may be defined as "the allotment of proportions of items of cost to cost centres or cost units". In other words, it is charging to a cost centre as fair share of an overheads. Where an item of overhead is common to various cost centres, it is allotted to different cost centres, proportionately on some equitable basis. Again taking the case of rent, as it cannot be allocated, it is apportioned to various departments on some equitable basis. Example in the ratio of area occupied. Similarly, salary of a general manager cannot be allocated wholly to anyone department as he attends in general to all the departments. It should, therefore, be apportioned on some equitable basis. Other items which generally cannot be allocated but are apportioned include fire insurance, lighting and heating, time keeping expenses, canteen expenses, medical and other welfare expenses etc.

Distinction between Allocation and Apportionment

The distinction between allocation and apportionment is important to understand. As seen above, the purpose of both cost allocation and cost apportionment is the identification or allotment of items of cost to cost centers or cost units. However, the main difference between the two procedures lies in that while allocation deals with whole items of cost, apportionment deals with proportions of item of cost. Allocation is a direct process but apportionment may be made only indirectly and for which suitable bases are to be selected. Whether an item of cost can be allocated or apportioned does not depend upon the nature of cost but upon the relation with the cost centre or cost unit to which it is to be charged.

Overheads should always be allocated, if possible. If an overhead cannot be allocated, it is apportioned, that will enable the overhead to be equitably shared between various production and service departments.

Allocation is a direct process of allotment of whole items of cost to cost units or cost centres but apportionment is an indirect method of distribution of proportions of items of cost to cost centres or cost units on some equitable basis of machine hours, labour hours or number of employees etc.

The guiding principle is not the nature of expenditure but its relation with the cost centre or cost units to which cost is to be allocated or apportioned (i.e. distributed).

For example, salary of a foreman is a direct charge (allocation) to the department in which he works but this cost has to be apportioned (distributed to the cost centres under that development on some equitable basis of machine hours or labour hours etc.)

Production and Service Departments

Departments are classified as either production or service department. A production department is one that engages in actual manufacture of the product by changing the shape, form or nature of the material worked upon or by assembling the parts into finished product. A service department, on the other hand, is one rendering the service that contributes in an indirect manner to the manufacture of the product but which does not itself change the shape, form or nature of material that is converted into the finished product. Examples are given below :

Production Departments	Service Departments
Weaving department	Purchasing department
Spinning department	Stores department
Crushing department	Time keeping department
Mixing department	Personnel department
Grinding department	Inspection department
Annealing shop	Canteen
Picking shop	Labour welfare department
Polishing department	Production control department
Finishing department	Internal transport department
Kiln burning shop	Tool room
Melting shop	Accounting department

Partly Producing Departments

There may be certain departments which are normally treated as service departments, but sometimes are required to undertake direct production work. These may be known as partly producing or partly service departments. For example, a carpentry shop which is mainly engaged in the work of repairs and maintenance of fittings and fixtures, is a service department but may be occasionally required to manufacture wooden boxes for packing of goods which may be charged direct to output. Similarly tool room, though a service department, may manufacture special tools against job orders. As these departments are sometimes engaged in direct manufacturing activities, they are called as partly producing departments.

Principles of Apportionment

Apportionment of overheads to various production and service departments is based on the following principles :

a) **Service or Use :** This is the most common basis of apportionment of overheads costs. It is based on the theory that greater the amount of service or benefit received by a department, the larger should be the share of the cost to be borne by that department. For example, rent is apportioned to various departments according to the floor space occupied, telephone cost according to the number of extension of telephones in each departments and so on.

b) **Survey method :** This method is used for those overhead costs that are not closely related to departments and whose remoteness necessitates an arbitrary distribution. For example, salary of general manager of a company may be apportioned on the basis of the results of a survey which may reveal that 30% of his salary should be apportioned to sales, 10% to administration and 60% to various producing departments. Similarly, lighting expenses may be apportioned on the basis of a survey of the number of lights, size, estimated hours of use etc.

c) **Ability to pay method :** This is based on the theory of taxation which holds that those who have the largest income should bear the highest proportion of tax burden. In overhead distribution, those departments which have the largest income may be charged the largest amount of overhead. This method is generally considered inequitable because it penalises the efficient and the profitable units of the business to the advantages of inefficient ones.

Basis of Apportionment

The following are some of the common basis of apportionment of overheads.

The following table indicates the various basis of apportionment for the usual items of factory overheads.

Item of Factory Overheads	Basis of Apportionment
1) Rent	Area or volume of building
2) Depreciation of Machinery	Percentage of original cost of machinery or machine hour rate
3) Power	Horse power multiplied by machine hours or kWH
4) Electric	Lighting Number of light points or area
5) Canteen expenses	Number of employees
6) Store-keeping and material handling	Number of stores requisitions
7) Indirect wages of maintenance	Estimated or actual time spent in department or inspection etc.
8) Delivery expenses	Weight volume or ton-kilometer.
9) Repairs of Plant	Value of Plant
10) Supervision	Direct wages
11) Fire Insurance	Value of Asset
12) Machine shop	Expenses Machine hours or labour hours
13) General Expenses	Direct wages or number of employees
14) Audit fees,	Sales or total cost
15) Maintenance of Building	Area or labour hours

Note : The basis of apportionment can be arrived at on a trial basis and reviewed annually.

It should be noted that some overheads in the above list can be apportioned on more than one basis. The choice of an appropriate basis is really a matter of judgement. For example, welfare expenses may be apportioned on the basis of employees or total wages. Similarly, lighting expenses may be apportioned on the basis of number of light points in each department or on the basis of technical estimates or on the basis of floor area.

Problem : 1

Naveen Co. Ltd., has three production departments X, Y and Z and two service departments, A and B. The following figures are extracted from the records of the company.

	Rs.		Rs.
Rent and Rates	5,000	General lighting	600
Indirect Wages	1,500	Power	1,500
Depreciation of Machinery	10,000	Sundries	10,000

The following further details are available.

	Total	X	Y	Z	A	B
Floor space (sq. ft.)	10,000	2,000	2,500	3,000	2,000	500
Light Points	60	10	15	20	10	5
Direct Wages (Rs.)	10,000	3,000	2,000	3,000	1,500	500
H.P. of Machines	150	60	30	50	10	--
Value of Machinery (Rs.)	2,50,000	60,000	80,000	1,00,000	5,000	5,000

Apportion the costs to various departments on the most equitable basis.

Solution

In the books of Naveen Co. Ltd.,

Primary Department Distribution Summary for the period ended......

Item	Basis of Apportionment	Total Rs.	X Rs.	Y Rs.	Z Rs.	A Rs.	B Rs.
Direct Wages	Actual	2,000	--	--	--	1,500	500
Rent and Rates	Floor space	5,000	1,000	1,250	1,500	1,000	250
General Lighting	Light point	600	100	150	200	100	50
Indirect Wages	Direct wages	1,500	450	300	450	225	75
Power	H.P. of Machines	1,500	600	300	500	100	--
Dep. of Machinery	Value of machines	10,000	2,400	3,200	4,000	200	200
Sundries	Direct Wages	10,000	3,000	2,000	3,000	1,500	500
Total Departmental Overheads		30,600	7,550	7,200	9,650	4,625	1,575

Re-apportionment of Service Department Costs (Secondary Distribution)

Once the overheads have been allocated and apportioned to production and service departments and totalled, the next step is to re-apportion the service department costs to production departments. This is necessary because our ultimate object is to charge overheads to cost units, and no cost units pass through service departments. Therefore, the costs of service department must be charged to production department which directly comes in contact with cost units. This is called secondary distribution.

The method of re-apportionment of service department costs is similar to apportionment of overheads discussed earlier. Some of the important bases of apportionment of service department costs are as follows:

Service Department	Basis of Apportionment
1) Storekeeping department	No. of requisitions or value or quantity of material of each department
2) Purchase department	Value of materials purchased for each department or number of purchase orders placed.
3) Time-keeping department, payroll department	Number of employees or total labour or machine hours.
4) Personnel department	Rate of labour turnover or number of employees in each department.
5) Canteen, welfare and recreation services	Number of employees and total wages.
6) Maintenance department	Number of hours worked in each department.

7) Inspection department — Direct labour hours or machine operating hours.
8) Drawing office — Number of drawings made or man-hours worked.
9) Internal transport service — Value or weights of goods transported, distance covered.

Thus, the cost service departments are re-apportioned on the basis of service rendered i.e. the benefits received by the beneficiary departments.

Methods of re-apportionment of service department costs

The various methods of re-apportionment of service department costs are summarised in this chart:

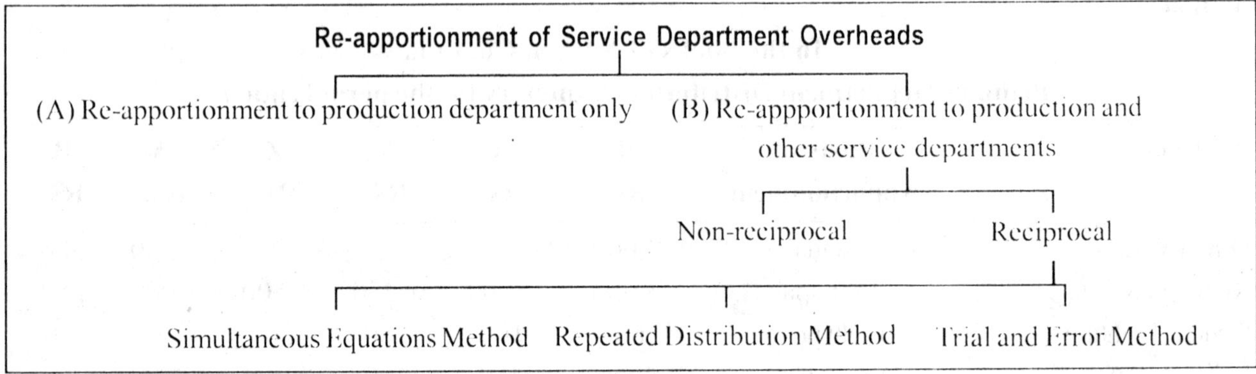

A) Re-apportionment only to Production Departments

In this case, cost of a service department is apportioned only to production departments without apportioning it to other service departments.

Problem : 2

Continuing illustration 1 by taking the total overhead as per departmental distribution summary and the following additional information, apportion the service department costs to production departments, ignoring inter-service department transfer.

	X	Y	Z
Number of employees	75	30	45
Value of material purchased	Rs.10,000	Rs. 8,000	Rs. 7,000

Further assume service department A is purchasing department and B is time keeping department.

Solution — **Secondary Distribution Summary**

Item	Basis of Apportionment	Total Rs.	X Rs.	Y Rs.	Z Rs.	A Rs.	B Rs.
Direct Wages	Actual	2,000	--	--	--	1,500	500
Rent and Rates	Floor space	5,000	1,000	1,250	1,500	1,000	250
General Lighting	Light point	600	100	150	200	100	50
Indirect wages	Direct wages	1,500	450	300	450	225	75
Power	H.P. of Machines	1,500	600	300	500	100	--
Dep. of Machinery	Value of machines	10,000	2,400	3,200	4,000	200	200
Sundries	Direct wages	10,000	3,000	2,000	3,000	1,500	500
Total Departmental Overheads		30,600	7,550	7,200	9,650	4,625	1,575

B) Re-apportionment to production as well as service departments

Quite often, a service department renders service not only on production department but also on other service departments. For example, maintenance department looks after not only the plant and machinery of production department but also the equipment of other service departments like power house, material handling, etc. Similarly, power house supplies electricity not only to production departments but also to canteen, maintenance departments etc.

This type of inter-service department apportionment may be either on reciprocal basis or non-reciprocal basis :

a) Re-apportionment on Non-reciprocal basis : This is done when service departments are not independent. In this method, the service departments are arranged in the descending order of their serviceability. The cost of the most serviceable departments i.e. the department which serves the largest number of departments is first apportioned to other service departments. The service departments whose services are the next largest number of departments is taken up next and its cost (including the prorated cost of the first service department) is apportioned to other service and production departments excepting the first service department. In the same way, while apportioning the third service department in this order, the first two service departments are ignored. This process is continued till the cost of the last service department is apportioned. It should be noted that the cost of the last service department is apportioned only to production department.

Problem : 3 The method has been illustrated with assumed figures.

Secondary Distribution Summary

	Production Departments			Service Departments				
Total	X	Y	Z	A	B	C	D	Total
Rs.	Rs.	Rs.	Rs.	Rs.	Rs.	Rs.	Rs.	Rs.
	8,000	7,250	5,600	1,200	1,000	800	1,500	25,350
	350	250	300	300	200	100	-1,500	
	300	250	200	150		-900		
	200	350	400	250	-1,200			
	600	700	600	-1,900				
25,350	**9,450**	**8,800**	**7,100**					

It is assumed that the descending order of serviceability of service departments is D.C.B. and A. This means service department D is the most serviceable department i.e. it renders service to the largest number of production as well as other service departments. It does not receive any service from other service department. Therefore cost of Rs.1,500 of service department D is apportioned to all other departments in the ratio it renders its services. The next more serviceable department is C which renders its services to all other departments except D. Therefore, its cost is apportioned which is next in the order of serviceability and lastly A's cost is apportioned.

b) Re-apportionment on Reciprocal basis : This method is used when service departments are mutually dependent. Thus, in the above example, position will be different if in addition to servicing departments, each service department also renders services to each other service department. For example, service department A renders service to B, C and D, service department B renders service to A, C and D department and so on. In such a case, until B's charge to A, C and D is known A, C and D cannot allot any cost to A. Thus, there are many unknown variable as the number of service departments. If two departments provide service to each other each department should be charged for the cost of services rendered by other.

There are three methods for breaking this vicious circle which are given below :

1) Simultaneous Equation Methods 2) Repeated Distribution Method 3) Trial and Error Method

1) Simultaneous Equations Method

In this method, the following algebric equation help in finding out the unknowns :

$X \quad a + by \qquad Y \quad a + bx$

This is illustrated below :

Problem : 4

In Illustratiion 1, the departmental distribution summary showed the following departments totals :

Departments	x	y	z	a	b
Amount Rs.	7,550	7,200	9,650	4,625	1,575

The costs service departments D and E are to be charged on the basis of the following percentage :

	X	**Y**	**Z**	**A**	**B**
A	20%	30%	40%		10%
B	40%	20%	30%	10%	

Find the total overheads of production department.

Solution

Let X denote total overhead of service department A Y denote total overhead of service department B

$X \quad Rs.\ 4{,}625 + \frac{10}{100}\ Y \qquad Y \quad Rs.\ 1{,}525 + \frac{10}{100}\ X$ or

$X \quad Rs.\ 4{,}625 + 0.10\ Y \qquad Y \quad 1575 + 0.10\ X$

Again multiplying equation (ii) by 10 to ultimate X and adding :

$10\ X - Y \quad Rs.\ 46{,}250 \qquad -10\ X + 100\ Y \quad Rs.\ 1{,}57{,}500 \qquad 90\ Y \quad Rs.\ 2{,}03{,}750$

$Y \quad \frac{Rs.\ 2{,}03{,}750}{99} \qquad \therefore\ Y \quad Rs.\ 2{,}058$

Substituting the value of Y in equation (i)

$10\ X - Rs.\ 2{,}058 = Rs.\ 46{,}250 \qquad 10\ X \quad Rs.\ 46{,}250 + Rs.\ 2{,}058 \quad Rs.\ 48{,}308$

$X = Rs.\ 4{,}830.8$ or Rs. 4,831 (Approx.) Thus, X Rs. 4,831 and Y Rs. 2,058.

Secondary Distribution Summary

Items	**Total**	**Production Departments**		
	Rs.	**X (Rs.)**	**Y (Rs.)**	**Z (Rs.)**
Total as per Primary Distribution Summary	24,400	7,550	7,200	9,650
Service Department A (Rs. 4,831)				
Less : 10% to Dept. B	4,348	966	1,450	1,932
Service Department B (Rs. 2,058)				
Less : 10 % to Dept. A	1,852	823	411	618
Total	**30,600**	**9,339**	**9,061**	**12,200**

This method of simultaneous equations gives accurate results. But when the number of service departments exceeds two, calculations becomes cumbersome.

2) Repeated Distribution Method

In this method, following steps are taken to apportion the service department costs :

1) The costs of the first service department are apportioned in the normal way according to the given percentages. This will close the amount of the first service department.
2) Then apply the given percentages to the apportionment of second service department costs which includes its own total plus amount apportioned from the first service department. This closes the account of the second service department but re-opens the account of the first service department.
3) The same procedure should be followed in the case of all other service departments.
4) The procedure should be repeated again starting with the first service department whose total now consists only of amounts apportioned from other service departments. In this way, service department costs keep on reducing with each process of distribution because each time a substantial amount is charged to the production departments.
5) This process is continued until the amounts involved become insignificant.

The method of Repeated Distribution Method will be applied as under : (Taking the figures of Problem i.e. Naveen & Co.

Secondary Distribution Summary

	Production Departments			**Service Departments**	
Items	**X (Rs.)**	**Y (Rs.)**	**Z (Rs.)**	**A (Rs.)**	**B (Rs.)**
Total as per Primary Summary	7,550	7,200	9,650	4,625	1,575
Department A	925	1,387	1,850	-4,625	463
Department B	815	408	611	204	-2,038
Department A	41	61	82	-204	20
Department B	9	4	7	--	(-) 20
Total 9,040	9,340	12,200	--	--	

Working Note : In the above solution, first of all the cost of service department A is apportioned to X, Y, Z and B in the ratio given. Then the cost of the service department B Rs. 2,038 (i.e. 1,575 + 463) has been apportioned to departments X, Y, Z and B in the given ratio Then Rs. 20 allotted to department B is distributed to departments X, Y, Z.

Nothing has been allotted to department A as the share of department is quite negligible. In this way, the entire costs of service departments A, and B are appportioned to production departments X, Y, and Z.

It should be noted that, unlike Simultaneous Equations method, this method produces approximate results. But the advantage of this method is that it can be conveniently applied where the number of service departments is more than two.

3) Trial and Error Method

In this method, the cost of first service department is apportioned to other service departments in the given ratio. The cost of the next service department is apportioned to first and other service departments. In this way, when the costs of all service departments has been apportioned, the process is repeated till the service department costs are negligible. This is illustrated below :

Problem : 5

The figure of the following problem1 have been taken

	Service departments	
	A (Rs.)	B (Rs.)
Total as per Primary Summary	4,625	1,575
Service department A (10% to B)		463
Service department A (10% to A)	204	2,038
Service department B (10% to B)		20
Service department A (10% to A)	2	
	4,831	**2,058**

Thus, the total costs of service departments A and B are Rs. 4,831 and Rs. 2,058 respectively. Now a Secondary Distribution Summary can be prepared in the same way as was done in Simultaneous Equation Method.

It will be seen that this is a modification of Repeated Distribution Method where production departments are initially ignored for the purpose of redistribution. Like Repeated Distribution Method, this method also gives approximate results and can be usually employed where the number of service departments is more than two.

ABSORPTION OF OVERHEADS

Introduction

After apportionment and re-apportionment of overheads to production departments, these can now be charged to cost units. In essence, the procedure is to take each production department and distribute its overheads among all cost units passing through that particular department. This is technically known as 'absorption' and is defined as charging of overheads to cost units.

Meaning of Absorption

We have seen in the earlier units, the methods of allocation and apportionment of overheads cost to cost centres. The next step is accounting of overhead is absorption of overheads in the cost of production i.e. recovery of overheads in the cost of production. All jobs, processes or service pass through one or more producing cost centre. The overhead expenses are ultimately charged to cost centres in such a manner that the cost of production of each includes an appropriate or equitable share of overheads of the cost centres. This method of apportionment of overhead expenses of the cost centres to cost units is called absorption of overheads. This is also known as application, levy recovery of overheads.

Overheads Absorption Rates

Overhead absorption rates are determined for the purpose of overheads in costs of job, process or products. There are several methods of determination of overhead absorption rates. These method will be discussed in this chapter at a later stage. The basic procedure followed in these methods is to divide the amount of overheads by the total number of units of the base selected. The base may be units of products, direct labour cost, labour hours, machine hours to direct material cost. The rate so determined is multiplied by the units of the base in each individual product or job to decide cost of the each unit. The rate is given by the following formula :

$$\text{Rate} \quad \frac{\text{Amount of overheads}}{\text{Quality or values of base}}$$

Amount of overheads absorbed in a product Units of the base x Overhead rate

Basic objectives of Fixation of Overhead rates

The basic objective of fixation of overhead rates are as follows :

1) To facilitate absorption of overhead to cost units on a logical basis.
2) To estimate overhead cost in advance of production.
3) To even out the fluctuations in the overhead rates.
4) To facilitate quick computation of cost of completion of production.
5) To help in prompt calculation of cost of work in progress.

Actual Rate

This rate is determined by dividing actual overheads incurred during the accounting period by actual quantity or value of base selected. The rate is calculated as follows :

$$\text{Actual Rate} = \frac{\text{Actual overhead expenses incurred during a certain period}}{\text{Actual quantity or value of the base related to production during a certain period}}$$

As far as possible, recovery of overheads should be done on actual basis. However, in practice it is not possible due to following reasons :

1) Actual rate can be determined only after the accounting period is over. This may delay determination of cost.
2) The incidence of some of the overhead expenses is not uniformly spread over all the accounting periods. Similarly, actual volume of activity is affected by seasonal and cyclic factors.
3) Actual rates do not provide any basis for cost control.

Pre-determined Rate

This rate is determined on the basis of budgeted overheads and the budgeted base for the period. It is calculated as follows :

$$\text{Pre-determined Rate} = \frac{\text{Budgeted overheads for the period}}{\text{Budgeted base for the period}}$$

Pre-determined rate facilitates computation of cost in advance. Quotation can be given in advance. This helps preparation of bills promptly. No extra clerical work is involved in determination of overhead rate in an organization where budgetary control system is adopted.

Blanket Rate

This is single or general overhead rate applicable to the whole factory. This is calculated as follows:

$$\text{Blanket Rate} = \frac{\text{Overhead cost for the entire factory}}{\text{Total quantum of the base selected}}$$

Blanket rate is suitable in those factories where only one major product is manufactured in a continuous process. It is also suitable where the work performed by every department is fairly uniform.

Multiple Rates

These are the rates for different departments in the factory. A separate rate is determined for each department. The rate is decided as follows :

$$\text{Overhead Rate} = \frac{\text{Overhead costs allocated and apportioned to each department cost centre or product}}{\text{Corresponding base}}$$

Multiple rates are determined where the product lines are varied, or machinery is used to a varying degree in different departments i.e. the conditions in the factory are not uniform. The incidence of overhead cost of each department is different. Under such circumstances, departmental rates are suitable.

Methods of Absorption

Following are the various methods of absorption adopted :

1) Labour Hour Rate Method
2) Machine Hour Rate Method
3) Percentage of Material Cost Method
4) Percentage of Labour Cost Method
5) Percentage of Prime Cost Method
6) Combined Machine Hour and Labour Hour Rate.

1) Labour Hour Rate Method

This is also referred to as production hour rate method. This method is adopted in those factories where labour is prominent. Labour hour rate is calculated for each category of workers. The expenses incurred other than wages paid to workers. On each category of workers are listed and totalled for a certain period. The amount is divided by the number of hours put in by all the direct workers during the period to get the rate. Following formula may be used to decide the rate :

$$\text{Direct Labour Hour Rate} = \frac{\text{Factory Overheads}}{\text{Direct Labour hours during a period}}$$

Effective working hours can be calculated by the following formula :

Effective working hours = No. of average workers employed during a given period x No. of hours for which the factory works during each day

Problem : 6

Calculate labour hour rate from the following :

1) Total number of workers	100	2) Working days in year	300
3) Number of hours per day worked	8	4) Idle time	5 %
5) Factory on cost	Rs.1,14,000	6) Office Rent	Rs. 1,600

Solution

1) Calculation of effective number of working hours in a year

= Total number of workers x Working days in a year x Number of hours per day worked.

=	100 workers x 300 days x 8 Hrs.....	2,40,000 Hrs.
	Less : Idle time 5 % of 2,40,000 Hrs.......	- 12,000 Hrs.
	Number of Labour Hours Worked	2,28,000 Hrs.

2) Calculation of Labour Hour Rate

$$= \frac{\text{Factory Overheads}}{\text{Number of Labour Hours Worked}} = \frac{\text{Rs. } 1,14,000}{\text{Hrs.} 2,28,000} = \text{Re. } 0.50 \text{ per labour hour}$$

(**N.B. :** Office Rent is a part of office overheads and hence not to be considered while calculating Total Factory Overheads).

Advantages

1) The rate takes into account the time factor.
2) It is suitable when most of the work is done by the labour.
3) It is not affected by the method of wage payment or the grade or rate of pay of workers.

Disadvantages

1) It does not take into account factors of production other than labour. This may lead to faulty distribution of overheads to the products.
2) Many concerns do not maintain any record of the time taken on job when the payment is not related to the time taken for the production. Hence, more clerical work is involved in determination of the rate.

2) Machine Hour Rate Method

This method of absorption is followed where work is performed predominantly on machines. The hourly machine rate is calculated department-wise. A single machine rate is unsuitable because of different types of machines may be used in various producing departments. In a department more than one rate may be computed in a department. A separate rate is calculated for each machine. Each machine or a group of machines constitutes a cost centre for the purpose of absorption of overhead expenses. The machine hour rate is determined by dividing the overhead costs pertaining to the machine cost centres by the number of effective machine hours likely to be worked during a period. The overhead cost consists of indirect expenses allocated or apportioned to the particular machine cost centre for which the machine hour rate is to be decided.

There are two ways of calculating the machine hour rate. As per first method, only indirect expenses directly or immediately connected with the operation of the machine are taken into account. E.g. power, depreciation, repairs, maintenance, insurance etc. The rate is calculated by dividing the total of these expenses by the number of operating hours of the machine during the stipulated period.

In addition to above expenses, there may still other manufacturing expenses such as Supervisor Charges, Shop Cleaning and Lighting. Consumable stores and Shop supplies, shop general labour, rent and rates etc. incurred for the department as a whole and hence not proportionate amount of such expenses applicable to the machine should be considered to decide the machine hour rate. Some people think that wages paid to the machine operator also should be considered while deciding the rate.

On the basis of the above discussion, it can be concluded that recovery of direct machine expenses without the proportion of the departmental expenses is likely to be more accurate than when these are a part thereof because general departmental expenses are connected with the actual operation of the machines.

Computation of Machine Hour Rate

a) Each machine or a group of machines is treated as a cost centre in order to identify the overhead expenses.
b) Machine overhead expenses are of two types viz. standing charges (fixed) and machine expenses (variable or running) standing charges.

These expenses remain constant. They do not vary with the use of machines. These expenses include rent, rates, supervision etc. The standing charges are estimated for a given period for every month. The estimated expenses divided by total working hours of a period will give an hourly rate for the standing charges.

Machine Expenses or Variable Expenses

These are the variable expenses which vary with the use of machines. These includes power, depreciation, repairs etc. The amount of machine expenses is divided by the normal working hours to give hourly rate to each item. Normal working hours are calculated by taking into account idle time for maintenance, setting up etc.

c) The sum of the standing rate and the machine expenses rate will give machine hour rate.

Basis for Apportionment of Expenses

The standing charges are apportioned to each machine on a suitable basis. Following chart gives the basis of apportionment of expenses :

Item of Expenses	Basis of Appportionment
1) Depreciation on the machine	Life of the asset or number of machine hours
2) Rent and rates	Area occupied by the machine
3) Lighting	No. of light points in the above mentioned area
4) Heating	Area occupied by the machine
5) Repairs and Maintenance	Actual allocation to the particular machine
6) Power	Actual allocation to the particular machine i.e. Horse power multiplied by Machine Hours
7) Insurance Premium	Machine value
8) Supervisory Labour	Time of Supervision
9) Miscellaneous Expenses	Actual or on any other reasonable basis
10) Operator Wages	Actual allocation

Hints for calculation of Machine Hour Rate

1) Machine Hour Rate is an actual or pre-determined rate of cost apportionment or overheads absorption, which is calculated by dividing the cost to be apportioned or absorbed by the number of hours for which a machine or machines are operated as per the ICMA definition. Machine Hour Rate is used where the cost centre is machine intensive and the work is predominantly on machine.
2) A single machine hour rate will not be sufficient and in such cases, different machine hour rates may be worked out depending on the make, type, size or capacity, wattage, horsepower, value function and other technical factors. Each group of machines constitute a cost centre for the purpose of overhead absorption. The overhead expenses of each machine are ascertained as above and machine hour rate is worked out on the basis of actual running hours of the machine. Every job product using such machine will be debited by the machine hours rate multiplied by the number of machine hours taken by such job or product. If the predetermined machine hours rate is required, it can be computed by dividing the estimated number of machine hours. Machine hour rates may be worked out separately for fixed and variable expenses. Idle time also is taken into account for arriving at the effective running hours.
3) A rate may be worked out with or without operator. Similarly it can be computed with or without operator. Similarly, it can be computed with or without set up time. Otherwise a separate rate also can be worked out for set-up time of machine. Combining these two or three above rates, we get a comprehensive machine hour rate.

Advantage of Machine Hour Rate Method

1) It is suitable where one operator uses several machines.
2) Under absorption of overheads indicates that the machines were idle.
3) It is the most appropriate method when machine is the main factor of production.
4) It is a scientific and logical method as it takes into account time factor.
5) Relative efficiencies of machine can be compared.
6) The management can understand the difference between usefulness of machine work and manual work.

Disadvantages of Machine Hour Rate

1) It leads to more clerical work in finding out the working hours of machines.
2) Expenses which are not proportional to the working hours of machine are not taken into account.

Disposal of Under and Over-absorption

The under or over-recovered amounts are disposed off in accordance with any of the following methods depending upon the circumstances :

1) **Use of supplementary rates :** Where the amount of under or over-absorbed overhead is not negligible, a supplementary overhead absorption rate is calculated to adjust this amount in the cost. However, adjustment is made in the cost of (i) work-in progress; (ii) finished stock, and (iii) cost of sales. In the case of under-absorption the overhead is adjusted by a plus rate since the amount is to be added whereas over-absorption is adjusted by a minus rate since the amount is to be deducted.

Example :	Predetermined overhead rate	Rs 5 per machine hour
	Actual machine hours	1,500
	Actual overheads	9,000
	Overhead-absorbed	1,500 x 5 = 7,500
	Under-absorption	Rs. 1,500 i.e. 9,000 - 7,500
	Supplementary rate	1,500 + 1,500 Rc 3,000

This is a plus rate because it is for under-absorbed overheads and will be used to add to the overhead already recovered.

2) **Writing off to costing Profit and Loss Account :** The method is used when the under or over-absorbed amount is quite negligible and it is not worth-while to absorb it by supplementary rates. Under-absorption due to abnormal factors like idle capacity, defective planning etc, is also transferred to costing Profit and Loss Account.

This method suffers from the shortcoming that stocks of work-in-progress and finished goods remain under or over-valued and are carried over to the next accounting period at such values.

3) **Carry over to the next year:** Under this method the under or over-absorbed amount is transferred to Overhead Reserve Account or Suspense Account for carry over to the next accounting year. This procedure is open to criticism on the ground that it is not logical to carry over the overhead of one year to the subsequent years for absorption. But, this method can be usefully employed where normal business cycle extends over more than one year and overheads are determined on a long-term basis.

Example : In a manufacturing unit, overhead was recovered at a pre-determined rate of Rs. 25 per man day. The total factory overhead expenses incurred and the man days actually worked were Rs. 41.50 lakhs and 1.50 lakhs days respectively.

Out of the 40,000 units produced during a period, 30,000 were sold. On analysing the reasons, it was found that 60% of the unabsorbed overheads were due to defective planning and the rest were attributable to increase in overhead costs.

How would unabsorbed overheads be treated in cost accounts ?

Solution

	Rs. (in lakhs)
Actual overhead expenses incurred	41.50
Overhead expenses absorbed (Rs 25 x 1.50 lakhs days)	(-) 37.50
Unabsorbed overheads	4.00

60% of this amount of unabsorbed overheads which is due to defective planning (controllable reasons) should be charged to costing Profit and Loss Account and the remaining 40% should be adjusted to the cost of sales and closing stock in the ratio of units sold and units in stock respectively.

Thus,

	Rs (in lakhs)
Thus, Charge to Costing Profit and Loss A/c (60% of Rs 4 lakhs)	2.40
Adjustment to the cost of sales 40% of Rs 4 lakhs Rs. 1.60 lakhs x $\frac{30,000 \text{ units}}{40,000 \text{ units}}$	1.20
Adjustment to closing stock Rs. 1.60 lakhs x $\frac{10,000 \text{ units}}{40,000 \text{ units}}$	0.40
Unabsorbed overhead	4.00

Example : A company absorbs overheads on pre-determined rates. For the year ending 31st December 2001, factory overhead absorbed were Rs. 3,66,250. Actual amount of overhead incurred totalled Rs. 4,26,890. The following figures are also derived from the trial balance :

Finished stock Rs.2,30,732 Cost of goods sold Rs.8,40,588 Work in progress Rs.1,41,480

Give two methods for the disposal of under-absorbed overhead and show the profit implications of each method.

Solution

Under absorbed overhead 4,26,890 - 3,66,250 Rs. 60,640

This under-absorbed amount may be disposed off by any of the following two methods.

a) Use of supplementary rate : Here under-absorbed amount will be charged to finished stock, cost of goods sold and work-in-progress.

$$\text{Supplementary Rate} \quad \frac{\text{Unabsorbed amount}}{\text{Total cost}} \times 100 \quad \frac{60,640}{12,12,800^*} \times 100 \quad 5\%$$

* 2,30,732 + 8,40,588 + 1,41,480 Rs. 12,12,800

The following journal entry will be made :

	Rs.	Rs.
Work-in progress Ledger Control A/c...... Dr.	7074.00	
Finished Goods Ledger Control A/c ....Dr.	11536.60	
Cost of Goods Sold A/c .... Dr.	42029.40	
To Factory Overhead Control A/c		60,640
(Being the apportment of under-absorbed factory overhead to work in progress, finished goods and cost of goods sold at a rate of 5% of cost)		

The cost of goods sold increased by Rs. 42029.40. Since this is debited to Profit & Loss A/c, the profit will decrease by this amount. On the other hand, credit to Profit & Loss A/c on account of increase in the value of closing stocks of work in progress and finished stock will be Rs. 18610.60 (i.e. Rs.7074 + 11536.60). Thus the net effect of using this method is that profit for the year will reduce by Rs. 23418.80 (i.e. Rs. 42029.40 - 18610.60).

b) Carry over to next year : Alternatively, entire amount of under-absorbed overhead may be carried over to next year. This will have no effect on the current year's profit or loss.

Overheads : (A summary at glance)

An overhead means Indirect cost. It is also 'On Cost' Overhead and are normally classified on the basis of functions i.e. Manufcturing Overheads, Administrative (office) Overheads, Marketing Overheads. Computation of administrative and marketing overheads per unit is simple where as computation of manufacturing overheads per unit is little complex.

Process Computing Manufacturing Overhead per unit :

Following are the five steps in this process :

a) Classification b) Collection c) Primary Distribution or Allocation

d) Secondary Distribution or Redistribution e) Absorption

a) **Classification :** Factory overheads incurred in the departments are classified into few major heads. e.g. Electricity, Maintenance, Power, Rent, Canteen Expenses etc.

b) **Collection :** All the production overheads incurred during the year, are recorded under appropriate heads. Such recording is called collection.

c) **Primary Distirbution or Allocation :** All such recorded overheads should be distributed among various departments using logical basis. Normally 'common overheads' are distributed. Specific overheads identified with specific department are to be allocated directly to such department.

d) **Secondary Distribution :** All overheads incurred in the service departments are to be distributed among the production department using logical basis.

e) **Absorption :** The final overheads of each production department are to be absorbed in the units produced i.e. 'Production overhead per unit' is calculated. Such production overhead may be used as 'Predetermined Overhead Rate' for submittng tender or for valuaing 'a job' to be done.

Problem : Following are the factory overheads incurred during 2003 - 2004

Factory rent	Rs. 90,000	Factory electricity	Rs. 30,000
Factory power	Rs. 60,000	Canteen Expenses	Rs. 45,000
Storage Expenses	Rs. 30,000	Maintenance Expenses	Rs. 24,000
Time-keeping Expenses	Rs. 6,000	Depreciation on plant	10 %

Following are the further details available :

20,000 Units were produced in 2003 - 2004. Compute the Factory Overhead per unit.

Particulars	Production Dep. I	Production Dep. II	Store	Time Keeping Dept	Maintenance Dept
Space (sq. feet)	2400	42200	600	600	900
Electric points	100	120	40	30	10
Power watts consumed	400	200	--	--	--
No. of employess	200	200	10	10	30
Cost of plant (Rs.)	3,00,000	5,00,000	--	--	--
Cost of Material Consumed (Rs.)	4,00,000	5,00,000	--	--	--

Solution

In the above example step no 1 (Classification) and 2 (Collection) are already completed. Now we have to work out step no. 3, 4 & 5

Step No. 3 : Primary Distribution or allocation over-heads.

Particulars	Basis for Distribution	Total (Rs.)	Production Dep. I	Production Dep. II	Store	Time Keeping Dept	Mainte-nance Dept
Factory Rent	Sq feet area (Total 9000 sq.f)	90,000	24,000	45,000	6,000	6,000	9,000
Factory Electricity	Electrcicity points (Total 300 points)	30,000	10,000	12,000	4,000	3,000	1,000
Factory power	Watts consumed (Total 600 W)	60,000	40,000	20,000	--	---	--
Canteen Expenses	No. of employees (Total 450)	45,000	20,000	20,000	1,000	1,000	3,000
Storing Exp.	Allocation	30,000	--	--	30,000	--	--
Mainteance	Allocation	24,000	--	--	--	--	24,000
Exp.	Allocation	6,000	--	--	--	6,000	---
	10% on cost	80,000	30,000	50,000	--	---	---
	Total	3,65,000	1,24,000	1,47,000	41,000	16,000	37,000

Step No. 4 : Redistribution of overheads of service departments to the production departments. Under this step,

Particulars	Basis for Redistribution	Production Dep. I	Production Dep. II	Store	Time Keeping Dept	Mainte-nance Dept
Overhead as per Primary distribution	Sq feet area (Total 9000 sq.f) Electricity points	1,24,000	1,27,000	41,000	16,000	37,000
Time Keeping Overhead	No. of Employees (20 : 20 : 1 : 3) i.e. 20/44,20/44,1/44,3/44	(+) 7,273	(+) 7,273	(+) 364	(-) 16,000	(+) 1,090
		1,31,273	1,54,273	41,364	NIL	38,090
Store Overhead	Cost of material consumed (4 : 5) i.e. 4/9, 5/9	(+) 18,384	(+) 22,980	(-) 41,364	---	---
		1,49,657	1,77,253	NIL	NIL	38,090
Maintenance Overhead	Cost of Plant (3 : 5) i.e. 3/8, 5/8	(+) 14,284	(+) 23,806	---	---	(-) 38,090
	Total	1,63,941	2,01,059	NIL	NIL	NIL

Note :- Time keeping department serves all the departments including stores & maintenance. Therefore these overheads are proportionately transferred to all departments.

Step No. 5 : Absorption of production overheads by each unit produced.

a) Production overhead per unit in production dept. I $= \frac{1,63941}{20,000}$ = Rs. 8,19

b) Production overhead per unit in production dept. II $= \frac{2,01,059}{20,000}$ = Rs. 10,05

d) Total production overhead per unit $= \frac{3,65,000}{20,000}$ = Rs. 18,25

Problem

With the following information work out the production hour rate recovery of overhead in depratments X,Y,Z,. (Continued Distribution Method)

Particulars	Total	Production Dep.			Service Depts.	
		X	Y	Z	A	B
Rent (Rs.)	12,000	2,400	4,800	2,000	2,000	800
Electricity (Rs.)	4,000	800	2,000	500	400	300
Indirect Exp.(Rs.)	6,000	1,200	2,000	1,000	800	1,000
Depreciation (Rs.)	5,000	2,500	1,600	200	500	200
Sundries (Rs.)	4,500	910	2,143	847	300	300
Estimated working hours		1,000 hrs	2,500 hrs	1,400 hrs		

Expenses of service departments A & B are apportioned as under :

	X	Y	Z	A	B
A	30 %	40 %	20 %	-	10 %
B	10 %	20 %	50 %	20 %	-

Solution

Overhead Distribution Summary (Continuous Distribution Method)

Particulars	Total	Production Depts.			Service Depts.	
		X	Y	Z	A	B
Rent (Rs.)	12,000	2,400	4,800	2,000	2,000	800
Electricity (Rs.)	4,000	800	2,000	500	400	300
Indirect Labour Exp. (Rs.)	6,000	1,200	2,000	1,000	800	1,000
Depreciation (Rs.)	5,000	2,500	1,600	200	500	200
Sundries (Rs.)	4,500	910	2,143	847	300	300
Total departmental expenses	31,500	7,810	12543	4547	4000	2600
Service Dept. A		(+) 1200	(+) 1600	(+) 800	(-) 400	(+) 400
		(30%)	(40%)	(20%)	(100%)	(10%)
Service Dept. B		9010	14143	5347	NIL	3000
		(+) 300	(+) 600	(+) 1500	(+) 600	(-)3000
		(10%)	(20%)	(20%)	(20%)	(100%)
Service Dept. A		9310	14743	6847	(+) 600	NIL
		(+) 180	(+) 240	(+) 120	(-) 600	(+) 60
		(30%)	(40%)	(20%)	(100%)	(10%)
Service Dept. B		9490	14983	6967	NIL	(+) 60
		(+) 06	(+) 12	(+) 30	(+) 12	(-0 60
		(10%)	(20%)	(50%)	(20%)	(100%)
Service Dept. A		9496	14995	6997	(+) 12	NIL
		(+) 04	(+) 05	(+) 02	(-) 12	(+) 01
		(30%)	(40%)	(20%)	(100%)	(10%)

		9500	15000	6999	NIL	(+) 01
Service Dept. B		--	--	(+) 01	NIL	(-) 01
Total	31500	9500	15000	7000	NIL	NIL
Working Hours.	---	1000	2500	1400	--	--
Rate per hours (Rs.)		9.50	6.00	5.00	--	--

MACHINE HOUR RATE METHOD

Problem 1

The following particulars relates to a new machine purchased.

Purchase price of the machine	Rs. 4,00,000
Rent and Rates per quarter	Rs. 15,000
Installation expenses	Rs. 20,000
Monthly lighting charges for the total area	Rs. 1,000
Estimated value of scrap at the end of 10th year	Rs. 20,000
Foreman's salary for the year	Rs. 30,000
Estimated life of the machine - 10 years	
(Annual insurance premium for the machine)	Rs. 3,000
Running of the machine in its lifetime	Hrs. 2,00,000
Estimated repairs and maintenance for the machine for a period of 12 months	Rs. 5,000
Machine occupies 25% of the total area.	
Consumable stores	Rs. 3,000 p.a.
Sundry supplies	Rs. 1,000 p.a.
Time devoted by the foreman - 1/6th of his time.	
Power consumption : 5 units per hour @Rs. 5 per 100 units.	

Solution

Calculation and Notes

1) Depreciation

$$\frac{\text{Purchase price of the machine + Installation expenses - Estimated value of scrap}}{\text{Estimated working life of the machine}}$$

$$\frac{\text{Rs. 4,00,000 + Rs. 20,000 - Rs. 20,000}}{\text{2,00,000 Hrs.}} \quad \frac{\text{Rs.4,00,000}}{\text{Hrs.2,00,000}} \quad \text{Rs. 2}$$

2) Rent and Rates

Rs. 15,000 x 4 Quarters x 25% Rs. 15,000

3) Lighting Charges

Rs. 1,000 x 12 months x 25% Rs. 3,000

4) Foreman's Salary

Rs. 30,000 x $\frac{1}{6}$ Rs.5,000

5) Repairs and Maintenance

$\frac{\text{Rs. 5,000}}{\text{20,000 Hrs.}}$ Rs.0.25

6) Power :

5 units x Rs. 0.05 Rs. 0.25

7) Standing charges :

$\frac{\text{Rs.30,000}}{\text{Hrs.20,000}}$ Rs. 1.50

In the books of a Company

Machine Hour Rate

Machine No. ----------

Department ---------

Particulars	**Per Year Rs.**	**Per Hour Rs.**
A) Standing Charges :		1.50
1) Rent and Rates	15,000	
2) Lighting Charges	3,000	
3) Foreman's Salary	5,000	
4) Insurance Premium	3,000	
5) Consumable Stores	3,000	
6) Sundry Supplies	1,000	
Total	30,000	
B) Machine Expenses :		
1) Depreciation		2.00
2) Repairs and Maintenance		0.25
3) Power		0.25
Machine Hour Rate		4.00

Problem : 2

From the following particulars, calculate Machine Hour Rate for a machine "Texmo".

Capital cost of the machine	Rs. 9,500
Rent and Rates of the shop per quarter	Rs. 900
Freight and installation charges	Rs. 1,500
Supervisor's salary per month	Rs. 400
Extimated scrap value after 10 years of working life	Rs. 1,000
General lighting charges per month	Rs. 300
Sundry supplies per year	Rs. 40
Monthly insurance premium	Rs. 30
Estimated cost of repairs and maintenance per annum	Rs. 200
Consumption of power 8 units per hour @ Rs. 5 per 100 units	
Effective running time per year,	Hrs. 2,000

Space occupied by the machine - 1/3rd of the floor shop.

Time devoted by the supervisor for Texmo' - 1/4th of his time.

Rent and Rates are to be apportioned in the ratio of floor space occupied by the machine on the floor shop. Out of 12 light points 4 points are being used for 'Texmo' machine.

Solution

Calculation and Notes

1) **Depreciation**

Capital cost of machine + Freight and Installation Charges :

Estimated Scrap Value

Estimated working life of the machine

$$= \frac{\text{Rs. } 9{,}500 + \text{Rs. } 1{,}500 - \text{Rs. } 1{,}000}{2{,}000 \text{ Hours} \times 10 \text{ years}} = \frac{\text{Rs. } 10{,}000}{\text{Hrs. } 20{,}000} = \text{Re. } 0.50$$

2) **Rent and Rates**

= Rs. 900 x 4 Quarters x $^1/_3$ = Rs. 1,200

3) **Supervisor's Salary**

= Rs. 400 x 12 months x $^1/_4$ = Rs. 1,200

4) **General Lighting charges**

= Rs. 300 x 12 months x $^1/_3$ = Rs. 1, 200

5) **Insurance Premium**

= Rs. 30 x 12 months = Rs. 360

6) **Repairs and Maintenance**

$$= \frac{\text{Rs.}200}{2{,}000 \text{ Hours}} = \text{Re. } 0.10$$

7) **Power**

= 8 units x Re. 0.05 = Re. 0.40

8) **Standing charges**

$$= \frac{\text{Rs.}4{,}000}{2{,}000 \text{ Hours}} = \text{Rs. } 2.$$

In the books of a Company

Machine Hour Rate for 'Texmo'

Machine No. ---------------

Department ---------------

Particulars	Per Year Rs.	Per Hour Rs.
A) Standing Charges :		2.00
1) Rent and Rates	1,200	
2) Supervisor's Salary	1,200	
3) General Lighting Charges	1,200	
4) Sundry supplies	40	
5) Insurance Premium +	360	
∴ Total	4,000	
B) Machine Expenses :		
1) Depreciation		0.50
2) Repairs and Maintenance		0.10
3) Power +		0.40
∴ Machine Hour Rate		3.00

Problem 3

Compute the machine hour rate for the Machine 'Fowerluba' from the following particulars.

1)	Cost of the machine	Rs. 52,500
2)	Machine fixation charges	Rs. 2,000
3)	Octroi duty on import of machine	Rs. 3,500
4)	Estimated scrap value at the end of 10th year	Rs. 5,500
5)	Estimated working life of the machine per annum	Hrs.3,000
6)	Estimated life of the machine 10 years	
7)	Rent,Rates and Taxes for the department	Rs. 28,500 p.a.
8)	Monthly insurance charges for the machine	Rs. 75 p.a.
9)	Electric lighting	Rs. 8,000 p.a.
10)	Consumable stores Rs. 50 per month	
11)	Cotton, waste, oil etc. Rs. 100 per quarter	
12)	Supervisor's salaries	Rs. 8,000p.a.
13)	Power - 13 units per hour @ Rs. 5 per 100 units	
14)	Repairs and Maintenance for the entire life of the machine	Rs. 18,000

Fowerluba occupies $1/_3$rd space of the total area of the shop. Out of the total number of light points in the shop are 20, only 4 points are used by this machine. The supervisor devotes ¼th of his time on this machine.

Solution

Calculation and Notes

1) Depreciation :

$$\frac{\text{Cost of the Machine} + \text{Machine fixation charges} + \text{Octroi duty} - \text{Estimated scrap value}}{\text{Estimated working life of the machine}}$$

$$\frac{\text{Rs. } 52,500 + \text{Rs. } 2,000 + \text{Rs. } 3,500 - \text{Rs. } 5,500}{3,000 \text{ Hours} \times 10 \text{ Years}} = \frac{\text{Rs. } 52,500}{\text{Hrs. } 30,000} = \text{Rs. } 1.75.$$

2) Rent, Rates and Taxes

$$\text{Rs. } 28,500 \times \frac{1}{3} = \text{Rs. } 9,500$$

3) Insurance charges

Rs. 75 x 12 months = Rs.900

4) Electric lighting

$$\text{Rs. } 8,000 \times \frac{4}{20} = \text{Rs. } 1,600$$

5) Consumable stores

Rs. 50 x 12 months = Rs.600

6) Cotton, Waste, oil etc.

Rs. 100 x 4 quarters = Rs. 400

7) Supervisor's salaries

$$\text{Rs. } 8,000 \times \frac{1}{4} = \text{Rs. } 2,000$$

8) **Repairs and Maintenance**

$\frac{\text{Rs.18,000}}{\text{30,000 Hrs.}}$ Re.0.60

9) **Power**

13 units X Re. 0.05 Rs. 0.65

10) **Standing charges**

$\frac{\text{Rs.15,000}}{\text{3,000 Hours}}$ Rs. 5

In the books of a Company

Machine Hour Rate for 'Fowerluba'

Machine No.----------

Department ----------

	Particulars	Per Year Rs.	Per Hour Rs.
A)	Standing Charges :		5.00
	1) Rent, Rates and Taxes	9,500	
	2) Insurance Charges	900	
	3) Electric Lighting	1,600	
	4) Consumable Stores	600	
	5) Cotton, Waste, Oil etc.	400	
	6) Supervisor's Salaries	2,000	
	∴ Total	15,000	
B)	Machine Expenses :		
	1) Depreciation		1.75
	2) Power		0.65
	3) Repairs and Maintenace		0.60
	∴ Machine Hour Rate		8.00

Problem 4

From the following data compute the machine hour rate to be charged in respect of jobs carried out during the month of March, 200X.

a) The cost of machine is Rs. 7,30.000, its anticipated residual value at the end of working life i.e. 15 years is Rs. 10,000.

b) Monthly running hours - 375, Hours spent on trial runs and job setting - 25, hours lost due to abnormal factors - 40, hours lost due to normal repairs and maintenance - 25, overtime hours worked to complete the job in time - 75.

c) Repairs and Maintenance Rs. 1,000

d) Salaries to Supervisors Rs. 8,000

e) Power Rs. 2,500

f) Sundry Shop Expenses Rs. 6,500

g) Departmental Overheads Rs. 4,000

h) Production Service Charges Rs. 1,500

i) Normal rate of wages per hour Rs. 40.00

j) Rate of overtime : 50 % extra over normal time wages.

Solution

Calculation and Notes

1) Calculation of effective working hours per month :

Monthly running hours		375
Less : Time allowed for -		
i) trial runs and job setting	25	
ii) normal repairs and maintenance	+ 25	-50
		325
Add : Time allowed for -		
i) Overtime		+ 75
∴ Effective Working Hours		400

Effective working hours per month - 400 hours

Effective working hours per year - 400 Hours x 12 months i.e. 4,800 Hours

2) Depreciation

$$\frac{\text{Cost of Machine - Residual value}}{\text{Estimated value}}$$

$$\frac{\text{Rs.7,30,000 - Rs. 10,000}}{\text{4,800 Hours X 15 Years}} \quad \frac{\text{Rs.7,20,000}}{\text{Hours 72,000}} \text{ Rs. 10}$$

3) Overtime Wages

75 Hours x Rs. 60 (i.e. 50% extra over normal time wages of Rs. 40 per hour) Rs. 4,500.

4) Repairs and Maintenance

$$\frac{\text{Rs.1,000}}{\text{400 Hrs.}} = \text{Rs. 2.50}$$

5) Power

$$\frac{\text{Rs.2,500}}{\text{400 Hrs.}} \quad \text{Rs. 6.25}$$

6) Standing Charges

$$\frac{\text{Rs.24,500}}{\text{400 Hrs.}} \quad \text{Rs. 61.25}$$

In the books of a Company

Machine Hour Rate for

Machine No. ---------

Department ---------

Particulars	Per Year Rs.	Per Hour Rs.
A) Standing Charges :		
1) Overtime chargas	4,500	61.25
2) Salaries to Supervisor's	8,000	
3) Sundry Shop Expenses	6,500	

4) Departmental. Overheads	4,000	
5) Production Service charges	1,500	
∴ Total	24,500	
B) Machine Expenses :		
1) Depreciation		10.00
2) Repairs and Maintenance		2.50
3) Power		6.25
∴ Machine Hour Rate		80.00

Problem 5

From the following particulars relating to a Machine, calculate Machine hour rate.

1) Original cost of the machine Rs. 19,000
Carriage and freight paid on purchase of mahine Rs. 1,200
Residual value of machine after ten years Rs. 200
Estimated life 10 years

In a year of 50 weeks the machine is operated for 48 hours, which includes 300 hours towards machine maintenance down-time and 100 hours towards setting up time.

2) Electric power used by the machine is 6 units per hour @ Rs. 5 per 100 units.
3) Repairs and Maintenance Rs. 75 per month
4) Two operators attend the machine during operation alongwith three other machines, their total wages including fringe benefits amounted to Rs. 800 per month.
5) General overheads attributable to this machine Rs. 600 per year
6) Rent and Taxes Rs. 1,500 p.a.

Solution

Calculation and Notes

1) **Calculation of effective working hours per annum :**

Estimated yearly working hours (50 Weeks X 48 Hours)		2,400
Less : Time allowed for -		
a) Machine-Maintenance down-time	300 hours	(-) 400
b) Seeting up time	+ 100 hours	
∴ Effective working hours	400 hours	2,000

2) **Depreciation**

$$\frac{\text{Original cost of machine + Carriage and Freight paid on purchase of machine - Residual value of machine}}{\text{Estimated working life of machine}}$$

$$\frac{\text{Rs.19,000 + Rs. 1,200 - Rs.200}}{\text{2,000 Hours X 10 Years}} = \frac{\text{Rs.20,000}}{\text{Hrs 20,000}} = \text{Re. 1}$$

3) **Electric Power**

6 units x Re. 0.05 Re. 0.30

4) **Repairs and Maintenance**

$$\frac{\text{Rs.75 X 12 months}}{\text{2,000 Hrs.}} \quad \text{Re. 0.45}$$

5) **Operators Wages**

$$\frac{\text{Rs.800 X 12 months}}{\text{4 machines}} \quad \text{Rs. 2,400}$$

In the books of a Company

Machine Hour Rate

Machine No ----------

Department ----------

Particulars	Per Year Rs.	Per Hour Rs.
A) Standing Charges :		2.25
1) Operators Wages	2,400	
2) General Overheads	600	
3) Rent and Taxes	1,500	
∴ Total	4,500	
B) Machine Expenses:		
1) Depreciation		1.00
2) Electric Power		0.30
3) Repairs and Maintenance		0.45
∴ Machine Hourt Rate		4.00

Problem 6

Calculate Machine Hour Rate from the following information relating to machine No.14.

Purchase price of the machine	Rs. 97,000
Repair charges - 50 % of depreciation	
Railway freight	Rs. 2,000
Lubricating oil @ 2per day of 8 hours (effective)	
Errection charges for the machine	Rs. 1,500
Consumable stores @Rs. 3 per day of 8 hours (effective)	
Estimated scrap value of machine after 10 years	Rs. 500
Estimated working hours 2,150 per annum	
Cost of Supervision	Rs. 1,500 p.a.
Hours lost due to normal tool setting	150
Rent and Taxes Rs. 11 per day of 8 hours (effective)	
Electric power	Rs. 1,000 p.a.

Labour cost of operating the machine No. 14 is to be ignored while calculating Machine Hour Rate.

Solution

Calculation and Notes

1) **Calculation of effective working hours per annum :**

Estimated working hours	2,150
Less : Hours lost due to normal tool-setting	- 150
∴ Effective Working Hours	2,000

2) **Depreciation**

$$\frac{\text{Purchase price of the machine + Railway Freight + Erection charges for the machine - Estimated Scrap Value}}{\text{Estimated working life of the Machine}}$$

$$\frac{\text{Rs.97,000 + Rs. 2,000 + Rs.1,500 - Rs.500}}{\text{2,000 Hours X 10 Years}} \quad \frac{\text{Rs.1,00,000}}{\text{Hrs 20,000}} \quad \text{Rs.5}$$

3) **Repair charges**

50 % of depreciation i.e. Rs. 5 Rs. 2.50

4) **Electric Power**

$$\frac{\text{Rs.1,000}}{\text{Hrs 2,000}} \quad \text{Re. 0.50}$$

5) **Standing charges**

$$\frac{\text{Rs.16}}{\text{8 Hours}} \quad \text{Rs. 2}$$

6) **Cost of Supervision as related to labour cost of operating the machine hence ignored while calculating machine hour rate.**

In the books of Company

Machine Hour Rate

Machine No.-------

Department -------

Particulars	Per years Rs.	Per Hour Rs.
A) Standing Charges :		2.00
1) Lubricating Oil	2.00	
2) Consumable Stores	3.00	
3) Rent and Taxes	11.00	
∴ Total	16.00	
B) Machine Expenses :		
1) Depreciation		5.00
2) Repair charges		2.50
3) Electric Power		0.50
∴ Machine Hour Rate		10.00

Questions for self study

1) Explain Accounting and Control of Overhead.
2) What is Departmentalisation of Overhead ? What is the need of departmentalisation of overheads?
3) What is meant by allocation of overheads? Distinguish between Allocation and Apportionment of overheads.
4) What are the principle basis or methods for apportionment of overhead expenses among departments ? Name the overheads and state which basis or method will be suitable.
5) What are the methods of distribution of Service department to Production department?
6) Write detailed note on Apportionment of Service Department overheads.
7) Write short notes on;
   i) Apportionment only to Production department
   ii) Apportionment to Production as well as Service department
   iii) Apportionment on non-reciprocal basis
   iv) Apportionment on re-control basis

v) Repeated Distribution Method

vi) Trial and Error Method.

8) What is meant by Overhead Absorption? How the overhead absorption rates are determined?

9) Explain :

i) Actual rate,

ii) Pre-determined rate,

iii) Blanket rate,

iv) Multiple rate, in connection with overhead absorption,

10) What is meant by absorption of overheads ? Explain various methods of absorption.

11) Write short notes on :

i) Labour hour rate method

ii) Machine hour rate method

12) write notes on "Computation of machine hour rate".

13) What is meant by Machine houre rate method ? What are its advantages?

14) While selecing the method of absorption explain the various circumstances under which a method is suitable.

15) Write short notes on:

i) Percentage of direct material cost method

ii) Percentage of direct labour method

iii) Percentage of Prime Cost method

16) Explain the terms :

(a) Under absorption of overheads and

(b) Over-absorption of overheads.

17) What is meant by under and over-absorption of overheads? Explain the causes of under and over-absorption of overheads.

18) Write short Note on : a) Cost unit and cost centre. b) Types of cost centres. c) Classification of overheads costs. d) Methods of segregating semi-variable costs e) Importance of Classifying costs into fixed and variable f) Methods of Allocating the standing order numbers. g) Allocation overheads. h) Basis of Apportionment.

19) Following information is available of a company.

Item		Production Department			Serice Departments		
		A	B	C	Office	Stores	Work Shop
Direct Wages	Rs.	20,000	25,000	30,000			
Direct Material	Rs.	30,000	35,000	45,000			
Indirect Material	Rs.	2,000	3,000	3,000	1,000	2,000	2,000
Indirect Wages	Rs.	3,000	3,000	4,000	10,000	10,000	5,000
Area in Sq. mtrs.		200	250	300	150	100	250
Book value of Machinery	Rs.	30,000	25,000	25,000	-	-	15,000
Total H.P. of Machine		15	20	25	-	-	5
Machine Hrs. Worked		10,000	20,000	15,000	-	-	5,000

General Expenses	Rs. 12,500
Rent	Rs. 1,050
Depreciation	15 % of Value of Machine
Power	Rs. 3,800
Light	Rs. 1,250

You are requested to prepare an overhead analysis sheet for the departments showing the apportionment of total cost of service departments to Production departments on appropriate basis.

20) Surabhi Ltd. is divided into two production departments A and B and two service departments X and Y. The following is the summary of overhead costs for a particular period.

	Rs.
Works Manager's Salary	4,000
Power	21,000
Contribution to P.F.	9,000
Plant Maintenance	4,000
Depreciation on Plant and Machinery	20,000
Rent paid	6,000
Canteen Expenses	12,000

Following information is available from the various departments.

Particulars	A	B	X	Y
No.of employees	16	8	4	4
Area in sq. meters	2,000	3,000	500	500
Value of plant (Rs.)	75,000	1,00,000	25,000	
Wages paid (Rs.)	40,000	20,000	10,000	5,000
H.P.Ratio	3	3	1	-

Apportion the cost to the various departments on the most suitable basis.

21) In Modern Enterprises there are three production department A,B,C and one service department. The following figures are available for one month of 25 working days of 8 hrs. each day. All departments work all these days with full attendance.

Expenses		**Service dept**	**Producation dept**		
		S	A	B	C
Power and Lighting		240	200	300	360
Supervisor's Salary	Rs. 2,000				
Rent	Rs. 500				
Welfare Exps.	Rs.600				
Other Exps		200	200	400	400
Supervisor's Salary		20%	30%	30%	20%
No. of workers		10	30	40	20
Floor area in sq. mt.		500	600	800	600
service rendered by Service Dept. to production. dept		-	50%	30%	20%

Calculate labour hour rate of the dept. A,B,and C.

22) The Nashik Enterprises Ltd. has three Production departments A,B,C, and two Service departments D and e.

The following figures are extracted from their records.

	Rs.
Rent and Rates	5,000
General Lighting	600
Indirect Wages	1,500
Power	1,500
Depreciation of Machinery	10,000
Sundries	10,000

The following furher details are available.

Particulars	Total	A	B	C	D	E
Floor space (Sq.ft)	10,000	2,000	2,500	3,000	2,000	500
Light Points	60	10	15	20	10	5
Direct Wages (Rs.)	10,000	3,000	2,000	3,000	1,500	500
H.P. of Machines	150	60	30	50	10	-
Value of Machinery	2,50,000	60,000	80,000	1,00,000	5,000	5,000
Working Hours	-	6,226	4,028	4,066	-	-

The expenses of D and E are allocated as follows :

Particulars	A	B	C	D	E
Dept. D	20%	30%	40%	-	10%
Dept E	40%	20%	30%	10%	-

Calculate the Labour Hour Rate for each of these departments. sundry expenses are to be allocated on the basis of direct wages. What is the total cost of article if material cost is Rs. 30 and it passes through Dept. A,B and C for 4, 5 and 3 hours respectively?

23) The primary distribution of expenses disclosed the following details in respect of Production departments P_1, P_2 and P_3 and Service department S_1 and S_2.

Department	P_1	P_2	P_3	S_1	S_2
Overheads (Rs.)	6,300	7,400	2,800	4,500	2,000

The services given by S_1 and S_2 are as below :

Department	P_1	P_2	P_3	S_1	S_2
S_1	40%	30%	20%	-	10%
S_2	30%	30%	20%	20%	-

Find out the overheads chargeable to Production departments by using Simultaneous equations method.

24) In Baramati Ltd., there are two Service departments P and Q and three Production departments A,B,and C. In april 2001, the department expenses were :

Department	A	B	C	P	Q
Rs.	75,000	60,000	50,000	12,000	10,000

The service department expenses are allotted on a percentage basis as follows :

Service Departments	Production Departments			Service depts.	
	A	B	C	P	Q
P	30	40	15	-	15
Q	40	30	25	5	-

Prepare a Statement showing the distribution of the two Service departments expenses to the three departments by (a) Simultaneous Equation Method, (b) Repeated Distribution Method.

25) Work out overhead recovery rate under Repeated distribution method and Simultneous distribution methods.

Primary Overheads :			
Production Departments		**Service Departments**	
A -	7,810	Transport P -	4,000
B -	12,540	Power Q -	2,700
C -	4,550		
D -	3,000		

Expenses of Service Departments are apportioned as under -

	A	B	C	D	P	Q
P	10%	30%	20%	20%	-	20%
Q	30%	20%	30%	10%	10%	-

Estimated Labour Hours : A - 900, B - 2,700, C - 1,500.

26) From the following particulars compute a Machine Hour Rate. Consider the base period as one year.

1. Name of Equipment - Crane
2. Date of Purchase - 1st April 2002
3. Make - L & T Co. Ltd., Mumbai
4. Cost of Equipment - Rs. 25,000/-
5. Power - Diesel 10 H.P.Engine
6. Estimate life - 10 yrs.
7. Depreciation - 15% p.a. on Original cost
8. Insurance - Rs. 25/- per quarter
9. Repairs - Rs. 50 per month
10 Consumable Stores (Oil, Grease etc.) - Rs. 150 per term of six months
11 Rent paid for space allotted to Crane - Rs. 125/- for 2 months
12 Overheads for 5 similar machines - Rs. 1,300 p.a.
13 Cost of Diesel per hour - Rs. 1.50
14 Hire purchase instalment paid for one year - Rs, 5,960/- including Rs.960 as interest.
15 Assume Crane works normally for 200hrs. per month but actually works for only 80% of the normal hrs.

27) From the following particulars compute Machine hour rate for a machine for the month of November, 2002.

	Per Annum Rs.
Rent and Taxes	12,000
(¼ space is occupied by the machine)	
Lighting and Heating	3,000
(10 workers are engaged in the department, out of them 4 are working on this machine	
Supervisor's Salary	6,000
(1/3 time is devoted for this machine)	
Insurance	600
Lubricants and Cotton waste	60

The cost of machine is Rs. 16,000/- and its scrap value is estimated at Rs. 1,000/-

From the past experience it has been ascertained

(a) that the working life of the machine is 20,000 hrs.

(b) that the machine will work 2,000 hours annually.

(c) that the estimated cost of repairs and maintenance is Rs. 1,000 for the whole life.

(d) that the machine consumes 4 units per hour, rate of power is 5 paise per unit.

28) The following particulars relate to processing machine treating a typical material :

1. The cost of machine — Rs. 10,000
2. Estimated life — 10 years
3. Scrap value — Rs. 1,000
4. Yearly working time — 2,200 hours
   (50 weeks of 44 hours each)
5. Machine maintenance — 200 hours p.a.
6. Setting up time estimated at 5% of total productive time is regarded as productive time.
7. Electricity is 16 units per hour @ 10 paise per unit
8. Chemical required weekly — Rs. 20
9. Maintenance cost per year — Rs. 1,200
10. Two attendants control the operations of machine together with 6 other machines.
    Their combined weekly wages are - — Rs. 140
11 Departmental overhead allocated to this machine per annum — Rs, 2,000

You are required to calculate the Machine Hour Rate.

29) The following expenses have been incurred in respect of a shop having 4 identical machines -

1. Rent and Rates — 9,000 p.a.
2. Power consumed by the shop @ 10 paise per unit — 4,800 p.a.
3. Repairs — 1,000 p.a.
4. Lighting for the shop — 1,800 p.a.
5. Attendants two each getting Rs. 60 p.m.
6. Supervisor Salary — 6,000 p.a.
7. Lubricants etc. per machine — 100 p.m.
8. Depreciation per machine — 900 p.a.
9. Hire-Purchase Instalment for the machiines (including Rs. 300 for interest)
10. Each machine consumes 10 units of power in an hour
    Calculate machine hour rate.

30) The following annual charges are incurred in respect of a machine in a shop where manual labour is almost nil and where work is done by means of five machines of exactly similar type of specifications.

		Rs.
1.	Rent and Rates (Proportional to the floor space occupied) for the shop	4,800
2.	Depreciation on each machine	500
3.	Repairs and Maintenance for the five machines	1,000
4.	Power consumed (as per meter) at 6 $^{1}/_{4}$ paise per unit for the shop	3,750
5.	Electric charges for the shop	540
6.	Attendants : there are two attendants for the five machines and they are each paid Rs. 60 p.m.	-
7.	Supervision : for the five machines there is one supervisor whose emoluments are Rs. 250 p.m.	-
8.	Sundry supplies for the shop	450
9.	Hire purchases instalments payable for machine (including Rs. 300 as interest)	1,200

The machines uses ten units of power per hour. Calculate the working hours for each machine in a year and also calculate machine hour rate.

31) In a Machine department of factory there are five identical machines from the particulars given below, prepare a machine hour rate for one of the machine -

1. Space of department 10,000 sq. meters.
2. Effective space occupied by this machine 2,000 sq. mts.
3. Cost of machine Rs. 20,000
4. Estimated scrap value of the machine Rs. 300/-
5. Effective life of machine 13 years/. Depreciation is to be charged at 7 1/2 % p.a. on original cost.
6. Normal running hours of machine 2000 hrs. p.a.
7. Power consumed by the machine as shown by meter Rs. 3,000 p.a.
8. Estimated repairs and maintenance throughout working life of the machine Rs. 5,200.
9. Sundry supplies including oil etc. charged direct to the machine amounted to Rs. 600 p.a. on an average.
10. Other expenses of the department are as follows :

	Rs.
Rent and Taxes	9,000
Lighting to be apportioned to workers employed	400
Supervision	1,250
Other charges	5,000

It is ascertained that the degree of supervision required by the machine 2/5th and 3/5th being devoted to other machines.

There are 16 workers in the department of which 4 attend to the machine and remaining to other machines.

* * * * *

Unit No. 3

MARGINAL COSTING, BUDGETARY CONTROL & STANDARD COSTING

MANAGERIAL DECISION MAKING TECHNIQUES

Decision-making is the essence of management since it may make or mar the success of the business as a whole. Decision making is a regular phenomenon of the business. In general decision making means taking the final step in deliberation before acting. In management world it means the process of choosing among alternative courses of action, since if there is no choice, there is no decision to make. A decision always involves a prediction. The function of decision-maker is, therefore, to select courses of action for the future. Marginal Costing, Budgetary control and standard costing are the important managerial decision making techniques used in management accounting.

Marginal costing (Variable costing)

Introduction

Every manufacturing concern would like to increase its profits by increasing volume of production which will automatically involve additional cost. Such a decision would require a detailed analysis of additional costs and its behavior as it has a direct bearing on the profitability of the concern. Any increase in the level of operation will diminish the firm's marginal profit if it is already at its optimum level of existing operation. However, such a decision would definitely prove financially worthy if there exists any unutilised operational capacity. Thus, to reach at an accurate decision, management must know how costs will react to changes in activity.

The analysis of cost behavioral reveals that the cost of a product can be divided into two major categories, the first is fixed cost and second is variable cost.

As we know that, fixed cost remains constant to a particular level of output whereas variable cost has tendency to change proportionally with a change in the level of output. The following example will further clear the concept.

ABC Company made sale of 20,000 units @ Rs. 1000 per unit during the year 2003-2004 with the following details of expenditure on production.

i) Raw material required to produce one unit of finished product 2 kg @ Rs. 2 per kg
ii) Wages Rs. 200 per unit
iii) Rent of factory Rs. 50,000 per annum.
iv) Salary of executive Rs. 5,00,000 per annum.

In the above-mentioned example, the costs of raw-material and wages change proportionately with the change in the level of output and, therefore are known as variable costs. Whereas the rent of factory and salary of executive are such costs that are not subject to change with the change in output. They remain constant at every level of output and as such are known as fixed costs. On account of this reason, it is illogical to apportion fixed costs to production. Marginal costing is the technique which deals with this concept.

Different terminology used for "Marginal Costing"

Marginal costing which is otherwise known as "variable costing" is used as a tool for decision-making by the management. Marginal Costing is also known as "direct costing" and this new concept is gaining wide popularity in the field of accounting. Marginal costing is a technique through which variable costs are taken into account for purposes of product costing, inventory valuation and other important management decisions. The term "marginal costing" is commonly used in U.K. and other European countries while the same is denoted as "direct costing" or "variable costing" in U.S.A.

Marginal costing is also known as variable/direct/differential/incremental cost. The term "marginal costing" seems to be inappropriate since is has an exclusive meaning in Economics. Under the above circumstances, the term 'variable costing' seems to be more appropriate and acceptable.

Concept of Marginal Cost

The term "marginal cost" is derived from the word "margin" which is a well known terminology in economics. As is used in economic parlance, the term "marginal cost" connotes the cost which arises from the production of additional increment of output.

The Institute of Cost and Works Accountants, London, in its publication "A Report of Marginal Costing" defines marginal cost as "the amount at any given volume of output by which aggregate costs are changed if the volume of output is increased or decreased by one unit". "Marginal Cost", according to the Institute of Chartered Accountants, England, "is the very expense (whether of production, selling or distribution) incurred by the taking of a particular decision."

Viewed from this angle, marginal costs in the short run will be synonymous with variable costs, i.e., prime costs and variable overhead; but in the long run the marginal costs will include fixed costs in planning production activities involving an increase in the production capacity. It is clear that the marginal costs are related to change in output under certain conditions.

Blocker and Weltmore defines Marginal Cost as "the increase or decrease in total cost which results from producing or selling additional or fewer units of a product or from a change in the method of production or distribution such as the use of improved machinery, addition or exclusion of a product or territory, or selection of an additional sales channel". Thus, marginal cost is the cost incurred by a company for the additional output.

Concept of Marginal Costing

Marginal costing is an accounting technique which ascertains marginal cost by differentiating between fixed or periodical, and variable costs. This technique aims to charge only those costs of the cost of the product that vary directly with sales volumes. Those costs would be direct material, direct labour, and factory overhead expenses, such as supplies, some indirect labour, and power. The cost of the product would not include fixed or non-variable expenses such as depreciation, factory insurance, taxes and supervisory salaries.

Marginal costing is defined by the National Association of Accountants, as follows :

"This method proposes that fixed factory expenses be classified as period expenses and be written off currently as is generally done with selling and administration expenses, and that only the variable costs become the basis of inventory value and profit determination."

According to the Institute of Cost and Management Accountants, London, Marginal costing is "the ascertainment of marginal costs and of the effect on profit, of changes in volume or type of output by differentiating between fixed costs and variable costs. In this technique of costing only variable costs are charged to operations, processes or products, leaving all indirect costs to be written off against profits in the period in which they arise".

In a nutshell, we can say that marginal costing is a costing technique that considers only the costs that vary directly with volume - direct materials, direct labour, and variable factory overhead and ignores fixed cost in additional output decisions. Thus, the technique of marginal costing lies in i) Differentiation between fixed and variable costs, ii) Ascertainment of marginal costs, and, iii) Finding out effect on profit due to change in volume or type or output.

Features of Marginal Costing

The concept of marginal costing is evolved on the main distinction between product cost and period cost. While product cost relates to the volume of output, the period cost is mainly concerned with the period of time.

Marginal costing considers all those manufacturing costs which vary directly with the volume of output as product costs. This is in contradiction to the traditional system of costing under which all manufacturing costs - fixed as well as variable - are treated as product costs. It should also be remembered that variability with the volume of production is the basis for the classification of costs into product and period costs.

Thus, marginal costing necessitates classification of costs into fixed and variable. Even the semi-variable costs have to be closely examined so as to separate fixed and variable components thereof depending upon the increase or decrease in the volume of output. Thus, the marginal costs focuses the effect of costs on the varying of output.

A pure marginal cost has the following four important characteristics

1) Under Marginal costing, all types of operating costs (factory, selling and administrative) are separated into fixed and variable components and are recorded separately.
2) Variable cost elements are handled as product costs i.e. they are charged to the product at the appropriate movements and follow the product through the inventory accounts, and thus become treated as expenses when the product is sold. Variable distribution costs normally are chargeable to product at or near the moment of sale, and thus do not become inclined in inventory values.
3) Fixed costs (including fixed factory overhead) are handled as period costs; i.e., they are written off as expenses in the period in which they are incurred. They do not follow the inventories through the accounts but rather are treated in the way which is traditional for selling and general administrative expenses.
4) Marginal costing is a method of recording as well as reporting costs. Unlike differential cost analysis and break even analysis which utilise traditional records, variable costing requires a unique method of recording cost transactions as they originally take place.

Therefore, marginal costing is a technique which deals with the effect on profits of changes in volume or type of output.

Difference between Marginal Costing & Absorption Costing

Marginal costing is based on the assumption that initial investment in productive factors and other facilities is required before commencement of production. For instance, a factory building is hired for which rent is paid regularly, plant is installed against which depreciation is charged periodically and payment is made towards factory insurance, property taxes, salary of plant manager and such other initial expenses. Thus, the fixed costs arising from the investment on the above items are not product costs, but period costs. By nature these costs must necessarily be incurred to establish a manufacturing unit and they will recur every year. More precisely, the principle underlying variable cost is that the fixed manufacturing overheads are not carried as part of the cost of the inventory; they are period costs and must be compared against revenue of that year. On the other hand absorption costing denotes that the manufacturing fixed overheads are part of the cost of inventory; they are product costs and must be compared with the revenue of that year in which sales are made.

It will be understood from the foregoing that much of the work of allocating overhead expenses in an absorption cost accounting system simply does not arise under marginal costing. Under marginal costing, it becomes unnecessary to allocate these expenses to departments, cost centres, or products.

In marginal costing the product is charged only with those costs that are directly affected by changes in volume, while under the absorption costing method period costs (fixed costs) or these are a function of time and are not affected by volume changes are also charged to the cost of production.

Under the absorption costing method, inventories will normally be reported at a higher figure than the marginal costing method. This is due to the fact that fixed costs, under the absorption method, are deferred by being included in the cost of goods inventory. This element of fixed cost will not be reported as a deduction from revenue until the goods are sold and then becomes an expense in the cost of goods sold section of the income statement. Under the marginal cost method, no fixed costs are differed; they are charged against revenue in the period in which they are incurred.

It should be noted that where the firm's operating capacity is different from the normal capacity, there will be capacity variance. This calls for certain adjustments before determining the gross margin. If the capacity variance is favorable, the amount is to be deducted from the total cost of goods manufactured and sold. But when the capacity variance is unfavorable, the amount is to be added.

It is clear from the following two formats (see fig 5.1 & 5.2) that every thing is common except the fixed manufacturing overheads form part of production costs with full costing whereas they are non-production costs in the case of variable costing. More precisely in treatment of overheads other than manufacturing viz., selling and administrative cost etc., is the same under both the techniques, fixed and variable.

Income Statement (Absorption Costing)

		Amount Rs.
Sales revenue (No. of units sold x selling Price)		
Less : Total cost of manufacturing :		______
Direct material cost	______	
Direct labour cost	______	
Variable manufacturing overhead	______	
Fixed manufacturing overhead	______	
Total cost of goods manufactured	______	______
Plus : Cost of inventory at the beginning of the year (No. of units x Total cost)		______
Less : Cost of inventory at the end of the year	______	
(No. of units x Total cost) Cost of goods manufactured and sold	______	______
Gross margin (Manufacturing - unadjusted)		______
Total + Capacity variance		+ ______
(+ favourable; - unfavourable)		______
Gross margin (adjusted)		
Less : Non-production Costs :		
Selling and distribution costs	______	
Administrative costs	______	
Other costs (specify)	______	______
Net income (before income-tax)	______	______
Less : Income tax	______	______
Net income (after taxes)		______

Fig. 4.1 The cost flow pattern of absorption costing

Income Statement (Variable Costing)

			Amount Rs.
Sales revenue (No. of units sold x selling price)			______
Less :	Variable costs (production costs) :		
	Direct material cost	______	
	Direct labour cost	______	
	Variable manufacturing overheads	______	
		______	
	Total cost of goods manufactured	______	
Plus :	Cost of inventory at the beginning of the year (No. of units x Variable cost)	______	
Less :	Cost of inventory at the end of the year (No. of units x Variable cost)	______	
		______	
	Cost of goods manufactured and sold		______
	Marginal contribution (Manufacturing)		______
			______
Less :	Variable non-production costs :		
	Selling and distribution costs	______	
	Administrative costs	______	______
	Other costs (specify)		
			______
	Marginal contribution (Final)		______
Less :	Fixed costs :	______	
	Fixed production costs		
	Fixed non-production costs (specify individual items)	______	______
		______	______
	Net income (before income-tax)		______
Less :	Income tax		______
			______
	Net income (after income-tax)		______
			______

Fig. 4.2 The cost flow pattern of variable costing

The following problem would clearly demonstrate the difference between these two methods.

Problem 1

ABC Industrial Ltd., Nashik, furnished the following details for the year ended 31st December, 2004 for preparing the Comparative Income Statement of the year under Marginal Costing and Absorption Costing :

Sales	:	2,000 Units at Rs. 200/Unit
Fixed Manufacturing Cost	:	Rs. 42,000
Variable Manufacturing Cost	:	2,100 Units at Rs. 120/Unit
Inventory at close	:	100 Units
Fixed selling and administrative expenses	:	Rs.10,000
Variable selling and administrative expenses	:	Rs. 14,000

ABC Industrial Ltd., Nashik
Income Statement
for the ended 31st Dec. 2004

Particulars	Rs	Rs.
a) **Under Absorption Costing :**		4,00,000
Sales 2,000 units at Rs. 200 each		
Less : Cost of sales		
Variable manufacturing costs		
2,100 units at Rs. 120 each	2,52,000	
Fixed manufacturing costs	42,000	
	2,94,000	
Less : Inventory at Close 100 units at rs. 14 each	14,000	2,80,000
		1,20,000
Gross Margin or Profit		
Less : Total selling and administrative Expenses - Fixed	10,000	
- Variable	14,000	24,000
		96,000
Net Income		

Working Notes

The cost of inventory at close, as well as the cost of each unit of inventory at close, have been calculated as follows :

Units manufactured	2,100
Units of inventory at close	100

Ratio of closing inventory to total production $\frac{100}{2,100} \quad \frac{1}{21}$

Cost of inventory at close = $\frac{1}{21}$ x Rs. 2,94,000 = 14,000

Thus, the cost of each unit of inventory at close = $\frac{\text{Rs. } 14,000}{100 \text{ units}}$ = Rs. 140 per unit

b) Under Marginal Costing

Particulars	Rs.	Rs.
Sales : 2,000 units at Rs. 200 each		4,00,000
Less : Variable cost of sales		
Variable Manufacturing Cost :		
2,100 units at Rs. 120 each	2,52,000	
Less : Inventory at close :		
100 units at Rs. 120 each	(-) 12,000	(-) 2,40,000
Variable Gross Margin		1,60,000
Less : Variable Selling and Administrative expenses		(-) 14,000
Operating Contribution Margin		1,46,000
Less : Fixed costs :		
Fixed Manufacturing costs	42,000	
Fixed selling and administrative expenses	10,000	(-) 52,000
Net Income		94,000

Working Notes

The cost of inventory at close as well as the cost of each unit of inventory at close have been calculated as follows :

The ratio of closing inventory to total production = $\frac{100}{2,100} = \frac{1}{21}$

Cost of inventory at close = $\frac{1}{21}$ x Rs. 2,52,000 = Rs. 12,000

Thus, the cost of each unit of inventory at close = $\frac{\text{Rs. } 12,000}{100 \text{ units}}$ = Rs. 120

Note : The difference of Rs.2,000 in the net income calculated under the two method; wholly due the difference between the cost of closing inventory which, under absorption costing is Rs. 14,000 and, under marginal costing, Rs. 12,000

Problem 2

From the following data prepare statements of cost according to both absorption costing and marginal costing system.

Particulars	Product X (Rs.)	Product Y (Rs.)
Sales	15,000	40,000
Direct material	6,000	18,000
Direct labour	4,000	7,000
Factory overheads :		
Fixed	3,000	3,000
Variable	1,000	2,500
Administrative overheads :		
Fixed	500	1,000
Selling Overheads		
Fixed	1,000	1,500
Variable	500	1,500

Solution

Statement of Cost and Profit (Absorption Costing)

Particulars	Product X (Rs.)	Product Y (Rs.)	Total (Rs.)
Sales (A)	15,000	40,000	55,000
Less : Cost of Sales :			
Direct Materials	6,000	18,000	24,000
Direct Labour	4,000	7,000	11,000
Factory overheads	4,000	5,500	9,500
Administrative overheads	500	1,000	1,500
Selling overheads	1,500	3,000	4,500
Total cost (B)	16,000	34,500	50,500
Net Profit (A + B)	(-) 1,000	5,500	4,500

Statement of Cost (Marginal Costing)

Particulars	Product X (Rs.)	Product Y (Rs.)	Total (Rs.)
Sales (A)	15,000	40,000	55,000
Less : Cost of Sales :			
Direct Materials	6,000	18,000	24,000
Direct Labour	4,000	7,000	11,000
Variable Factory overheads	1,000	2,500	3,500
Variable selling overheads	500	1,500	2,000
Total (B)	11,500	29,000	40,500
Contribution (A-B)	3,500	11,000	14,500
Less : Fixed Cost			
(Factory Administration and selling)	4,500	5,500	10,000
Net Profit	(-) 1,000	5,500	4,500

When fixed costs are not traceable to different products, then the statement of cost will be prepared after contribution margin as under.

Statement of Cost (Marginal Costing)

Particulars	Product X (Rs.)	Product Y (Rs.)	Total (Rs.)
Sales (A)	15,000	40,000	55,000
Less : Cost of Sales :			
Direct Materials	6,000	18,000	24,000
Direct Labour	4,000	7,000	11,000
Variable Factory overheads	1,000	2,500	3,500
Variable selling overheads	500	1,500	2,000
Total (B)	11,500	29,000	40,500
Contribution (A-B)	3,500	11,000	14,500
Less : Fixed Cost			
(Factory Administration and selling)	—	—	10,000
Net Profit			4,500

Determination of Marginal Cost (Segregation of Semi Variable Costs or Semi-Variable overhead Expenses (SVOHEs)

Costs, according to their reactions to changes in volume, are classified as fixed, variable, or semi variable. But the utility of marginal costing depends on the segregation of total costs only into variable and fixed costs. Total costs include a significant portion of semi-variable element. Therefore, the effective application of marginal costing depends to a large extent upon the accuracy with which semi-variable costs are segregared into variable and fixed elements. A number of methods are available for segregation of semi-variable costs into variable and fixed costs.

The important methods are as under

1) Comparison by period or level of activity method
2) Equation method
3) Range method
4) Analytical method
5) Scattergraph method
6) Least squares method

1) Comparison by Period or Level of Activity Method

In this method the level of output at two levels is compared with corresponding level of expenses. Since the fixed costs remain constant, the variable costs are arrived at by the ratio of change in expense to change in output. Therefore, variable element.

i) Variable Overhead Expenses per unit (included in SVOHEs) $\frac{\text{Difference in SVOHEs}}{\text{Difference in output}}$

Or

ii) Variable element $= \frac{\text{Change in amount of expenses}}{\text{Change in activity of quantity}}$

This method is simple as it is clear from following problem but is not scientific and accurate method.

Problem 3

The ABC Ltd. submits the following information in respect of semi-variable costs.

During the month of July 2005 the production was 20,000 units only. Calculate the amount of fixed variable and total semi-variable expenses for the month.

Month	Production Units	Semi-variable costs (Rs.)
Jan. 2005	25,000	1,50,000
Feb. 2005	15,000	1,32,000
March 2005	40,000	2,00,000
April 2005	30,000	1,70,000
May 2005	50,000	2,30,000
June 2005	35,000	1,90,000

Solution

Taking the level of activity of any two months, say March and May, the variable costs may be calculated as follows :

Month	Production Units	Semi-variable (Rs.)	Fixed (Rs.)	Variable (Rs.)
March	40,000	2,00,000	80,000*	1,20,000*
May	50,000	2,30,000	80,000**	1,50,000**
Difference	10,000	30,000		

Therefore, variable element $= \dfrac{\text{Change in amount}}{\text{Change in quantity}} = \dfrac{\text{Rs. }30,000}{10,000} =$ Rs. 3.00 per unit

* Variable overheads for March = 40,000 x Rs.3.00 = Rs.1,20,000

∴ Fixed Overheads for March = Rs. 2,00,000 - Rs.1,20,000 = Rs.80,000

** Overheads for May has been computed accordingly.

Calculation of fixed, variable and total semi-variable costs of 20,000 units for the month of July 2005 :

Variable overheads for July = 20,000 x Rs. 3.00	= Rs.	60,000
Fixed overheads	= Rs.	80,000
Total semi-variable overheads	Rs.	1,40,000

2) Equation Method

When cost and output figures for only two periods are given or available, equation method may also be used. Here, the straight line or liner equation is used. The equation used for this purpose is as follows.

$$Y = MX + C$$

where Y = Total semi-variable cost;

M = Variable cost per unit;

X = Output; and

C = Fixed cost included in semi-variable cost.

It is now possible to segregate the fixed and variable portions with the use of the above given equations with respect to two periods.

Problem 4

Taking the figures for July and August from problem 3

January 2005 : 1,50,000 = 50,000 M + C (i)

February 2005 : 1,32,000 = 30,000 M + C (ii)

Subtracting (i) from (ii) we get 18,000 = 20,000 M

M = 1.80

Putting value of M in (i) 1,50,000 = 50,000 x 1.80 + C

1,50,000 = 45,000 + C

C = Rs. 1,05,000

3) Range Method or High & Low Method

This is also known as High or Low method. In this method the levels of highest and lowest expenses are compared with one another and related to output attained in those periods. This method assumes a linear cost behaviour pattern between these two points; that is costs for all intermediate volumes are assumed to fall along a straight line. Thus, it is similar to the two method except that only the highest and lowest points are considered amount of various levels. In other words we can say that this method is an improvement over the comparison and the equation methods as it can be used even when the data are given for more than two periods. Once the selection of the periods is made then either the comparison method or the equation method can be used. Because after the selection of periods, the same procedure as per the comparision or equation method is used.

Problem 5

Considering the highest and lowest production from problem 3

Month	Production Units	Semi-variable (Rs.)	Fixed (Rs.)	Variable (Rs.)
Feb. 2005	15,000	1,32,000	90,000*	42,000*
May 2005	50,000	2,30,000	90,000**	1,40,000**
Difference	35,000	98,000		

Variable element = $\frac{98,000}{35,000}$ = Rs. 2.80 per unit

* Variable overheads for August = 15,000 x Rs. 2.80 = Rs. 42,000

∴ Fixed overheads for August = 1,32,000 - 42,000 = Rs. Rs. 90,000

Accordingly the fixed and variable overheads for May 2005 has been calculated.

Calculation of fixed, variable and semi-variable overheads of 20,000 units for the month of July 2005

Variable overheads for July = 20,000 x Rs. 2.80 = Rs. 56,000

Fixed overheads = Rs. 90,000

Total semi-variable overheads = Rs. 1,46,000

4) Analytical Method

This method considers the degree of variability for each item of semi-variable expenses. Some semivariable items have a 40 per cent variability while other may have 60 per cent variability. This method is easy to calculate but there are difficulties in estimating the degree of variability of expenses.

Problem 6

Taking the amount of any month of problem 3 say April and assuming a 60 percent degree of variability, the analysis shall be as under :

Variable element	60 percent of Rs. 1,70,000	1,02,000
Fixed element	1,70,000 - 1,02,000	68,000

Fixed element will remain constant, whereas variable element will vary according to variation in production.

Thus, for July, fixed element is Rs. 68,000 and variable portion $\frac{1,02,000}{60,000}$ x 20,000 Rs. 34,000

Therefore, the total semi-variable expenses for 20,000 units (34,000 x 2) Rs.68,000 + Rs.68,000 Rs.1,36,000

5) Scatter graph method

The segregation of semi-variable overheads into fixed and variable overheads can also be done graphically, i.e., in the scatter chart a "line of best fit", could be drawn through the observations and extended to the value of axis, thus indicating the fixed cost. This method is widely used in practice.

In the graph, horizontal line represents the output or the levels of activity and the vertical axis represents the costs. Let us use the following figures to construct a scatter graph and to segregate the Semi Variable costs (SVCs).

Output (Units)	10,000	15,000	20,000	25,000	30,000
SVCs (Rs.)	30,000	40,000	35,000	50,000	45,000

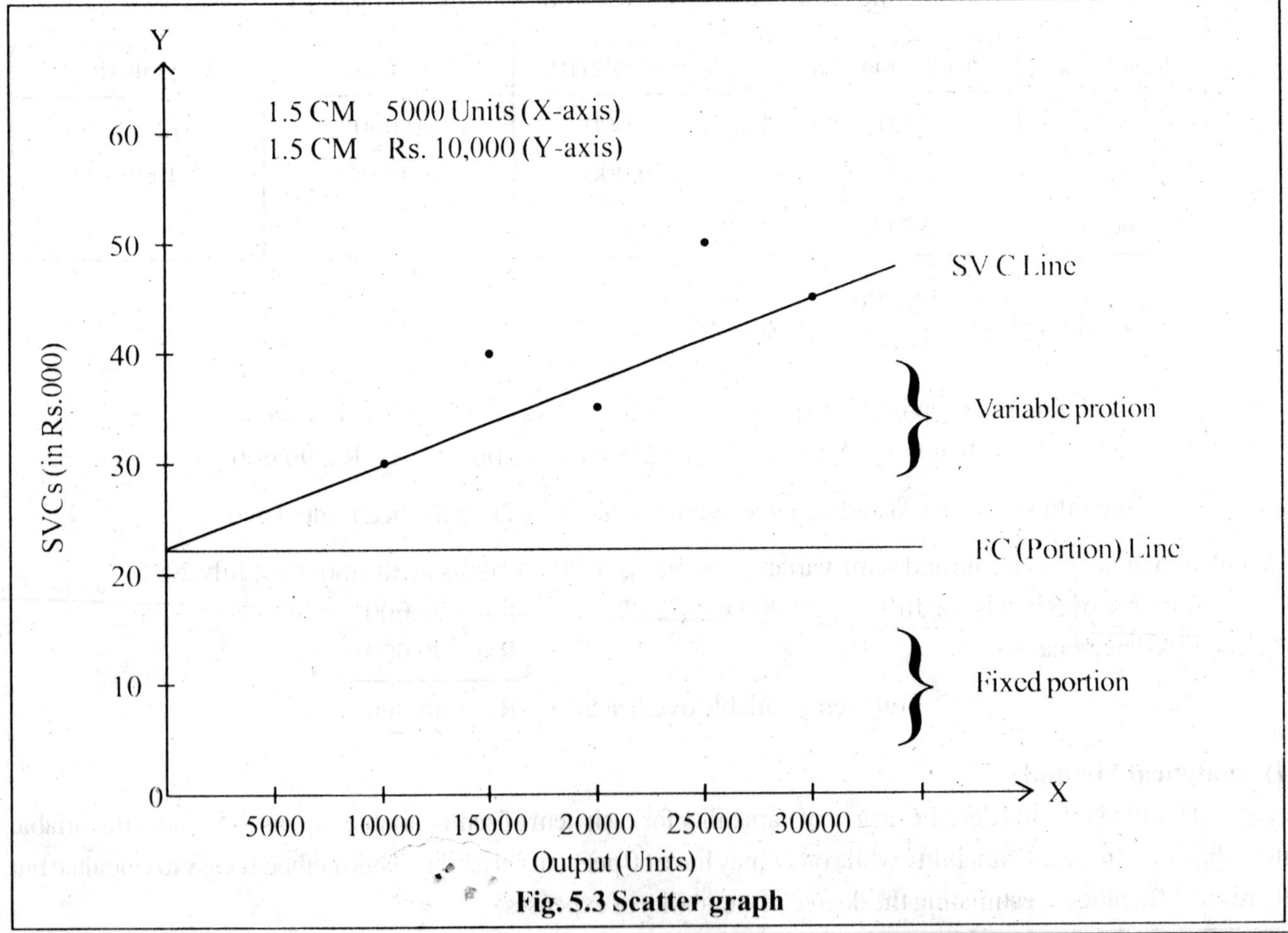

Fig. 5.3 Scatter graph

From the above figure (5.3), it becomes obvious that by fitting a line and extending the same till it touches the vertical axis, here we can find out the fixed element included in the SVS (Rs.22,500) The SVC at any level of activity minus the fixed element (as computed above) represents the variable portion included in the SVCs at that level of activity.

6) Least Squares Method

This method is an improvement over the scattergraph method.

Under this method the statistical technique of fitting an equation with the help of a number of observations is used to segregate semi-variable cost.

We know the straight line equation Y = MX + C where 'C' represents the fixed element and 'M' the degree of variability.From this basic equation, and given a set of observation, two simultaneous linear equations can be used to determine the fixed cost element and the variable cost element per unit of activity. The linear equations are:

$\Sigma Y = Na + b\Sigma X$ (i) $\Sigma XY = a\Sigma X + b\Sigma n^2$ (ii)

where

X = Number of units; Y = Total cost at a given production level

N = Number of observations; a = Fixed cost

b = Variable cost

The application of the least squares method can be further clear from the study of the example given below

Problem 7

ABC Ltd. submits the following information for a six months period ended on 30th June 2005.

Month	Production (Units)	Semi-variable costs (Rs.)
January 2005	20,000	20,000
Febuary 2005	40,000	30,000
March 2005	60,000	40,000
April 2005	80,000	50,000
May 2005	1,00,000	60,000
June 2005	1,20,000	70,000

Calculate the amount of fixed and variable element in semi variable cost.

Month	Production (Units)	Semi-variable expenses (Rs.)	X^2	XY (Rs.)
January 2005	20,000	20,000	4,00,000	4,00,000
Febuary 2005	40,000	30,000	16,00,000	12,00,000
March 2005	60,000	40,000	36,00,000	24,00,000
April 2005	80,000	50,000	64,00,000	40,00,000
May 2005	1,00,000	60,000	100,00,000	60,00,000
June 2005	1,20,000	70,000	144,00,000	84,00,000
Total	Σx = 4,20,000	Σy = 2,70,000	Σx^2 = 3,64,00,000	Σxy = 2,24,00,000

N	6	Σx	4,20,000
Σy	2,70,000	Σx^2	3,64,00,000
Σxy	2,24,00,000		

Substitute these values in the two linear equations, we have

$\Sigma y = Na + b\Sigma x$ Rs. 2,70,000 = 6a + 4,20,000 b (i)

$\Sigma xy = a\Sigma x + b\Sigma X^2$ Rs. 2,24,00,000 = 4,20,000 a + 3,64,00,000 b (ii)

In order to solve the equations, it will be necessary to eliminate one of the terms. The "a" term can be eliminated by multiplying equation (i) by 70, and then subtracting it from equation (ii), we get,

Rs. 2,24,00,000 = 420 a + 3,64,00,000 b

Rs. 1,89,00,000 = 420 a + 2,94,00,000 b

Rs. 35,00, 000 = 70,00,000 b

$$b = \frac{35,00,000}{70,00,000} = \text{Rs. } 0.50$$

Solve for 'a' by substituting Rs. 0.50 for 'b' in either equations.

Rs. 2,70,000 = 6a ÷ 4,20,000 x 0.50

Rs. 2,70,000 = 6a + 2,10,000

6a = 2,70,000 - 2,10,000 = 60,000

a = Rs. 10,000 fixed cost

The computation for 'a' and 'b' establish the values for the fixed and variable components in the semi-variable costs. Using the calculated values, a = Rs. 10,000 fixed cost per month and b = Rs. 0.50 variable cost per unit, the composition of the semi-variable cost could be shown as follows :

4,20,000 units @ 0.50 per unit	= Rs. 2,10,000	(variable cost)
6 months @ Rs. 10,000 per month	= Rs. 60,000	(fixed cost)
Total Semi-variable cost	= Rs. 2,70,000	

Role of contribution

In marginal costing, contribution has greater significance. The justification for contribution lies in the fact that when two or more products are manufactured by a single unit, the apportionment of fixed costs to different product under marginal costing is simplified. Contribution represents the difference between sales and variable cost of sales and it is often referred to as "Gross Margin". It can be considered as some sort of fund from which all fixed costs are to be met. Again, the difference between contribution and fixed cost represents either profit or loss as the case may be.

The concept of 'contribution' is of immense use in fixing the selling prices, determining the break even point, selecting the product mix for profit maximisation and also ascertaining the profitability of the products departments etc.

The difference between the marginal cost of the various products manufactured and their respective selling price is the contribution which each product makes towards fixed or period costs and profit. According to Watter W. Bigg. "Contribution may be defined as the difference between sales value and the marginal cost of sales, and no net profit arises until the contribution equal the fixed overheads. When this level of output is achieved, the business is said to breakeven as neither profit nor loss occurs. Production in excess of that necessary to breakeven will result in a profit equivalent to the excess units multiplied by the "contribution" per unit. Conversely, a loss is sustained if output is less than that required to break-even, amounting to the short-fall of units multiplied by the contribution." Thus, contribution is the difference between product revenue and variable cost of product. It represents the excess of sales over marginal cost (variable cost) that is the amount to meet fixed cost and profit expectation of an organisation. It can be calculated as under.

i) Contribution = Sales - Variable Cost

Or

Contribution (per unit) = Selling price - variable cost per unit

ii) Contribution = fixed cost + profit / loss

Suppose total sales revenue is Rs. 1,50,000, variable cost is Rs. 60,000 and sale in terms of units is 1,000 then contribution will be :

Contribution = Rs. 1,50,000 - Rs. 60,000 = Rs. 90,000

OR

Contribution (per unit) = 150 - 60 = Rs. 90

Marginal Cost Equation : (Relationship between Marginal cost & Contribution)

The analysis of marginal cost statement and the contribution above reveals that :

i) Sales (-) Marginal cost = Contribution

ii) Fixed cost (+) Profit = Contribution

By combining the above two equations, we get the fundamental marginal cost equation.

Sales - Marginal Cost = Fixed Cost + Profit / Loss Or S - V = F + P/L

The marginal cost equation has practical utility in the sense that if any three factors of the above equation are known, the fourth can be easily found out or computed.

Contribution and Profit

A product sells at Rs. 50 has a variable cost of Rs. 30 and during the period ended 30 June 2005, 2,000 units were sold. Fixed costs for that period amounted to Rs. 25,000. The contribution and profit would be calculated, as shown in following table.

Particulars	per unit (Rs.)	2,000 units (Rs.)	% of sales
Selling Price	50	100,000	10
Less : Variable costs	30	60,000	60
Contribution	20	40,000	40
Less : Fixed costs		25,000	
Profit		15,000	

From the above table it can be observed that the contribution goes towards the recovery of the fixed overheads and profit. Marginal costing is a technique which can be used as part of the decision making process to show the effect of changes possible changes in demand and / or selling prices and / or variable costs. It can for example, be used to identify the most profitable projects; in make or buy decision making or in deciding whether or not to accept a special contract. Variable costs include only those costs which can be identified with and traced to products, e.g. direct labour, direct materials, direct expenses and variable overheads. The fixed costs are those which cannot be identified with and traced to the products. They tend to vary more with time than output, and are treated as period costs. This means that the fixed costs are not included in Product costs. They are simply written off, in total, against the total contribution (s) generated from the sale of all the firms's products, for the period in which they were incurred : see Fig. 5.5. This treatment of fixed costs also means that because they are not included in product costs they are carried forward into the future as part of the valuation of the stocks of work in progress and finished goods.

Rs.000	Products	A	B	C	D	Total Rs.
Contribution		20	34	36	20	110
Less : Fixed costs						78
		Profit				32

Fig. 5.5 A multi-product environment

Problem 8

Compute the amount of fixed cost from the information given below :

Sales	:	Rs. 2,40,000
Variable cost	:	Rs. 1,20,000
Profit	:	Rs. 60,000

Solution

As per marginal cost equation,

$$S - V = FC + P / L$$

$$2{,}40{,}000 - 1{,}20{,}000 = FC + 60{,}000$$

$$1{,}20{,}000 = FC + 60{,}000$$

$$(-)\ FC = 60{,}000 - 1{,}20{,}000$$

$$(-)\ FC = (-)\ 60{,}000$$

$$FC = Rs.\ 60{,}000$$

Profit Volume Ratio (P/V Ratio)

The profit / volume ratio also knows as 'contribution ratio' or 'marginal ratio' expresses the relationship between contribution and sales. In other words, it is the contribution per rupee of sales. The P/V ratio may be expressed as under.

$$P/V\ ratio = \frac{Contribution}{Sales} \times 100 \quad or \quad \frac{Contribution\ per\ unit}{Selling\ price\ per\ unit} \times 100$$

$$Sales = \frac{Contribution\ (FC + Profit)}{P/V\ ratio} \quad OR \quad Contribution = Sales - P/V\ ratio$$

Since contribution is equal to sales minus (-) variable cost and also represents the amount of fixed cost and profit expectations, therefore, P/V ratio can also be expressed as

i) P/V ratio $= \frac{\text{Sales - Variable cost}}{\text{Sales}} = \frac{S - V}{S}$

ii) P/V ratio $= \frac{\text{Fixed Cost + Profit}}{\text{Sales}} = \frac{F + P}{S}$

As discussed earlier, the fixed cost remains constant in the short term period, therefore any increase in contribution after the recovery of fixed cost would result straight way in the increase of profit. Thus,

$$\text{P/V Ratio} = \frac{\text{Change in Profit / Contribution}}{\text{Change in Sales}}$$

Problem 9

Compute (i) P/V ratio, (ii) Fixed Cost, and (iii) Sales Volume to earn a profit of Rs. 1,20,000 from the following information :

Sales	:	1,50,000
Profit	:	15,000
Variable Cost	:	80%

Solution

Sales = 1,50,000

Variable cost = 80% = $\frac{80}{100}$ x 1,50,000 = Rs. 1,20,000

i) P/V ratio $= \frac{S - V}{S} \times 100 = \frac{1,50,000 - 1,20,000}{1,50,000} \times 100 = 20\%$

ii) Contribution = F C + P

30,000 = FC + 15,000

(-) FC = 15,000 - 30,000

(-) FC = (-) 15,000 FC = Rs. 15,000

iii) Sales $= \frac{FC + P}{\text{P/V ratio}} = \frac{15,000 + 15,000}{20} \times 100 =$ Rs. 1,50,000

Proof:

Sales	=	1,50,000
Less : V.C (80%)	–	1,20,000
Contribution	=	30,000
Less: F.C	=	15,000
Profit	=	15,000

Problem 10

Assuming that the cost structure and selling prices remain the same in period (i) and (ii), find out the P/V ratio.

Periods	Sales (Rs.)	Total cost (Rs)
I[st] Quarter	2,80,000	2,50,000
IInd Quarter	3,20,000	2,80,000

Solution

Period	Sales (Rs.)	Total Cost (Rs.)	Profit (Rs.)
I[st] Quarter	2,80,000	2,50,000	30,000
IInd Quarter	3,20,000	2,80,000	40,000

$$\text{P/V ratio} = \frac{\text{Change in Profit}}{\text{Change in sales}} \times 100 = \frac{10,000}{40,000} \times 100 = 25\%$$

Merits & Demerits of Marginal Costing

According to National Association of Accountants Marginal Costing (Direct Costing) has the following merits and demerits

Merits (Benefits)

1) Cost-volume-profit relationship data wanted for profit planning purposes are readily obtained from the regular accounting statements. Hence management does not have to work with two separate sets of data to relate one to the another.
2) The profit for a period is not affected by changes in absorption of fixed expenses resulting from building or reducing inventory. Other things remaining equal (e.g., setting prices, costs, sales mix) profit move in the same direction as sales, when marginal costing is in use.
3) Manufacturing cost and income statements in the marginal cost follow management's thinking more closely than does the absorption cost from these statements. For this reason, management finds it easier to understand and the use marginal cost reports.
4) The impact of fixed costs on profits is emphasized because the total amount of such cost for the period appears in the income statement.
5) Marginal income figures facilitate relative appraisal of products, territories, classes of customers and other segments of the business without having the result obscured by allocation of joint fixed costs.
6) Marginal costing ties in with such effective plans for cost control as standard costs and flexible budgets. In fact, the flexible budget is an aspect of marginal costing and many companies thus use marginal costing methods for this purpose without recognising them as such.
7) Marginal cost constitutes a concept of inventory cost which corresponds closely with the current out - of pocket expenditure necessary to manufacture the goods.

Demerits of Marginal Costing

1) Difficulty may be encountered in distinguishing fixed costs. In particular, certain semivariable costs may fall in a border line area and more or less arbitrary classification may be considered necessary in order to arrive at a practical determination of fixed and variable components.
2) Complete manufacturing cost is not determined in the process of costing production and supplementary allocation of fixed overheads on normal or some other volume base must be made to provide product costs of or long-range pricing and other long range policy decisions.
3) Serious taxation problems may be encountered if a change is made from full cost to marginal cost for costing inventory and definite rulings are not available for guidance.

In the light of the merits and demerits of marginal costing it can be concluded that this will prove to be an effective tool in the hands of management wherever it can be applied fruitfully. At the same time, it must be remembered that both marginal costing and absorption costing are equally important - variable costing for internal reporting and absorption costing for external users.

Break - Even Analysis (Cost-Volume - Profit Analysis)

Break-even analysis establishes the relationship between costs and profit with sales volume. It represents a specific method of presenting and studying the inter-relationship between costs, volume and profits. It also helps in the determination of that volume of sales at which costs and revenues are in equilibrium. The equilibrium point is often referred to as the 'break even point'. The break even point may be defined as that point of sales volume at which the total revenue is equal to the total cost. Briefly, it is a no-profit, no-loss point. It should be remembered that the break even point is purely incidental to the CVP analysis. If all costs are assumed to be variable with sales volume, the break-even point would be at zero sales. On the other hand, if all costs remain fixed, profits would vary disproportionately with sales and the BEP would be at a point where total sales revenue and fixed cost are in equilibrium.

Meaning & Definition of Break Even Point

Break-even analysis is a costing technique that helps executives in profit planning. The narrow interpretation of break-even analysis limits to the study of break-even point. The break-even point is defined as the volume of activity at which total sales revenue exactly equals total costs of the output produced or sold. Since, at this level of operation sales revenue is adequate to cover all costs to manufacture and sell the product leaving no amount as profit, and therefore, this level is also known as no profit no loss level. Thus, in a situation where total costs of the output consist of only variable costs, the break-even point would be at zero of operation.

Break-even analysis need not be limited merely to seeking the break-even point. In broader sense, break-even analysis refers to the study of relationship between cost, volume, and profit at different levels of sales or production which in technical terminology is known as cost-volume-profit analysis. Cost-Volume-Profit Analysis as a planning tool analyses the inhernt relationship between prices, cost structure, volume and profit. Ahmad Belkooni defines cost-volume-profit analysis as "an examination of cost and revenue behavioral patterns and their relationships with profit. The analysis separates costs into fixed and variable components and determines the levels of activity where costs and revenues are in equilibrium".

According to Schmiedicke and Nagy, "cost-volume-profit analysis is an analytical technique which uses the degrees of cost variability for measuring the effect of changes in volume or resulting profits. Such analysis assumes that the plant assets of the firm will remain the same in the short-run, therefore, the established level of fixed cost will also remain unchanged during the period being studied."

We define cost-volume-profit analysis as a mature model to study the inter-related relationship between cost, price and profit structure of a company. It is a formal profit planning approach based on established relationship between different factors affecting profit. The usual starting point in such an analysis is the determination of the company's break-even point. Thus, break-even analysis forms just one component of the total system of Cost-Volume-Profit Analysis.

One of the important steps in CVP or break-even analysis is that of segregation of costs into fixed and variable costs. If the break-even point is to occur, it becomes essential that the business enterprise has some variable costs and some fixed costs.

Basic Technique (Determination of BEP)

The BEP can be determined by the two following methods.

1. Algebric methods. (Mathematical)
   a) Contribution margin technique and b) Equation technique.
2. Graphic presentation.
   a) Break-even chart and b) Profit volume graph.

The break-even point can be computed for a firm manufacturing single product only, in terms of units of product The BEP is reached when the total proceeds of units sold are equivalent to the total cost incurred-fixed and variable. Each unit of the product sold will cover its variable cost and leave the remainder which is known as the contribution, to cover the fixed costs. The break-even point will occur when adequate units are sold so that total contribution would become equivalent to the total fixed costs. More precisely, contribution per unit, while total contribution is equal to unit contribution multiplied by the total units sold. The profit of the unit is obtained by subtracting the fixed cost from the total contribution. The following equation can easily be remembered.

Unit Contribution = Selling price per unit - Variable Cost per unit.

Total contribution = Unit Contribution x Number of units sold.

Profit = Total contribution - Fixed Costs.

1) Algebric methods

a) Contribution Margin Technique

As has been stated earlier, contribution per unit represents the difference between selling price per unit and variable cost thereof and the profit represents the difference between the total contribution and the fixed costs. The BEP is reached when the total proceeds of units sold are equivalent to the total costs incurred - fixed and variable.

On an analysis of the above two statements it would be clear that the BEP is reached when the profit is zero or more precisely when the total contribution is exactly equivalent to the fixed costs. The same thing can be represented in the form of equations as given below :

$$\text{BEP (Units)} = \frac{\text{Fixed Cost}}{\text{Marginal Contribution per unit}} \quad \text{(or)} \quad \frac{\text{F C}}{\text{MC per unit}} \qquad (1)$$

$$\text{BEP (Rs.)} = \text{BEP (Units) x Selling Price per unit} \qquad (2)$$

OR

$$\text{BEP (Rs.)} = \frac{\text{Fixed Cost}}{\text{Profit Volume Ratio}} \quad \text{(or)} \quad \frac{\text{FC}}{\text{P/V Ratio}} \qquad (3)$$

$$\text{P/V Ratio} = \frac{\text{Marginal Contribution per unit}}{\text{Selling Price per unit}} \qquad (4)$$

From the above it is clear that Equation (3) is only the derivative of Equation (1) Multiplying both the numerator and the denominator with the common factor of sales, the following equation is obtained :

$$\text{BEP (Rs.)} = \frac{\text{Fixed Cost x Sales}}{\text{Sales - Variable Cost}} \quad \text{(or)} \quad \frac{\text{FC x S}}{\text{S - VC}} \qquad (5)$$

Again by dividing both the numerator and the denominator of the equation (5) by the common factor of sales, the following equation is obtained.

$$\text{BEP (Rs.)} = \frac{\text{Fixed Cost}}{1 - \dfrac{\text{Variable cost}}{\text{Sales}}} \quad \text{(or)} \quad \frac{PC}{1 - \dfrac{VC}{S}} \qquad (6)$$

Despite the existence of the numerous formulae, it should be remembered that the following three formulae are always adopted for calculating the breakeven point of the business rather than drawing a chart for ascertaining the same.

$$\text{(i) BEP} = \frac{FC \times S}{S - VC} \quad \text{(or)} \quad \frac{FC}{\text{P/V Ratio}} \quad \text{(or)} \quad \frac{PC}{1 - \dfrac{VC}{S}}$$

Under mathematical approach, break-even can easily be computed by engaging the technique of unit contribution which is developed on the basis of marginal cost equation as discussed earlier.

The equation can be stated as follows :

Sales = Variable cost + Fixed Cost + Profit

As the break-even point, profit is absent, therefore, the same equation for this purpose can be rewritten as follows :

Sales = Variable Cost + Fixed Cost

or

Sales - Variable Cost = Fixed Cost

or

Contribution = Fixed Cost

The study of the above equation reveals that sales revenue of each unit leaves a certain amount in the shape of contribution margin to meet fixed costs. Thus, in order to work out the required number of units to break-even (where the amount of contribution will be sufficient to cover total fixed cost) the total fixed cost must be divided by the unit contribution. Accordingly, the break even point can be calculated in terms of units by using the following equation :

$$\text{Break-even point (in terms of units)} = \frac{\text{Fixed Cost}}{\text{Unit contribution margin}} = \frac{FC}{SP-VC}$$

where :

BEP	=	Break-even point	FC	=	Total fixed cost
SP	=	Selling price per unit	VC	=	Variable cost per unit

On the same basis, the break-even point in terms of rupees can be computed with the help of the equation as given under :

$$\text{BEP (in terms of rupees)} = \frac{FC}{CMR}$$

where, FC = Total Fixed Cost

CMR = Contribution margin ratio

Where the selling price and variable cost per unit is not readily available, the following equation is applied to compute break-even point.

$$\text{BEP (in terms of rupees)} = \frac{\text{FC}}{\text{P/V ratio}}$$

where

FC = Total Fixed Cost P/V Ratio = Profit/Volume ratio.

Problem 11

Calculate break-even point from the following information :

Fixed cost	:	Rs. 1,200
Variable cost	:	Rs. 5,000
Sales in rupees	:	Rs. 7,000
Sales in units	:	1,000

Solution

$$\text{BEP (in units)} = \frac{\text{FC}}{\text{SP-VC}} = \frac{1,200}{7 - 5} = 600 \text{ units}$$

$$\text{BEP (in rupees)} = \frac{\text{FC}}{\text{CMR*}} = \frac{1200}{0.285} = \text{Rs. } 4200$$

$$\text{*CMR} = \frac{\text{SP - VC}}{\text{SP}} = \frac{7 - 5}{7} = 0.285$$

Working Note :-

$$\text{i) Calculation of variable Cost} = \frac{5,000}{1,000} = \text{Rs. } 5.00$$

$$\text{ii) Calculation of selling price (per unit)} = \frac{7,000}{1,000} = \text{Rs. } 7.00$$

Problem 12

Compute break-even point from below given information :

Fixed Cost	:	Rs. 3,600
Variable cost	:	Rs. 15,000
Sales	:	Rs. 21,000

Solution :

The break - even point will be calculated with the help of P/V ratio.

$$\text{BEP (in rupees)} = \frac{\text{FC}}{\text{P/V ratio}} = \frac{3,600}{28.57 / 100} = \frac{3,600}{28.5} \times 100 = \text{Rs. } 12,600$$

Working Note

Calculation of profit/volume ratio

$$\text{P/V ratio} = \frac{\text{Contribution}}{\text{Sales}} \times 100 = \frac{6,000}{21,000} \times 100 = 28.57\ \%$$

Graphic presentation of BE chart

The break-even analysis can also be demonstrated graphically, which is commonly known as break-even chart. A break-even chart is a graphic approach to the study of the relationship of cost, revenue and profit. The graphic instead of algebric approach is often used because it tends to be more easily understood by persons whose acquaintance with mathematics is minimal and because it provides an immediate view of variable costs fixed costs and profit at any level of activity.

Information for constructing a break-even chart can be obtained from the income statement of the concern. However, the total cost i.e., fixed cost, variable cost, and semi variable cost must be separated only into two categories of costs : Fixed-cost and Variable-cost. A brief description of these costs follows :

i) Fixed Cost : Fixed costs are the costs which remain fixed for all practical purposes to a certain level of activity. Once that level of activity is increased, the fixed cost will also increase to a specific degree. Examples of such costs are : Cost of plant and machinery, salaries, rent etc. These costs are shown on the graph by means of a straight line.

ii) Variable Cost : These cost vary in proportion to output. This means that they increase directly with the volume of production. Cost of material, wages, carriage, etc. are some examples of variable cost. For graphic application, these costs will be aggregated with the fixed cost.

iii) Semi-variable cost: Semi-variable costs possess the characteristics of both fixed and variable costs. These costs demand special attention from the management in splitting them into fixed and variable costs.

Constructing a breakeven chart :

(I) The traditional breakeven chart (graph)

Problem 13

Construct a breakeven chart, using the following information :

Output	:	1,25,000 units
Sales	:	Rs. 15,00,000
Variable cost	:	Rs 12,50,000
Fixed cost	:	Rs. 21,00,000

First we will have to draw up our chart and then insert the sales line (see Figure 5.6) Next we will draw the fixed cost line which runs parallel to the base of the chart (i.e. the output) (see Figure 5.7)

Finally, we include the variable costs by adding them on to the fixed costs. This line is drawn from Rs. 1,00,000 at 0 output to Rs. 93,50,000 at 1,25,000 output.

This line is the total cost line, i.e. fixed cost Rs. 1,00,000 plus variable cost Rs. 2,50,000 = Rs 3,50,000 total cost (see Figure 5.8)

Having completed our breakeven chart (Figure 5.8) we can read off the breakeven point at Rs. 200,000 sales and costs and 50,000 output, the point at which costs and revenue (sales/income) are equal, i.e. where the sales line crosses the total cost line (see table 5.1)

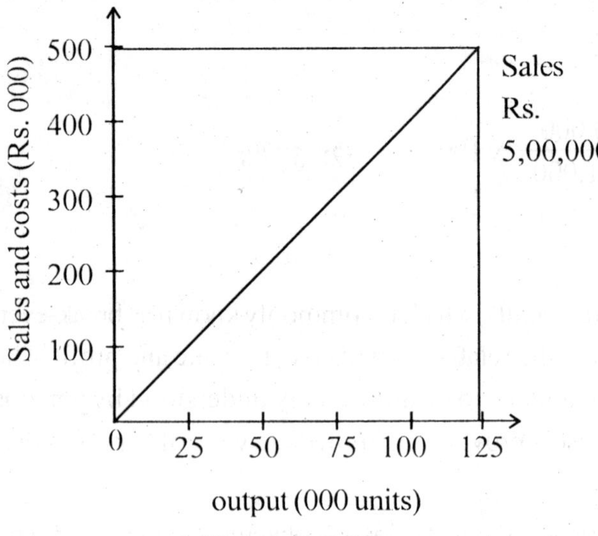

Figure 4.6 Sales

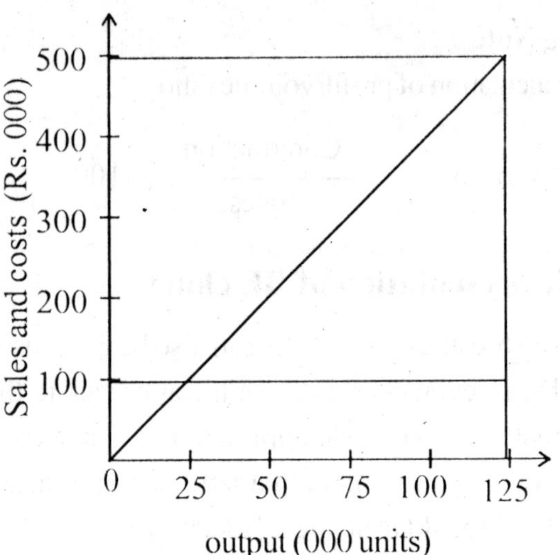

Figure 4.7 Sales and fixed costs

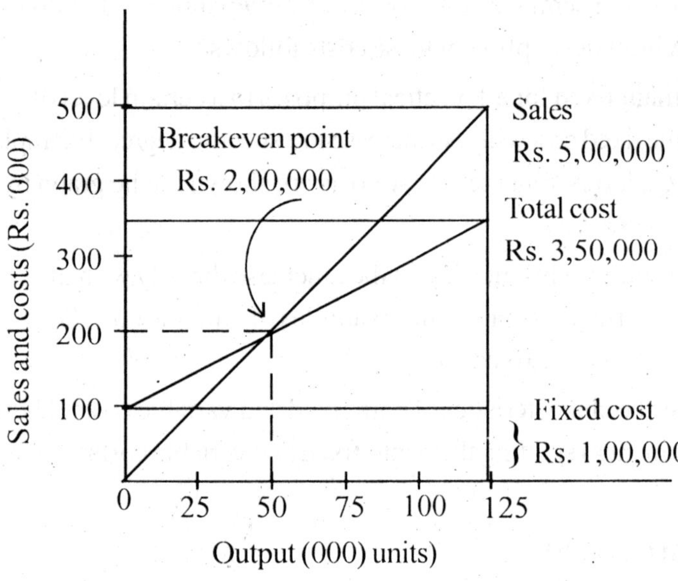

Figure 4.8 Breakeven point

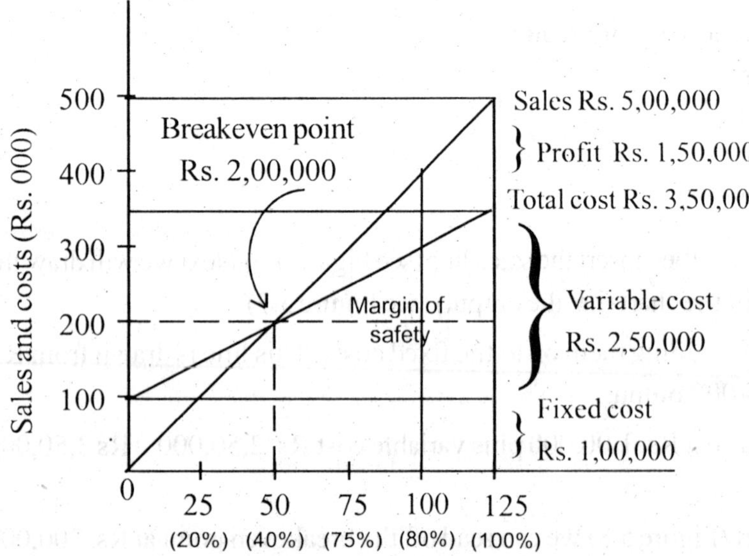

Figure 4.9 Conventional Break even chart

After taking a closer look at the chart which we will so complete lastly show the following information (fig.5.9)

1) The logic of the calculations involved can be followed as per the right hand side of the chart, i. e. sales Rs. 5,00,000 less total cost Rs. 3,50,000 profit Rs. 1,50,000, total cost Rs. 3,50,000 variable cost Rs. 2,50,000 + fixed cost Rs. 1,00,000
2) Above the breakeven point we make a profit, below it we make a loss.
3) The margin of safety is the difference between the breakeven point and the selected output / level of activity. This indicates the extent to which the level of activity must fall before a loss making situation is reached.
4) The base of the chart can be expressed either in terms of output or level of activity.
5) By projecting a vertical line from the base line, e.g. at 1,00,000 units output (80% level of activity) we can use the chart to read off the fixed cost, total cost and sales applicable to this particular level of activity. We can see that the vertical line drawn from 1,00,000 units output (80% level of

activity) cuts the fixed cost line at Rs. 1,00,000 the total cost line at Rs. 3,00,000 and the sales line at 4,00,000. The gap between sales and total cost of Rs. 1,00,000 represents the profit which should be achieved at the 80% level of activity. (see Table 5.2)

	Per unit (Rs.)	125,000 units (Rs.)
Sales	4	5,00,000
Less : Variable cost	2	2,50,000
Contribution	2	2,50,000 (50% profit volume ratio)
Less : Fixed Cost		1,00,000
Profit		Rs. 1,50,000

Breakeven point = Fixed cost ÷ PV ratio = Rs. 1,00,000 x $\frac{100}{50}$ = Rs. 2,00,000

or

$= \frac{\text{Fixed Cost}}{\text{Contribution per unit}} = \frac{\text{Rs. } 1,00,000}{\text{Rs. } 2} =$ 50,000 Units

Table 5.1 : Calculating the breakeven point

	Rs.
Contribution from 100,000 units @ Rs. 2 per unit	2,00,000
Less : Fixed cost	1,00,000
Profit	Rs. 1,00,000

Table 5.2 : A profit proof using marginal costing

(II) The contribution breakeven chart (graph)

The contribution breakeven chart is an alternative way of showing the information which is used to construct our traditional breakeven chart. Using the same information as problem 5.13 we will look at its construction in two phases. Firstly, we draw up the chart and then insert the sales line and the variable cost line, both of which are drawn from the base line point (see fig. 5.10)

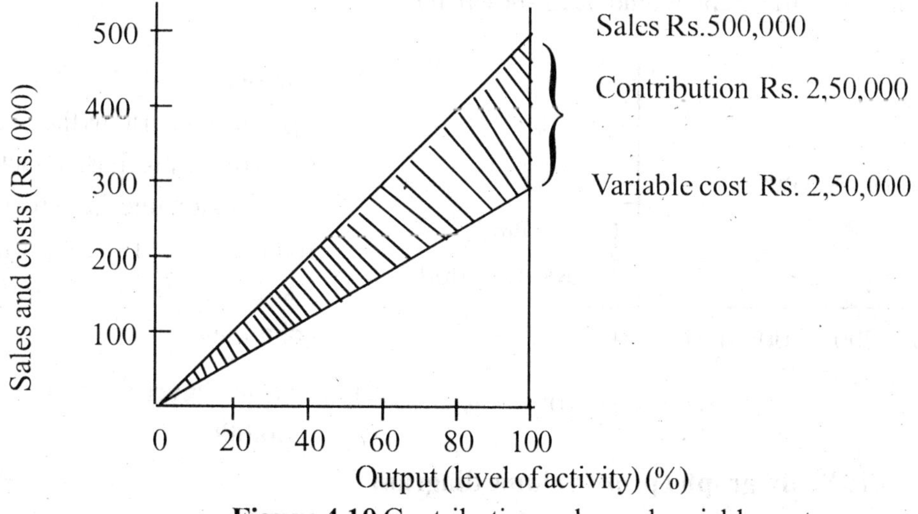

Figure 4.10 Contribution, sales and variable cost

This income breakeven chart (figure 5.10) illustrates that sales Rs. 5,00,000 less variable cost Rs. 2,50,000 = contribution Rs. 2,50,000. The principal advantage of this chart is that it shows, very clearly, the contribution which is being generated at different levels of activity.

The fixed costs of Rs. 1,00,000 are then added to the variable costs and the total cost line drawn from 1,00,000 at 0% level of activity to 3,50,000 at 100% level of activity; the fixed costs are plotted parallel to the variable costs (See figure 5.11)

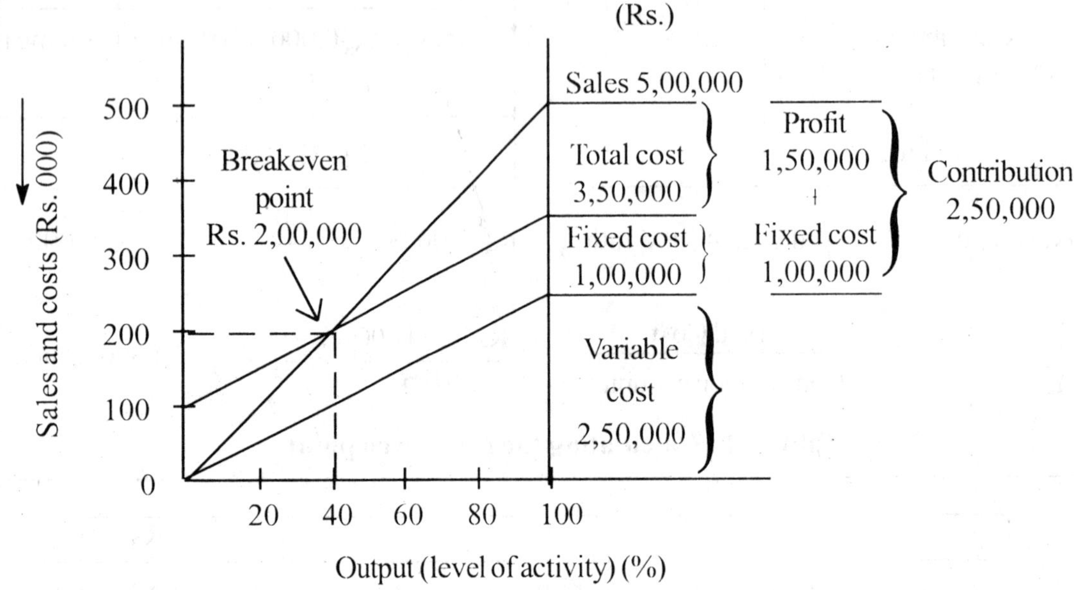

Figure 4.11 Contribution breakeven chart

Observations :-

1) This chart shows that below the breakeven point the fixed costs are not being covered. When the contribution generated has covered fixed costs, the remainder is profit.

2) The final contribution breakeven chart (Figure 5.11) illustrates that the contribution, Rs. 2,50,000 less fixed cost Rs. 1,00,000 = profit Rs. 1,50,000

(III) The profit graph/profit volume diagram

This is an alternative type of breakeven chart and help to understand the profit volume ratio more clearly. To draw it you need to know any two of the three figures : fixed cost, profit and breakeven point. Again using the same figures as in example 5.13 the graph would be as shown in Figure 5.12

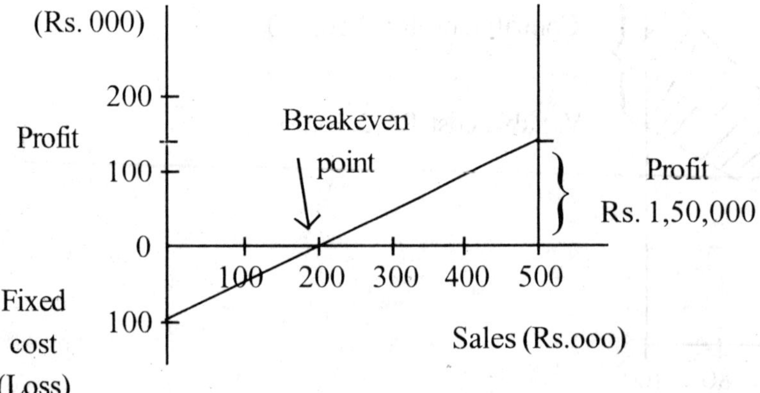

Figure 4.12 Profit graph / profit volume diagram

Observations :

1) The line which joins the fixed costs to the profit is, in fact, the contribution line, i.e. it represents fixed cost Rs. 1,00,000 + profit Rs. 1,50,000 = Rs. 2,50,000 contribution.

2) The breakeven point is again Rs. 2,00,000.

Problem 14

From the following particulars relating to the Ahemadnagar Engineering Construction Ltd. Ahemadnagar Draw a break-even chart, and indicate the BEP therein :

Particulars	Rs	Rs
Sales (10,000 units at Rs. 20 per unit)		2,00,000
Variable Costs :		
Direct Material	30,000	
Direct Labour	50,000	
Factory Overheads	20,000	
Administrative and selling overheads	20,000	1,20,000
		80,000
Contribution		
Fixed Costs		
Factory overheads	20,000	
Administrative and Selling overheads	20,000	40,000
Net Profit		40,000

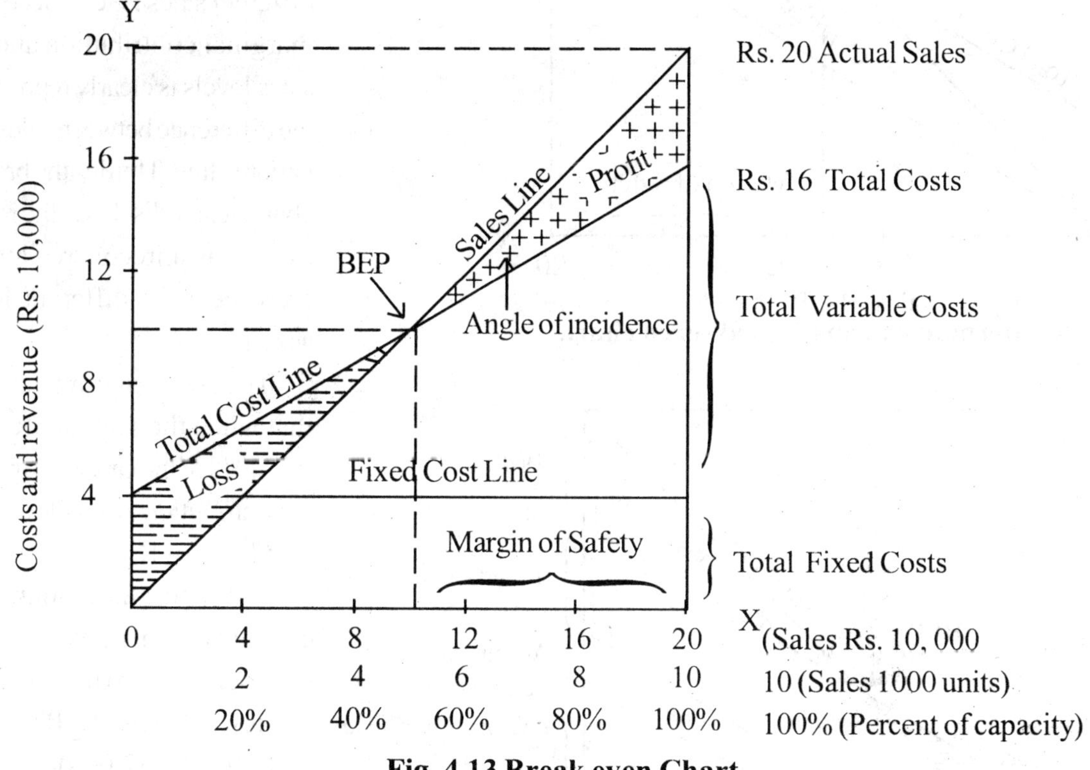

Fig. 4.13 Break even Chart

In fig. 4.13 the fixed cost line is represented as the horizontal line parallel to the X axis, whereas the variable cost line is represented by the area covered between the total cost and the fixed cost. The point of intersection between the sales and the total cost lines represents the break-even point indicated as BEP. It acquires at a sales volume of 5,000 units and total sales worth Rs. 1,00,000 (5,000 x Rs. 20). The angle formed by the intersection of sales line and the total cost line is called the angle of incidence. The greater the angle of incidence, the lower will be the break-even point and vice-versa. While the area to the right of the break-even point represents the profit area, that to left of it represents the loss area which only reveals the uncovered fixed costs. The excess of actual sales over the break-even sales is known as the margin of safety.

Alternative Form

In Fig. 5.13 the fixed costs line is drawn first, starting from the fixed cost point. This focuses attention on the fact that fixed cost remains constant for different levels of sales. An alternative method of constructing the break-even chart is to draw the variable cost line followed by the total cost line from the fixed cost point. This total cost line will be parallel to the variable cost line. The alternative form of break-even chart is represented in Fig. 5.14.

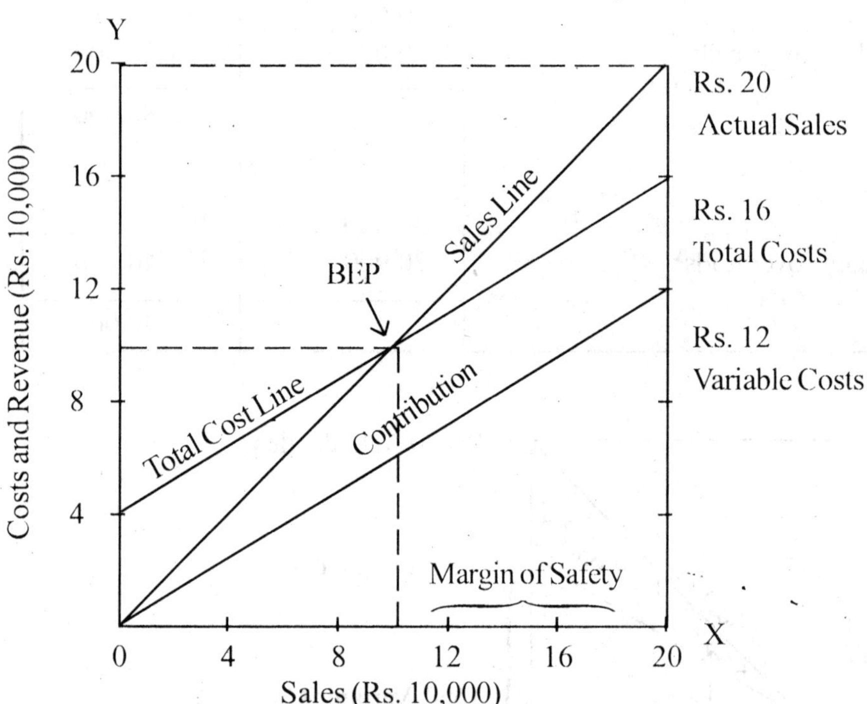

Fig. 4.14 Alternative form of break-even chart.

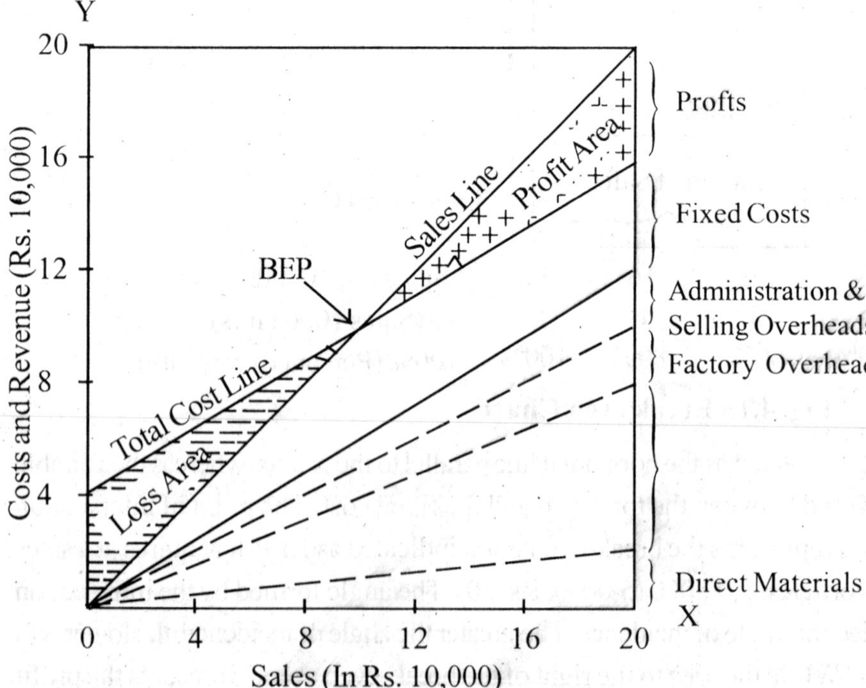

Fig. 4.15 Alternative break-even chart.

The alternative form of break-even chart discloses certain additional information not given by the first form. The fixed costs are indicated by the intercept of the total cost line on the vertical axis. There are three distinctive benefits of the alternative form. Firstly, the variable costs are shown for different sales levels. Secondly, the marginal contribution at different sales levels is clearly represented by the difference between sales line and variable line. Thirdly, the break-even chart clearly discloses the recovered as well as unrecovered amount of fixed costs at different levels of activity.

It can be seen from the Fig. 4.14 that when the sales are Rs. 80,000 (i.e. 40% of the capacity) the amount of contribution available to cover the fixed cost of Rs. 40,000 is only Rs. 32,000. Thus, the amount of fixed cost left unrecovered which represents loss to the business unit at this level of sales is Rs. 8,000 (Rs. 40,000 - Rs. 32,000)

The third alternative is to construct a break-even chart portraying all the details of the components of fixed as well as variable costs as shown in Fig. 4.15

Margin of Safety

The margin of safety represents the difference between actual sales and break-even sales. In fig. 5.13 the margin of safety is indicated as Rs.1,00,000 the difference between actual sales of Rs. 2,00,000 and the break-even sales of Rs. 1,00,000. It can also be calculated by the following formulae :

$$\text{Margin of Safety} = \text{Profit} \div \frac{\text{Sales - Variable Cost}}{\text{Sales}} \quad \text{(or)} \quad \frac{\text{Profit}}{\text{P/V Ratio}}$$

The margin of safety represents the extent to which sales can decline before the business unit sustains a loss. Larger the margin of safety, safer it will be for the business unit. A lower margin of safety will result for the business unit which has a low P/V Ratio. When both the margin of safety and the P/V Ratio are low, the management should either increase the selling price without adversely affecting the sales volume or reduce the variable cost by effecting improvements in the manufacturing process.

Problem 15

ABC Ltd., Nashik manufactures 5,000 units with the existing plant and premises. An analysis of cost accounts indicates that:

i) The expenditure on fixed overheads is Rs. 1,000. ii) The varibale costs are 60 p. per unit.

iii) Selling price per unit is Re.1

The management is anxious to increase production and ascertain that the following increase in fixed expenses will occur if production is increased.

Exceeding 5,000 units and not exceeding 10,000 units - Rs. 2,000 per annum.

Exceeding 10,000 units - Rs. 2,000 per annum.

Incorporate the above information in a break-even chart.

Solution

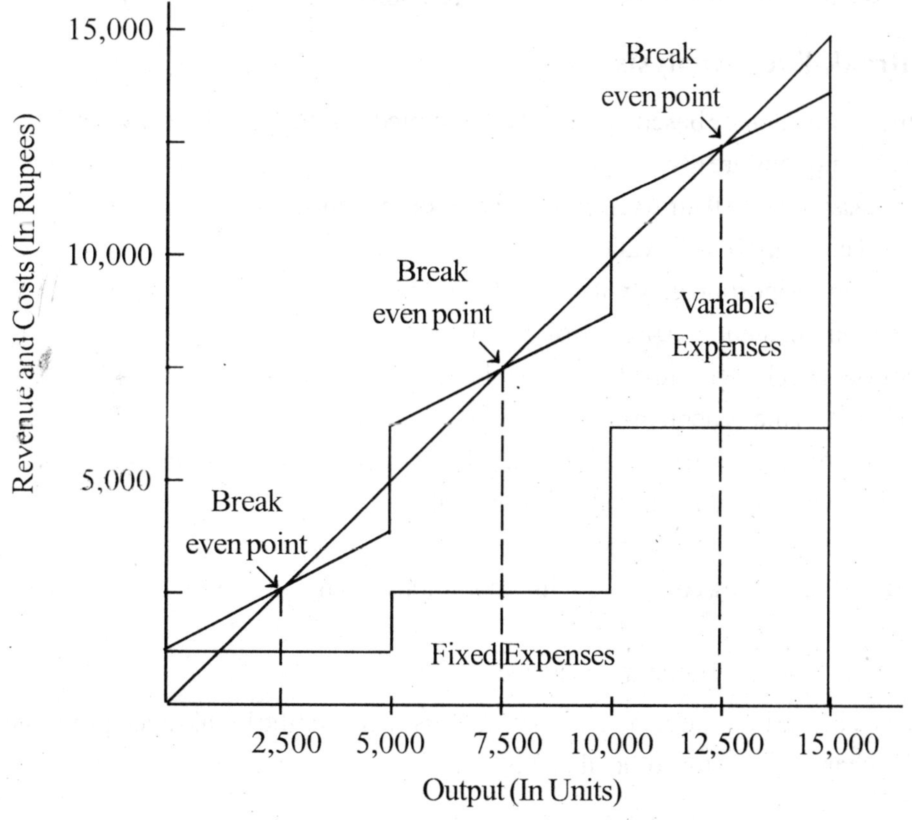

Fig. 4.16 Break-even chart.

Mathematical Verification

BEP at sales of 5,000 units variable costs remain at 60 p. per unit, fixed overheads at Rs. 1,000 and selling price at Re. 1 per unit.

i) $BEP = \frac{PC \times S}{S - VC}$ S = 5,000 x Re. 1 = Rs. 5,000
PC = Rs. 1,000 & VC = 5,000 x 60p = Rs. 3,000

$= \frac{Rs. 1,000 \times Rs. 5,000}{Rs. 5,000 - Rs. 3,000} = \frac{Rs. 50,00,000}{Rs. 2,000} = Rs. 2,500$

ii) BEP at sales of 10,000 units, costs remain at 60p. per unit, fixed overheads at Rs. 3,000 and selling price at Re. 1 per unit.

$BEP = \frac{PC \times S}{S - VC}$ S = 10,000 x Re. 1 = Rs. 10,000
PC = Rs. 3,000 & VC = 10,000 x 60p = Rs. 6,000

$= \frac{Rs. 3,000 \times Rs. 10,000}{Rs. 10,000 - Rs. 6,000} = \frac{Rs. 3,00,00,000}{Rs. 4,000} = Rs. 7,500$

iii) BEP at sales of 15,000 units, costs remain at 60p. per unit, fixed overheads at Rs. 5,000 and selling price at Re. 1 per unit.

$BEP = \frac{PC \times S}{S - VC}$ S = 15,000 x Re. 1 = Rs. 15,000
PC = Rs. 5,000 & VC = 15,000 x 60p = Rs. 9,000

$= \frac{Rs. 5,000 \times Rs.15,000}{Rs. 15,000 - Rs. 9,000} = \frac{Rs. 7,50,00,000}{Rs. 6,000} = Rs. 12,500$

Assumptions of Break-Even Analysis

Cost - Volume profit data are based upon certain assumed conditions which are rarely found in practice. Some of these basic assumptions are given below :

1) Costs can be classified into their fixed and variable components.
2) The principle of cost variability is valid.
3) Variable costs vary proportionately with the volume changes.
4) Fixed costs remain constant irrespective of the level of activity.
5) Selling price does not change with the volume changes.
6) There is no change in the general price level.
7) There is only one product or in the case of multiple products sales mix remains constant.
8) There is synchronisation between production and sales.
9) Productivity per worker remains constant.
10) Revenue and costs are being compared with a common activity base, e. g., units produced or sales value of production.
11) Plant capacity and efficiency remain unaffected.

It is clear that a change in any one of the above factors will alter the break-even point such that profits are effected by changes in factors other than volume.

Usefulness of CVP or BEP Analysis

Break-even analysis is considered to be the most useful technique of profit planning and control. It is an important device to explain the relationship between cost, volume and profit. The usefulness of the break-**even** analysis is as follows :

1) It is simple tool employed to graphically represent complicated accounting data.
2) It is a more useful diagnostic tool.
3) It provides basic information facilitating further studies on improving the profit.
4) It is also used for analysing the risk implication of alternative actions.
5) It is useful in marketing strategies also.

The break-even analysis serves as a useful tool for considering the risk implications of alternative actions. The problem of risk evaluation can be solved by considering the effects of the alternative actions on break-even point. While taking a decision, the business unit should not only consider the profits arising from the alternatives but also the probability of reaching the break-even point.

Limitations of Break-Even Analysis

1) The application of break-even analysis to a multi-product firm becomes very difficult.
2) Since the break-even analysis is a short-run concept, it has a limited application in the long-range planning.
3) The break-even tool is a static tool with very limited practical application.
4) It is very difficult if not impossible to separate costs into fixed and variable components.
5) The assumption that the total fixed cost remains constant over the entire volume range does not stand to reason.

Margin of Safety (In the form of equation)

The amount by which the current volume of sales exceeds the break-even sales volume, either in units or rupees represents margin of safety. This is the difference between the total sales figures and the amount of sales at break-even point. It indicates the extend to which sales may decrease before the company suffers a loss. A margin a safety is calculated as follows :-

$$M/S = S_A - S_B \quad \text{OR} \quad MoS = AS - BS$$

where,

M/S = Margin of safety		MoS =	Margin of safety
S_A = Actual volume of sales		AS =	Actual volume of sales
S_B = Break-even volume of sales		Bs =	Break-even volume of sales

Margin of safety may be expressed as a percentage based either on units or rupee value. For this purpose, the following formulas are used :

$$\text{M/S (in rupees)} = \frac{\text{Profit}}{\text{P/V Ratio}} \qquad \text{M/S (in units)} = \frac{\text{Profit}}{\text{Contribution per unit}}$$

The high margin of safety is the sign of prosperity of the business. A low margin would indicate high fixed cost. Such a critical situation calls for :-

i) Increase in selling price
ii) Decrease in variable costs
iii) Replacement of existing product line by a more profitable line, and
iii) Increase in volume of production.

Problem 16

Compute Margin of Safety of Surya Ltd From the information given below :-

Selling price	:	Rs. 8 per unit
Variable cost	:	Rs. 5 per unit
Fixed cost	:	Rs. 45,000
Sales (current)	:	25,000 units p.a.

Solution

i) M/S (in rupees) = $S_A - S_B$ = Rs. 2,00,000 - Rs. 1,20,000 = Rs. 80,000

ii) M/S (in units) = 25,000 units - 15,000 units = 10,000 units

OR

iii) M/S (in rupees) $= \frac{\text{Profit}}{\text{P/V Ratio}} = \frac{30,000}{37.5} \times 100 =$ Rs. 80,000

iv) M/S (in units) $= \frac{\text{Profit}}{\text{Contribution per unit}} = \frac{30,000}{3} =$ 10,000 units

Working Note

I. Marginal Cost Statement

Output : 25,000 units

Particulars	Amount Per unit (Rs.)	Total (Rs.)
Sales	8	2,00,000
Less : Marginal cost	5	1,25,000
Contribution	3	75,000
Less : Fixed cost	--	45,000
Profit	--	30,000

II. Calculation of P/V ratio :

$$\text{P/V ratio} = \frac{\text{Contribution}}{\text{Sales}} \times 100 = \frac{75,000}{2,00,000} \times 100 = 37.5 \text{ per cent}$$

III. Calculation of Break-even Point

$$\text{BEP} = \frac{\text{Fixed cost}}{\text{SP - VC}} = \frac{45,000}{8 - 5} = \frac{45,000}{3} = 15,000 \text{ units}$$

$$\text{BEP (in rupees)} = \frac{\text{FC}}{\text{OMR}} = \frac{45,000}{3/8^*} = \frac{45,000}{3} \times 8 = \text{Rs. } 1,20,000$$

$$^*\text{C.M.} = \frac{\text{SP - VC}}{\text{SP}} = \frac{8 - 5}{8} = 3/8$$

Practical Problems

Problem 1

A factory manufacturing printing machines has the capacity to produce 600 machines per annum. The marginal (variable) cost of each machine is Rs. 300 and each machine is sold for Rs. 375. Fixed overheads are Rs. 30,000 per annum. Calculate the break-even points for output and sales.

Solution

$$\text{Break-even point (for output)} = \frac{FC}{SP-VC} = \frac{30{,}000}{375-300} = \frac{30{,}000}{75} = 400 \text{ machines}$$

$$\text{Break-even point (for sales)} = \frac{FC}{CM} = \frac{30{,}000}{0.20} = \text{Rs. } 1{,}50{,}000$$

Working Note

Calculation of contribution Margin (CM)

$$CM = \frac{SP - VC}{SP} = \frac{375 - 300}{375} = \frac{75}{375} = 0.20$$

Problem 2

Calculate (i) Break-even point, and (ii) Margin of safety from the information given below :-

Sales	:	Rs. 1,50,000
Variable costs	:	Rs. 1,20,000
Fixed costs	:	Rs. 15,000

Solution

In this problem selling price and variable cost per unit cannot be calculated, therefore, break-even point is calculated with the help of following formula.

i) $$BEP = \frac{FC}{P/V \text{ ratio}} = \frac{15{,}000}{20\%\ *} = \text{Rs. } 75{,}000$$

* Calculation of P/V ratio :

$$P/V \text{ ratio} = C/S \times 100 = \frac{30{,}000}{1{,}50{,}000} \times 100 = 20 \text{ per cent}$$

ii) $$M/S = S_A - S_B = \text{Rs. } 1{,}50{,}000 - \text{Rs. } 75{,}000 = \text{Rs. } 75{,}000$$

Problem 3

From the following particulars, find out the break-even point and the selling price per unit if the break-even point is reduced to 6,000 units.

Variable cost per unit	:	Rs. 15
Fixed expenses	:	Rs. 54,000 p.a.
Selling Price per unit	:	Rs. 20

Solution

I) Calculation of Break Even Point

i) BEP (in units) $= \dfrac{FC}{SP-VC} = \dfrac{54,000}{20-15} = \dfrac{54,000}{5} = 10,800$ units

ii) BEP (in rupees) $= \dfrac{FC}{CM\ *} = \dfrac{54,000}{0.25} = 2,16,000$

* Calculation of Contribution Margin

CM $= \dfrac{SP - VC}{SP} = \dfrac{20 - 15}{20} = \dfrac{5}{20}$ 0.25

II) Calculation of selling price when break-even point is reduced to 6,000 units.

BEP $= \dfrac{FC}{SP - VC}$ OR BEP $\dfrac{FC}{\text{Contribution per unit}}$

By transportation, we have

Contribution per unit $= \dfrac{FC}{BEP} = \dfrac{54,000}{6,000} =$ Rs. 9

Selling price per unit = V.C + Contribution = Rs. 15 + 9 Rs. 24

Problem : 4

From the following information calculate the break-even point and the turnover required to earn a profit of Rs. 60,000

Fixed overheads	:	Rs. 42,000
Variable cost	:	Rs. 4 per unit
Selling price	:	Rs. 10 per unit

If the company is earning a profit of Rs. 60,000 express the Margin of Safety available to it.

Solution

I) Calculation of Break-even point

i) BEP (in units) $= \dfrac{FC}{SP-VC} = \dfrac{42,000}{10 - 4} = \dfrac{42,000}{6} = 7,000$ units

ii) BEP (in rupees) $= \dfrac{FC}{CM*} = \dfrac{42,000}{0.60} =$ Rs. 70,000

* Calculation of contribution margin

CM $= \dfrac{SP - VC}{SP} = \dfrac{10 - 4}{10} = \dfrac{6}{10}$ 0.60

II) Calculation of turnover required to earn a profit of Rs. 60,000

i) Desired turnover (output) $= \dfrac{\text{Fixed cost + Desired profit}}{\text{SP - VC}}$

$$\frac{\text{Rs. } 42{,}000 + \text{Rs. } 60{,}000}{10\text{-}4} = \frac{1{,}02{,}000}{6} = 17{,}000 \text{ units}$$

ii) Desired turnover (in rupees) $= \dfrac{\text{Rs. } 42{,}000 + \text{Rs. } 60{,}000}{0.60} = \dfrac{1{,}02{,}000}{0.60} = 1{,}70{,}000$ units

III) Calculation of margin of safety when the profit is Rs. 60,000

M/S (in units) = S_A-S_B = 17,000 - 7,000 = 10,000 units

M/S (in rupees) = S_A-S_B = 1,70,000-70,000 = RS. 1,00,000

Problem 5

From the following data calculate break-even point

		Rs.
Selling price per unit	:	20.00
Trade discount	:	10%
Direct Material	:	6.00
Direct labour cost per unit	:	4.00
Fixed overheads	:	20,000

Variable overheads 100 percent on direct labour cost. If sales are 10 percent and 15 percent above the break-even volume, determine the net profit.

Solution

Marginal Cost Statement

	(Rs.)	(Rs.)
Selling price per unit	20.00	
Less : 10% trade discount	2.00	18.00
Less : Variable cost :		
Direct material cost per unit	6.00	
Direct labour cost per unit	4.00	
Variable overheads	4.00	14.00
Contribution per unit		4.00

I) Calculation of Break-even point :

i) Break-even point (in units) $= \dfrac{\text{FC}}{\text{SP-VC}} = \dfrac{20{,}000}{18\text{-}14} = \dfrac{20{,}000}{4} = 5{,}000$ units

ii) Break-even point (in rupees) $= \dfrac{\text{FC}}{\text{C M *}} = \dfrac{20{,}000}{4/18} = 20{,}000 \times 18/4 =$ **Rs. 90,000**

* Calculation of Contribution Margin

$$CM = \frac{SP-CV}{SP} = \frac{18 - 14}{18} = 4/18$$

II) When sales is 10 per cent above BEP

Contribution	= 4 x 5,500**	=	Rs. 22,000
Fixed cost		=	(-) Rs. 20,000
Net profit		=	Rs. 2,000

III) When sales is 15 per cent above BEP

Contribution	= 4 x 5,750***	=	Rs. 23,000
Fixed cost		=	(-) Rs. 20,000
Net profit		=	Rs . 3,000

** Calculation of sales 10 per cent above BEP

Break-even sales	=	5,000
Add : 10 per cent	=	500
		5,500 units

*** Calculation of sales 15 per cent above BEP

Break-even sales	=	5,000
Add: 15 per cent	=	750
		5,750 units

Problem 6

Gold Mart Co. estimates that next year their profit will be Rs. 50,000. A budgeted fixed cost amounted to Rs. 2,50,000 and Sales are Rs. 9,00,000. Find out BEP (Sales).

Solution

$$\text{BEP (Sales)} = \frac{\text{Fixed cost}}{\text{Contribution}} \times \text{Sales}$$

But,

$$\text{Contribution} = \text{Fixed Cost} + \text{Profit}$$

$$\text{BEP (Sales)} = \frac{\text{Fixed Cost}}{\text{Fixed Cost} + \text{Profit}} \times \text{Sales}$$

$$= \frac{\text{Rs. } 2,50,000}{\text{Rs.} 2,50,000 + \text{Rs. } 50,000} \times \text{Rs. } 9,00,000$$

$$= \frac{\text{Rs. } 2,50,000}{\text{Rs. } 3,00,000} \times \text{Rs. } 9,00,000$$

$$= \text{Rs. } 7,50,000 / -$$

Problem 7

Calculate BEP (Sales) from the following data:

P/V Ratio 40%, Profit Rs. 10,000 (25% of Sales)

Solution

1) Calculation of sales

If Rs. 25 profit   Rs. 100 Sales

∴ Rs. 10,000   ?

$$\frac{\text{Rs. } 10{,}000 \times \text{Rs. } 100}{\text{Rs. } 25}$$

Rs. 40,000

2) Calculation of Fixed Cost

Where,

Contribution   Fixed Cost + Profit

∴   Fixed Cost   Contribution - Profit

But,   Contribution   Sales x P/V Ratio

∴   Fixed Cost   (Sales x P/V Ratio) - Profit

(Rs. 40,000 x 40%) - Rs. 10,000

Rs.16,000 - Rs. 10,000

Rs. 6,000

BEP(Sales) : $$\frac{\text{Fixed Cost}}{\text{P/V Ratio}}$$

$$\frac{\text{Rs. } 6{,}000}{40\ \%} \qquad \text{Rs.} 6{,}000 \times \frac{100}{40} \qquad \text{Rs. } 15{,}000$$

Problem 8

Calculate BEP (Sales) from the following :

	Rs.
Fixed Cost	80,000
Sales	2,00,000
Variable Cost per unit	4
Selling Price per unit	20

Solution

1) Calculation of P/V Ratio:

Where,

$$\text{P/V Ratio} = \frac{\text{Contribution per unit}}{\text{Selling price per unit}} \times 100$$

But,

$$\text{Contribution per unit} = \text{Selling price per unit} - \text{Variable cost per unit}$$

$$\therefore \quad \text{P/V Ratio} = \frac{\text{Selling price per unit} - \text{Variable cost per unit}}{\text{Selling price per unit}} \times 100$$

$$= \frac{\text{Rs. } 20 - \text{Rs. } 4}{\text{Rs. } 20} \times 100$$

$$= \frac{\text{Rs. } 16}{\text{Rs. } 20} \times 100 = 80\%$$

2) **Calculation of BEP (Sales)**

Where,

$$\text{BEP (Sales)} = \frac{\text{Fixed Cost}}{\text{P/V Ratio}}$$

$$= \frac{\text{Rs. } 80{,}000}{80\%} = \text{Rs. } 80{,}000 \times \frac{100}{80}$$

$$= \text{Rs. } 1{,}00{,}000$$

Problem 9

From the following cost data, calculate BEP (Sales)

	Rs.
Turnover	20,000
Profits	2,000
Direct Materials and Labour	12,000

Solution

1) **Calculation of Total Contribution**

Where,

Contribution = Sales - Variable Costs

= Rs. 20,000 (i.e. Turnover) - Rs. 12,000 (i.e. Direct Materials and Labour)

= Rs. 8,000

2) **Calculation of Fixed Cost**

Where,

Contribution = Fixed Cost + Profits

Fixed Cost = Contribution - Profits

= Rs. 8,000 - Rs. 2,000

= Rs. 6,000

3) **Calculation of P/V Ratio**

Where,

$$\text{P/V} = \frac{\text{Contribution}}{\text{Sales}} \times 100$$

$$= \frac{\text{Rs. } 8{,}000}{\text{Rs. } 20{,}000} \times 100 = \frac{2}{5} \times 100 = 40\%$$

BEP (Sales)

$$= \frac{\text{Fixed Cost}}{\text{P/V Ratio}} = \frac{\text{Rs. }6{,}000}{40\%} = \text{Rs. }6{,}000 \times \frac{100}{40}$$

= Rs. 15,000

Problem 10

Abhinav Industries, a medium scale unit has budgeted the following sales, costs and selling price per unit.

Sales units	Total Costs Rs.	Selling price per unit Rs.
12,000	90,000	15
10,000	78,000	15

Find out,

a) P/V ratio, b) BEP (Units and Sales)

Solution

1) Calculation of Variable Cost per unit

Difference between the total costs of two volumes of production is caused by variable costs as the fixed costs are not related to the volume of production. Hence, an increase of Rs.12,000 in total costs (Rs. 90,00- Rs. 78,000) is the increase in Variable Cost which is due to the increase in output by 2,000 units (12,000 units - 10,000 units).

∴ Variable Cost per unit : $= \frac{\text{Total increase in Variable Cost}}{\text{Total increase in output}}$

$= \frac{\text{Rs.}12{,}000}{\text{Units }2{,}000} =$ Rs.6 per unit.

2) Calculation of Profit

Where,

Sales = Total Cost + Profit

∴ Profit = Sales - Total cost

(i) = (12,000 units x Rs. 15) - Rs. 90,000

= Rs. 1,80,000 - Rs.90,000

= Rs. 90,000

(ii) = (10,000 units x Rs.15) - Rs. 78,000

= Rs. 1,50,000 - Rs. 78,000

= Rs. 72,000

3) Calculation of Fixed Cost

Where, Contribution = Fixed Cost + Profit

But, Contribution = Sales - Variable cost

∴ Sales - Variable Cost = Fixed Cost + Profit

∴ Fixed Cost = (Sales - Variable Cost) - Profit

(i) = (12,000 units x Rs. 15 -12,000 units x Rs. 6) - Rs. 90,000

= (Rs. 1,80,000 - Rs. 72,000) - Rs. 90,000 = Rs. 1,08,000 - Rs. 90,000

= Rs. 18,000

= (10,000 units x Rs. 15 - 10,000 units x Rs. 6) - Rs. 72,000

= (Rs.1,50,000 - Rs. 60,000) - Rs.72,000 = Rs.90,000 - Rs.72,000
= Rs. 18,000

a) **P/V Ratio** = $\frac{\text{Contribution}}{\text{Sales}} \times 100$

But,

Contribution = Sales - Variable Cost

P/V Ratio = $\frac{\text{Sales - Variable Cost}}{\text{Sales}} \times 100$

(i) = $\frac{\text{Rs. 1,80,000 - Rs. 72,000}}{\text{Rs. 1,80,000}} \times 100$ = $\frac{\text{Rs.1,08,000}}{\text{Rs.1,80,000}} \times 100$

= 60%

(ii) = $\frac{\text{Rs. 1,50,000 - Rs. 60,000}}{\text{Rs. 1,50,000}} \times 100$ = $\frac{\text{Rs.90,000}}{\text{Rs.1,50,000}} \times 100$

= 60%

b) **BEP(Units)** = $\frac{\text{Fixed Cost}}{\text{Contribution per unit}}$

But,

Contribution per unit = Selling price per unit - Variable cost per unit

∴ BEP (Units) = $\frac{\text{Fixed Cost}}{\text{Selling price per unit - Variable cost per unit}}$

= $\frac{\text{Rs. 18,000}}{\text{Rs. 15 - Rs. 6}}$ = $\frac{\text{Rs.18,000}}{\text{Rs.9}}$ = 2,000 units

BEP (Sales) = $\frac{\text{Fixed Cost}}{\text{P/V Ratio}}$

= $\frac{\text{Rs. 18,000}}{60\%}$ = Rs. 18,000 x $\frac{100}{60}$

= Rs. 30,000

OR

= $\frac{\text{Fixed Cost}}{\text{Selling price per unit - Variable cost per unit}}$ x Selling price per unit

= $\frac{\text{Rs. 18,000}}{\text{Rs. 15 - Rs. 6}}$ x Rs.15 = $\frac{\text{Rs.18,000}}{\text{Rs.9}}$ x Rs. 15

= 2,000 units x Rs. 15

= Rs. 30,000

Problem 11

From the following particulars calculate.

(i) Contribution per unit

(ii) P/V Ratio

(iii) BEP (units and in rupees)

(iv) What will be the selling price per unit if BEP is brought down to 25,000 units ?

Fixed expenses Rs. 1,50,000, Selling price per unit Rs. 15, Variable Cost per unit Rs. 10.

Solution

(i) Contribution per unit

Selling price per unit - Variable cost per unit

Rs. 15- Rs. 10

Rs. 5

(ii) P/V Ratio

$$\frac{\text{Contribution per unit}}{\text{Selling price per unit}} \times 100$$

$$\frac{Rs.5}{Rs.15} \times 100 \qquad \frac{1}{3} \times 100 \qquad 33\,{}^{1}/_{3}\%$$

(iii) BEP (in rupees)

$$\frac{\text{Fixed Cost}}{\text{P/V Ratio}}$$

$$\frac{Rs.1,50,000}{33\,{}^{1}/_{3}\%} \qquad \frac{Rs.1,50,000}{{}^{1}/_{3}} \qquad Rs.\ 1,50,000 \times \frac{1}{3}$$

Rs. 4,50,000

BEP (units)

$$\frac{\text{Fixed Cost}}{\text{Contribution per unit}}$$

$$\frac{Rs.1,50,000}{Rs.5} \quad 30,000 \text{ units}$$

(iv) Selling price per unit

where,

BEP (units) $\frac{\text{Fixed Cost}}{\text{Contribution per unit}}$

∴ Contribution per unit $\frac{\text{Fixed Cost}}{\text{BEP (Units)}}$ $\frac{Rs.1,50,000}{\text{Units } 25,000}$

Rs. 6 per unit

Selling price per unit Variable cost per unit + Contribution per unit

Rs. 10 + Rs. 6

Rs. 16

Problem 12

Find out the selling price per unit if BEP is to be brought down to 9,000 units

	Rs.
Marginal cost per unit	75
Fixed Cost	2,70,000
Market price per unit 100	

Solution

1) Calculation of Contribution per unit :

Where,

BEP (units) $\frac{\text{Fixed Cost}}{\text{Contribution per unit}}$

$\therefore$ Contribution per unit = $\frac{\text{Fixed Cost}}{\text{BEP (Units)}}$

= $\frac{\text{Rs.2,70,000}}{\text{9,000 units}}$ = Rs. 30 per unit

2) Calculation of Selling Price per unit :

Where,

$\therefore$ Contribution per unit = Selling price per unit - Variable cost per unit

$\therefore$ Selling price per unit = Contribution per unit + Variable cost per unit

= Rs. 30 + Rs. 75

= Rs. 105 per unit

Problem 13

Find out the actual sales from the following information:

	Rs.
Fixed Cost	8,000
Profits	2,000
BEP (Sales)	40,000

Solution

Let 'A' be the actual sales

Then,

BEP (Sales) = $\frac{\text{Total Fixed Cost}}{\text{Total Contribution}}$ x A

But,

Total Contribution = Fixed Cost + Profit

$\therefore$ BEP (Sales) = $\frac{\text{Total Fixed Cost}}{\text{Fixed Cost + Profit}}$ x A

$\therefore$ Rs. 40,000 = $\frac{\text{Rs. 8,000}}{\text{Rs.8,000 + Rs.2,000}}$ x A

$\therefore$ Rs. 40,000 = $\frac{\text{Rs. 8,000}}{\text{Rs.10,000}}$ x A

$\therefore$ Rs. 40,000 = 0.8 A

$\therefore$ A = $\frac{\text{Rs. 40,000}}{0.8}$ = Rs. 40,000 x $\frac{10}{8}$ = $\frac{\text{Rs. 4,00,000}}{8}$

= Rs. 50,000

$\therefore$ Actual Sales = Rs. 50,000

Problem 14

From the following cost data calculate :

a) BEP (units)

b) BEP (units) if selling price is reduced by 10%.

c) Selling price per unit if BEP is 8,000 units

Fixed Cost - Rs. 1,00,000 Variable cost per unit - Rs. 10, Selling price per unit - Rs. 20.

Solution

a) BEP (units) = $\frac{\text{Fixed Cost}}{\text{Contribution per unit}}$

But,

Contribution per unit = Selling price per unit - Variable cost per unit

∴ BEP (units) = $\dfrac{\text{Fixed Cost}}{\text{Selling price per unit - Variable cost per unit}}$

= $\dfrac{\text{Rs. 1,00,000}}{\text{Rs.20 - Rs.10}}$ = $\dfrac{\text{Rs. 1,00,000}}{\text{Rs.10}}$ = 10,000 units

b) BEP (units) if selling price is reduced by 10%

Original selling price per unit - Reduction by 10% = New selling price per unit.

Rs 20 - Rs. 2 = Rs.18

BEP (units) : $\dfrac{\text{Fixed Cost}}{\text{Contribution per unit}}$

But,

Contribution per unit = Selling price per unit - Variable cost per unit

BEP (units) = $\dfrac{\text{Fixed Cost}}{\text{Selling price per unit - Variable cost per unit}}$

= $\dfrac{\text{Rs. 1,00,000}}{\text{Rs.18 - Rs.10}}$ = $\dfrac{\text{Rs. 1,00,000}}{\text{Rs.8}}$ = 12,500 units

c) Selling price per unit if BEP is 8,000 units

Let X' be the selling price per unit.

Where,

BEP(units) = $\dfrac{\text{Fixed Cost}}{\text{Contribution per unit}}$

But,

Contribution per unit = Selling price per unit Variable cost per unit

∴ BEP (units) = $\dfrac{\text{Fixed Cost}}{\text{Selling price per unit - Variable cost per unit}}$

∴ 8,000 units = $\dfrac{\text{Rs. 1,00,000}}{\text{X - Rs.10}}$

∴ 8,000 unit sx (X - Rs. 10) = Rs. 1,00,000

∴ 8,000 X - Rs. 80,000 = Rs. 1,00,000

∴ 8,000 X = Rs. 1,00,000 + Rs. 80,000

X = $\dfrac{\text{Rs. 1,80,000}}{\text{8,000 units}}$ = Rs. 22.50

∴ Selling price per unit = Rs. 22.50

Problem 15

From the following cost data of Onida Co. Ltd., calculate BEP (units) and also new BEP (units) if selling price is reduced by 10%

	Rs.
Direct materials per unit	3
Depreciation on Plant and Machinery	1,00,000
Basic Labour per unit	1.50
Salaries to Staff - Middle Level	80,000
Prime cost expenses per unit	0.50
Workshop Rent	20,000
Value of Turnover per unit	10

Solution

(i) Calculation of Variable Cost per unit :

	Rs.
Direct Materials per unit	3.00
Add : Basic Labour per unit	+ 1.50
Add : Prime Cost expenses per unit	+ 0.50
∴ Total Variable Cost per unit	5.00

(ii) Calculation of Total Fixed Cost :

	Rs.
Depreciation on Plant and Machinery	1,00,000
Add : Salaries of Staff	+ 80,000
Add : Workshop Rent	+ 20,000
∴ Total Fixed Cost	2,00,000

BEP (units) $= \dfrac{\text{Fixed Cost}}{\text{Contribution per unit}}$

But,

Contribution per unit = Selling price per unit - Variable cost per unit

∴ BEP(units) $= \dfrac{\text{Fixed Cost}}{\text{Selling price per unit - Variable cost per unit}}$

$= \dfrac{\text{Rs. 2,00,000}}{\text{Rs.10 - Rs.5}} = \dfrac{\text{Rs. 2,00,000}}{\text{Rs.5}} = 40{,}000$ units

Calculation of new BEP (units) if selling price is reduced by 10% :

Original selling price per unit - Reduction by 10% = New selling price per unit

Rs. 10 - Rs. 1 = Rs. 9

BEP (units) $= \dfrac{\text{Fixed Cost}}{\text{Contribution per unit}}$

But, Contribution per unit = Selling price per unit - Variable cost per unit

∴ BEP (units) $= \dfrac{\text{Fixed Cost}}{\text{Selling price per unit - Variable cost per unit}}$

$= \dfrac{\text{Rs. 2,00,000}}{\text{Rs.9- Rs.5}} = \dfrac{\text{Rs. 2,00,000}}{\text{Rs.4}} = 50{,}000$ units

Problem 16

The Burma-Shell Ltd. has submitted the following data :

	Rs.
Selling price per unit	20
Variable cost per unit	16
Total Fixed Cost	20,000

Calculate BEP (units). Also calculate the effect on BEP (units) if

a) Selling price is increased by Re. 1

b) Selling price is decreased by Re. 1

c) Variable cos is increased by Re. 1

d) Variable cost is decreased by Re. 1

e) Fixed cost is increased by Rs. 5,000

f) Fixed cost is decreased by Rs. 5,000

Solution

BEP (units) : $= \frac{\text{Fixed Cost}}{\text{Contribution per unit}}$

But,

Contribution per unit = Selling price per unit - Variable cost per unit

$\therefore$ BEP (units) $= \frac{\text{Fixed Cost}}{\text{Selling price per unit - Variable cost per unit}}$

$= \frac{\text{Rs.}20{,}000}{\text{Rs.}20 - \text{Rs.}16} = \frac{\text{Rs. }20{,}000}{\text{Rs.}4} = 5{,}000 \text{ units}$

Calculation of effect on BEP (units) if

a) **Selling price is increased by Re. 1**

Original Selling Price per unit + Increase by Re. 1 = New Selling Price per unit

Rs. 20 + Re. 1 = Rs.21

BEP (units) $= \frac{\text{Fixed Cost}}{\text{Selling price per unit - Variable cost per unit}}$

$\frac{\text{Rs.}20{,}000}{\text{Rs.}21 - \text{Rs.}16} = \frac{\text{Rs. }20{,}000}{\text{Rs.}5} = 4{,}000 \text{ units}$

b) **Selling price is decreased by Re. 1**

Original Selling Price per unit - Decrease by Re. 1 = New Selling Price per unit

Rs. 20 - Re. 1 = Rs. 19

BEP(units) $= \frac{\text{Fixed Cost}}{\text{Selling price per unit - Variable cost per unit}}$

$\frac{\text{Rs.}20{,}000}{\text{Rs.}19 - \text{Rs.}16} = \frac{\text{Rs. }20{,}000}{\text{Rs.}3} = 6{,}667 \text{ units}$

c) **Variable cost is increased by Re. 1**

Original Variable Cost per unit + Increase by Re.1 = New Variable Cost per unit

Rs. 16 + Re.1 Rs. 17

BEP (units) $= \frac{\text{Fixed Cost}}{\text{Selling price per unit - Variable cost per unit}}$

$\frac{\text{Rs.}20{,}000}{\text{Rs.}20 - \text{Rs.}17} = \frac{\text{Rs. }20{,}000}{\text{Rs.}3} = 6{,}667 \text{ units}$

d) **Variable Cost is decreased by Re. 1**

Original Variable Cost per unit - Decrease by Re. 1 = New Variable Cost per unit

Rs. 16 - Re.1 = Rs. 15

BEP (units) $= \frac{\text{Fixed Cost}}{\text{Selling price per unit - Variable cost per unit}}$

$\frac{\text{Rs.}20{,}000}{\text{Rs.}20 - \text{Rs.}15} = \frac{\text{Rs. }20{,}000}{\text{Rs.}5} = 4{,}000 \text{ units}$

e) **Fixed Cost is increased by Rs. 5,000**

Original Fixed Cost	Increase by	New Fixed Cost
Rs.20,000	Rs. 5,000	Rs.25,000

BEP (units) $= \frac{\text{Fixed Cost}}{\text{Selling price per unit - Variable cost per unit}}$

$$\frac{Rs.25,000}{Rs.20 - Rs.16} \quad \frac{Rs.\ 25,000}{Rs.4} \quad 6,250 \text{ units}$$

f) **Fixed Cost is decreased by Rs. 5,000**

Original Fixed Cost	Decrease by	New Fixed Cost
Rs.20,000	Rs. 5,000	Rs.15,000

$$\text{BEP (units)} \quad \frac{\text{Fixed Cost}}{\text{Selling price per unit - Variable cost per unit}}$$

$$\frac{Rs.15,000}{Rs.20 - Rs.16} \quad \frac{Rs.\ 15,000}{Rs.4} \quad 3,750 \text{ units}$$

Problem 17

A Company prepared the following budget estimated for the year 200X-2001.

Sales	15,000 units
Fixed Cost	Rs. 34,000
Sales Value	Rs. 1,50,000
Variable cost per unit	Rs. 6

You are required to calculate,

(A)P/V Ratio, BEP (Sales) and Margin of Safety

(B) Also calculate the effect of the following.

(i)decrease of 10% in selling price

(ii)increase of 10% in variable cost.

Solution

Selling price per unit $\frac{\text{Sales value}}{\text{Sales units}}$ $\frac{Rs.\ 1,50,000}{15,000 \text{ units}}$ Rs. 10

A) **(1) P/V Ratio** $\frac{\text{Contribution per unit}}{\text{Selling Price per unit}} \times 100$

But, Contribution per unit Selling price per unit - Variable Cost per unit

$\therefore$ P/V Ratio $\frac{\text{Selling price per unit - Variable cost per unit}}{\text{Selling price per unit}} \times 100$

$$\frac{Rs.10 - Rs.6}{Rs.10} \times 100 \quad \frac{Rs.\ 4}{Rs.10} \times 100 \quad 40\%$$

BEP(Sales) $\frac{\text{Fixed Cost}}{\text{P/V Ratio}}$

$$\frac{Rs.\ 34,000}{40\%} \quad Rs.\ 34,000 \times \frac{100}{40} \quad Rs.\ 85,000$$

3) **Margin of Safety**

Actual Sales - BEP (Sales)

Rs. 1,50, 000 - Rs. 85,000

(15,000 units x Rs. 10)

Rs. 65,000

(i) Decrease of 10% in Selling Price

Original Selling Price unit - Decrease of 10%	New Selling Price per unit
Rs. 10 - Re. 1	Rs.9

1) **P/V Ratio**

$$= \frac{\text{Contribution per unit}}{\text{Selling Price per unit}} \times 100$$

But, Contribution per unit = Selling Price per unit - Variable Cost per unit

∴ P/V Ratio = $\frac{\text{Selling price per unit - Variable cost per unit}}{\text{Selling price per unit}} \times 100$

$$= \frac{\text{Rs.9 - Rs.6}}{\text{Rs.9}} \times 100 = \frac{\text{Rs. 3}}{\text{Rs.9}} \times 100 = 33\tfrac{1}{3}\%$$

3) **BEP (Sales)**

$$= \frac{\text{Fixed Cost}}{\text{P/V Ratio}}$$

$$= \frac{\text{Rs. 34,000}}{33\tfrac{1}{3}\%} = \frac{\text{Rs.34,000}}{\tfrac{1}{3}} = \text{Rs. 34,000} \times \tfrac{3}{1}$$

= Rs. 1,02,000

3) **Margin of Safety**

= Actual Sales - BEP (Sales)

= Rs. 1,35,000 - Rs. 1,02,000

= Rs. 33,000

ii) **Increase of 10% in Variable Cost**

Original Variable Cost per unit + Increase of 10 % = New Variable Cost per unit

Rs. 6 + Re.0.60 = Rs.6.60

1) **P/V Ratio**

$$= \frac{\text{Contribution per unit}}{\text{Selling Price per unit}} \times 100$$

But, Contribution per unit = Selling Price per unit - Variable cost per unit

P/V Ratio = $\frac{\text{Selling price per unit - Variable cost per unit}}{\text{Selling price per unit}} \times 100$

$$= \frac{\text{Rs.10 - Rs.6.60}}{\text{Rs.10}} \times 100 = \frac{\text{Rs.3.40}}{\text{Rs.10}} \times 100 = 34\%$$

2) **BEP (Sales)**

$$= \frac{\text{Fixed Cost}}{\text{P/V Ratio}}$$

$$= \frac{\text{Rs. 34,000}}{34\%} = \text{Rs. 34,000} \times \frac{100}{34}$$

= R. 1,00,000

3) **Margin of Safety**

= Actual Sales - BEP (Sales)

= Rs. 1,50,000 - Rs. 1,00,000

= Rs. 50,000

Problem 18

Reliance Industries provides the following information for the year 200X - 20001.

	Rs.
Sales	2,00,000
Variable Cost	1,00,000
Fixed Cost	50,000

A) Find P/V Ratio, BEP (Sales) and Margin of Safety.

B) Also calculate the effect of the following.

i) 10% increase in selling Price

ii) 5% decrease in variable cost

iii) 20% decrease in selling price

iv) 10% decrease in fixed cost

Solution

A) (1) **P/V Ratio** $= \dfrac{\text{Contribution}}{\text{Sales}} \times 100$

But, Contribution = Sales - Variable Cost

P/V Ratio $= \dfrac{\text{Sales - Variable Cost}}{\text{Sales}} \times 100$

$= \dfrac{\text{Rs. 2,00,000 - Rs.1,00,000}}{\text{Rs.2,00,000}} \times 100 = \dfrac{\text{Rs.1,00,000}}{\text{Rs.2,00,000}} \times 100$

= 50%

2) **BEP (Sales)** $= \dfrac{\text{Fixed Cost}}{\text{P/V Ratio}}$

$= \dfrac{\text{Rs. 50,000}}{50\%} = \text{Rs. 50,000} \times \dfrac{100}{50} = \text{Rs. 1,00,000}$

3) **Margin of Safety**

= Actual Sales - BEP (Sales)

= Rs. 2,00, 000 - Rs.1,00,000

= Rs.1,00,000

B) (i) **10% increase in selling price :**

Original Selling Price + Increase by 10% = New Selling Price

Rs.2,00,000 + Rs. 20,000 = Rs.2,20,000

1) **P/V Ratio**

$= \dfrac{\text{Contribution}}{\text{Sales}} \times 100$

But, Contribution = Sales - Variable Cost

∴ P/V Ratio $= \dfrac{\text{Sales - Variable Cost}}{\text{Sales}} \times 100$

$= \dfrac{\text{Rs. 2,20,000 - Rs.1,00,000}}{\text{Rs.2,20,000}} \times 100 \quad \dfrac{\text{Rs.1,20,000}}{\text{Rs.2,20,000}} \times 100$

= 54.54%

2) **BEP (Sales)** $= \dfrac{\text{Fixed Cost}}{\text{P/V Ratio}}$

$= \dfrac{\text{Rs. 50,000}}{54.54\%} = \text{Rs.50,000} \times \dfrac{100}{54.54}$

= Rs.91,676

3) Margin of Safety

= Actual Sales - BEP (Sales)

= Rs.2,20,000 - Rs. 91,676

Rs.1,28,324

ii) 5% decrease in Variable Cost

Original Variable Cost - Decrease by 5% = New Variable Cost

Rs. 1,00,000 - Rs. 5,000 = Rs.95,000

1) P/V Ratio

$$= \frac{\text{Contribution}}{\text{Sales}} \times 100$$

But,

Contribution = Sales - Variable Cost

$$\therefore \quad \text{P/V Ratio} = \frac{\text{Sales - Variable Cost}}{\text{Sales}} \times 100$$

$$= \frac{\text{Rs. } 2{,}00{,}000 - \text{Rs.}95{,}000}{\text{Rs.}2{,}00{,}000} \times 100 = \frac{\text{Rs.}1{,}05{,}000}{\text{Rs.}2{,}00{,}000} \times 100$$

= 52.5%

2) BEP (Sales)

$$= \frac{\text{Fixed Cost}}{\text{P/V Ratio}}$$

$$= \frac{\text{Rs. } 50{,}000}{52.5\%} = \text{Rs.}50{,}000 \times \frac{100}{52.5}$$

= 95,238

3) Margin of Safety

= Actual Sales - BEP (Sales)

= Rs. 2,00,000 - Rs. 95,238

= Rs. 1,04,762

iii) 20% decrease in Selling Price

Original Selling Price - Decrease by 20% = New Selling Price

Rs. 2,00,000 - Rs. 40,000 = Rs. 1,60,000

1) P/V Ratio: $= \frac{\text{Contribution}}{\text{Sales}} \times 100$

But,

Contribution = Sales - Variable Cost

$$\therefore \quad \text{P/V Ratio} = \frac{\text{Sales - Variable Cost}}{\text{Sales}} \times 100$$

$$= \frac{\text{Rs. } 1{,}60{,}000 - \text{Rs.}1{,}00{,}000}{\text{Rs.}1{,}60{,}000} \times 100 = \frac{\text{Rs.}60{,}000}{\text{Rs.}1{,}60{,}000} \times 100$$

= 37.5%

2) BEP (Sales)

$$= \frac{\text{Fixed Cost}}{\text{P/V Ratio}}$$

$$\frac{Rs.\ 50,000}{37.5\%} \quad Rs.\ 50,000 \times \frac{100}{37.5}$$

Rs. 1,33,333

3) **Margin of Safety**

Actual Sales - BEP (Sales)

Rs. 1,60,000 - Rs. 1,33,333

Rs. 26,667

iv) 10% decrease in Fixed Cost

Original Fixed Cost - Decrease by 10% New Fixed Cost

Rs. 50,000 - Rs. 5,000 Rs. 45,000

1) P/V Ratio :

$$\frac{Contribution}{Sales} \times 100$$

But, Contribution Sales - Variable Cost

∴ P/V Ratio

$$\frac{Sales - Variable\ Cost}{Sales} \times 100$$

$$\frac{Rs.\ 2,00,000 - Rs. 1,00,000}{Rs. 2,00,000} \times 100 \quad \frac{Rs. 1,00,000}{Rs. 2,00,000} \times 100$$

50%

2) **BEP (Sales)**

$$\frac{Fixed\ Cost}{P/V\ Ratio}$$

$$\frac{Rs.\ 45,000}{50\%} \quad Rs. 45,000 \times \frac{100}{50} \quad Rs. 90,000$$

3) **Margin of Safety**

Actual Sales - BEP (Sales)

Rs. 2,00,000 - Rs. 90,000

Rs. 1,10,000

Problem 19

From the following cost data you are required to calculate,

a) BEP (units and sales)

b) Sales required to earn a profit of Rs. 54,000

Selling Price per unit Rs. 18, Contribution per unit Rs. 6 and Fixed Cost Rs.84,000

Solution

a) **BEP (Units)**

$$\frac{Fixed\ Cost}{Contribution\ per\ unit} \quad \frac{Rs.84,000}{Rs.6} \quad 14,000\ units$$

BEP (Sales)

$$\frac{Fixed\ Cost + Profit}{P/V\ Ratio} \times Selling\ Price\ per\ unit$$

$$\frac{Rs.84,000}{Rs.6} \times Rs.\ 18 \quad 14,000\ units \times Rs.\ 18$$

Rs. 2,52,000

Calculation of P/V Ratio

$$\text{P/V Ratio} = \frac{\text{Contribution per unit}}{\text{Selling Price per unit}}$$

$$= \frac{\text{Rs.}6}{\text{Rs.}18} \times 100 = \frac{1}{3} \times 100 = 33\frac{1}{3}\%$$

b) **Sales required to earn a profit of Rs. 54,000**

$$\text{P/V Ratio} = \frac{\text{Contribution}}{\text{Sales}}$$

But,

$$\text{Contribution} = \text{Fixed Cost} + \text{Profit}$$

$$\therefore \quad \text{P/V Ratio} = \frac{\text{Fixed Cost} + \text{Profit}}{\text{Sales}}$$

$$\therefore \quad \text{Sales} = \frac{\text{Fixed Cost} + \text{Profit}}{\text{P/V Ratio}}$$

$$= \frac{\text{Rs. }84{,}000 + \text{Rs.}54{,}000}{33\frac{1}{3}\%} = \frac{\text{Rs.}1{,}38{,}000}{\frac{1}{3}} = \text{Rs. }1{,}38{,}000 \times \frac{1}{3}$$

$$= \text{Rs. }4{,}14{,}000$$

Decision making based on Marginal Costing

Decision making is an regular phenomenon of the business. Managers have to analyse the relevant costs and other related factors to take right decisions. The decision criterion most often used are cost minimisation, profit maximisation, and contribution maximisation.

The accounting world slowly accepted the idea that the accounting information for decision is different from the accounting information recorded in the books of cost and financial accountant. For short-term decision making absorption costing may give totally misleading decision information. Say for example, the total cost of a cosmetic article is Rs. 40, made up of Rs. 28 as variable cost and Rs. 12 as fixed cost. The sales manager is having difficulty in selling the article and a customer has offered Rs. 32 each. The following positions may be observed :

i) If there is no other customer for the article, Rs. 32 may be better than nothing and the product may be sold on short-term basis to improve his income.

ii) If the company has spare capacity, it may be possible to manufacture and sell more of the cosmetic article, if customers are willing to pay Rs. 32 each for extra article. As the contribution per unit will increase by Rs. 4 for each article, the profit will increase marginally by Rs 4 for each unit manufactured and sold.

iii) In absorption costing terms, the product makes a loss of Rs. 8 per article but if the sales demand is less or market share is lost, the loss would be substantial and the total fixed cost of the concern will remain the same.

Thus for short-term decisions or decision affecting the use of spare capacity absorption costing fails to guide management in proper decision making. In marginal costing, when costs are analysed into variable and fixed, a suitable decision for short-term is possible.

Thus, the most useful contribution of marginal costing is the assistance that it render to the management in vital decision making. This is to say that, marginal costing is an invaluable aid to management decision making. Specific areas where marginal costing proves its worth in decision making process are given on next page :

Specific Decision making areas

Marginal costing is an effective tool for decision making and it is used in the following areas of managerial problems :

a) Pricing Decision.
b) Sales mix Decision.
c) Make or Buy Decision.
d) Selection of suitable method of production.
e) Plant shut down decision.
f) Profit planning.

a) Pricing Decision

Pricing decision has been a serious problem for managers as the strategy of pricing depends upon many factors. The interaction of supply and demand tends to determine price, as so too does the cost of production, but neither is different; the nature and degree of competition varies from period to period and demand positions also do not remain constant. However, marginal costing is useful tool to deal with such situations Managers often use this technique to make a decision concerning the price at which a product should be sold.

The marginal cost approach to pricing of products is based on the following formula :

Selling price - Marginal cost = Contribution.

In the long run, the selling prices must cover the total cost otherwise the profit cannot be earned. But the technique of marginal costing is of great help in fixing selling prices under special conditions like the following :

i) In times of competition.
ii) In times of trade depression.
iii) In accepting additional orders for utilising spare plant capacity.
iv) In exploring foreign markets.

This under special circumstances like the trade depression or competition, if selling prices are higher than marginal cost, the production should not be stopped. This is because fixed costs will have to be incurred irrespective of whether production is continued or not, and continuing the production will help in reducing the amount of loss.

As a note of caution, fixation of selling price below total cost should be made only on a short term basis.

Problem 20

Marginal Cost : Rs. 28 per unit. Fixed cost : Rs. 4,00,000.

Selling price : Rs. 32 per unit and 50,000 units can be sold at this price.

The cost per units is -

		Rs.
Marginal Cost (50,000 x 28)	=	14,00,000
Fixed cost	=	+ 4,00,000
Total cost	=	18,00,000

$$\text{Cost per unit} = \frac{18,00,000}{50,000} = \text{Rs. } 36$$

Thus although the selling price does not cover the total cost, yet it is wise to continue to produce and sell because such a step will reduce the loss (on account of fixed cost) that will be incurred if production is stopped. If production is stopped, the loss would be Rs. 4,00,000 (the amount of fixed cost), but if production is continued, the loss will be as follows :

		Rs.
Sales (50,000 x 32)	=	16,00,000
Less : Total cost (marginal cost & fixed costs)	=	18,00,000
Loss	=	2,00,000

Thus simply by continuing to produce and sell at below total cost, the loss has reduced by Rs. 2,00,000 than when production is stopped. (Rs. 2,00,000)

Problem 21

Datar computers Ltd., deals in computer goods and submits the following information in respect of the goods manufactured by it.

Selling price per unit	:	Rs. 10
Variable cost per unit	:	Rs.4
Fixed overheads	:	Rs. 40,000
Units produced	:	75,000

The company is expected to reduce the selling price in order to meet the competition. You are requested to calculate the level of output to maintain present level of profit if the proposed reduction in prices is 10 per cent, 15 per cent and 20 per cent.

Solution :

Marginal Cost Statement

(No. of Units : 75,000)

Particulars	Present Price	Price Reduction		
		10%	15%	20%
	(Rs.)	(Rs.)	(Rs.)	(Rs.)
Sales	7,50,000	6,75,000	6,37,500	6,00,000
Less : Marginal Cost	(-) 3,00,000	3,00,000	3,00,000	3,00,000
Contribution	4,50,000	375000	3,37,500	3,00,000
Less Fixed cost	(-) 1,50,000	1,50,000	1,50,000	1,50,000
Profit	3,00,000	2,25,000	1,87,500	1,50,000
Contribution per unit	6.00	5.00	4.50	4.00

Profit to be maintained at Rs. 3,00,000

Contribution to be earned = Desired profit + Fixed Cost = Rs. 3,00,000 + 1,50,000 = Rs. 4,50,000

$$\text{Number of units required to be sold at different levels of price reduction} = \frac{\text{Total contribution to be earned}}{\text{Contribution per unit}}$$

Hence,

$$\text{At 10 percent reduction} = \frac{\text{Rs. } 4,50,000}{\text{Rs. } 5.00} = 90,000 \text{ units}$$

$$\text{At 15 percent reduction} = \frac{\text{Rs. } 4{,}50{,}000}{\text{Rs. } 4.50} = 1{,}00{,}000 \text{ units}$$

$$\text{At 20 percent reduction} = \frac{\text{Rs. } 4{,}50{,}000}{\text{Rs. } 4.00} = 1{,}12{,}500 \text{ units}$$

b) Sales Mix decision :

Sales mix denotes the proportion in which various products are sold or produced. The problem of selecting a profitable mix of sales thus arises only when a business enterprise has a variety of product lines and each making a contribution of its own. Any change in sales mix also results in the change in profit position. The technique of marginal costing informs the management regarding the most profitable sales mix. The most profitable sales mix is one which yields the largest overall contribution.

Problem 22

ABC Manufacturing Company gives you the following information.

	Product A (Rs.)	**Product B (Rs.)**
Fixed overhead : Rs. 10,000 p.a.		
Direct materials	20	25
Direct labour @ Re. 1 per hour	10	15
Variable overhead (100% of direct labour)		
Selling price	60	100

You are required to present a statement showing the marginal cost of each product and recommend which of the following sales mixes should be adopted :

a) 900 units of A and 600 units of B

b) 1800 units of A only

c) 1200 units of B only

d) 1200 units of A and 400 units of B

Solution :

Marginal Cost Statement

	Product A Rs.	Product B Rs.
Direct materials	20	25
Direct labour	10	15
Variable overhead	10	15
Marginal cost	40	55
Contribution	20	45
Selling price	60	100

Statement of Contributions and Profits of different Sales Mixture

Sales mix	Contribution per unit Rs.	Contribution Rs.	Total contribution Rs.	Fixed cost Rs.	Profit Rs.
(a) A : 900 units	20	18,000			
B : 600 units	45	27,000	45,000	10,000	35,000
(b) A- 1800 units	20	36,000			
B - Nil	45	Nil	36,000	10,000	26,000
(c) A - Nil	20	Nil			
B - 1200 units	45	54,000	54,000	10,000	44,000
(d) A-1200 units	20	24,000			
B-400 units	45	18,000	42,000	10,000	32,000

Thus sales mix (c) is recommended as it yield the highest profit of Rs. 44,000. This is because contribution per unit of B is more than that of A and, therefore, any sales mixture that takes into account the maximum number of units of B would be more profitable.

Problem 23

ABC Ltd. submit the following information of costs in respect of its two products :

	Product X (per unit)	Product Y (per unit)
Direct Material	Rs. 25	Rs. 30
Direct Wages	Rs. 15	Rs. 20
Variable overheads	Rs. 15	Rs. 20
Fixed Overheads	Rs. 15,000 per annum	
Selling price	Rs. 75	Rs. 125

You are required to recommend the management the profitable sales mix from the below mentioned alternatives :

a) 300 units of X and 200 units of Y

b) 600 units of X

c) 800 units of Y

d) 100 units of X and 300 units of Y

Solution

Marginal Cost Statement

	X (Rs.)	Y (Rs.)
Selling price per unit	75	125
Less : Variable cost		
Direct Material	25	30
Direct Wages	15	20
Variable overheads	15	20
Marginal Cost	55	70
Contribution	20	55

Statement of Sales Mixtures

	X (Rs.)	Y (Rs.)	Total (Rs.)
a) 300 units of X and 200 Units of Y			
Contribution : X (300 x 20) & Y (200 x 55)	6,000	11,000	17,000
Less : Fixed overheads			15,000
Profit			2,000
b) 600 units of X			
Contribution (600 x 20)	12,000		12,000
Less : Fixed overheads			15,000
Profit / Loss			(-) 3,000
c) 800 Units of Y			
Contribution (800 x 55)		44,000	44,000
Less : Fixed overheads			15,000
Profit			29,000
d) 100 Units of X and 300 Units of Y			
Contribution X (100 x 20) & Y (300 x 55)	2,000	16,500	18,500
Less : Fixed cost			15,000
Profit			3,500

Comments :

As the sales mixture (c) i. e., 800 units of Y gives maximum profit, it is recommended.

C) Make or Buy Decisions

Marginal cost analysis renders useful assistance when a decision has to be taken by the management as to whether a component part should be manufactured internally or purchased from an outside firm. This is particularly so when a component part is available in the market at a price below firm's own total cost. Such a decision can be arrived at by comparing the outside price with firm's own marginal cost. On the face of it, since the only extra cost to manufacture the component is the marginal cost, then the amount by which this falls below supplier's price, is the saving that arises in making. Therefore, it will be profitable to buy from outside only when supplier's price is below firm's own marginal cost.

This decision, from economic point of view, requires accurate calculations involving the concepts of differential costing and opportunity cost. This problem can be solved with the help of incremental analysis as is clear from Example given below.

Problem 24

In its manufacturing operations, Sucheta Co. Ltd., uses a component 'WWS' that can be purchased from a supplier for Rs. 20 per unit. The same component 'WWS' is manufactured by Sucheta Ltd., at the following unit cost :

Direct Material	:	Rs. 10.00
Direct Labour	:	Rs. 12.00
Variable overheads (125% of Direct Labour)	:	Rs. 15.00
Fixed overhead (75% of Direct Labour)	:	Rs. 09.00
Total unit cost	:	Rs. 46.00

Give your suggestion whether to make or buy this component.

Solution

If the component 'WWS' is purchased it will cost Rs. 40 per unit. However the purchasing cost should not always be compared with the full cost of internal manufacture, which amounts to Rs. 46. For short run decision-making purpose, fixed overheads will remain constant regardless of the alternative chosen. Therefore, the outside purchase price should be compared only with internal manufacturing costs that can be avoided if the outside purchase is made. These avoidable cost include :

Direct Material	:	Rs. 10.00
Direct Labour	:	Rs. 12.00
Variable overheads	:	Rs. 15.00
Total avoidable costs (per unit)	:	Rs. 37.00

Thus, total avoidable costs of Rs. 37.00 per unit is less than Rs. 40.00 outside purchase price. Therefore it is suggested that Sucheta Company Ltd., should continue to manufacture the components 'WWS'

Problem 25

Manufacture of product A takes 20 hours of machine No. 101. It has a selling price of Rs. 150 and marginal cost of Rs. 110. A component part Y could be made on machine no. 101 in 4 hours. The marginal cost of component part is Rs. 9 of which supplier's price is Rs. 15.

Should one make or buy component Y. Assume machine time is the key factor.

Solution

Contribution per unit A = Rs. 150 - 110 = Rs. 40

Contribution per unit of key factor i. e. machine hour $= \frac{\text{Rs. } 40}{20 \text{ hrs}} =$ Rs. 2 per hour

If component Y takes 4 hours, the loss of contribution is Rs. 8 (i.e. 4 hrs 180 x Rs. 2)

The total cost to make will be Rs. 9 + Rs 8 = Rs. 17.

This is more than supplier's price of Rs. 15 and so it is better to buy than to make component Y.

If, however, there was some unutilised machine capacity, then there would be no loss of contribution and so the making cost would only be its marginal cost i. e. Rs. 9. In such a case, it would be economical to make the product than to buy it.

D) Selection of a Suitable Method of Production

Sometimes the management is confronted with the problem of choosing from amongst alternative methods of production. For example, a new product may have been developed and the management is faced with the problem of determining the best method of production i.e. whether to employ a machine or to produce entirely by hand labour. Similarly, management may have to decide whether to employ an ordinary machine or an automatic machine. The management should select the method which gives the largest contribution (i.e. the lowest marginal cost), keeping in view the limiting factor. It can be better explained with the help of example given below :

Problem 26

	Machine A	Machine B
Total machine hours per annum	3,000 hrs.	3,000 hrs.
Production per hour	5 units	8 units
	(Rs.)	(Rs.)
Selling price per unit	100	100
Material per unit	35	35
Labour per unit	15	10
Variable overheads per unit	25	35
Marginal cost per unit	75	80
Contribution per unit	25	20
Contribution per hour	125	160
Contribution per annum	3,75,000	4,80,000

Comments :

Apparently, machine B is more profitable, provided there is no other factor to be considered.

E) Plant Shut Down Decisions

The management under certain circumstances, might feel that plant should be shut down i.e. closing down the business is better than operating at a loss, but a marginal costing analysis may prove that this is not so.

This type of situation usually arises when sufficient business cannot be secured.

This type of decision may be either (i) temporary suspension of production activities, or (ii) permanent closing down of production.

Temporary suspension of activities is a short term concept. The object is usually to stop operations until trade depression has passed. The problem before management is when should operations be suspended, or in other words, how long should operations be continued. The answer to this problem is that if products are making a contribution towards fixed cost, then generally speaking, production should not be suspended. This is so because continuing production will help minimising loss which would be incurred if plant is shut down Thus, the information needed to solve this type of problem involves a comparison between probable loss at a given level of output and the loss that would be suffered if production is suspended temporarily.

Problem 27

A manufacturing company supplies you the following information :

Normal capacity of plant	:	10,000 units
Fixed cost	:	Rs. 2,00,000
Marginal cost per unit	:	Rs. 150
Estimated selling price	:	Rs. 160
Estimated sales volume at this selling price	:	5,000 units

Solution

Marginal Cost Statement

Total sales (5,000 units x Rs. 160	8,00,000
Less : Marginal cost (5,000 units x Rs. 150)	7,50,000
Contribution	50,000
Fixed cost	2,00,000
Loss	(-) 1,50,000

If plant is shut down the loss due to fixed charges would be Rs. 2,00,000, whereas if plant is operated, the loss would only be Rs. 1,50,000. This is because selling price is above the marginal cost and is making a contribution towards fixed cost.

Sometimes, certain items of fixed cost are also not incurred when plant is not operating. In such cases, in order to continue production, contribution should be of the size which exceeds the difference between the following:

a) Fixed cost when plant is operating b) Fixed cost when plant is closed down.

Examples of fixed cost items which may be avoided by closing down operation are skilled labour and management salaries. The longer the period involved for shut down, the larger is the total of avoidable fixed cost likely to be.

F) Profit Planning

Profit planning is a function of management requiring a thorough knowledge of the inter-relationship of selling prices, sales volume, variable costs and fixed costs. Marginal costing with the help of cost-volume-profit analysis guides management about the profit position at various levels of output so that management can operate the business at optimum level, where profit is the maximum. Thus marginal costing is optimum level, where profit is the maximum. Thus marginal costing is quite a useful tool in planning profits so that an adequate return on capital employed is ensured. The profit planning potential of marginal costing is illustrated which can be better explained with the help of example given below :

Problem 28

A manufacturer of plastic boxes makes an average profit of Rs. 5.00 per piece on a selling price of Rs. 29.00 by producing and selling 60,000 pieces at 60% of potential capacity. His cost of sales is:

		Rs.
Direct material	:	Rs. 8.00
Direct wages	:	Rs. 2.00
Factory overhead	:	Rs. 12 (50% fixed)
Selling overhead	:	Rs. 2 (75% fixed)

During the current year, he intends to produce the same number of units, but anticipates that :

a) Fixed cost will go up by 10% b) Material and labour cost will go up by 5% each.

c) Selling price will remain unchanged.

Under these circumstances, he obtains an offer for a further 20% of his capacity. What minimum price you would recommend for acceptance to ensure an overall profit of Rs. 3,20,000?

Solution

Budgeted Statement for the Current Year Prior to Acceptance of 20 % Excess order

	Per piece (Rs.)	Total (Rs.)
Sales	29.00	17,40,000
Direct material	8.40	50,40,000
Direct labour	2.10	12,60,000
Variable factory overhead	6.00	3,60,000
Variable selling overhead	0.50	30,000
Marginal cost	17.00	10,20,000
Contribution	12.00	7,20,000

	Rs.	Rs.
Fixed cost		
Factory overhead	3,60,000	
Add 10 %	36,000	3,96,000
Selling overhead	90,000	
Add 10%	9,000	99,000
Total fixed overhead		4,95,000

Profit = Contribution - Fixed cost = 7,20,000 - 4,95,000 = 2,25,000

Planned profit = 3,20,000

Increase in profit or contribution expected = 3,20,000 - 2,25,000 = 95,000

	Rs.
Marginal cost of additional 20,000 pieces (order for 20% capacity) i.e., 20,000 x Rs.17.00	3,40,000
Add : Additional profit Desired	95,000
Total sales expected	4,35,000

Selling price per unit = 4,35,000 ÷ 20,000 = 21.75

Practical Problems

Problem 1

The following figures are obtained from XYZ Company Ltd., having four branches :

	I (Rs.)	II (Rs.)	III (Rs.)	IV (Rs.)	Total (Rs.)
Sales	2,00,000	3,20,000	2,40,000	2,80,000	10,40,000
Less : Costs Variable cost	2,20,000	2,40,000	80,000	80,000	6,20,000
Fixed cost (Apportioned)	20,000	1,60,000	40,000	40,000	2,60,000
	2,40,000	4,00,000	1,20,000	1,20,000	8,80,000
Profit (+) / Loss (-)	(-) 40,000	(-) 80,000	(+)1,20,000	(+)1,60,000	(+)1,60,000

The management is planning to close branch II immediately as loss shown is maximum. After that branch I will be closed. You are requested to advice management in this regard.

Solution

Marginal Cost Statement

	I (Rs.)	II (Rs.)	III (Rs.)	IV (Rs.)	Total (Rs.)
Sales Less : Marginal costs	2,00,000 2,20,000	3,20,000 2,40,000	2,40,000 80,000	2,80,000 80,000	10,40,000 6,20,000
Contribution	(-) 20,000	80,000	1,60,000	2,00,000	4,20,000
Less : Fixed cost					2,60,000
Profit					1,60,000

Comments (observations) :

From the above marginal cost statement, it is clear that branch I, has negative contribution and therefore, requires immediate closure. However, branch II has a contribution amounting to Rs. 80,000 and as such should be continued otherwise the total profits would be reduced by Rs. 80,000.

Problem 2

The following information in respect of product X and product Y of Gurunanak Limited is obtained :

	Product X (Rs.)	Product Y (Rs.)
Selling price	2000	1280
Material	800	800
Direct labour (Rs. 5.00 per hour)	40 hrs.	8 hrs.
Variable overheads (100 per cent of direct wages)		
Fixed overheads	60,000	

Present the above information to show the profitability of products during labour shortage.

Solution

Comparative Marginal Cost Statement

	Product X (Rs.)	Product Y (Rs.)
Sales	2000	1280
Less : Variable costs		
Material	800	800
Direct labour	200	40
Variable overheads	200	40
Marginal Cost	1200	880
Contribution (per unit)	800	400

$$\text{Profitability} = \frac{\text{Contribution}}{\text{Key factor}} \quad \text{Or} \quad \frac{\text{Contribution}}{\text{Labour hours}}$$

Profitability for X product = $\frac{800}{40 \text{ hours}}$ = Rs. 20 per hour

Profitability for Y product = $\frac{400}{8 \text{ hours}}$ = Rs. 50 per hour

Problem 3

A factory produces 24,000 units. The cost sheet gives the following information :

		Rs.
Direct material	:	1,20,000
Direct wages	:	84,000
Variable overheads	:	48,000
Semi-variable overheads	:	28,000
Fixed overheads	:	80,000
Total cost		3,60,000

The product is sold at Rs. 20 per unit.

The management proposes to increase the production by 3,000 units for sales in the foreign market. It is estimated that the semi-variable overheads will increase by Rs. 1,000. But the product will be sold at Rs. 14 per unit in the foreign market. However, no additional capital expenditure will be incurred. The management seeks your advice as a cost accountant. What will you advise them ?

Solution

Marginal Cost Statement

	Total (Rs.) (24,000 units)	Per unit (Rs.)
Sales	4,80,000	20.00
Direct materials	1,20,000	5.00
Direct wages	84,000	3.50
Variable overheads	48,000	2.00
Marginal cost	2,52,000	10.50
Contribution	2,28,000	9.50

If production of additional 3,000 units is undertaken for sale in the foreign market, the position of cost and profit will be as follows :

		Total (Rs.) (3,000 units)	Per unit (Rs.)
	Additional Sales	42,000	14.00
Less :	Marginal cost	31,500	10.50
	Additional contribution	10,500	3.50
Less :	(Increase in semi-variable overheads)	1,000	
	(Net addition to profit)	9,500	

Acceptance of this offer for sale in the foreign market at Rs. 14 per unit will yield an additional profit of Rs. 9,500. Therefore, the offer should be accepted.

Problem 4

The following production / sales mix is capable of achievement in a factory.

i) 2,000 units of product A and 2,000 units of product C.

ii) 4,000 units of product B.

iii) 1,000 units of product A, 2,000 units of product B and 1,600 units of product C.

Cost per unit is as follows :

	A	B	C
Direct materials	Rs. 20	Rs. 16	Rs. 40
Direct wages	Rs. 8	Rs. 10	Rs. 20

Fixed cost is Rs. 20,000 and variable overheads per unit of A, B and C are Rs. 2, Rs 4 and Rs. 8 respectively. Selling prices of A, B and C are Rs. 36, Rs 40 and Rs. 100 per unit respectively. Determine the marginal contribution per unit of A, B, and C and the profit resulting from product mixes (i), (ii) and (iii).

Solution

Marginal Cost Statement

	Per unit of products		
	A Rs.	B Rs.	C Rs.
Selling price	36	40	100
Direct material	20	16	40
Direct wages	8	10	20
Variable overhead	2	4	8
Marginal cost	30	30	68
Contribution	6	10	32

Statement Showing Comparative Profitability

Sales mix	Contribution	Total Contribution	Fixed cost	Profit
(i) A 2,000 units	12,000			
C 2,000 units	64,000	76,000	20,000	56,000
(ii) B 4,000 units	40,000	40,000	20,000	20,000
(iii) A 1,000 units	6,000			
B 2,000 units	20,000			
C 1,600 units	51,200	77,200	20,000	57,200

Comments : The sales mix (iii) is the most profitable as it yields the highest amount of profit of Rs. 57,200.

Problem 5

X Ltd. Produces part No. 201 of an article. The cost of making part No. 201 is given below :

	Cost of making part No. 201	
	Per unit (Rs.)	10,000 units (Rs.)
Direct Materials	1	10,000
Direct Labour	8	80,000
Variable Overhead	4	40,000
Fixed Overhead charged	5	50,000
Total cost	18	1,80,000

Another manufacturer offers to sell X Ltd. the same part for Rs. 16 per unit.

The analysis of fixed overhead charged showed that Rs. 30,000 represents (such costs like depreciation, insurance, allocated executive salaries etc.) those costs that will continue regardless of the decision.

Should the X Company Ltd. make or buy the part ?

Solution

It is obvious that X Ltd. should buy. But if the key factor, that is, how best to utilise the available facilities taken into account is then the decision will be different.

Suppose the capacity now used to make parts will become idle if the parts are purchased.

The relevant computations follow :

	Per unit		Total	
	Make Rs.	Buy Rs.	Make Rs.	Buy Rs.
Direct Materials	1		10,000	
Direct Labours	8		80,000	
Variable Overhead	4		40,000	
Fixed Overhead that can be avoided by not making	2		20,000	
	15	16	1,50,00	1,60,000
Difference in favour of making	Re.1		Rs. 10,000	

The above analysis of cost indicates that making the parts is a better choice in absence of the alternative use of released facilities.

Decision Making - Relevant Costs

Relevant Costs (Meaning & Features)

Relevant costs are pertinent costs, related solely to a particular decision. These are specific costs which get changed in the short-run as a result of some management decision. Costs and benefits which are independent of a decision are not relevant and will not be considered while making that decision. Drury defines them as "future cash flows which will differ between the various alternatives being considered." In essence, these are "future differential costs." Thus, the two characteristic features of relevant costs are :

i) Expected future costs : Relevant costs are prospective in nature. These are projected costs over the future life of assets. These are forward-looking based on expected factor for the planning period. Selection of one alternative over another does not affect the past cash flows. Current fixed costs, which will not change irrespective of the decision are hardly significant. These are sunk or historical costs. Since decisions are made unto the future circumstances, they must also include anticipated costs.

Relevant costing no doubt, is the modification and extention of marginal costing it is not exactly the same. There are material points of difference.

Relevant costs are future costs and arise as a direct consequence of a decision. Relevant costs are cash flows and non-cash item such as depreciation, notional charges, absorbed fixed overheads which do not reflect additional cash flows should be ignored. A distinction between relevant and irrelevant costs is as follows.

Relevant costs	**Irrelavant costs**
1) Marginal or variable costs (V)	1) General or absorbed fixed cost.
2) Additional or specific or unavoidable fixed costs. (FC) OR Differential or Incremental costs.	2) Committed costs
3) Opportunity costs (D) (where alternative choices exist)	3) Sunk or past costs (having no relevancy in the future)

Problem 29

Mr. X a retail trader, finds at the beginning of an accounting year that there is a stock of Rs. 10,000 (at cost) of maxi skirts which are outdated and have to be sold as scrap (Alternative I) for Rs. 2,000 or remake them incurring a cost of Rs. 5,000 and sell at Rs. 8,000 (Alternative II).

You are required to :

a) to prepare a statement showing net profit or loss of each alternative, for decision making, and

b) to prepare a statement under relevant cost approach to make a decision by the management.

Solution

	Alternative I		Alternative II	
	Rs.	Rs.	Rs.	Rs.
Sales		2,000		8,000
Less : Opening stock	10,000		10,000	
Remaking costs	--	10,000	5,000	15,000
Loss		8,000		7,000

Thus, alternative II is preferable as the loss could be reduced by Rs. 1,000 (from Rs. 8,000 in Alternative I to Rs. 7,000 in Alternative II)

b) In this case the value of opening stock is a sunk cost and is irrelevant for making a and so it can be omitted considering opportunity cost the position can be shown in Alternative I as follows :

Alternative I

	Rs.
Sales (as scrap)	2,000
Less : Opportunity cost	
(benefit foregone in not availing Alternative II)	3,000
Net disadvantage	1,000

Alternatively, the position can be shown with Alternative 2 as follows :

Alternative II

		Rs.
Sales (after remaking)		8,000
Remaking cost	5,000	
Opportunity cost	2,000	7,000
(benefit foregone in not availing Alternative I)		
Net advantage over Alternative I		1,000

Thus, in relevant cost approach, the opening stock becomes sunk cost (irrelevant) whereas opportunity cost is taken into consideration for decision-making.

ii) Different in different alternatives : Only costs that differ among various alternatives are relevant to a decision. These are different between each of the alternative courses of action. Differential costs are defined as "the amount of difference (increase or decrease) in cost expected from one alternative compared to the amount expected from another." Thus, it is obtained by subtracting the cost of one alternative from the cost of other alternative. For example, when management is considering a change in the level of production, differential cost will be calculated by subtracting the cost at lower level of production from that of a higher level. This can be explained by the problem given below.

Problem 30

Output (Units)	Alternative I 10,000 Rs.	Alternative II 15,000 Rs.	Differential Cost 5,000 Rs.
Material	80,000	1,00,000	20,000
Labour	24,000	30,000	6,000
Variable overhead	16,000	20,000	4,000
Fixed overhead	20,000	22,000	2,000
	1,40,000	1,72,000	32,000

Thus, in order to produce additional 5,000 units, additional cost is Rs. 32,000 (i.e. 1,72,000 - 1,40,000). In other words, differential cost for 5,000 units is Rs. 16,000. It should be noted that in this example, if additional output does not involve any additional fixed cost to be incurred, the differential cost will be equal to marginal variable cost. Thus, when fixed costs remain constant, the differential cost is synonymous with the variable costs of producing the n-units. It is for this reason that differential cost is sometimes referred to as marginal cost. Sometimes the term incremental cost is also interchangeably used with differential cost. Incremental cost means only an increase in cost from one alternative to another generally such costs are differential costs.

The two elements, or criteria of costs that differ among alternatives are : a) Incremental costs, and b) Opportunity costs. Both are added with a view to choosing between the competing schemes. These are being taken up for a detailed discussion.

Incremental costs : In effect, differential cost are incremental costs. These are the additional costs of manufacturing and marketing new products. These would not be incurred if the firm does not proceed with the project. These represent a change in aggregate costs that accompany the addition or deletion of a batch or block of output. If total costs do not change as a result of a decision, the incremental cost would be zero. They are thus avoidable or out-of-pocket costs, and need be compared with differential revenue. Unless incremental revenue exceeds the incremental costs, the proposed decision is not good enough.

Opportunity costs : The opportunity cost of a decision is the net benefit of the best alternative that is foregone. It is represented by the potential revenue that might be earned if the contemplated action were not implemented. It is cost of one course of action in terms of the opportunities, which are relinquished or given up to carry on that action. In fact, these are shadow prices, not collected within the accounting system. These are not paid out in cash of a third party. They are imputed in terms of a measurable advantage of a lost opportunity. It is important to note opportunity costs only apply to the use of scarce resource. Where resources are not scarce, no sacrifice exists from using these resources.

Application & Use of Relevant Costing :

The, relevant costing principles give a fresh and refreshing insight. It clearly indicates the minimum price which must be charged to cover variable costs. It reveals the most profitable lines in all conditions of trade. It does this by showing the contribution each product makes towards fixed costs and profit.

The typical situations in which relevant costing is useful are the following short-run, special ad hoc, or non-routine decision. The term short-run is applied to decision horizons over which capacity will be unchanged. This is generally taken as one year. Short term decision effect cash flow for such a short period that the time value of money is immaterial.

i) Capacity utilisation.
ii) Selection of a plant, replacement of existing machine with a newer model.
iii) Introduction of a new product.
iv) Accepting tender, exploring possibilities of foreign market.
v) Alternative course of action.
vi) Sell a partially completed product or process the product further.
vii) Make or buy decisions.
viii) Pricing decisions.
ix) Maintaining a desired level of profit.
x) Selection of suitable product mix.
xi) Dropping a product line.

For decision-making, as choice between alternative mix, replacement, etc. orthodox system cannot be used with advantage, as fixed or irrelevant cost distorts the analysis. This is the special domain of Marginal Costing. In planning Marginal Costing is thus more helpful. In preparation of Budget too. Marginal Analysis is more helpful, as it is not vitiated by allocation of different types of fixed overheads. For control purpose too, the Marginal Analysis is more dependable, as a person is responsible for direct expenses under him and not for expenses occurring elsewhere and allocated on different bases on which he has no control whatsoever. Of course, from control point of view Standard Costing is superior to Marginal Costing.

In the short-run, the time horizon is conventionally limited to one year. The plant capacity, therefore, remains unchanged. The objective function is of "maximising contribution margin". For such non-routine, adhoc problem - solving, relevant costing principles are utilised. These examine both revenue and cost effects. But in some cases, only costs may be looked into as revenues remain unaffected by the decision choice.

Questions for Self Study

1) What is marginal costing ? What are the main features of marginal costing ?
2) Define marginal costing and Distinguish it from absorption costing.
3) What is variable cost ? Explain the four important characteristics of pure marginal cost.
4) Explain the important methods which are available for segregation of semi-variable costs.
5) Write short notes on : i) Level of activity method ii) Range method iii) Analytical method iv) Equation method v) Scattergraph method vi) Least squares method.
6) What is the role of contribution in marginal costing ?
7) What is marginal costing ? Give its merits and demerits ?
8) Define break-even analysis and explain its managerial uses ?
9) Critically evaluate the assumptions underlying the break-even analysis ?
10) Draw a break even chart with illustrative figures. What are the uses of these charts ?
11) What are the advatages and disadvantages of break-even analysis ?
12) What is margin of safety ? and what does it indicate?
13) "Marginal costing is an effective tool for decision making and it is used in solving managerial problems". Elucidate.
14) Identify the various problems in which marginal costing is effective tool for decision making.
15) Define Relevant cost and describe its important featares.
16) What is ment by Relevant costing ? Explain the uses of Relevant costing.
17) Explain the technique of marginal costing and state its importance in decision making.
18) Explain what is meant by "Break-even Analysis". Discuss the assumptions underlying the technique and its uses.
19) What do you understand by break-even analysis ? Explain its significance as a tool of profit planning.
20) What is cost-benefit analysis ?
21) "Cost-Volume-Profit relationship provides the management with a simplified framework for an organisation which is thinking on a number of problems." Discuss.
22) Explain the principles underlying "make or buy" decision.
23) Your boss is looking over a break-even chart which you have constructed to portray the cost-volume-profit relationship of a proposed plan of operation. He comments. "The chart only tells me, the more we sell, the more profit we make." What is your reply ?
24) "Marginal Costing is the administrative tool for the management to achieve higher profits and efficient operation." Discuss.
25) "Differential costs are basically 'special purpose' cost applicable only to a set of circumstances." Do you agree with this statement ? To what extent will it be prudent to take major policy decision regarding selling prices based on differential costs alone. Give reasons for your answer.

Practical Problemes for Self Study

1) Aloba Ltd. manufactures and sells four types of products under the brand names of A, B, C, and D. The sales mix in value comprise 33 1/3 %, 412/3%, 16 2/3 % and 8 1/3 % of products A, B, C, and D respectively. The total budgeted sales (100%) are Rs. 60,000 per month. Operating costs are :.

Variable costs :

Product	A	:	60%	of selling price
Product	B	:	68%	of selling price
Product	C	:	80%	of selling price
Product	D	:	40%	of selling price

Fixed cost Rs.14,700 per month.

a) Calculate the break-even point for the products on over-all basis.

b) It has been proposed to change the sales mix as follows, the total sales per month remaining Rs. 60,000.

Product	A	:	25 %
Product	B	:	40%
Product	C	:	30%
Product	D	:	5%

Assuming that the proposal is implemented, calculate the break-even point.

2) An analysis of costs of Gogate plastic ltd. led to the following information.

Cost of Elements	Variable Costs (% of Sales)	Fixed Cost. (Rs.)
Direct Materials	32.8 %	
Direct Labour	28.4 %	
Factory Overheads	12.6 %	1,89,900
Distribution Expenses	4.1 %	58,400
Administrative Expenses	1.1 %	66,700

Budgeted Sales for the next year are Rs. 18,50,000. You are required to determine :

i) the break-even Sales Volume ii) the profit at the budgeted Sales Volume

iii) the profit, if actual sales a) drop by 10 percent b) increase by 5 percent of budgeted sales.

3) The following data relate to the operations of Bharat Manufacturers Limited for the year ending 31st March, 2005 (Rs. 000)

Units Produced		600
Units Sold		500
Direct Material Cost Incurred	Rs.	900
Direct Labour Cost Incurred	Rs.	300
Variable Factory Overhead Incurred	Rs.	750
Fixed Factory Overhead Incurred	Rs.	1,200
Selling and Administrative Expenses (Fixed)	Rs.	275
Raw Material Inventory - Beginning	Rs.	6
Raw Material Inventory - Ending	Rs.	100
Work-in-Process Inventories - Beginning & Closing		Nil
Finished Goods Inventory - Beginning		Nil

You are required to prepare Income Statements using absorption and Variable costing mehtods.

4) From the following information extracted from the books of XYZ. Ltd., Trichy, manufacturing Automatic Washing Machines, calculate the break-even point using the algebric mehtod.

i) Fixed overheads remain constant at Rs. 40,000
ii) Variable overheads at the present level of output stand at Rs. 1,20,000
iii) Selling price of one washing machine is Rs. 2,000
iv) Number of washing machines produced and sold is 100

5) From the following data, calculate (i) P/V ratio, (ii) Profit when sales are Rs. 20,000 and (iii) New break-even point if selling price is reduced by 20 per cent.

Fixed expenses	:	Rs. 4,000	Break-even point	: Rs. 10,000

6) Calculate :
i) The amount of fixed expenses ii) The number of units to be produced to break-even.
iii) The number of units to earn a profit of Rs. 5,00,000 iv) The profit with sales of Rs. 10,00,000

The company's sales turnover and profit during two period were as follows :

	Sales (Rs.)	Profit (Rs.)
Period I	20,00,000	2,00,000
Period II	30,00,000	4,00,000

7) The following figures for profit and sales are obtained from the account of great ABC Ltd.

Year	Sales (Rs.)	Profit (Rs.)
2002-2003	2,00,000	20,000
2004-2005	3,00,000	40,000

Calculate :
a) P/V ratio; b) Fixed cost; c) Profit at sales of Rs. 40,000 d) Break-even sales and
e) Sales to earn profit of Rs. 50,000

8) From the following results of a company determine by how much the value of sales must be increased for the company to break-even.

Net sales	:	Rs. 16,00,000	Fixed cost	:	Rs. 8,00,000
Variable cost	:	Rs. 9,60,000			

Use a break chart to illustrate the case.

9) The selling price of a product was Rs. 100 per unit as against the variable cost of Rs. 50 per unit. The total fixed costs were Rs. 1,00,000. Calculate the effect of a reduction in price by Rs. 20 per unit on the P/V ratio, Break-even point, and Margin of Safety if 4,000 units were produced and sold.

11) The P/V ratio of product x is 20%. The cost per unit at 50% capacity is : material Rs. 15, labour Rs. 8, variable overheads Rs. 2 and fixed overheads Rs. 5.
a) Determine selling price for quotation if same Gross Profit percentage is to be earned.
b) What should be the selling price if same net profit percentage on the sale is to be maintained as before, assuming activity will increase to 75% capacity, if the order is accepted.

12) Sales of two products are Rs. 1,00,000 and Rs. 1,50,000 with P./V of 25% and 20% respectively. The fixed overheads of the organization are Rs. 75,000. To avoid loss, which is being presently incurred, it is proposed to increase activity as capacities are sufficient.
Calculate the percentage of increase required
a) of each, assuming the level of activity in the other will remain same,
b) of the line which will be better, assuming that market is not key factor of the organization.
c) of both the lines, assuming that resistance to increase sales is same in both the lines.

BUDGETARY CONTROL

Introduction

Control is one of the important functions of management. The main object of control is to bring to light the variations between the standards set and performance and then to take necessary steps to prevent the occurrence of such variations in future. It is the process through which managers assure that actual activities confirm to planned activities. The concept of control system originated in the field of engineering but it has been adapted to management in course of time.

Meaning of control

Control aims to detect and correct deviations in a system's state in order to achieve the desired (standard) state. In the words of E.F.L. Brech, "control is checking current performance against predetermined standards contained in the plans, with a view to ensuring adequate progress and satisfactory performance.".

According to George R. Terry, "controlling is determining what is being accomplished, that is evaluating the performance and if necessary, applying corrective measures so that the performance take place according to plans." To draw an analogy, it is like thermostat in an air conditioning system.

Lorange, Morton and Ghoshal, define the spectrum of organisational planning and control as a three-tier construction comprising strategic planning and control, tactical planning and control, and operational planning and control as depicted in fig. 4.1.

As per the three tiers of organisational planning and control indicated in fig. 4.1. be in agreement with the three levels of management popularly known as top management, middle management and lower management in the content of a private sector organisation.

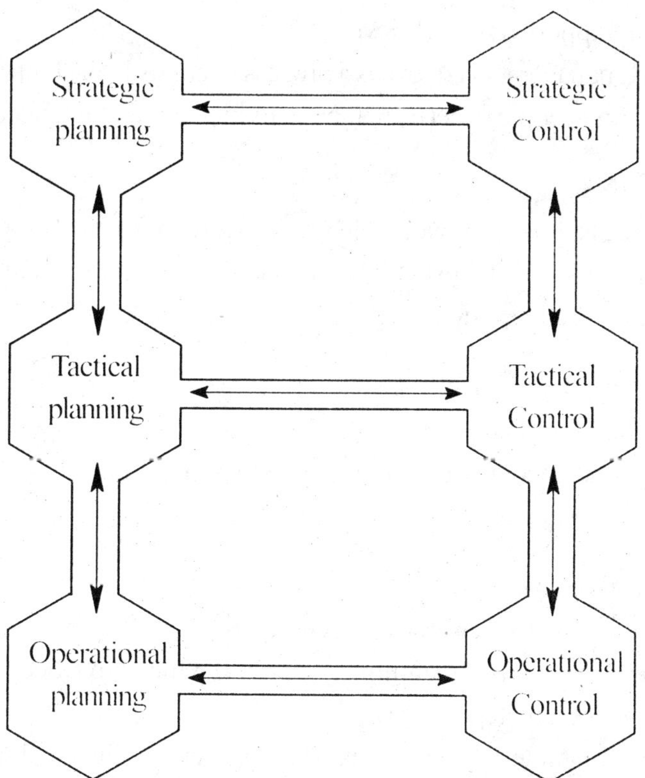

Fig 4.1. Spectrum of organisational planning and control

Basic Concepts of Management Control

Management control is regular, not occasional and tends to be a rhythmic activity. It follows a definite pattern and time table, month after month and year after year.

As per Anthony and Dearden the term management control is defined as "Management control is the process by which managers assure that the resources are obtained and used efficiently and effectively in the accomplishment of the organisation's goals."

Characteristics of Management Control

With the help of above definition we may pinpoint important characteristics of management control as follows :

a) Management control is intended to help in the achievement of organisational goals.

b) Management control is a process of actions such as programing, budgeting, accounting, analysing, evaluating, monitoring and reporting the performance of individual heads of sub-divisions or units in an organisation.

c) Management control is exercised by the Coordinating agency, which in a private sector organisation, is the top management.

d) Management control is concerned both with the efficiency and effectiveness of performance.

e) Management control is focused on controlling the performance of individual managers rather than organisation as a whole.

f) Management control is focused on all operations of a sub-division or unit of an organisation.

g) Management control often used as integrated, financial, futuristic and historical information, even approximations sometime.

h) Management control works with weekly, monthly or yearly time frames.

i) Management control has to work with diverse information generated through management Information system (MIS) and Decision Support system (DSS).

In short, we can say that, management control is a process of control by which a management attempts to carry out its strategies by motivating people to perform their activities and making necessary corrections.

Steps in a control process

Control is a very important process through which managers ensure that actual activities confirm to planned activities. It involves three basic steps : a) establishment of standards , b) measurement and comparison of results against standards and, c) taking corrective action.

Need for control

A control system is needed for three purposes :

a) to measure progress, b) to uncover deviations and c) to indicate corrective action.

Control Techniques

All control techniques can be broadly divided into two :

a) Old control techniques b) New control techniques.

a) ***Old control techniques :*** Old control techniques are those which have been used by managers. Important techniques under this categories are :

i) budgeting ii) cost accounting iii) break even analysis iv) financial statements & ratio analysis v) auditing vi) reports vii) rules and personal observation

Budget is most widely used among the old techniques.

b) New control techniques : The new control techniques are Programme Evaluation and Review Technique (PERT) and Critical Path Method (CPM) and Human Resources Accounting (HRA)

PERT and CPM illustrate the task involved in a project. Under both the techniques, a project is decomposed into activities and then all activities are integrated in a highly logical sequence to find the shortest time required to complete the entire project.

The concept of human resources accounting is of recent origin. Working on the idea that human assets in an organisation are on less important than its materials assets. Human resource accounting refers to the method of reflecting the rupee value of human assets in the company's balance sheet.

Budget & Budgetary Control

Meaning

A budget is a plan which relates to a definite period of time and which is expressed in quantitative terms. It is thus a predetermined statement which incorporates the policy of the management during a given period and serve as a standard for comparing the actual results. Thus a budget is a tool in the hands of the management which serves as a guide to all the employees in achieving their goals, objectives and targets.

A budget can help us in planning and coordination with all the employees, and departments, but the most important factor is that it is used for control purposes at all levels of management.

Difference Between Budget and Budgetary Control

There is a difference between budget and budgetary control. As we have seen, a budget is a quantitative statement prepared in advance and keeping it as the base, the actuals are compared. Budgetary control on the other hand means use of the budgets. Thus budgetary control involves use of the budgeting techniques to help the management for carrying out the various functions viz. planning, organising, coordinating and controlling the activities of a business.

The budgetary technique includes :

a) Establishment of budgets for each department.

b) Variance analysis is done for taking suitable action.

c) To see that the mistakes of the past are not repeated in future.

d) Comparing the budgets with the actuals which is known as variance.

According to ICMA, England, Terminology, a budget is " a financial and/or quantitative statement, prepared and approved prior to a defined period of time, of the policy to be pursued during that period for the purpose of attaining a given objective."

Budgetary control is defined by ICMA, England Terminology as "the establishment of budget relating to the responsibilities of executives to the requirements of a policy and the continuous comparison of actual with the budgeted results, either to secure by individual action the objectives of that policy, or to provide a basis for its revision.

Purpose of Budgetary Control

The technique of budgetary control is extensively used in the modern business world. Most of the business failures are due to lack of proper planning, flanning helps us to know in advance whether to start a business or not, whether to continue a business or not and also to indicate the various constraints and limiting factors in business which may be faced during operation of the business.

Budgetary control also tells us in advance about the dangers which one has to face in business, their remedies and solutions.

Objectives of Budgetary Control

Generally budgetary control is concerned with three aspects viz, planning, co-ordination and control. All these factors depend on one another and hence we cannot isolate them.

a) ***Planning :*** A budget is nothing but a plan. Without planning any modern business cannot function, planning is related to production, sales, stocks, requirement of labour, etc. The advantage of planning is that we can anticipate the problems before hand. Planning through budgetary control is necessary at all levels of management in which there is the process of thinking which enables to provide new idea to the management.

b) ***Co-ordination :*** It means co-operation by the different people in the organisation to achieve the common goal. To have co-ordination, there should be proper communication. Communication can be through the budgets. Planning helps co-ordination and hence if the planning is good, there is effective co-ordination. A detailed budgetary control system is one where the plans are written down and these plans are circulated to all the levels of management.

c) ***Control :*** It ensures that the goals of the management as stated in the budgetary control system have been achieved. For this fixing of standards is necessary. Thus through the budgets the standards are fixed which enables the management to control the activities so that the goals are achieved. Thus through budgetary control, we can compare the standards with the actuals and the analysis of the variances is possible and corrective action taken whereever necessary.

It encourages research and development as budgetary control schedules are usually based on past experience.

Uses / Advantages of Budgetary Control

a) It locates the inefficient areas and persons in the business.

b) It helps to increase the efficiency, reduce wastages and control costs.

c) It helps to co-ordinate the activities of the various employees, departments and thus helps to achieve the goal of the management.

d) With the help of budgeting, the responsibilities of the managers can be fixed for planning, so that they can think of future, anticipate and be prepared to meet the challenges ahead.

e) Maximization of profits is possible through budgeting.

f) It helps to introduce the standard costing technique.

g) It helps to ensure cash flow and hence bank credit can be obtained.

h) It creates cost consciousness in the minds of all the employees in the organisation.

i) Authority can be delegated and responsibilities fixed.

j) It rewards the efficient workers and the managers can show their efficiency by achieving the goals fixed by the management through the budgets.

k) It ensures that the capital of the firm is utilized in a proper way and that there is no misutilization of funds.

l) Vital decisions can be taken by the management based on the budgets.

m) Actual results can be compared with the budgets so that corrective action can be taken in time.

n) It is like a barometer which enables us to study the changes in the business conditions.

Limitations of Budgetary Control

Though we have seen many advantages of budgetary control it suffers from many deficiencies also. Hence the persons using the budgets should be careful and should be fully aware of the limitations. The following are the limitations :

a) ***Budgetary Control does not replace management :*** It cannot replace the management because in business all vital decisions have to be taken by the management.

b) ***Too much reliance on budgets is harmful :*** Budgetary control is only a technique and tool in the hands of the management. To execute the budget, all the employees must take active part and co-operate with one another so that the budgetary goal can be achieved. But the budgets should not be taken as the only means through which the business should run. Though sometimes, through budgetary control, it is possible to have success in business, it should not be depended upon totally.

c) ***Less Flexibility :*** A budgetary control system should be more flexible and should be changed according to the changing circumstances. The alternative systems should be added, deleted, improved, replaced or compared with the present system of budgetary control.

d) ***Budgets are based on estimated figures :*** Budgets are prepared in anticipation of various factors. These factors are estimated by seeing the past and forecasting the future. Hence forecasting is done which may or may not happen in actual life. Thus, it is not an exact prediction of figures, but based on estimates.

e) ***Costly System :*** The installation of the system and its execution is an expensive affair. This is because specialized persons have to be appointed and extra costs have to be incurred for carrying out the operations. Hence small scale units cannot go in for budgetary control system.

f) **Budgetary control deals with quantitative data only :** In budgetary control system, only the figures are considered and hence qualitative i.e. the facts are not considered. For example if worker is inefficient, we should analyse the various reasons for his inefficiency as he may be inefficient because of the conditions (environment) where he works are not suitable to his health. Here budgets are of no use because, budgets will only measures his efficiency in terms of quantity produced and will not consider other factors.

Requirements of good Budgeting System

The following are the requirements of a good budgeting system :

a) ***Sound Organisation :*** A good organisation is necessary to carry out the plans and policies of the management. It means that the organisational structure should be such that each one knows what the management expects from him and also his responsibilities.

b) ***Cost Factor :*** The cost benefit analysis should be made before the budget is introduced. It means that the cost of operation of the budget should be less than the benefits derived from it.

c) ***Interpersonal Relationship :*** The management should develop interpersonal relationship, which means that the management should be able to know the personal difficulties of the executives and managers in implementing the budgets. This will ensure that the budget is not imposed on anyone without studying his ability to undertake the responsibility.

d) ***Systematic Accounting Systems :*** It is necessary so that the management can hold the concerned person responsible in the organisation in terms of monetary consideration.

e) ***High Profits :*** The main aim or goal of the management should be to earn maximum profits and this factor should be kept in mind while preparing the budget.

f) ***Goals should be achievable :*** The management should fix the goals in such a way that they should be attainable. Otherwise there will be confusion in the organisation.

g) ***Constant Review :*** Constant review of the performance should be made to evaluate the actual results as compared to the budgets so that corrective action can be taken at the right time.

h) ***Fixing up of Responsibilities and preparation of budget :*** It should be noted that the person who will execute the budgets should be made responsible for its preparation.

i) ***Budget committee :*** A budget committee is necessary to carry out the policies effectively so that the committee consisting of the directors and the executives of various departments are responsible for its implementation.

j) ***Involvement of Top management :*** Unless the top management co-operates in implementing the budget in true spirit, the budgetary control system cannot be successful. It means that the top management should carry out the plans and policies strictly as laid down in the budget.

Procedure in Budget preparation : Organisation & Administration.

When control through budgets is desired the budgetary control organisation has to be busy with the following preliminaries :

a) Establishment of budget centres.
b) Preparation of an organisation chart.
c) Preparation of adequate accounting records.
d) Formation of Budget Committee.
e) Preparation of Budget manual.
f) Fixation of Budget period.
g) Determination of governing factors.

a) ***Establishment of budget centres :*** A budget centre is a section of the organisation of an undertaking defined for the purposes of budgetary control. Budget centres should be clearly defined and established, for each of which a budget will be set with the help of the head of departments concerned e.g. labour budget, production cost budget etc. by the accountant in conjunction with production manager and other executives.

b) ***Preparation of an organisation chart :*** An organisation chart when properly drafted will show the functional responsibilities of each member of management and ensure that he knows his position in the organsiation and his relationship to other members. The organisation chart may have to be adjusted to ensure that each centre is controlled by an appropriate member of the staff.

Specimen of Organisation Chart (which can be modified according to circumstances) is given below :

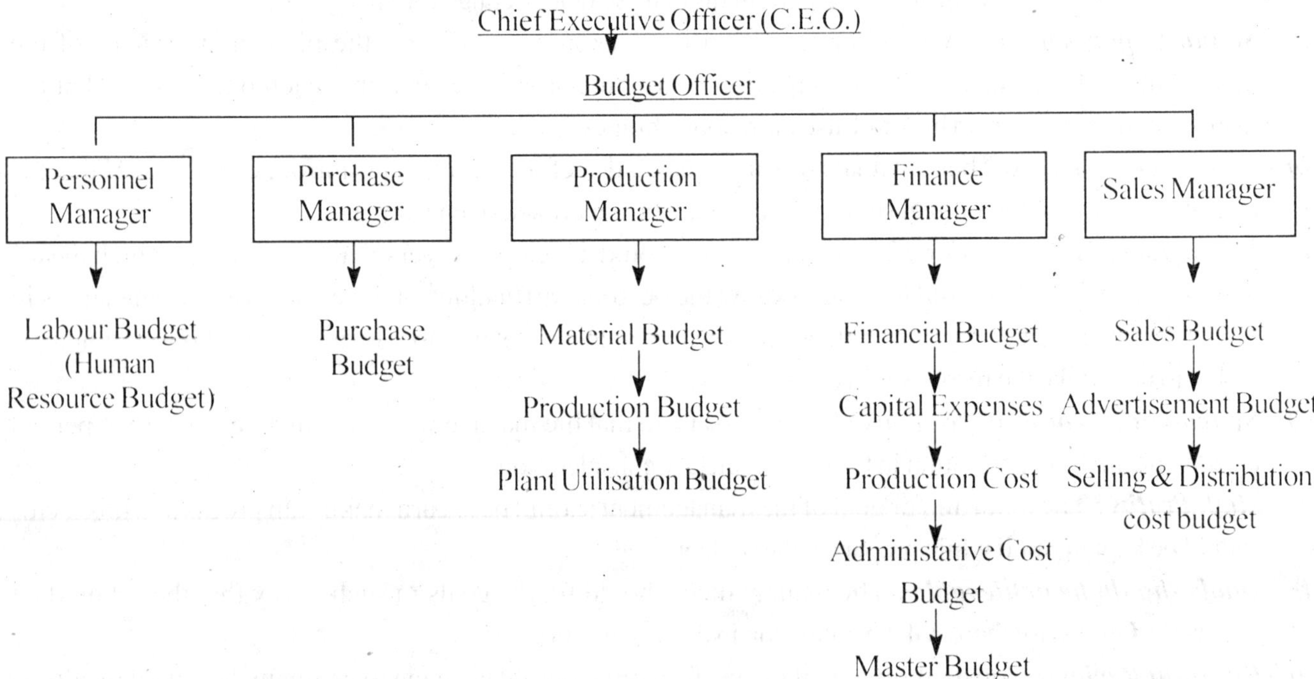

c) ***Preparation of adequate accounting records :*** It is essential that the accounting system should be able to record and analyse the transactions involved. An "accounts code" should be maintained which may linked with the budget centres for establishment of budgets and finally control through budgets.

d) ***Formation of Budget Committee :*** In small sized organisations a budget officer may establish budget & co-ordinate all the work involved, but in large organisations a budget committee consisting of chief executive, budget officer and heads of departments or budget centres, is established. The main functions of a budget committee are as follows :

i) To accept and scrutinise all budgets.

ii) To decide about overall policy to be followed.

iii) To suggest revision of functional budgets, whereever necessary.

iv) To approve finally revised budgets.

v) To receive and deal with budget and comparative statements,

vi) To recommend action to be taken under different situations.

e) ***Preparation of 'Budget Manual' :*** A budget manual is a document setting out the responsibilities of the persons engaged in, the routine of, and the forms and records required for budgetary control, A budget manual helps in standardising methods and procedures and the risk of overlapping of function is eliminated.

f) ***Fixation of 'budget' period :*** A budget period is the period of time for which a budget is prepared and employed. Except in case of Capital Expenditure Budget, the budget period is generally the accounting year subdivided into 4 quarters or 12 months.

g) ***Determination of governing factors :*** A governing factor or key factor or principal budget factor is that factor the extent of whose influence must first be assessed in order to ensure that functional budgets are reasonably capable of fulfilment. The key factor serves as a starting point for preparation of budget. Generally, sales become the key factor, but other factors of production, such as men, material, machine, capital etc. may also be the governing factors.

Fixed and Flexible Budgets

Fixed Budget

Fixed budgets are prepared for only one level of activity under the same conditions. It is an unchangeable budget which is drawn on the assumption that the level of activity will remain the same. Hence the changes in the expenses due to changes in the conditions are not provided for in this budget. Thus a fixed budget becomes useful when the actual level of activity is equal to the budgeted level of activity. However in real life, the level of activity and business conditions due to the internal constraints as well as external factors like changes in the demand, piece, shortage of materials, cut in the electricity, etc. go on changing. Thus a fixed budget is not that successful because it does not consider the variable, semi-variable and fixed costs as separate items and also does not consider changes in costs due to change in the level of activity. The reasons why fixed budgets are not considered to be useful are given below :

i) In fixed budgets the management become helpless as they cannot do anything beyond the budget. Now we can define a fixed budget as one "which is designed to remain unchanged irrespective of the level of activity actually attained. "ICMA, London Terminology.)

   In case of fixed budgets if the actual level differs widely as compared to the fixed budget, we find large variances.

ii) In the real life we find that the cost of material, labour and overheads go on changing. Hence fixed budgets are not useful because these changes do not have any effect on the budgeted figures.

iii) Since it is fixed in nature, it is not suitable for long-term planning.

Flexible Budget

ICMA. London Terminology defines a flexible budget as "one which by recognising the difference between fixed, semi fixed and variable costs, is designed to change in relation to the level of activity attained." Thus a flexible budget is one which is designed to change according to the level of activity actually achieved. The budgeted figures can be changed according to the changing conditions. Hence a flexible budget is just the opposite of a fixed budget. Thus it is more elastic, practical and useful in the real life. These budgets are prepared for the purpose of cost control.

Flexible budget are prepared in the following cases :

i) Where the business depends upon some scarce material.

ii) Where the exact demand cannot be estimated e.g. in new business.

iii) Where the business depends upon nature e.g. rainfall

iv) In some business where the sales cannot be predicted.

v) Where sufficient labour force is necessary for running the business smoothly.

Preparation of Flexible Budgets

Flexible budget can be prepared in the following manner :

At first a number of fixed budgets are prepared for each manufacturing budget centre. Within the limits of these budgets, the flexible budgets are prepared. In flexible budgets clear differences are drawn between fixed, semi-fixed and variable costs.

There are three methods of preparing flexible budgets :

a) Tabular Method b) Charting method c) Ratio method .

a) ***Tabular Method :*** In this method a table is prepared wherein different capacities are shown in horizontal columns and the budget, the budgeted figures are shown against different capacities in the vertical columns. The expenses are recorded as variable, semi variable and fixed. Various capacity levels showing different volumes of production are shown in the flexible budgets.

b) ***Charting method :*** In this method, the expenses are analysed according their nature or behaviour, i.e. variable, semi variable and fixed. The budgeted expenses are prepared and these are plotted on a graph paper against different levels of activity. The budgeted expenses relating to the level of activity actually attained can be read from this chart.

c) ***Ratio method :*** If the activities of a company are standardised and the expenses are of uniform nature, most of the expenses can be worked out as percentage of level of activity. The method is that the common costs are estimated. For the normal production i.e. the normal level of activity. From this we can work out various ratios which show the relationships of each expenses with increase in the each level of activity. The budgeted cost for any level of activity can be ascertained by using these ratios.

Uses of Flexible budget

a) It is more realistic and has great practical utility in the business.

b) The efficiency of the managers can be measured.

c) It helps to control the costs.

d) It is more realistic than a fixed budget because a fixed budget deals with only one level of activity of condition.

e) The figures in a flexible budget can be changed according to the change in the volume of activity.

Proforma of a Flexible Budget

FLEXIBLE BUDGET

Normal Level of Activity : 70% Period ending :-

Units	Capacity		
	40%	70%	90%
	Rs.	Rs.	Rs.
1) **PRIME COST :**			
Direct Material	---	---	---
Direct Labour	---	---	---
Direct Expenses	---	---	---
2) **VARIABLE OVERHEADS** :			
Indirect Material	---	---	---
Indirect Labour	---	---	---
Repairs and Maintenance	---	---	---
3) **MARGINAL COST** (1+2)	---	---	---
4) **SALES**	---	---	---
5) **CONTRIBUTION** (4-3)	---	---	---
6. **FIXED COSTS**	----	---	---
Production	----	---	---
Administration	----	---	---
Selling and Distribution	----	---	---
7. **PROFIT/LOSS (5-6)**	----	---	---

Practical Problems on Flexible Budgets

Problem 1

A factory produces 20,000 units. The budgeted expenses are given below :

	Per Unit (Rs.)
Raw Material	75
Direct Labour	20
Direct Expenses	25
Overheads	15
Fixed overheads (Rs. 2,00,000)	20
Administrative expenses (Fixed)	10
Selling expenses (10% fixed)	15
Distribution expenses (25% fixed)	20
Total cost per unit	200

You are required to prepare a budget for 15,000 and 10,000 units.

Solution

Flexible Budget

Particulars	20,000 Units		15,000 Units		10,000 Units	
	Per Unit	Amount	Per Unit	Amount	Per Unit	Amount
Production Expenses						
Raw Material	75.00	15,00,000	75.00	11,25,000	75.00	7,50,000
Direct Labour	20.00	4,00,000	20.00	3,00,000	20.00	2,00,000
Overheads	15.00	3,00,000	15.00	2,25,000	15.00	1,50,000
Direct Expenses	25.00	5,00,000	25.00	3,75,000	25.00	2,50,000
Fixed Overheads (Rs. 2,00,000)	20.00	4,00,000	26.67	4,00,000	40.00	4,00,000
Administrative Expenses	10.00					
Fixed		2,00,000	13.33	2,00,000	20.00	2,00,000
Selling Expenses						
Variable	13.50	2,70,000	13.50	2,02,500	13.50	1,35,000
Fixed	1.50	30,000	2.00	30,000	3.00	30,000
Distribution Expenses						
Variable	15.00	3,00,000	15.00	2,25,000	15.00	1,50,000
Fixed	5.00	1,00,000	6.67	1,00,000	10.00	1,00,000
Total Cost of Sales	200.00	40,00,000	212.17	31,82,500	236.50	23,65,000

Problem 2

The following is the information given by Someshwar Industries for 50% production (10,000 units):

Raw Materials	Rs. 100 per unit
Direct Labour	Rs. 80 per unit
Direct Expenses	Rs. 20 per unit
Factory Expenses	Rs. 1,00,000 (40% fixed)
Administrative Expenses	Rs. 50,000 (50% variable)

Prepare a flexible budget for production capacity at 80% and 100%

Solution

Flexible Budget

Capacity Units	50% (Rs.) 10,000	80% (Rs.)16,000	100% (Rs.)20,000
Raw Materials	10,00,000	16,00,000	20,00,000
Direct Labour	8,00,000	12,80,000	16,00,000
Direct Expenses	2,00,000	3,20,000	4,00,000
Factory Expenses :			
Variable - 60%	60,000	96,000	1,20,000
Fixed - 40%	40,000	40,000	40,000
Administrative Expenses :			
Variable - 50%	25,000	40,000	50,000
Fixed - 50%	25,000	25,000	25,000
Total Cost	21,50,000	34,01,000	42,35,000

Problems 3 : From the following information, prepare a flexible budget at 60% and 80% capacity

Particulars	70% Capacity (Rs.)
Variable Overheads :	
Indirect Material	5,000
Indirect Labour	15,000
Semi-Variable Overheads :	
Electricity	50,000
Variables - 60 %	
Fixed - 40%	
Repairs & Maintenance	5,000
Variable - 65 %	
Fixed - 35 %	
Fixed Overheads	
Salaries to Staff	10,000
Depreciation on machine	14,000
Insurance of machines	6,000
Total Overheads	1,05,000

The company estimated the Direct Labour hours to be worked at 70% capacity as 1,40,000 hours. Also calculate the overhead recovery rate at 60% 70% and 80% capacities

Solution :

Flexible Budget for the period

Capacity % Units	60% 1,20,000 Rs.	70% 1,40,000 Rs.	80% 1,60,000 Rs.
Variable Overheads			
Indirect Materials	4285	5000	5714
Indirect Labour	12,857	15,000	17,142
Semi-Variables Overheads			
Electricity (Rs. 50,000)			
Variable 60%	25,714	30,000	34,285
Fixed 40%	20,000	20,000	20,000
Repairs & Maintenance (Rs. 5000)			
Variable -65%	2,785	3,250	3,714
Fixed- 35%	1,750	1,750	1,750
Fixed Overheads			
Salaries to Staff	10,000	10,000	10,000
Dep. on machines	14,000	14,000	14,000
Insurance on machines	6,000	6,000	6,000
Total Overheads	97,391	1,05,000	1,12,605
Estimated direct labour hrs.	1,20,000	1,40,000	1,60,000
Overhead recovery rate (On the basis of direct labour hour)	Rs. 0.81	Rs. 0.75	Rs. 0.70

Note : Overhead recovery rate per Direct Labour hour is calculated as follows :

Capacities	60%	70%	80%
Total overheads / Total Direct Labour hrs.	$\frac{97,391}{1,20,000}$ = Rs. 0.81	$\frac{1,05,000}{1,40,000}$ = Rs. 0.75	$\frac{1,12,605}{1,60,000}$ = Rs. 0.70

Problem 4

Bajarang Ltd. works at 50% capacity and manufactures 2,000 units of gas stoves. The price per stove is Rs. 2,000 while the cost per stove is Rs. 1,700 at 50% capacity. The company furnishes you with the following details:

Particulars	Cost per unit (Rs.)
Material	700
Labour	400
Works Overheads (30% fixed)	500
Administrative Overheads (80% fixed)	100
Total Cost	1,700

Prepare a Flexible Budget at 50%, 70% and 90% capacities and determine the profits when at 70% capacity material cost goes up by 3% and the selling price falls by the same percentage. At 90% capacity the material cost is increased by 5% and there is a corresponding reduction in the selling price by 5%.

Solution :

Flexible Budget

Capacities	50%		50%		50%	
Units	2000		2800		3600	
Particulars	**Per Unit Rs.**	**Total Rs.**	**Per Unit Rs.**	**Total Rs.**	**Per Unit Rs.**	**Total Rs.**
Sales	2,000	40,00,000	1,940	54,32,000	1900	68,40,000
Material	700	14,00,000	721	20,18,800	735	26,46,000
Labour	400	8,00,000	400	11,20,000	400	14,40,000
Works overheads						
Variable 70%	350	7,00,000	350	9,80,000	350	12,60,000
Fixed 30%	150	3,00,000	107.14	3,00,000	83.33	3,00,000
Admn. Overheads						
Variable - 20%	20	40,000	20	56,000	20	72,000
Fixed -80%	80	1,60,000	57.14	1,60,000	44.44	1,60,000
Total Cost	1700	34,00,000	1655.28	46,34,800	1632.77	58,78,000
Profit	300	6,00,000	284.72	7,97,200	267.23	9,62,000

Problem 5

Raghuwanshi Ltd. produce computer hardware. The fixed overheads are estimated at Rs. 1,00,000. The semi-variable overheads are Rs. 50,000 at 100% capacity i.e.10,000 units. The semi-variable expenses vary in stages of Rs. 4,000 for each change in output of 1000 units. Selling price per unit is Rs. 70.

The estimated cost per unit is as under :

Direct Material : Rs. 15 Direct Wages : Rs. 10 Direct Expenses :Rs. 4 Variable Overheads : Rs. 6

You are required to prepare a flexible budget at 50%, 70% 90% and 100% capacities.

Solution :

From the problem it can be seen that data for 100% capacity is given. Hence we have to calculate the figures of 50%, 70% and 90% capacities based on 100% capacity figures.

Flexible Budget for the period...... $\frac{\text{Normal Activity}}{\text{100\% (10,000 units)}}$

Capacity	50%	70%	90%	100%
Units	5,000	7,000	9,000	10,000
	Rs.	Rs.	Rs.	Rs.
Sales	3,50,000	4,90,000	6,30,000	7,00,000
Direct Material	75,000	1,05,000	1,35,000	1,50,000
Direct Wages	50,000	70,000	90,000	1,00,000
Direct Exps.	20,000	28,000	36,000	40,000
Prime Cost	**1,45,000**	**2,03,000**	**2,61,000**	**2,90,000**
Overheads :				
Variable	30,000	42,000	54,000	60,000
Semi-variable	30,000	38,000	46,000	50,000
Fixed	1,00,000	1,00,000	1,00,000	1,00,000
Total Cost	**3,05,000**	**3,83,000**	**4,61,000**	**5,00,000**
Profit	**45,000**	**1,07,000**	**1,69,000**	**2,00,000**

Problem 6 :

The statement given below gives the flexible budget at 60% capacity. Prepare a tabulated statement giving the budget figures at 75% capacity and 90% capacity.

Where no indication has been given make your own classification of expenses between fixed and variable overhead.

Expenses	At 60% Capacity (Rs.)
Direct Materials	1,60,000
Direct Labour	40,000
Indirect Materials and Spares	48,000
Depreciation	60,000
Indirect Labour	40,000
Rent	12,000
Electric Power (40% Fixed)	8,000
Repairs and Maintenance (40% Variable)	20,000
Insurance of Machinery	12,000

Solution

Working Notes

1) Semi-variable overheads - Electricity

Fixed Portion = 40% of Rs. 8000 = 3,200

Variable portion at 60% capacity = 8000-3200 = 4,800

Variable portion at 75% capacity = $\frac{4800}{60} \times 75 = 6,000$

Total cost = Fixed Cost portion + Variable cost portion

Total electricity at 75% capacity = 3,200 + 6,000 = 9,200

Variable portion of electricity at 90% capacity = $\frac{4,800}{60} \times 90 = 7,200$

Total electricity cost 90% capacity = 3,200 + 7,200 = Rs. 10,400

2) Repairs & Maintenance

Fixed portion of cost - 60% of 20,000 = 12,000

Variable portion at 60% capacity - 40% of 20,000 = 8,000

Variable portion at 75% capacity = $\frac{8000}{60\%} \times 75\%$ = 10,000

a) Total maintenance and repairs at 75% capacity = 12,000 + 10,000 = Rs. 22,000

Variable portion of cost at 90% capacity = $\frac{8000}{60\%} \times 90\%$ = Rs. 12,000

Total repairs and maintenance cost at 90% capacity = 12,000 + 12,000 = 24,000

Fixed Budget

Expenses	Basis	60%	75%	90%
(A) Variable cost				
Direct Material	100% variable	1,60,000	2,00,000	2,40,000
Direct Labour	100% variable	40,000	50,000	60,000
Indirect Materials & Spares	100% variable	48,000	60,000	72,000
Indirect Labour	100% variable	40,000	50,000	60,000
(B) Semi-Variable Overheads				
Electric Power	40% fixed 60% variable	8,000	9,200	10,400
Repairs & Maintenance	60% Fixed 40% variable	20,000	22,000	24,000
(C) Fixed Overheads				
Depreciation	100% fixed	60,000	60,000	60,000
Rent	100% fixed	12,000	12,000	12,000
Insurance	100% fixed	12,000	12,000	12,000
	Total	**4,00,000**	**4,75,200**	**5,50,400**

Problem 7

With the help of following data at 80% capacity draw up a Flexible Budget for overhead expenses and determine the overhead rates at 70% and 90% plant capacity.

	At 80% Capacity (Rs.)
Variable Overheads :	
Indirect Labour	12,000
Stores including spares	4,000
Semi - Variable Overheads :	
Power (30% Fixed, 70% variable)	20,000
Repairs and Maintenance (60% Fixed, 40% Variable)	2000
Fixed Overheads :	
Depreciation	11,000
Insurance	3,000
Salaries	10,000
Total Overheads	62,000

Esitmated Direct Labour Hours at 80 % capacity : 1,24,000 Hrs.

Solution: **In the books of Company-Flexible Budget**

Normal Activity....... **Capacity : 80 %**

Production (Units)		--	--	--
Capacity %		70	80	90
		Rs.	Rs.	Rs.
Variable Overheads :		10,500	12,000	13,500
Indirect Labour		3,500	4,000	4,500
Stores including spares				
Semi - Variable Overheads :				
Power	Rs. 20,000			
a) Fixed 30%	Rs. 6,000	6,000	6,000	6,000
b) Variable 70%	Rs. 14,000	12,250	14,000	15,750
Repairs & Maint	Rs. 2,000			
a) Fixed 60%	Rs. 1,200	1,200	1,200	1,200
b) Variable 40%	Rs. 800	700	800	900
Fixed Overheads				
Depreciation		11,000	11,000	11,000
Insurance		3,000	3,000	3,000
Salaries		10,000	10,000	10,000
Total Overheads		58,150	62,000	65,850
		Total Overheads / **Direct Labour hours**		
		Rs.58,150	Rs. 62,000	Rs. 65,850
Overhead Recovery Rate (on the basis of direct labour hours)		Hrs. 1,08,500	Hrs. 1,24,000	Hrs. 1,39,500
		Rs 0.536	Rs. 0.500	Rs. 0.472

Master Budget

A Master budget is the summary of all the functional budgets taken together. The Master Budget is finally approved, adopted and implemented by the management. Thus when all the functional budgets are prepared and consolidated into a master budget we can get the :

a) Budgeted Profit and Loss Account.

b) Budgeted Profit and Loss Appropriation Account.

c) Budgeted Balance Sheet

Thus a Master Budget shows an overall business plan and contains the financial statements which we prepare as usual. But the only difference between a Master budget and the financial statement is that in case of a Master Budget, the budgeted figure i.e. estimated amounts are taken , while in case of the financial statements prepared by the Account department, the past data is considered i.e. the accounts are prepared from the vouchers for which the expenses have already been incurred.

The Master budget is prepared by the Budget Committee on the basis of the consolidated functional budgets. When the Master budget is approved by the management, it becomes the business plan of the company.

When the functional budget have been drawn up, a Master budget can be built up by summarising all the functional budgets and expressing and incorporating them under Budgeted Profit and Loss Account and a Budgeted Balance Sheet. Such Master Budget must contain the budgeted profit and loss account for the current year as well as for previous year showing clearly why there has been a change.

The following specimen of budgeted profit and loss account and the budgeted balance sheet, provides the summary of all revenue accounts and the summary of all capital items respectively.

MASTER BUDGET (Figures are imaginary)

A) Budgeted Profit and Loss account for the year ending 31st March 200X

Items	Budget Period		Budget Period	
	Amount Rs.	Percent %	Amount Rs.	Percent %
Sales	50,000	100	40,000	100
Less : Cost of production	30,000	60	24,800	62
Gross Profit (A)	20,000	40	15,200	38
Less : Operating Expenses				
Administrative	2,500	5	2,200	5.5
Selling and Distribution	3,500	7	3,000	7.5
Advertisemt	1,000	2	1,000	2.5
Total (B)	7,000	14	6,200	15.5
Operating Profit (A - B)	13,000	26	9,000	22.5
Add : Other income (Investments)	600	1.2	600	1.5
Net Profit before Tax	13,600	27.2	9,600	24.0

Note : Appropriations are not shown in this account.

B) Budgeted Balance - Sheet

Liabilities	Budgeted Year (Rs.)	Previous Year (Rs.)	Assets	Budgeted Year (Rs.)	Previous Year (Rs.)
Share Capital			**Fixed Assets (Net)**		
Equity Shares	1,25,000	1,25,000	Buildings	90,000	1,00,000
Reserves & Surplus			Plant & Machinery	22,500	25,000
General Reserves	25,000	25,000	Furniture & Fixtures	22,500	25,000
Profit and Loss	22,500	17,500	**Current Assets**		
Current Liabilities			Stocks	19,000	20,000
Creditors	11,500	25,000	Debtors	10,000	12,500
			Cash & Bank	20,000	10,000
	1,84,000	**1,92,500**		**1,84,000**	**1,92,500**

Operational & Functional Budgets

A functional budget is one which relates to any of the functions of an organisation, e.g. sales, production, personnel etc. The Master budget is prepared based on the functional budget. Generally the following are the functional budgets prepared :

a) Sales budget
b) Selling and Distribution cost budget .
c) Production budget
d) Production cost budget
e) Plant Utilization budget
f) Capital expenditure budget
g) Purchase budget
h) Personnel budget
i) Administrative cost budget
j) Research and Development cost budget

If all the above budget are preapared, it is possible to consolidate them and prepare the budgeted profit & Loss Account and the budgeted Profit and Loss Appropriation Account.

The next step would be to prepare the Cash budget and Budgeted Balance sheet .

Purchase Budget

This budget is prepared to show the purchases to be made during the budget period.
It includes the direct and indirect materials to be purchased and also the services required by the management. In case of trading business where the finished goods are purchased for resale, the purchase budget should take into account the requirements of finished goods which are to be resold. The purchase budget is either shown in terms of quantity or money.

The purchase budget is mainly based upon

a) Sales budget
b) Production cost budget
c) Estimated requirements of raw materials, supplies or brought out components.
d) Maximum, Minimum and Economic Order Quantity.

The purpose of preparing the purchase budget are

a) To estimate the cash requirement for the purchases to be made during the budget period
b) To enable the Purchase department to chalk out its plans for timely purchases.

Practical Problems

Problem 1

In a company the Sales Executive expects to sale 60,000 units of Water Cooler for the year 200X. For producing one water cooler the Production Manager has estimated the requirements of raw materials as :

A - 4 Units

B - 6 Units

The opening and closing balances of the finished good and raw materials estimated are as follows :

Item	Opening balance at the beginning of the next Year (Units)	Closing Balance at the end of the next Year (Units)
A	10,000	11,000
B	15,000	17,000
Finished goods	8,000	11,000

Prepare a Purchase Budget showing the quantities of materials to be purchased

Solution :

First we have to prepare the Production Budget and from this we can estimate the purchases and draw the Purchases Budget as shown below ;

Production Budget for the year 200X

Item	Units
Estimated Sales for the year	60,000
Add: Closing balance (estimated)	11,000
	71,000
Less: Opening balance (estimated)	8,000
Estimated Production	**63,000**

Purchase budget for the year 200X

Item	Material A Units	Material B Units
Annual requirement of Materials		
A : 63,000 x 4	2,52,000	
B : 63,000 x 6		3,78,000
Add : Stock to be maintained at the end of the year	11,000	17,000
	2,63,000	**3,95,000**
Less: Stock at the beginning of the year	(-) 10,000	(-) 15,000
Quantity to be purchased	**2,53,000**	**3,80,000**

Problem 2

Nashik Soap Factory uses the combination of two materials X and Y which constitute 75% and 25% of the total output in units. They estimate a sale of 500 quintals of soap during the month of July 200X. The estimates for the opening and closing stocks are as follows.

Item	Opening Stock Quintals	Closing Stock Quintals
X	100	140
Y	80	300
Finished Goods	70	90

The expected purchase price of the two materials were :

X : Rs. 600 per Quintal   Y : Rs. 500 per Quintal

Prepare

a) Production Budget   b) Material Consumption Budget   c) Purchase Budget (showing cost)

Solution

a) Production Budget

	Quintals
Sales (estimated)	**500**
Add: Closing Stock	90
	590
Less: Opening Stock	70
Production (quintats)	**520**

b) Material Consumption Budget

	Materials X	Materials Y
Ratio in proportion of 520 quintals (3:1)	390	130

(c) Purchase Budget

	X	Y
Material required for production	390	130
Add. Closing Stock	140	300
	530	430
Less: Opening Stock	(-) 100	(-) 80
Material to be purchased	430	350
Purchase price per quintal	Rs.600	Rs.500
Cost (430 x 600) (350 x 500)	2,58,000	1,75,000
Total Cost	**Rs. 4,33,000**	

Production Budget

This budget is prepared after the sales budget because the sales to be made are estimated in the sales budget so that how much quantity should be produced can be known. Thus, a production budget is one which is an estimate for the quantities of goods to be purchased during the budget period. It is expressed either in units or standard hours. The following factors should be taken into consideration while preparing the production budget.

(a) Forecast of sales
(b) Requirement of stock to be maintained
(c) Plant capacity
(d) Spares and components to be purchased
(e) Make or buy decisions
(f) Production cycle
(g) Production policy of management.

Production budget can be drawn in the following way

Particulars			Product	
			Unit A	Unit B
	Sales		....	....
Add:	Closing Stock	(+)	....	....
			....	....
Less:	Opening Stock	(-)	....	....
	Production		....	....

An analysis of the above factors will suggest the amount of goods that can be produced within the factory. If the calculated production is less than the budgeted sales, then the firm will not be in a position to maintain the sales budget and earn sufficient profits for which potential exists. In such a situation, the firm should explore the following possibilities before taking a final decision on production budget.

1. Can the inventory level be reduced ?
2. Can the plant utilization capacity be increased or additional plant installed to fill the gap ?

Problem 1

OCL India Ltd. has budgetd sales as under :

Months	Black Cement	White Cement
July 2005	5,000	2,000
August	10,000	4,000
September	12,000	5,000
October	15,000	6,000
November	13,500	5,000
December	10,000	6,550
January 2006	12,000	5,000
	77,500	33,550

The company maintains inventory equal to half of the sales for next month and there is no work-in-progress at the end of any month.

Prepare the production Budget for the half year ending on 31-12-200X.

Solution

In the Books of OCL India Co.Ltd.
Production Budget
for the half year ending 31-12-200X

	Product Y		July	August	Sept.	Oct.	Nov.	Dec.
	Black Cement							
	Budgeted Sales		5,000	10,000	12,000	15,000	13,500	10,000
Add:	Closing Inventories		5,000	6,000	7,500	6,750	5,000	6,000
	(50% of next month)	+						
			10,000	16,000	19,500	21,750	18,500	16,000
Less:	Opening Inventories	-	2,500	5,000	6,000	7,500	6,750	5,000
	Budgeted Production		7,500	11,000	13,500	14,250	11,750	11,000
	White Cement							
	Budgeted Sales		2,000	4,000	5,000	6,000	5,000	6,550
Add:	Closing Inventory	+	1,000	2,500	3,000	2,500	3,275	2,500
			3,000	6,500	8,000	8,500	8,275	9,050
Less:	Opening Inventory	-	1,000	1,000	2,500	3,000	2,500	3,275
	Budgeted Production		2,000	5,500	5,500	5,500	5,775	5,775

Problem 2

Padmini Ltd. estimates its quaterwise sales as under:

1st Quarter	IInd Quarter	IIIrd Quarter	IVth Quarter	Vth Quarter
1,00,000 (Units)	1,20,000 (Units)	1,32,000 (Units)	1,44,000 (Units)	1,68,000 (Units)

The Opening Stock was 20,000 units. The company has decided to keep Closing Stock equal to 1/12th of the sales of the sales of the next quarter. Show what should be the production in each quarter for the current year?

Solution

1. Note that there are four quarters in a year. The Vth quarter is shown of the next year for calcuation of the Closing Stock. Hence, in the Production cost budget only 4 quartes should be taken.
2. The Closing Stock of each year becomes the Opening Stock of the next year.

In the Books of Padmini Ltd.
Production Budget (Units)
for the quarter ended ....

	Particulars		1st Unit	IInd Unit	IIIrd Unit	IVth Unit
	Sales		1,00,000	1,20,000	1,32,000	1,44,000
Add:	Closing Stock	(+)	10,000	11,000	12,000	14,000
			1,10,000	1,31,000	1,44,000	1,58,000
Less:	Opening Stock	(-)	20,000	10,000	11,000	12,000
∴	**Estimated Production**		**90,000**	**1,21,000**	**1,33,000**	**1,46,000**

Production Cost Budget

This budget is prepared after the Production Budget. This budget shows the details of the estimated costs which are required to be incurred as per the quantities shown in the production budget. The details include materials cost, labour cost, and overheads. The overheads again include variable, semi-variable and fixed costs. The costs are classified and analysed according to the products or departments.

The production cost budget depends upon:

(a) Production budget (b) Estimated increase in wages, salaries and expenses.

(c) Estimated increase / decrease in the price of raw materials and other supplies.

Proforma of the Prodution Cost Budget

Production Cost Budget

	Periods	
	Department	**Total**
Units to be produced as per production budget		
Costs :		
(a) Direct Material	....	
(b) Direct Labour	....	
(c) Direct Expenses	....	....
(d) Factory Overheads		
Variable	....	
Semi-variable	....	
Fixed	....	
Total	....	....
(e) Production Cost (a+b+c+d)	....	....

Problem 1

Rajdoot Co Ltd. gives the following production costs,

Particulars	Rs.	Rs.
Direct Material Cost		1,50,000
Direct Labour Cost		80,000
Factory Overheads :		
Variable	50,000	
Fixed +	25,000	75,000

The estimates made by the Production Manager for the next year about the various changes are as below:

(a) Production will rise by 10%

(b) There will be decrease in labour cost by 2% due to more efficiency of the labourers.

(c) Direct material price will increase by 5%.

Draw a Production Cost Budget.

Solution

Working Notes

1. Production will rise by 10% = Rs.1,50,000 + 10% of Rs.1,50,000

   Hence, Direct Material Cost = Rs.1,65,000

But again Direct Material price will increase by 5% which means,

If 100 - 105

$\therefore$ Rs. 1,65,000 - ? $= \frac{105}{100} \times \frac{\text{Rs. } 1,65,000}{1} = \text{Rs. } 1,73,250$

2. Direct labour cost will decrease by 2%. Hence, first 10% rise in production,

= Rs. 80,000 + 10% of Rs. 80,000

= Rs. 88,000

If 100 = 98

$\therefore$ Rs.88,000 = ? $= \frac{\text{Rs. } 88,000}{100} \times \frac{98}{1} = \text{Rs. } 86,240$

In the Books of Rajdoot Co.Ltd.

Production Cost Budget

for the year ended ....

	Particulars		Original Budget Rs.	Revised Budget Rs.
	Direct Material		1,50,000	1,73,250
Add :	Direct Labour	(+)	80,000	86,240
	Prime Cost		2,30,000	2,59,490
Add :	Factory Overheads :			
	(i) Variable		50,000	55,000
	(ii) Fixed	(+)	25,000	25,000
	Total Cost		3,05,000	3,39,490

Problem 2

The following information has been made available from the records of Siemens India Ltd. for the last six months of 2004 (and the sale of only January 2005) in respect of Product A

(a) The units to be sold in different months are :

	Units		Units
July	1,100	August	1,100
September	1,700	October	1,900
November	2,500	December	2,300
January	2,000		

(b) There will be no work-in-progress at the end of any month.

(c) Finished units equal to half of sales for the next month will be in Stock at the end of every month (including June).

(d) Budgeted Production and Production Cost for the year ending 31-12-2004

Production (Units)	22,000
Direct Material per unit	Rs. 10.00
Direct Wages per unit	Rs. 4.00
Total Factory Overheads apportioned to product	Rs. 88,000

Prepare

(a) A Production Budget for each of the last six months of 2004

(b) A summarised production cost budget for the same period.

Solution

In the Books of Siemens India Ltd.

(a) Production Budget for six months ended 31-12-2004

Particulars	July	August	Sept	Oct	Nov	Dec
Sales (in units)	1,100	1,100	1,700	1,900	2,500	2,300
Add : Closing Stock half of sales for the next month	550	850	950	1,250	1,150	1,000
	1,650	1,950	2,650	3,150	3,650	3,300
Less : Opening Stock last months Closing Stock	550	550	850	950	1,250	1,150
Production in units	**1,100**	**1,400**	**1,800**	**2,200**	**2,400**	**2,150**

(b) Production Cost Budget for six months ended 31-12-2004

Production for six months (July to Dec.) =

= (1,100 + 1,400 + 1,800 + 2,200 + 2,400 + 2,150 units) = 11,050 units

	Particulars		Rs.
	Direct Materials @ Rs.10 per unit		1,10,500
Add :	Direct Wages @ Rs.4 per unit	(+)	44,200
Add :	Factory Overheads (88,000 x 1/2)	(+)	44,000
	Total Production Cost		**1,98,700**

Sales Budget

A Sales Budget is a statement expressed in physical quantities or/and values of anticipated sales during a specified period of time. Sales forecasting is the basic step in the preparation of a sales budget. It is done by sales department under the charge of a Sales Manager in consultation and co-operation with the Budget Controller. The forecasting of sales is not an easy job. It requires a lot of skill and knowledge in the techniques of sales forecasting, collection of relevant facts and figure and an understanding of business environment in which the firm is placed. The techniques of sales forecasting for new products are different from those used for established products.

In case of established products, historical data relating to sales quantities and expenditure on sales campaign are available within the firm. The sales department also possesses good knowledge about its market share, nature of competition, availability of substitutes, consumers preferences etc. The sales data for the last few years are compiled in a form which is known as "Time Series" which is statistically dealt to fit a trend line and extrapolate the sales figures for future. This technique is quite simple and widely used by business firms for the purpose of sales forecasting. However, it can be profitably used only if the Time Series do not show violent fluctuations and corrections are rightly made for seasonal and stochastic variations.

The amount of sales in any given period is much affected by the amount spent on advertisement and other sales promotion techniques. A study of correlation between expenditure on advertisement and amount of sales in different time periods will reveal the degree of impact of advertising cost on amount of sales. Thus, sales should be predicted only after due consideration to the advertisement budget for the period for which sales budget is being prepared.

It is the first budget which is prepared in most of the organisation, Sales budget is the most diffcult budget and the success of budget system of the whole organisation depends upon the sales budget. A sales budget indicates the number of units, to be sold, at what price and what types of products are to be sold.

The Sales Manager is responsible for the preparation of the sales budget. He is supported by the salesmen and also the market research department. While preparing the sales budget the following factors are considered :

(a) Post Sales Cost
(b) Future economic, industrial and market conditions
(c) Threat of competition
(d) Amount to be spent on advertisement.
(e) Intutuion of the Sales Manager.
(f) Profitability of the product.
(g) Market research studies.
(h) Pricing policies.
(i) Competitions
(j) Plant capacity
(k) Sales trends of other joint products if any.

The consideration of prevailing and expected economic environment within and outside the industry is essential before any decision on budgeted sales is taken. The management should give proper valuation in their estimation for sales for factors such as the structure of national income, Government fiscal and monetary policies, industrial policy, import-export policy, demographic structure etc, in so far as they influence the demand for firm's products.

In a modern age of competition, sales is generally a limiting factor. In case of certain products, sales may not be a constraint and the estimated sales might be much higher than the production facilities available within the firm. Under such a situation, the possibilities of increasing production should be found out and the production budget can be prepared first.

The data of budgeted sales can be arranged in a number of ways. They can be grouped according to commodity, territory or salesman-wise. Consider the following form of a sales budget according to commodity-wise.

Proforma of Sales Budget (Specimen)

Sales Budget
for the six months ending 30th June, 200X

Months	Product A		Product B		Total	
	Quantity	Value	Quantity	Value	Quantity	Value

Problem 1

Titan Ltd. has estimated the sales of three products O, P and Q. Following are the particulars of the three products.

Product

	O	P	Q
Quantities	5,000 units	10,000 units	15,000 units
Selling price per unit	Rs.1,500	Rs.2,000	Rs.2,500

Prepare a Sales Budget.

Solution

In the Books of Titan Ltd.
Sales Budget
for the year ended period .....

Product	Budgeted SalesUnits	Selling Price per unit	Value of Sales
		Rs.	Rs.
O	5,000	1,500	75,00,000
P	10,000	2,000	2,00,00,000
Q	15,000	2,500	3,75,00,000
Total	30,000	----	6,50,00,000

Problem 2

United Brew Ltd. sells its products in two regions i.e.Mumbai and Thane of the two products X and Y. The budgeted sales for the six months ended 30th june 200X in each of the areas i.e.Mumbai and Thane are as follows :

Mumbai	X	2,000 Units
	Y	1,000 Units
Thane	X	1,500 Units
	Y	1,200 Units

The actual sales for the period ended 30th June 200X were as follows :

Mumbai	X	2,500 Units
	Y	1,100 Units
Thane	X	1,600 Units
	Y	1,200 Units

The budgeted selling price and the actual price per unit were the same which are as follows :

For	X	by 8 per Unit
	Y	by 5 per Unit

From the market survey report it is found that the sales of both the products can be increased over the budgeted units of 30th June 200X for the next six months ending 31-12-200X as given below :

Mumbai	X	by 500 Units
	Y	by 200 Units
Thane	X	by 100 Units
	Y	by 80 Units

Prepare Sales Budget for six months for the period ended 31st December 200X. Also prepare the budgeted and actual sales for the period ended 30th June 200X.

In the Books of United Brew Ltd.

		Budget 31-12-200X			Budget 30-06-200X			Actual 30-06-200X		
Region	Product	Quantity Units	Rate Rs.	Amount Rs.	Quantity Units	Rate Rs.	Amount Rs.	Quantity Units	Rate Rs.	Amount Rs.
Mumbai	X	2,500	8	20,000	2,000	8	16,000	2,500	8	20,000
	Y	1,200	5	6,000	1,000	5	5,000	1,100	5	5,500
	Total	3,700	-	26,000	3,000	-	21,000	3,600	-	25,500
Thane	X	1,600	8	12,800	1,500	8	12,000	1,600	8	12,800
	Y	1,280	5	6,400	1,200	5	6,000	1,200	5	6,000
	Total	2,880	-	19,200	2,700	-	18,000	2,800	-	18,800
	X	4,100	-	32,800	3,500	-	28,000	4,100	-	32,800
	Y	2,480	-	12,400	2,200	-	11,000	2,300	-	11,500
	Total	6,580	-	45,200	5,700	-	39,000	6,400	-	44,300

Problem 3

Voltas Ltd. sell two products X and Y. The following estimates are given for the year 200X.

Sales Budget (Units)

Particulars	1st Quarter Rs.	IInd Quarter Rs.	IIIrd Quarter Rs.	IVth Quarter Rs.
Product X	1,00,000	1,40,000	90,000	1,20,000
Product Y	90,000	1,20,000	1,00,000	1,10,000

Product X is sold @ Rs.100 per unit, while product Y is sold @ Rs.200 per unit. Satyam Traders incurs selling and distribution expenses @ 3% of the sales value. Bad debts amount to 1% of the sales value.

You are required to prepare a Sales Budget for the year 200X.

Solution

In the Books of Voltas Ltd.

Sales Budget

for the year 200X

(Rs.in thousands)

Particulars	1st Quarter Rs.	IInd Quarter Rs.	IIIrd Quarter Rs.	IVth Quarter Rs.	Total Rs.
Product X	10,000	14,000	9,000	12,000	45,000
Product Y (+)	18,000	24,000	20,000	22,000	84,000
Total Sales	**28,000**	**38,000**	**29,000**	**34,000**	**1,29,000**
Less : Selling and Distribution Expenses @ 3% of Sales value	840	1,140	870	1,020	3,870
Bad Debts @ 1% of sales value (+)	280	380	290	340	1,290
	1,120	1,520	1,160	1,360	5,160
Net Sales	**26,880**	**36,480**	**27,840**	**32,640**	**1,23,840**

Problem 4

Wimco Ltd. manufactures two types of cement known as 'Black' and 'White'. The cement is sold in the three states of Rajasthan, Haryana and Punjab through stock dealers. From the following data relating to budget period ended on 30th June, 200X and the adjoining information, you are required to prepare a Sales Budget for 6 months period beginning from 1st July and ending on 31st December, 200X.

Commodity	Territories					
	Rajasthan		Punjab		Haryana	
	Budgeted	Actual	Budgeted	Actual	Budgeted	Actual
Black Cement	25,000	24,000	20,000	18,000	10,000	10,000
White Cement	15,000	12,000	10,000	10,000	5,000	4,500
Total	40,000	36,000	30,000	28,000	15,000	14,500

Other Information

1. The construction activity is expected to go up by 10% and accordingly the demand in all states except in Punjab, is likely to increase in the budget period. The Sales Department visualises a decrease in sales by 5% in Punjab.
2. The company has decided to appoint few more dealers in Rajasthan and it forecasts an additional sales of 5,000 bags of black cement through the new dealers.
3. With a vigorous advertisement campaign, the demand in Haryana for both black and white cement is likely to increase by 20% in addition to the 10% as pointed out above.
4. The company expects to make direct supplies to local bodies in the states of Rajasthan and Haryana. It proposes to sell 2,000 bags of black cement in each of these states.
5. Adequate production facilities exist and there is no limiting factors.
6. The selling price per bag is estimated at Rs. 60 and 100 for black and white cement respectively.

Solution

In the Books of Wimco Ltd.

Sales Budget

for the six months ended 31-12-200X

Territories	For 1st Jan. to 30th June 200X				For 1st July to 31st Dec. 200X			
	Black Cement (Bags)		White Cement (bags)		Budgeted for six months			
	Budgeted	Actuals	Budgeted	Actuals	Black	White	Black	White
	Black	Black	White	White	(Bags)	(Bags)	(Rs.)	(Rs.)
Rajasthan	25,000	24,000	15,000	12,000	33,000	13,200	20,04,000	13,20,000
Punjab	20,000	18,000	10,000	10,000	17,100	9,500	10,26,000	9,50,000
Haryana	10,000	10,000	5,000	4,500	15,000	5,850	9,00,000	5,85,000
Total	**55,000**	**52,000**	**30,000**	**26,500**	**65,000**	**28,550**	**39,30,000**	**28,55,000**

Statement of Sales Forecast (Bags)

Sales	Rajasthan		Punjab		Haryana	
	Black	White	Black	White	Black	White
Present Sale	24,000	12,000	18,000	10,000	10,000	4,500
Increase due to construction activity (10% of existing)	+2,400	+1,200	-	-	+1,000	+450
Estimated decrease for Punjab (5%)	-	-	(-)900	(-)500	-	-
Additional sales by new dealers	+5,000	-	-	-	-	-
Increase due to massive advertising campaign (20% of existing)	-	-	-	-	+2,000	+900
Direct Supplies	+2,000	-	-	-	+2,000	-
Total	33,400	13,200	17,100	9,500	15,000	5,850

Problem5

Yashwant Traders sells two products viz. Bee and Dee. The following are the estimates regarding sales during 200X

Particulars	First Quarter Units	Second Quarter Units	Third Quarter Units	Fourth Quarter Units	Total Units
Product-Bee	9,000	23,000	30,000	80,000	1,42,000
Product-Dee	8,500	7,500	5,500	8,500	30,000

Both the products are sold on seasonal basis. Product=Bee tends to sell better in summer while Product-Dee sells better in winter. Product-Bee is sold @ 10 per unit whereas Product-Dee @ Rs. 20 per unit. Past experiences reveal that the firm is unable to realise 1% of their total sales value and spends 2% of it for carriage and 3% of it for advertising purposes. Prepare a Sales Budget for the year 200X incorporating the above mentioned information.

Solution

In the Books of Yeshwant Traders
Sales Budget
for the year 200X

Particulars	First Quarter Rs.	Second Quarter Rs.	Third Quarter Rs.	Fourth Quarter Rs.	Total Rs.
Actual Sales :					
(i) Product Bee @ Rs.10 per unit	90,000	2,30,000	3,00,000	80,000	7,00,000
(ii) Product Dee- @ Rs.20 per unit (+)	1,70,000	1,50,000	1,10,000	1,70,000	6,00,000
∴ **Total Sales Value (A)**	**2,60,000**	**3,80,000**	**4,10,000**	**2,50,000**	**13,00,000**

Less : Selling and Distribution Expenses					
(i) Bad Debts - @ 1% of Total Sales Value	2,600	3,800	4,100	2,500	13,000
(ii) Carriage Outward - @ 2% of Total Sales Value	5,200	7,600	8,200	5,000	26,000
(iii) Advertisement - @ 3% of Total Sales Value	7,800	11,400	12,300	7,500	39,000
∴ **Total Expenses (B)**	**15,600**	**22,800**	**24,600**	**15,000**	**78,000**
∴ **Total Sales (A -B) (C)**	**2,44,400**	**3,57,200**	**3,85,400**	**2,35,000**	**12,22,000**

Cash Budget

Cash budget is the forecast of cash position for a particular period. Cash budget is prepared after all the functional budgets are prepared. Cash budget is important because unless there is liquid cash, the budgeted profit has no meaning. Cash budget is prepared either weekly or monthly.

Necessity of Cash Budget

a) To get the working capital easily from the banks and for smooth running of the business.

b) To enable the top management to make necessary arrangements of cash in case of emergency.

c) To invest excess cash.

d) To know the exact amount of cash required for the business.

Cash budgeting helps the companies to plan for dividend and interest payments. It also help in ascertaining the cash requirements for future years. When a company requires more long-term capital, cash budget helps in planning for such long-term capital requirements. The management comes to know which type of capital is required to be raised e.g. equity capital, or fixed deposits from the public or from Banks and financial institutions. If there is no cash budgeting, the management will have to run for finance and borrow from sources which are more expensive.

Methods of Preparation of Cash Budget

There are three methods of preparing cash budget.

A) Receipts and Payments Method. B) Adjusted Profit and loss Method

C) The Balance Sheet Method

Usually, the first method i.e. the Receipts and payments method is used for short-term cash budget. The other two methods mentioned above are used for long-term cash budgets.

A) Receipt and Payment Method

According to this method. Cash Budget includes all the cash receipts whether they are on revenue account or capital account. Similarly all expected capital and revenue expenditures are brought in a cash budget. The accruals i.e. income earned but not received and expenditure due but not paid are excluded from the cash budget. Thus a cash budget is a sort of cash account which records cash receipts and cash payments and shows expected cash balance at the end of the budget period. The information for cash budget is derived from other budgets. For example, the sales budget will provide the amount of sales and the receipts from sales and realization from debtors can be estimated by taking into account the terms of sales. The raw materials purchase budget, labour budget and overheads budget will provide information relating to payments for raw materials, wages and overhead charges.

The management can forecast payments on account of capital expenditure, tax, dividend etc. The difference of cash receipts and cash payments, for a period is either positive or negative, which is carried to next period.

In this method, all the cash receipts which are expected to be received and all the cash payments which are expected to be made are taken into account. Thus the cash balance will represent the difference between the total cash receipts expected (including the opening cash balance) and the total cash payments to be made.

The following are the sources and application of cash.

Sources

a) From customers (debtors). This can be ascertained from the Sales budget. The terms and conditions of sale, lag in payments and other factors should be considered while estimating the cash receipts.

b) Cash receipts from other sources viz. Dividends received, interest on investments, rent received, sale of investments, sale of fixed assets etc.

Application

a) Cash payments for purchase of raw materials, payment of wages and other expenses are estimated from the various budgets viz. Purchase budgets, personnel budget and overhead / expenses budget. The suppliers credit period, terms and conditions of purchases, cash discount allowed, lag in payment of wages, etc. should be considered.

b) Cash payments of capital expenditure can be ascertained from the capital expenditure budget.

c) Cash payments for dividends, income tax etc.

Problem 1

From the following budget prepare Cash Budget for 3 months Febuary to April 2005

Months	Sales	Purchases	Wages	Overheads.
January	85,000	48,000	10,000	12,500
February	90,000	52,000	11,000	13,500
March	1,20,000	60,000	14,000	15,000
April	1,30,000	62,000	14,000	16,000

Other Information

1) 20% sales is for cash and the remaining amount is realised in the month following that of sales.
2) Suppliers supply raw materials at one months credit.
3) Wage-bill is paid in the first week of next month.
4) Overheads are paid in cash.
5) Monthly rent payment is Rs. 1,000
6) Advance Income Tax of Rs. 15,000 is payable in April.
7) Bonus of Rs. 10,000 is payable to workers in Feb.
8) Plant costing Rs. 80,000 is due to be installed in Feb. The bill will be paid in March.
9) Interest on 12% 50,000 debentures is realised in Feb. and August every year.
10) Cash balance on Ist Feb. Rs. 5,000

Solution

Cash Budget for the 3 Months Period (Febuary to April 2000)

	Febuary	March	April
Receipts			
Opening balance	5,000	11,500	(- 51,500)
Cash sales	18,000	24,000	26,000
Collection from debtors (80% of 85,000)	68,000	72,000	96,000
Debenture Interest (6 months)	3,000	--	--
Total	94,000	1,07,500	70,500
Payments			
Purchases	48,000	52,000	60,000
Wages	10,000	11,000	14,000
Overheads	13,500	15,000	16,500
Rent	1,000	1,000	1,000
Bonus	10,000	--	--
Income Tax	--	--	15,000
Plant	--	80,000	--
Total	82,500	1,59,000	1,06,000
Closing Balance	11,500	(- 51,500)	(- 35,500)

B) Adjusted Profit and Loss Method

Under this method the profit as shown in the Profit and Loss Account prepared in the conventional manner forms the basis for cash forecast. The profit is adjusted by adding back to in the non-cash items such as depreciation, outstanding expenses, other provisions etc. The other items which increase the total cash inflows are the increase in share capital, debenture and loans, current liabilities (creditors) and decrease in fixed assets, debtors and stock etc. Out of the total cash-inflows calculated as above, the items which results in cash outflow are subtracted to arrive at the cash position at the end of the period. The items which reduce the cash position are accrued incomes, advance payments, dividend payment, redemption of debentures and loans, decrease in creditors, payment for fixed assets, increase in debtors and stock etc. This method of cash forecast may also be called as the Cash Flow Statement method as the net income as per the conventional income Statement is converted into a cash flow forecast. These are main sources of information for cash forecast as per this method and the profit and loss account and balance sheet. This method is suitable to prepare a long-period cash budget.

Problem 2

From the following Balance Sheet and Projected Profit and Loss Account, prepare the Cash Budget according to adjusted Profit and Loss Account method.

Balance Sheet
for the Year Ended on 31st Dec., 2004

Liabilities	Rs.	Assets	Rs.
Share Capital	1,50,00,000	Land and Buildings	1,25,000,00
General Reserve	0,50,00,000	Plant and Machinery	80,000,00
Profit and Loss A/c.	0,25,00,000	Furniture and fixtures	0,15,000,00
Debentures	0,80,00,000	Sundry debtors	0,75,000,00
Creditors	1,00,00,000	Stock	50,00,000
Bills Payable	0,20,00,000	Bills Receivable	10,00,000
Outstanding Salaries	0,3,00,000	Prepaid Rent	3,00,000
		Cash at bank and in hand	70,00,000
	4,28,000,000		4,28,000,000

Projected Profit and Loss Account for the Year Ended on 31st December, 2005

		Rs.		Rs.
To Opening Stock		50,00,000	By Sales	3,00,00,000
To Purchases		2,25,00,000	By Closing Stock	45,00,000
To Gross Profit C/d.		70,00,000		
		3,45,00,000		3,45,00,000
To Salaries	10,00,000			
Less : last years			By Gross profit b/d.	70,00,000
outstanding	(-) 3,00,000			
	7,00,000			
Add : outstanding	+ 1,00,000	8,00,000		
To commission		1,50,000		
To Rent	9,00,000			
Add : last years				
prepaid	(+) 3,00,000	12,00,000		
To Interest		8,00,000		
To Establishment charges		2,50,000		
To Advertising expenses		2,00,000		
To Depreciation :				
Plant & Machinery	8,00,000			
Land & Building	6,00,000			
Furniture	1,50,000	15,50,000		
To Net Profit		20,50,000		
		70,00,000		70,00,000
To Dividend		30,00,000	By Net Profit (31.12.2004)	25,00,000
To General Reserve		10,00,000	By Profit for 2005	20,50,000
To Balance carried		5,50,000		
		45,50,000		45,50,000

On 31st Dec. 2004 the position of some of the items was as under :

Share capital	:	2,00,00,000
Debentures	:	1,00,00,000
Creditors	:	80,00,000
Debtors	:	90,00,000
Bills Payable	:	25,00,000
Bills Receivable	:	8,00,000
Purchase of Plant and Machinery during 2004	:	28,00,000
Purchase of Furniture and Fixtures	:	21,50,000

Solution

Cash Budget (Adjusted Profit & Loss Method)
for the year ended on 31st December, 2005

Cash Balance (31.12.2004)			70,00,000
Add :			
Net Profit for 2005		20,50,000	
Depreciation :			
Plant and Machinery	8,00,000		
Land and Building	6,00,000		
Furniture	1,50,000		
		15,50,000	
Decrease in prepaid rent		3,00,000	
Decrease in stock		5,00,000	
Decrease in bills receivable		2,00,000	
Increase in bills payable		5,00,000	
Issue of share capital		50,00,000	
Issue of debentures		20,00,000	(+)1,21,00,000
			1,91,00,000
Less :			
Purchase of plant & machinery		28,00,000	
Purchase of furniture & fixtures		21,50,000	
Dividend		30,00,000	
Decrease in outstanding salaries		2,00,000	
Increase in debtors		15,00,000	
Decrease in creditors		20,00,000	(-) 1,16,50,000
Cash Balance as on 31st December 2005			74,50,000

C) Balance Sheet Method

As per this method a projected Balance Sheet is prepared in which cash balance is not an estimated item but a difference between total projected assets and total estimated liabilities. In other words, the excess of projected assets over projected liabilities represents cash balance. If the liabilities are more than the assets, the balance shows the overdraft.

Problem 3

Using the data of illustration No.2 prepare a projected Balance Sheet as on 31st December 2005 to show the Cash position as on that date :

Solution

Projected Balance Sheet as on 31st December, 2005

Liabilities	Rs.	Assets		Rs.
Share capital	2,00,00,000	Land and Buildings	1,25,00,000	
Debentures	1,00,00,000	Less : Depreciation	6,00,000	
				1,19,00,000
General Reserve	60,00,000	Plant & Machinery	80,00,000	
Profit & Loss A/c.	5,50,000	Less : Depreciation	8,00,000	
Creditors	80,00,000		72,00,000	
		Add : Purchases	28,00,000	1,00,00,000
Bills Payable	25,00,000			
Outstanding salaries	1,00,000	Furnitures & Fixtures	15,00,000	
		Less : Depreciation	1,50,000	
			13,50,000	
		Add : Purchases	21,50,000	35,00,000
		Debtors		90,00,000
		Bill Receivable		8,00,000
		Stock		45,00,000
		Cash and Bank Balance (Balancing figure)		74,50,000
	4,71,50,000			4,71,50,000

Proforma of Cash Budget

(I) Cash Budget for the period........

	January (Rs.)	February (Rs.)	March (Rs.)	Total (Rs.)
Particulars				
Opening Balance of Cash	----	----	----	----
Receipts :				
Cash Sales	----	----	----	----
Receipts from Debtors	----	----	----	----
Issue of Shares and Debentures, Dividends etc	----	----	----	----
Total (a)	----	----	----	----
Payments :				
Cash Purchases	----	----	----	----
Creditors	----	----	----	----
Wages	----	----	----	----
Capital Expenditure	----	----	----	----
Dividend Payable	----	----	----	----
Interest Payable	----	----	----	----
Income-Tax Payable	----	----	----	----
Total (b)	----	----	----	----
Closing Cash Balance (a-b)	----	----	----	----

(II) Proforma of Cash Budget (Under Rolling Period Basis)

Budget & Actual Comparision Month - 1		ITEMS	Month 1	Month 2	Month 3
Budget	Actual				
		A. Sales Receipts			
		1. Cash Sales & advances			
		2. Sundry Debtors Collection			
		3. Cash Subsidies, Rebate etc.			
		Total (A)			
		B. Operating Distribution			
		1. Cash Purchases & Advances			
		2. Sundry Creditors payment			
		3. Wages, Salaries etc.			
		4. Rent, Electricity etc.			
		5. Selling Expenses			
		6. Administrative Expenses			
		7. Tax paid (Income Tax)			
		Total (B)			
		C. Cash Flow through Operations (A-B)			
		D. Miscellaneous Receipts (interest, rent, royalties etc.)			
		E. Capital Receipts			
		1. Debenture Issues			
		2. Term Loans			
		3. Issue of share capital			
		4. Sale of assets			
		Total (E)			
		F. Non Operating Distributions			
		1. Interest & Financial Cost			
		2. Donations			
		3. Dividends			
		4. Capital Expenditures			
		5. Debt redemptions			
		Total (F)			
		G. Net cash flow (C+D+E-F)			
		Add : Opening Balance			
		Cash Position			
		Less : Minimum Cash Required			
		Bank Loan (Increase) / decrease			
		Cumulative Bank Position (Drawing Power)			

Practical Problems

Problem 1

Prepare a Cash Budget for 3 months for January, February and March 2005 from the following particulars.

2004 / 2005 (Month)	Credit Sales (Rs.)	Purchases (Rs.)	Wages (Rs.)
November 2004	1,00,000	80,000	5,000
December 2004	90,000	70,000	6,000
January 2005	1,10,000	1,00,000	4,500
February 2005	60,000	1,25,000	5,500
March 2005	80,000	1,30,000	7,000

40% of the credit sales will be realised in the month following the sale and the remaining 60% in the second month following. The creditors will be paid in the month following the purchases. Interest of Rs. 5000 will have to be paid in the month of February 2005. Income tax of Rs.15,000 will have to be paid in the month of March 2005. Wages are paid in the same month.

The opening balance of cash as on 1.1.2005 was Rs. 20,000

Solution

Working Notes

a) Sales amounts are calculated for January 2005 as below :

60% of balance amount of sales is received in the second month. Hence sales before two months should be considered which are Rs. 1,00,000 (November 2004)

$\therefore$ 60% of Rs. 1,00,000 = Rs. 60,000

40% of sales is received in the next month. Hence previous months sales should be considered which are Rs. 90,000 (December 2004)

$\therefore$ 40% of Rs. 90,000 = Rs. 36,000

Similar calculations are done for February and March 2005 budgets.

b) Creditors are paid in the following month which means purchases are paid for in the next month.

c) In the month of March there is minus balance of cash, which means that the management should make necessary arrangements for meeting the estimated cash shortage.

d) Closing balance at the end of the month becomes the opening balance for the next month .

Cash Budget for the period ended 31st March 2005

Particulars	January (Rs.)	February (Rs.)	March (Rs.)
Cash Balance b/f	20,000	41,500	29,000
Receipts :			
Sales : 60% (2nd month)	60,000	54,000	66,000
40% (1st month)	36,000	44,000	24,000
Total (a)	**1,16,000**	**1,39,500**	**1,19,000**
Payments :			
Creditors	70,000	1,00,000	1,25,000
Wages	4,500	5,500	7,000
Interest	---	5,000	---
Income-Tax	---	---	15,000
Total (b)	**74,500**	**1,10,500**	**1,47,000**
Cash Balance (a - b)	**41,500**	**(+) 29,000**	**(-) 28,000**

Problem 2

Hindustan Machine Tools Ltd. wants to avail overdraft facility with Bank of India for the period October-December 2005, for meeting the orders. From the following particulars prepare a cash budget and find out the amount of overdraft facility required.

2005, Month	Credit Sales (Rs)	Purchases (Rs)	Wages (Rs)
July	1,30,000	1,60,000	14,000
August	2,10,000	1,55,000	15,000
September	2,20,000	1,80,000	18,000
October	3,00,000	3,20,000	15,000
November	1,50,000	2,20,000	17,000
December	1,50,000	3,50,000	16,000

The credit sales are realised as below :

a) 50% of the amount in the second month following, and balance

b) 50% of the amount in the third month following the sales.

The creditors for purchases are paid in the months following the month of purchase.

The bank pass book shows a balance in the current account as on 30th September 2005 as Rs. 10,000.

Solution :

Cash Budget for the period ended December 2005

Particulars	October (Rs.)	November (Rs.)	December (Rs.)
Opening Balance of cash	10,000	(-) 15,000	(-) 1,37,000
Receipts :			
Sales :			
50% (2nd month)	1,05,000	1,10,000	1,50,000
50% (3rd month)	65,000	1,05,000	1,10,000
Total Receipts (a)	**1,80,000**	**2,00,000**	**1,23,000**
Payments :			
Purchases (creditors)	1,80,000	3,20,000	2,20,000
Wages	15,000	17,000	16,000
Total Payments (b)	**1,95,000**	**3,37,000**	**2,36,000**
Closing balance (a-b)	**(-)15,000**	**(-)1,37,000**	**(-)1,13,000**

Note : Calculation of Sales Receipts for October 2005 as follows :

50% after 2 months (August)	1,05,000
50% after 3 months (July)	65,000
Total credit sales receipts	**1,70,000**

Problem 3

Prepare a Cash Budget for the three months ended 30th September 2005 based on the following information : Cash and Bank on 1st July 2005 Rs. 25,000 Salaries and wages estimated monthly Rs. 10,000. Interest payable August 2005 Rs.5000.

Estimated	June (Rs.)	July (Rs.)	August (Rs.)	September (Rs.)
Cash Sales	--	1,40,000	1,52,000	1,21,000
Credit Sales	1,00,000	80,000	1,40,000	1,20,000
Purchases	1,60,000	1,70,000	2,40,000	1,80,000
Other Expenses	--	20,000	22,000	21,000

Credit Sales are collected 50% in the month sales are made and 50% in the month following. Collections from credit sales are subject to 5% discount if payment is received during the month of purchases and 2 ½ % if payment is received in the following month. Creditors are paid either on a "prompt" or 30 days basis. It is estimated that 10% of the creditors are in the "prompt" category.

Solution

Working Notes

a) Receipts from Debtors for the month of July

Previous month : Rs. 50,000 less 2½ %	=	Rs. 48,750
Current month : Rs. 40,000 less 5%	=	Rs. 38,000
		Rs. 86,750

Similarly for August and September 2005

b) Payments to Creditors for the month of July

Rs. 1,60,000 x 90%	=	Rs. 1,44,000
Rs. 1,70,000 x 10%	=	Rs. 17,000
		Rs. 1,61,000

Cash Budget for three months ended 30th September 2005.

Particulars	July (Rs.)	August (Rs.)	September (Rs.)
Receipts :			
Opening balance of cash	25,000	60,750	1,04,250
Cash sales	1,40,000	1,52,000	1,21,000
Credit Sales (realisation)	86,750	1,05,500	1,25,250
Total receipts (a)	**2,51,750**	**3,18,250**	**3,50,500**
Payments :			
Creditors for purchases	1,61,000	1,77,000	2,34,000
Salaries and Wages (monthly)	10,000	10,000	10,000
Interest payable (August)	-	5,000	-
Other Expenses	20,000	22,000	21,000
Total Payments (b)	**1,91,000**	**2,14,000**	**2,65,000**
Balance (a-b)	**60,750**	**1,04,250**	**85,500**

Problem 4

ABC company wishes to arrange overdraft facility with its bankers during the period April to June 2005 when it will be manufacturing mostly for stock. Prepare a cash-budget for the above period from the following data, indicating the extent of bank facilities the company will require at the end of each month :

Month	Sales (Rs.)	Purchases (Rs.)	Wage (Rs.)
February 2005	1,80,00,000	1,24,80,000	12,00,000
March 2005	1,92,00,000	1,44,00,000	14,00,000
April 2005	1,08,00,000	2,43,00,000	11,00,000
May 2005	1,74,00,000	2,46,00,000	10,00,000
June 2005	1,26,00,000	2,68,00,000	15,00,000

b) 50% of Credit Sales are realised in the month following the sale and the remaining 50% in the second month following the sale. Creditors are paid in the month following the month of purchase.

c) Cash at Bank on 1.4.2005 (estimated) Rs. 25,00,000

Solution

Cash Budget for April, May and June 2005

	April (Rs.)	May (Rs.)	June (Rs.)
Estimated Opening Balance	25,00,000	53,00,000	(-) 51,00,000
Receipts : From Debtors (for sales)	1,86,00,000	1,50,00,000	1,41,00,000
Total Receipts	**2,11,00,000**	**2,03,00,000**	**90,00,000**
Estimated Payments :			
Creditors for purchase of previous month	1,44,00,000	2,43,00,000	2,46,00,000
Wages for previous month	14,00,000	11,00,000	10,00,000
Total Payments	**1,58,00,000**	**2,54,00,000**	**2,56,00,000**
Balance on hand	53,00,000	--	--
Bank Overdraft	–	**(-) 51,00,000**	**(-)1,66,00,000**

Note

It is assumed that wages are paid on monthly basis on the first and very next month.

Working : Debtors realised as under

April 2005	
50% of February Sales	= Rs. 90,00,000
50% of March Sales	= Rs. 96,00,000
Total	= Rs. 1,86,00,000
May 2005	
50% of March Sales	= Rs. 96,00,000
50% of April Sales	= Rs. 54,00,000
Total	= Rs. 1,50,00,000
June 2005	
50% of April Sales	= Rs. 54,00,000
50% of May Sales	= Rs. 87,00,000
Total	= Rs. 1,41,00,000

Problem 5

Make out a Cash Budget of ABC Co. for April, May & June from the following information.

Months	Sales Rs.	Purchases Rs.	Wages Rs.	Expenses Rs.
January (Actual)	80,000	45,000	20,000	5,000
February (Actual)	80,000	40,000	18,000	6,000
March (Actual)	75,000	42,000	20,000	6,000
April (Budgeted)	90,000	50,000	24,000	7,000
May (Budgeted)	85,000	45,000	20,000	6,000
June (Budgeted)	80,000	35,000	18,000	5,000

Additional Information :

1) The advance income tax is payable in June Rs. 20,000/-
2) Plant is to be purchased in April and Rs. 10,000/- to be paid for the same in the month of April.
3) Rent of Rs. 300/- payable each month is not included in expenses.
4) 10% of purchases and 10% of sales are on cash basis.
5) Credit purchases are paid after one month & credit sales are collected after two months.
6) The time lag in wages and expenses is half month.
7) Cash and Bank balances on April 1 are estimated at Rs. 13,000/-

Solution

Cash Budget of ABC Company
For a Period of 3 months ending June

Problem 6

	April Rs.	May Rs.	June Rs.
Opening Cash & Bank Balance	13,000	11,400	9,100
Receipts :			
Cash Sales	9,000	8,500	8,000
Collection from Debtors	72,000	67,500	81,000
Total Cash Available (A)	94,000	87,400	98,100
Payments :			
Cash Purchases	5,000	4,500	3,500
Payment of suppliers	37,800	45,000	40,500
Wages	23,000	22,000	19,000
Expenses	6,500	6,500	5,500
Rent	300	300	300
Advance Income Tax			20,000
Plant	10,000		
Total Payments	82,600	78,300	88,800
Closing Cash Balance (A-B)	11,400	9,100	9,300

From the following information and the assumption that the balance in hand on 1st Jan 2005 is Rs.72,500 prepare a Cash Budget :

Assume that 50% are cash sales. Assets are to be acquired in the month of Feb. and April. Therefore,

Month	Sales	Materials	Wages	Selling & disc.cost	Production cost	Administration cost
January	72,000	25,000	10,000	4,000	6,000	1,500
February	97,000	31,000	12,100	5,000	6,300	1,700
March	86,000	25,500	10,600	5,500	6,000	2,050
April	88,600	30,600	25,000	6,700	6,500	2,260
May	1,02,500	37,000	22,000	8,500	8,000	2,500
June	1,08,700	38,800	23,000	9,000	8,200	2,580

provision should be made for the payment of Rs. 8,000 and Rs. 25,000 for the same. An application has been made to the bank for the grant of a loan of Rs. 30,000 and it is hoped that it will be received in the month of May. It is anticipated that a dividend of Rs. 35,000 will be paid in June; Debtors are allowed one month's credit. Sales Commission @ 3% on larger is to be paid. Creditors (for goods or overheads) grant one month credit.

Solution

Cash Budget

	Jan.	Feb.	Mar.	Apr.	May	June	Total
Receipts :							
Cash Sales	36,000	48,500	43,000	44,300	51,250	54,350	2,77,400
Debtors	--	36,000	48,500	43,000	44,300	51,250	2,23,050
Bank Loan	--	--	--	--	30,000	--	30,000
Total	**36,000**	**84,500**	**91,500**	**87,300**	**1,25,550**	**1,05,600**	**5,30,450**
Payments :							
Materials	--	25,000	31,000	25,500	30,600	37,000	1,49,100
Wages	10,000	12,100	10,600	25,000	22,000	23,000	1,02,700
Selling Overheads	--	4,000	5,000	5,500	6,700	8,500	29,700
Prod. Overheads	--	6,000	6,300	6,000	6,500	8,000	32,800
Adminis. Overheads	--	1,500	1,700	2,000	2,200	2,500	9,900
Capital Expenditure	--	8,000	--	25,000	--	--	33,000
Dividend	--	--	--	--	--	35,000	35,000
Commission	2,160	2,910	2,580	2,658	3,075	3,261	16,644
	12,160	**59,510**	**57,180**	**91,658**	**71,075**	**1,17,261**	**4,08,844**
Excess of receipts	23,840	24,990	34,320	--	54,475	--	1,21,606
Excess of payments	--	--	--	4,358	--	11,661	--
Balance b/f.	72,500	96,340	1,21,330	1,55,650	1,51,292	2,05,767	1,94,106
Balance c/f.	**96,340**	**1,21,330**	**1,55,650**	**1,51,292**	**2,05,767**	**1,94,106**	**3,15,712**

Problem : 7

A newly started Faster Co., Ltd. wishes to prepare cash budget from January. Prepare a cash budget for the first six months from the following estimated revenue and expenses :-

Month	Total sales (Rs.)	Materials (Rs.)	Wages (Rs.)	Overheads	
				Production (Rs.)	Selling and distrn. (Rs.)
Jan.	20,000	20,000	4,000	3,200	800
Feb.	22,000	14,000	4,400	3,300	900
Mar.	24,000	14,000	4,600	3,300	800
Apr.	26,000	12,000	4,600	3,400	900
May	28,000	12,000	4,800	3,500	900
June	30,000	16,000	4,800	3,600	1,000

Cash balance on 1st January was Rs. 10,000 A new machine is to be installed at Rs. 30,000 on credit, to be repaid by two equal instalments in March and April.

Sales commission @ 5% on total sales is to be paid within the month following actual sales.

Rs. 10,000 being the amount of 2nd call may be received in March. Share premium amounting to Rs. 2,000 is also obtainable with 2nd call.

Period of credit allowed by suppliers	2 months
Period of credit allowed to customers	2 month
Delay in payment of overheads	1 month
Delay in payment of wages	1/2 month

Assume cash sales to be 50% of total sales.

Solution

Faster Co. Ltd. Cash Budget For the period : Jan. to June

Details	Jan. Rs.	Feb. Rs.	Mar. Rs.	April Rs.	May Rs.	June Rs.
A. Balance b/d.	10,000	18,000	29,800	20,000	6,100	8,800
B. Receipts :						
Cash Sales (50%)	10,000	11,000	12,000	13,000	14,000	15,000
Debtors		10,000	11,000	12,000	13,000	14,000
Capital			10,000			
Share premium			2,000			
(A + B) Total	20,000	39,000	64,800	45,000	33,100	37,800
C. Payments :						
Materials			20,000	14,000	14,000	12,000
Wages	2,000	1,200	4,500	4,600	4,700	4,800
Production overhead		3,200	3,300	3,300	3,400	3,500
Selling & distribn.		800	900	800	900	900
Commission		1,000	1,100	1,200	1,300	1,400
Plant			15,000	15,000		
(C) Total	2,000	9,200	44,800	38,900	24,300	22,600
Balance c/d (A+B-C)	18,000	29,800	20,000	6,100	8,800	15,200

Problem : 8

Prepare a cash budget for the three months ending 30th June, 200 x from the information given below :

Months	Sales (Rs.)	Materials (Rs.)	Wages (Rs.)	Overheads (Rs.)
February	14,000	9,600	3,000	1,700
March	15,000	9,000	3,000	1,900
April	16,000	9,200	3,200	2,000
May	17,000	10,000	3,600	2,200
June	18,000	10,400	4,000	2,200

b) Credit terms are :

Sales / Debtors - 10% of the credit sales 50% of the credit sales are collected next month and the balance in the following month.

Creditors	-	materials	2 months
	-	wages	1/4 month
	-	overheads	1/2 month

c) Cash and bank balance on 1st April 200X is expected to Rs. 6,000

d) Other relevant information is :

i) Plant and machinery will be installed in February 200X at a cost of Rs. 96,000. The monthly installment of Rs. 2,000 is payable from April onwards.

ii) Dividend @ 5% on preference share capital of Rs. 2,00,000 will be paid on 1st June.

iii) Advance to be received for sale of vehicles Rs. 9,000 in June.

iv) Dividends from investments amounting to Rs. 1,000 are expected to be received in June.

v) Income tax (advance) is to be paid in June.

Solution

Working Note : (i)

Month	Calculation	Collection from sales / debtors		
		April	May	June
February	(14,000 - 10 % of 14,000) x 50%	6,300	--	--
March	(15,000 - 10 % of 15,000) x 50%	6,750	6,750	--
April	(10 % of 16,000)	1,600	--	--
	(16,000 - 10 % of 16,000) x 50%	--	7,200	7,200
May	10 % x 17,000		1,700	--
	(17,000 - 10 % of 17,000) x 50%			7,650
June	(10% x 18,000)			1,800
		14,650	15,650	16,650

ii) Wages : 75 % of the current month + 25% of previous month.

iii) Overheads : 50% of the current month + 50% of previous month.

Cash budget - April, May and June - 200x

Particulars	April	May	June	Total
A. Opening balance	6,000	3,950	3,000	12,950
B. Receipts				
Sales / debtors : note (i)	14,650	15,650	16,650	46,950
Dividend			1,000	1,000
Advance against sale of vehicle			9,000	9,000
Total	14,650	15,650	26,650	56,950
C. Payments				
Creditors for materials note (ii)	9,600	9,000	9,200	27,800
Wages : note (iii)	3,150	3,500	3,900	10,550
Overheads	1,950	2,100	2,250	6,300
Capital expenditure	2,000	2,000	2,000	6,000
Dividend on preference share			10,000	10,000
Income-tax advance			2,000	2,000
Total	16,700	16,600	29,350	62,650
D. Surplus (deficit) (B-C)	(2,050)	(950)	(2,700)	(5,700)
Closing balance (A-D)	3,950	3,000	300	7,250

Problem : 9

From the following information given to you, prepare a cash budget for the months June to September, 2005

Month	Sales (Credit) (Rs.)	Purchase (Credit) (Rs.)	Wages (Expenses) (Rs.)	Factory Expenses (Rs.)	Administrative (Expenses) (Rs.)	Selling Expenses
2005 April (Actual)	30,000	15,000	3,000	1,150	1,060	500
May (Actual)	35,000	20,000	3,200	1,225	1,040	550
June (Budgeted)	25,000	15,000	2,500	990	1,100	600
July (Budgeted)	30,000	20,000	3,000	1,050	1,150	620
August (Budgeted)	35,000	22,500	2,400	1,100	1,220	570
Sept. (Budgeted)	40,000	25,000	2,600	1,200	1,180	710

Additional Information

1) The customers are allowed a credit period of 2 months.
2) A dividend of Rs. 10,000 is payable in September 2005.
3) Capital expenditure to be incurred : Plant to be purchased for Rs. 5,000 in June, 2005 and a vehicle is to purchased on 1st August 2005 and payments are to be made for it in monthly instalments of Rs. 2,000 each, starting from August 2005.
4) The creditors allow a credit of 2 months.

5) Wages are paid on the 1st of the next month.

6) Lag in payment of other expenses is one month.

7) Balance of cash on 1st June 2005 is estimated as Rs. 15,000

Solution

Cash Budget for June 2005 to Sept 2005

	June Rs.	**July Rs.**	**Aug. Rs.**	**Sept. Rs.**
Opening Cash Balance	15,000	18,985	28,795	30,975
Receipts :				
Collection from Customers	30,000	35,000	25,000	30,000
Total Cash Available (A)	45,000	53,985	53,795	60,975
Payments :				
Payment to creditors	15,000	20,000	15,000	20,000
Wages	3,200	2,500	3,000	2,400
Factory Expenses	1,225	990	1,050	1,100
Administrative Expenses	1,040	1,100	1,150	1,220
Selling Expenses	550	600	620	570
Dividend	--	--	--	10,000
Plant Purchased	5,000	--	--	--
Vehicle Purchased	--	--	2,000	2,000
Total Payments (B)	26,015	25,190	22,820	37,290
Closing Cash Balance (A-B)	18,985	28,795	30,975	23,685

Questions for Self-Study

1. Clearly bring out the meaning of Budget, Budgeting and Budgetary Control.
2. What do you mean by Budgetary Control? Suggest a suitable organisation for efficient Budgetary Control System.
3. Disucss the objective, advantages and limitations of Budgetary Control System.
4. What are the different types of functional budgets which are prepared by a large scale manufacturing concern? Explain the method of preparation of a Sales Budget or a Cash Budget.
5. What do you understand by a Flexible Budget? How does fixed cost per unit vary in case of a budget for varying levels of activity?
6. Define Cash Budget. Show neatly with the help of a proforma how it is prepared?
7. Explain the various types of Budget.
8. Write short notes on :

(i)	Sales Budget	(ii)	Purchase Budget
(iii)	Production Budget	(iv)	Cost of Production Budget
(v)	Cash Budget	(vi)	Flexible Budget
(vii)	Fixed Budget	(viii)	Sales Budget
(ix)	Types of Budget	(x)	Objectives of Budgetary Control

Problem 1 The following budget estimates are available from Monica Industries Ltd. working at 50% capacity.

Variable Costs	Rs. 50,000
Semi-variable Costs	Rs. 25,000
Fixed Costs	Rs. 10,000

You are required to prepare a budget for 80% capacity assuming that semi-variable expenses increases by 10% for every 20% increase in capacity.

Problem 2 In a factory, a cost centre works at 60% capacity and the following overhead expenses are incurred.

Particulars	**Rs.**
Salary of Supervisor	2,000
Salary of Assistant supervisor	1,000
Wages of workers	5,000
Repairs of machines	8,000
Spoiled work	2,500
Oils and lubricants	2,000
Depreciation on machine	10,000
	30,500

Prepare a Flexible Budget for 75%, 100% and 125% capacities.

Problem 3 Kumaran Mohan Ltd produces a consumer product. The estimated costs per unit are given below:

Raw Material	Rs. 500
Direct Labour	Rs. 300
Factory Overhead	Rs. 400 (30% fixed)
Administrative overheads	Rs. 200 (60% fixed)
Cost per unit	Rs. 1,400

The selling price per unit is Rs. 1,800. At 50% capacity it produces 5,000 units. Find out the profits when it works at 60% and 80% capacity.

Notes :

(i) The cost per unit of Rs. 1,400 is at 50% capacity.

(ii) At 60% capacity raw material cost increases by 3% and selling price falls by 3%.

(iii) At 80% capacity raw material cost increases by 4% and selling price falls by 5%.

Draw a proforma of a Flexible Budget using imaginary figures for 50%, 60% and 70% capacity levels.

Problem 4 Prepare a Production Budget for 3,000 and 2,000 units capacities assuming that administration expenses remain constant at all levels of output. The budgeted expenses for production of 4,000 units are:

Particulars	Rs. Per Unit
Raw Materials	80
Direct Labour	30
Variable overheads	20
Fixed Overheads (Rs. 80,000)	10
Variable Overheads (Direct)	4
Selling Expenses (10%Fixed)	15
Administration Expenes (Rs. 40,000)	5
Distribution Expenses (25% Fixed)	6
	170

Problem 5 A company estimates the sales of 25,000 units of a product for the year 200X. The raw material to be required are A - 3 units and B - 4 units. The opening and closing balances of finished goods and raw materials are estimated as follows:

Items	Opening Balance at the beginning of next year (Units)	Closing Balance at the end of year (Units)
A	8,000	10,000
B	10,000	14,000
Finished goods	5,000	18,000

Prepare Purchase Budget showing the quantities of materials to be purchased.

Problem 6 Ramalal and Co. sells two products X and Y. The following are the estimates for the year 200X. Sales Budget (Units)

	Ist Quarter	IInd Quarter	IIIrd Quarter	IVth Quarter
Product X	50,000	60,000	40,000	1,10,000
Product Y	40,000	50,000	70,000	1,00,000

Product X is sold at Rs. 8 per unit while Product Y is sold at Rs. 15 per unit.

Ramalal incurs Selling and Distribution Expenses @ 2% of the Sales value. Bad debts amount to 1% of the Sales value. Prepare a Sales Budget for the year 200X.

Problem 7 From the following particulars prepare a Cash Budget for January, February and March 200X in a tabular form

Months		Sales	Purchases	Wages	Expenses
October	2004	1,00,000	50,000	15,000	6,000
November	2004	90,000	45,000	19,000	5,000
December	2004	80,000	40,000	24,000	7,000
January	2005	85,000	42,500	22,000	5,000
February	2005	95,000	50,000	18,000	6,000
March	2005	90,000	45,000	20,000	5,000

Further information :

(i) 5% of the purchases and 10% of the sales are for cash.

(ii) Credit allowed to customers is 1/2 months.

(iii) Creditors for purchases are paid in month following the month of purchases.

(iv) Wages are paid every 15 days

(v) Opening Balance of cash as on January 2005 is Rs. 15,000

Problem 8 From the following particulars prepare a Cash Budget for the quarter ended 30-6-200X

	Actual			Budgeted		
	January Rs.	**February Rs.**	**March Rs.**	**April Rs.**	**May Rs.**	**June Rs.**
Sales	1,00,000	1,00,000	95,000	1,20,000	1,15,000	1,10,000
Purchases	50,000	45,000	48,000	50,000	45,000	30,000
Wages	30,000	25,000	28,000	30,000	25,000	20,000
Expenses	4,000	5,000	5,000	8,000	6,000	4,000

Further Information :

(i) 50% of the purchases and sales are for cash

(ii) Debtors are realised after one month

(iii) Creditors are paid after two months

(iv) Payment of wages made after one week

(v) Expenses are paid after one month

(vi) Rent of Rs. 5,000 per month not considered in expenses

(vii) Income-tax payable in April Rs. 1,500

(viii) Cash balance as on 1st April, 2005 was Rs. 1,500

Problem 9 The following is the estimated data for six months - March 200X to August 200X of a company

Months 200X	Credit Sales Rs.	Credit Purchases Rs.	Wages Rs.	Manufacturing Expenses Rs.	Office Expenses Rs.	Selling Expenses Rs.
March	50,000	35,000	9,000	5,000	1,500	1,500
April	54,000	39,000	8,500	4,000	2,000	4,000
May	58,000	32,000	9,500	4,500	3,500	4,500
June	50,000	35,000	8,000	3,000	1,000	3,500
July	55,000	38,000	7,900	5,500	1,500	4,500
August	60,000	36,000	8,200	4,400	2,500	4,000

Other Information :

(i) A machine valued at Rs. 20,000 will be supplied by supplier in June 200X when 20% will have to be paid against delivery and the remaining balance to be paid after 4 monthys

(ii) Credit Period .... Allowed to customers .... 1 month

Allowed by suppliers .... 2 month

(iii) Tax too be paid in advance Rs. 10,000 in March 200X

(iv) Lag in payments .... Manufacturing expenses 15 days

.... All other expenses 30 days

Prepare a Cash Budget.

STANDARD COSTING

Indroduction

The concept of control which is the third and final link in the managerial process refers to the process of ensuring the accomplishment of predetermined plans. Such a control over the destiny of an enterprise is accomplished through a widely used technique called "Standard Costing".

In ordinary language, the standard forms a yard-stick that is used to measure weight, quantity, quality and value. It is a measure of acceptable cost performance of a given activity under controlled conditions. The controlled conditions means a situation where every activity of the task is performed as per predetermined way and procedure. Thus, a standard cost is a scientific predetermination of what a unit cost of product should be.

Concept of Standard Costing

Standard costing is an important accounting-oriented tool which keeps the cost at a minimum level by planning and controlling costs of each unit produced. Under this system, the cost of each unit is predetermined on some scientific basis and arrangement are made for costs not exceeding pre-determined standard.

In the words of W.W. Bigs standard costing is a system of costing where "a comparision is made of the actual cost with a pre-arranged standard and the cost of any deviations (called variances) is analysed by causes. This method permits management to investigate the reasons for these variances and to take suitable corrective action. It is, therefore, a system of cost control as well as cost ascertainment".

According to the Institute of Cost and Work Accounants, London, "standard costs are prepared and used to clarify the final results of a business, particularly by measurement of the variations of actual costs from standard costs and the analysis of the causes of variations for the purpose of maintaining efficiency by executive action."

M.C. Shukla and T.S. Grewal state

"Standard costing is a system which seeks to control the cost of each unit or batch through determination before hand of what should be the cost and then its comparison with actual costs". In short, standard costing is a procedure under which predetermined costs are used to measure the efficiency of production. If refers to the determination of standard costs and their application to managerial problems particularly those problems relating to product costs, and departmental cost control. Thus, under standard costing system predetermined costs are carefully computed which are then compared with actual cost to aid in cost control.

Standard costs are part of cost accounting system whereby standard costs are incorporated directly and formally into the manufacturing accounts. Standards are performance expectations. Standards may be defined as measured quantity which should be obtained in connection with some particular operation or activity. Precisely standard costing is a control device and not a separate method of product costing. It can be used with any method of product costing, job costing or process costing.

Logical dissimilarity between Estimated, Standard and Budgeted Costs

Even it might appears that standard and estimated costs are the same, some dissimilarity exists. An estimated cost are determined on basis of the average past performance and therefore, can be regarded as a reasonable assessment of what the cost "will be".

On the other hand, standard costs are the costs that would be incurred under the most efficient operating conditions and are forecast before the manufacturing process begins. Thus, it is carefully predetermined costs used as performance criteria - a measure what a cost should be. Whereas budgeted costs are viewed as future costs (prediction, estimates, forecasts) that are formally combined into an integrated plan of action. It is the standard cost per unit of the budgeted quantity to be produced during a particular period.

Establishment of Cost Standards

The effectiveness of standard cost as a technique wholly depends upon the establishment of the very cost standards. Care should be taken in setting the standards considering all relevant factors such as the employees, their attitudes and abilities, the extent of control exercised over their operations and so on.

There are several methods adopted for fixing the standards such as engineering estimates, observed behaviour, predicted behaviour and desired behaviour. The standard cost in a particular situation is based on two or more of these bases.

When cost standards are determined on the basis of engineering estimates, it is but proper to consider the specifications of the machinery for accurartely ascertaining the standard relationship between a given unit of output and a given unit of input. On the basis of such technical specifications cost standards can be fixed. The cost standards so fixed, represent only what can be accomplished.

Another technique employed for establishing cost standards is the past experience. Here, the principle involved is to consider the past achievement as standard for the future. Of course, the past can provide a reliable guide for the future as long as the processes and procedures of the past remain unchanged. If changes occur in the processes and procedures, the observed behaviour can no longer provide a reliable basis for establishing cost standards.

When certain technological changes are expected to take place they are likely to have profound influence on the cost estimates. In such cases the predicted behaviour which represents what is most likely to happen, can be used for setting cost standards. This calls for a minor adjustment to historical standard cost.

Desired behaviour

The desired behaviour can also be taken as the basis for setting cost standards. The term "desired behaviour" represents what the management actually desires. Again, the desire of the management in turn, reflects the experience of similar concerns or the industry as a whole.

It is clear that there are several techniques available for establishing cost standards. But, the final basis adopted for the purpose depends on the management's judgement. The management should be careful while setting the standards. The standards so set are very attainable with reasonable efforts. When standards set are very high, they will be difficult to achieve resulting in all round demoralization. On the other hand, if the standards set are very low, there may not be adequate motivation to achieve them. Hence, it is essential that the standards set in manufacturing organisation should be easily attainable standards.

Steps involved in Standard Costing

Standard costing system involve the following steps :

i) Determination of standard cost for each element of cost - direct material, direct labour, and overhead;
ii) Recording of both standard and actual costs in appropriate books of accounts:
iii) Computation of variance between standard cost and actual cost;
iv) Analysis and investigation of the variances; and
v) Feed correction and suggest modification where required. Corrective actions are taken to ensure that future performance will be in accordance with pre-determined-standards.

The standard cost of a product consists of :

i) **Quantitative Facts :** Standard quantity of given material, standard labour hours for specified operations, and standard machine hours for the stated machines to be used.

ii) **Price Factors :** Standard cost per rupee and per hour, by which the standard quantities are converted to the standard product costs.

The quantitative factors are based on engineered specifications tempered by experience, and vice versa whereas prices used are typically those which are expected to be representative of actual prices during the period for which the standards are established.

For control purposes, the various actual activities of a period; such as quantity of each type of material used, labour hours worked, and machine hours involved, as well as units of goods produced, are multiplied by appropriate unit standard cost to establish standard cost totals for work performed by job or process, and by department. The actual costs of these activities are then compared with the standard costs and the resulting variances are examined as to cause;

i) To aid the interpretation of financial results for the period;
ii) To fix the responsibility for non-standard performance; and
iii) To focus attention on areas in which cost improvement should be sought.

The Standard Costing System

The standard costing system is designed to furnish management with a measure that will help in making decisions regarding the efficiency of operation. A sound standard costing system comprises of following main activities, namely,

i) Establishment of cost centre;
ii) Determination of quality of standard;
iii) Organization of standard costing;
iv) Setting of standards;
v) Actual cost accumulation and
vi) Analysis of variance.

i) Establishment of Cost Centre

The standard costing system begins with the establishment of the cost centre which is usually a process, or an operation or an item of equipment etc. It is unit of activity within the factory to which costs may be practically and equitably assigned. Performance is assessed by comparing the actual costs with the performance standard, which shows the costs the centre should have incurred, given their actual activity.

ii) Determination of Quality of Standard

Standard may be broadly classified into four types. They are : (a) Ideal Standards (b) Normal Standards (c) Basic Standards & (d) Attainable Standards.

a) **Ideal Standards :** Ideal standards are set at the level of maximum efficiency, representing conditions that can seldom if ever be attainable. Such a standard fails to pay any attention to normal materials spoilage and idle labour time. This type of standard can be used as standard of perfection rather than a standard for the measurement of practical results because conditions that satisfy ideal standards are extremely rare. Ideal standards are more effective for direct material costs and usage. The application of ideal standard makes various accounts less significant for control purposes.

b) **Normal Standards :** Normal standards are the standards that can be achieved by efficient working and efficient management. Such standards are set after taking into consideration the conditions that are expected to prevail over a long period of time sufficient to reflect the effects of seasonal and cyclical fluctuations. These standards are of great significance for manufacturing overhead expenses.

c) **Basic Standards :** Basic standards provide a measuring scale for performance over a long period of time. Such standards are not influenced by any change in material prices and labour rates and therefore, remain unchanged for a number of years. Basic standards are useful for such items of expenditure that are fixed in nature.

d) **Attainable Standards :** Attainable standards based on past performance, can be achieved with reasonable effort. Perhaps the standards should be somewhat lower than what can be achieved by earnest effort. Such standards are set as closely as possible to that level which represents anticipated conditions. They allow for usual production problems, such as down time for maintenance, employee errors, or occasional inventory shortages. These standards are more realistic and satisfactory and thus represent desirable performance. Attainable standards are particularly useful in setting price standards for materials and labour.

iii) Organization of Standard Costing

The efficiency of a standard costing system largely depends upon the accuracy and reliability of the standards. In the past the job of standard setting was the responsibility of the cost accountant. However, keeping in view the dynamic conditions of the present business, it requires the combined thinking and expertise of all persons who have responsibility over prices and quantities of inputs. Against this background, almost in every big organization, at present, this function is discharged by a standard committee comprising of representatives from various concerned departments of the organization. The said committee establishes and monitors standards for various costs and activities and is also responsible for changing and updating the standards when required.

iv) Setting of Standards

The important components of standard costing system is the setting of standards to be used for evaluation of actual results.

The term standard cost refers to cost that should reasonably be incurred in the manufacture of a product. The main components of standard costs are :

1) Standard direct material cost

2) Standard direct labour cost and

3) Manufacturing overheads.

1) Standard direct material cost

The standard direct materials cost of a product incurred depends on price and quantity standards. It can be ascertained by application of the following formula :

Standard Direct Material Cost = Standard price of direct material x Standard quantity of direct material

a) Standard Price of Direct Material : One of the important ingredient of cost is the cost of direct material used in the manufacture of goods. An important element of cost control is the price paid for the purchase of material. Another essential of cost control is that the price paid should be reasonable. The material price standard refers to the price which should be reasonably paid for a particular direct raw material under the most favorable possible conditions. But the most favorable possible conditions will differ from firm to firm depending upon the circumstances of each case. It implies, therefore, that direct material price standard should be set for each firm and not for the industry as a whole.

The standard price of the direct material should include all the components of the amount spent in the acquisition of a particular material. Where the prices differ for the goods of the same quality, the standard should be set based on the lowest price. Again, where the supplier who is prepared to sell the material at a lowest price, is not a reliable one, there is no real savings to the firm. In such cases, higher prices charged by more reliable suppliers will form the basis for fixing the standard price. While fixing the standard price of direct material, freight charges and import duties should be considered wherever applicable. Another related aspect to be considered is that of discounts available for the purchase of materials. This includes quantity discounts which are granted for purchase of goods in bulk and cash discounts which are allowed for prompt payment. The effect of discounts is lowering of the costs and hence, the standard price.

b) Standard Quantity of Direct Material : The quantity of direct material is another important factor affecting the cost of direct material. For setting the standard cost of direct material. the quantity of materials used for the production of a particular product should also be standardized. The standards of the quantity of consumption of raw materials is referred to as standard quantity of materials or material usage standards. Such standards can be determined on the basis of the following factors :

I) The input-output relationship between raw-materials and final products based on observation of actual experience and

II) The inherent loss of materials in the productive processes such as shrinkage, evaporation, weight losses due to scrapping and smoothing etc.,

The total standard direct material cost is computed by multiplying the standard price with the standard quantity of direct material.

2) Standard Direct Labour Cost

The second component of the total standard cost is standard direct labour cost. It is calculated by multiplying the labour standard rate by the labour standard time.

Labour Standard Rate

The payment made to labour for carrying out production represents wages. The wages are calculated either on time basis (monthly, weekly or daily) or on piece basis (per piece of production). The term standard labour rate refers to the conventional standard wage rate only, i.e. in case of the time wage payment only. In fact, these standard labour rates come into force either as a result of the management policy or due to negotiation between management and trade unions. Moreover, there will be several wage rates depending upon the degree of skill, the inherent risk involved, seniority and so on. Thus, it is clear that the labour standard rates are quite different from material standard price. It should be remembered that the standard labour rates are not under the control of the management.

Labour Standard Time

The quantum of labour is measured in terms of the time consumed for the completion of the particular piece of work. Hence, labour standard time refers to the total time which particular operation should take. This is based on the observation of actual operation and critical evaluation of the whole performance. Time and motion studies provide a popular example of this type. It is on this basis the labour standard time is determined. While doing so some allowance must be given, since human beings are not mechanical devices and cannot utilise the entire time for production purpose. At the same time, it should also be remembered that while setting the standards no allowance is made for prolonged periods of illness of the workers.

Overhead Standards

Another component of cost standard is overhead. There is a basic difference between the material and labour standards and overhead standards. For the material and labour, standards are set on the basis of price and quantity standards. This only establishes the functional relationship that exists between the number of units of a product and the quantities of material and labour required for producing the same with the underlying fact that each material has its standard price and each worker has a standard wage rate. But no such functional relationship exists between the units produced and the total overhead cost. Even that part of the manufacturing overhead which varies with the volume of production cannot be directly related to production in the same way as direct material and direct labour. Therefore, the determination of overhead standards is completely different from that of direct material and direct labour.

The overheads are classified into (a) variable and (b) fixed. The standard variable overhead is fixed directly per unit of volume. The volume of measure refers to some measure of input such as direct labour cost or hours. Standard fixed rates, on the other hand are usually fixed at some volume representative of the firm's operations over a longer period.

Such standards are set after careful study of cost volume analysis.

v) Actual Costs Accumulation

The establishment of standards is followed by the accumulation of actual costs which are then compared with standards in performance reports. For accumulating actual manufacturing costs firms use either a job order system or a process cost system. The application of standard costing gets much information from the cost data than is possible with just actual costs. A sound system of standard costing will help management in determining the type of required cost data and in reporting such data.

vi) Analysis of Variance

Variance may be defined as the difference between the actual cost (AC) and the standard Cost (SC). But the variance analysis is the process of analysis of variance of sub-dividing the total variance in such a way that management can fix the responsibility for the divergence from the standard performance. If AC is less than SC, it is considered to be a sign of efficiency and the difference is termed as "favourable" variance. On the other hand, if AC is more than SC, it is considered to be a sign of inefficiency and the difference is termed as "unfavourable" variance. Favourable variance is also referred to as "positive variance" while unfavourable variance is also known as "negative variance".

It should also be borne in mind that the words favourable/positive and unfavourable/negative merely indicate the deviation of variance from the SC, they need not be construed as good or bad from the point of view of the firm. A real quantitative evaluation can be effected only after determining the causes for the variance. Again, the final result is also affected by the type of standards predetermined by the firm. For, if the set standards are reasonable and accurate and are revised from time to time, according to the changed circumstances, any deviation would reflect true deviation. On the other hand, if the expected standards are not reasonable and accurate, the deviations will be distorted.

Variances, as a control technique, are computed only to fix the responsibility for the deviation from the SC and thus ensure perfect control over the standard cost. For purposes of control, variances are classified into "controllable" and "uncontrollable" variances.

If a variance can be located with the responsibility of a particular individual, it is considered to be a "controllable" variance. If variances arise from causes beyond the control of the responsible individuals, it is considered to be "uncontrollable". For instance an increase in the price of materials and increase in the wage rates, are often referred to as "uncontrollable" variance, whilst excessive inputs of material in production and more than standard hours taken by direct labourers provide example of "controllable" variance. This distinction between controllable and uncontrollable variance is important. This facilitates careful analysis of the controllable variance and reporting to the management so as to enable it to implement corrective action as and when needed.

Cost Control Using Standard Costing

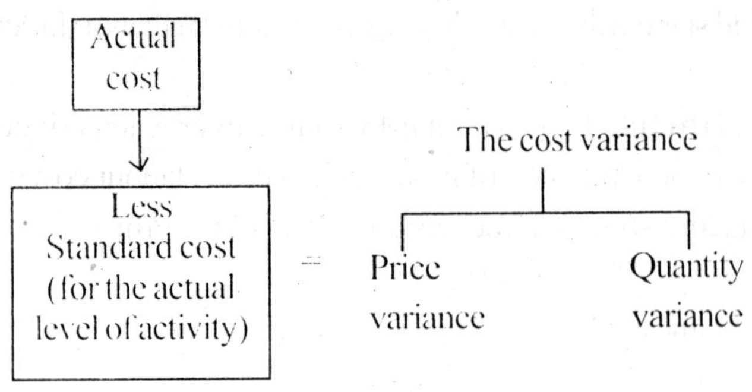

Fig Variance analysis

Control in standard costing is achieved by variance analysis. Figure should help you to understand how variance analysis works. At the end of the period under review the actual cost is compared with the predetermined standard cost for the actual level of activity which was attained. This difference is known as the total or cost variance. All variances are the result of two factors, price and quantity. Thus, the total or cost variance can be subdivided into that part of the variance which arises from price differences and that part which arises from differences in quantities. The names of these subversions may cause confusion, but the principles remain unchanged. Table No.8 should make the position a little clear.

Table : Variances : materials, labour, overheads and sales

	Total / cost variance	**Price variance**	**Quantity variance**
Materials	Material cost variance	Material price variance	Material usage variance
Labour	Labour cost variance	Labour rate variance	Labour efficiency variance
Overheads	Overheads cost variance	Overheads expenditure variance	Overheads volume or efficiency variance
Sales	Sales margin variance	Sales margin price variance	Sales margin volume variance

Advantages of Standard Costing

The important advantages of standard costing technique are enumerated below :

1) It provides continual incentive for management to keep costs and performance in tune with predetermined objectives. The comparison between actual costs and the predetermined standards are much more effective than comparisons between current actual costs and actual costs of prior periods.
2) Under standard system, variances are determined normally at the end of the month, or even weekly basis to allow for more timely action in correcting inefficiencies.
3) Standard costing system involves less clerical efforts than other costing systems because actual costs are recorded and accumulated by cost centre rather than by job.
4) Standard costing system makes possible for the management to pay more attention to weak areas that require control as it follows the principle of management by exception.
5) Prices can be determined in anticipation of the actual production as standard costs for various inputs are already available.
6) The standard costing system makes possible to determine and compare the efficiency of various operations.
7) It eliminates wastage by detecting variances and suggesting corrective measures for them.
8) It ensures better control as the workers are known about the performance criteria and naturally they take more interest in the work to achieve the standard.

9) It brings about an improvement in production methods as it requires a continuous detailed examination of all important functions of the concern. It also results in reduction of costs.

Limitations of Standard Costing

In order to reap the maximum benefits of standard costing, the costing department should keep the following points in their mind. Because, these can be considered as precautions to be taken while implemeating standard costing technique. If organisation fails to take, note of these, the same will act as limitations. The following are the limitations attached to standard costing system.

1) Fixation of standard is not possible for every type of work or operation.
2) Wrong standards may result in wastage of time, money, and energy.
3) Standard must be reviewed from time to time; otherwise they loose importance for our purpose.
4) Determination of actual cost is must for certain purposes. For example, preparation of cash budget, reconciliation of cost and financial accounts etc.
5) These is a difficulty in classifying the variances into controllable and non-controllable.
6) Since the setting up of standards require high degree of technical proficiency and skill, it is alleged that the adoptation of standard costing is a costly and time consuming exercise.

However, it should be remarkable that, despite the above limitations, a standard costing system is must for efficient control. The standards must be fixed and implemented properly.

Basic Variances

Variances may be segregated by department, by cost and by elements of cost, e.g. price and quantity. It is common experience that different industries make use of different variances. Despite the existence of a number of variances the following are some basic variances found in practice.

1) Direct Material Variance
2) Direct Labour Variance
3) Variable Overhead Variance
4) Fixed Overhead Variance
    a) Based on units
    b) Based on standard hours.

Basically, there are two different types of variances : **Price variance** and **Volume variance.** The price variances is closely related to the price of materials, rates of labour, expenditure on overheads or selling price of products. The volume variance has some thing to do with quantity and is related to quantity of units in terms of raw materials consumed, number of hours worked or number of products sold.

Classification of variances

Classification of variances based on price variances

1) Material Price Variance
2) Labour Price Variance
3) Variable Overhead Expenditure Variance
4) Fixed Overhead Expenditure Variance
5) Sales Price Variance

Classification of variances based on quantity

1) Materials Usage Variance
2) Labour Efficiency Variance
3) Fixed Overhead Volume Variance
4) Sales Volume Variance

It is clear that the cost variance comprises both price variance as well as volume variance. Again, for sales there is a total variance called sales value variance comprising the total of price variance and volume variance.

The need of the management cannot be met fully by the basic variances which merely provide information regarding the extent of change in the volume. The management should also ascertain the causes for such changes, so that they can initiate corrective action whenever needed. Keeping this view, a simple variance analysis may be extended as given below :

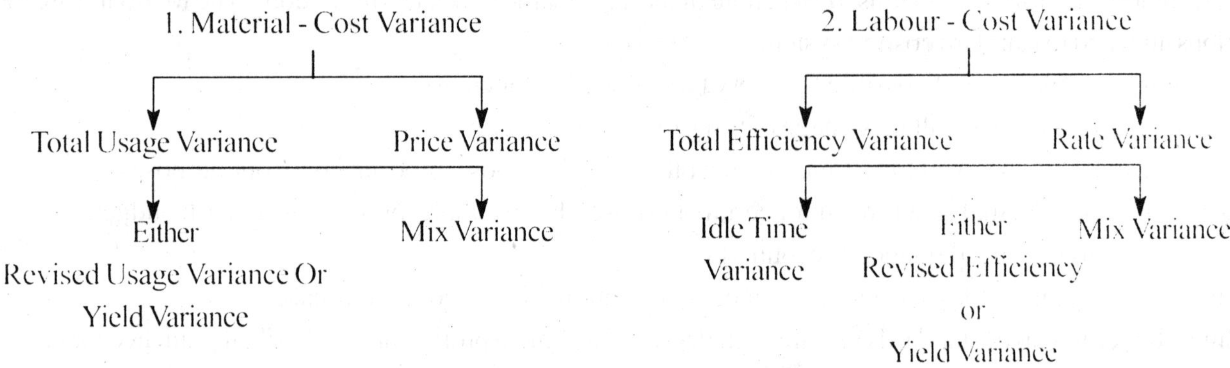

3. Variance Overheads - Cost Variance - Expenditure Variance

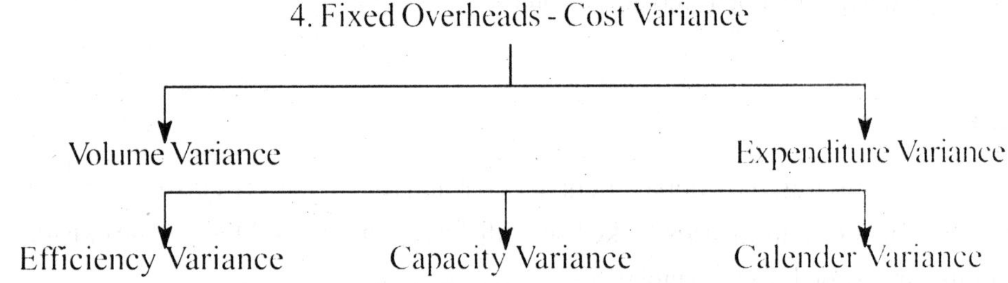

Material Variance (MV)

Material variances are commonly referred to as material cost variance (MCV). The MCV represents the difference between the standard cost of standard quantity of materials of actual output and the actual cost of materials consumed.

Symbolically

Material Cost Variance (MCV) = Standard Cost (SC) - Actual Cost (AC)

From the above, it is clear that the MCV depends on two factors, viz., the price paid for material and the actual quantity of materials used. Accordingly, the MCV which represents a total variance can be divided into two sub-variances :

a) Material Price Variance (MPV) b) Material Usage/Quantity Variance (MUV)

a) Material Price Variance (MPV))

MPV Occurs when the actual price paid for the materials used is different from the standard price. The MPV is calculated by multiplying the difference between the standard unit price and the actual unit price paid for the materials used by the actual number of units or quantity of materials used in production.

Symbolically

Material Price Variance = Actual Quantity / Number of Units Purchased (Standard Price - Actual Price)

MPV = AQ (SP - AP)

It should be remembered that, in the absence of specific information the actual number of units purchased can be considered synonymous with those used in production.

MPV is caused by any one or combination of the factors such as changes in the price of materials, excessive freight charges, increase in the rates of taxes and customs duty, failure to avail cash discount or off-season low price, buying uneconomic quantities and the like. From the above, it is clear that the purchasing department may not always be held responsible for paying higher or lower than the standard price, since some of the factors devolve on persons outside the purchase department. It is but proper to institute a detailed analysis for the MPV and then attribute the responsibility for such variance to the concerned department / departments other than purchasing.

b) Material Usage / Quantity Variance (MUV)

The material usage / quantity variance (MUV), the second component of MCV, measures the extent of utilization of materials in production. The MUV represents the difference between the actual quantity consumed in production and the standard quantity that should have been used for actual output. The MUV is calculated by multiplying the standard unit price of materials with the difference between the actual quantity of material and the standard quantity.

Symbolically

Material Usage Variance (MUV) = Standard Price)SP) (Standard Quantity (SQ) - Actual Quantity- AQ)

The MUV arises due to any one or combination of the factors such as carelessness in the handling of materials by workers, wastage due to inefficient production methods or unskilled/untrained employees, low quality of materials used, pilferage and spoilage due to poor storage, maintenance, use of defective materials causing excessive consumption and the like. The overall responsibility for the MUV lies with the production personnel. But this should not be taken as a general rule always, as in the case of MPV. For instance, a favourable MUV may arise solely on account of substitution of above standard materials resulting in less wastage than was anticipated. Viewed from another angle, the purchase of above standard materials will definitely result in unfavourable MPV, since higher quality materials will cost more.

Classification of MUV

Where more than one type of material is used in the manufacture of products in a factory, MUV can be further sub-divided into "Material Mix Variance" (MMV) and "Material Yield Variance" (MYV).

Material Mix Variance (MMV)

This is component of material usage/quantity variance and hence, it is also called material mix sub-variance. This arises due to difference between the standard and actual composition of mix. The MMV occurs only where more than one type/grade of raw materials or combination of materials is used and when quantities issued to production differ from pre-determined standard mix. MMV is calculated by multiplying the standard price per unit of materials with the difference between actual proportion of those materials in actual quantity used and the standard proportions of those materials in actual quantity used. The standard proportions of materials in the actual total quantity used are referred to as "Revised Standard Quantity" (RSQ)

Symbolically

Material Mix Variance (MMV) = Standard Unit Price (SP) (Revised Standard Quantity (RSQ) - Actual Quantity) - AQ

A favourable variance would arise, when the Revised Standard Quality (RSQ) is more than the Actual Quantity (AQ) and vice versa.

Material Revised Usage Variance (MRUV)

The word "Revised" is prefixed to 'usage variance' only to denote the residue left after segregating material mix variance. In other words, it represents that portion of material total usage variance which is attributable to causes other than the difference between the standard and actual proportion of actual quantity used. MRUV is calculated by multiplying the standard price per unit of material with the difference between the standard proportion of different types of materials in the standard quantity and the standard proportion of those materials in actual quantity used.

Symbolically

Material Revised Usage Variance MRUV =

Standard Unit Price SP (Standard Quantity (SQ) - Revised standard Quantity - (RSQ)

A favourable variance would arise, if the standard quantity is more than the Revised Standard Quantity and vice varsa.

Material Yield Variance (MYN)

In all process industries, "loss in production" is usually inevitable. This loss is classified into two types as 'normal' and 'abnormal'. The normal loss is taken into consideration while determining the standard for normal expected output or yield. Quite frequently, the actual yield differs from the standard yield due to abnormal loss sustained in the different processes of production. This difference is designated as "Yield Variance".

The yield variance represents that portion of the Material. Total Usage Variance which arises as a result of difference between the standard yield and the actual yield obtained. Again, the standard yield represents that output which should have resulted from the actual input of materials based on the standard expectations. It should also be rememberd that while yield variance represents output vaiance other variances like price, usage and mix variances are input variances. MYV is calculated by multiplying the standard material cost per unit of output with the difference between the standard yield and the actual yield.

Symbolically :

Material Yield Variance MYV =

Standard Material Cost (SMC) per unit of output (Standard Yield (SY)-Actual Yield (AY))

Diagrammatic Representation of Material Variance

I. Where one type of material is used

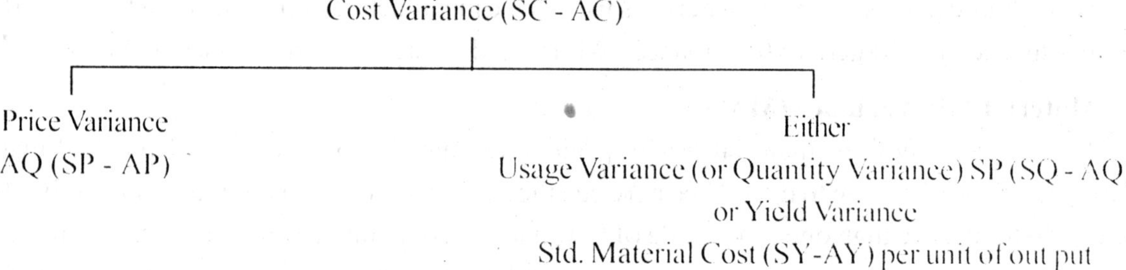

Verification : Cost Variance = Price Variance + Either Usage or Yield Variance

II. Where more than one type of material is used.

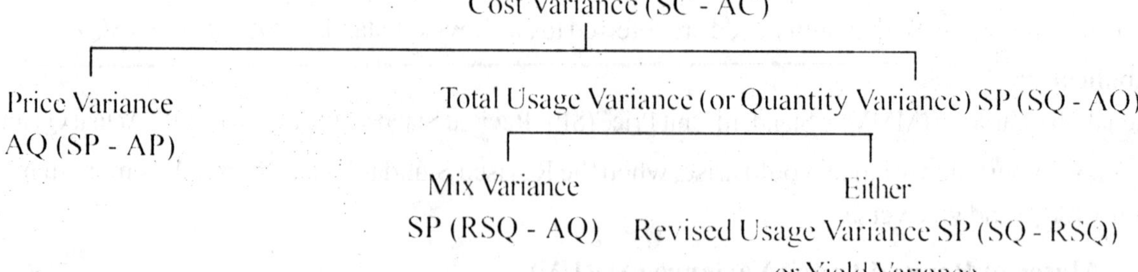

Verification : Cost Variance = Price Variance + Mix Variance + Either Revised Usage Variance or Yield Variance

Material Cost Variance (MCV)

Material cost variance represents the differences between the actual costs and the standard costs of materials for a specified output. The actual cost is computed by multiplying actual price with the actual quantity of material and in the same way standard cost is computed by multiplying the standard price with the standard quantity of material. Cost analysts can also develop other variances of Material cost to meet specialised purposes of management. However such variance may either be related to price, quantity or to the combination of price and quantity. Material cost variance can be expressed in abbreviated form as shown below :

MCV = (SP x SQ) - (AP x AQ)

where SP = Standard price SQ = Standard Quantity

AP = Actual Price AQ = Actual Quantity

Note: Standard quantity should be taken for actual output.

Practical Problems

Problem 1

Compute Material Cost Variance for a output of 200 units from the information given below:

Standard quantity	=	3 kg per unit of output
Standard price	=	Rs.4 per kg
Actual quantity consumed	=	550 kg
Actual price	=	Rs. 6 per kg

Solution

Material Cost Variance = (Total Standard Cost - Total Actual Cost)

MCV = (SP x SQ) - (AP x AQ)

= (4 x 600) - (6 x 550)

= Rs.900 unfavourable

Material Price Variance (MPC) :

The material price variance attempts to measure the variation between the actual cost of material and the standard cost expected to be paid for the material. It reflects the actual unit cost of material above or below the standard unit cost, multiplied by the actual quantity of function will attain standard price. The payment of lower prices by the purchasing department for a given quantity would result in favourable material price variance and thereby maintaining the required standard; whereas purchasing department will fail to meet the standard if it pays higher prices that will reflect an unfavourable material price variance. The material price variance is computed as follows :

Material Price Variance (MPV) = (Standard Price (SP) - Actual Price(AP)) x Actual quantity (AQ)

Problem 2

Calculate Material Variance from the information as given in Problem 01.

Solution

Material Price Variance = (Standard Price - Actual Price) x Actual quantity

MPV = (4 - 6) x 550

= Rs.1100 unfavourable.

Material Usage Variance (MUV)

Material usage variance is deviation caused from the standard due to difference in quantities used. It indicates the actual quantity of direct materials used above or below the standard price.

Material Usage Variance (MUV) = (Standard quantity (SQ) - Actual quantity(AQ)) x Standard price (SP)

This variance can also be calculated as follows :-

Material Usage Variance (MUV) =

(Standard price of standard quantity (SPSQ) - Standard price of Actual quantity (SPAC))

Problem 3

With the help of information as given in problem 1, calculate material usage variance

Solution

Material usage variance	=	(Standard quantity - Actual quantity) x Standard price
MUV	=	(600 - 550) x 4 = Rs. 200 Favourable
or MUV	=	(Standard price of standard quantity - Standard price of actual quantity)
	=	2400 - 2200 = Rs.200 Favourable

Problem 4

Suba an engineering industrial enterprise manufactured 100 items of product 'MCC' compute material cost variances from the information given below:

Standard quantity	:	2 kg per item	Actual quantity	:	3 kg per item
Standard price	:	Rs.10 per kg	Actual price	:	Rs. 8 per kg

Solution

Material cost variance	=	(Standard cost - Actual cost)		
MCV	=	(SQ x SP) - (AQ x AP)		
	=	(200 x 10) - (300 x 8)	=	Rs.400 unfavourable
Material price variance	=	(Standard price - Actual price) x Actual quantity		
MPV	=	(10 - 8) x 300	=	Rs.600 Favourable
Material Usage variance	=	(Standard quantity - Actual quantity) x Standard price		
MUV	=	(200 - 300) x 10	=	Rs.1000 unfavourable

Verification :

MCV	=	MPV + MUV
Rs.400 (U)	=	Rs.600 (F) + Rs.1000 (U)
Rs.400 (U)	=	Rs.400 (U)

Presentation of Material Cost Variance by graph

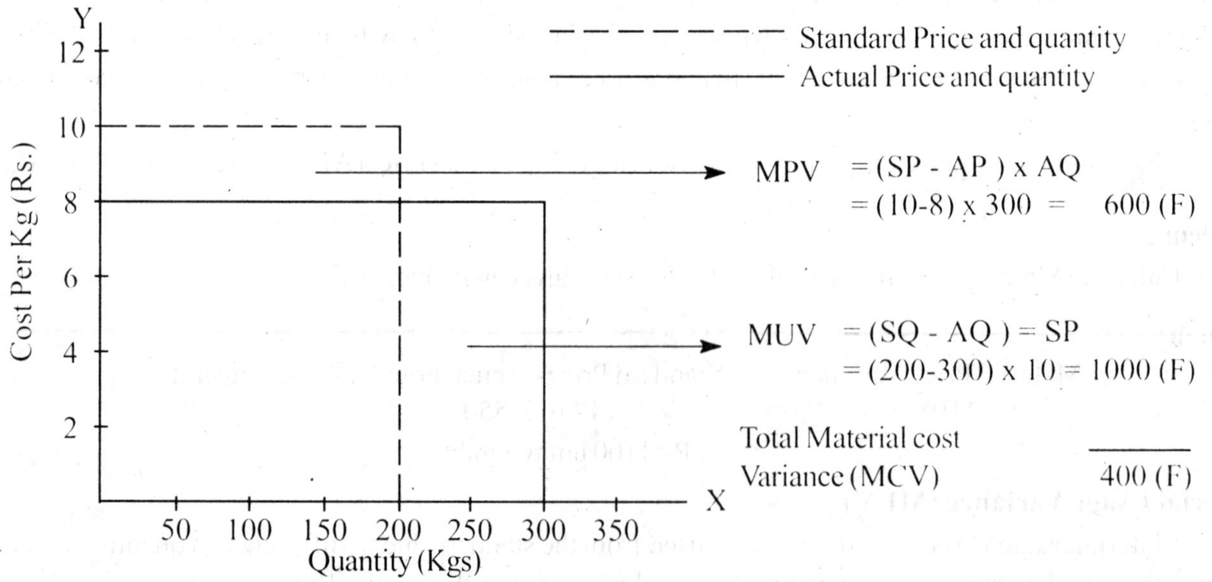

Sub- Variances of Material Usage Variance :

i) Material Mix Variance; ii) Material Revised Usage Variance; and iii) Material yield variance.

This variance can be expressed by the following formulas :

1. Material mix variance = (Standard cost of standard mix - Standard cost of actual mix)

2. Material mix variance = (Revised standard mix of actual input - Actual mix x Standard price)

The revised standard mix is computed with the help of following formula :

$$\text{Revised Standard mix} = \frac{\text{Standard quantity of a particular material}}{\text{Total standard quantity}} \times \text{Total actual Quantity}$$

Problem 5

Compute material mix variance from the information given below :

Material	Standard			Actual		
	Quantity (kg.)	Price (Rs)	Value (Rs)	Quantity (kg.)	Price (Rs)	Value (Rs)
A	60	12	720	50	9	450
B	40	6	240	40	9	360
C	30	9	270	40	12	480
	130	--	1230	130	--	1290

Solution

The computation of material mix variance requires, Revised standard quantity which are calculated as under :

$$\text{Material Revised Standard Quantity} = \frac{\text{Standard quantity of the particular material}}{\text{Total standard quantity}} \times \text{Total actual quantity}$$

$$\text{Material A} = \frac{60}{130} \times 130 = 60 \text{ kg}$$

$$\text{Material B} = \frac{40}{130} \times 130 = 40 \text{ kg}$$

$$\text{Material C} = \frac{30}{130} \times 130 = 30 \text{ kg}$$

The above results clearly reveal that the revised standard mix are equal to the standard mix. Under such a situation formula for the calculation of material mix is the same as for calculation of material usage variance.

Material mix variance (MMV) = (SQ - AQ) x SP

For Material A = (60 - 50) x 12 = Rs. 120 (F)

For Material B = (40 - 40) x 06 = 0

For Material C = (30 - 40) x 09 = Rs. 90 (UF)

= Rs. 30 (F)

Here, we found that difference in material mix is the only cause responsible for material usage variance. However when standard weight and actual weight of material mix varies, the quantity variance shall be due to mix accompanied by other reasons. Under such a situation Material Usage Variance (MUV) would be equal to Material Mix Variance (MMV) and revised Material Usage Variance (RMUV).

Revised Material Usage Variance (RMUV) =

(Standard quantity (SQ) - Revised Standard quantity (RSQ)) x Standard price (SP)

The variance will be favourable if standard quantity is greater than Revised standard quantity and vice versa.

Note : Generally Revised Material Usage Variance is calculated only when question is silent about the output because under such a situation it is not possible to calculate Material Yield Variance. Otherwise Revised Material Usage Variance is not usually calculated.

Problem 6

Calculate a) Material Usage Variance, b) Material Mix Variance and c) Material Revised Usage variance from the following information.

Material	Standard			Actual		
	Quantity (kg.)	Price (Rs)	Value (Rs)	Quantity (kg.)	Price (Rs)	Value (Rs)
EXX	70	15	1050	80	12	960
YA	30	18	540	40	21	840
	100		1590	120		1800

Solution

Material Usage Variance (MUV)	=	(SQ - AQ) x SP		
For material EXX	=	(70 - 80) x 15	=	150 (UF)
For material YA	=	(30 - 40) x 18	=	180 (UF)
Total MUV	=		=	330 (UF)
Material Mix Variance (MMV)	=	(RSQ - AQ) x SP		
For material EXX	=	(84 - 80) x 15	=	60 (F)
For material YA	=	(36-40) x 18	=	72 (UF)
Total MMV	=		=	12 (UF)
Revised Usage Variance	=	(SQ- RSQ) x SP		
For material EXX	=	(70-84) x 15	=	210 (UF)
For material YA	=	(30 - 36) x 18	=	108 (UF)
Total RUV	=		=	318 (UF)

Verification

Material Usage Variance	=	Material Mix Variance + Material Revised usage Variance
330 (UF)	=	12 (UF) + 318 (UF)
330 (UF)	=	330 (UF)

Material Yield Variance

Material Yield variance is calculated with the help of the following formula :

Material Yield Variance (MYV) = (Standard yield - Actual yield) x Standard Rate.*

Or

MYV = (Standard Loss of actual mix - Actual loss of actual mix) x standard cost per unit

$$* \text{ Standard Rate} = \frac{\text{Standard cost of standard mix}}{\text{Net standard output}}$$

Problem 7

ABC Ltd. which has adopted standard costing furnishes the following information

Material	Standard			Actual		
	Quantity (kg.)	Price (Rs)	Value (Rs)	Quantity (kg.)	Price (Rs)	Value (Rs)
X	60	15	900	55	18	990
Y	40	12	480	45	12	540
	100		1380	100		1530
Less	10			20		
	90		1380	80		1530

Calculate Material Yield Variance.

Solution

Material Yield Variance (MYV) = (Standard yield - Actual yield) x Standard rate

MYV = (90 - 80) x 15.33 = 153.3 Unfavourable

As mentioned earlier, Material yield variance can also be calculated on the basis of standard loss and actual loss like :

MYV = (Standard Loss of actual mix - Actual loss on actual mix) x (standard cost per unit)

MYV = (10 - 20) x 15.33 = 153.3 Unfavourable

Calculation of standard rate :

$$\text{Standard Rate} = \frac{\text{Standard cost of standard mix}}{\text{Net standard output}} = \frac{1380}{90} = \text{Rs. } 15.33$$

Problem 8

The standard cost shows the following details relating to the materials needed to produce 1 kg of groundnut oil:

Quantity of groundnut required	:	3 kg.
Price of groundnut	:	Rs.2.50 per kg.
Actual production data		
Production during the week	:	1,000 kg.
Quantity used	:	3,500 kg.
Price of groundnut per kg.	:	Rs.3

Calculate:

a) Material cost variance; b) Material price variance: and c) Material usage variance.

Solution

a) Material cost variance = (Standard quantity for actual output x standard price) - (Actual quantity x Actual price)

= (3,000 x Rs.2.50) - (3,500 x Rs.3) = Rs.3,000 Adverse.

b) Material price variance = (Standard price - Actual price) x Actual quantity

= (Rs.2.50 - Rs.3) x 3,500 = Rs.1,750 Adverse.

c) Material usage variance = (Standard quantity for actual output - Actual quantity) x Standard price

= (3,000 - 3,500) x Rs.2.50 = Rs.1,250 Adverse

Alternative method

Solution by the worksheet method

(1)	(2)	(3)
Applied input at Std. Price and Std. quantity	Flexible budget input a Std. Price and actual quantity	Actual input incurred (Actual quantity x Actual Price)
(Rs.2.5 x 3000)	(Rs.2.50 x 3500)	Rs. (300 x 3500)
= Rs.7,500	= Rs.8,750	= Rs.10,500

Material Usage Variance	Material Price Variance
Rs.1,250 (A)	Rs.1,750 (A)

Total material cost Variance Rs.3000 (A)

Problem 9

From the following, you are required to calculate:

a) Material Price Variance. b) Material Usage Variance. c) Material Cost Variance.

Quantity of material purchased	:	3,000 units.
Value of material purchased for	:	Rs.9,000.
Standard of quantity of material required for one tonne of finished product:25 units.		
Standard rate of material	:	Rs.2 per unit.
Opening stock of material	:	100 units.
Closing stock of material	:	600 units.
Finished production during the period	:	80 tonnes.

Solution

Standard quantity of material required for actual production = 80 x 25 = 2,000 units.

Actual quantity of material used. = Opening Stock + Material purchased - Closing Stock

= 100 + 3,000 - 600 = 2,500 units.

Standard Price per unit = Rs.2

Actual Price per unit = Rs.9,000/3,000 units = Rs.3.

(a) Material price variance = (Std. Price - Actual Price) x Actual Qty.

= (Rs.2 - Rs.3) x 2,500 = Rs.2,500 (A)

(b) Material usage variance = (Std. Qty - Actual Qty) x Std. Rate

= (2,000 - 2,500) x Rs.2 = Rs.1,000 (A)

(c) Material cost variance = (Total Std. Cost - Total Actual Cost)

= (SP x Std. Qty) - (AP x A. Qty)

= (Rs.2 x 2,000 - Rs.3 x 2,500) = Rs.3,500 (A).

Verification

MCV = MUV + MPV

Rs.3,500 (A) = Rs.2,500 (A) + Rs.1,000 (A)

Rs.3,500 (A) = Rs.3,500 (A)

Problem 10

From the following information calculate,

(1) Material Cost Variance

(2) Material Price Variance and

(3) Material Usage Variance

		Standard	Actual
Quantity of Material	:	5,000 units	5,500 units
Price per unit	:	Rs. 2	Rs. 3

and verify results.

Solution

1. **Material Cost Variance : (SQ x SP) - (AQ x AP)**

= (Standard Quantity x Standard Price) - (Actual Quantity x Actual Price)

= (5,000 units x Rs. 2) - (5,500 units x Rs. 3)

= Rs. 10,000 - Rs. 16,500

= Rs. 6,500 (Adverse)

2. **Material Price Variance : (SP - AP) x AQ**

= (Standard Price - Actual Price) x Actual Quantity

= (Rs. 2 - Rs. 3) x 5,500 units

= Re. 1 x 5,500 units

= Rs. 5,500 (Adverse)

3. **Material Usage Variance : (SQ - AQ) x SP**

= (Standard Quantity - Actual Quantity) x Standard Price

= (5,000 units - 5,500 units) x Rs. 2

= 500 units x Rs. 2

= Rs. 1,000 (Adverse)

Verification, MCV = MPV + MUV

Material Cost Variance = Material Price Variance + Material Usage Variance

Rs. 6,500 (A) = Rs. 5,500 (A) + Rs. 1,000 (A)

Problem 11

From the following information calculate,

(1) Material Cost Variance

(2) Material Price Variance

(3) Material Usage Variance

and also verify the results.

Material	Standard Quantity	Standard Price	Actual Quantity	Actual Price
	kgs.	Rs.	kgs.	Rs.
X	100	4	120	3
Y	150	5	180	4
	250		300	

Solution

1. **Material Cost Variance : (SQ x SP) - (AQ x AP)**

= (Standard Quantity x Standard Price) - (Actual Quantity x Actual Price)

Material X = (100 kgs x Rs. 4) - (120 kgs x Rs. 3)
= Rs. 400 - Rs. 360
= Rs. 40 (Favourable)

Material Y = (150 kgs x Rs. 5) - (180 kgs x Rs. 4)
= Rs. 750 - Rs. 720
= Rs. 30 (Favourable)

2. **Material Price Variance : (SP - AP) x AQ**

= (Standard Price - Actual Price) x Actual Quantity

Material X
= (Rs. 4 - Rs. 3) x 120 kgs
= Re. 1 x 120 kgs
= Rs. 120 (Favourable)

Material Y
= (Rs. 5 - Rs. 4) x 180 kgs
= Re. 1 x 180 kgs
= Rs. 180 (Favourable)

3. **Material Usage Variance : (SQ - AQ) x SP**

= (Standard Quantity - Actual Quantity) x Standard Price

Material X = (100 kgs - 120 kgs) x Rs. 4
= 20 kgs x Rs. 4
= Rs. 80 (Adverse)

Material Y = (100 kgs - 120 kgs) x Rs. 4
= 30 kgs x Rs. 5
= Rs. 150 (Adverse)

Verification, MCV = MPV + MUV

Material Cost Variance	=	Material Price Variance + Material Usage Variance
Material X	=	Rs. 40 (F) = Rs. 120 (F) + Rs. 80 (A)
Material Y	=	Rs. 30 (F) = Rs. 180 (F) + Rs. 150 (A)

Problem 12

The standard cost of a product is,
35% of Material A @ Rs.20 per kg.
65% of Material B @ Rs.25 per kg.

The standard loss estimated in the production is 10%. During 200X, 100 kgs. of Material A @ Rs. 15 per kg. and 120 kgs. of Material B @ Rs. 30 per kg. were used. The actual production which turned out good was 180 kgs.

Calculate,

(1) Material Cost Variance
(2) Material Price Variance
(3) Material Usage Variance

and also verify the results.

Solution

Calculation and Notes

(A) **Calculation of Standard quantity of material :**

	Total estimated output	100 kgs.
	Less : Standard loss estimated (i.e. 5%)	- 10 kgs
∴	Effective standard output	90 kgs.

Material 'A' :

If 90 kgs. = 35 kgs

180 kgs = ?

$$= \frac{180 \text{ kgs} \times 35 \text{ kgs}}{90 \text{ kgs}}$$

= 70 kgs

Material 'B' :

If 90 kgs. = 65 kgs

180 kgs = ?

$$= \frac{180 \text{ kgs} \times 65 \text{ kgs}}{90 \text{ kgs}}$$

= 130 kgs

1. **Material Cost Variance : (SQ x SP) - (AQ x AP)**

= (Standard Quantity x Standard Price) - (Actual Quantity x Actual Price)

Material A : (70 kgs x Rs. 20) - (100 kgs x Rs.15)

= Rs. 1,400 - Rs. 1,500

= Rs. 100 (Adverse)

Material B : (130 kgs x Rs. 25) - (120 kgs x Rs. 30)

= Rs. 3250 - Rs. 3600

= Rs. 350 (Adverse)

2. **Material Price Variance : (SP - AP) x AQ**

= (Standard Price - Actual Price) x Actual Quantity

Material A : (Rs. 20 - Rs. 15) x 100 kgs

= Rs. 5 x 100 kgs

= Rs. 500 (Favourable)

Material B : (Rs. 25 - Rs. 30) x 120 kgs

= Rs. 5 x 120 kgs

= Rs. 600 (Adverse)

3. **Material Usage Variance : (SQ - AQ) x SP**

= (Standard Quantity - Actual Quantity) x Standard Price

Material A : (70 kgs - 100 kgs) x Rs. 20

= 30 kgs x Rs. 20

= Rs. 600 (Adverse)

Material B : (130 kgs - 120 kgs) x Rs. 25

= 30 kgs x Rs. 25 = Rs.250 favourable

Verification, MCV = MPV + MUV

Material Cost Variance = Material Price Variance + Material Usage Variance

Material A = Rs. 100 (A) = Rs. 500 (F) + Rs. 600 (A)

Material B = Rs. 350 (A) = Rs. 600 (A) + Rs. 250 (F)

Problem 13

The following particulars derived from the cost records are made available from which you are required to find out,

(1) Material Cost Variance

(2) Material Price Variance and

(3) Material Usage Variance

Opening stock of material	Nil
Closing stock of Material	1,000 units
Standard quantity of material required per ton of output	50 units
Standard price of material per unit	Rs. 1.50
Quantity of materials purchased	5,000 units
Amount of materials purchased	Rs. 10,000
Quantity produced	100 tons

Also verify your results

Solution

Calculation and Notes

(A) Calculation of Standard Quantity of Materials

= Standard Quantity of materials required per ton of output x Quantity produced

= 50 units x 100 tons

= 5,000 units.

(B) Calculation of Actual Quantity used :

= Opening Stock + Purchases - Closing Stock

= Nil + 5,000 units - 1,000 units

= 4,000 units.

(C) Calculation of Actual Price per unit :

$$= \frac{\text{Amount of Materials purchased}}{\text{Quantity of Materials purchased}}$$

$$= \frac{\text{Rs.}10{,}000}{5{,}000 \text{ unit}} = \text{Rs. 2 per unit}$$

1. Material Cost Variance : (SQ x SP) - (AQ x AP)

= (Standard Quantity x Standard Price) - (Actual Quantity x Actual Price)

= (5,000 units x Rs. 1.50) - (4,000 units x Rs. 2)

= Rs. 7,500 - Rs. 8,000

= Rs. 500 (Adverse)

2. Material Price Variance : (SP - AP) x AQ

= (Standard Price - Actual Price) x Actual Quantity

= (Rs. 1.50 - Rs. 2) x 4,000 units

= Re. 0.50 x 4,000 units

= Rs. 2,000 (Adverse)

3. **Material Usage Variance : (SQ - AQ) x SP**

= (Standard Quantity - Actual Quantity) x Standard Price

= (5,000 units - 4,000 units) x Rs. 1.50

= 1,000 units x Rs. 1.50

= Rs. 1,500 (Favourable)

Verification, MCV = MPV + MUV

Material Cost Variance = Material Price Variance + Material Usage Variance

Rs. 500 (A) = Rs. 2,000 (A) + Rs. 1,500 (F)

Problem 14

From the following cost information calculate.

(1) Material Cost Variance

(2) Material Price Variance

(3) Material Usage Variance

Standard		Actual	
Material for 70 kgs.	Finished	Output	2,10,000 kgs.
Product-	100 kgs.	Materials used	2,80,000 kgs.
Price of Material -	Re.1 per kg	Cost of Materials -	Rs. 2,52,000

Verify the results.

Solution

Calculation and Notes

(A) Calculation of Standard Quantity required for Actual Output :

(Standard Input, Standard Output Ratio)

100 kgs. : 70 kgs.

If 70 kgs. output = 100 kgs. output

2,10,000 kgs. = ?

$$= \frac{2,10,000 \times 100}{70}$$

= 3,00,000 kgs.

(B) Calcualtion of Actual Price per kg. :

$$= \frac{\text{Actual Cost of Materials}}{\text{Actual Quantity of Materials used}}$$

$$= \frac{\text{Rs.}2,52,000}{2,80,000 \text{ kgs.}}$$

= Re. 0.90 per kg.

1. **Material Cost Variance : (SQ x SP) - (AQ x AP)**

= (Standard Quantity x Standard Price) - (Actual Quantity x Actual Price)

= (3,00,000 kgs x Rs. 1) - (2,80,000 kgs x Rs. 0.90)

= Rs. 3,00,000 - Rs. 2,52,000

= Rs. 48,000 (Favourable)

2. **Material Price Variance : (SP - AP) x AQ**

= (Standard Price - Actual Price) x Actual Quantity

= (Re. 1 - Rs. 0.90) x 2,80,000 kgs

= Re. 0.10 x 2,80,000 kgs.

= Rs. 28,000 (Favourable)

3. **Material Usage Variance : (SQ - AQ) x SP**

= (Standard Quantity - Actual Quantity) x Standard Price

= (3,00,000 kgs - 2,80,000 kgs) x Re. 1

= 20,000 kgs x Rs. 1

= Rs. 20,000 (Favourable)

Verification, MCV = MPV + MUV

Material Cost Variance = Material Price Variance + Material Usage Variance

Rs. 48,000 (F) = Rs. 28,000 (F) + Rs. 20,000 (F)

Problem 15

Calculate Material mix Variance from the following details,

Material	Standard Quantity units	Actual Quantity units	Standard Price per unit Rs.
A	60	50	15
B	50	40	13
C	40	45	12

Since material A was in short supply, it was decided to reduce its consumption by 12 units and increase the consumption of material B and material C by 7 units and 5 units respectively.

Solution

Calculation and Notes :

(A) Calculation of Standard Revised Mix :

Material A : 60 units - 12 units = 48 units

Material B : 50 units + 7 units = 57 units

Material C : 40 units + 5 units = 45 units

Material Mix Variances : (SRM - AM) x SP

= (Standard Revised Mix - Actual Mix) x Standard Price

Material A : (48 units - 50 units) x Rs. 15

= 2 units x Rs. 15

= Rs. 30 (Adverse)

Material B : (57 units - 40 units) x Rs. 13

= 17 units x Rs. 13

= Rs.221 (Favourable)

Material C : (45 units - 45 units) x Rs. 12

= NIL x Rs. 12

= NIL

Problem 16

The standard mix to produce one unit of product is as follows :

Material A : 60 units @ Rs. 15 per unit		= Rs. 900
Material B : 80 units @ Rs. 20 per unit		= Rs. 1,600
Material C : 100 units @ Rs. 25 per unit		= Rs. 2,500
Total	240 units	Rs. 5,000

During the month of January, 200X 10 units were actually produced and the consumption was as follows :

Material A : 640 units @ Rs. 17.50 per unit		= Rs. 11,200
Material B : 950 units @ Rs. 18 per unit		= Rs. 17,100
Material C : 870 units @ Rs. 27.50 per unit		= Rs. 23,925
Total	2,460 units	Rs. 52,225

You are required to calculate

(1) Material Cost Variance

(2) Material Price Variance

(3) Material Usage Variance

(4) Material Mix Variance

Solution

Calculation and Notes

(A) Calculation of Standard Quantity of Material for actual production :

Material A -

If 1 unit = 60 units

10 units = ? $\frac{10 \times 60}{1}$ = 600 units

Material B -

If 1 unit = 80 units

10 units = ? $\frac{10 \times 80}{1}$ = 800 units

Material C -

If 1 unit = 100 units

10 units = ? $\frac{10 \times 100}{1}$ = 1,000 units

1. Material Cost Variance : (SQ x SP) - (AQ x AP)

= (Standard Quantity x Standard Price) - (Actual Quantity x Actual Price)

Material A : (600 units x Rs. 15) - (640 units x Rs.17.50)

= Rs. 9,000 - Rs. 11,200

= Rs. 2,200 (Adverse)

Material B : (800 units x Rs. 20) - (950 units x Rs. 18)

= Rs. 16,000 - Rs. 17,100

= Rs. 1,100 (Adverse)

Material C : (1,000 units x Rs. 25) - (870 units x Rs. 27.50)

= Rs. 25,000 - Rs. 23,925

= Rs. 1,075 (Favourable)

2. Material Price Variance : (SP - AP) x AQ

= (Standard Price - Actual Price) x Actual Quantity

Material A : (Rs. 15 - Rs. 17.50) x 640 units

= Rs. 2.50 x 640 units = 1,600 (Adverse)

Material B : (Rs. 20 - Rs. 18) x 950 units

= Rs. 2 x 950 units

= Rs. 1,900 (Favourable)

Material C : (Rs. 25 - Rs. 27.50) x 870 units

= Rs. 2.50 x 870 units

= Rs. 2,175 (Adverse)

3. Material Usage Variance : (SQ - AQ) x SP

= (Standard Quantity - Actual Quantity) x Standard Price

Material A : (600 units - 640 units) x Rs. 15

= 40 units x Rs. 15

= Rs. 600 (Adverse)

Material B : (800 units - 950 units) x Rs. 20

= 150 units x Rs. 20

= Rs. 3,000 (Adverse)

Material C : (1,000 units - 870 units) x Rs. 25

= 130 units x Rs. 25

= Rs. 3,250 (Favourable)

4. Material Mix Variance : (SRM - AM) x SP

(i) Calcuation of standard mixing proportion between A, B and C -

A	B	C
600 units	800 units	1,000 units
$\frac{3}{12}$	$\frac{4}{12}$	$\frac{5}{12}$

(ii) Calculation of total actual quantity consumed :

= Material A + Material B + Material C

= 640 units + 950 units + 870 units

= 2,460 units

(iii) Calculation of Standard Revised Mix :

= Actual Quantity Consumed x Standard Mixing Proportion

Material A :	2,460 units x 3/12	= 615 units
Material B :	2,460 units x 4/12	= 820 units
Material C :	2,460 units x 5/12	= 1,025 units

= (Standard Revised Mix - Actual Mix) x Standard Price

Material A : (615 units - 640 units) x Rs. 15

= 25 units x Rs. 15

= Rs. 375 (Adverse)

Material B : (820 units - 950 units) x Rs. 20

= 130 units x Rs. 20

= Rs. 2,600 (Adverse)

Material C : (1,025 units - 870 units) x Rs. 25

= 155 units x Rs. 25

= Rs. 3,875 (Favourable)

Verification, MCV = MPV + MUV

Material Cost Variance	=	Material Price Variance + Material Usage Variance
Material A	:	Rs. 2,200 (A) = Rs. 1,600 (A) + Rs. 600 (A)
Material B	:	Rs. 1,100 (A) = Rs. 1,900 (F) + Rs. 3,000 (A)
Material C	:	Rs. 1,075 (F) = Rs. 2,175 (A) + Rs. 3,250 (F)

Problem 17

From the following information compute the following material variances and verify the results.

(1) Material Cost Variance (2) Material Price Variance

(3) Material Usage Variance (4) Material Mix Variance

Materials	Standard		Actual	
	Quantity	Price	Quantity	Price
	kgs.	Rs.	kgs.	Rs.
X	40	10	20	35
Y	20	20	10	20
Z	20	40	30	30
	80		60	

Solution

1. **Material Cost Variance : (SQ x SP) - (AQ x AP)**

= (Standard Quantity x Standard Price) - (Actual Quantity x Actual Price)

Material X - (40 kgs x Rs. 10) - (20 kgs x Rs. 35)

= Rs. 400 - Rs. 700

= Rs. 300 (Adverse)

Material Y - (20 kgs x Rs. 20) - (10 kgs x Rs. 20)

= Rs. 400 - Rs. 200

= Rs. 200 (Favourable)

Material Z - (20 kgs x Rs. 40) - (30 kgs x Rs. 30)

= Rs. 800 - Rs. 900

= Rs. 100 (Adverse)

2. **Material Price Variance : (SP - AP) x AQ**

= (Standard Price - Actual Price) x Actual Quantity

Material X - (Rs.10 - Rs. 35) x 20 kgs

= Rs. 25 x 20 kgs

= Rs. 500 (Adverse)

Material Y - (Rs. 20 - Rs. 20) x 10 kgs

= NIL x 10 kgs

= NIL

Material Z - (Rs.40 - Rs. 30) x 30 kgs

= Rs. 10 x 30 kgs

= Rs. 300 (Favourable)

3. **Material Usage Variance : (SQ - AQ) x SP**

= (Standard Quantity - Actual Quantity) x Standard Price

Material X = (40 kgs - 20 kgs) x Rs. 10

= 20 kgs x Rs. 10

= Rs. 200 (Favourable)

Material Y = (20 kgs - 10 kgs) x Rs. 20

= 10 kgs x Rs. 20

= Rs. 200 (Favourable)

Material Z = (20 kgs - 30 kgs) x Rs. 40

= 10 kgs x Rs. 40

= Rs. 400 (Adverse)

Material Mix Variance : $\textbf{SP} \times \left(\frac{\textbf{TAQ}}{\textbf{TSQ}} \times \frac{\textbf{SQEM}}{\textbf{1}} - \textbf{AQEM} \right)$

$$= \text{Standard Price} \times \left(\frac{\text{Total Actual Quantity}}{\text{Total Standard Quantity}} \times \frac{\text{Standard Quantity of each material}}{1} - \text{Actual Quantity of each material} \right)$$

Verification, MCV = MPV + MUV

$$\textbf{Material X} = \text{Rs. } 10 \times \left(\frac{60 \text{ kgs.}}{80 \text{ kgs.}} \times \frac{40 \text{ kgs.}}{1} - 20 \text{ kgs.} \right)$$

= Rs. 10 x (30 kgs. - 20 kgs.)

= Rs. 10 x 10 kgs.

= Rs. 100 (Favourable)

$$\textbf{Material Y} = \text{Rs. } 20 \times \left(\frac{60 \text{ kgs.}}{80 \text{ kgs.}} \times \frac{20 \text{ kgs.}}{1} - 10 \text{ kgs.} \right)$$

= Rs. 20 x (15 kgs. - 10 kgs.)

= Rs. 20 x 5 kgs.

= Rs. 100 (Favourable)

$$\textbf{Material Z} = \text{Rs. } 40 \times \left(\frac{60 \text{ kgs.}}{80 \text{ kgs.}} \times \frac{20 \text{ kgs.}}{1} - 30 \text{ kgs.} \right)$$

= Rs. 40 x (15 kgs. - 30 kgs.)

= Rs. 40 x 15 kgs.

= Rs. 600 (Adverse)

Verification, MCV = MPV + MUV

Material Cost Variance = Material Price Variance + Material Usage Variance

Material X : Rs. 300 (A) = Rs. 500 (A) + Rs. 200 (F)

Material Y : Rs. 200 (F) = NIL + Rs. 200 (F)

Material Z : Rs. 100 (A) = Rs. 300 (F) + Rs. 400 (A)

Problem 18

Calculate different material variances from the following data and verify the results.

Material		Standard Mix	Actual Mix
X	:	70 kgs. @ Rs. 2 per kg.	60 kgs. @ Rs. 2 per kg.

: 30 kgs. @ Rs. 4 per kg. 50 kgs. @ Rs. 5 per kg.

100 kgs. 110 kgs.

Solution

1. Material Cost Variance : (SQ x SP) - (AQ x AP)

= (Standard Quantity x Standard Price) - (Actual Quantity x Actual Price)

Material X = (70 kgs x Rs. 2) - (60 kgs x Rs.2)

= Rs. 140 - Rs. 120

= Rs. 20 (Favourable)

Material Y = (30 kgs x Rs. 4) - (50 kgs x Rs. 5)

= Rs. 120 - Rs. 250

= Rs. 130 (Adverse)

2. Material Price Variance : (SP - AP) x AQ

= (Standard Price - Actual Price) x Actual Quantity

Material X = (Rs. 2 - Rs. 2) x 60 kgs

= NIL x 60 kgs

= NIL

Material Y = (Rs. 4 - Rs. 5) x 50 kgs

= Re. 1 x 50 kgs

= Rs. 50 (Adverse)

3. Material Usage Variance : (SQ - AQ) x SP

= (Standard Quantity - Actual Quantity) x Standard Price

Material X : (70 kgs - 60 kgs) x Rs. 2

= 10 kgs x Rs. 2

= Rs. 20 (Favourable)

Material Y : (30 kgs - 50 kgs) x Rs. 4

= 20 kgs x Rs. 4

= Rs. 80 (Adverse)

4. Material Mix Variance : (SRM - AM) x SP

(i) **Calculation of standard mixing proportion between X and Y -**

X : Y

70 kgs. : 30 Kgs.

$$\frac{7}{10} : \frac{3}{10}$$

(ii) Calculation of total actual quantity consumed -

= Material X + Material Y

= 60 kgs. + 50 kgs.

= 110 kgs.

(iii) Calculation of Standard Revised Mix -

= Actual Quantity Consumed x Standard Mixing Proportion

$$\text{Material X} = 110 \text{ kgs.} \times \frac{7}{10} = 77 \text{ kgs.}$$

Material Y = 110 Kgs. x $\frac{3}{10}$ = 33 kgs.

= (Standard Revised Mix - Actual Mix) x Standard Price

Material X = (77 kgs. - 60 kgs.) x Rs. 2

= 17 kgs x Rs.4

= Rs. 68 (Adverse)

Verification MCV = MPV + MUV

Material Cost Variance = Material Price Variance + Material Usage Variance

Material X : Rs. 20 (F) = NIL + Rs. 20 (F)

Material Y : Rs. 130 (A) = Rs. 50 (A) + Rs. 80 (A)

Problem 19

From the following information calculate -

(1) Material Cost Variance (2) Material Price Variance

(3) Material Usage Variance (4) Material Mix Variance

and verify your results.

Material	Standard			Actual		
	Quantity kgs	Price Rs	Value Rs	Quantity kgs	Price Rs	Value Rs
X	50	2.00	100	40	5.00	200
Y	30	3.00	90	20	3.00	60
Z	20	4.00	80	30	3.00	90
	100		270	90		350

Solution

1. **Material Cost Variance : (SQ x SP) - (AQ x AP)**

= (Standard Quantity x Standard Price) - (Actual Quantity x Actual Price)

Material X - (50 kgs x Rs. 2) - (40 kgs x Rs.5)

= Rs.100 - Rs. 200

= Rs. 100 (Adverse)

Material Y - (30 kgs x Rs. 3) - (20 kgs x Rs. 3)

= Rs. 90 - Rs. 60

= Rs. 30 (Favourable)

Material Z - (20 kgs x Rs. 4) - (30 kgs x Rs. 3)

= Rs. 80 - Rs. 90

= Rs. 10 (Adverse)

2. **Material Price Variance : (SP - AP) x AQ**

= (Standard Price - Actual Price) x Actual Quantity

Material X - = (Rs.2 - Rs. 5) x 40 kgs

= Rs. 3 x 40 kgs

= Rs. 120 (Adverse)

Material Y - (Rs. 3 - Rs. 3) x 20 kgs

= NIL x 20 kgs

= NIL

Material Z - (Rs.4 - Rs. 3) x 30 kgs

= Rs. 1 x 30 kgs

= Rs. 30 (Favourable)

3. **Material Usage Variance : (SQ - AQ) x SP**

= (Standard Quantity - Actual Quantity) x Standard Price

Material X = (50 kgs - 40 kgs) x Rs. 2

= 10 kgs x Rs. 2

= Rs. 20 (Favourable)

Material Y = (30 kgs - 20 kgs) x Rs. 3

= 10 kgs x Rs. 3

= Rs. 30 (Favourable)

Material Z = (20 kgs - 30 kgs) x Rs. 4

= 10 kgs x Rs. 4

= Rs. 40 (Adverse)

4. **Material Mix Variance :** $SP \times \left(\frac{TAQ}{TSQ} \times \frac{SQEM}{1} - AQEM \right)$

$$= \text{Standard Price} \times \left(\frac{\text{Total Actual Quantity}}{\text{Total Standard Quantity}} \times \frac{\text{Standard Quantity of each material}}{1} - \text{Actual Quantity of each material} \right)$$

Material X = $\text{Rs. } 2 \times \left(\frac{90 \text{ kgs.}}{100 \text{ kgs.}} \times \frac{50 \text{ kgs.}}{1} - 40 \text{ kgs.} \right)$

= Rs. 2 x (45 kgs. - 40 kgs.)

= Rs. 2 x 5 kgs.

= Rs. 10 (Favourable)

Material Y = $\text{Rs. } 3 \times \left(\frac{90 \text{ kgs.}}{100 \text{ kgs.}} \times \frac{30 \text{ kgs.}}{1} - 20 \text{ kgs.} \right)$

= Rs. 3 x (27 kgs. - 20 kgs.)

= Rs. 3 x 7 kgs.

= Rs. 21 (Favourable)

Material Z = $\text{Rs. } 4 \times \left(\frac{90 \text{ kgs.}}{100 \text{ kgs.}} \times \frac{20 \text{ kgs.}}{1} - 30 \text{ kgs.} \right)$

= Rs. 4 x (18 kgs. - 30 kgs.)

= Rs. 4 x 12 kgs.

= Rs. 48 (Adverse)

Verification, MCV = MPV + MUV

Material Cost Variance = Material Price Variance + Material Usage Variance

Material X : Rs. 100 (A) = Rs. 120 (A) + Rs. 20 (F)

Material Y : Rs. 30 (F) = NIL + Rs. 30 (F)

Material Z : Rs. 10 (A) = Rs. 30 (F) + Rs. 40 (A)

Problem 20

From the following data calculate-

(1) Material Cost Variance (2) Material Price Variance

(3) Material Usage Variance (4) Material Mix Variance

Raw Material	Standard	Actual
X	40 units @ Rs. 50 per unit	50 units @ Rs. 50 per unit
Y	60 units @ Rs. 40 pr unit	60 units @ Rs. 45 per unit
Total	100 units	110 units

Also verify the results.

Solution

1. **Material Cost Variance : (SQ x SP) - (AQ x AP)**

= (Standard Quantity x Standard Price) - (Actual Quantity x Actual Price)

Material X - (40 units x Rs. 50) - (50 units x Rs.50)

= Rs.2,000 - Rs. 2,500

= Rs. 500 (Adverse)

Material Y - (60 units x Rs. 40) - (60 units x Rs.45)

= Rs. 2,400 - Rs. 2,700

= Rs. 300 (Favourable)

2. **Material Price Variance : (SP - AP) x AQ**

= (Standard Price - Actual Price) x Actual Quantity

Material X - (Rs.50 - Rs.50) x 50 units

= NIL x 50 units

= NIL

Material Y - (Rs.40 - Rs.45) x 60 units

= Rs. 5 x 60 units

= Rs. 300 (Adverse)

3. **Material Usage Variance : (SQ - AQ) x SP**

= (Standard Quantity - Actual Quantity) x Standard Price

Material X = (40 unit - 50 units) x Rs. 50

= 10 units x Rs. 50

= Rs. 500 (Adverse)

Material Y = (60 units - 60 units) x Rs. 40

= NIL x Rs. 40

= NIL

4. **Material Mix Variance : (SPM - AM) x SP**

(a) Calculation of standard mixing proportion between X and Y -

X : Y

40 units : 60 units

$$\frac{2}{5} : \frac{3}{5}$$

(b) Calculation of total actual quantity consumed -

= Material X + Material Y

= 50 units + 60 units

= 110 units

(c) Calculation of Standard Revised Mix -

= Actual Quantity Consumed x Standard Mixing Proportion

Material X = 110 units x $\frac{2}{5}$ = 44 units

Material Y = 110 units x $\frac{3}{5}$ = 66 units

= (Standard Revised Mix -Actual Mix) x Standard Price

Material X = (44 units - 50 units) x Rs. 50

= 6 units x Rs. 50

= Rs. 300 (Adverse)

Material Y = (66 units - 60 units) x Rs. 40

= 6 units x Rs. 40

= Rs. 240 (Favourable)

Verification, MCV = MPV + MUV

Material Cost Variance = Material Price Variance + Material Usage Variance

Material X : Rs. 500 (A) = NIL + Rs. 500 (A)

Material Y : Rs. 300 (A) = Rs. 300 (A) + NIL

Labour Variance

The direct labour or wage variance is similar to direct material variance. But for the change of name, they are parallel to the material variances in concept and calculation. Whenever difference occurs between the standards specified for direct labour and the actual, labour variances arise necessitating their investigation and remedy. The following are the principal labour variances calculated in practice :

1) Labour Rate Variance 2) Labour Efficiency Variance 3) Labour Cost Variance

4) Labour Mixture Variance 5) Labour Yield Variance 6) Labour Idle Time Variance

1) Labour Rate Variance :

Labour rate variance is similar to the material price variance, and is the cost of having paid and actual wage higher or lower than standard rate. It is the difference between the standard rate of pay and the rate paid for the actual hours worked. Since labour rate variance equals the time taken multiplied by the difference between the standard and actual wage rate, the following formula emerges :

LRV = (SR - AR) x AH

where, SR = standard wage rate per hour,

AR = actual wage rate per hour,

AH = actual direct labour hours worked.

If the standard rate is higher than the rate, it shall result in favourable variance and vice versa.

Problem

Standard wage rate	:	Rs. 4 per hour
Standard hours	:	400
Actual hours	:	380
Actual wage rate	:	Rs. 5 per hour

Calculate wage rate variance.

Solution

Labour Rate Variance = (Standard Rate - Actual rate) x Actual Time

= (Rs. 4 - Rs. 5) x 380 = Rs. 380 (Adverse)

2) Labour Efficiency Variance

Labour efficiency variance, also called the labour usage or quantity variance, is the difference between the standard hours and the actual hours worked times the standard wage rate. It is the cost of using excess or less hours over the standard hours allowed for the units of products produced. Since labour efficiency variance equals standard wage rate multiplied by the difference between the standard labour hours specified and the actual labour hours expended, the formula is :

Labour Efficiency Variance = (Standard time for actual output - Actual time) = (SH - AH) x SR

where, SH = standard hours

AH = actual hours

SR = standard wage rate per hour.

Using the figures contained in Example 1 above, this variance will be as under :

= (400 - 380) x Rs. 4 = Rs. 80 (Favourable)

The labour efficiency variance may be due to the following reasons :

i) Inaccurate selection of employees, ii) inadequately trained operatives,

iii) labour turnover, i.e. constant training and breaking-in of new employees,

iv) inferior working conditions, v) overtime hours,

vi) length of production run, vii) interruptions or delays in work,

viii) changes in method of production, ix) inaccurate recording of time or output,

x) higher rates of wages during seasonal or emergency operations.

3) Labour Cost Variance

Total direct labour costs depend on the wage rate paid and the number of hours worked. Similar to the material cost, labour cost variance is the difference between the total standard amount of labour and the actual amount of labour times the respective wage rates. In simple words, it is the difference between the standard cost of direct labour and the actual cost expended for it. The formula for the purpose is :

Labour Cost Variance (LCV) = (Std. Rate x Std. Time for Actual Output) - (Actual Rate x Actual Time)

Or

= Standard Cost for Actual Output - Actual Cost

It should be noted that the labour rate and labour efficiency variances must equal the total labour cost variance. Using the figures contained in Example 1 above, labour cost variance would be :

= (Rs. 4 x 400) - (Rs. 5 x 380) = Rs. 300 (Adverse)

Verification

Labour cost variance = Labour rate variance + Labour efficiency variance

Rs. 300 (A) = Rs. 380 (A) + Rs. 80 F)

Problem 1

From the data given below calculate each of the variances for the two departments :

	Dept. X	Dept. Y
Actual gross wage	Rs. 2,050	Rs. 1,740
Standard hours produced	8,000	6,000
Standard rate per hour	30 paise	35 paise
Actual hours worked	8,200	5,800

Solution

Labour Cost variance = (SR x SH) - (AR x AH)

Dept. X = 30 x 8,000 - 25 x 8,200 = Rs. 350 Favourable

Dept. Y = 35 x 6,000 - 30 x 5,800 = Rs. 360 Favourable

Labour Rate variance = (SR - AR) x AH

Dept. X = (30 - 25) x 8,200 = Rs. 410 Favourable

Dept. Y = (35 - 30) x 5,800 = Rs. 290 Favourable

Labour Efficiency variance = (SH - AH) x SR

Dept. X = (30 - 25) x 8,200 = Rs. 410 Favourable

Dept. Y = (35 - 30) x 5,800 = Rs. 290 Favourable

Verification

Labour cost variance = Labour rate variance + Labour Efficiency variance + Idle time variance (if any)

Dept. X = Rs. 350 (R) = Rs. 410 (F) + Rs. 60 (A) = Rs. 350 (F)

Dept. Y = Rs. 360 (F) = Rs. 290 (F) + Rs. 70 (F) = Rs. 360 (F)

Note : Actual Wage Rate = $\frac{\text{Actual gross wages paid}}{\text{Actual hours worked}}$

Dept. X = $\frac{2,050}{8,200}$ = 25 paise Dept. Y = $\frac{1,740}{5,800}$ = 30 paise

Labour Mix Variance

Labour mix variance is like materials mix variance and is a part of labour efficiency variance. It arises when there is a change in the labour composition during a particular period. It is calculated in the same manner as the material mix variance and; hence, also called gang composition variance. The following formulae are applicable.

Labour Mix Variance = Standard Cost of Std. Composition - Standard Cost of Actual Composition.

In case there is a change in the labour composition due to shortage of one category of labour, but there is no change in the total standard time and actual time spent, then :

Labour Mix variance = Std. Cost of Revised Std. Composition - Standard Cost of Actual Composition.

In case standard are revised and total standard time of labour differs from the actual time of labour

Labour Mix Variance = (Revised Standard time - Actual Time) x Standard Rate

$$\text{where, Revised standard time} = \frac{\text{Total time of actual workers}}{\text{Total time of std. workers}} \times \text{Standard Time}$$

Problem 2

Data relating to a job are as thus :

Standard rate of wages per hour	:	Rs. 10
Standard hours	:	300
Actual rate of wages per hour	:	Rs. 12
Actual hours	:	Rs. 200

Your are required to calculate :

a) Labour Cost Variance b) Labour Rate Variance, and c) Labour Efficiency Variance.

Solution

a) Labour Cost Variance = (Standard Rate x Standard Time) - (Actual Rate x Actual Time)
= (Rs. 10 x 300) - (Rs. 12 x 200) = Rs. 600 (Favourable)

b) Labour Rate = (Standard Rate - Actual Rate) x Actual Time Variance
= (Rs. 10 - Rs. 12) x 200 = Rs. 400 (Adverse)

c) Labour Efficiency = (Standard Time - Actual Time) x Standard Rate
= (300 - 200) x Rs. 10 = Rs. 1,000 (Favourable)

Problem 3

The standard time for unit component X is given below :

Standard hours per unit	:	15
Standard rate	:	Rs. 4 per hour
The actual data and related information are as under	:	
Actual production	:	1,000 units
Actual hours	:	15,300 hours
Actual rate	:	Rs. 3.90 per hour

Calculate : a) Labour cost variance, b) Labour efficiency variance, and c) Labour rate variance.

Solution

a) Labour cost variance = (SR x SH - AR x AH)
= (4 x 15,000 - 3.90 x 15,300) = Rs. 330 (F)

b) Labour efficiency variance = (SH - AH) x SR
= (15,000 - 15,300) x Rs. 4 = Rs. 1,200 (A)

c) Labour rate variance = (SR - AR) x AH
= (Rs.4 - Rs. 3.90) x 15,300 = Rs. 1,530 (F).

Verification

Labour efficiency variance + Labour rate variance = Labour cost variance
Rs. 1,200 (A) + Rs. 15,300 (F) = Rs. 330 (F).

Alternative method

Solution by the Worksheet Method

Applied Inputs standard labour rate (SR) allowed for actual output times standard hours (SH)	Flexible budget inputs standard labour rate (SR) times actual hours (AH) used	Actual inputs actual labour rate (AR) times actual hours (AH) used
(SR x SH)	(SR x AH)	(AR x AH)
(Rs. 4 x 15,000 hrs.)	(Rs. 4 x 15,200 hrs.)	Rs. 3.90 x 15,300 hrs.
= Rs. 60,000	= Rs. 61, 200	= Rs. 59,670

Labour Efficiency Variance	Labour Rate Variance
Rs. 1,200 (A)	Rs. 1,530 (F)

Total Labour Cost Variance Rs. 330 (F)

Problem 4

A gang of workers normally consists of 30 men, 15 women and 10 boys. They are paid at standard rates as under :

Man : Rs. 0.80
Woman : Rs. 0.60
Boy : Rs. 0.40

In a normal working week of 40 hours, the gang is expected produce 2,000 units of output.

During the week ended 31st December, the gang consisted of 40 men, 10 women and 5 boys. The actual wages paid were @ Rs. 0.70, Rs. 0.65 and 0.30 respectively 1,600 units were produced.

Calculate : a) Wage Variance; b) Wage rate variance, c) Labour efficiency variance
d) Gang composition variance, (i.e. labour mix variance,) & e) Labour revised efficiency variance.

Solution

Type of worker	Standard			Actual		
	Hours	Rate	Amount	Hours	Rate	Amount
Men	30 x 40 = 1,200	0.80	960	40 x 40 = 1,600	0.70	1,120
Women	15 x 40 = 600	0.60	360	10 x 40 = 400	0.65	260
Boys	10 x 40 = 400	0.40	160	5 x 40 = 200	0.30	60
Total	2,200		1,480	2,200		1,440

Hours = No. of workers x Weekly hours

a) Wages Variance (Labour Cost Variances) = (Standard Cost of Actual output) - (Actual Cost)
= 1,184 - 1,440 = Rs. 256 (Adverse)

$$\text{SC of actual output} = \frac{1,600}{2,000} \times 1,480 = \text{Rs. } 1,184$$

b) Labour Rate Variance = (SR - AR) x AH

Men	=	(0.80 - 0.70) x 1,600	=	Rs. 160 (Favourable)
Women	=	(0.60 - 0.65) x 400	=	Rs. 20 (Adverse)
Boys	=	(0.40 - 0.30) x 200	=	Rs. 20 (Favourable)
		LRV	=	Rs. 160 (Favourable)

c) Labour Efficiency Variance = (SH - for actual output - AH) x SR

Men	=	(960 - 1,600) x 0.80	=	Rs. 512 (A)
Women	=	(480 - 400) x 0.60	=	Rs. 48 (F)
Boys	=	(320 - 200) x 0.40	=	Rs. 48 (F)
		LEV	=	Rs. 416 (A)

Standard hours for actual output are calculated as follows :

Men $= \frac{1,200}{2,000} \times 1,600 = 960$ Women $= \frac{600}{2,000} \times 1,600 = 480$

Boys $= \frac{400}{2,000} \times 1,600 = 320$

d) Labour Mix Variance (Gang - composition variance) = (Revised Standard hours - Actual hours) x Standard Rate

Men	=	(1,200 - 1,600) x 0.80	=	Rs. 320 (A)
Women	=	(600 - 400) x 0.60	=	Rs. 120 (F)
Boys	=	(400 - 200) x 0.40	=	Rs. 80 (F)
		LMV	=	Rs. 120 (A)

Revised Std. hrs. are total actual hours i.e., 2,200 hrs. in the standard proportion for men, women and boys. This is given in the table above.

e) Labour Revised Efficiency Variance = (Std. hours for actual output - Revised Std. hrs.) x Std. Rate

Men	=	(960 - 1,200) x 0.80	=	Rs. 192 (A)
Women	=	(480 - 600) x 0.60	=	Rs. 72 (A)
Boys	=	(320 - 400) x 0.40	=	Rs. 32 (A)
		LREV	=	Rs. 296 (A)

Verification

Wage Variance	=	Rate Variance + Efficiency Variance
Rs. 256 (A)	=	Rs. 160 (F) + Rs. 416 (A)
Efficiency Variance	=	Mix Variance + Revised Efficiency Variance
Rs. 416 (A)	=	Rs. 120 (A) + Rs. 296 (A)

Labour Idle Time Variance

It arises due to abnormal circumstances like strike, lock-outs, power failures, etc., and is calculated as under :

Idle Time Variance = Idle hours x Standard hourly rate

For example, in a factory's idle time recorded was 40 hours and workers were paid Rs. 15 per hour. Thus variance would be 40 hours x Rs. 15 = Rs. 600.

This variance will be always unfavorable.

Labour Yield Variance

It is just like material yield variance. It is the difference between the standard labour output and actual output or yield. It is calculated as below :

Labour Yield Variance = (Std. Production for Actual Mix - Actual Production) x Std. cost per unit.

If the actual production is more than standard production, the difference would be a favorable variance and vice versa. However, it should be noted that the figure would be negative.

Problem 5

Standard production	:	200 units
Actual production	:	180 units
Standard wage rate	:	Rs. 15 per hour
Standard time	:	2 hours per unit.

Solution

Labour yield would be :

Standard cost per unit	=	2 hours x Rs. 15	=	Rs. 30
Labour Yield Variance	=	(200 - 180) x Rs. 30	=	Rs. 600 (A).

Problem 6

From the following records of Apollo Bolt Nut Manufacturing Company you are required to compute material and labour variances :

An input of 100 kg. of material yield to a standard out put of 10,00,000 units.

Standard price per kg. of material = Rs. 20

Actual quantity of material issued and used by production department 10,000 kg.

Actual price per kg. of material	:	Rs. 21 per kg.
Actual output	:	9,00,000 units
Number of employees	:	200
Standard wage rate per employee per day	:	Rs. 40
Standard daily output per employee	:	100 units
Total number of days worked	:	50 days

(Idle time paid for and included in the above half day for each employee)

Actual wage rate per day.	:	Rs. 45

Solution

Material Cost Variance = (SQ x SP - AQ x AP)

= (9,000 x 20) - (10,000 x 21) = Rs.30,000 (A)

$$SQ = \frac{100 \text{ kg}}{10,000} \times 9,00,000 \text{ units} = 9,000 \text{ kg.}$$

a) Material Price Variance = (SP - AP) x AQ

= (20 - 21) x 10,000 = Rs. 10,000 (A)

b) Material Quantity Variance = (SQ - AQ) x SP

= (9,000 - 10,000) x 20 = Rs. 20,000 (A)

$$\text{Man-days required for actual output} = \frac{9,00,000 \text{ units}}{100} = 9,000 \text{ man-days}$$

Idle time	=	$\frac{1}{2}$ of 200	=	100 days
Actual Man-days	=	200 x 50	=	10,000
c) Labour Cost Variance	=	Standard Cost - Actual Cost		
	=	(9,000 x 40) - (10,000 x 45)	=	Rs. 90,000 (A)
d) Labour Rate Variance	=	(SR - AR) x Actual days		
	=	(40 - 45) x 10,000	=	Rs. 50,000 (A)
v) Labour Efficiency Variance	=	(Std. days - Actual days) x SR		
	=	(9,000 - 10,000) x 40	=	Rs. 40,000 (A)
vi) Idle Time Variance	=	Idle time x SR		
	=	100 days x Rs. 40	=	Rs. 4,000 (A)

Problem 7

The standard time rate for a unit component are given as follows:

Standard hours per unit	Hrs. 15
Standard rate per hour	Rs. 4

The actual data and related information are as follows:

Actual production	1,000 units
Actual hours	15,300 hours
Actual rate per hour	Rs. 3.90

Calculate,

(1) Labour Cost Variance

(2) Labour Rate Variance

(3) Labour Efficiency Variance and

verify the results.

Solution

Calculation and Notes

(A) Calculation of standard labour hours for actual production

If 1 unit = 15 Hours

∴ 1,000 units = ?

$$= \frac{1{,}000 \text{ units} \times 15 \text{ Hours}}{1 \text{ unit}}$$

= 15,000 Hours

1. **Labour Cost Variance : (SH x SR) - (AH x AR)**

= (Standard Hours x Standard Rate) - (Actual Hours x Actual Rate)

= (15,000 Hours x Rs.4) - (15,300 Hours x Rs.3.90)

= Rs.60,000 - Rs.59.670

= Rs.330 (Favourable)

2. **Labour Rate Variance : (SR - AR) x AH**

= (Standard Rate - Actual Rate) x Actual Hours

= (Rs.4 - Rs.3.90) x 15,300 Hrs.

= Re.0.10 x 15,300 Hrs.

= Rs.1,530 (Favourable)

3. **Labour Efficiency Variance : (SH - AH) x SR**

= (Standard Hours - Actual Hours) x Standard Rate

= (15,000 Hours - 15,300 Hours) x Rs.4

= 300 Hours x Rs.4

= Rs.1,200 (Adverse)

Verification, LCV = LRV + LEV

Labour Cost Variance = Labour Rate Variance + Labour Efficiency Variance

Rs.300 (F) = Rs.1,530 (F) + Rs.1,200 (A)

Problem 8

From the following particulars relating to a production order calculate,

(1) Labour Cost Variance

(2) Labour Rate Variance

(3) Labour Efficiency Variance

Also verify the results.

Standard hours per unit	Hrs. 20
Standard rate per hour	Rs. 5
Actual production	2,000 units
Actual hours	30,000 hours
Actual rate per hour	Rs. 4

Solution

Calculation and Notes

(A) Calculation of standard labour hours for actual production :

If 1 unit = 20 Hours

2,000 units = ?

$$= \frac{2{,}000 \text{ units} \times 20 \text{ Hours}}{1 \text{ unit}}$$

= 40,000 Hours

1. **Labour Cost Variance : (SH x SR) - (AH x AR)**

= (Standard Hours x Standard Rate) - (Actual Hours x Actual Rate)

= (40,000 Hours x Rs.5) - (30,000 Hours x Rs.4)

= Rs.2,00,000 - Rs.1,20,000

= Rs.80,000 (Favourable)

2. **Labour Rate Variance : (SR - AR) x AH**

= (Standard Rate - Actual Rate) x Actual Hours

= (Rs.5 - Rs.4) x 30,000 Hrs.

= Re.1 x 30,000 Hrs.

= Rs.30,000 (Favourable)

3. **Labour Efficiency Variance : (SH - AH) x SR**

= (Standard Hours - Actual Hours) x Standard Rate

= (40,000 Hours - 30,000 Hours) x Rs.5

= 10,000 Hours x Rs.5

= Rs.50,000 (Favourable)

Verification, LCV = LRV + LEV

Labour Cost Variance = Labour Rate Variance + Labour Efficiency Variance

Rs.80,000 (F) = Rs.30,000 (F) + Rs.50,000 (F)

Problem 9

From the following information calculate for each department

(1) Labour Cost Variance

(2) Labour Rate Variance

(3) Labour Efficiency Variance

Also verify the results.

	Departments	
	X	**Y**
Gross wages - direct	Rs. 28,080	Rs.19,370
Standard hours produced	Hrs. 8,640	Hrs. 6,015
Standard rate per hour	Rs. 3	Rs. 3.40
Actual hours worked	Hrs. 8,200	Hrs. 6,345

Solution

Calculation and Notes

(A) Calculation of Actual Rate per hour

$$\frac{\text{Gross Wages - Direct}}{\text{Actual Hours Worked}}$$

Dept. X $\frac{\text{Rs.28,080}}{\text{Hrs. 8,200}}$ = Rs. 3.4243902

Dept. Y $\frac{\text{Rs.19,370}}{\text{Hrs. 6,345}}$ = Rs. 3.0527974

(1) Labour Cost Variance : (SH x SR) - (AH x AR)

= (Standard Hours x Standard Rate) - (Actual Hours x Actual Rate)

Dept. X = (8,640 Hours x Rs.3) - (8,200 Hours x Rs.3.4243902)

= Rs.25,920 - Rs.28,080

= Rs.2,160 (Adverse)

Dept. Y = (6,015 Hours x Rs.3.40) - (6,345 Hours x Rs.3.0527974)

= Rs.20,451 - Rs.19,370

= Rs.1,081 (Favourable)

2. Labour Rate Variance : (SR - AR) x AH

= (Standard Rate - Actual Rate) x Actual Hours

Dept. X = (Rs.3 - Rs.3.4243902) x 8,200 Hrs.

= Re.0.4243902 x 8,200 Hrs.

= Rs.3,480 (Adverse)

Dept. Y = (Rs.3.40 - Rs.3.052794) x 6,345 Hrs.

= Re.0.347206 x 6,345 Hrs.

= Rs.2,203 (Favourable)

3. Labour Efficiency Variance : (SH - AH) x SR

= (Standard Hours - Actual Hours) x Standard Rate

Dept. X = (8,640 Hours - 8,200 Hours) x Rs.3

= 440 Hours x Rs.3

= Rs.1,320 (Favourable)

Dept. Y = (6,015 Hours - 6,345 Hours) x Rs.3.40

= 330 Hours x Rs.3.40

= Rs.1,122 (Adverse)

Verification, LCV = LRV + LEV

Labour Cost Variance = Labour Rate Variance + Labour Efficiency Variance

Dept. X = Rs.2,160 (A) = Rs.3,480 (A) + Rs.1,320 (F)

Dept. Y = Rs.1,081 (F) = Rs.2,203 (F) + Rs.1,122 (A)

Problem 10

The following information relates to cost labour records of Ajmera Company.

Payroll allocation to Direct wages, Rs.4,000. Time card analysis shows that 3,700 hours were worked on production lines. Production reports for the period showed that 1,600 units have been completed each having standard labour hour times of 2 hours and a standard labour rate of Rs.1 per hour.

Calculate labour variances and check your answer.

Solution

(A) Calculation of Standard Cost of actual production

= 1,600 units x 2 Hours x Re.1

= Rs.3,200

(B) Calculation of actual labour rate per hour

$$= \frac{\text{Total Direct Wages}}{\text{Actual Hours Worked}} = \frac{\text{Rs.4,000}}{\text{3,700 Hrs.}} = \text{Rs. 1.081}$$

(C) Calculation of Standard Hours

= Units completed x Standard Labour Hour per unit

= 1,600 units x 2 Hours

= 3,200 Hrs.

1. Labour Cost Variance : (SH x SR) - (AH x AR)

= Standard Cost - Actual Cost

= (Standard Hours x Standard Rate) - Actual Hours x Actual Rate

= Rs.3,200 - Rs.4,000

= Rs.800 (Adverse)

2. Labour Rate Variance : (SR - AR) x AH

= (Standard Rate - Actual Rate) x Actual Hours

= (Re.1 - Rs.1.081) x 3,700 Hrs.

= Rs.300 (Adverse)

3. **Labour Efficiency Variance : (SH - AH) x SR**

= (Standard Hours - Actual Hours) x Standard Rate

= (3,200 Hours - 3,700 Hours) x Re.1

= 500 Hours x Re.1

= Rs.500 (Adverse)

Verification, LCV = LRV + LEV

Labour Cost Variance = Labour Rate Variance + Labour Efficiency Variance

Rs.800 (A) = Rs.300 (A) + Rs.500 (A)

Problem 11

From the following cost data calculate the labour variances and verify the results :

Standard time per unit		Hrs. 10
Standard rate per hour		Rs. 5
Actual production		1,000 units
Actual hours paid	11,000 Hrs.	
Less : Idle time	- 500 Hrs.	
Production time		Hrs. 10,500

The actual labour payment was made @ Rs.6 per hour.

Calculate,

(1) Labour Cost Variance

(2) Labour Rate Variance

(3) Labour Efficiency Variance and

Solution

Calculation and Notes

(A) Calculation of standard labour hours for actual production

If 1 unit = 10 Hours

1,000 units = ?

$$= \frac{1{,}000 \text{ units} \times 10 \text{ Hours}}{1 \text{ unit}}$$

= 10,000 Hours

1. **Labour Cost Variance : (SH x SR) - (AH x AR)**

= (Standard Hours x Standard Rate) - (Actual Hours x Actual Rate)

= (10,000 Hours x Rs.5) - (11,000 Hours x Rs.6)

= Rs.50,000 - Rs.66,000

= Rs.16,000 (Adverse)

2. **Labour Rate Variance : (SR - AR) x AH**

= (Standard Rate - Actual Rate) x Actual Hours

= (Rs.5 - Rs.6) x 11,000 Hrs.

= Re.1 x 11,000 Hrs.

= Rs.11,000 (Adverse)

3. **Labour Efficiency Variance : (SH - AH) x SR**

= (Standard Hours - Actual Hours) x Standard Rate

= (10,000 Hours - 10,500 Hours) x Rs.5

= 500 Hours x Rs.5

= Rs.2,500 (Adverse)

Verification, LCV = LRV + LEV + ITV

Labour Cost Variance = Labour Rate Variance + Labour Efficiency Variance + Idle Time Variance

Rs.16,000 (A) = Rs.11,000 (A) + Rs.2,500 (A) + Rs.2,500 (A)

Problem 12

Using the following cost information calculate,

(1) Labour Cost Variance

(2) Labour Rate Variance

(3) Labour Efficiency Variance

(4) Idle Time Variance

Also verify your results.

Gross direct wages	Rs.3,000
Standard hours produced	Hrs. 1,600
Standard rate per hour	Rs. 1.50
Actual hours worked	Hrs. 1,500

(Out of which hours not worked i.e. abnormal idle time are 50 Hrs.)

Calculation and Notes

(A) Calculation of Actual Rate per hour

$$\frac{\text{Gross Direct Wages}}{\text{Actual Hours Worked}} = \frac{\text{Rs.3,000}}{\text{1,500 Hrs.}} = \text{Rs. 2 per hour}$$

(1) Labour Cost Variance : (SH x SR) - (AH x AR)

= (Standard Hours x Standard Rate) - (Actual Hours x Actual Rate)

= (1,600 Hours x Rs.1.50) - (1,500 Hours x Rs.2)

= Rs.2,400 - Rs.3,000

= Rs.600 (Adverse)

(2) Labour Rate Variance : (SR - AR) x AH

= (Standard Rate - Actual Rate) x Actual Hours

= (Rs.1.50 - Rs.2) x 1,500 Hrs.

= Re.0.50 x 1,500 Hrs.

= Rs.750 (Adverse)

(3) Labour Efficiency Variance : (SH - AH) x SR

= (Standard Hours - Actual Hours) x Standard Rate

= (1,600 Hours - 1,450 Hours) x Rs.1.50

= 150 Hours x Rs.1.50

= Rs.225 (Favourable)

(4) Idle Time Variance : (IT x SR)

= Idle Time x Standard Rate

= 50 Hours x Rs. 1.50

= Rs.75 (Adverse)

Verification, LCV = LRV + LEV + ITV

Labour Cost Variance = Labour Rate Variance + Labour Efficiency Variance + Idle Time Variance

Rs.600 (A) = Rs.750 (A) + Rs.225 (F) + Rs.75 (A)

Problem 13

Calculate different labour variances from the following cost data :

Standard time per unit	10 Hours.
Standard rate per hour	Rs.4
Actual production	1,100 units
Hours Taken - Production	11,500 Hours.
Add : Idle Time	+ 500 Hours.
Total	12,000 Hours.

Payment of Rs. 60,000 was made @ Rs.5 per hour.

Solution

Calculation and Notes

(A) Calculation of standard labour hours for actual production

If 1 unit = 10 Hours

1,100 units = ?

$$= \frac{1,100 \text{ units x } 10 \text{ Hours}}{1 \text{ unit}}$$

= 11,000 Hours

1. **Labour Cost Variance : (SH x SR) - (AH x AR)**

= (Standard Hours x Standard Rate) - (Actual Hours x Actual Rate)

= (11,000 Hours x Rs.4) - (12,000 Hours x Rs.5)

= Rs.44,000 - Rs.60,000

= Rs.16,000 (Adverse)

2. **Labour Rate Variance : (SR - AR) x AH**

= (Standard Rate - Actual Rate) x Actual Hours

= (Rs.4 - Rs.5) x 12,000 Hrs.

= Re.1 x 12,000 Hrs.

= Rs.12,000 (Adverse)

3. **Labour Efficiency Variance : (SH - AH) x SR**

= (Standard Hours - Actual Hours) x Standard Rate

= (11,000 Hours - 11,500 Hours) x Rs.4

= 500 Hours x Rs.4

= Rs.2,000 (Adverse)

(4) **Idle Time Variance : (IT x SR)**

= Idle Time x Standard Rate

= 500 Hours x Rs. 4

= Rs.2000 (Adverse)

Verification,

LCV	=	LRV + LEV + ITV
Labour Cost Variance	=	Labour Rate Variance + Labour Efficiency Variance + Idle Time Variance
Rs.16,000 (A)	=	Rs.12,000 (A) + Rs.2,000 (A) + Rs.2,000 (A)

Problem 14

From the following details calculate,

(1) Labour Cost Variance

(2) Labour Rate Variance

(3) Labour Efficiency Variance

(4) Labour Mix Variance

Material	Standard			Actual		
	Hours	Rate Rs.	Amount Rs.	Hours	Rate Rs.	Amount Rs.
X	30	5	150	32	5	160
Y	40	4	160	32	4.25	136
Total	70		310	64		296

Solution

1. **Labour Cost Variance : (SH x SR) - (AH x AR)**

= (Standard Hours x Standard Rate) - (Actual Hours x Actual Rate)

Material X = (30 Hours x Rs.5) - (32 Hours x Rs.5)

= Rs.150 - Rs.160

= Rs.10 (Adverse)

Material Y = (40 Hours x Rs.4) - (32 Hours x Rs.4.25)

= Rs.160 - Rs.136

= Rs.24 (Favourable)

2. **Labour Rate Variance : (SR - AR) x AH**

= (Standard Rate - Actual Rate) x Actual Hours

Material X = (Rs.5 - Rs.5) x 32 Hours.

= Rs.NIL x 32 Hrs.

= NIL

Material X = (Rs.4 - Rs.4.25) x 32 Hours.

= Rs.0.25 x 32 Hrs.

= Rs.8 (Adverse)

3. **Labour Efficiency Variance : (SH - AH) x SR**

= (Standard Hours - Actual Hours) x Standard Rate

Material X = (30 Hours - 32 Hours) x Rs.5

= 2 Hours x Rs.5

= Rs.10 (Adverse)

Material Y = (40 Hours - 32 Hours) x Rs.4

= 8 Hours x Rs.4

= Rs.32 (Favourable)

4. **Labour Mix Variance : (SRH - AH) x SR**

(Standard Revised Mix - Actual Mix) x Standard Rate

(a) **Calculation of standard mixing proportion between X and Y**

X	:	Y
30 Hours	:	40 Hours
$\frac{3}{7}$	:	$\frac{4}{7}$

(b) Calculation of total actual hours worked :

= Material X + Material Y

= 32 Hours + 32 Hours

= 64 Hours

(c) **Caculation of standard revised hours**

= Actual hours worked x Standard mixing proportion

Material X = 64 Hours x $\frac{3}{7}$ = 27.42 i.e. 27 Hours

Material Y = 64 Hours x $\frac{4}{7}$ = 36.57 i.e. 37 Hours

= (Standard Revised Hours - Actual Hours) x Standard Rate

Material X = (27 Hours - 32 Hours) x Rs.5

= 5 Hours x Rs.5

= Rs.25 (Adverse)

Material Y = (37 Hours - 32 Hours) x Rs.4

= 5 Hours x Rs.4

= Rs.20 (Favourable)

Verification, LCV = LRV + LEV

Labour Cost Variance = Labour Rate Variance + Labour Efficiency Variance

Material X = Rs.10 (A) = NIL + Rs.10 (A)

Material Y = Rs.24 (F) = Rs.8 (A) + Rs.32 (F)

Problem 15

The following are the details of a job which is expected to be complete within 50 weeks.

Grade of workers	Standard		Actual	
	Number of workers	Weekly wage rate per workers Rs.	Number of workers	Weekly wage rate per worker Rs.
Skilled	80	75	70	80
Semi-skilled	40	50	40	60
Unskilled	50	35	50	20

55 weeks were taken to complete the job, Calculate -

(1) Labour Cost Variance

(2) Labour Rate Variance

(3) Labour Efficiency Variance

(4) Labour Mix Variance

and verify your results.

Solution

Calculation and Notes

Statement showing Standard and Actual Labour Cost

Grade of workers	Standard			Actual		
	Weekly Hours	Rate Rs.	Amount Rs.	Weekly Hours	Rate Rs.	Amount Rs.
Skilled	80 x 50 = 4,000	75	3,00,000	70 x 55 = 3,850	80	3,08,000
Semi-skilled	40 x 50 = 2,000	50	1,00,000	40 x 55 = 2,200	60	1,32,000
Unskilled	50 x 50 = 2,500	35	87,500	50 x 55 = 2,750	20	55,000
Total	8,500		4,87,500	8,800		4,95,000

1. **Labour Cost Variance : (SH x SR) - (AH x AR)**

= (Standard Hours x Standard Rate) - (Actual Hours x Actual Rate)

Skilled = (4,000 Hours x Rs.75) - (3,850Hours x Rs.80)

= Rs.3,00,000 - Rs.3,08,000

= Rs.8,000 (Adverse)

Semi-skilled = (2,000 Hours x Rs.50) - (2,200 Hours x Rs.60)

= Rs.1,00,000 - Rs.1,32,000

= Rs.32,000 (Adverse)

Unskilled = (2,500 Hours x Rs.35) - (2,750 Hours x Rs.20)

= Rs.87,500 - Rs.55,000

= Rs.32,500 (Favourable)

2. **Labour Rate Variance : (SR - AR) x AH**

= (Standard Rate - Actual Rate) x Actual Hours

Skilled = (Rs.75 - Rs.80) x 3,850 Hours.

= Rs.5 x 3,850 Hrs.

= Rs.19,250 (Adverse)

Semi-skilled = (Rs.50 - Rs.60) x 2,200 Hours.

= Rs.10 x 2,200 Hrs.

= Rs.22,000 (Adverse)

Unskilled = (Rs.35 - Rs.20) x 2,750 Hours.

= Rs.15 x 2,750 Hrs.

= Rs.41,250 (Favourable)

3. **Labour Efficiency Variance : (SH - AH) x SR**

= (Standard Hours - Actual Hours) x Standard Rate

Skilled = (4,000 Hours - 3,850 Hours) x Rs.75

= 150 Hours x Rs.75

= Rs.11,250 (Favourable)

Semi-skilled = (2,000 Hours - 2,200 Hours) x Rs.50

= 200 Hours x Rs.50

= Rs.10,000 (Adverse)

Unskilled = (2,500 Hours - 2,750 Hours) x Rs.35

= 250 Hours x Rs.35

= Rs.8,750 (Adverse)

4. Labour Mix Variance : (SRH - AH) x SR

= (Standard Revised Hours - Actual Hours) x Standard Rate

(a) Calculation of standard Revised Hours -

$$= \frac{\text{Standard Time per grade}}{\text{Total Standard Time}} \times \text{Total Actual Time}$$

Skilled $= \frac{4{,}000 \text{ Hours}}{8{,}500 \text{ Hours}} \times 8{,}800 \text{ Hours} = 4{,}141 \text{ Hours}$

Semi-skilled $= \frac{2{,}000 \text{ Hours}}{8{,}500 \text{ Hours}} \times 8{,}800 \text{ Hours} = 2{,}071 \text{ Hours}$

Unskilled $= \frac{2{,}500 \text{ Hours}}{8{,}500 \text{ Hours}} \times 8{,}800 \text{ Hours} = 2{,}588 \text{ Hours}$

= (Standard Revised Hours - Actual Hours) x Standard Rate

Skilled = (4,141 Hours - 3,850 Hours) x Rs.75

= 291 Hours x Rs.75

= Rs.21,825 (Favourable)

Semi-skilled = (2,071 Hours - 2,200 Hours) x Rs.50

= 129 Hours x Rs.50

= Rs.6,450 (Adverse)

Unskilled = (2,588 Hours - 2,750 Hours) x Rs.35

= 162 Hours x Rs.35

= Rs.5,670 (Adverse)

Verification,

LCV	=	LRV + LEV
Labour Cost Variance	=	Labour Rate Variance + Labour Efficiency Variance
Skilled	:	Rs.8,000 (A) = Rs. 19,250 (A) + Rs. 11,250 (F)
Semi-skilled	:	Rs.32,000 (A) = Rs. 22,000 (A) + Rs. 10,000 (A)
Unskilled	:	Rs. 32,500 (A) = Rs. 41,250 (F) + Rs. 8,750 (A)

Questions for Self - Study

1) Define standard cost and distinguish it from estimated cost.
2) What do you mean by standard costing ? What are its advantages ?
3) Explain the concept of standard costing.
4) Explain the main activities related to a sound standard costing system.
5) What do you mean by variances ? Explain the different categories of cost variances.
6) What do you mean by material cost variance ? Explain the classification of material cost variances into different categories with suitable illustrations.

7) Distinguish between material price variance and material wage variance with suitable examples.

8) Define labour cost variance and explain the possible reasons for labour rate variance, labour efficiency variance and idle time variance.

9) What is overhead variance ? What are the different types of overhead variance ? How are they calculated and dealt with ?

10) Write short notes on :

a) Concept of standard costing,
b) Establishment of standard costing,
c) Steps involved in standard costing
d) The standard costing system
e) Standard Direct Material cost
f) Standard Quantity of Direct Material
g) Overhead standard
h) Direct material variance
i) Standard costing
j) Direct labour variance
k) Labour price variance
l) Labour cost variance
m) Material mix variance
n) Material yield variance,

Practical Problems for Self Study

1) Standard Price : Rs. 6 per kg.
Actual Price : Rs. 8 per kg.
Standard Quantity : 1,000 kg.
Actual Quantity Used : 900 kg.
Calculate material price variance

2) Calculate the material mix variance from the following particulars

Standard mix for product		Actual mixture of product	
Product A :	60 kg. @ Rs. 5 kg.	Product A :	80 kg. @ Rs. 4 kg
Product B :	40 kg. @ Rs. 10 kg.	Product B :	20 kg @ Rs. 8 kg
Total	100	Total	100

3) From the following data, calculate the material mix variance :

Materials	Standard Qty.	Rate (Rs.)	Actual Qty.	Rate (Rs.)
A	160	10.00	128	9.50
B	80	8.00	112	9.00
	240		240	

Due to shortage of material A, it was decided to reduce consumption of A by 15% and increase consumption of material B by 30 %

4) The standard mix and actual mix for producing an article is given below :

Standard Raw Material	Actual Raw Material
A 60 Units @ Rs. 10	80 Units @ Rs. 12
B 90 Units @ Rs. 20	60 Units @ Rs. 25
150	140

Calculate the material price variance, material usage variance and material mix variance.

5) From the following data of a factory, calculate :

a) Material Cost Variance; b) Material Price Variance: and c) Material usage Variance.

Items of Material	Standard Units	Rate	Actual Units	Rate
A	300	1.00	300	0.80
B	600	0.50	340	0.60
C	900	0.80	900	1.00

6) The standard cost of chemical mixture is :

40% material A at Rs. 20 per kg. & 60% material B at Rs. 30 per kg

A standard loss of 10% is expected in production. During a period there is used :

90 kg. material A at a cost of Rs. 18 per kg.

110 kg. material B at a cost of Rs. 34 per kg.

The weight produced is 182 kg. of good product.

Calculate

a) Material price variance b) Material mix variance

c) Material yield variance d) Material cost variance

7) ABC Ltd. manufacturing LXE by mixing three raw materials for every batch of 100 kgs. of LXE, 125 kgs of raw materials are used. In March 2004, 60 batche were prepared to produce an output of 5,000 kgs of LXE. The standard and actual particulars for March, 2004 are us under.

Raw Material	Standard		Actual		Quantity of Raw Materials
	Mix %	Price per kg.(Rs.)	Mix %	Price per kg. (Rs.)	Purchased kg.
A	50	20	60	21	5,000
B	30	10	20	8	2,000
C	20	5	20	6	1,200

Calculate :

a) Material Cost Variance b) Material Price Variance

c) Material Mix Variance d) Material Yield Variance

8) The following information is received from a manufacturing company for the month of March.

	Budgeted	Actual
Variable overheads	Rs. 25,200	Rs. 27,500
Labour hours	Rs. 11,200	Rs. 11,000
Production units	5,600	5,400

Calculate variances :

a) Expenditure b) Efficiency c) Cost Variance

9) ABC Company sets 30 hours at a wage rate of Rs. 4 per hour for a given task. The given task was completed within 7 days with daily working of 4 hours. Compute labour efficiency variance.

10) CTBT engaged 75 workers at an average rate of Rs. 3 per day. The work was completed within 4 days. The standard cost set for the specified work amount to Rs. 850. Compute Labour Cost Variance.

11) ABC Co. Ltd. sets five hours as labour time standard for processing one unit of product XX at a standard direct labour rate of Rs. 5 per hour. During the month of May, the company used 6,000 actual direct labour hours at Rs. 4 per hour to process 1,000 units of product VX Compute Labour Cost Variances.

12) Calculate Labour Mix Variance from the following :

	Standard			Actual		
	Hours (Rs.)	Rate (Rs.)	Amount	Hours (Rs.)	Rate (Rs.)	Amount
Men	600	3	1800	550	4	2200
Women	800	2	1600	850	1.50	1275
	1400		3400	1400		3475

13. Calculate

(a) Material Cost Variance(b) Material Price Variance

(c) Material Usage Variance from the following particulars

Material	Standard Quantity	Standard Price	Actual Quantity	Actual Price
X	15 kg.	Rs. 5	18 kg.	Rs. 4
Y	20 kg.	Rs. 4	24 kg.	Rs. 3

14. The standard mix of a product is as follows

Material	Units	Price per unit
A	30	20 ps
B	20	15 ps
C	50	30 ps

Standard loss in production 10 %

There is actual production of 8,000 units from 90 mixes during July 2004

The actual purchase and consumption of materials during July 2004 were

Material	Units	Price per unit
A	2,500	25 ps
B	1,600	10 ps
C	4,500	40 ps

Compute the various material variance

15. Compute

(a) Labour Cost Variance

(b) Labour Rate Variance

(c) Labour Efficiency Variance

Standard hours per unit	25
Standard rate	Rs.5 per hour
Actual production	3,000 units
Actual hours	20,000 Hours.
Actual rate	Rs.4 per hour

16. From the following particulars calculate the various labour variances :

Standard time per unit		10 hours per unit
Standard rate		Rs.5 per hour
Actual production		1,500 units
Actual time taken (hours)	18,000	
Idle time (hours)	1,000	
Total	19,000 hours	

The actual wages paid was Rs.1,14,000 at the rate of Rs.6 per hour.

17. A medium scale unit worked for 50 hours a week. It has 100 workers. The following are the other details.

Standard rate per hour	Rs. 2
Standard output per gang hour during a week	400 units
10 workers were paid	Rs. 1.00 per hour
15 workers were paid	Rs. 1.50 per hour
75 workers were paid	Rs. 2.00 per hour

The actual production was 20,500 units

Calculate the labour variances

18. From the data given below, calculate labour variances for the two departments.

	Department A	Department B
Actual gross wages (direct)	Rs. 2,000	Rs. 1,800
Standard hours produced	8,000	6,000
Standard rate per hour	30 ps.	35 ps.
Actual hours worked	8,200	5,800

19. In a factory, 100 workers are engaged and the average rate of wages is 50 ps. per hour. Standard working hours per week are 40 and the standard performance is 10 units per gang hour.

During a week in March, wages paid for 50 workers were at the rate of 50 paise per hour, 10 workers at 70 paise per hour and 40 workers at 40 paise per hour. Actual output was 380 units.

The factory did not work for five hours due to break-down of machinery. Calculate appropriate labour hour.